Extraordinary acclaim for

American Pharaoh

Mayor Richard J. Daley: His Battle for Chicago and the Nation

by Adam Cohen and Elizabeth Taylor

"Cohen and Taylor put Daley in historical perspective. . . . If you want to understand the most beautiful and most corrupt city of mid-twentieth-century America, and the power that urban machines once had, you could not do better than to read this gripping book." — David L. Chappell, *Newsday*

"Briskly written, authoritative, and thoroughly honest."
— Steve Neal, *Chicago Sun-Times Book Week*

"Readers likely will find that they have revisited a place from their and this nation's past. *American Pharaoh* isn't just about Daley and the city he grew up in and ran for more than twenty years. It is the gritty reality of how it feels to be inside a melting pot. It is a modern history lesson that takes us from the Irish immigration in the mid-1800s through the Civil Rights Era of the '60s." — Robert T. Nelson, *Seattle Times*

"This is a myth-shattering portrait of Mayor Daley the elder. . . . *American Pharaoh* is an eye-opening work that enthralls the reader from page 1."
— Studs Terkel, author of *Working* and *My American Century*

"This fine biography speaks to our time as well as to memory. . . . Cohen and Taylor know Chicago, byways and all, and they tell a good story. Their detailed account of personalities and events never lets us forget the grander drama of Daley's public life, its bright successes shadowed by elements of tragedy." — Wilson Carey McWilliams, *San Francisco Chronicle*

"Cohen and Taylor's book stands as the one indispensable source on Daley, the argument-starter and the argument-settler. . . . *American Pharaoh* accomplishes the odd feat of leaving its readers with a more positive impression of Daley than they probably used to have while also being, page by page, quite anti-Daley. . . . A fascinating and admirably complete biography."
— Nicholas Lehmann, *New Republic*

"Until now, the definitive chronicle of Mayor Richard J. Daley's two-decade reign over Chicago has been Mike Royko's *Boss*, published in 1970, when Daley was still very much in power. The intervening years have permitted the authors of this hefty new biography a cooler perspective. Cohen and Taylor hit all the high points while also sketching a compelling social history of mid-century Chicago." — *The New Yorker*

"A fascinatingly detailed civic biography. . . . Through the prism of the public housing issue and throughout *American Pharaoh*, the authors do an excellent job of exposing the tragic racial history of postwar America. . . . Cohen and Taylor have written history as it did unfold, clear-eyed and astringently." — David C. Ward, *Boston Book Review*

"Superb. . . . Daley's story is vividly told by Cohen and Taylor in what is not only the best full-scale investigation of the Daley reign but one of the finest political biographies of recent years. . . . Highly recommended." — Karl Helicher, *Library Journal*

"A masterly biography. . . . Indeed, the patronage and favoritism afforded by big-spending government at all levels (and the waste and corruption it entails) drive the rhythm of this book: an insistent ostinato of greed and power." — John Lilly, *American Spectator*

"Worth the attention of anyone interested in big-city politics." — Larry King, *USA Today*

"Cohen and Taylor are fastidiously fair to the famous mayor and do not take sides. No edge and no attitude adorn this encyclopedic saga of the fifty wards. Like their subject, the authors take Chicago very seriously. To anyone interested in America or its cities, Chicago is fascinating. Art, commerce, political power, and race are part of the city's story, especially race. . . . *American Pharaoh* is fast-paced, comprehensive, and written well enough to evoke the sights and sounds of a great city in turbulent times." — Martin F. Nolan, *Washington Monthly*

"Engrossing and massively detailed. . . . *American Pharaoh* is a vital and necessary work that students of American political history are likely to consult for decades to come." — Andrew O'Hehir, *Salon.com*

AMERICAN PHARAOH

MAYOR RICHARD J. DALEY:
HIS BATTLE FOR CHICAGO
AND THE NATION

*Adam Cohen
and
Elizabeth Taylor*

LITTLE, BROWN AND COMPANY

Boston New York London

Originally published in hardcover
by Little, Brown, May 2000
First Back Bay paperback edition, May 2001

Library of Congress Cataloging-in-Publication Data
Cohen, Adam (Adam Seth)
American pharaoh : Mayor Richard J. Daley: his battle for Chicago and the nation /
by Adam Cohen and Elizabeth Taylor. — 1st ed.
p.   cm.
Includes bibliographical references and index.
ISBN 0-316-83403-3 (hc) / 0-316-83489-0 (pb)
1. Daley, Richard J., 1902–1976.   2. Mayors — Illinois — Chicago — Biography.
3. Chicago (Ill.) — Politics and government — 1951–   4. United States — Politics and
government — 1945–1989.   I. Taylor, Elizabeth (Elizabeth Joel)   II. Title.
F548.54.D34 C64 2000
977.3'11043'092—dc21
[B]
99-042157

10   9   8   7   6   5   4   3   2   1

Book design by Bernard Klein

Q-FF
Printed in the United States of America

Beverly Cohen and Stuart Cohen
and
Barbara Taylor and James, William, and Caroline Kaplan

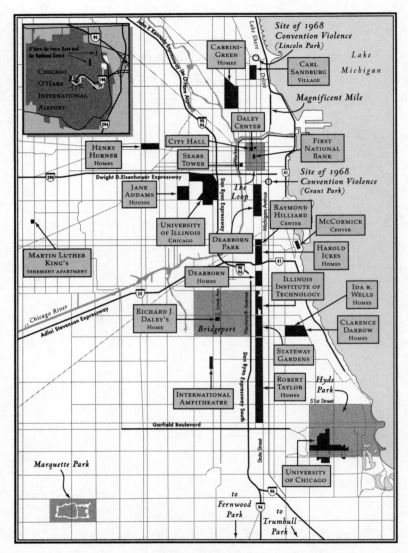

Daley's Chicago

"This is Chicago, this is America."

—Richard J. Daley, press conference, August 29, 1968

Contents

AMERICAN PHARAOH

Prologue

As Chicago mayor Richard J. Daley prepared to talk to Walter Cronkite on August 29, 1968, a CBS News camera panned across the empty floor of the Democratic National Convention. The news reports from the convention so far had been grim and bloody, filled with footage of the Chicago police charging into crowds of unarmed anti-war demonstrators, swinging clubs and breaking heads. The elderly, the young, and innocent bystanders of all kinds had been attacked by Daley's army in blue — some were teargassed, others had their skulls cracked, and still others were shoved through plate-glass windows. Daley, the wily machine boss who ruled Chicago like a feudal preserve, was being portrayed in the national media as a homegrown American tyrant: just the night before, Senator Abraham Ribicoff of Connecticut had stood at the podium and decried, to a nationwide television audience, the "Gestapo tactics" being used on the streets of Chicago.

But as the CBS camera scanned the International Amphitheatre, it found no sign of this tyrannical Daley. The protest signs that filled the streets were absent from the hall: all the camera picked up were banners, lovingly hung from the rafters by machine foot soldiers, praising Chicago's embattled leader. "World's Greatest Mayor! Richard J. Daley," exclaimed one, signed "14th Ward Regular Democratic Organization, Edward M. Burke, Committeeman." Nor could the camera find any of the thousands of demonstrators who were loudly denouncing Daley and the Chicago police for engaging in unprovoked violence. The only nondelegates admitted to the galleries were precinct captains and patronage workers, who waved American flags and held placards reading "We love Mayor Daley" and "Police Keep Up the Good Work."[1]

Against this carefully crafted backdrop, Daley arrived in the CBS anchor booth and took a seat beside Cronkite. Like most of the media covering the convention, Cronkite had been outraged by the violence of the past week, and had been vocal in his criticism of the Chicago police. In the next few minutes, before a television audience of millions, it seemed that Daley would be gently torn apart by America's most beloved newsman. As the TV camera rolled, the two men warily exchanged pleasantries. Cronkite declared that CBS had received hundreds of telegrams and "a lot of phone calls" taking Daley's side over the recent violence. "I can tell you this, Mr. Daley, that you have a lot of supporters around the country as well as in Chicago," Cronkite said. Daley assured Cronkite that, through his nightly news broadcasts, he was a "constant visitor" in the Daley home. Then Daley brought the casual conversation to an abrupt halt. Accustomed to being in control, the mayor produced a typewritten statement and — defying the traditions of the on-air interview — began reading an uncompromising defense of the Chicago police and of himself.[2]

The anti-war demonstrators who had converged on Chicago were nothing less than terrorists, Daley said sternly. "They came here equipped with caustics, with helmets, and with their own brigade of medics," he read, his voice a mixture of midwestern flatness and working-class rough edges. "They had maps locating the hotels and routes of buses for the guidance of terrorists from out of town." The truth was, it had been the demonstrators who had been violent and the police who had been the victims, Daley insisted — the media were just too biased to report the clashes fairly. "How is it that you never showed on television, Walter, the crowd marching down the street to confront the police?" Daley asked. "You show it after . . . it happens. Is the television industry interested in this violence? I'd like to have them show the fifty-one policemen who were injured, some of them severely." Cronkite offered up a hesitant defense of his news-gathering colleagues. "Maybe the police take care of their own and get them out of the way when they're wounded," the newsman suggested. "They don't take care of them," Daley snapped. "They're lying on the street like everyone else."[3]

Daley was not finished putting his gloss on the week's events. The leaders of the anti-war movement were Communists, Daley insisted — David Dellinger, leader of the National Mobilization to End the War in Vietnam, had even visited Hanoi. Why, Daley wanted to know, had none of this been reported in the media? "Can't you get their record?" Daley asked, again impatient. "Anyone can get their record." Cronkite gently raised a point much on the minds of his colleagues: that among those injured by the Chicago police had been thirty-two members of the press. But Daley had a quick retort. "Many of them are hippies themselves," he explained. "They're a part of this movement. Some of them are revolutionaries and they want these things to happen. There isn't any secret about that." Finally, Daley announced that he was going to share with Cronkite something "that I never said to anyone." He had received intelligence reports in recent weeks that "certain people" planned to assassinate the presidential candidates and Daley himself. "I didn't want what happened in Dallas or what happened in California to happen in Chicago," Daley said, invoking the shootings of John Kennedy in 1963, and Robert Kennedy only a few months before the convention. "So I took the necessary precautions."[4]

Most of what Daley told Cronkite was simply untrue. The young men and women who had descended on Chicago were upset about the Vietnam War and critical of the way the country was being run, but few of them were actually Communists. The vast majority of reporters injured by the Chicago police were professional newsmen with no ties to the anti-war movement. And if there were actual plots to assassinate the presidential candidates during convention week, they were never mentioned again, and no one was ever arrested or prosecuted. As for a threat to assassinate Daley, he admitted himself in the course of the interview that it was a common enough occurrence — "I've had that constantly," he noted — and it certainly provided no justification for raging attacks against unarmed civilians. Most egregious of all was Daley's attempt to blame the hundreds of anti-war demonstrators for being beaten up by the Chicago police. By week's end, more than one hundred civilians would be hospitalized and hundreds more treated by mobile medical units. A few months after the convention, a blue-ribbon panel appointed by President Johnson would carefully sift through the evidence, examining video evidence and evaluating three thousand eyewitness accounts. The panel would conclude that Daley's officers had engaged in an unjustified "police riot."[5]

Millions of Americans watching the interview at home were waiting for Cronkite to challenge Daley's self-serving account. But that confrontation never came. In the face of the mayor's bluster and strength of purpose, Cronkite folded. The veteran newsman, who had been deeply troubled by the events of the past week, let Daley's wildest assertations stand. And to the amazement of many viewers, Cronkite concluded the interview with an ingratiating anecdote. He told Daley he had recently driven back to his hotel with several other people, and they had all commented on "the genuine friendliness of the Chicago Police Department." Daley had gone into the interview a subject of national scorn, but he had emerged with a public relations triumph. As one CBS executive said dejectedly when it was over: "Daley took Cronkite like Grant took Richmond."[6]

The defeated CBS news staff were hardly the first people to underestimate Daley. It had happened to him all his life. Daley was born in 1902 in the gritty, working-class neighborhood of Bridgeport on Chicago's South Side. He was bereft of the usual attributes of promising youth. He was not academically gifted, charismatic, or articulate. (Indeed, later in life he would be known for his colorful malapropisms. "The policeman is not there to create disorder," he said after the convention violence. "The policeman is there to preserve disorder.") What Daley did begin with was an Irish-Catholic background, making him part of the city's politically ascendant ethnic group; extraordinary personal drive; and a keen understanding of how to amass and wield power.

Daley was a masterful politician — perhaps the shrewdest retail politician in U.S. history. Like Stalin, he understood the enormous personal power that could come from presiding over a strong party apparatus. Daley skillfully worked his way up the ranks of Chicago's mighty Democratic machine, quietly forging the citywide coalition that elected him party boss in 1954. Daley presided over a Central Committee made up of ward committeemen from each of the city's fifty wards. Through them, he commanded an army of 3,400 precinct captains spread out over every block of the city, and dispensed 40,000 patronage jobs. Patronage workers who came through on election day kept their jobs. Those who failed to turn out the vote were "vised," or fired, and replaced with someone who would try harder. The machine's leadership was made up of Daley's fellow Irish-Catholics, but its genius was that it included most of the city — blacks, Jews, Poles, even organized crime. Within a year of becoming Democratic boss, Daley ousted Chicago's well-meaning but politically naive mayor and installed himself in City Hall.

Daley, who served as mayor of Chicago from 1955 until his death in 1976, was the most powerful local politician America has ever produced. He possessed a raw political might that today, in an age when politics is dominated by big money and television, is hard to imagine. He personally slated, or selected, candidates for every office, from governor to ward committeeman. A generation of governors, U.S. senators, congressmen, state legislators, and aldermen owed Daley their political careers. When he wanted something from them — whether it was a congressman's vote on the national budget or a patronage position in the county sheriff's office — he almost always got it. (And when he did not, he could be ruthless: one of the brightest stars on the Chicago political scene in the 1960s lost his seat on the Cook County Board for refusing to side with the machine on a vote over a garbage dump.) But Daley's influence reached far beyond the borders of his city and state. His control over the large and well-disciplined Illinois delegation made him a kingmaker in selecting Democratic candidates for president — he was, Robert Kennedy once declared, "the whole ball game."

To what end did Daley use all of this power? He reigned in an era rich with ideological leaders. Martin Luther King Jr. was battling for civil rights, and George Wallace was fighting for segregation; Eugene McCarthy was campaigning to end the Vietnam War, and President Johnson was struggling to win it. Daley had an ideology of his own: the flinty conservatism that prevailed in Bridgeport and in much of white ethnic, working-class America in the 1950s and 1960s. A devout Catholic and loyal machine member, he believed deeply in authority. He favored the strong over the weak, the establishment over dissidents. Daley liked presidents, business leaders, and powerful in-

stitutions; he was offended by anti-war protesters, civil rights protesters, and hippies, who sought to influence policy without doing the
hard work of prevailing at the ballot box. Daley believed that poor
people should pull themselves up by their bootstraps, as his Bridgeport neighbors struggled to do. And he believed in racial separation,
of the kind that prevailed in his own neighborhood. Blacks stayed in
the Black Belt to the east of Wentworth Avenue, and whites stayed
to the west.

Those were Daley's views, but his agenda in office was less complicated: he was motivated first and foremost by a drive to accumulate and retain power. That was the way of the Chicago machine,
and it was Daley's — make deals and share the wealth with the Church
or the syndicate, with black political leaders or anti-black neighborhood organizations, and with anyone else whose votes would
help elect the machine's candidates. Daley's primary test of a political
cause was whether it would increase or decrease his power. He chose
candidates who would win, and who would pull the rest of the machine slate into office with them. He formed alliances with politicians who could deliver votes, and ruthlessly cut them off when they
were no longer useful — or when they became so strong that they
posed a threat.

Daley came to see the great liberal crusades of the 1950s and
1960s — civil rights, the War on Poverty, the anti-war movement —
as a threat to his power, and he battled against all of them. His focus
was Chicago, but his power and influence were such that he ended
up quietly shaping the national agenda. Nowhere was this more true
than on civil rights. Daley was elected at the dawn of the civil rights
era: it was during his first year as mayor that Rosa Parks refused to
move to the back of a Montgomery, Alabama, city bus. The civil
rights movement first took hold in the South, where Jim Crow en-
shrined racial segregation in the law books, but its implications for
Chicago were substantial. The city was in the midst of a demographic revolution when Daley took office. The city's black population was reaching record levels, as trainloads of blacks fled their hard
lives in the rural South for the promise of a better life in northern
cities.

Chicago under Daley became America's major northern civil
rights battleground. After his success in the South, and after winning

the Nobel Peace Prize, Martin Luther King Jr. decided to take his movement to the North — and he chose Chicago as the place to start it off. King moved into a tenement on Chicago's South Side for eight months in 1966 and spearheaded the Chicago Campaign, personally leading open-housing marches into the city's white neighborhoods. Daley responded to King's drive with a brilliant campaign of his own. Daley did not make the same mistake so many southern governors and mayors had: he refused to let the movement cast him as the villain in its drama. In the end, Daley's handling of the Chicago Campaign would have far-reaching effects on the civil rights movement across the country. Daley also played a key role in preserving racial segregation in education, both in Chicago and nationally. Chicago's public schools were nearly as segregated as the southern schools that were being ordered by federal courts to integrate. Daley fought back attempts to integrate Chicago's public schools, and took on the federal government when it tried to force school desegregation on the city.

Daley was also a leading opponent of President Johnson's War on Poverty, and again his victory was felt far beyond Chicago. Daley did not share Johnson's moral commitment to using government programs to lift the disadvantaged up from poverty, but his greatest objections were political. Johnson's poverty programs incorporated the liberal notion of "maximum feasible participation," which meant that poor people should have as much control as possible over how poverty programs were run. Daley saw these programs as a threat to the machine, because they put money and power in the hands of independent community activists. Daley's response to the War on Poverty would be felt not only in Chicago, but in Washington and across the country.

Daley emerged on the national scene in 1968 as an icon of working-class resentment toward the anti-war movement and the youth-oriented counterculture. Daley's opposition was in large part political. The anti-authoritarian spirit behind the movement was a threat to machine politics, which was built on a foundation of blind obedience. Daley understood that when power shifted to the grassroots level and to the streets, political bosses like him would suffer. In fact, his fears about the direction the anti-war activists were leading the Democratic Party would be borne out in the aftermath of the

1968 convention. Daley and his delegates were not seated in the 1972 convention: the party voted instead to recognize a ragtag group of liberals and blacks as the official Illinois delegation. The schism that emerged in Chicago in 1968 would haunt the Democratic Party, and national politics, for decades to come.

In the end, however, Daley's most lasting legacy was the cause he devoted most of his life to: building the modern city of Chicago. When he took office in 1955, Chicago was spiraling downward. The city's middle-class was beginning to flee for the suburbs, their path paved by low-cost government mortgages and newly laid highways. Businesses were also headed for outlying areas, drawn by cheaper land and lower taxes. At the same time, poor blacks were flooding into the city from the rural South. Middle-class white areas were "flipping" rapidly and becoming black slums. Daley used his power to reverse Chicago's decline. His City Hall worked hard to develop the city's infrastructure and buttress its downtown business district. Daley built or helped build Chicago's superlative institutions — O'Hare International Airport, the world's busiest; Sears Tower, the world's tallest; and the Dan Ryan Expressway, the world's widest. Under Daley, an impressive new crop of skyscrapers went up downtown and filled out the city's skyline. Daley convinced a reluctant University of Illinois to build a campus in Chicago, giving the sons and daughters of the city's working class access to affordable college education close to home. And he built the Civic Center, a massive complex of government buildings, and McCormick Place, the world's largest exhibition space. Daley also presided over the rise of North Michigan Avenue's Magnificent Mile, one of the nation's grandest upscale retailing districts.[7]

Daley's modern Chicago was built, however, on an unstated foundation: commitment to racial segregation. He preserved the city's white neighborhoods and business district by building racial separation into the very concrete of the city. New developments — housing, highways, and schools — were built where they would serve as a barrier between white neighborhoods and the black ghetto. Daley worked with powerful business leaders to revitalize downtown by pushing poor blacks out, replacing them with middle-class whites. But Daley's most striking accomplishment was Chicago's deeply troubled public housing projects. Daley used public housing as a repository for thousands of blacks who might otherwise have ended up moving into white neighborhoods.[8] He built new public housing in the form of densely packed high-rise towers, and he placed them in Chicago's black ghettos. Many of these projects ended up along a single street in the South Side ghetto. The State Street Corridor, as it came to be known, remains today the densest concentration of public housing in the nation. Daley was also responsible for the final touch: routing the Dan Ryan Expressway to follow the neighborhood's traditional racial boundary. The fourteen-lane Dan Ryan separated the State Street Corridor from the white, working-class neighborhoods of the South Side — including Daley's own neighborhood of Bridgeport.

Daley may well have saved Chicago. He reigned during an era in which suburbanization, crime, and white flight were wreaking havoc on other midwestern cities. Detroit, Kansas City, Cleveland, and Saint Louis were all prosperous, middle-class cities when Daley took office, and all declined precipitously after World War II. In a twenty-five-year period after the war, Detroit lost one-third of its *Fortune* 500 companies; by the mid-1970s, it had become the nation's murder capital, with twice as many killings per capita as any other large American city. That never became Chicago's fate. In large part due to Daley, the city's downtown business district expanded at the same time Detroit's was collapsing, and much of its sprawling white, working-class "Bungalow Belt" remained intact.[9]

Daley created a city that, in the famous phrase, worked. The question was, for whom did it work? Daley championed working-class, ethnic neighborhoods like his own beloved Bridgeport, and fought to preserve and expand Chicago's now-thriving downtown. But for every middle-class neighborhood he saved, there was a poor neighborhood in which living conditions worsened. For every downtown skyscraper that kept jobs and tax dollars in the city, there was a housing project tower that confined poor people in an overcrowded ghetto. Over time, the Daley-era housing projects turned into "vertical ghettos," rife with crime and social dysfunction. Today, Chicago is the nation's most racially segregated large city: about 90 percent of black Chicagoans would have to move for the city to be integrated.

Chicago is one of America's wealthiest cities but, remarkably, nine of the nation's ten poorest census tracts are in Chicago's housing projects. Most of these are in the State Street Corridor.[10]

During the civil rights era, Chicago blacks often referred to Mayor Daley as "Pharaoh." Civil rights activists saw Daley as an oppressor and a taskmaster — as an unrelenting Ramses to Martin Luther King's Moses. Daley was a pharaoh in this sense, but also in others. He ruled over his empire with pharaonic power, the kind of absolute power that few American politicians have ever wielded. His twenty-one-year reign over Chicago was of dynastic proportions. And like the pharaohs of old, Daley built a city and filled it with awesome monuments — an imposing legacy that, for good and for bad, has survived long after his death, and that will likely continue to carry out his will for generations to come.

1

A Separate World

Richard Joseph Daley was a product of the bloody world of the Chicago slaughterhouses. Chicagoans of his day, both Catholics and non-Catholics, located themselves by referring to their local parish — they came from Saint Mary's or Saint Nicholas's. Daley came from Nativity of Our Lord, the parish church of his childhood, where he would be eulogized seventy-four years later. Nativity was founded in the mid-1800s to serve the poor Irish-Catholic laborers who were flooding the area to work in the growing meatpacking industry. The church's simple stone building stood at the corner of 37th and Union, on the fringes of the South Side neighborhood of Bridgeport and hard up against a vast expanse of cattle-slaughtering facilities. Standing on the steps after Mass, young Daley could smell the fetid mixture of manure and blood that wafted over from the sprawling Union Stock Yards to the south. The gurgling in the background was the cackle of "Bubbly Creek," a torpid offshoot of the Chicago River that got its name from the fermenting animal carcasses and offal in its slow-moving waters. If Nativity seemed like an unlikely place for spiritual repose, it had once been worse. The church's first home had actually been in the former J. McPherson livery stables. The name "Nativity" was a reference to the fact that the church, like Christ, had been born in a stable — an attempt to put a holy gloss on grim surroundings. Nativity's new building had a pleasant interior, including ornate stained-glass windows, but nothing could make up for the harsh reality of geography. Daley's spiritual home was located just a few hundred feet from what one parish history called "the greatest and bloodiest butcher shamble in the world."[1]

The whole city of Chicago had a reputation for coarseness and for lacking the style and sophistication of older cities like Philadelphia or Boston. "Having seen it, I urgently desire never to see it again," Rudyard Kipling wrote after visiting in 1889. "It is inhabited by savages." Chicago was the industrial capital of the Midwest, a tough town dominated by factories that belched black smoke. Theodore Dreiser, who roamed the city as a reporter, marveled in his book *Newspaper Days* at the "hard, constructive animality" of the rougher parts of Chicago. It was not uncommon, he found on his rounds, to come across men standing outside ramshackle homes "tanning dog or cat hides." The Chicago of this era was a town in which displaced farmhands and struggling immigrants competed for space in ramshackle tenements and rooming houses, and hooligans roamed the streets. Block after block of "disorderly houses" did a brisk business corrupting hordes of guileless young girls, like Dreiser's Sister Carrie, who arrived daily from small towns in a desperate search for a better life. And it was Chicago saloonkeepers who invented the Mickey Finn, a chloral hydrate–laced drink slipped to solitary patrons so they could be easily robbed. "The New York Tenderloin," journalist Lincoln Steffens wrote, "was a model of order and virtue compared with the badly regulated, police-paid criminal lawlessness of the Chicago Loop and its spokes." Chicago's moral climate was shaped by Al Capone and the Saint Valentine's Day Massacre, and by the ignominy of the 1919 Chicago White Sox — the team that shocked the nation by fixing the World Series. "Chicago is unique," journalist A. J. Liebling would conclude after visiting for a year to research a book. "It is the only completely corrupt city in America." Loving Chicago, Nelson Algren once said, was like loving a woman with a broken nose.[2]

Even by the standards of turn-of-the-century Chicago, Daley's neighborhood was a grim place. It was Chicago's first slum, known in its early days by the evocative name Hardscrabble. It was settled in the 1830s and 1840s by the Irish "shovelmen" who built the nearby Illinois & Michigan Canal, many working for whiskey and a dollar a day. The area was renamed Bridgeport in the 1840s, when a low bridge was built across the Chicago River at Ashland Avenue, forcing barges to unload on one side and reload on the other. When the canals were completed, Bridgeport's dirty work of canal-building gave way to the even less savory trade of animal slaughter. Chicago killed and prepared for market much of the livestock raised in the farm states surrounding it. Leading the nation in slaughterhouses, it was truly — as Carl Sandburg observed — "hog butcher for the world." In the mid-1800s, Chicago slaughterhouses were being forced out of the congested downtown, and they found the vast expanses south of Bridgeport an ideal place to relocate. The area had sweeping tracts of open land, and a steady supply of water from the Chicago River available to use in the slaughtering and treatment processes. It was also near railroad tracks, which meant that once the cattle arrived from the countryside, they would not need to be led through the city streets on their way to the slaughter. In 1865, several slaughterhouses that once operated in downtown Chicago combined to form the Union Stock Yards, an enormous collection of meat-processing plants that dominated the area just south of Bridgeport.[3]

Upton Sinclair, whose novel *The Jungle* exposed the horrific world of the Chicago slaughterhouses, captured the unsavory surroundings in which Daley grew up. There were "so many cattle no one had ever dreamed existed in the world," Sinclair wrote. "The sound of them here was as of all the barnyards of the universe; and as for counting them — it would have taken all day simply to count the pens." Young Daley used to watch as the animals were driven down Archer Avenue to their demise, and he and his friends would gawk at the remnants that showed up in Bubbly Creek. Thousands of Daley's neighbors labored in the slaughterhouses, their workdays an uninterrupted assembly line of killing. Pigs with chains around their hind legs were hooked to a spokeless wheel, which hoisted the squealing animals into the air and carried them by overhead rail across the length of the building, where a man covered in blood cut their throats by hand. The blood that drained out was collected for use as fertilizer. Then the hog, often still squirming with life, was dropped into a vat of boiling water. Cattle were treated no better. It was hard, dispiriting work. Daley's neighbors were the workers Sinclair told of, those who fell prey to the chemicals used to pickle the meats, which caused "all the joints" of their fingers to "be eaten by the acid, one by one." Coming of age in this violent world, Daley was robbed of any illusions early.[4]

As its original name suggested, Bridgeport was a hardscrabble place. The neighborhood's earliest residents had lived in wooden shanties along the Chicago River that sank into the muddy soil of the riverbank. It was a wild region, where wolves ran free in the early years of Daley's childhood. The predominant form of housing, after residents gained the wherewithal to move beyond wooden shanties, was the humble "bungalow," a staple of working-class Chicago architecture. These long and narrow houses, or "shotgun-shacks," were a big step up from the squalid accommodations along the river, but they were still cheap housing for people who could not afford better. These small bungalows, on not-much-larger lots, were usually home to large immigrant families that would have been crowded in twice the space. Years after Daley was elected mayor, his wife would recall the cramped conditions of her childhood bungalow, in a neighborhood adjoining Bridgeport. "There were 10 children in our family and we only had one bathroom but somehow we all managed," Sis Daley told a newspaper reporter cheerfully.[5]

Bridgeport was, as much as any neighborhood in Chicago, a world apart. It lay on the geographical fringes of the city, five miles from downtown, on land that had only recently been incorporated. And it was separated on all sides by imposing barriers: the Chicago River to the north, the stockyards to the south, Bubbly Creek to the west, and wide railroad tracks — and then a black ghetto — to the east. Ethnic groups had divided Chicago according to an unwritten peace treaty. Germans settled on the North Side, Irish on the South Side, Jews on the West Side, Bohemians and Poles on the Near Southwest Side and Near Northwest Side, and blacks in the South Side Black Belt. Bridgeport was more diverse than most Chicago neighborhoods: it was home to several different white Catholic immigrant groups. But this only meant that Bridgeport was itself divided into ethnic enclaves. Most of its Poles were concentrated in northwest Bridgeport, west of Halsted Street, the traditional boundary line between Irish and non-Irish Bridgeport. Lithuanians also lived predominantly in the northwest, with Morgan Street separating them from the Poles. Germans and Bohemians were more spread out, but they too stayed mainly on the non-Irish side of Halsted. It is a reflection of how ethnically divided Bridgeport was that in 1868 the "index of dissimilarity" — the most commonly used measure of residential segregation — between its Lithuanians and Irish was .96, indicating almost complete separation. In turn-of-the-century Bridgeport, a block or two meant a world of difference. Tom Donovan, who would later become Daley's patronage chief, grew up at 39th and Lowe Avenue, only a few blocks from Daley's home at 35th and Lowe. But it was one parish over — Saint Anthony's, rather than Nativity of Our Lord — so, Donovan insisted, "I didn't grow up in his neighborhood." Even Bridgeport's Irish were divided up into sub-neighborhoods: the northwest Bridgeport Irish; the Dashed Irish, who lived along upper Union Avenue, once named Dashed Avenue; the Canaryville Irish, who lived in the marshy far-south end of the neighborhood; and, just north of Canaryville, the little rectangle of land around Nativity of Our Lord Church known as Hamburg.[6]

Daley's deepest loyalties were to this small Irish-Catholic village-within-a-village. Hamburg was no more than a few square blocks, stretching from 35th Street down to the stockyards at 39th Street, and bounded by Halsted Avenue on the west and the railroad tracks along Wentworth Avenue on the east. Its major institution was Nativity, which like all Catholic churches of the time was as much a center of communal life as a place of worship. Archbishop James Quigley, who led the Chicago Archdiocese from 1903 to 1915, had decreed that "a parish should be of such a size that the pastor can know personally every man, woman, and child in it,"[7] and this was certainly the case in tiny Nativity Parish. The annual parish fair — which featured gambling games, booths selling oyster stew, and a Hibernian band playing in the corner — was almost a family gathering.[8] Hamburg also had an array of secular institutions tying its residents together. The 11th Ward offices, headquarters of one of the most important units of the city's powerful Democratic machine, were located on Halsted Avenue at 37th Street. Directly across Halsted was the neighborhood saloon, Schaller's Pump, which many said was the real headquarters of the 11th Ward Democrats. Young residents had an institution of their own, the Hamburg Athletic Club, a combination of sports club, adjunct to the political machine, and youth gang. Hamburg was a tight little world inhabited by people who shared a religion, an ethnicity, and a common set of values, and who were mistrustful of those who lacked these bonds. Though it was in the middle of a large city, Hamburg was "not only a separate neighborhood, but . . . a separate world — a small town on a compact . . . scale."[9]

By one well-established formulation, a neighborhood is a "place to be defended." For all its seeming solidity, Irish-Catholic Hamburg was already in decline even at the time of Daley's birth. Nativity Parish was losing congregants, declining from 2,800 to 1,200 in the early years of the century, and beginning to encounter financial troubles. Throughout Daley's childhood, other ethnic groups were growing in size and drawing closer to Hamburg: formerly Irish Lawler Avenue, a mere four blocks west of Daley's childhood home, was renamed "Lithuanica" as the Lithuanian population around it grew. Mr. Dooley, the fictional creation of the great Irish-American journalist Finley Peter Dunne, expressed Bridgeport's fears of being engulfed by fast-encroaching ethnic rivals. In Dunne's columns in the *Chicago Daily News,* Mr. Dooley was the Irish-born keeper of a Bridgeport saloon. In 1897, five years before Daley's birth, Mr. Dooley was already bemoaning the fact that "th' Hannigans an' Leonidases an' Caseys" were moving out to greener pastures, "havin' made their pile," and "Polish Jews an' Swedes an' Germans an' Hollanders" had "swarmed in, settlin' on th' sacred sites." The most telling sign of Bridgeport's "change an' decay," Mr. Dooley said, was the selection of "a Polacker" to tend the famous "red bridge," which joined Bridgeport to the rest of the city, thereby placing control of the neighborhood in the hands of a non–Hibernian. It was the rising tide of black immigration, though, that Bridgeporters found most worrisome. Daley's youth coincided with the start of an unprecedented migration, as southern blacks moved north to take industrial jobs in the Northeast and Midwest. Most of the blacks flooding into Chicago were settling in the South Side Black Belt, just a few blocks east of Bridgeport, and the ghetto was always threatening to move closer. By the time Daley was born, many Bridgeporters had decided that their tough little neighborhood, with its workaday bungalows and slaughterhouse ambience, was best left to the new ethnic groups that were engulfing it on all sides. Irish residents of Hamburg who had the money — like Mr. Dooley's Hannigans, Leonidases, and

Caseys — were already moving out to more attractive and prestigious neighborhoods where the lawns were larger and the air did not smell of blood. But despite all sense and logic, Daley's family, and later Daley himself, remained intensely loyal to their small Irish-Catholic village. Daley never moved out and, it might be said, he spent a lifetime defending it.[10]

Daley was born in a simple two-flat at 3502 South Lowe on May 15, 1902. Daley's father, Michael, was the second of nine children born to James E. Daley, a New York–born butcher, and Delia Gallagher, an immigrant from Ireland. Like most Irish-American immigrants, Daley's forebears came to the country as part of the Great Potato Famine migration, which caused more than two million Irish to expatriate between 1845 and 1850. Though not brought over in chains, these Irishmen and Irishwomen were torn from their land and forced to emigrate by extraordinarily cruel circumstances. Before the famine ended, perhaps one-quarter of Ireland's population of eight million had died of starvation and disease. Many survivors headed for America. Their journey across the ocean, made in aptly named "coffin ships," was perilous. Passengers often succumbed to "ship fever," a kind of typhus, along the way. It was a migration of refugees fleeing a country they held dear, often forced to leave loved ones behind. Family legend has it that Daley's grandfather began his own journey when he went to market in Cork with his brother to sell pigs and, with the few shillings he made on the sale, boarded the next ship for America.[11]

Growing up in Bridgeport, Daley could not have avoided hearing about the horrors of the "Great Starvation." Adults in the neighborhood, some of whom had seen the suffering firsthand, passed on to the children lurid tales of skeletons walking the countryside, and peasant women dying in the fields. These famine stories were invariably laced with bitter accounts of how the hated British had exported wheat and oats out of the country while the Irish starved. In the course of his childhood, Daley learned the whole tragic history of his people — the centuries of rule as a conquered territory, the rebellions brutally put down, the absentee landlordism that drove farmers into poverty, and the language all but obliterated.[12]

The America Daley's grandparents immigrated to rescued them

from famine, but it was far from welcoming. The flood of Irish arriving in the nation's large cities produced a feverish outpouring of anti-Catholic sentiment. Protestant ministers preached about the threat posed by a Catholic Church they referred to by epithets like "The Scarlet Lady of Babylon" and "The Whore of Rome." And the American reading public devoured incendiary anti-Catholic books like the infamous novel *Artful Disclosures,* an "exposé" of convent life in which a nun describes forced sexual relations with priests, frequent orgies, and the murder of nuns who refused to submit.[13] This anti-Catholic fervor found political expression in the Know-Nothing Party, which in the elections of 1854/55 won seventy-five seats in Congress. In newspapers and popular magazines, a stereotype soon emerged of Irish immigrants as shiftless and prone to drink, with a dangerous propensity for brawling, gambling, and other lowlife pastimes. "Who does not know that the most depraved, debased, worthless, and irredeemable drunkards and sots which curse the community are Irish Catholics?" the *Chicago Tribune* asked in 1855. The Irish were regarded as particularly disposed to crime. "Scratch a convict or a pauper," the *Chicago Post* declared in 1898, and "the chances are that you tickle the skin of an Irish Catholic at the same time — an Irish Catholic made a criminal or a pauper by the priest and politicians who have deceived him and kept him in ignorance, in a word, a savage, as he was born."[14]

America reserved some of the lowest rungs on the economic and social ladder for the new Irish immigrants. Signs proclaiming "No Irish Need Apply" were common. Advertisements for housekeepers often specified "Protestant girls" only, because young Irish-Catholic women, as one account had it, were "the daughters of laborers, or needy tradesmen, or persecuted, rack-rented cotters, they are ignorant of the common duties of servants in respectable positions." Irish men, for their part, were largely relegated to the jobs native-born whites would not take. They were the laborers who carved out the canals, laid the railroad tracks, and dug the ditches — often at great personal cost. As one Irish-American lamented at the time: "How often do we see such paragraphs in the paper as an Irishman drowned — an Irishman crushed by a beam — an Irishman suffocated in a pit — an Irishman blown to atoms by a steam engine — ten, twenty Irishmen buried alive by the sinking of a bank — and other like casualties and perils to which honest Pat is constantly exposed in the hard toils for his daily bread."[15]

Coming of age in Bridgeport, Daley absorbed a keen understanding of Ireland's long years of "misery, suffering, oppression, violence, exploitation, atrocity, and genocide." And he felt deeply the discrimination that, even in America, his countrymen experienced. Hard as it may be to imagine now, one of the major forces driving Daley — born in a working-class Irish-Catholic neighborhood in a city run by wealthy Protestants — was something as basic as "an aspiration for full-class citizenship." Later in life, after he had taken control of the Chicago Democratic machine and been elected mayor, Daley spoke at an Irish-American dinner at Chicago's venerable Conrad Hilton Hotel. "I can't help thinking of your mothers and fathers and grandparents who would never have been allowed in this hotel," Daley declared. The lace-curtain Irish crowd laughed, but Daley did not. "I want to offer a prayer for those departed souls who could never get into the Conrad Hilton." Daley's childhood catechism of Irish deprivations left him convinced that no group had suffered as his kinsmen had suffered. In the 1960s, when Daley was turning a deaf ear to the civil rights movement, one liberal critic opined: "I think one of the real problems [Daley] has with Negroes is understanding that the Irish are no longer the out-ethnic group."[16]

Daley spent his childhood in conditions a distinct notch above the world of his grandfathers. He was born just as Chicago's Irish immigrants were making the hard transition from "shanty Irish" to the more respectable echelons of the lower middle class. Daley's father, Michael, was a sheet-metal worker and a business agent for his union. The Daleys fit in well in a neighborhood whose beliefs were few but deeply cherished: the Catholic Church, family, labor unions, and the White Sox, who played at Comiskey Park, just a few blocks away from the Daley home.

In the teeming Irish-Catholic world of Hamburg, Daley was a rarity: an only child. He and his parents were, perhaps because there were only three of them, an unusually closely knit family. Michael Daley, a wiry man who almost always sported a derby, was a man of few words. If Daley did not learn ambition or politics at his father's knee, he did acquire one of the mannerisms that would serve him best in his career: speaking little and keeping his own counsel. "Part of the mystique of Richard Daley is that no one ever seems to know precisely what he thinks," one observer has written. Daley's taciturn ways may have been sheer political strategy, but they were also the prevailing character trait in the Daley household. "I think the reason he's always had trouble talking," an old Bridgeport neighbor recalled, "was that there weren't any other children in his home, and his parents were quiet people." Daley's father also taught him respect for authority and reverence for the government. Years later, when his own mayoral authority was questioned by civil rights protesters, Daley would invoke a lesson he learned from his father at the funeral parade for Governor Edward Dunne. "There is the governor of Illinois, son," Daley recalled his father saying to him. "Take off your hat."[17]

Lillian Dunne Daley was eight years older than Daley's father, and she had a far stronger personality. Students of Irish history contend that as families left the land and moved to cities, gender roles changed, and women began to play a more dominant role. Mrs. Daley was one of this new breed, the "powerful and autocratic Irish matron." She was an active force in the church. Once, a young priest new to the parish wanted to start a bingo game, but was too shy to bring it up. Mrs. Daley advised him to raise it at an upcoming meeting of churchwomen. When the priest said in an uncertain voice that he wanted to start bingo, Mrs. Daley shouted out, "And we all do, too!" applauding, and carrying along the other women in the group. In addition to her work at Nativity of Our Lord, Mrs. Daley was a committed suffragist — not a usual cause for women in Bridgeport — and even took her son along to marches in support of the franchise for women. It is a measure of how formidable a force Lillian Daley was that a spectator would recall that as the Daley family walked by, a neighbor pronounced with dark Irish humor, "Here they come now, the Father, the Son, and the Holy Ghost!" Daley remained close to his mother her entire life, never moving more than a block away. Years later, as mayor, Daley would nod and wipe a tear from his eye when a women's float at a Chicago Saint Patrick's Day parade waved a banner saying, "The Mayor's Mother Was a Suffragette!"[18]

Mrs. Daley had high hopes that her only son would end up somewhere better than the stockyards or a South Side sheet-metal union

hall. She always dressed Daley more formally than his contempo-
raries, in suits with neckties, which made him look like a little
adult — an extravagance made easier by the fact that the family had
only one child to clothe. Young Daley often sported a handkerchief
and he was, according to one family friend, the only child in Bridgeport at the time who owned pajamas. Whether it came from his parents or from somewhere within, Daley had a strong work ethic from
a very young age. His first childhood job was selling newspapers at
the corner of 35th and Wallace. Daley also made the rounds of the
city's streetcars, riding to the end of the line as he walked up and
down the aisle selling papers. These early jobs provided Daley with
spending money, but they also trained him for his future career. "I
think selling newspapers is a good thing for kids," Daley would say
later. "They learn how to handle themselves with people." Daley also
worked Saturday mornings, starting at 7:00, running up and down
stairs to make deliveries for a peddler who sold vegetables door-to-
door from a horse-drawn wagon. Bridgeport was a neighborhood in
which many parents expected nothing more of their children than
for them to match their own modest achievements. Lillian Daley,
however, always made it clear she wanted more. This pressure to succeed was a constant in Daley's life as long as his mother lived. Shortly
before her death, after Daley won the Democratic nomination for
the powerful post of Cook County sheriff, Lillian Daley made it
clear that she was unimpressed. "I didn't raise my son to be a policeman," she told a friend. She also had another reason for opposing his
run for sheriff. Gilbert Graham, a priest and a friend of the family,
recalls that she complained to her son: "You're going to have to put
people to death." Earl Bush, Daley's longtime press secretary, suspects
Mrs. Daley had an entirely different career path in mind for her only
child. "I don't think [Mrs. Daley] naturally thought of her son as
being a politician," says Bush. "I think she would have preferred him
to become a priest."[19]

Daley attended parochial school at Nativity, where he became an
altar boy and stayed through graduation. In that era, the Catholic
Church expected its parishioners to send their children to parochial
school, and most complied. By one estimate, as many as 90 percent
of Bridgeport's Catholic children attended church schools. The Daleys, like many Catholic parents, probably feared the non-Catholic

world around them. The Catholic press of this era was filled with cautionary tales of Catholic parents who had entrusted their children to Protestant-dominated public schools. An article in the *Irish World and American Industrial Liberator,* extreme but not entirely atypical, told the tale of a ten-year-old child whipped "black and blue" in a Boston public school "for refusing to read the King James Version" of the Bible. The story all but omitted the fact that the incident had occurred fifty years earlier, but it reflected the deep mistrust many Irish-Catholic parents held for the public school system.[20]

Daley's parochial school education emphasized the basics: reading, writing, arithmetic, and the catechism. But as much as anything he learned in the formal curriculum, his eight years there helped instill in him many of the Irish-Catholic values he would carry with him throughout his life. Parochial school education was a prolonged education in submission to authority. Daley's patronage coordinator, Matt Danaher, who grew up in Bridgeport, once told of serving as an altar boy for a monsignor at Nativity of Our Lord Church. "I said to him one morning, 'We're all set, Father,'" Danaher recalled. "He walked over, looked at the clock and said, 'It's one minute to 6.' And then he said, 'How would you like to hang for one minute.' He was always a perfectionist." And the nuns were, as countless Catholic memoirs have attested, often tyrants in habits. One chronicler of a parochial school in a parish not far from Bridgeport wrote that "children were sometimes asked to kneel on marbles, or eat soap, or scrape gum from the hallway stairs." The curriculum at Nativity emphasized memorization, penmanship, and rote learning. The Catholic catechism drilled into Daley in religion class was, of course, the ultimate form of rote learning, reducing almost every question students could have about God or man to a memorized short answer. It was the ideal education for a young man who might find his way to a career in machine politics, where success lay in unquestioningly performing the tasks set out by powers above. But it was less helpful as training for a leader who would need to think independently and adapt himself to changing times.[21]

In school and out, Daley absorbed his neighborhood's conservative values and flinty self-reliance. Bridgeport, with its legions of slaughterhouse workers marching off to their bloody and dangerous jobs each day, was a community dedicated to the virtues of industry. No

Bridgeporter with any pride would rely on others for his daily bread: success came through constant toil and pulling oneself up by one's own bootstraps. The Catholic Church had its charities, but the overwhelming ethic in neighborhoods like Bridgeport was that except in the most dire cases of family death or illness it was an embarrassment to accept alms. "Poor people didn't look to anybody for help or assistance," observed the superintendent of Bridgeport's parochial schools in the 1930s. Mr. Dooley tells of the down-on-his-luck laborer Callaghan who nevertheless musters the strength of character to tell the Saint Vincent de Paul almsgivers to "Take ye'er charity, an' shove it down ye'er throats." If the Callaghans had things tough, it was because this earthly life was a hard one.[22]

The pre–Vatican II Catholicism in which Daley was raised impressed on him a keen sense of man's fallen state, and of the inevitability of sin. Man had to struggle hard against the influence of evil, which could be warded off only "if one chose the path of dutifulness and care, if one made sure by doing this twice over and respecting authority, if one closed off the energies of rebellion inside oneself." It was an education that bred a wary, even skeptical view of one's fellowman — a character trait Daley would carry with him through life. "He's like a fellow who peeks in the bag to make sure the lady gave him a dozen buns," a profile of Daley in the *Chicago Daily News* once observed. And it was an environment that left Daley with a lifelong skepticism of idealists of all kinds — whether they were reformers working to clean up machine politics or civil rights activists hoping to change hearts and minds on the question of race. These utopians all proceeded from an unduly optimistic vision of man's perfectibility. "Look at the Lord's Disciples," Daley would later say in response to a charge of corruption in City Hall. "One denied Him, one doubted Him, one betrayed Him. If our Lord couldn't have perfection, how are you going to have it in city government?"[23]

Daley was an obedient student, but not a particularly gifted one. He was "a very serious boy," his teacher Sister Gabriel recalled. "A very studious boy. He played when he played. He worked when he worked. And he prayed when he prayed." In 1916, after graduating from Nativity, Daley enrolled at De La Salle Institute, a three-year Catholic commercial high school known as "the Poor Boy's College." De La Salle was located at 3455 South Wabash, in a poor black neighborhood on the "wrong" side of the racial dividing line separating Bridgeport from the black neighborhoods to the east. Daley's commute brought him into closer physical proximity with the blacks who lived across the railroad tracks, but it did nothing to break down the psychological barriers that still separated him and his classmates from their black neighbors. De La Salle regarded its location in a black neighborhood as an unfortunate trick of fate, and it made no effort to introduce its young charges to their neighbors. "The school was surrounded by tenements and by low life," a history of De La Salle, prepared by the school itself, states bluntly. "It was a white school as an island surrounded by a black sea." Daley traveled to De La Salle in a pack of his fellow Bridgeporters, and quickly made his way out of the neighborhood when school let out.[24]

De La Salle, founded by an Irish immigrant from the Christian Brothers Order named Brother Adjutor of Mary, had a highly practical approach to educating the children of the Catholic working class. Brother Adjutor believed the best training for a young man with few advantages was intensive instruction in business. De La Salle's curriculum combined Catholic religious studies with commercial courses, including typing, bookkeeping, and business law. The school had actual "counting rooms," and other lifelike replicas of business settings, for students to begin acting out the financial jobs they would one day hold. Daley continued to be a diligent but unremarkable student. One classmate remembered him as "a hard worker . . . maybe a little above average." Brother Adjutor's educational philosophy worked well for Daley: the business skills he acquired at De La Salle were of considerable help later in life, when his financial skills proved to be a critical factor in his rise up the ranks of the machine. Like Nativity, De La Salle instilled the importance of unquestioning obedience. The Christian Brothers, imposing figures in long black robes and stiff white collars, instructed with a strictness that at times crossed the line to brutal. "They were good teachers," one of Daley's classmates recalled, "but if you got out of line, they wouldn't hesitate to punch you in the head."[25]

De La Salle's real strength was its extensive efforts to get jobs for its graduates. Most young Irish-Catholic boys coming of age in places like Bridgeport in the early 1900s never made it out of the working class. But De La Salle opened up another world, a white-collar alternative, for its students. As graduation neared, its faculty operated as a kind of Irish-Catholic educational machine — mirroring the Irish-Catholic political machine — in which Brother Adjutor and other instructors drew on their contacts in the business world to find jobs for the "Brother's Boys." Brother Adjutor's reference letters were similar to the ones precinct captains were writing in clubhouses across the city. Because of "the necessity of giving our students a good start in life," went one, "I have for many years past strenuously exerted myself to secure for them good positions in the leading mercantile houses of this and other cities." The school's combination of commercial training and methodical Irish-Catholic networking was a powerful engine for thrusting working-class boys into the upper echelons of the city's power structure. When Daley was elected mayor, he would be the third consecutive mayor educated at De La Salle. The school also produced numerous aldermen, including two from Daley's own graduating class, and many prominent businessmen. A commemorative book boasted, with only some hyperbole, that "The battle of Waterloo was won on the playing fields of Eton" but "the business leaders of Chicago were trained in the Counting Rooms of De La Salle." As an adult, Daley would remember De La Salle warmly as a place that "taught us to wear a clean shirt and tie and put a shine on your shoes and be confident to face the world." Daley worked after school and on weekends. When classes let out at 3:30 every day, he traveled to the Loop to wrap packages and act as a department store messenger until the early evening. He also worked on bakery wagons and joined the drivers' union.[26]

When Daley was not at school or working, he spent much of his free time at the Hamburg Athletic Club, which met in a nondescript clubhouse at 37th and Emerald, just a few blocks from his home. Hamburg was one of many such clubs in Chicago at the time — others had names like "Ragen's Colts," "the Aylwards," and "Our Flag" — that were part social circle, part political organization, and part street gang. The athletic clubs placed a premium on toughness and loyalty. The Ragen's Colts' motto could have belonged to any of them: "Hit me and you hit two thousand." Young men like Daley often ended up on the wrong end of the local policeman's billy club. "All they wanted to do was just beat you over the head," Daley would later say, revealingly, about the policemen of his youth. When they were not testing the limits of the law, Hamburg Athletic Club members actually engaged in a few athletic activities. The clubs organized their own competitive sports leagues, sponsored outings to professional sporting events, and even held picnics and dances. Daley excelled in the Hamburg Athletic Club's sports program — not as a participant but as a manager of others. "Dick often came to practice carrying his books," recalled a union official who was once the mascot of the Hamburg Athletic Club baseball team. "He was a very busy guy, but he took his job as a manager seriously. He made line-ups, booked the games, and ran the team on the field during games."[27]

Clubs like Hamburg also served as the first rung of the Democratic machine. Most were sponsored by machine politicians, who contributed to their treasuries and took a personal interest in their members. The clubs, for their part, did political work in the neighborhood during election season. The "Ragen" of Ragen's Colts was Cook County commissioner Frank Ragen, who paid the rent on the clubhouse and underwrote many of the club's other expenses. Hamburg's patron was Alderman Joseph McDonough, a rising star in the Democratic machine. Hamburg had a long history as a training ground for machine politicians. Among its alumni was Tommy Doyle, president of the club in 1914, who challenged Bridgeport's twenty-year-incumbent alderman and won. The club had served as a powerful political base for Doyle, providing him with an army of 350 campaign workers. Four years later, when Doyle moved on to higher office, McDonough inherited his aldermanic seat. Clubs like Hamburg were also valuable because their members were willing and able to apply force on behalf of their sponsors. It was a useful service, since Chicago political campaigns had a way of getting rough. A fierce battle for ward committeeman in the "Bloody 20th" Ward in 1928 ended with one candidate killed gangland-style and his opponent put on trial for the killing. It was common for election judges to be beaten up on election day, or kidnapped and not released until the voting — and the vote stealing — was completed. "Politics ain't bean-bag," Mr. Dooley said in one of his most famous pronouncements. " 'Tis a man's game, an' women, childer, cripples an' prohybitionists 'd do well to keep out iv it." For a young man in Bridgeport with political ambitions, the Hamburg Athletic Club was a good place to start out. Daley was elected president of the club in 1924, at age twenty-two, a post he held for the next fifteen years.[28]

Another prime function of the athletic clubs was defending their narrow stretch of turf from outsiders. Before World War II, Chicago was divided into ethnic enclaves that were bitterly mistrustful of their neighbors on all sides. When an Irish neighborhood adjoined a Slavic one, or a Polish neighborhood adjoined a Scandinavian one, the fault lines were clear and the animosities barely restrained. For Bridgeport, the great dividing line was Wentworth Avenue, which separated it from the black neighborhoods to the east. Bridgeport's fears were exacerbated by the fact that the population in the black ghetto was expanding rapidly as a result of migration from the South. At any moment, it seemed, the black neighborhoods to the east might expand and grow large enough to overrun Bridgeport. The intensity of Bridgeport's racial feelings would be laid bare decades later by a small but brutally revealing incident. It was June 1961, just weeks after busloads of Freedom Riders had been beaten up in the segregated bus stations of the South. The old Douglas Hotel on the black South Side had caught fire, and eighty residents had suddenly been made homeless. Red Cross volunteers had arrived on the scene and — unaware of Bridgeport's racial sensitivities — evacuated the refugees to temporary quarters in Bridgeport's Holy Cross Lutheran Church, a few blocks from Daley's home. Word spread quickly, and almost immediately a crowd of jeering whites was standing outside the church demanding the removal of the black fire victims. "They threatened to break windows in the church and screamed obscenities I can't repeat," Helen Constien, the pastor's wife, said afterward. "They threatened to destroy the church if we didn't get the Negroes out of the building." The Red Cross quickly took the black fire victims out of Bridgeport.[29]

The work of patrolling the South Side's racial borders was often taken care of by gangs like Daley's Hamburg Athletic Club. Because of these gangs' propensity for violence, blacks who walked through neighborhoods like Bridgeport did so at their peril. It was a lesson that black children growing up on the South Side absorbed with their ABC's, but newly arrived blacks who wandered into the area from outside could be caught unaware, often with dire results. In 1918, the poet Langston Hughes made the mistake of walking west across Wentworth Avenue into the heart of the white South Side. It was Hughes's first Sunday in Chicago — he was a high school student at the time — and he "went out walking alone to see what the city looked like." Hughes returned to the black side of Wentworth with black eyes and a swollen jaw, having been beaten up by an unidentified Irish street gang — it is lost to history whether it was the Hamburg Athletic Club — "who said they didn't allow niggers in that neighborhood."[30]

Blacks have lived in the Chicago area longer than any group but Native Americans. "Chicago's first white man," the old Chicago saying has it, "was a Negro." The man in question was Jean Baptiste du Sable, a Haitian black who built a trading post at the mouth of the Chicago River in 1779 to trade with the Potawatomi Indians. The city's black population grew slowly at first: black migration into Illinois was limited until the Civil War by laws that barred blacks, both slave and free, from settling in the state. Despite the legal prohibitions, enough fugitive slaves followed the Underground Railroad to Chicago in the 1840s and 1850s that it came to be known among pro-slavery polemicists as a "sink hole of abolition." By the 1870s, Illinois blacks had the franchise, and in 1876 Chicago sent a black representative to the Illinois legislature. Chicago had 3,700 black residents — 1.2 percent of the total population — when, as legend had it, Mrs. O'Leary's cow kicked over the lantern that started the Great Chicago Fire of 1871. By the turn of the century, blacks still numbered only 30,000. Although they were starting to concentrate in a small "Black Belt" on the South Side, even as late as 1915 blacks were still living in virtually every part of Chicago.[31]

Daley's childhood coincided with one of the nation's most far-reaching social transformations: the Great Migration of blacks from the rural South to the urban North. With the start of World War I, the booming wartime economy in the North faced a severe labor shortage, as the war cut off the flow of European immigrants. Realizing that there was a ready supply of workers in the rural South, where agricultural automation was fast reducing the need for black farm laborers, northern recruiters spread out across the Deep South. Many northern cities were competing for these black workers, but Chicago had a unique advantage. The *Chicago Defender,* the nation's leading black newspaper, was widely read throughout the South, and it painted an especially rosy picture of the high-paying jobs and good life that awaited black migrants in Chicago's factories and slaughterhouses. "MILLIONS TO LEAVE SOUTH," a banner headline in the January 6, 1917, *Chicago Defender* declared. "Northern Invasion Will Start in Spring — Bound for the Promised Land." To many southern blacks living in conditions of extreme poverty and chafing under the oppression of Jim Crow, Chicago and the other large northern cities became a "glorious symbol of hope." Even blues singers from the era got caught up in the spirit:

> I used to have a woman that lived up on a hill
> I used to have a woman that lived up on a hill
> She was crazy 'bout me, ooh well, well, cause
> I worked at the Chicago Mill.[32]

The trip itself was not difficult. The Illinois Central Railroad, dubbed the "Fried Chicken Special" for the homemade lunches carried by the migrants, provided easy passage from New Orleans through the cotton fields of the Mississippi Delta and on up to Chicago. A half-million southern blacks made the journey north between 1916 and 1919 alone, and another million followed in the 1920s. Large numbers of blacks headed to New York, Detroit, and Cleveland, but as one Mississippi migrant recalled, "the mecca was Chicago."[33]

As the city's black population soared, blacks were increasingly concentrated in a distinct ghetto — the South Side's Black Belt. Many of the southern migrants pouring into the Illinois Central Railroad Station clutched the addresses of friends and family who lived in the Black Belt, and those who arrived with no plans were generally steered in that direction. By 1920, the Black Belt — an area roughly bounded by 26th Street to the north, 55th Street to the south, State Street to the west, and Lake Michigan to the east — was home to about 85 percent of the city's blacks. "[S]egregation has been increasing," Swedish sociologist Gunnar Myrdal wrote of Chicago in *An American Dilemma,* his classic survey of American race relations. "[E]ven the upper class Negroes whose ancestors lived in Chicago on terms of almost complete social equality with their white neighbors are now forced into Negro ghettos and are hardly differentiated from the impoverished Negro just arrived from the South." The upside of this racial segregation was that a remarkable African-American world began to take shape on the South Side. The stone-front houses and apartment buildings along once-white avenues like South Parkway and Michigan Boulevard now housed black teachers, lawyers, and other pillars of the black middle class. And the Black Belt's business districts were filled with black-owned stores and black doctors' and lawyers' offices. "Why should Negro doctors and dentists give a damn that most white folks would rather die than let skilled black fingers repair their vital organs?" St. Clair Drake and Horace Cayton wrote in *Black Metropolis,* their 1945 study of Chicago's "Bronzeville." "The Negro masses were gradually learning to trust their own professional men and would some day scorn to enrich white physicians at the expense of their own. Why beg white stores and offices to rescue educated colored girls from service in the white folks' kitchens and factories? Negroes were learning to support their own businesses, and some day colored entrepreneurs would own all the stores and offices in the Black Belt; cash registers and comptometers and typewriters would click merrily under lithe brown fingers." The Black Belt provided Chicago's blacks with a measure of control over their own lives, and some refuge against the unfriendly white city outside its borders. But the sad reality was that it remained badly overcrowded and desperately poor, with high illness and mortality rates; a high percentage of residents on relief; a high crime rate; inadequate recreational facilities; lack of building repairs; accumulated garbage and dirty streets; overcrowded schools; and high rates of police brutality.[34]

In white Chicago, the Great Migration produced a response that ranged from wariness to undisguised panic. The Chicago newspapers ran inflammatory headlines such as "Half a Million Darkies from Dixie Swarm to the North to Better Themselves" and "Negroes Arrive by Thousands — Peril to Health." Articles in the city's three leading papers — the *Tribune,* the *Daily News,* and the *Herald Examiner* — generally overstated the size of the migration, and focused on the new arrivals' purported sickness, criminality, and vice. White Chicagoans worked to prevent the migrants from moving into white neighborhoods. One South Side neighborhood association captured the exclusionary spirit sweeping white Chicago when it declared that "there is nothing in the make-up of a Negro, physically or mentally, which should induce anyone to welcome him as a neighbor." In April 1917, the Chicago Real Estate Board met and — concerned about what officials described as the "invasion of white residence districts by the Negroes" — appointed a Special Committee on Negro Housing to make recommendations. On this committee's recommendation, the board adopted a policy of block-by-block racial segregation, carefully controlled so that "each block shall be filled solidly and . . . further expansion shall be confined to contiguous blocks." Three years later, the board took the further step of voting unanimously to punish by "immediate expulsion" any member who sold property to a black on a block where there were only white owners.[35]

If white Chicago as a whole turned a cold shoulder to the new black arrivals, Daley's Irish kinsmen were particularly unwelcoming. The Irish and blacks had much in common. Ireland's many years of domination at the hands of the British resembled, if not slavery, then certainly southern sharecropping — with Irish farmers working the land and sending rent to absentee landlords in England. The Irish were dominated, like southern blacks, through violence, and lost many of the same civil rights: to vote, to serve on juries, and to marry outside their group. Indeed, after Cromwell's bloody invasion in the mid-1600s, not only were Irish-Catholics massacred in large numbers, but several thousand were sent in chains to the West Indies, where they were sold into slavery. But these similar histories of oppression did not bring Chicago's Irish and blacks together. Much of the early difficulty stemmed from rivalry between two groups relegated to the lowest levels of the social order. As early as 1864, a mob of four hundred Irish dockworkers went on a bloody rampage against a dozen blacks they regarded as taking jobs from unemployed Irishmen. The *Chicago Tribune* — whose WASP management had little affection for Irish-Catholics — argued that this kind of anti-black violence was particularly the province of Irish-Americans. "The Germans never mob colored men from working for whoever may employ them," the *Tribune* declared. "The English, the Scotch, the French, the Scandinavians, never molest peaceable black people. Americans never think of doing such a thing. No other nationality consider themselves 'degraded' by seeing blacks earning their own living by labor."[36]

Nor was the Catholic Church a force for racial tolerance during these tense times. The Church had more reason to fear the black influx than other white institutions. Unlike some faiths, Catholicism is firmly rooted in geography: Catholics' relationship to their Church is determined by the parish in which they reside. Catholics "ascribe sacramental qualities to the neighborhood," one historian has explained, "with the cross on top of the church and the bells ringing each day before Mass as visual and aural reminders of the sacred." Protestants and Jews who saw blacks moving into their neighborhoods could move to the suburbs, taking their houses of worship with them or joining new ones when they settled in. But for Catholics, the ties to the land were greater, and the threat of losing their parish more deeply felt. "[E]verything they have been taught to value, as Catholics and Americans, is perceived as at risk," wrote a reporter in Cicero, describing the racial siege felt by a parish there. "The churches and schools they built would become empty, the neighborhood priests, if any were left, would become missionaries. . . ." In 1917, the same year the Chicago Real Estate Board endorsed new steps to preserve racial segregation, Chicago's Archbishop George Mundelein declared that Saint Monica's Parish would henceforth be reserved for the city's black Catholics. Since Mundelein had in the past opposed "national" parishes on principle, it seemed clear that his intention was to keep the races separate within the Church.[37]

The demographic pressures kept mounting as trainload after trainload of blacks arrived from the South — and it was not clear how much longer these new migrants could be squeezed into the borders of the overcrowded Black Belt. The end of World War I had brought the return of black soldiers, many of whom were less willing to accept racial discrimination back home after they had risked their lives for their country. And Chicago had just reelected William Thompson, a mayor many whites felt they could not trust to keep blacks from moving into their neighborhoods. Republican Thompson's close ties to the black community, and his record number of black appointees, had led resentful whites to dub his City Hall "Uncle Tom's Cabin." The racial backlash growing in white neighborhoods was palpable, and word began to spread in the black community that whites were plotting some kind of bloody attack to reassert their control of the city — perhaps even an invasion of the Black Belt designed to drive blacks out of Chicago.[38]

On July 27, 1919, these tensions exploded when six black teenagers went swimming in the wrong part of Lake Michigan. Young Eugene Williams drifted too close to a "white" beach on the South Side, and drowned after being hit by a rock thrown by a white man standing on the shore. False rumors spread rapidly through both the white and black communities. Blacks reported that a policeman had held a gun on a black crowd while whites threw stones; whites spread word that it was a white swimmer who had drowned after being hit by a rock thrown by a black. Five days of bloody riots ensued, from July 27 to July 31, followed by another week of intermittent violence. White gangs roamed the South Side, attacking blacks indiscriminately, and whites drove through the Black Belt shooting at blacks out of car windows. Black gangs wandered through black neighborhoods, beating up white merchants. In the end, it took the state militia and a driving rainstorm to bring about a tense peace. But before the hostilities had died down, 23 blacks and 15 whites had been killed, and another 537 injured, two-thirds of them black.[39]

The seventeen-year-old Daley was, at the very least, extremely close to the violence. Bridgeport was a major center of riot activity: by one estimate, 41 percent of all the encounters occurred in and around Daley's neighborhood. South Side youth gangs, including the Hamburg Athletic Club, were later found to have been among the primary instigators of the racial violence. "For weeks, in the spring and summer of 1919, they had been anticipating, even eagerly awaiting, a race riot," one study found. "On several occasions, they themselves had endeavored to precipitate one, and now that racial violence threatened to become generalized and unrestrained throughout Chicago, they were set to exploit the chaos." The Chicago Commission on Human Relations eventually concluded that without these gangs "it is doubtful if the riot would have gone beyond the first clash." It is also clear that Joseph McDonough, patron of the Hamburg Athletic Club and later Daley's political mentor, actively incited the white community at the time of the riots. McDonough was quoted in the press saying that blacks had "enough ammunition . . . to last for years of guerrilla warfare," and that he had seen police captains warning white South Side residents: "For God's sake, arm. They are coming; we cannot hold them." At the City Council, McDonough told police chief John J. Garrity that "unless something is done at once I am going to advise my people to arm themselves for protection."[40]

Was Daley himself involved in the bloody work of the 1919 race riots? His defenders have always insisted he was not, arguing that it would have been more in character for him to be attending to "his studies" or "family affairs" while much of the Irish-Catholic youth of Bridgeport were out bashing heads. But Daley's critics have long "pictur[ed] him in the pose of a brick-throwing thug." It strains credulity, they say, for Daley to have played no part in the riots when the Hamburg Athletic Club was so heavily involved — particularly when he was only a few years away from being chosen as the group's president. Daley's close ties to McDonough, who played an inflammatory role, also argue for involvement. Adding to the suspicions, Daley always remained secretive about the riots, and declined to respond to direct questions on the subject. It was a convenient political response that allowed Daley to play both sides of the city's racial divide: whites from the ethnic neighborhoods could believe that Daley was a youthful defender of the South Side color line, while blacks could choose to believe the opposite. Daley's role, or lack of role, is likely lost to history, in part because the police and prosecutors never pursued the white gang members who instigated the violence. At the least, it can be said that Daley was an integral member of a youth gang that played an active role in one of the bloodiest antiblack riots in the nation's history — and that within a few years' time, this same gang would think enough of Daley to select him as its leader.[41]

After graduating from De La Salle in 1919, Daley took a job with Dolan, Ludeman, and Company, a stockyards commission house. Daley once said that as children he and his friends were always drawn to the slaughterhouses, "being city kids fascinated with farm animals." Daley woke at 4:00 A.M. each day to walk from his parents' house to the yards. In the mornings, he moved cattle off trucks and weighed them. In the afternoons, he put his De La Salle skills to work in the firm's offices, writing letters, taking dictation, and handling the books. Later in his career, Daley would regale political audiences with tales of his days as a stockyards "cowboy." He presented himself as something of a South Side John Wayne, probably overstating the amount of derring-do his job required, and certainly omitting the grim brutality of the work.[42]

Bridgeport's traditional employment trinity consisted of the stockyards, government work, and politics — with a select few going off to the priesthood. Daley once said that his ambition early in life had been to become "another P. D. Armour," but it must soon have become clear to him that a career in the stockyards would likely have been low-paying and unsatisfying. Daley could have joined the many Bridgeporters who took patronage jobs with government bodies like the Park District or signed on as police officers. But that route also held little promise and fell far short of the accomplishments his mother had been grooming him for. Politics was another matter entirely. A young man with political ambitions could hardly have started out better than being born in Bridgeport. Bridgeport lay in the heart of the Irish South Side, in the powerful 11th Ward. The 11th was one of Chicago's famous "river wards," the bloc of working-class and slum wards along the Chicago River that were the mainstay of Chicago's Democratic machine. These wards — which were at odds with Chicago's Protestant Republican establishment — regularly produced the machine's margins of victory, and their leaders controlled the Cook County Democratic Organization's Central Committee. Of all the river ward neighborhoods, Bridgeport was in a class of its own: it would soon come to be known as the "mother of mayors." Starting in 1933, this small South Side neighborhood would send three successive residents to City Hall — Edward Kelly, Martin Kennelly, and Daley — who would rule the city for forty-three years. Daley was coming of age just as Bridgeport's machine politicians were rising to new heights of power.

In addition to being lucky in his place of birth, Daley had the right ethnic background for a career in Chicago politics. An old Chicago adage holds that "the Jews own it, the Irish run it, and the blacks live in it." It was an exaggeration on all three counts. But if the Irish did not run Chicago — most of the businesses, banks, and newspapers were in Protestant hands — they did dominate the Democratic machine out of all proportion to their numbers. Chicago was far from the only city to fall under the sway of Irish politicians. As early as

1894, Yankees were decrying the "Irish conquest of our cities," and listing the Irish Democratic party bosses who had seized the reins of municipal power from Boston to San Francisco. It is one of the great puzzles of American political life that almost all of the great political bosses — including New York's William "Boss" Tweed, Kansas City's Tom Pendergast, Boston's James Michael Curley, and, of course, Daley — have been Irish. The Irish had an advantage of timing: they arrived in the United States in one of the earliest migrations, making them one of the most established ethnic groups. They also spoke English and were familiar with America's British-style political system. And unlike Central European and Eastern European immigrants who often carried ethnic rivalries with them from the old country, the Irish had no enemies among their fellow immigrants. "A Lithuanian won't vote for a Pole, and a Pole won't vote for a Lithuanian," said one old-time Chicago politician. "A German won't vote for either of them — but all three will vote for [an Irishman]."[43]

It has also been suggested that the Irish have a particular aptitude for machine politics. Edward Levine, in his classic study *The Irish and Irish Politicians,* argued that the Irish were naturally "given to politics."[44] Daniel Patrick Moynihan pointed out in *Beyond the Melting Pot* that the structure of the political machine, with its rigid hierarchies and respect for seniority, in many ways paralleled "[t]he Irish village . . . a place of stable, predictable social relations in which almost everyone had a role to play, under the surveillance of a stern oligarchy of elders, and in which, on the whole, a person's position was likely to improve with time. Transferred to Manhattan, these were the essentials of Tammany Hall." The Irish disposition toward political machines may also derive from a traditional need for unofficial forms of government. In eighteenth-century Ireland, the penal laws made Catholicism illegal. In response, the Irish created their own informal mechanisms for taking care of their own. It was an outlook that translated easily to America's Protestant-dominated cities. This new land might be filled with employers whose hiring policies bore the hated words "No Irish Need Apply," charity workers who looked down their noses at the Irish poor, and judges who regarded the Irish as an incorrigible race. But the political machine would provide. Moynihan has also argued that disreputable machine practices like vote theft, patronage hiring, and kickbacks — he lumps

them together under the rubric of "indifference to Yankee propri-
eties" — were commonplace in eighteenth-century Ireland. Irish
landed aristocrats sold the votes of their tenants and bought seats in
Parliament long before the Tweeds and Daleys of the New World.
"The great and the wealthy ran Ireland politically like Tammany Hall
in its worst days," noted one scholar. "Had they not sold their own
country for money and titles in the Act of Union with England and,
as one rogue said, thanked God they had a country to sell?"[45]

By the time of Daley's birth, the Irish political ascendancy was already well under way. As early as the 1830s, complaints were being
heard that the city's Irish population wielded too much political
power. Irish influence grew over the next few decades, as immigration from Ireland surged. The Irish suffered a setback in the municipal elections of 1855, when Know-Nothing Party candidate Levi D.
Boone, grandson of frontiersman Daniel Boone, was elected mayor
and his fellow Nativists took control of the City Council. During its
brief reign, Boone's regime passed a law barring immigrants from
city jobs. But Irish political influence soon resumed its steady rise.
After the City Council elections of 1869, the Irish held 15 of the 40
seats. And Irish politicians had an influence beyond their numbers. In
the 1890s, by one estimate, 24 of the 28 most influential aldermen
of the decade were Irish. In 1905, when Daley was three, Chicago
elected Edward Dunne, its first Irish-Catholic mayor. The first mayoral candidate to break through the WASP stranglehold on city government, Dunne was a populist hero in neighborhoods like Daley's.
"It was taking your life in your hands to campaign against Dunne in
Bridgeport or Back of the Yards," a turn-of-the-century mayor once
said.[46]

Daley's route into the Democratic machine was through a Hamburg
Athletic Club connection: the club's sponsor, Bridgeport alderman
Joseph ("Big Joe") McDonough. McDonough was elected alderman
in 1917 at the age of twenty-eight, and ward committeeman the following year. With the two most important ward positions his, Mc-
Donough was indisputably the most powerful Democrat in the 11th
Ward. McDonough, a three-hundred-pound former Villanova University football hero, was a colorful neighborhood institution, known
for eating an entire chicken for lunch. McDonough ran a saloon,

owned a real estate firm, and served as vice president of an auto-mobile sales company. The clout he held as a result of his politi-cal offices contributed to the bottom lines of each business. But he was beloved in the 11th Ward for taking care of his people: one depression-era Christmas, McDonough single-handedly passed out 5,600 baskets of food for the needy. Bridgeport was filled with young men who would have jumped at the chance to apprentice them-selves to the powerful McDonough. No doubt some of these men were more intelligent, better educated, and more charismatic than Da-ley. But these were not the important qualities for a budding machine politician. Daley was a plain-speaking, Irish-Catholic son of Bridge-port, who had proven through his presidency of the Hamburg Athletic Club that he could earn the respect of his peers. He also benefited from the premium the machine placed on the traditional vir-tues: discretion, sobriety, plodding hard work, fitting in, and a willing-ness to follow orders. McDonough selected Daley to be his personal assistant, appointed him to serve as a precinct captain, and invited him to work in the 11th Ward Organization. Daley worked as a pre-cinct captain in the mayoral election of 1919 and the presidential elec-tion of 1920.[47]

The Chicago machine that Daley signed on with was a remarkable political organization. It was formally the Cook County Democratic Organization, reflecting its true sphere of influence — beyond the Chicago city limits and into the surrounding suburban ring, which made up the rest of Cook County. At the top of the machine was the county chairman, or party boss, who was elected by ward com-mitteemen from the city's fifty wards, along with a smaller number of committeemen from the suburban townships. The machine was as rigidly hierarchical as the Catholic Church that most of its members belonged to. The county chairman presided like a secular cardinal, and beneath him were ward committeemen — the political equiva-lent of parish priests — who controlled their own geographical realms. Each of the fifty wards had its own Democratic ward organi-zation, with its own headquarters, budget, slate of candidates, and army of workers. Daley was one of more than three thousand precinct captains, spread out across the fifty city wards, who were re-sponsible for the machine's performance at the block level. Like the Catholic Church, the machine offered its members not just a structure, but a worldview and a moral code. One academic who studied the Chicago machine concluded that it was guided by what he called the "regular ethic." Among the tenets of the regular Democrat's creed: (1) Be faithful to those above you in the hierarchy, and repay those who are faithful to you; (2) Back the whole machine slate, not individual candidates or programs; (3) Be respectful of elected officials and party leaders; (4) Never be ashamed of the party, and defend it proudly; (5) Don't ask questions; (6) Stay on your own turf, and keep out of conflicts that don't concern you; (7) Never be first, since innovation brings with it risk; and (8) Don't get caught. Another scholar of Chicago politics summed up the machine ethic more concisely in a book title: *Don't Make No Waves, Don't Back No Losers.*[48]

The chairman of the Cook County Central Committee held the ultimate power, but it was ward committeemen like McDonough who did most of the machine's day-to-day work. Ward committeemen slated, or picked, candidates for ward offices from alderman down — and like McDonough, they not infrequently ended up as both ward committeeman and alderman. They were also in charge of distributing patronage to precinct captains and other ward workers, a difficult, sensitive, and time-consuming task. "A committeeman gets a phone call and is told, 'I've got three crossing guards, one sanitation worker,'" said a committeeman with the Cook County Democratic Organization. "'Do you want them?' 'How soon do you have to know?' he asks. 'I'll call you tomorrow.' You call back and say, 'I want two crossing guards. I can't use three. The sanitation worker — yes, I want that. Here are the names.' The girl says, 'Send them in to get their yellow slips,' and they go in to get their yellow slips." Being ward committeeman could be lucrative work, particularly for those who had law firms or insurance agencies on the side. Benjamin Lewis, a 24th Ward committeeman who was shot to death in the early 1960s under mysterious circumstances, once boasted that the post was worth $50,000 a year in insurance work alone. In exchange for his power and opportunity for enrichment, a committeeman was responsible for ensuring that his ward met the vote totals that the machine boss expected. Ward committeemen who failed to deliver on election day risked being "vised," as the machine lingo put it, or fired, and replaced by someone who would do better.[49]

Daley's new position of precinct captain made him a soldier in Mc-
Donough's 11th Ward army, and put him in charge of a unit of about
four hundred to five hundred voters. Precinct captains were the
prime practitioners of the retail politics that was the stock in trade of
the old urban machines. A precinct captain was expected to form a
close personal relationship with every voter in his territory; the machine relied on these personal contacts — rather than the strength of
its candidates in a given year — to win. "I never take leaflets or mention issues or conduct rallies in my precinct," a Chicago precinct
captain once explained. "After all, this is a question of personal
friendship between me and my neighbors." To forge these connections, precinct captains were expected to be out in their neighborhoods virtually every night, attending community meetings, putting
in hours in the ward office, or visiting voters in their homes. "I
found that those who related to people and were sincere in trying to
help their neighbors in the community turned out to be the best
captains," one ward committeeman once said. Jake Arvey, committeeman from the heavily Jewish 24th Ward, required his precinct
captains to belong to a synagogue or church, and to fraternal organizations like the Knights of Columbus or B'Nai Brith. "Sure, I was
looking for votes," Arvey says. "But, in the process, I made them
charity-minded, civic-minded, culture-minded, and sensitive to the
needs of other people." In his last mayoral campaign in 1975, Daley
delivered a tribute to the underappreciated precinct captain. He "is as
honest as the rest of us and he's a better neighbor than most of us,
for partisan reasons," Daley said. "He has solicitude for the welfare of
the family on his block, especially if they are a large family with de-
pendable political loyalties. He gets your broken-down uncle into the
county hospital. . . . He's always available when you're in trouble."[50]

As a young precinct captain, Daley spent countless hours each
week in one of Bridgeport's great institutions: the 11th Ward headquarters. Daley's new world had the feel of a Hibernian social club.
One non-Irish Bridgeport native recalled how he felt when he stopped
by for a political event. "In a short time the office was packed with
precinct captains and workers — all Irish," he says. "Outside of one
Italian and myself, I saw nothing but red hair, freckles, and green eyes.
I met an old high school chum who is now a helper in a precinct and
who works at City Hall. I asked him how one can get into the orga-

nization. He smiled and said, 'The first thing you have to do is be Irish!'" During election season, the 11th Ward was a campaign war room, where strategy was mapped out, precinct canvasses were analyzed, and campaign literature was handed out for distribution throughout the ward. The rest of the year, it functioned as a combination of constituent-service office and community center.[51]

In the 11th Ward offices, and every other ward office across the city, the machine dispensed favors systematically in exchange for political support. Priority treatment went to political and financial backers of the machine, and to those who came with a referral from their precinct captain — the kind of solid citizen that ward workers referred to as "one of our people." But since the granting of favors was a form of outreach to the community, any ward resident not known to be actively hostile to the machine was eligible for help. Complaints about city services, like missing stop signs or irregular garbage pickups, were easily handled. If a constituent had his water cut off, a single phone call from the ward office to the water department could get it restored. The ward organization had volunteer lawyers available in the evenings to provide free legal advice on everything from immigration paperwork to criminal law problems. Precinct captains like Daley could find summer jobs for neighborhood youth, arrange scholarships to the University of Illinois, and even get constituents hospital care or glass eyes. "Everybody needs a favor sometimes, but some people are too dumb to ask for it," a saloonkeeper-alderman from the 43rd Ward once reflected. "So I say to my captains, 'If you notice a hole on the sidewalk in front of a fellow's house, call him a week before election and ask him if he would like it fixed. It could never do any harm to find out.'"[52]

Machine politicians were adept at taking credit for every favor they dispensed — so voters would remember on election day. When machine aldermen contacted city agencies for their constituents, they requested written responses. Letters agreeing to take the requested action were sent to the alderman, so he could in turn pass the good news on to the voter. Letters of refusal went directly from the agency to the constituent. Machine officials often took more than their share of credit. When one alderman got a stop sign installed at a dangerous intersection, he sent a letter to every registered voter in his ward claiming that it was the machine's doing — even though it began with local block associations, who had conducted a petition drive for the sign. Sometimes the machine took credit less formally. If the organization succeeded in intervening with the water department and getting a voter's water restored, one machine operative says, "on election day the precinct captain would ask you about your water."[53]

Working as a precinct captain in the 11th Ward organization, Daley got an ideal introduction to the craft of machine politics. In the weeks before an election, the precinct captains were expected to canvass each home in their precinct at least twice to find out which way every voter was leaning — an early forerunner of the opinion poll. A captain was expected to be able to predict his vote almost exactly; missing by more than ten or so votes could result in a reprimand. A few days before the election, the precinct captain reported the results of the canvass to his ward committeeman. The committeeman, in turn, delivered the aggregated numbers for his ward to the machine boss. In addition to giving the machine a preview of how things looked for the election, the precinct-by-precinct canvass allowed captains to familiarize themselves with the individual circumstances of every voter. A captain could find out which of his voters were wavering and needed further persuasion, which needed transportation to the polls, and which would need to be reminded to vote. He could also learn which voters were determined to vote Republican, and therefore should not be encouraged to vote. A captain's machinations to maximize the Democratic vote in his precinct could be quite elaborate. Just before the 1939 mayoral election, an Italian family with six voting-age members moved into Arvey's 24th Ward. The precinct captain paid them regular visits, discussing over red wine how they planned to vote. "Six votes is an awful lot," noted Arvey. But the captain soon realized that the head of the household was related to a leading Chicago Republican. When the captain asked him to vote in the Democratic primary, he refused. "I can't do that!" he said. "My cousin is a Republican committeeman. How would it be if I voted in the Democratic primary?" After the captain pursued the family for a month, a compromise was arrived at. The man and his wife, who shared a last name with the cousin, could vote Republican. The man's two daughters and sons-in-law, who had different names, would vote the straight Democratic ticket.[54]

On election day, precinct workers often turned to more blatant forms of persuasion. Precinct captains handed out turkeys, nylons, and cash in exchange for votes. A captain from the poor West Side 27th Ward was once convicted of buying votes for one dollar a head. In the South Side 4th Ward, a newspaper reporter observing the voting caught a precinct worker handing out bags of groceries. "We gotta get these voters out any way we can," the worker explained. On skid row, precinct captains often lured winos with free liquor. The fact that bars were legally closed on election day worked in the machine's favor: many alcoholics considered the few minutes it took to vote a small price to pay to make the shakes go away. Clory Bryant, who ran for alderman in the early 1960s against the machine's candidate, saw the effect of the machine's generosity toward voters firsthand. "I had asked a neighbor of mine was she going to vote for me," Bryant says. "As a matter of fact, I says, 'I know you'll vote for me.' And she said, 'No, I'm afraid I can't, because my alderman always gives me a Christmas tree for my vote. And I know you can't afford to go around buying these many trees.'" Bryant did not get her neighbor's vote. The machine also did favors for neighborhood organizations that could help it win votes. The West Side 25th Ward Organization used to give regular donations to the thirty-five churches in the ward. One election day, the ward boss arrived at a polling place located in the basement of St. Roman's Church. The priest was handing out coffee and doughnuts. Asked what he was doing, the priest responded, "What the hell do you think I'm doing? I'm trying to get some Democratic votes." Ward organizations also wielded the stick in order to round up votes. Captains in black precincts frequently told voters they would lose their government benefits if they failed to vote a straight Democratic ticket. "Every welfare recipient is afraid to oppose the wishes of the precinct captain," the pastor of a Mennonite church once complained. "Everyone living in public housing is afraid. They have been told that the machine alderman is the one who ensures them living quarters." It was not an idle threat. Welfare programs were so rule-bound at the time, and enforcement was so arbitrary, that a determined precinct captain often could get a voter's benefits cut off if he really wanted to. Saying hello to the precinct captain at the polls every year also came in handy when a public-housing recipient's refrigerator or stove broke down.[55]

*   *   *

In addition to his position as precinct captain, Daley was now working for McDonough in his City Council office. The job of "secretary" to an alderman was not glamorous. Daley was one of a corps of glorified gofers. But McDonough was a garrulous, old-style politician who liked to spend most of the workday at the saloon or the racetrack. He was more than willing to have the hardworking and detail-oriented Daley plow through the draft bills and proposed budgets that regularly crossed his desk. Working at the City Council, particularly for such a lackadaisical alderman, gave Daley a chance to observe city government up close. It also put Daley in the political mix, letting him make personal connections with machine politicians from across the city. Daley's work for McDonough fit a pattern he followed throughout his career: he apprenticed himself to powerful men and made himself indispensable by taking on dull but necessary jobs. "I'll tell you how he made it," Daley's friend-turned-rival Benjamin Adamowski once said. "He made it through sheer luck and by attaching himself to one guy after another and then stepping over them."[56]

In 1923, Daley began taking pre-law and law school classes four nights a week at DePaul University. Getting a law degree while juggling work and political responsibilities would ultimately take Daley more than a decade. "Daley was a nice fellow, very quiet, a hard worker, and always neatly dressed," a fellow student, who would later be appointed a judge by Daley, recalled. "He never missed a class and always got there on time. But there was nothing about him that would make him stand out, as far as becoming something special in life. Even then, he misused the language so that you noticed it. He had trouble expressing himself and his grammar wasn't good." But Daley succeeded in law school by the same plodding persistence he brought to every task he undertook. "I always went out dancing every night, but Dick went home to study his law books," recalled a friend from youth who later went on to head the plumbers' union. "He would never stop in the saloon and have a drink."[57]

Daley's career progressed as his patron, McDonough, moved up through the political ranks. In 1930, the machine slated McDonough for county treasurer, and when he was elected he brought Daley along as his deputy. As county treasurer, McDonough was even less conscientious than he had been as an alderman. The dry financial work of the county treasurer's office offered McDonough even less reason than the City Council had to remain at his desk. While his boss frequented racetracks and speakeasies, Daley applied the skills he had acquired in the De La Salle counting rooms to the county treasury. In his new job, Daley learned the intricacies of local government law and municipal finance, and how to work a budget. And he saw firsthand how a government office operates when it is inextricably tied to a political machine. He learned how the machine larded the county treasurer's office with patronage appointees who were hired for their political work. And he saw how it ensured that county funds were deposited with bankers who contributed to the campaigns of machine candidates.[58]

While Daley was toiling away at night law school, he met Eleanor Guilfoyle at a neighborhood ball game. Her brother Lloyd, a friend of Daley's, made the introduction. "Sis," as she would always be known, came from a large Irish-Catholic family in the neighboring Southwest Side community of Canaryville. She had graduated from Saint Mary High School and was working as a secretary at a paint company and caring for an invalid mother when Daley asked her out on their first date, to a White Sox game. "We had a very happy courtship," Sis once recalled. "I used to meet him after law school and go to the opera." "Of course I knew Dick was bound to succeed — even when I first met him," she would say later. "Anyone who would work in the stockyards all day long, then go to school at night was determined to get ahead." Daley pursued marriage as he pursued everything else in his life — carefully, even ploddingly. Their courtship lasted for six years, until he had finished law school and had begun to establish himself professionally. The couple married on June 17, 1936, when Daley was thirty-four and Eleanor was twenty-eight. It was three years after his graduation, and the same year that he entered into a law partnership with an old friend, William Lynch, the politically minded son of a Bridgeport precinct captain.[59]

A House for All Peoples

The Democratic machine that Daley had joined was largely the invention of a Bohemian immigrant named Anton Cermak. Cermak was born in 1873, outside Prague, and came to America at the age of one. His family settled in Braidwood, a coal town sixty miles southwest of Chicago. As a teenager, Cermak headed for the big city and settled in Lawndale, a West Side neighborhood where Russian and Polish Jews and Bohemian Christians lived together in relative harmony. Cermak supported himself as a peddler, selling kindling from a horse-drawn wagon, but he was drawn to politics and quickly showed an aptitude for it. Cermak was a leader of his tightly knit Czech community, and with its backing was elected to the state House of Representatives in 1902. He was also helped early in his career by another important constituency: supporters of alcohol. In turn-of-the-century Chicago, the battle between Prohibitionists and "wets" was the defining political schism. Cermak's zealous anti-Prohibition advocacy quickly earned him the nickname the "voice of liquor." As he rose to greater power, the liquor interests — notably a powerful saloonkeepers' trade association — always remained at the heart of his political base.[1]

The most important thing big liquor did for Cermak — more important than providing financial and electoral support — was to introduce him to ethnic coalition politics. Like many divisive political issues, Prohibition was a proxy for deeper social insecurities. The anti-liquor cause drew its strongest support from native-born Americans, and many Chicago immigrants regarded it as a thinly veiled assault on them and their way of life. Chicago's badly fragmented immigrant community — divided by language, religion, and in many cases Old World enmities — united in opposition to this blue-blooded assault on their neighborhood saloons. In 1906, the German-language newspaper *Abendpost* brought Chicago's disparate immigrant groups together into a pro-liquor coalition. This alliance eventually grew into the United Societies for Local Self-Government, a multi-ethnic lobbying group. By 1919, United Societies had more than one thousand ethnic organizations and one-quarter of a million people affiliated with it. Cermak was the group's secretary and its leading spokesman, which put him at the forefront of the most powerful pan-ethnic political coalition Chicago had ever experienced. Cermak had by now begun to shift his own political focus away from Springfield and back to Chicago. In 1922, after two decades in the state legislature, he was elected president of the Cook County Board of Commissioners. It was a powerful post, as was reflected in the nickname he soon acquired — "the mayor of Cook County."[2]

Cermak had discovered the power of ethnic coalition-building at a particularly opportune moment. By 1930, the city's population had soared to 3.3 million and its ethnic composition was changing rapidly. Immigrants were flooding into the city, and white Protestant families had begun fleeing to the surrounding suburbs. Nearly two-thirds of Chicago's population was now either foreign-born or born to immigrant parents. Chicago's political power was starting to shift from a Protestant monolith to a more eclectic assortment of ethnic groups, many divided from each other by language and religion. More than ever, there was a need for a leader who could unite these groups into a coherent political force. Cermak, fresh from his success with United Societies, decided to build a political organization to serve as a "house for all peoples." He began with a solid base in his own Czech community, and had strong ties to the city's Germans. He also was on good terms with the city's Jews — as president of the Cook County Board, he had created a kosher section of the county poorhouse — and enlisted Moe Rosenberg and Jake Arvey of the 24th Ward organization to the cause. Ethnic coalition building serves many larger purposes including, as political scientists have noted, the important work of managing conflict among competing groups. But in Cermak's case, panethnic politics also served his own personal ambitions. As a member of one of the city's smaller ethnic groups, he would not have gone far simply as a Bohemian politician. Cermak's "house for all peoples" gave him the opportunity to appeal for the votes of all of Chicagoans. The genius of Cermak's approach became clear in 1928, when Democratic Party chairman George Brennan died. Brennan had been heir to the city's old Irish Democratic organization, and all other things being equal, another Irishman would likely have been chosen to succeed him. But Cermak drew on his multiethnic support to wrest away the party machinery from the Irish. The first real test of Cermak's new style of politics came in 1931, when he accepted the Democratic nomination to run for mayor.[3]

Chicago's Republican mayor, William Hale Thompson, was a colorful combination of populist, political boss, and friend to the city's criminal element. "Big Bill" Thompson was born in 1867 into Boston's Brahmin aristocracy. His family moved to Chicago a year after his birth, and his father quickly built a real estate fortune. Thompson had an itinerant youth, running away from home to avoid attending Yale University. When Thompson returned to Chicago, he discovered politics, running for alderman in 1900 and winning. Two years later, he was elected to a seat on the influential Cook County Board. In time, he attracted the attention of leaders of Chicago's fledgling Republican machine, who were looking for a mayoral candidate. He "may not be too much on brains," an influential Republican declared, "but he gets to the people." Thompson beat a reform candidate in the 1915 Republican mayoral primary, and with strong support from Germans, Swedes, and blacks went on to win the general election. He brought a quirky charisma with him to City Hall. Chicago's new mayor thought nothing of putting aside municipal business to organize an expedition to photograph a reputed tree-climbing fish. Thompson's most enduring contribution to Chicago politics, however, was the introduction of large-scale patronage and graft to city government. The newspapers wasted little time in coining a new word — "Thompsonism" — for the corruption and scandal that had settled on City Hall. Thompson's patronage-backed Republican machine fast became a formidable force in both city and state politics. But its influence was short-lived: the defections started among middle-class Chicagoans, who were becoming disaffected over reports of corruption in government. Thompson also lost working-class voters by his support of Prohibition, which more than 80 percent of Chicagoans opposed in a 1919 referendum. In 1923, after two terms, Thompson decided not to run again, and he was succeeded by a Democrat. After four years out of office, Thompson was elected to a third term in 1927, but just barely, winning 50.4 percent of the vote.[4]

The Thompson-Cermak race got nasty quickly. Thompson had long been haunted by rumors linking him to Al Capone and other prominent Chicago gangsters. During the election, the rumors gained strength, after one of Thompson's top city officials, a friend of Capone's, was indicted for conspiring with merchants to cheat the people out of $54 million by the use of short weights. Despite his own scandals, Thompson accused Cermak of being in league with bootleggers and gamblers, and charged that he had "saved six million out of a $10,000 salary." But Thompson saved his most pointed attacks for Cermak's humble origins. It would be an embarrassment, Chicago's WASP mayor declared, for the city to be led by "Pushcart Tony," an immigrant who had gotten his start selling firewood. "He don't like my name," Cermak replied. "It's true I didn't come over on the Mayflower, but I came over as soon as I could." With the ethnic changes that had overtaken Chicago, Cermak's side was where the votes were. He ended up winning, but Thompson's critics felt vindicated when, after Cermak's death, one of his many safe-deposit boxes was discovered to hold $1,466,250 in cash.[5]

The victorious Cermak continued shoring up his "house for all peoples." As mayor, he reached out to the city's Irish, an important political constituency that was still smoldering over being ousted from political power by a Bohemian. Cermak tapped Irish-Catholic politician Pat Nash to succeed him as chairman of the Democratic Party. The move was well received among Irish Democrats, but it was largely for show: Cermak continued to exercise the powers of Democratic boss. The one group that continued to resist joining the Democratic machine was Chicago's black population, who traditionally voted Republican, the party of Lincoln, the emancipator. In the 1931 mayoral race, the five wards, out of fifty, that went for Thompson all had substantial black populations.[6]

Cermak moved into City Hall early — on April 9, 1931, two days after the election and thirteen days before his inauguration — and undertook a systematic decimation of the Republican patronage army. He fired up to three thousand temporary workers, many of them blacks who had done precinct work for Thompson, and declared war on the South Side gambling and prostitution rackets that had generously supported black Republican elected officials. The Black Belt was turned upside down in the early months of Cermak's mayoralty, as the police swooped in. Cermak admitted freely that he was turning on the heat because the black community had made the mistake of throwing its lot in with the Republicans. "On Friday and Saturday nights, the police stations were crowded with Negroes that had been arrested in gambling raids," recalled a longtime Republican ward committeeman. "And when the aldermen would try to intercede for them, they would be told, 'The minute you people find out there's something besides the Republican Party, come back and talk to us.' That was one way to make them Democrats, and he did." At the very least, it was a start. The real black political realignment was still a few years away, and it would be triggered by national, not local, politics.[7]

Cermak maintained that the new organization he was building could be a seemingly paradoxical entity: a reform-minded political machine. "The period of the backroom . . . is gone," he told reporters. "From now on everybody in the organization will have a voice in its management." Cermak believed hard work and strict discipline could replace the corruption that usually propped up political machines. One of his favorite aphorisms was that "only lazy precinct captains steal votes." Cermak founded a party newspaper, the *Public Service Leader,* that printed each ward organization's performance in the most recent election. The *Leader* claimed it had developed a "scientific mathematically exact grading of the vote-getting machinery in each of Chicago's fifty wards." The paper's analysis considered vote margins, turnout percentages, and percentage of straight Democratic voters. Cermak's rigorous attention to detail injected into the machine, from its earliest days, an obsession with the smallest elections and with turning out every possible vote.[8]

Cermak's work in building the Chicago machine was cut short by an incident that instantly made him a footnote to American presidential history. Not long after his election as mayor, Cermak contracted dysentery from sewage that had seeped into the luxury hotel he was living in on South Michigan Avenue, and he traveled to Miami Beach to recuperate. On February 15, 1933, Franklin D. Roosevelt stopped in town on his way back from a fishing trip in the Bahamas. Cermak showed up at a Roosevelt appearance to pay his respects. When he was done delivering remarks from an open car, Roosevelt motioned Cermak over to talk. Their conversation had barely begun when an Italian immigrant named Giuseppe Zangara fired a revolver in Roosevelt's direction, missing him but hitting Cermak and four other bystanders. Cermak, who fell into Roosevelt's arms, had stopped a bullet that could have struck the president-elect. According to Cermak lore, as he sped to the hospital, he said to Roosevelt: "I'm glad it was me instead of you." Most people who knew Cermak, however, deemed the sentiment out of character. A sometime journalist named John Dienhart, who traveled with Cermak and advised him on public relations, later said that he made up the quote. "Jesus," Dienhart said. "I couldn't very well have put out a story that Tony would have wanted it the other way around."[9]

Before Cermak had succumbed to his bullet wounds in a Miami Beach hospital, the jockeying was already under way back in Chicago to succeed him as mayor. The obvious choice was Nash, the powerful alderman Cermak had named to take over the Democratic machine. But the seventy-year-old Nash pronounced himself too old and took himself out of the running. Jake Arvey, alderman from the mighty 24th Ward, was another possibility. But with Henry Horner, another Jew, having just been elected governor, the ethnic politics were wrong. "Nash thought and I agreed with him," Arvey said later, that "to have a governor of Illinois Jewish, and a mayor of Chicago Jewish, at that time would have been rubbing it in to the Irish." In fact, with Cermak out of the way, the Irish political bosses were more than ready to put an Irishman back in City Hall. Nash had a candidate in mind, a good friend and Bridgeport native named Edward Kelly, who held the improbable position of chief engineer for the Metropolitan Sanitary District. But there was a problem: Illinois law provided that when the mayor left office the City Council had to appoint someone from its own ranks to fill the vacancy. Nash got around the restriction by pushing new legislation through in Springfield that made nonaldermen eligible to be selected.[10]

With the backing of Nash and the Democratic machine, Kelly was named mayor of Chicago by the City Council. Kelly, the eldest of nine children of a policeman who had emigrated from Ireland during the Civil War, had dropped out of school after the fifth grade to help support his family. He had worked at an array of menial jobs, including a $4-a-week stint carrying beer buckets on long poles to men on lunch break at the Armour cannery. But Kelly found his calling when, at age eighteen, he took a job with the Chicago Sanitary District. He first assignment was chopping down trees along the canal with an ax. Forty years later, he had risen to chief engineer, and presided over a vast municipal agency. The tall, athletically handsome Kelly had managed to do some good in his obscure but influential position. Most notably, he had presided over the transformation of Grant Park into a lush expanse of green in the middle of downtown, earning himself the nickname "Father of the Lakefront." But what brought Kelly to Nash's attention was not his impressive rise from poverty, or his accomplishments in government. Nash's family owned a sewer contracting firm, and it had done well under Kelly's regime at the Sanitary District. Arrangements of this kind had made Nash wealthy — he had one of the ten highest incomes in Chicago in 1925. Kelly had also prospered, despite the handicap of earning only a civil-service salary. From 1926 to 1928, Kelly somehow brought in an income of $450,000, a windfall that did not escape the notice of his political foes. During a tough primary campaign in 1936, an opponent responded to Kelly's sneer that he was not a politician that "if to amass a huge fortune on a modest salary is to be a politician, I am not a politician."[11]

The rise of Edward Kelly at first looked like a significant setback to Daley's own political hopes. Daley's political standing depended on his ward committeeman and boss, McDonough, but McDonough's best connections had died along with Cermak. It was unclear where McDonough, and therefore Daley, would fit into the new Kelly-Nash regime that now controlled the city. McDonough was despondent about the recent turn of events, and began to wonder if he had a future in politics. But thirty-one-year-old Daley kept up his hard work for McDonough and continued to plug away at his law school studies.

Kelly turned out to be a surprise as mayor. Nash had selected him because of his willingness to hand out sweetheart deals and patronage jobs, and he more than lived up to Nash's expectations in this regard. But Kelly was also a progressive political force during troubled times. His fourteen years in office included some of the worst years of the Great Depression. The national economic crisis caused thousands of people to board the railroad cars that passed through devastated industrial towns and dust bowl farm regions, heading to Chicago in search of a livelihood. In the face of this influx, the city's relief expenditures soared from $11 million in 1931 to $35 million in 1932, and Chicago began to teeter on the edge of bankruptcy. A "Hooverville" sat on the edge of the Loop, with streets named "Prosperity Road" and "Hard Times Avenue." Kelly responded by passionately embracing the New Deal. "Roosevelt," he liked to say, "is my religion." Kelly forged a strong relationship with the White House, and worked with Washington bureaucrats to bring desperately needed federal jobs to Chicago. Of course, Kelly and Nash gained as well: the federal jobs added considerably to the supply of patronage positions available for the machine faithful. The nation's economic hard times ended up being good for the Chicago machine. "They had more to work with," longtime Republican committeeman Bunnie East recalled. "They had more jobs, more money, and they had a Democratic president . . . [who] was very kind to them as far as government jobs and government contracts were concerned."[12]

Chicago's Democratic machine was now at a crossroads. With Kelly and Nash in charge, it seemed that Cermak's "house for all peoples" might revert to an old-style Irish political machine. But Kelly and Nash decided instead to continue in the Cermak tradition, making a point of filling important offices with Poles, Germans, and Jews. Kelly was also succeeding in one area where Cermak had done poorly: integrating black Chicagoans into the machine. While Cermak had relied primarily on sticks, Kelly held out an array of carrots. Kelly made a point of going to Soldier Field for the annual Wilberforce–Tuskegee football game — a red-letter day on black Chicago's calendar — and he banned the movie *Birth of a Nation,* a glorification of the early days of the Ku Klux Klan. Kelly also spoke to blacks in terms they could identify with: the millionaire mayor received enthusiastic responses from South Side audiences when he recalled the days when his mother scrubbed floors in the mansions of Hyde Park.[13]

Mayor Kelly's appeal to Chicago blacks was based on substance as well as symbolism. In 1943, he established Chicago's Commission on Human Relations, and three years later he set up a civil rights unit in the corporation counsel's office. Kelly also took pioneering stands in favor of equal opportunity in housing and education. When Kelly learned that branch schools had been set up to separate white and black pupils in Morgan Park, a Far South Side neighborhood, he ordered the Board of Education to end the segregation. He stood his ground even after white students staged a walk-out. The *Chicago Defender* lauded Kelly for his stand in favor of school integration, declaring that the mayor had earned "the respect and confidence of every citizen of every color and creed whose mind is not blinded by hate, prejudice, and bigotry." At the same time, Kelly offered an olive branch to the black gambling operations that had been Cermak's special target. The same police that had conducted aggressive raids under the previous mayoral administration now had firm orders to hold back. The new, warmer relations between gambling operations and City Hall were reflected in a 1934 *Chicago Daily News* report that the machine was now taking in $1 million a month from illicit vice, and that precinct captains, particularly in the black wards, were running gambling houses.[14]

Kelly's outreach to Chicago's black community came against the backdrop of a major party realignment occurring in black America. The Great Depression pushed many Americans into the Democratic camp: Franklin D. Roosevelt was elected in 1932 with roughly 60 percent of the vote, and he swept Democrats into office with him at every level. Although blacks were among the nation's worst off citizens, many were reluctant to abandon the party of Lincoln for a Democratic Party in which the segregationist Dixiecrat wing was so strong. In Roosevelt's landslide 1932 victory, blacks gave him only 32 percent of their votes. Once in office, though, Roosevelt quickly began to win black voters over with his evident compassion for the victims of hard times. His New Deal initiatives — the NRA, the CCC, the WPA, and other programs designed to get Americans working again — earned him considerable gratitude in the black community. Roosevelt was regarded as a kind of secular savior by many blacks — "Let Jesus lead you and Roosevelt feed you!" was one black preacher's rallying cry. In 1936, Roosevelt took 49 percent of the black vote, and four years later he won 52 percent. This black movement toward the Democratic Party was helped along by the fact that the party was beginning to break with its southern wing and express greater support for civil rights. In 1944, after Roosevelt endorsed equal opportunity for all races and an end to the poll tax, his national share of the black vote jumped to 64 percent. In 1948, after Hubert Humphrey's civil rights platform was adopted at the Democratic National Convention and President Truman issued his order integrating the armed forces, 75 percent of black America voted Democratic at the presidential level.[15]

In large part because of Mayor Kelly's efforts, Chicago blacks began to defect to the Democratic Party slightly ahead of the national trend. In 1934, the Democratic machine embarked on a mission of virtual lèse majesté, challenging the South Side's legendary three-term Republican congressman, Oscar DePriest. The first black elected to Congress since 1901, DePriest was a heroic figure to blacks across the country. He battled tirelessly against segregation and in support of black institutions such as Howard University. But for all of DePriest's popularity and good works, it was becoming increasingly hard to be a black Republican. It also hurt him that he was a loyal party man, who regularly voted against the New Deal programs that were so popular with his constituents. In an outcome that marked a sea change in the city's politics, a black Democrat, Arthur Mitchell, took DePriest's seat. Any doubts that the movement toward the Democrats was real were dispelled the following year when Kelly ran for reelection. Days before the voting, black Republicans turned out for a massive pro-Kelly rally in Congressional Hall. "Lincoln is dead," a former Republican alderman told the crowd. "You don't need no ghost from the grave to tell you what to do when you go to the polls Tuesday." The Democratic ticket, with Kelly at the top, swept the black South Side, taking more than 80 percent of the vote.[16]

This political realignment led to the birth of a remarkable political organization: the black submachine. This new force in Chicago politics was the product of two contrary instincts on race. The Kelly-Nash machine believed firmly in Cermak's pragmatic vision of serving as a "house for all peoples." But at the same time, the reality was that Chicago in the 1930s and 1940s was not prepared for a truly integrated political machine. Chicago was not as racially divided as the Jim Crow South, but in many ways it came close. As late as 1946, a restaurant that served customers of both races on an equal basis was so rare that one was given an award by the Chicago Commission on Human Relations. Marshall Field, the prominent downtown department store, had a policy against hiring black employees until 1953. The black submachine balanced these competing interests in inclusion and separation. It was a fully functioning part of the larger Chicago Democratic machine, delivering votes for the machine ticket and receiving political patronage in return. But it was also a world apart, headed by its own black political boss, who supervised legions of black ward committeemen, precinct captains, and election-day workers — and who reported to the boss of the citywide white machine.[17]

The first and only boss of the black submachine was William Levi Dawson. Dawson was born in Albany, Georgia, on April 26, 1886, a son of the segregated South and grandson of a slave. Dawson's father, a barber, had a sister who was raped by a white man. When Dawson's father retaliated against the man, the family was forced to leave Georgia. Dawson attended Fisk University, graduating in 1909 magna cum laude. During the summers, he earned his tuition and board by working as a bellhop and porter in Chicago, at the train station and at the old South Side Chicago Beach Hotel. After college, Dawson served in World War I with the 365th Infantry in France, where he was wounded and gassed during the Meuse-Argonne campaign. After the war, he returned to Chicago, where he attended law school. He joined the bar in 1920 and soon began practicing law.[18]

Dawson was, in physical terms, an unprepossessing man. He had a wooden leg and a pencil-thin mustache, and he looked enough like a political hack to seem right at home behind a battered desk in the Near South Side's 2nd Ward political office. But Dawson was far more intelligent and widely read than most of the Chicago machine politicians he spent his life working among. He could recite classical poetry from memory, and he was a jazz aficionado whose collection of Jelly Roll Morton, Count Basie, and Duke Ellington albums was among the finest on the South Side. But Dawson's true genius lay in his mastery of human nature. "God gave me the key to understand men and to know them," Dawson once said. "If you learn how to handle men . . . you can get what you want."[19] As far as Dawson rose — and he would for years be the nation's most powerful black elected official — he never lost touch with the common man. Dawson spoke the language of the black South Side, most of whose residents had made the same journey he had up from the rural South. "Walk along, little children," Dawson used to say when he wrapped up a speech at his headquarters on Indiana Avenue, "and don't get weary, 'cause there's a big camp meeting at the end of the road."[20]

Dawson began his political career as a Republican. In the days when the Republican Party still controlled Chicago's black wards, Dawson started out as a precinct aide, moved to the 2nd Ward, and in 1933 was elected alderman with the backing of the powerful Congressman DePriest. Dawson would have had a bright future as a Republican, except that during the New Deal all of his constituents were becoming Democrats. Dawson tried, at first, to resist the tide. He ran for Congress as a Republican in 1938, but despite campaign literature that pleaded with voters to "Vote the Man — Not the Party," Democrat Arthur Mitchell held on to the seat. Dawson's political future was mapped out for him the following year when a Democratic lawyer took his aldermanic seat away. Unable to beat the Democrats, Dawson decided to join them.[21]

Just as Dawson was preparing to jump ship, Kelly and Nash were looking for established black leaders to represent the machine in the city's black wards. The need was particularly dire in Dawson's own 2nd Ward. The Democratic ward committeeman for the 2nd Ward was a white man who was loathed by his black constituents. It was hard to blame blacks for being dissatisfied with him: when meeting with constituents at the ward office, he talked to every white in the room first, and then held what he called "colored folks hour" for the blacks who remained. He also made a point of giving his most lucrative patronage positions to whites who lived outside the ward.[22] Kelly and Nash were worried that blacks would shift back to the Republican Party or, more dangerous still, start their own Democratic organization. Before the end of the year, they offered the position of Democratic 2nd Ward committeeman to Dawson, who eagerly accepted.[23]

With this new lease on political life, Dawson immediately set to work consolidating his power. His biggest obstacle was that he held only one of the two major political positions in the ward — Alderman Earl Dickerson had the other. Kelly and Nash were happy to have the two men serve as coleaders of the ward, but Dawson regarded that arrangement as intolerable. He schemed to undermine Dickerson every way he could think of, including "forgetting" to invite his rival to important meetings. But Dawson's biggest advantage in this intra-ward battle was that Dickerson was serving as president of the Chicago Urban League and had begun speaking out in favor of civil rights. Though Kelly was relatively supportive on the issue of racial discrimination, there was no room in the Democratic machine for a politician who put civil rights ahead of loyalty to the organization. Dickerson's worst run-in with the machine leadership came when he opposed a bill in the City Council favored by Mayor Kelly, because it would not have barred unions from discriminating on the basis of race. Dawson, who steered clear of the race question, rose in the machine's estimation as Dickerson fell. In 1942, Congressman Mitchell decided not to run for reelection, and both Dawson and Dickerson wanted his seat. Not surprisingly, the machine backed the compliant Dawson over the "race man" Dickerson, and Dawson won the Democratic primary handily. Dawson still had a tough race against a Republican, and Dickerson's support may have made the difference. Dawson had promised Dickerson that, in return, he would back him for reelection. But once Dawson was elected to Congress, he quietly brought a machine ally named William Harvey down to City Hall to seek Mayor Kelly's blessing. With the backing of Kelly and the machine, Harvey defeated the double-crossed Dickerson and put the 2nd Ward aldermanic seat firmly under Dawson's control.[24]

With his home ward now secure, Dawson began to turn his attention to neighboring wards that were in racial transition. In these, the racial change usually came to the machine hierarchy from the bottom up. White ward committeemen generally kept their jobs, but they added more and more black precinct captains, in some cases creating a virtual mini–black submachine at the ward level. In the Near South Side 6th Ward, the longtime white ward committeeman adapted to the racial transition by segregating his precinct captains along racial lines and designating a black man named Emett Paige to serve as de facto boss over the black precinct captains. "Paige would call the black precincts together, sort of herded them together, and anything of reference to blacks getting jobs, problems of the blacks, would be referred to 'Doc' Paige," recalled one machine member. "[H]e was a big, talkative black guy with a lot of personality — hail-fellow-well-met, a person who could be used to corral the blacks. It was a means whereby [the white ward committeeman] didn't have to be bothered by the blacks. He'd say, 'Go see Doc Paige, whatever you want.'" This system worked while the wards were still racially mixed, but as they became almost all black, the machine began to look for black ward committeemen to lead them. Dawson used his influence with the machine leadership to get his allies appointed as ward committeemen. In the 3rd Ward, Dawson persuaded Nash to appoint an old army buddy as ward committeeman. And Dawson had his eye on several other wards that were ripe for takeover, his ultimate goal being to build an empire that encompassed the entire black South Side.[25]

The question of where Daley's patron, "Big Joe" McDonough, would fit into the new Kelly-Nash Democratic machine was never fully answered. McDonough died unexpectedly on April 25, 1934, at the age of forty-five. Even his obituary candidly conceded that he was "no angel," but McDonough was sincerely mourned, especially in Bridgeport. A well-attended requiem Mass was held at Nativity of Our Lord, and newspapers printed the names of more than one hundred federal, state, and city officials who had been named honorary pallbearers. Daley had the greater honor — and far more onerous responsibility — of serving as one of McDonough's eight "active pallbearers." He and the other seven undertook the task of hoisting McDonough's three-hundred-pound body toward its eternal reward. Once McDonough's body was interred, Daley's future was in considerable doubt. The death of one man had left him deprived of a ward committeeman, alderman, employer, and political mentor.[26]

The upside to the death of a machine politician was that it created vacancies to fill. McDonough's departure opened up three positions for which Daley could reasonably put in a bid. Daley was more than qualified to move up to county treasurer, since he had already been doing the job in everything but name. But he lacked the prominence and political connections to get a position of that magnitude. Nash ended up selecting his own cousin, a criminal lawyer who represented the likes of Al Capone, to succeed McDonough. Daley was kept on, however, as deputy. Daley also failed to get the machine's nod for the aldermanic seat McDonough had held on to when he was elected county treasurer. The machine summoned a four-term congressman, an alumnus of the Hamburg Athletic Club, who returned from Washington willingly, on the self-evident principle that the chance to be a Chicago alderman — and to partake of the patronage and back-room deal making that came with the position — was a step up from Congress. The final position McDonough left behind, ward committeeman for the 11th Ward, was the most logical one for Daley. The new ward committeeman would be selected from among the 11th Ward precinct captains, and in his eleven years of service Daley had been as hardworking and ambitious as any. But the machine selected Hugh "Babe" Connelly, a saloonkeeper and bookie eleven years older than Daley, to be the next ward committeeman.[27]

As it turned out, the former congressman did not remain 11th Ward alderman for long. Even in the hard-drinking ranks of Bridgeport's Irish politicians, he had stood out. Within a year of his return from Washington, his health gave out and he was dead at the age of forty-eight. Responsibility for filling the vacancy fell to the ward committeeman, and Connelly followed a revered Chicago tradition when he appointed himself. Daley kept his disappointment to himself, and proceeded to forge a close alliance with the increasingly powerful Connelly. By virtue of his ties to Connelly and his substantial government service, Daley was regarded as someone with a bright future, and a leading contender for the next vacancy to open up. Daley continued to toil away at the county treasurer's office while he waited. His break came soon enough, with another 11th Ward death. One of the three state representatives who represented Bridgeport in Springfield died on October 19, 1936, just fifteen days before the 1936 elections. A Republican, he ran unopposed as part of a not uncommon deal between 11th Ward Democrats and Republicans that sent two Democrats and one Republican to the legislature from the district. To much of Bridgeport, the most interesting aspect of his passing was that he had summoned a priest to his deathbed and married his secretary of twenty years, who then inherited hundreds of thousands of dollars from him. But to Daley, what mattered was that the death had left a Bridgeport legislative seat in an unusual state of limbo. The Republicans tried to substitute another candidate, but the Democratic-controlled state election board ruled that it was too late to reprint the ballots. As a result, neither party was officially fielding a candidate, and the election would have to be decided by write-in votes.[28]

Daley quickly announced his candidacy and rallied the support he had been building up in Bridgeport for years. Babe Connelly, the ward committeeman, supported Daley and put the 11th Ward Democratic Organization to work for him. Daley also enlisted his old Hamburg Athletic Club gang to turn out voters. Daley's well-organized campaign was a success — he defeated his Republican-supported opponent. Because the vacancy on the ballot was a Republican one, Daley had to be written in as a Republican, and he therefore won his first elected position as a Republican. When Daley arrived in Springfield, legislative rules required him to sit on the Republican side of the aisle. It was only after his friend and fellow legislator Benjamin Adamowski made a motion to let Daley sit as a Democrat that he was allowed to cross over and rejoin his party.

The Springfield that awaited Daley in 1936 was a town of surprising decadence. Nestled among the wheat fields and grain silos of central Illinois was a state capital culture that revolved around good-time women, free-flowing liquor, and lobbyists who carried wads of cash into dinner meetings with legislators. Many young legislators quickly found themselves caught up in the city's corrupting ways. "In Springfield you could tell real fast which men were there for girls, games and graft," Adamowski would say later. Daley was not one of them. He was, as even his worst enemies would readily concede, straitlaced when it came to sex and alcohol. During Daley's years in Springfield, he spent much of his time back in Chicago, where he and Sis were building a family. Their first child, Patricia, was born on Saint Patrick's Day, 1937. In 1939, after the birth of a second daughter, Mary Carol, the Daleys built a seven-room bungalow at 3536 South Lowe — the same block Daley had been born on. Other children came in quick succession: Eleanor, Richard, Michael, John, and William, who was born in 1949. Daley was devoted to Sis, and had low regard for the many politicians he saw all around him breaking their marital vows or drinking heavily. Later, when Daley was mayor, the story was told of a Daley administrator who was getting drunk one night when he received a phone call at the bar. "This is Mayor Daley. Your wife is rather upset. I think you better get home," said the voice at the other end. "I don't know how he knew where I was," the hapless appointee said later. "But, of course, I went home right away."[29]

Nor was Daley tempted by the special-interest money that flowed so freely. In those days, the legislative calendar was larded with "fetcher" bills. These were bills drafted for the express purpose of posing financial damage to any of the well-funded special interests that sent lobbyists to Springfield. When a fetcher bill was introduced, a little ritual was enacted: lobbyists duly showed up with cash-filled envelopes which they handed out to legislators, and the bill mysteriously disappeared. But cash-filled envelopes did little for Daley. It was clear even at this early stage of his career that Daley was driven to pursue power, not money. Still, if Daley did not personally get caught up in the corruption of the capital, he felt no obligation to speak out against it. "Daley's moral code was emerging" in Springfield, the newspaper columnist and Daley critic Mike Royko would later say. "Thou shalt not steal, but thou shalt not blow the whistle on anybody who does."[30]

Daley conceived of his role in Springfield as a simple one: following the orders of the Democratic machine back in Chicago. As he had in every previous job, Daley relied on "hard work, a disposition to do what he was told, and a willingness to dive into the most mundane details of governance to set himself apart." While less serious lawmakers crammed into the saloons and cadged drinks off lobbyists, Daley holed up with draft bills and budget documents. "Most of the time he kept to himself, stayed in his hotel room, and worked hard," Adamowski recalled. Along with Abraham Lincoln Marovitz, another state senator from Chicago, Daley and Adamowski used to walk up and down Springfield talking endlessly about legislative business. The topic was frequently Daley's greatest preoccupation, finance. "Dick Daley knew more about budgets than anyone else," recalled one representative. "Even as a first-termer, people went to him to ask questions about the budget."[31]

As a legislator, Daley had no trouble finding ways to make himself useful to Mayor Kelly and the Democratic machine. Chicago always had a great deal at stake in Springfield. With the depression raging, Kelly's agenda consisted chiefly of New Deal–style legislation to advance the economic interests of his poor and working-class constituents. By doing the machine's bidding, Daley ended up being something of a progressive force in the capital. He introduced bills to replace the state's sales tax, which fell disproportionately on the poor, with individual and corporate income taxes. Despite Daley's best efforts, the bill failed. Daley was also an early supporter of the school lunch program, and backed legislation to make it more difficult for people to be evicted from their homes. And he pushed for a law to make it easier for Chicago city government to take over and improve substandard properties. "One building without tenants, with the windows out, generally run down, can blight an entire block or neighborhood," Daley said in support of the bill. "This bill is a forerunner to rebuilding the blighted areas of Chicago and to stop the formation of new blighted areas." Daley could claim one major achievement during his time in the legislature: he shepherded through the law that created the Chicago Transit Authority out of Chicago's bankrupt Chicago Surface Lines and the Chicago Rapid Transit System. Daley was a machine operative during his years in Springfield, but an unusually effective one. It was perhaps the highest praise he could aspire to when a political columnist called Daley "probably the best exhibit of the hard-working, decent, honest organization politician that the Kelly machine can produce."[32]

The machine began bestowing its own generosity on Daley almost as soon as he arrived in Springfield. On December 10, 1936, the deputy Cook County controller died, and Daley was appointed to fill the vacancy while continuing to serve in the legislature. The new job kept Daley in close touch with Chicago politics during his sojourn in the wilderness of Springfield. It also had a more practical benefit: joining a long line of machine double-dippers, Daley earned another $6,000 a year in salary to spend on his growing family. Within two years, the death of another machine politician helped to advance Daley's career. When the state senator for the district that included Bridgeport died, the machine tapped Daley to move up to the higher chamber. On February 1, 1938, Daley led a field of nine candidates in the Democratic primary, and in the November general election, he beat his Republican opponent by almost 3 to 1. After three years in the state senate, Daley was elected minority leader, with the support of the body's large contingent of machine Democrats. Only thirty-eight, he was the youngest party leader in the history of the Illinois Senate.[33]

Daley's legislative agenda consisted of more than just New Deal programs and slum improvement: he spent much of his time promoting the parochial interests of the Kelly-Nash machine. Even in a body that seemed to function only to meet the needs of lobbyists and political operators, Daley stood out for his forthright commitment to the interests of the Chicago machine. One Daley tax reform, which he tried to pass four times, would have allowed Cook County residents to appeal their tax bills directly to the county assessor, rather than proceed through the court system. It might have made appeals simpler for taxpayers, but its greatest beneficiary would have been the ward committeemen and aldermen who could then use their ties to the highly political county assessor's office to reduce the taxes of their friends and supporters. Daley was also doing the machine's bidding when he crusaded to revise the state's divorce laws to make the state's attorney part of every divorce. The change would have given the state's attorney's office a five-dollar fee for every divorce action filed in Cook County, generating revenue and work for an office that was usually filled by the machine and that employed an army of Democratic patronage workers. The machine also looked to Daley for help with electoral issues that came up in Springfield. Daley tried and failed in 1943 to enact a redistricting plan that would have given Cook County representatives majority control in the state legislature. And in 1944, when the Republican-controlled state senate seemed close to passing a resolution condemning a fourth term for Roosevelt, it was Daley who organized the Democrats to block a roll call vote. Daley also served as the designated defender of the machine's extensive system of political patronage, fighting off Republican attempts to scrutinize the peculiar hiring practices that were rampant in Chicago and Cook County government offices. When the Republicans called for an inquiry into the Civil Service Protective Association of Chicago, Daley fought them to a draw by calling instead for an investigation of the Republican-run state civil service agency.[34]

Daley's years in Springfield continued the two constants in his political rise: learning about the minute workings of government, and ingratiating himself to the machine. It also gave him an opportunity to hone his political skills, teaching him how to build coalitions, field requests from lobbyists and constituents, and — not least — handle reporters. Not long after Daley arrived in Springfield, the *Chicago Tribune* ran a small story about the Cook County Board agreeing to pay a ten-dollar bounty to two hunters who had killed wolves inside the county limits. The chairman of the wolf bounty committee said the pelts should be examined, since the county had once been accused of paying a wolf bounty on five police dogs. "Having served with the state legislature last year," Daley was quoted in the paper as responding, "I consider myself an authority on wolves. I will certify that the pelts on which we are paying belonged to two timber wolves." It was a good line, but not one calculated to ingratiate himself with his Springfield colleagues. Daley wrote to the newspaper the following day "emphatically" denying that he had made the statement attributed to him, and demanding a retraction. The paper does not appear to have retracted the story, but Daley learned a lasting lesson about the perils of talking too freely to the press.[35]

Federally funded public housing is a product of the early days of the New Deal. During Franklin Delano Roosevelt's breakneck First Hundred Days in 1933, Congress enacted the National Industrial Recovery Act, which laid the groundwork for a public housing program. The act authorized the Housing Division of the Public Works Administration to buy and condemn property, and to build housing on it. Public housing was sold to a skeptical Congress by emphasizing its most conservative aspects: that it would clear slums and create work for unemployed members of the building trades. But to its creators, the public housing program was about something more idealistic. It was intended to be "more than a means of providing shelter for those unable to pay a fair, or economic, rent," one New Dealer wrote. "It is a visible proof that this is a country which believes in the dignity of all human beings, a living testimonial to the America for which Jefferson, Jackson, Lincoln and Roosevelt dreamed and fought." The PWA started off with a program of fifty-one "demonstration projects" to be built around the country at a cost of $134 million.[36]

No part of the country was more desperately in need of this new federal housing than Chicago. The housing available to poor Chica-

goans during the Great Depression rivaled any city's in scarcity, di-
lapidation, and dangerousness. Chicago's housing inadequacies traced
back to the Great Fire of 1871, which destroyed 17,000 buildings —
one-third of the city's total — and made 100,000 people homeless.
The City Council responded to the devastation by passing a law per-
mitting the construction of temporary wooden structures as emergency housing. But the emergency was never declared to have
ended, and this kind of shoddy housing continued to be common
well into the 1900s. Chicago's grim housing situation was made considerably worse by the depression. The city's population was growing rapidly, with much of the growth coming in the form of an
influx of displaced farmworkers and rural families. But just when the
need was greatest, new housing construction had all but ground to a
halt. In 1933, the worst year of all, only twenty-one new apartment
units were built in the entire city. At the same time, with more than
700,000 Chicagoans out of work and one-third of workers earning
$1,000 or less, much of the city's population was facing eviction
from their private-market apartments. Depression-era Chicago was
littered with "Hoovervilles" and "Hobovilles," squalid outposts that
the homeless fashioned out of scrap lumber and tar paper. Hard
times had also introduced a new form of civil disturbance, the eviction riot, in which friends and neighbors attempted forcibly to
prevent bailiffs from serving eviction papers. In one heated eviction
riot on the South Side, three demonstrators were killed when
police squared off against a crowd of 2,000 trying to stop an African-
American family from being removed from its home. Recognizing
its desperate straits, the Roosevelt administration was generous to
Chicago when the time came to apportion the first round of public
housing. Of the first fifty-one demonstration projects built by the
PWA, it was decided that Chicago would get three: Julia C. Lathrop
Homes on the North Side, Trumbull Park Homes on the Far South
Side, and Jane Addams Homes on the West Side.[37]

With Roosevelt's support, Congress enacted the United States
Housing Act of 1937, which authorized the United States Housing
Authority to underwrite construction and maintenance of public
housing. The new law also called for local governments to establish
their own housing authorities to manage public housing projects and

plan new ones. Cities around the country reacted to the program —
and to the promise of large federal subsidies — with enthusiasm.[38]

The Chicago Housing Authority was established in 1937, and to
run it Mayor Kelly appointed a housing activist named Elizabeth
Wood. Wood was an unusual government bureaucrat. She had been
born in Nara, Japan, the daughter of a Christian lay missionary.
When she was five, her family came back to America because of her
father's failing eyesight. On their return, he became a professor of
natural history at Illinois Wesleyan University. Wood's parents could
not afford to send her away for college. "We were just plain poor,"
she once recalled. So she enrolled at Illinois Wesleyan as a biology
major, taking some of her father's classes. She worked a series of odd
jobs — teaching violin for fifty cents a lesson, doing bacteriological
testing for a milk company — to pay for a senior year at the University of Michigan. Wood went on to earn bachelor's and master's degrees in rhetoric at the University of Michigan, and took a position
teaching English at Vassar College, in upstate New York. She headed
back to the Midwest to pursue a doctorate in English at the University of Chicago, but she remained restless in academia.[39]

Wood embarked on a series of short-lived undertakings, including
writing a novel, before stumbling into a job doing promotional writing for a Chicago housing project. Her lifelong interest in public
housing was born. She worked briefly as a caseworker for United
Charities, but found that her ability to bring about meaningful reform was limited. "It was a spit-in-the-ocean job," Wood would later
recall. "You could work your heart out and kids still got TB or starved,
rats still bit babies and youngsters still ended up in Juvenile Court. I
got out of it as soon as I could." The more poverty and deprivation
she encountered, the more convinced she became that the root cause
of these ills was the deficient conditions under which people lived.
"I really got a terrible feeling," she once said, "for the folly of pouring funds for medical and psychiatric treatment into families that live
in the slums, without taking the people out of these surroundings."
When Chicago's Council of Social Agencies began to shift its focus
toward housing issues, Wood became head of its housing committee. She went on to serve, from 1933 to 1937, as the first executive
secretary of the Metropolitan Housing Council, and as executive

secretary of the Illinois Housing Board. She left when Mayor Kelly named her to head the Chicago Housing Authority.[40]

Wood did not fit easily into the earthy male world of Chicago politics. As a woman heading a big-city housing authority from the 1930s to the 1950s, she was an anomaly. An early profile of her in the *Chicago Tribune* marveled that "45 male engineers, designers, and department heads call her 'boss' and like it!" As much as her gender, Wood's bearing set her apart from the rough-hewn men who ran Chicago. An ocean of cultural distance separated the barely literate aldermen from the refined author of *Afterglow,* Wood's psychological novel about a complicated mother-daughter relationship. "When people get to calling me names now — and a lot of people do — they bring up that book and also teaching poetry at Vassar," Wood once complained. "Those are pretty black marks for a public servant to have on his record." But for all of her refined ways, Wood brought a scientist's discipline to her job and had an impressive knowledge of the technical details of housing. "She may have taught poetry at Vassar, but she could read a blueprint faster than most people could read a comic strip," recalls the director of research for the CHA under Wood.[41]

From the very beginning, Wood was on a collision course with the city's political establishment. She never succeeded in forging good relationships with the city's most powerful aldermen, and even Mayor Kelly, who liked Wood and strongly backed her up, was not close to her. "Kelly admired and respected what I stood for, but he hated to talk to me," Wood once said. "We didn't talk the same language." She often sent her leading staff adviser to meet with the mayor, since he was able to "talk the language of the street." But what really distinguished Wood from the politicians around her was her unadulterated idealism, a quality that quickly earned her the nickname "the Jane Addams of public housing." Wood was guided in her work by the conviction that "houses work magic," and that good housing provides poor people "ladders to climb." Her constituency was not the machine politicians but the poor mothers and children crammed into the city's crumbling tenement houses and slum shacks. "These people have social pressures to face when they read newspaper advertising, or pass a downtown store window and see how a living room or kitchen can be furnished — while their own living space does not provide enough room so all the family can eat together at one time," Wood said. "Give these people decent housing and the better forces inside them have a chance to work. Ninety-nine percent will respond."[42]

Wood's idealism led her to refuse steadfastly to let her agency hire, contract, or select workers or tenants on the basis of patronage. To aldermen whose grip on power depended on finding jobs and providing favors to their supporters, her stand was unacceptable. "They really hate us," she told a reporter toward the end of her tenure. "They'd love to have that gravy." Most unforgivable of all, Wood strongly believed in using public housing to promote racial integration. "I think it came out of the Christian ideology in which she was raised," says a CHA division chief under Wood. "She did it not out of a sense of noblesse oblige, but because it was the right thing to do." Wood herself lived on Drexel Avenue in a neighborhood with many blacks. And she regularly invited black friends to her home for dinner parties, which was not common at the time. To the great frustration of her critics, Wood received unwavering support from City Hall for her racially progressive policies. City Council leader John Duffy complained that "[u]nder Kelly, the Housing Authority submitted a proposal and that was it."[43]

For all of the liberal impulses behind it, federal public housing was never meant to disrupt the nation's racial status quo. Southerners were a powerful force in Congress, and supporters of public housing understood that requiring it to be racially integrated would have doomed it to defeat. Time and again, congressional liberals compromised on integration in order to get more units of housing. "[I]t is in the best interests of the Negro race that we carry through the housing program as planned," Illinois senator Paul Douglas told his fellow liberals in one debate over a proposed nondiscrimination clause, "rather than put in the bill an amendment which will inevitably defeat it, and defeat all hopes for rehousing four million persons." When the public housing program began, the federal government's solution to the thorny issue of race was the Neighborhood Composition Rule, developed by interior secretary Harold Ickes himself. The regulatory rule stated that the racial mix of tenants in a new public housing project had to match the racial composition of the residents who had previously lived on the site. The Neighborhood

Composition Rule had the virtue of seeming to sidestep the whole question of race by simply maintaining the status quo. But it put local public housing authorities in the business of monitoring the race of all of their applicants and tenants. And like many such pronouncements from Washington, it proved extremely difficult to implement out in the field.[44]

It was clear from the beginning of Chicago's public housing program that virtually every decision relating to race would be fraught with controversy. Chicago's three "demonstration projects" were ready for occupancy in early 1938, and the CHA had to make its first decisions about racial composition. There was no debate about Lathrop Homes and Trumbull Park Homes: both were located in all-white sections of the city, and under the Neighborhood Composition Rule their first tenants would be exclusively white. But Jane Addams Homes was located on a site that had previously had a small black population. The CHA initially admitted twenty-six black families to the 1,027-unit project, but after a dispute over the calculations and the threat of a lawsuit, the agency raised the number of black units to sixty. In 1941, the CHA opened a fourth housing project, Ida B. Wells Homes, in an all-black neighborhood on the South Side. The housing situation for blacks was so dire that the CHA received ten applications for each of the project's 1,662 apartments. It was an indication of just how strong feelings ran about race and public housing that even this all-black project in an all-black neighborhood stirred up a racial firestorm. Residents of nearby white neighborhoods sued to shift Ida B. Wells a half-mile deeper into the black ghetto. When the suit failed, white homeowners in the area added restrictive covenants to their deeds in an attempt at racial containment.[45]

As the CHA built more housing projects, the racial balancing act became more complicated. Four more projects went up during World War II. Two of these presented no difficult racial issues. One was located between 31st and 32nd streets off Lithuanica Avenue, a short walk from Daley's home. In addition to having an entirely white tenant population, this project was designed as two-story row houses, virtually indistinguishable from the private housing around it. Another all-white project, built in a lightly populated industrial area, was also easily dealt with. But when the CHA set out to find tenants for the other wartime projects — Francis Cabrini Homes and

Robert Brooks Homes — it was confronted with the practical limits of the Neighborhood Composition Rule. Cabrini was built on the Near North Side, on the site of an old slum called "Little Sicily" that had some black residents mixed in among the Sicilians. Applying the Neighborhood Composition Rule, the CHA determined that occupancy of the project would be 80 percent white and 20 percent black. But it proved difficult to attract the full complement of whites to public housing in a racially changing neighborhood, and there were far too many black applicants. The CHA tried to surpass the 20 percent quota for blacks, but backed down when white residents resisted. As a temporary measure, it decided to leave 140 units unoccupied, but when it became clear that the missing whites would never be found, the CHA departed from the 80–20 ratio. By 1949, the project was 40 percent black.[46]

At Brooks Homes, the CHA had even less luck attracting white tenants. Brooks had been built on a site that was 80 percent black, and the CHA wanted to fill 20 percent of the units with whites. But it soon became clear that few whites were eager to move into public housing in an overwhelmingly black neighborhood. The CHA soon gave up its effort to attract white tenants and allowed Brooks to become entirely black. The CHA's fifth wartime project, Altgeld Gardens on the Far Southwest Side, suggested what may have been the only easy solutions to the racial issues associated with public housing. Altgeld was designed as an all-black project, so the CHA did not need to worry about attracting white tenants. And to speed construction, the CHA had built it on a 137-acre tract of vacant land in a remote part of the Far South Side–Lake Calumet industrial area. It was so far from any existing neighborhood, white or black, that there was no one around to complain about it.[47]

After nearly a decade in the state legislature, Daley was ready to return to Chicago. He wanted to spend more time with his family back in Bridgeport and, equally important, he was ready to redirect his ambitions toward Chicago politics. Daley's current patron, Mayor Kelly, was in political trouble. Kelly had stepped in as head of the Democratic machine on the death of Pat Nash. The move had allowed him to consolidate political power — and to fend off other factions that were looking to take over the machine — but it had also

cost him in popular support. Kelly's administration already had a reputation for corruption and for being too close to the machine. His
decision to tear down entirely the wall between City Hall and the
clubhouse hurt him with many voters. Kelly was also being blamed
for a series of school, police, and organized crime scandals that had
struck the city. Not least, he was rapidly losing popularity among
white ethnic voters because of his support for Elizabeth Wood and
the issue of open housing.[48]

Mayor Kelly had a great deal riding on the 1946 elections. He
needed a slate of Democratic candidates that could come through for
the machine, including a strong candidate for county sheriff to replace the incumbent, who was barred by law from succeeding himself. Kelly needed that rare ideal of a machine candidate: someone
with enough of an appearance of integrity to appeal to nonmachine
voters, but who could nevertheless be counted on to use his office to
advance the machine's interests, and to continue to employ the hundreds of Democratic Party workers who were currently on the sheriff's office payroll. Daley seemed like the perfect choice. He had won
a reputation for honesty and hard work in Springfield — the *Chicago
Daily News* had pronounced Daley one of the Democrats' "brightest
stars." Yet Kelly knew better than anyone how completely Daley had
subordinated himself to the interests of the machine. With Kelly's
backing, the machine slated Daley for county sheriff.[49]

If Daley seemed like a good choice for the machine, it was less
clear how good the job of county sheriff would be for Daley. Even
by the low standards of Cook County politics of that time, the sheriff's office was notorious for its levels of patronage and graft. County
sheriffs had been known for acquiring a quick personal fortune in
the one term that the law allowed them, and then retiring wealthy.
"Knowledgeable people had a rule of thumb at that time that if
a sheriff couldn't step out of office four years later with a clear
$1,000,000 in his pocket, he just wasn't trying," a Chicago journalist
has observed. Because of this history of corrupting its occupants, the
office of county sheriff was generally considered a career-ender. Daley
might become the rare sheriff who was able to raise the ethical standards of the office, but his friends and political allies were troubled
by his decision to accept the nomination. "When I got back from
the service and found out he was going to run for sheriff, I couldn't

believe it," recalled Benjamin Adamowski, who had been off fighting in World War II. "I told him: 'What in the hell do you want to do that for? You can't help but get dirty in that office. Everybody does.'" Daley told Adamowski that Mayor Kelly wanted him to run, and that Daley's law partner, William Lynch, thought it would be a good idea. "But he wanted it," Adamowski said. "He would have run for anything, he was that eager for it, that hungry for power.'" Lillian Daley also advised Daley against running for sheriff, pronouncing the post unworthy of her son. But Daley's beloved mother died during the campaign, before she could see how wise her counsel turned out to be.[50]

The 1946 campaign for county sheriff was a fierce one. Daley's Republican opponent, Elmer Michael Walsh, attacked him for his ties to Kelly and the Democratic machine. "'D' is for Daley and also for doubles on the payroll," Walsh told a Republican women's organization on the Far South Side. "He draws one salary as state senator and another as deputy county controller. Here is another example of how the present city and county administrations fail to give the public dollar value. Nephews, aunts and even cousins have been uncovered feeding upon the spoils of the Kelly machine." Daley responded with platitudes. At the birthplace of the National Temperance Union, he warned an audience of women about the dangers of underage drinking. "Boys and girls often go wrong when allowed to frequent disreputable resorts where liquor is sold to minors." More potently, Daley showed his talent for building coalitions and collecting endorsements. Adamowski, who had a strong following in the city's Polish wards, chaired a lawyers' committee for Daley. And William A. Lee, head of Local 734 of the Bakery Drivers Union, and president of the Chicago Federation of Labor, headed a labor committee for Daley. As the Democratic candidate, Daley started out with strong support in the black wards, and he courted black voters during the campaign by speaking out against racially restrictive covenants.[51]

Daley could not control the national political trends, however, and 1946 was shaping up as a disastrous year for the Democratic Party. President Truman had come into office on a wave of goodwill when he took over after Roosevelt's death, but eighteen months later, America found itself wracked by inflation, meat shortages, and red scares. A consensus was emerging that Truman was a bumbling incompetent, and his approval ratings had skidded to 32 percent, a 50 percent drop in the space of a year. New York impresario Billy Rose was promoting W. C. Fields for president in 1948 on the logic that "If we are going to have a comedian in the White House, let's have a good one." The best thing Truman could do to help Democratic candidates in the 1946 elections, national party leaders told him, was to hide in the White House. Daley did what many Democrats across the country were doing — distanced himself from Truman and told audiences that he still believed in "those policies for which Franklin D. Roosevelt was the great spokesman." But when election day arrived, Democratic candidates were trounced from coast to coast. The Republicans took control of the House 246–188 and the Senate 51–45, the first time they had held both houses of Congress since the 1920s. Senator Styles Bridges of New Hampshire exulted that "[t]he United States is now a Republican country." The aggressively Republican *Chicago Tribune* declared the Democratic defeat to be the nation's greatest victory since Appomattox.[52]

The Chicago Democratic machine was dragged down in this national Democratic rout, and Daley was no exception. Losing to the Republican Walsh seemed like a significant setback at the time, but it probably worked out for the best. Daley was never tempted to test the million-dollar rule of thumb, and he could not be faulted, as county sheriffs always were, for looking the other way as organized crime ran its gambling operations and loan-sharking rackets with impunity. Nor would the loss be held against him personally, since the entire Democratic ticket had been defeated. Daley still had his position as deputy comptroller for Cook County, which made him the machine's point man on large county contracts — and gave him a platform from which to plan his next move.[53]

With the end of World War II, the Chicago Housing Authority's job was becoming even more complicated. Thousands of discharged soldiers were streaming into Chicago, and the city was scrambling to find room for them in converted barracks, trailers, and Quonset huts. There was strong popular sentiment to do better for these returning national heroes, and the City Council quickly allocated millions of dollars to build new veterans' housing. To get the housing built quickly, Mayor Kelly directed that it be constructed on sites already owned by the Park District, the Sanitary District, and the Board of Education. As it happened, most of this land was in outlying white sections of the city. The CHA found itself in a bind. About 20 percent of the veterans needing public housing were black, and federal law required that they receive a proportionate share of new apartments. But the Neighborhood Composition Rule, which required public housing to reflect the racial mix of the surrounding community, dictated that the new housing be almost entirely white. Something had to give, and in 1946 the CHA abandoned the Neighborhood Composition Rule. Liberated from the constraints of the rule, Elizabeth Wood and her staff were free to pursue racially integrated housing with the new veterans' projects. The CHA developed a list of twenty-two sites for the new housing, and most were in white areas.[54]

When whites learned that public housing was coming to their neighborhoods — and that 20 percent or more of the residents might be black — they reacted with barely disguised panic. Racially integrated living was something that few of them had any experience with, and something that struck most of them as implausible. Most were convinced that integrated public housing would be the end of their neighborhoods, causing whites to flee for the suburbs and allowing blacks to take their place. It was a frightening prospect for working-class whites who had large stakes, both financial and emotional, in their neighborhoods. Elected officials from the neighborhoods targeted by Wood rose up in opposition to the CHA's plans for veterans' housing. "Some of the housing people are on the square but there are as many more who are interested in stirring up trouble," said City Council finance chairman John Duffy, who represented the heavily Irish 19th Ward on the Far Southwest Side. "By putting up a project in every section of Chicago they could infiltrate Negroes," Duffy charged, the CHA was trying to "stir up trouble and keep the pot boiling — never let it stop." To appease its critics in the white neighborhoods, the CHA decided to keep many of the smaller projects entirely white. Black veterans would be limited to the largest of the new projects, and even these would start out with an informal cap of 10 percent. Wood also insisted on careful screening of the applicants. In selecting black tenants for public housing, the CHA looked particularly for former military officers with combat records, and wives known to be good housekeepers.[55]

In late 1946, Airport Homes opened in an all-white Southwest Side neighborhood near Midway Airport. The CHA made clear from the outset that the 185-unit project was going to house both black and white veterans, but the neighborhood had other ideas. The CHA admitted 125 white veterans to the project, but before it could complete the more probing background checks it applied to black veterans, the community acted. White residents from the area helped themselves to keys to the vacant apartments and simply moved in. The surrounding neighborhood, caught up in anti-integration fervor, vocally supported the white squatters. Presented with a racial crisis, the CHA decided to try to work out an accommodation with the neighborhood. It allowed white squatters who were legally eligible for public housing to remain, but it required those who were not to vacate their apartments. The ineligible tenants moved out only when it was clear that a court would order them to leave.[56]

Wood and the CHA were determined to fill the newly vacant apartments with black veterans. On December 5, 1946, the CHA tried to move two black families into Airport Homes. It would prove to be the start of "an era of hidden violence and guerrilla warfare" in Chicago. The two black men who were chosen to break the color line at Airport Homes both had distinguished war records: one had seen combat in the Pacific and the other had fought in the Battle of the Bulge and been awarded four battle stars. Despite their war service, both were greeted with violent protests at Airport Homes. The CHA's strategy had been to move the families in at noontime, when most of the neighborhood men would be at work. But the neighborhood women, most of whom were at home, proved more than able to defend their turf. A crowd of two hundred dirt- and rock-throwing demonstrators, primarily middle-aged women, surged on the truck delivering the families' household furnishings, breaking its windows with rocks, and forcing the new tenants and their moving men to run to safety in the housing project office. It took four hundred policemen to restore the peace. The following day, the protests continued. Demonstrators turned over a police car, and police responded by cracking heads with nightsticks. As the violence raged at

Airport Homes, Wood announced that seven black families had changed their minds and asked to be removed from the waiting list. While the Mayor's Commission on Human Relations warned that the city was moving toward mob law, the CHA found that it could no longer locate any black veterans willing to move into Airport Homes. The project remained all white.[57]

For the next veterans' project the CHA sought to integrate, Fernwood Park Homes on the Far South Side, Wood personally attended a community meeting in May 1947 to emphasize that her agency did not intend to be defeated again. Wood's assertion that "we must invite them all in the exact order of their application and on the basis of their need" was not well received by the audience of 350 white residents from the neighborhood. The local alderman, Reginald DuBois, spoke after Wood and blamed her and the CHA for integration. "I believe that Negroes would not ask to be assigned to this project if they were not pushed to do so," DuBois said. "We all want to protect our homes, and the people of this community will put up a stout fight."[58]

Wood did not back down. On August 13, 1947, the CHA began to move the first fifty-two families, eight of them black, into Fernwood Park. A mob of five thousand white demonstrators was on hand to greet the new black tenants. The crowd returned night after night, engaging in intermittent acts of violence and trying to drive the black tenants out. The police sent seven hundred officers to hold the mob in check. Eventually, the white resisters realized they would not succeed in driving the black tenants out. Still, the protests took their toll and opposition grew to Wood and the CHA. Alderman DuBois, one of the leaders of this backlash, introduced a resolution in the City Council declaring that the CHA "persists in theories of housing which are shared by no other representative local government agencies in Chicago, and are not in accord with those of a great majority of citizens."[59]

Defeat was the one unforgivable sin in machine politics. When the organization slate lost, the machine leadership saw its power ebb, and lower-ranking members lost their jobs and the ability to put food on the table. Although the 1946 losses were part of a national rout for the Democrats, machine leaders insisted that Mayor Kelly step down as party boss. When the Cook County Central Committee met in June to select a new chairman, the Irish politicians who controlled the selection process divided into warring factions. The committee compromised on Jacob Arvey, ward committeeman from the West Side's heavily Jewish 24th Ward. Arvey made an ideal caretaker because of his relative powerlessness. An Irishman would necessarily have belonged to one of the rival Irish factions, and once installed in office would give his camp effective control over the machine. Poles were a large enough ethnic bloc that if one became boss, it might be impossible to wrest control of the machine back for the Irish. But Jews were a less powerful voting bloc, and their influence was waning, as they fled old machine neighborhoods for the suburbs or for wealthier reform wards along the lakefront. Arvey could be counted on to run the machine competently and could be pushed aside when one Irish faction or the other gained the upper hand.

A child of Russian immigrants, Arvey was born on La Salle Street in 1895. He attended the Chicago Hebrew Institute, and worked his way through night law school by covering settlement-house basketball games for the weekly *Jewish Sentinel*. Arvey began his political career in 1914, when one of his law professors ran for judge in the 24th Ward. When he graduated, he took a five-dollar-a-week clerk job at a law firm, and began working in politics on the side. Arvey rose through the ranks of the 24th Ward political organization, becoming a precinct captain, and then campaign manager for a ward committeeman who in 1923 exercised his slate-making prerogatives to install the twenty-seven-year-old Arvey as alderman from the 24th Ward. A decade later, Arvey became ward committeeman himself. Arvey took control of the 24th Ward at an opportune moment. Jewish Chicagoans had only a loose identification with the Democratic Party until the early 1930s, when Roosevelt and the New Deal turned Jews across the country into committed Democrats. Just as Arvey became ward committeeman, the 24th Ward was becoming one of the Democrats' strongest wards in Chicago — and in the nation. In 1936, it went for Roosevelt over Alf Landon by the remarkable margin of 26,112 to 974. Even President Roosevelt was impressed, telling Arvey that Chicago's 24th was "the No. 1 ward in the entire Democratic Party."[60]

The first item on Arvey's agenda as party boss was deciding how to handle the mayoral election of 1947. Mayor Kelly wanted to run for reelection, but the voters had turned against him. Kelly was widely regarded as too corrupt, even by the prodigious standards of Chicago mayors. Record levels of patronage hiring appeared to be interfering with the functioning of the public schools. And Kelly had happily looked the other way as the Chicago police took payoffs to let the syndicate operate its various gambling and prostitution rings unimpeded. "The truth is," one political observer wrote at the time, "Chicago's municipal affairs are shot through with political knavery, overt and concealed corruption . . . inefficiency and fakery." The machine leaders had nothing against corruption, but under Mayor Kelly it had been so blatant and artless that it seemed clear it would produce another anti-machine backlash at the polls. Equally problematic, Kelly was hurting the machine with white voters because of his support for racial integration. Arvey and a few other machine leaders had decided to assess Kelly's strength by conducting informal public opinion polls, approaching voters at neighborhood movie theaters, and calling them at home to ask them about the mayor. Arvey's poll takers heard, particularly from Irish voters, a consistent theme: that Kelly was "too good to the niggers." Armed with this evidence of the mayor's low standing with the Chicago electorate, Arvey persuaded Kelly not to seek reelection.[61]

The machine leaders were in a "demoralized state," Arvey recalled, as they looked around for a candidate to hold on to City Hall. They wanted someone with strong reform credentials, who could help throw off the cloud of scandal that had settled on city government. And their casual polling indicated that they would be best off with someone who did not share Mayor Kelly's politically unpopular views on race. The man they turned to was businessman and civic leader Martin Kennelly. Kennelly was a Bridgeport-born, Irish-Catholic bachelor who lived with his widowed sister in a luxury apartment on the North Side. He had made a considerable fortune founding a moving company, and was an active supporter of the Red Cross and DePaul University. The tall, silver-haired Kennelly at least looked like the part the machine was casting him for: A. J. Liebling would later observe that he resembled "a bit player impersonating a

benevolent mayor." The machine's calculated attempt to embrace reform — or, at least, the appearance of reform — was a success. In
the 1947 mayoral election, Kennelly beat a lackluster Republican
opponent, Russell Root, taking 59 percent of the vote.[62]

Daley was by now a powerful force — perhaps the most powerful —
in 11th Ward Democratic politics. As long as he lacked the title of
ward committeeman, though, he had no standing in the machine
hierarchy. Daley was eager to make the move up, but there was a
problem. The 11th Ward already had a ward committeeman, Daley's
old patron, Hugh "Babe" Connelly. Daley and Connelly had been
friends back when they both served as apprentices to Joe Mc-
Donough. When Abraham Lincoln Marovitz was off fighting in World
War II, Daley sent his old friend a letter assuring him that "Babe
Connelly and all the boys from the Hamburg A[thletic] A[ssociation]
wish you well and say hello." Connelly had consistently supported
Daley's ambitions, slating him for the state legislature and promoting
him for higher office. But now Connelly stood in his way, and he
was weak. He had recently been defeated by a Republican when he
ran for reelection to a fourth term as alderman, and he was in poor
health. On October 24, 1947, Daley convened a meeting of the 11th
Ward precinct captains at Saint John's School Hall just up the street
from his home. Connelly was too ill to attend. When the meeting
was over, Connelly was out as ward committeeman and Daley was in.
Romantics like to portray the Chicago Democratic machine as a political community in which people stood by their friends and loyalty was
rewarded. But the reality was much harsher. "Babe was always pushing Daley out front," Benjamin Adamowski said later. "He sent him
to Springfield, pushed him for the better jobs. Then, when Daley
got a chance, he squeezed Connelly out." Daley was a shrewd vote
counter, and one of his tactics in cobbling together his 11th Ward
majority was striking a deal with the Polish precinct captains, who
had been gaining influence in the 11th Ward. After he became ward
committeeman, Daley repaid his Polish supporters by slating Stanley
Nowakowski to run for alderman in the next election. Nowakowski
won the seat back for the Democrats, and the hapless Babe Connelly — who had now been stripped of both his alderman and ward
committeeman posts, along with his health — retreated to Florida. [63]

The Democrats' national prospects in the 1948 elections looked almost as bleak as they had in 1946. Trying to build on his success with Kennelly, Arvey once again sought out candidates with an aura of reform. In a single election year, Arvey slated two little-known men who would go on to become among the leading statesmen of their generation. For governor, Arvey selected Adlai Stevenson, a civic-minded lawyer whose grandfather had served two terms as a U.S. representative before becoming Grover Cleveland's vice president. To run for the Senate, Arvey slated Paul Douglas, a liberal alderman and University of Chicago economist. Knowing that the machine "had a tough fight," Arvey said, he looked for candidates who would "enhance the image of the organization." He found, he said, that "there was nobody that could question Douglas's open-mindedness, his lack of subservience to the organization, his independence, his integrity. And the same with Stevenson." Finding reform candidates to carry the Democratic banner worked as well for the machine in 1948 as it had a year earlier. Both Stevenson and Douglas won statewide and — more important for the machine — ran up impressive margins in Chicago. Arvey's shrewd slating decisions may have provided reverse coattails for President Truman, who carried Illinois by only 33,612 votes in his come-from-behind victory over Thomas E. Dewey.[64]

The machine's triumph in the 1948 elections turned out to be a victory for Daley. In the quid pro quo world of machine politics, he was suddenly in a strong position: Stevenson owed his election to Arvey, and Arvey needed the support of the powerful 11th Ward Democratic Organization to remain as boss. Daley prevailed on Arvey to sponsor him for state director of revenue, and on December 21, 1948, Governor-elect Stevenson made the appointment, declaring, "I need him in my show." As in his past promotions, Daley's rise was due not only to machine influence, but to his specialized knowledge of the workings of government. Daley had a solid legal and financial background, and brought with him the detailed knowledge of state budgets he had acquired in his years in the legislature. "Daley . . . is expected to be an ace on Stevenson's staff in helping guide the legislative programs over the hurdles ahead," the *Chicago Tribune* declared.[65]

The one drawback of Daley's new job was that the governor's staff worked out of the state capital of Springfield. Daley and Sis now had seven children, and he was reluctant to spend so much time away from home. He also could not afford to absent himself from the clubby political world of Chicago. Daley was by now forty-six, and if he was going to rise any further up the ranks of the machine, he would have to do it soon. The convenient arrangement Daley worked out with Stevenson was that he would work out of the State of Illinois building in downtown Chicago, diagonally across the street from City Hall. Daley got considerable political mileage out of being director of revenue. He was able to make some changes in how government operated, and then receive credit for them. One of his reforms was a new tax tabulation system that made it easier to catch delinquents, which was immediately praised in the newspapers. Daley also used his state office as a bully pulpit from which to speak out in favor of fiscal reform. Addressing the Business and Professional Women's Club, Daley held forth on the need for tax reform to distribute the tax load more fairly. Daley's prestigious position — in the cabinet of a respected reform-minded governor — also helped lift him above the mundane world of Chicago machine politics. The Daley that the public saw was Governor Stevenson's innovative revenue chief — not Daley the ward committeeman, a position he held on to, who spent evenings in the 11th Ward offices doling out favors.[66]

In July of 1949, Congress enacted landmark public housing legislation. The new law provided funding for 810,000 new units of government-subsidized housing to be built across the country. The need for the new building was real. After ten years of depression and another four of world war, the nation's housing stock was more depleted than ever. Chicago's shortfall was particularly dire: it had 1,178,000 families but only 906,000 standard units available to house them. In some cities, like New York, local housing authorities began building public housing almost as quickly as funding could be secured. But in Chicago, the politics was more complicated. A political cartoon in the *Chicago Sun-Times* showed an Uncle Sam figure towering over Chicago with his arms filled with public housing, with the caption: "Where Do You Want It?" That was the critical question. To most white aldermen, the new housing looked like an invitation to Elizabeth Wood and the CHA to build public housing for blacks in white neighborhoods. To prevent this from happening, the chairman of the City Council housing committee convinced the state legislature to pass legislation in 1948 giving the Chicago City Council the power to approve or disapprove all sites selected by the CHA.[67]

The same day Congress passed the new act, the CHA delivered to Mayor Kennelly an ambitious proposal for building 400,000 new units of public housing over the next six years. The difficult part was deciding where to recommend that the new units be located. Wood and her staff knew by now that every project they tried to locate in a white neighborhood would set off a political firestorm. But they were too committed to integrated housing to propose that all of the new units be built in the black ghetto. On November 23, 1949, the CHA formally submitted its proposal for the first seven sites, which contained 10,000 units of housing. The City Council held hearings on the sites that raged on for four days, with 160 speakers squaring off for and against the proposed sites. When the fighting was over — one observer said that the seven hills of Rome had generated less discussion than these seven sites — the City Council handed the CHA a stern rebuff. The aldermen approved two sites located in black neighborhoods near existing public housing, but rejected the remaining five sites. Unwilling to trust the CHA to identify additional sites, the City Council established its own subcommittee to evaluate possible locations. These aldermen took a raucous bus trip across the city in search of sites. The subcommittee joked in its wanderings around the city about how many public housing units it would place in the wards of the few white aldermen who supported Wood and the CHA. Benjamin Becker, a Jewish alderman from the North Side, was a particular target of the anti-integration aldermen. They also floated the idea — which they eventually abandoned — of locating a housing project on the University of Chicago's tennis courts, as a payback to liberal Hyde Park alderman Robert Merriam. The proposal that emerged from the bus tour turned out to be no more viable than the CHA's plan. Where the CHA had taken too little account of politics, the subcommittee's plan seemed to be concerned with nothing else. Civic groups and newspaper editorial boards assailed the "bus tour sites" as irresponsible, and accused the City Council of treating public housing as "a nuisance to be swept into odd corners here and there or hidden behind industrial ruins."[68]

With the site-selection process at a standstill, Mayor Kennelly called on the City Council to negotiate directly with the CHA. Two leading aldermen, John Duffy and William Lancaster, seized on the opportunity to develop an alternative plan. Their proposal, which came to be known as the Duffy-Lancaster Compromise, included a mix of sites. Eight sites, representing 10,500 units of housing, would be built in poor black areas. Another seven sites, with about 2,000 units of housing, would be on vacant land outside the ghetto. To proponents of integration, the Duffy-Lancaster Compromise did not seem like much of a compromise at all. The *Chicago Defender* declared that it was "calculated to continue the ghetto and strengthen the spirit of segregation." Elizabeth Wood and the CHA tried to block the Duffy-Lancaster Compromise, and Wood traveled to Washington to urge the Public Housing Administration to rule that it violated federal nondiscrimination requirements. But the federal agency approved the plan with only minor modifications. At the time, the Duffy-Lancaster Compromise was regarded as a substantial blow to the ideal of integrated public housing. But the truth was, despite its heavy use of ghetto sites, it was a compromise: a significant number of public housing units were actually built outside the black ghetto. In just a few years, the city's anti-integration forces would not feel they needed to compromise at all.[69]

State director of revenue Richard J. Daley, freshly installed in his downtown Chicago offices, was already casting around for his next position. It would often be said of Daley, later in life, that he loved Chicago so much that the only job he ever wanted was to be its mayor. It paints an admirable picture, but it is not true. Daley spent most of his career looking for any job that would move him up another rung on the political ladder and give him more power. In May 1947, the newspapers were reporting that the "political grapevine" favored Daley for U.S. attorney. In December, they were saying that Daley was a likely candidate for Cook County state's attorney if the incumbent's health continued to fail him. And a year later, the *Chicago Tribune* was reporting that the "[s]oft-spoken but persistent Richard

J. Daley" was angling to be slated for the powerful position of Cook County Board president. Daley was not alone in wanting the machine's backing for the board presidency, which was coming open in 1950. Dan Ryan, a sitting member of the board, and Alderman John Duffy, of the Duffy-Lancaster Compromise, also wanted to be considered.[70]

Daley tried to rig the nominating process in his own favor. The machine's slate-making committees were traditionally limited to sitting ward committeemen, but Daley argued that the rules should be changed to allow both Governor Stevenson and Mayor Kennelly to participate. Daley's strategy was not hard to discern. He must have known that Stevenson, his employer, would support him. But the machine would not go along with this change in the procedures. "I know that the mayor and the governor don't want to be pictured as political bosses," Arvey said, speaking out against Daley's proposal. Other machine leaders were more blunt in their insistence that high-minded reformers like Stevenson and Kennelly had no business helping to choose the machine's candidates. "What the hell does Stevenson know about ward committeemen?" state senator William "Botchy" Connors asked. "You're likely to get three or four members of the Chicago Crime Commission on the ticket if you let these guys name the candidates." Daley also proposed that candidates should be allowed to serve on the slate-making committee, which would have allowed him to be present as a representative of the powerful 11th Ward. In the end, Daley was foiled in his attempts to stack the slate-making committee, and he lost the nomination to Duffy. He was "bitterly disappointed," the *Chicago Tribune* reported, at being passed over.[71]

Daley's disappointment did not last long. Just two weeks later, the machine slate-makers had the chance to choose a candidate for another powerful Cook County post. The county clerk died on January 3, 1950, and a successor had to be named. Once again, Daley campaigned energetically for the job. He managed to get Mayor Kennelly to call Jake Arvey in Miami Beach to urge the machine to slate him. Daley also got Governor Stevenson to announce his support. Daley made his pitch to the slate-making committee in machine headquarters at the Morrison Hotel, recounting his years of service as deputy comptroller, Senate minority leader, and state director of revenue — as well as his years of loyal service to the machine as precinct captain and ward committeeman. On January 9,

1950, Daley was slated for the job, filling the interim position until an election could be held.[72]

The duties of the county clerk were mundane. Daley's main responsibilities were issuing marriage licenses, recording deaths and births, and maintaining vital statistics. But it was a good political stepping-stone for someone of Daley's ambitions. As a candidate for county clerk, Daley would have to run countywide — a chance to redeem himself with the countywide electorate that had rejected him for sheriff. The county clerk also controlled hundreds of patronage positions. That gave Daley, as they said in the Chicago machine, clout. As county clerk, Daley immediately went to work mastering the minutiae of his office. Because he was serving as county clerk on an interim appointment, he would have to stand for election in a matter of months in order to hold on to the position. Daley implemented an array of improvements designed to curry favor with the voters. Some of his changes were low profile: he published the first calendar of law cases for the county court. Others were more visible. One of Daley's most ingratiating innovations was his overhaul of the way in which his office dispensed marriage licenses. He installed microfilm machines for birth and marriage certificates, cutting the wait time for these documents from days to a matter of minutes. He also increased the number of staff devoted to processing marriage licenses, which both helped speed up the process and created new patronage positions for him to fill. And he ordered his marriage-license clerks to wear uniform beige jackets. "The new jackets should start altar-bound couples on their trip a little more cheerful," Daley declared. Daley included a message from the county clerk with every new license: "May I very warmly and sincerely congratulate you on your marriage, and may it be a long and happy one."[73]

The 1950 election, in which Daley had to run for his own full term as county clerk, was a grim one for Chicago Democrats. A few months before the voting, U.S. Senator Estes Kefauver's Committee to Investigate Organized Crime in Interstate Commerce arrived in town. The committee's star witness was Captain Daniel "Tubbo" Gilbert, the Democratic nominee for Cook County sheriff — or, as he was dubbed by the newspapers, "The World's Richest Cop." Gilbert tried to explain how he managed to accumulate $360,000 in negotiable securities, among other holdings, on a modest police salary. He claimed to have been a successful gambler, wagering on everything from stocks and bonds to baseball games and elections. Asked by the committee's counsel whether his gambling was legal, the police captain conceded that, "Well, no. No, it is not legal." The Kefauver committee met in secret, but the *Chicago Sun-Times* got hold of a transcript and splashed Gilbert's words across the front page. Predictably, Gilbert ended up losing to his little-known Republican opponent by 370,000 votes, and dragging down most of the Democratic ticket with him, including U.S. Senator Scott Lucas, the majority leader and a key congressional ally of President Truman.[74]

Daley's race for his own term as county clerk was hard fought. His Republican opponent, 7th Ward alderman Nicholas Bohling, ran a spirited anti-machine campaign. Daley had served as the "errand boy, the mouthpiece of the Kelly-Nash-Arvey machine in the legislature at Springfield," Bohling charged, and the machine now "owned" him. The centerpieces of Daley's defense were endorsements from Stevenson and Douglas, two machine-made politicians who were nevertheless able to confer a mantle of reform. Despite the Democratic rout, Daley ended up defeating Bohling by 147,000 votes. There was no obvious explanation for why Daley had run so strongly, and rumors circulated after the election that he had won as a result of a carefully crafted sellout. Republicans allegedly agreed to "trim" — or hold back support for — Bohling in exchange for the machine's trimming John Duffy, the Democratic candidate for Cook County Board president. The scenario had a certain plausibility. Machine boss Arvey wanted to see Daley elected, and he and Daley both had good reason to want to see Duffy defeated. A bitter battle was looming for control of the machine. Arvey's tenuous hold on power was being challenged by a group that included Duffy; 14th Ward alderman Clarence Wagner; Judge James McDermott, a former 14th Ward alderman and county treasurer; and 19th Ward committeeman Tom Nash, a cousin of former boss Pat Nash who had gone over to the other side. If Duffy were elected to the patronage-rich position of president of the county board, it would have given a considerable boost to the Wagner-McDermott-Duffy faction in the battle for control of the machine. From Daley's perspective, a victory for himself and a defeat for his rival Duffy was the best possible outcome.[75]

After the machine's poor showing in the 1950 elections, the anti-

Arvey forces were ready to make their move. Arvey had survived as boss for three years through a series of shrewd slating decisions — primarily, running Kennelly for mayor in 1947 and Stevenson and Douglas statewide in 1948 — but when he slated "Tubbo" Gilbert, his luck finally ran out. The powerful ward committeemen who controlled the machine decided that Arvey's interim chairmanship should come to a close. It was easy enough for the machine's warring factions to decide that Arvey was out. The more difficult question was who would take his place. The Wagner-McDermott-Duffy-Nash faction would clearly be fielding a candidate, and Daley wanted to run against them as the choice of the Arvey wing. Daley approached Arvey to ask for his support. "But Dick, I thought you wanted to run for mayor," Arvey responded. Daley said that he did. "Well, then, you shouldn't be county chairman," Arvey said. "People will say you're a boss." Daley promised Arvey that he would step down as party leader if he ever became mayor, and Arvey agreed to support him.[76]

The battle to succeed Arvey would be waged in the Democratic Cook County Central Committee — the Chicago machine's version of the Politburo. The Central Committee was made up of committeemen from all fifty of Chicago's wards, along with another thirty township committeemen representing suburban parts of Cook County. It was not a committee of equals: each committeeman's vote was weighted according to how large a Democratic vote he had produced in the previous election. The ward committeeman from a strong machine ward like the 24th might cast fifteen thousand votes in the Central Committee, while a township committeeman might cast only a few thousand. As a practical matter, power was concentrated in a few ward committeemen from wards where the machine ran strongly, and elected officials whose offices gave them large numbers of patronage positions.[77]

The two factions battling for control of the machine looked a lot alike: both were comprised primarily of South Side, Irish-Catholic machine loyalists. Beneath the similarities, however, lay a deep antipathy. The Arvey-Daley camp, heir to the old Kelly-Nash organization, was more politically liberal. Arvey, a child of impoverished Jewish immigrants, was a New Dealer at heart. He had used his office to move the machine in a more progressive direction: his greatest legacy would be the political careers of Stevenson and Douglas. The Wagner-McDermott-Duffy-Nash group, for its part, would have been happy to dump Senator Douglas before the next election, and might well have tried to force Governor Stevenson out when he ran for reelection. But the real fault lines between the two groups were cultural and personal. The Wagner-McDermott-Duffy-Nash faction was an alliance of two powerful groups of South Side Irish — the 19th Ward and the 14th. The 19th Ward was an enclave of upwardly mobile Irish-Americans who had left working-class areas like Bridgeport for middle-class enclaves like Morgan Park and Beverly. To Daley and his neighbors, they were the "lace-curtain Irish," bitterly resented for looking down on their less successful brethren. These were the sort of Irish people, it was said in Bridgeport, who had fruit in the house when no one was sick. The 14th Ward, centered on the Back of the Yards area adjoining the 11th Ward, was culturally closer to working-class areas like Bridgeport. But 14th Ward politicians had a long-standing rivalry with the nearby 11th Ward, which made them natural allies of the 19th Ward faction.[78]

When the time came to settle the issue, neither side had the votes to win the chairmanship. The committeemen decided to elect another caretaker boss, but this time one who would serve only through the 1952 presidential election. The two factions settled amicably on Joseph Gill, who was both Municipal Court clerk and ward committeeman from the 44th Ward on the North Side. The sixty-five-year-old Gill was the oldest member of the Cook County Democratic Committee, and was considered unlikely to try to stay on past his agreed-upon retirement date. Gill had been a noncombatant in the battles between the machine's rival camps, and both regarded him as neutral. For Daley, the selection of Gill was a disappointment, eased somewhat by the fact that he was elevated to first vice chairman, inching him ever closer to the top job. When the maneuvering was complete, Senator Douglas invoked a well-known hymn on Daley's behalf. "I do not ask to see the distant scene," Douglas said, quoting John Henry Cardinal Newman. "One step is enough for me."[79]

CHAPTER 3

Chicago Ain't Ready for Reform

After three years in office, Kennelly was turning out to be an ineffectual and not particularly popular mayor. Content to preside over ceremonial functions, he let the rapacious and independent-minded leaders of the City Council — the so-called Gray Wolves — plunder the city coffers. Kennelly's ineptitude had become a citywide joke: one police captain testified at a City Council hearing that "the only thing [the moving company owner turned mayor] learned in the moving business is never to lift the heavy end." Unfortunately for the machine, the one cause Kennelly pursued with determination and effectiveness was political reform. He had steadily whittled away at the patronage system, the machine's lifeblood, taking 12,000 jobs away from the ward bosses and turning them into civil-service positions. Kennelly had also put teeth in the civil-service system by appointing reformer Stephen Hurley to head the Civil Service Commission. Hurley was wise to all of the machine's tricks — hiring "temporary" employees to get around civil-service hiring lists, "forgetting" to schedule civil service exams, and changing job titles to wiggle out of civil service rules. Kennelly's anti-patronage campaign had an impact. In the days of Kelly and Cermak, ward committeemen and aldermen each had about 285 jobs to dispense at their discretion. By the end of Kennelly's first term, they had only a handful of jobs. The machine leaders were by now openly referring to Kennelly as "Snow White" and plotting his downfall.[1]

As damaging as Mayor Kennelly's war on patronage was to his political future, it was another moralistic campaign that more directly led to his undoing. Kennelly had worked throughout his first term to rein in two revered institutions in black Chicago: policy wheels and jitney cabs. "Policy" was an immensely popular, if illegal, lottery-like gambling game. It was divided into a variety of "pools," which had evocative names like "Harlem," "Monte Carlo," and "Royal Palm." Each pool issued its own "slips," inscribed with different combinations of numbers. Players selected a combination of numbers and placed their bets at any of the "policy stations" scattered in barbershops, shoe-shine parlors, or basements throughout the South Side ghetto. Policy operators selected winning combinations, or "gigs," by drawing numbered balls out of drum-shaped containers.[2] Jitney cabs were another great, illegal South Side institution. In Chicago, as in much of the country, big taxi companies operated cabs with white drivers who drove almost exclusively in white neighborhoods. That left black neighborhoods with jitney cabs, unofficial taxis that were generally owned and driven by blacks. In many parts of the Black Belt, they were the closest thing there was to public transportation.

Policy and jitneys were not merely popular on the South Side — they were big business. There were, by one estimate, 4,200 policy stations spread across the South Side, handling bets from 100,000 people a day. The policy wheels were "as efficient and as well run as any marble-lined bank or brokerage house on LaSalle Street and many times more profitable," one historian observed.[3] They also provided thousands of well-paying runner, clerk, and cashier jobs for black Chicagoans, who faced an otherwise grim employment market. "Sometimes the girls could make $20 a week," one study reported. "There isn't a laundry in the city or a kitchen in Hyde Park where a girl without learning could earn $20 for a week's work." The jitneys were also an important source of jobs for black workers, and they were a critical part of the ghetto infrastructure: for many blacks, they were the only means of getting to grocery stores and doctor appointments.[4]

The policy wheels also contributed a great deal of money to the black submachine, particularly William Dawson's 2nd Ward Democratic Organization. Both the policy wheels and jitney cabs had operated for years with the protection of black politicians. Dawson and the machine defended the black policy wheels against both police extortion and the white syndicate, which tried repeatedly to extend its gambling empire into the black wards. Each time the Al Capone mob bribed a police captain to let white mobsters move in, Dawson had gone to Mayor Kelly and got the captain transferred out of the ward. But Mayor Kennelly, as part of his reform program, directed his police to undertake a massive crackdown on illegal activity in the black neighborhoods. The black community was outraged. Kennelly's edict was doing real harm to black Chicagoans — jitney cabdrivers were being thrown out of work, and employees of the policy wheels were being arrested. Kennelly was also violating the long-standing tradition of allowing black leaders to determine what illegal activity would be allowed in the black wards. Not least, many blacks suspected that for all of his good-government talk, Kennelly was simply clearing the way for white organized crime to replace black organized crime. "If anybody is to profit out of gambling in the Negro community, it should be the Negro," William Dawson fumed. "I want the money my people earn to stay in the Negro community." Dawson resolved to put a stop to Mayor Kennelly's incursions.[5]

Dawson's response to Kennelly was the indignation of a classic black "welfare" politician. In his book *Negro Politics,* James Q. Wilson divided black leaders of the pre–civil rights era into two types: those who pursued "status" for the black community and those who pursued "welfare." Status leaders, many affiliated with groups like the NAACP and the Urban League, devoted themselves to uplifting the social standing of the race — integrating neighborhoods and public facilities, or pushing for equal employment opportunity. That was not Dawson. Well into the 1940s, much of Chicago was racially segregated, and blacks were as a rule barred from white hotels, bars, soda fountains, taxis, and bowling alleys. But Dawson was best known in civil rights circles for the battles he failed to join — like the 1946 protests at Chicago's aptly named White City Roller Skating Rink, challenging its policy of denying admission to blacks. When Dawson did take a stand on integration, he was liable to oppose it. Chicago's leading black politician outraged the NAACP and his black congressional colleagues in 1956 by coming out against a federal bill to end segregation in public schools. He argued that requiring integration could endanger federal funding to public schools, which he viewed as more important. And during the 1960 presidential campaign, Dawson served on the civil rights issues committee of John F. Kennedy's presidential campaign — known as the Civil Rights Section. The first thing Dawson tried to do was get the name changed. "Let's not use words that offend our good Southern friends, like 'civil rights,'" he told the group's first meeting. His office in the campaign headquarters was quickly dubbed "Uncle Tom's Cabin." Dawson's primary loyalty was to his political organization, not his race — and when the two were in conflict, the Democratic machine always won. "You would not expect Willie Mays to drop the ball just because Jackie Robinson hit it," Dawson liked to say.[6]

Dawson was doing the machine's bidding when he opposed civil rights, but he also had his own self-interested reasons for opposing the status goals of civil rights activists. The black submachine that he led owed its existence to racial segregation, and Dawson's personal political power derived from his ability to mine the rich lode of Democratic votes in the black wards. The Black Belt was growing as a result of racial segregation, and as it grew Dawson incorporated more wards into the black submachine. If the status leaders got their way and achieved racial integration, black voters would disperse across the city — and would end up on the tally sheet of white ward committeemen. Civil rights activism had another practical drawback: it threatened to destroy the black submachine's monopoly on black politics. Now, the only candidates in the black wards were put up by the machine, and they had no significant opposition. If the black community divided over integration, civil rights supporters might run their own slate of candidates and turn every election into a referendum on racial progress. Whatever civil rights activism meant for the race — and Dawson remained skeptical on this point — it spelled disaster for the black submachine.[7]

To his critics, Dawson's civil rights record made him "perhaps *the* classic Uncle Tom politician," currying favor with the white power structure by selling out his own people. But Dawson vehemently rejected the label, insisting that he was more in the tradition of Booker T. Washington, who taught his politically dispossessed black followers the pragmatic gains that came from working within the system. "Yes, they called Booker T. an Uncle Tom," Dawson once said. "But today the bust of Booker T. Washington is displayed in the Hall of Fame. Congress has just approved an appropriation to help preserve his birthplace for posterity while the names of his detractors have long since been forgotten." In fact, Dawson's career is too complex to dismiss with the epithet "Uncle Tom." Having grown up in the Jim Crow South, and having been forced to flee his hometown in a Faulknerian scenario involving interracial rape and revenge, he knew at least as well as his critics how bad things were for blacks. In his speeches, he occasionally alluded to these racial wounds. "Were it my desire," he once told an audience at Ohio's historically black Wilberforce University, "I could cite to you from my own personal knowledge incidents which would chill the blood within you, whip your temper into a frenzy, and fan the fires of your wrath into a devastating flame on which reason and judgment would be quickly consumed and give place to bitter vengeance and unbridled retaliation." Rather than unleashing this spirit of "unbridled retaliation," Dawson believed in working through the political process for incremental gains. For years, he had a sign over his desk with Reinhold Niebuhr's Serenity Prayer: "God grant me the serenity to accept the things I cannot change; courage to change the things I can; and wisdom to know the difference." For Dawson, these words were a racial credo.[8]

What Dawson believed in was welfare politics: jobs, money, and favors. Dawson went downtown to the Democratic machine headquarters just as the white ward committeemen did, demanding patronage, and because he delivered on election day, the machine gave it to him. Dawson and the submachine did not get the same number of patronage jobs as his white counterparts did, and the black submachine's positions were generally low-level ones. In 1955, when blacks were 19 percent of the Chicago population, and regularly gave machine candidates more than 70 percent of their votes, they had only 5 percent of judgeships and no city commissioners. Still, in the impoverished black wards Dawson represented, even the lowliest patronage jobs were prized. "He'd take a hundred menial jobs over ten judgeships," observed historian Dempsey Travis. "He counted numbers." Dawson and his precinct captains were also able to dole out favors, just as white machine politicians did — calling the city to get garbage picked up or intervening with a judge to get a young person out of a scrape with the law. And until Kennelly's crackdown on the policy wheels and jitney cabs, the machine had always given Dawson a measure of autonomy over the black wards — allowing him, as the saying went, to "stand between the people and the pressure." Kennelly's decision to go after the jitneys and policy wheels was an attack on this autonomy, and on Dawson's ability to deliver for his followers on a classic welfare issue.[9]

Dawson was in a strong position to make his displeasure about Kennelly's actions known. He was, by now, a substantial figure in the Democratic Party. He had risen in Congress to become chairman of the committee that would later be called Government Operations, the first black to serve as chairman of a regular House committee. In 1948, he had headed up the Negro division of the Democratic National Committee, raising money and hitting the hustings in black neighborhoods across the country. Far more important, though, was his power at the local level. Dawson's submachine was in the process of extending its reach to include five majority-black wards that, along with the River Wards, were the machine's most productive. Dawson knew that he and his voters had played a large part in putting Kennelly in City Hall — it was only Kennelly who seemed to have forgotten it. Before the 1951 election, Dawson exploded at Kennelly, in a meeting that immediately became part of Chicago's political lore. "Who do you think you are? I bring in the votes. I elect *you*. *You* are not needed, but the votes are needed. I deliver the votes to you, but you won't talk to *me?*" Many white machine leaders felt as Dawson did, bitterly resentful that Kennelly wanted them to back him for reelection at the same time as he was turning their patronage jobs into civil-service positions.[10]

Had the machine been more united, it might have ousted Kennelly before he could win a second term. But with the bitter power struggle between the Arvey-Daley and Wagner-McDermott-Duffy-Nash factions still unresolved, the machine could not agree on an alternative candidate. Dawson and the other ward committeemen allowed Kennelly one more term, but they were not enthusiastic about it. "We as troops knew there was something wrong at the top," said a Dawson precinct captain during Kennelly's reelection campaign. "In any good organization its members can just about get the temperament or the feel of there being something rotten in Denmark. . . . We were just dragging our feet." Kennelly was reelected in 1951, but he failed to realize what even Dawson's foot soldiers had figured out: that his second term as mayor would be his last.[11]

The 1952 Democratic National Convention was held in Chicago, in the International Amphitheatre, just a few blocks from Daley's home. Joseph Gill, whose reign as party boss was scheduled to end after the 1952 presidential election, went out in a burst of glory, by presiding over the convention. The delegates nominated Adlai Stevenson for president — the favorite son of Illinois, and of the Chicago machine, which had plucked him from obscurity four years earlier. Stevenson's nomination was marred only by the fact that most people at the convention knew in their hearts that he had little prospect of defeating Dwight D. Eisenhower, the World War II general who would be carrying the Republican banner. In fact, Eisenhower's appeal was so broad that Jake Arvey had initially tried and failed to recruit the unaligned hero to run for the Democratic nomination.[12]

The Democratic convention was also notable as the site of an odd outburst of Daley ambition. When Stevenson got the nomination, it created a vacancy at the top of the statewide ticket. Edward J. Barrett, Illinois secretary of state and a Chicagoan, was eager to get the Chicago machine's nomination for governor. He approached Daley on the convention floor, in the presence of several witnesses, and asked for his support. "Without any hesitancy, Daley answered, 'Absolutely,' and we shook hands on it," Barrett said afterward. "He said I should be the man and that he would be with me." But the Monday morning after the convention ended, Daley told reporters that he was throwing his own hat in the ring. "I'm available," he said from his county clerk's office. "Many people have suggested that my background of legislative leadership and as state revenue director under Governor Stevenson would fill the bill." Daley was undeniably going back on his word, and in reporting it the *Tribune* noted that Daley "had been considered a backer of Barrett." When Stevenson threw his support behind his lieutenant governor, Sherwood Dixon, it was clear that Daley had no chance of winning the nomination. Three days after announcing his interest in running, Daley was insisting the whole matter had never occurred. "I am not, and was not, a candidate for the nomination for governor," Daley said. It was just as well that Daley did not get the nomination. Eisenhower was elected in a landslide, rolling up a 400,000-vote victory even in Stevenson's home state. Dixon lost to Republican William Stratton in the statewide Republican rout.[13]

With the elections over, the maneuvering to replace Gill as machine boss heated up. Daley, now the vice chairman, remained eager for the position. The Wagner-McDermott-Duffy faction put Judge McDermott forward as its candidate. McDermott's supporters had considerable pull but the Arvey-Daley faction looked to be slightly stronger — particularly by the critical measure of patronage positions. As county clerk, Daley himself controlled hundreds of patronage jobs. The retiring boss, Gill, who was backing Daley, had another large army of patronage workers working for him in the Municipal Court clerk's office. And another Daley supporter, Municipal Court bailiff Al Horan, doled out both patronage jobs and lucrative insurance and bonding work. The cold war between the two factions finally broke out into open warfare on July 8, 1953, when Gill formally submitted his resignation to the Cook County Democratic Central Committee.[14]

The meeting at the Morrison Hotel began with vice chairman Daley reading Gill's resignation letter. The script then called for Daley to be nominated and elected. But the Wagner-McDermott-Duffy-Nash faction, knowing it did not have enough votes to prevail, pursued a different strategy. After almost two hours of debate, Wagner moved to adjourn the proceedings for two weeks. His unspoken plan was to use the extra time to round up additional support for McDermott. When Daley emerged from the meeting, reporters waiting outside were incredulous at the turn of events. "They didn't give it to you?" asked one reporter, who, on the basis of that morning's *Tribune,* had expected to be interviewing the new machine boss. Daley, his eyes moist, shook his head and explained. "Clarence [Wagner] stopped it," Daley said. "Gill calls for a motion to nominate me and Clarence gets up and says 'Now, wait a minute. Let's not be hasty.' And there was a big argument and we didn't get to vote."[15]

Wagner decided to go off on a fishing trip to Canada while McDermott and Duffy tried to win over wavering committeemen.

Wagner and friends, including state senator Donald O'Brien, packed into a city-owned Cadillac and headed north until Wagner crashed the car over an embankment. Wagner died, though all his passengers survived. "It's hard to know, even now, what actually happened," O'Brien said later, "but those highways up there are full of curves, and I think that Clarence mistook a small dirt road that went off into the woods for a turn in the highway." Daley had already built his career on a series of well-timed deaths, but none was more convenient for him than this one.[16]

McDermott did not give up his quest immediately. "I know that [the Daley forces] have the shiv out for me," he declared, "but I think it looks pretty good for us." But with the powerful Wagner dead, he soon realized that there was no chance of defeating Daley. "In the interest of my party and to bring about unity and harmony, I have requested those committeemen who advanced my name to withdraw it," McDermott said the day before the county committee was to meet for its vote. On July 21, the fifty-one-year-old Daley was voted in as the new chairman of the Cook County Democratic Central Committee. Daley rose to thank McDermott for "putting the unity and harmony of the party first." Then he made the kind of implausible assertion he liked to offer whenever he won a new office: "I have made no deals or commitments to anyone, nor will I."[17]

Daley's victory over McDermott was widely hailed as a victory for progressivism and reform within the machine. The comparatively liberal *Sun-Times* welcomed Daley as "an associate of the more enlightened progressive wing of the Democratic Party," and said his challenge would be to convert the machine's "old-timers" to his way of thinking. The hard-core Republican *Tribune* declared that "[o]ne result of Daley's election will be to continue the New Deal color of the Democratic organization, with semireform overtones." Daley was already being mentioned as a candidate for mayor in 1955, and some observers wondered if he was hurting himself by becoming head of the machine. It would make him an easy target for opponents who wanted to charge him with bossism. But the political reality was that if the Wagner-McDermott-Duffy group had seized control of the machine, it is unlikely Daley would ever have received the Democrat nomination for mayor. Daley insisted that the point was moot. Two days after winning the chairmanship, he appeared on television to declare that he would seek reelection as county clerk. Daley promised that he would support Mayor Kennelly for reelection in 1955, "if the mayor is interested in being a candidate."[18]

After the Duffy–Lancaster Compromise, it was clear that the tide had turned forcefully against integrated public housing. The CHA began to lose some of its key integrationists. Elizabeth Wood's top staff member had been forced out when Mayor Kennelly took office. Within months of the City Council's vote on the Duffy–Lancaster plan, two of the strongest supporters of integration resigned from the CHA board of directors.[19]

With site selection resolved by the Duffy–Lancaster plan, the battle over race in public housing shifted to tenant selection. Many of the CHA's public housing projects remained racially segregated. There were a number of all-white projects — including Trumbull Park Homes, Lawndale Gardens, Lathrop Homes, and Bridgeport Homes — reflecting the all-white neighborhoods in which they had been built. And others were all black, including Ida B. Wells Homes and Altgeld Gardens. The CHA had announced a policy of nondiscrimination in 1952, under which blacks would be admitted to the all-white projects. But top CHA officials later admitted that the board had ordered the agency to continue to exclude blacks from these projects. It was a secret policy, Wood would later charge, identical to "the discredited 'separate but equal' doctrine which the Dixiecrats have used to support segregation." Wood tried to resist the board policy by continuing to recommend blacks for the city's all-white projects, but her candidates were routinely rejected.[20]

The next white public housing project to be besieged by racial unrest was Trumbull Park Homes, in the Far South Side neighborhood of South Deering. The all-white project was accidentally integrated in the summer of 1953, when the project's administrative staff mistakenly gave Betty Howard and her family an apartment. Howard was a black woman with an extremely light complexion, whose application listed her as living in a neighborhood that was not identifiably black. Because Mr. Howard was a veteran, the CHA waived its customary home visit, and therefore did not meet the rest of the family. With no clear indications that the Howards were black, Trumbull Park's housing clerk assumed they were white and approved their application. The Howard family moved into the project on July 30. It was not until the following week that Trumbull Park's manager called the city with some troubling news — Mrs. Howard, the manager reported, "might be Negro."[21]

Word of the unwelcome new neighbors spread quickly through Trumbull Park. On August 5, a crowd of about fifty white teenagers gathered at the Howards' apartment, yelling threats and throwing rocks and bricks. Four days later, the angry mob had grown to more than one thousand. They threw rocks, bricks, and sulfur candles through the Howards' windows, forcing them to board them up with plywood. The Howards lived as virtual prisoners in their home, as the white-looking Mrs. Howard escaped for occasional trips for food and other supplies. By week's end, forty-one protesters had been arrested, twenty injured, and a round-the-clock vigil of 250 police officers was needed to keep the peace. The mob at Trumbull Park was a mixture of white ethnic groups — Irish, Slavs, Poles, and Italians — with no one group predominating. The *Chicago Defender* would note of the white mobs that "although there was no unity in the language backgrounds, they had a common . . . hatred for Negroes." The Trumbull Park mob enforced a fierce racial solidarity: within a month of the Howards' arrival, a white-owned liquor store that served blacks was set on fire. Adding to the feeling of terror, bombs exploded regularly in the area around the Howards' apartment.[22]

South Deering's whites were convinced that the black incursion into Trumbull Park Homes was only the first step in a campaign of racial infiltration. Blacks would soon start using the neighborhood's parks and playgrounds. Then they would begin buying up private homes in the neighborhood. In no time at all, the whites believed, "the whole thing will be Black and they will buy at their own price." When the housing battle was won, blacks would begin taking away white jobs at the nearby Wisconsin Steel Works, which had started hiring blacks only during the labor shortages of World War II. The great underlying fear for many South Deering residents — as it was in the Deep South — was interracial dating and miscegenation. "White people built this area [and] we want no part of this race mixing," the *South Deering Bulletin* declared. According to one fair-housing investigator who had been sent into South Deering, neighborhood residents were saying that "it won't be long now and Negroes and whites intermarrying will be a common thing and the white race will go down hill." In fact, the investigator reported, no doubt with some exaggeration, that South Deeringites lately talked "about nothing else."[23]

Tensions in South Deering ratcheted up in the fall, after Wood announced plans to move another three black families into Trumbull Park. The rabidly anti-integrationist South Deering Improvement Association stirred up opposition among neighborhood residents, cheered on by the hate-filled reportage of the *South Deering Bulletin*. Elected officials from the area aimed their most inflammatory rhetoric at the CHA. The local alderman denounced Wood for seeking to "cause racial tension" and demanded her resignation. Another, from a nearby ward, joined in, declaring that "there's vindictiveness and revenge in this picture because we have pinkoes in the CHA." On October 13, 1953, the day the three new families were scheduled to move in, the police presence was increased to twelve hundred and the new tenants were brought in "in a caravan under police escort." About two hundred protesters were on hand, pelting the new arrivals with an array of projectiles, but the police were able to contain the conflict. The CHA instituted a brief moratorium on new black tenants to quell the demonstrations, but in February 1954, the housing authority once again began moving small numbers of black families into Trumbull Park Homes, without prior announcement, under heavy police guard.[24]

The Howards moved out of Trumbull Park on May 3, 1954, after it was determined that they did not meet the project's income requirements. But by the time they left, another ten black families were living in the project. Over the summer, the battle of Trumbull Park shifted to the actual park. On June 22, a mob of whites attacked two blacks who were trying to play ball in the park. When blacks came to the park on July 10 to use a baseball diamond, the police had nearly four hundred officers on hand to keep the peace. Still, a riot broke out, and police ended up arresting fifteen white demonstrators and one black baseball player. The Trumbull Park disturbances, which started out as a neighborhood controversy, were increasingly gaining national attention. On July 4, 1954, Eric Sevareid devoted his entire CBS news review, *American Week,* to the conflict.[25]

Adding to her political troubles, Elizabeth Wood had continued to flout the machine on personnel matters. The reform-minded Wood always refused to hire the patronage workers that other agency heads understood they had to make room for. As long as Mayor Kelly was protecting her, there was little the machine could do but complain. But without a strong patron in City Hall, Wood found herself increasingly being "subjected to the opposition and attack of persons and interests who would wish the situation otherwise," she said. Wood's strong stand against patronage and favoritism had made headlines in the spring of 1953, when she refused to hire one particularly well-connected office-seeker: Richard Daley's cousin, John M. Daley. Kennelly had urged the CHA to hire John Daley as the agency's general counsel, no doubt in an effort to curry favor with the county clerk and powerful 11th Ward committeeman, and to enlist his support for a third term as mayor. John Daley was approved by the CHA, but Wood refused to make the appointment. She told the press he was not even technically qualified for the job, since he had only five years of legal experience, while the CHA's rules required that the general counsel have eight. Wood also pointed out that Daley had graduated 183rd in a law school class of 193. "Up to now, the commissioners have taken pride in the fact that the CHA has been untainted by politics," Wood said. "The commissioners do not set a very good example for the staff when they make a political appointment of this nature." Daley eventually withdrew himself from consideration. Wood was, of course, correct about Daley's utter lack of qualification for the job, but he chose to present himself as a victim of bias against Irish-Catholics at the hands of the patrician Wood. "As a young American," Daley said in a statement, "I thought I would be entitled to the same fair play that any person, regardless of race, color, creed, religion, or nationalistic origin, is entitled to."[26]

It was time for the machine to choose its candidates for the 1954 elections, Daley's first slating decision since becoming boss of the machine. Slating was inherently undemocratic. Rather than give the voters a choice among candidates in a primary election, the Cook

County Democratic Central Committee selected the Democratic Party's nominees. The actual selection process was even more autocratic: Daley, in his capacity as machine boss, handpicked a subcommittee of ward committeemen who served as a slating committee. The slating committee joined Daley in meeting with and evaluating candidates seeking the machine's support. The interview process under Daley, a reform member of the Central Committee recalled, was far from substantive:

> The candidate would come forward and make a speech, and answer some very perfunctory questions. Usually, there are two questions. One, "If you were not to be slated for the office you seek, would you accept slating for any other office?" And the right kind of a guy would be expected to say, "I'm a loyal Democrat, and if, in the wisdom of this committee, I'm chosen for some other post, I can assure you that every bit of energy and talent that I have will be devoted," and so on. Another question is, "If you are not slated, will you support the guy that is slated?" And you are supposed to say, "I will be disappointed if I were not chosen, but I am a loyal Democrat and I will support whomever you choose." And another question is, "Will you support the candidate of the party after the primary against the Republican opponent?" And you say, "Of course I will."

Daley's handpicked committee always followed his lead, slating whomever he wanted on the ticket. The slate chosen by the committee was later presented to the full Central Committee for ratification, but that was a mere formality. "Ordinarily there was no discussion at all," one participant observed. "I don't think I can remember a time when there was anyone but myself who spoke against anybody. When I did, the hostility was unbelievable.'"[27]

The greatest dilemma confronting Daley in 1954 was whether to reslate Senator Paul Douglas. Douglas had distinguished himself as an outspoken liberal in his six years in the Senate, where he had championed labor unions in their battle against the Taft-Hartley Act, fought for civil rights, and advocated higher capital gains and corporate taxes. Douglas's forthright stands had won him enemies among Chicago conservatives, including the *Chicago Tribune* editorial board. Daley defied the critics and reslated Douglas, though probably not for ideological reasons. In slating the top of a ticket, Daley's primary consideration was always how strongly the candidate would run and what kind of coattails he would provide for machine candidates lower down the ballot. Daley expected that Douglas, a fairly popular incumbent, would run strongly in Chicago, and would help the rest of the ticket. He also understood, as Arvey had, the practical value of running "good government" candidates for the top offices. There was no harm in selecting a reformer for an office like U.S. senator, since it was not a position that carried a significant number of patronage jobs with it. And Daley knew that a reform candidate for senator or governor could help the machine elect its candidates for positions like county clerk — offices that came with considerable patronage, and were therefore of real importance. Daley also understood the value of keeping on good terms with independent voters. He knew that as powerful as the machine was, it had to reach out to unaffiliated voters to win citywide and countywide offices. Men like Douglas and Stevenson could lend the machine their credibility and help to reach these voters. A year later, when Daley was running for mayor and trying to convince voters he was not a machine hack, his close ties to Douglas would prove invaluable.

Daley also wanted a "blue-ribbon" candidate to run for Cook County sheriff. The voters were well aware how corrupt this office had been over the years, and they had registered their unhappiness four years earlier by roundly rejecting the hapless "Tubbo" Gilbert. Daley decided to try to win the office back from the Republicans by slating a candidate who would be so clearly qualified and nonpolitical as to be above reproach. Just as Arvey had found Douglas on the University of Chicago faculty, Daley found Joseph Lohman, a well-regarded criminologist who looked nothing like a typical machine candidate for sheriff. Lohman did not want to enter politics, and only after Daley met with Lohman personally did he agree to run.

When the time came to launch the 1954 campaign, Daley quickly demonstrated his skill at political organization. He instituted weekly meetings of all the machine candidates, something that had never been tried before, to coordinate campaign strategy. And he broadcast a fifteen-minute nightly "Democratic News Report to the People," which precinct captains were encouraged to tune in to so they would know the official party line on important issues. Daley also inaugurated a speakers' bureau, which arranged appearances by candidates and surrogates at citizens' groups and neighborhood organizations across the city and into the suburbs. Since Daley held a countywide position, he understood better than most machine politicians the importance of cultivating suburban voters. He also saw sooner than most the increasing influence the fast-growing suburbs would have on Cook County politics. Daley began to meet regularly with the thirty Democratic township committeemen, the suburban equivalent of ward committeemen, and drew them more closely into the day-to-day operations of the machine.

Daley was himself a candidate for reelection as county clerk, opposed by North Side Republican alderman John J. Hoellen. Daley began campaigning immediately after the April primary, not waiting for the traditional Labor Day kickoff. His primary focus was ward organizations, and he instructed each ward office to schedule at least three meetings at which candidates could speak to precinct captains and other machine workers, who would turn out voters on election day. Daley also experimented with some of the populist rhetoric he would employ a year later in his campaign for mayor. "Special interests dominate the Republican party nationally and locally," Daley told a kickoff rally of the machine faithful at the Morrison Hotel. "For too long a time — much too long — Illinois has been represented by a majority of reactionary special interests Congressmen." To help with fund-raising, he brought in a charismatic Democratic senator from Massachusetts named John F. Kennedy to speak at a $100-a-plate dinner at the Conrad Hilton Hotel.[28]

Daley made a concerted effort during the campaign to raise his public profile through the increasingly important medium of television. He eagerly appeared on the local NBC show *City Desk*. To smooth his rough Bridgeport edges, he took diction lessons through the Northwestern University speech department. Even with this expert advice, however, Daley still badly mangled syntax and vocabulary, at times fading into incomprehensibility. At a televised roundtable, he was asked whether he would serve out his term if reelected or whether he might run for mayor in a year. "Well . . . that question is highly problematically and loaded, as you know," Daley responded.

He added that the question, which seemed straightforward enough, "had too many contingencies and too many possibilities for any intelligent man to answer it at the present time." Despite Daley's weak performance on television, he won reelection as county clerk handily.[29]

Daley's reelection campaign had all the markings of a dry-run for a mayoral race the following year. Most tellingly, he seemed to be quietly working to undermine Mayor Kennelly. Party regulars had never liked Kennelly, but some viewed him as a necessary evil — a reformer they needed to keep their hold on City Hall. Kennelly was, for better or worse, an integral part of the machine's operations. This changed, however, once Daley became machine boss. Kennelly's views were no longer considered in slating decisions, and the mayor was suddenly frozen out of the traditional preelection precinct captains' luncheons and from the traditional round of "speak for the ticket" rallies at the ward offices. When a Daley loyalist was asked about Kennelly not being invited to the precinct captains' luncheons, he responded that "Kennelly's not a committeeman" — something that had been equally true in years when he had been invited. These attempts to push Kennelly out bore all the hallmarks of a classic Daley betrayal. Kennelly had consistently supported Daley. Desperate to be slated for county clerk in 1950, Daley had Kennelly call Arvey to lobby for him. The same year, when Daley was maneuvering to be slated for Cook County Board president, Kennelly was one of the allies Daley tried to sneak onto the slating committee. On October 31, 1954, Daley declared, "I am not and never was a candidate for mayor." He was, he insisted, only "a candidate for the important office of County Clerk" — words of reassurance to help lull his old ally Kennelly into a false sense of security.[30]

With the drive to push Elizabeth Wood out gaining force, Kennelly's housing coordinator recommended that the CHA board commission a study of the agency's operations. On his recommendation, the board retained a consulting firm. Wood was frozen out of the consultants' information-gathering process, and when the firm completed its report it recommended abolishing her position of executive secretary and replacing it with a new position of executive director. Wood's supporters at the CHA were convinced that the consultants' report was designed to provide the board with nominally objective reasons for doing what it had already decided to do. "All that stuff about Elizabeth not being a good administrator was phony," says the former CHA director of research. "It was what the board wanted them to say."[31]

At an August 23 meeting, the CHA commissioners gave Wood a copy of the report. They informed her that they had taken the consultants' advice to create a new position, executive director, and had filled it with retired army lieutenant-general William Kean. Kean would run the CHA. Board chairman John Fugard said he hoped that Wood would stay on to handle "the social aspect of housing in which she excels." Wood requested and was granted a meeting with Mayor Kennelly. In a sharply worded statement days after that meeting, she attacked the CHA board for the new restructuring "without prior notice to or consultation or discussion with me." She was being stripped of her authority, she charged, because of differences between herself and the board over race:

> [T]he most significant and dramatic area of conflict has been on the subject of race relations and segregation. The truth is that the differences that have arisen between the Commissioners and the Executive Secretary have been related primarily to the issue of the elimination of segregation in public housing and the opening of all public housing projects in the City of Chicago to Negro and white persons without discrimination or segregation.

Wood went on to accuse the board of paying "lip-service" to open housing "while privately issuing instructions thwarting those policies." The CHA refused to admit blacks to all-white projects, she charged, "despite repeated protests on my part." With black families in the white Trumbull Park project living "in a state of fear and isolation, subject to constant harassment," Wood said, that housing project had "become the shame of Chicago and the shame of the Nation." Most dramatically, Wood went on television and attacked Kennelly for his weak support for open housing. "I don't think that the city administration has ever adopted a clear cut policy on the integration of races in housing," she declared on a local news show, only an hour after attending a closed meeting with the CHA board.[32]

The day after Wood made her public statements, the CHA board met in special session and voted unanimously to fire her effective the following day. The board contended that she was being fired for making irresponsible statements to the press, including charging board members with "illegal and immoral motives" in connection with the integration of public housing. But Wood stuck by her own interpretation: "My feeling is that the racial question lies under my problems," she said. The *Chicago Defender* agreed, headlining a story: "Action Labeled Victory for Mob." Wood was quickly hailed by supporters of open housing as a martyr to the cause. Four members of a CHA citizens' advisory committee on racial matters, which included representatives from the *Chicago Defender,* the NAACP, and the National Conference of Christians and Jews, resigned to protest her removal. The black Baptist Ministers Conference of Chicago denounced her ouster, and one local pastor gave a sermon entitled "Elizabeth Wood and Her Enemies." Wood's backers formed an Emergency Committee on the Chicago Housing Authority, which asked the State Housing Board to investigate, and held a testimonial for her on October 28, 1954, at the 8th Street Theatre, at which she was praised for her "fearless leadership and selfless service" in her seventeen years with the CHA.[33]

After she left office, Wood continued to attack the CHA for supporting racial segregation. "In no field," she said, "is the program of nondiscrimination so bloody, so ruthless, as in the field of housing." Before long, Wood moved to New York, where she became a housing consultant. In 1961, she wrote a report for the Citizens Housing and Planning Council of New York urging that public housing be designed with built-in lounges, candy stores, and even pubs. She told the *New York Times,* which put her recommendations on its front page, that these social accommodations were necessary to avoid the "army barracks" feel of most projects, in which residents are deprived of the physical space to socialize with their neighbors. Wood also traveled to India for the Ford Foundation, as part of a team advising a Calcutta metropolitan governmental body on planning issues. Her most eloquent later writings, though, were on the importance of racial and economic integration in housing. In *The Balanced Neighborhood,* she proselytized for what she called "good heterogeneity" in urban planning, her vision of a residential environment that provides for "meaningful contacts between unlike members of a community as a result of shared community facilities." Exiled from Chicago, she continued to issue the same warning she delivered shortly before being forced out at the CHA: "The next generation will have to cure the slums created by this generation's official blindness."[34]

Wood always blamed the political forces in the Democratic machine and the City Council for her ouster, says a former staff member who spoke with her after she left. The CHA board was weak, she explained, and important decisions were essentially forced on it by the mayor and the City Council, which is to say the Democratic machine. Though Daley was still eight months away from becoming mayor when Wood was forced out, he may have played a significant role in her dismissal. Daley had as much motive as anyone to want Wood out. He was strongly opposed, on principle, to using public housing to integrate white neighborhoods, and Wood's plans hit especially close to home, since she had announced plans to move blacks into Bridgeport Homes, only blocks from Daley's house. Wood's insistence on running a "clean" agency was particularly problematic for Daley, since he was the head of a political machine that relied for its survival on its ability to find jobs for patronage workers. Her refusal to hire Daley's cousin was the most personal affront, and it is likely that Daley would have been especially unhappy with the way the incident played out in the press.[35]

Daley was in a good position to influence the situation if he desired. He had already been chairman of the Cook County Democratic Central Committee for eight months when the consultants' report on the CHA was commissioned, and for more than a year when Wood was removed. As party boss, he had considerable influence over the mayor, the City Council, and the CHA board. Daley also had close ties to James Downs, the Kennelly housing coordinator who commissioned the report and played a key role in ousting Wood. The NAACP Chicago chapter president said Wood's removal was an "expertly engineered coup . . . masterminded" by Downs, and one of Wood's former staffers called Downs "the evil genius behind it all" and suspected Daley may have been an important force acting on Downs. "Downs was a running dog for the political system, which at that time was Daley," says Edward Holmgren, a former assistant to Elizabeth Wood. Daley proved happy enough with Downs that when he was elected mayor a year later, Downs became his first housing and redevelopment coordinator and one of his most trusted advisers.[36]

With former military man William Kean now in charge, the CHA dramatically changed course. Wood's aggressive attempts to use the agency to promote racial integration were replaced by obedience to the city's political establishment. Kean set forth the CHA's new direction in his first statements to the press. Asked if he would take a new approach to the Trumbull Park Homes situation, Kean said he did not know enough to comment, but that in any case he would not be the one to ask, "because the commissioners issue policy to me." As it turned out, Kean lost little time in revising Wood's racial policies and calling a halt to the CHA's efforts to integrate all-white projects like Trumbull Park and Bridgeport Homes.[37]

As for the integrated projects, Wood's successor undid her efforts to promote "managed integration." Wood had grasped that with racial animosities running as high as they were in 1950s Chicago, housing projects had to be integrated with great care. She worked hard to introduce blacks into majority white projects without exceeding the "tipping point" at which whites would move out and abandon the project so that it became entirely black. She also tried to keep the racial mix in projects in white neighborhoods sufficiently white to make them acceptable to the surrounding community. Leclaire Courts, for example, had been built in a predominantly white neighborhood, over loud protests from its neighbors. Wood had carefully managed its racial composition, holding black occupancy to between 10 percent and 15 percent and making a concerted effort to replace departing whites with new white families. It was an approach that by today's standards seems troubling, and perhaps illegal, since it apportioned housing on the basis of race, and often meant that blacks would have to wait longer for housing than similarly situated whites. But Wood's tactics were intended to promote integrated housing in a highly segregated city. When her successor took office, he decreed that integration would no longer be managed. Kean did not hold open the apartments of departing whites until new white tenants could be found. As a result, projects that had been racially integrated soon became segregated. Leclaire Courts, for example, had 315 whites and 40 black tenants in 1953. After Wood's departure, when whites moved out they were replaced by blacks. Before long, it was virtually all black.[38]

By abandoning managed integration, the CHA effectively decided that Chicago's public housing would become housing for blacks. Over the next twenty-five years, whites fled projects like Trumbull Park and Cabrini-Green. By 1969, fully 99 percent of the tenants in the CHA's family housing would be black. In addition to ending Wood's dream of integrated public housing, the new policies ensured that white politicians would fiercely resist allowing any new projects to be built in their districts "Now the aldermen could say self-righteously, 'We can't give you another site in our area; look at what you will do with it,'" recalls one of Wood's aides. "And so no further sites were given."[39]

The CHA also abandoned Wood's careful attention to tenant selection. Some of Wood's criteria in evaluating tenants seem, by today's standards, to be inappropriate. It is hard to imagine bureaucrats today evaluating the housekeeping skills of applicants for government benefits, and no doubt civil libertarians would file a lawsuit if they did. But the animating principle behind Wood's tenant-selection process was that housing projects would only be healthy communities when careful thought was given to what kind of tenants would be allowed to move in. "It takes only a very few, very antisocial people to make a floor or a building or a project unsatisfactory to parents who are concerned about their children," she once said. Wood's tenant-selection process was abandoned not out of concern for civil liberties, but because the CHA was no longer concerned about the kind of communities that were being created. "The biggest problem after 1954, housing project tenants told me, was the breakdown in tenant selection . . . no real belief that you had to select self-respecting families," recalls Wood's aide. The chronically unemployed, convicted criminals, and gang members were all ushered into the projects, and hardworking tenants who wanted a healthier environment for their children moved out.[40]

On December 1, 1954, Kennelly announced that he would be running for reelection the following spring. Asked by a reporter if he had notified the machine of his plans, Kennelly said cheerfully that he intended to call Daley as soon as the press conference was over. If

Kennelly still did not grasp the depth of his troubles with the machine, he was one of the few people active in Chicago politics who missed it. "It is symbolic of the difficulties that have arisen between the mayor and the party machine that only after handing his announcement to the press did he telephone the news to Richard J. Daley," the *Chicago Daily News* explained for him on its editorial page the next day. "It is this aloofness which angers and alienates the ward committeemen." The aloofness ran in both directions. Asked if he would attend the opening of Kennelly's reelection headquarters in his capacity as party leader, Daley offered a curt response: "No, I have to take my kids to Santa Claus."[41]

Daley was evasive about whom he intended to support. "I expect the Democratic mayoral primary to attract the most able men in our great city," he said. "I have been asked as chairman of the Democratic Party just whom the Democratic Party will endorse. Obviously, I cannot answer that question because I do not know. The Democratic Party will meet and discuss all candidates, and it will select the best candidate." Daley was being unduly modest about the role he would play in the process. As he had done a year earlier, Daley would appoint the slate-making committee that would choose the machine's candidates, and he would be sure to stack it with men who could be counted on to follow his lead. Daley named Joe Gill, his predecessor as boss and a reliable ally, as chairman. He appointed Barnet Hodes, Jake Arvey's law partner, and Michael McDermott, committeeman from the 13th Ward on the Southwest Side, whose day job was chief clerk in Daley's county clerk's office. And Daley named submachine leader Bill Dawson. Dawson was not as much of a Daley crony as other members of the committee — that would come later — but Daley had been assiduously cultivating him, stopping by his district office at 35th and Calumet on a regular basis for visits on his way home from the Loop. At the least, Daley knew that Dawson was a reliable anti-Kennelly vote, since he had vowed four years earlier that the mayor's current term would be his last.[42]

Reports were by now rampant that Daley himself was on the verge of entering the mayoral race. Daley fueled the speculation. Asked if he would be making a presentation to the slate-making committee, Daley said he would "if asked to make one." Asked if he would run for mayor, Daley responded: "That's up to the slate committee." On December 15, 1954, Kennelly walked from City Hall to the smoke-filled rooms of the Morrison Hotel and read a prepared statement to the slate-making committee in which he assured them that "[w]henever there has been conflict between the interests of the public and personal or political considerations, my decisions have been made upon the basis of what is good for the city and its citizens — and what benefits the city benefits the Democratic Party." His stony-faced audience was buying none of it. When Kennelly was through reading, he said to Gill, who at Daley's behest chaired the committee, "You invited me, I'll be glad to answer any questions." But no one spoke up. "Is there anything you want me to explain?" the mayor asked. "No," Gill responded. Kennelly looked from one ward committeeman to the next, and saw that he was not going to win them over. "I presume it's unanimous?" he asked. "They gave me a fast deal," he would complain later.[43]

Most ominous of all for Kennelly's prospects was the fact that Daley had sat in on the proceedings, even though he was not on the committee. "My office as chairman is next door to the room where the committee is meeting," Daley explained. "I pop in now and then." In contrast to Kennelly's brief appearance, Daley met with the committee for two hours. The slating committee later insisted it had "seriously" considered Kennelly, Adamowski, and others, but it unanimously voted to draft Daley. It had been a foregone conclusion that the committee would choose Daley, but it was not certain it would be unanimous. The unanimity indicated that the anti-Daley factions were beginning to reconcile themselves to Daley's leadership, and that Daley would have the support of a united machine in the primary.[44]

The machine's official line was that Daley had been "drafted" to run for mayor. Daley played his part in the little drama, exclaiming that the draft was "a great honor, and I never dreamed it could happen to me." He said he would need time to decide whether he would be willing to run. Two days later, to the surprise of absolutely no one, in a prepared statement, Daley said he would accept the draft, "[a]lthough I have not sought this honor." The slate-making committee's nomination was technically only a recommendation that was forwarded to the full Cook County Democratic Central Committee. Frank Keenan, the powerful Cook County assessor and Kennelly's newly appointed campaign manager, delivered a passionate speech to this larger group in favor of renominating the mayor. In the end, Daley won 47–1, with Kennelly winning only Keenan's vote.[45]

Kennelly was not about to give up City Hall without a fight. "It is already evident that the 'draft' is building to a hurricane of resentment against boss rule," Kennelly declared. "The question is whether the people of Chicago will rule or be ruled by the willful, wanton inner circle of political bosses at the Morrison Hotel." As an embattled candidate taking on the machine, Kennelly started to show a spirit he never exhibited as mayor. Five of the ward committeemen who voted for Daley in the Democratic Central Committee held city jobs. Kennelly demanded their resignations; two were forced out just two days before Christmas. Kennelly also stopped putting patronage workers recommended by the party bosses on the city payroll, and vowed to fire all non-civil-service city employees who campaigned against him in the upcoming election. Though Kennelly had lost the machine, he was not without supporters. The business community — a traditional antagonist of the machine — threw its weight behind his candidacy. And in an editorial headlined "The Man They Dumped," the *Chicago Tribune* — another longtime machine opponent — lauded Kennelly as a public servant who "hasn't regarded service to the party organization as his first duty in office."[46]

The Democratic primary was complicated further when Benjamin Adamowski, Daley's old friend from Springfield, entered the race on an anti-machine platform. Adamowski is one of the great might-have-beens of Chicago politics, and someone whose career stands in dramatic counterpoint to Daley's plodding but utterly effective ascent up the machine ranks. Adamowski was born into machine politics to a far greater degree than Daley. He was the oldest of nine children of Max Adamowski, a three-hundred-pound Polish immigrant saloonkeeper and organization alderman from Little Poland, on the near North Side. Adamowski earned a law degree from DePaul University in 1928, and took a job as examiner of titles for the Cook County recorder of deeds. But he was too ambitious to remain in the county bureaucracy for long. In 1931, at the age of twenty-five, he was elected to the state House of Representatives. After the election, Adamowski submitted his resignation as examiner of titles. The

Cook County recorder of deeds, a good machine politician, tried to talk Adamowski into staying on. The machine liked having legislators on its payroll, and the legislators — who earned as little as $1,750 a year — were usually grateful for a second salary. But Adamowski decided to take a more independent path, spurning the machine's offer and opening a law office on LaSalle Street instead.

In the legislature, Adamowski put even more distance between himself and his father's political machine. While Daley was doing the bidding of Mayor Kelly and the Democratic Organization, Adamowski aligned himself with the liberal, reformist governor Henry Horner, Kelly's rival in the statewide Democratic Party. It was not a good career move — as Daley understood, the machine could do more for an ambitious Chicago politician than an unaffiliated governor could — but Adamowski was acting on principle. As a legislator, Adamowski was a force to be reckoned with. He was a man of unusual intelligence and a skilled orator, whom one University of Chicago philosopher called the "Daniel Webster of the West." After rising to majority leader, Adamowski left the legislature and returned to Chicago to become Mayor Kennelly's corporation counsel. Adamowski took the job because he believed Kennelly was prepared, despite his machine backing, to usher in a new age of reform for Chicago. After three years, Adamowski resigned, disillusioned by the degree to which the machine bosses continued to have their way at City Hall. "Kennelly was just a nice guy," Adamowski said later. "He should never have been mayor of Chicago. He should have been a cardinal or a monsignor. He was that kind of person."[47]

As the 1955 election approached, Adamowski felt he had seen enough of Daley and Kennelly to know that he could do a better job as mayor than either of them. The question for Adamowski was how he could outpoll a well-known two-term mayor and the head of the powerful Democratic machine. Adamowski was convinced that Kennelly would drop out of the race. "My experience with him was that in a contest, he'd back off," he said. Then, in a one-on-one race against Daley and the machine, Adamowski believed he could win by combining the anti-machine vote with his following in the city's large Polish community. The problem with Adamowski's plan was that Kennelly remained steadfast, and Chicago's first contested mayoral race in modern times ended up as a three-man race.[48]

The ugly tone the election would take became clear on December 29, 1954, the day nominating petitions were due. In Chicago, candidates were listed on the ballot in the order in which the city clerk received their petitions. This top spot was coveted because so many voters routinely pulled the lever beside the first recognizable name. The city clerk's office opened at 8:30 A.M., and Kennelly's Corporation counsel, John Mortimer, arrived in the outer office at 7:45 A.M. to deliver the petitions. He patiently waited for the office to open, confident that Kennelly would be first on the ballot. Somehow, though, Daley's men managed to enter through a side door and get their petitions time-stamped at 8:13 A.M., while Kennelly's followed by three minutes. Kennelly's camp protested foul play but was unable to push Daley off the top of the ballot.[49]

Daley was less successful in an attempt to strong-arm the Cook County Board. Word leaked out on December 30 that Daley had applied "extreme pressure" to the Democratic board members to slash the budget of county assessor Frank Keenan, the most prominent elected official backing Kennelly. Daley's attempt to undermine Keenan was rebuffed at a closed-door meeting at which Daley and board president Daniel Ryan reportedly almost came to blows. Daley later denied he had ever approached the board on the subject, saying that "the woods are full of rumors these days" and "a lot of people are trying to spread rumors to hurt Dick Daley."[50]

Daley's campaign was run out of the machine's headquarters in the old Morrison Hotel. The offices of the Cook County Democratic Organization were prosaic in appearance. "An out-of-town conventioneer . . . would think he had stumbled into the local sales office of a business firm that distributed literature and brochures advertising the company's product," one student of the Chicago machine wrote some years later about its offices, which by then had moved to the LaSalle Hotel. "There are no smoke-filled rooms reeking of cigars (Chairman Daley does not smoke), no jangling batteries of telephones, no authentic characters out of *The Last Hurrah* lounging around. . . . Except for a large Buddha-like photograph of a Chairman Daley, smiling enigmatically down on all who enter, and pictures of the local candidates at election time on the walls, the decor is typical of any business office in the Loop." In Daley's campaign for mayor, the main emphasis was on coordinating the efforts of, and providing backup to, the fifty ward organizations that would do the real work of turning out voters on election day. "What do they do over at the Morrison?" Jake Arvey once asked rhetorically. "Actually, the Morrison is just like any sales organization trying to sell its product and straighten out its problems. Setting up an organization in a ward where we're weak. Then there's the matter of literature — deciding on it, distributing it, getting it into the hands of four or five thousand precinct captains. Then there's organized labor. Labor and fraternal groups are for you but you've got to see to it that they do the work, get special literature, and so on." Daley's strategists at the Morrison were responsible for those functions that had to be performed on a citywide basis — sending out speakers to community groups across the city, organizing the big downtown rallies, and hosting the massive pre-election precinct captain luncheons. Machine headquarters also told the ward committeemen how many votes they were expected to deliver, and mediated conflicts between rival factions in a ward. "It's a full-time job, eight-thirty to six at night," said Arvey. "That's what makes an organization."[51]

Daley's run for mayor was a tour de force of old-style machine politics. He spent relatively little time introducing himself to actual voters, and almost none working out plans for the city or positions on controversial issues. Classic machine campaigns like Daley's were focused on gearing up the machine to work as efficiently as possible on election day. Daley spent much of his time meeting with the city's fifty ward committeemen and building personal relationships with as many of the three thousand precinct captains — he always pronounced it "presint captains" — as he could. Daley knew that if he could fire them up, they would in turn fire up their voters. Although he was not an eloquent man, Daley had a rare ability to reach party workers with what has been called his "I'm witchoo treatment."[52]

Daley traveled around the city and spent countless hours visiting with machine workers in the ward organizations. "We will continue to carry the message as the early Christians did," he liked to say, "by word of mouth." Daley knew how to speak the language of the neighborhoods. He asked after the workers' families, talked with the men about the White Sox, and with the women about church and children. When he delivered prepared remarks, Daley spoke "as a good father, good neighbor, and good citizen." And like any good politician, he could deliver a well-worn joke. "There was a fellow who was hard of hearing, and he had been doing a lot of drinking," went one of Daley's favorites. "So he went to see Doctor Hughes, over at Thirty-seventh and Wallace, and the doc told him, 'Pat, I'm telling you this: If you keep up your drinking, you'll lose your hearing.' Well, the fella came back in a month, and he says, 'Well, Doc, I'll tell you, I been enjoying what I been drinking so much more than what I been hearing that I thought I'd just keep on drinking.'" Daley fine-tuned his message to the personalities and ethnic politics of particular wards. At a 25th Ward Democratic Organization rally, presided over by Alderman Vito Marzullo, Daley was introduced as someone who "will recognize the Italian-Americans and other nationality groups in Chicago."[53]

Daley's campaign also made great use of a Chicago machine tradition — massive luncheons and rallies for the precinct captains. These meetings were held in the large downtown hotels and various civic centers around the city. Red, white, and blue bunting hung down from the balconies, photographs of the candidates were strategically placed around the auditorium, and thousands of hardworking machine loyalists hooted and hollered from their seats as a parade of speakers rose to the podium to heap praise on even the most mediocre member of the machine slate. On Valentine's Day 1955, candidate Daley spoke to an audience of almost five thousand of the machine's best workers gathered at the Civic Opera House. As a brass band struck up "For He's a Jolly Good Fellow," the party faithful — crammed into 3,700 seats and jamming the aisles — waved "Daley" placards and roared their approval for five uninterrupted minutes. A chorus sang "Back of the Yard," in tribute to Daley's 11th Ward. As Arvey spoke, Daley moved through the exuberant mass of humanity, surrounded by a wedge of family and uniformed ushers. He waved and grinned at the crowd, which was by now calling out "Dick!" and cheering wildly. When he got to the podium, Daley told the machine workers that their calling was a noble one. "My opponent says, 'I took politics out of the schools; I took politics out of this and I took politics out of that.' I say to you: There's nothin' wrong with politics. There's nothing wrong with good politics. Good politics is good government." In Daley's speeches, the Chicago machine took on an almost religious quality — as if he were confusing it with the other Irish-Catholic, hierarchical institution that loomed so large in his life, the Catholic Church. "I am proud to be the candidate of this organization," he told a rally of precinct captains at the Morrison Hotel. "No man can walk alone." For the black precinct captains, Daley often hauled out Congressman Bill Dawson to do some country-style preaching. "If we were not successful we'd be just an organization," Dawson told one group of the submachine faithful at a rally during the 1955 mayoral election. "May we always be a machine!" Before he was done, an audience member shouted from the balcony, "Pour it on!"[54]

Daley's ministrations to the Democratic foot soldiers had an electrifying effect. "This election has revived the whole damn party," North Side alderman Paddy Bauler would say after the primary. "It's fired up the precinct captains like they ain't been in thirty years. My guys are going all out for Daley in the general election. They like a guy who takes care of them." Mayor Kennelly, who had been the machine's candidate twice but never bothered to understand machine politics, never grasped the significance of Daley's work in the ward organizations. He believed that politics was about standing up for the right principles, and he was convinced that if the voters were told of his views on such issues as civil-service reform, they would naturally support him over Daley. "Television is our precinct captain," a Kennelly aide boasted during the campaign. But Daley understood Chicago politics far better than Kennelly ever would. "Can you ask your television set for a favor?" he responded.[55]

Daley's campaign benefited from some of the machine's more unsavory practices. The machine's patronage army — government workers who knew that their jobs were at stake — went into battle for Daley in this election as they had never battled before. And the campaign was flush with campaign money extracted by the machine from its usual sources. Companies doing business with the city and county kicked back thousands of dollars, knowing that failure to do so could mean the end of their government contracts. Daley, who subscribed to his own version of Tammany Hall leader George Washington Plunkitt's famous distinction between "honest graft" and "dishonest graft," saw nothing wrong with the kickbacks. "A real crook, in the eyes of Daley, was somebody who'd take the $5,000 for himself," said Lynn Williams, a township committeeman and member of the Cook County Democratic Central Committee. "A fellow who would ask someone to make a $5,000 contribution to the party was a loyal party worker." The machine also had a tradition of charging "assessments" to each of the ward organizations for the cost of a citywide campaign. Ward organizations came by this money in a variety of legal and illegal ways, including forcing patronage workers to give back 1 percent to 2 percent of their salaries, shaking down businesses for zoning variances, and siphoning off protection money from illegal activities in the ward. During the campaign, an unidentified man appeared on TV with his back to the camera to say that fully 10 percent of the city's illegal gambling revenues went to politicians in the form of "juice money." This year, much of that juice money would be used to turn out voters for Daley.[56]

Daley's supporters were not above using violence or threats to intimidate the opposition. In the final days of the 1955 campaign, an anti-machine aldermanic candidate in the South Side 6th Ward — a hotly contested ward the black submachine was trying to move into — had to dive into his basement window for cover when he was shot at outside his home. A month earlier, Dawson had asked him to withdraw from the race. And just days before the primary, the 11th Ward alderman whom Daley had handpicked after his defeat of Babe Connelly — Stanley Nowakowski — was charged with threatening a campaign worker who allegedly pulled down some of his signs. "They told me I'd better watch myself going home, and to lay off, or we'll take care of you once and for all," said Frank Serafini, owner of the Automatic Heating and Equipment Company. "They said they had Daley's okay on it."[57]

Kennelly declared that his reelection battle was a fight of "the people against the bosses." He told a luncheon audience at the City Club on January 31, 1955, that he had won the enmity of the machine because he had moved employees out of the patronage system and into civil service. Twice as many civil-service exams were held during his two terms as mayor, he said, as in any other comparable period in Chicago history. A machine alderman had approached him six months earlier, he said, and told him he could have the party's backing if he dumped the Civil Service Commission chairman. "With me, dumping is an ugly word," Kennelly said. "Why would I do it? He was doing a good job. All we tried to do was live up to the law we were sworn to uphold. The pressure to 'go easy' was very great. It still is." At a February 6 candidates' forum at Temple Sholom on Lake Shore Drive, Daley exploded when Adamowski and Kennelly accused him of having fixed the machine's nominating process. "The hocus-pocus is over," Adamowski said. "He can't deny that he picked the committee to run him for mayor." Daley seethed as Kennelly added to the point. "[T]hey gave me three minutes and 56 seconds to tell about what has been done in eight years, how the city government has been improved," the mayor said. At this, Daley jumped up in a rage. "The mayor took two minutes," Daley shouted. "He could have had all day if he wanted it! Nobody stopped him! He could have had all afternoon." When Kennelly told the audience about how he had spotted Daley "almost hidden on the sofa" while the slate-making committee met, Daley jumped up to the microphone only to be blocked by the female moderator.[58]

Kennelly was helped in his anti-machine crusade by a well-timed scandal. The newspapers were reporting that Alderman Benjamin Becker, the machine's candidate for city clerk, had been sharing zoning case fees with an attorney and former 40th Ward machine operative. It was classic machine-style corruption: the powerful elected official who extracted a favor from city government in exchange for a kickback. The alderman refused to respond to the allegations, saying he was "not going to be tried in the newspapers," and he argued that only the Chicago Bar Association, not the press or the public, was in a position to evaluate the charges. The bar association was willing to conduct an inquiry, but the organization's president said there was no guarantee it would be completed before the primary. Pressure mounted to dump Becker from the ticket, but Daley stood by his running mate. "Don't you think this man is entitled to a fair trial in accordance with American tradition?" Daley demanded. Employing a technique Daley would use time and again in his career, he lashed out at those making the accusations. "There are false charges and malicious remarks being made about us," he told a rally of ward committeemen. "Where is the proof? Where are the facts behind the rumors? I have not heard of the facts because there are no facts!"[59]

Daley's shrewder, and ultimately more effective, strategy for blunting the anti-machine charges against him was to wrap himself in the mantle of reform. Following the model of Arvey's shrewd slating of

Stevenson and Douglas, Daley convinced a respected reform lawyer who had been an important backer of Douglas in 1948 and 1954 to lead a "Volunteers for Daley" committee to rally nonmachine Democrats to the cause. At the same time, Daley drew on his own long association with Stevenson, leader of Illinois reformers and the man *Time* magazine had recently called "the nation's top Democrat." Breaking his rule against endorsing in primaries, Stevenson backed Daley. He was acting, he said, out of "personal respect and friendship," but there were more practical reasons at work. The Chicago machine had launched Stevenson's political career, and he would need its backing when he sought the 1956 Democratic nomination for president. Win or lose in the race for mayor, Daley would be head of the machine when that decision was made. Daley also convinced Douglas, the machine's other loyal reformer, to endorse him. At a February 4 rally of party workers at the Morrison Hotel, Douglas spoke of his respect and admiration for Daley and the entire machine. "On the basis of my own experience, I have never been treated more honorably by any group than by the Democratic organization here in Cook County," Douglas declared. "[T]hey having stood by me when I was under fire, I believe unjustly, I think I should testify to the truth now when they are under fire." As with Stevenson, any genuine warm feelings Douglas may have had for the machine were mixed with an appreciation of its practical value to his career. Douglas had lost the 1942 Senate primary when he ran without the machine's backing, and was elected to the Senate six years later when the machine was with him. Keeping company with distinguished reformers like Stevenson and Douglas, Daley almost seemed to be moving beyond the machine. To further support this impression, he pledged that if he were elected mayor, he would step down as head of the machine. Daley said he had offered to resign on December 20, when the machine slated him for mayor, but that the machine leadership had convinced him to stay on. If he were elected mayor, though, he would resign his party post to "devote my full time and attention to the duties of the mayor's office." Convincing though it sounded at the time, it was not a promise he intended to keep.[60]

While Kennelly and Adamowski wanted to make the election a referendum on bossism, Daley tried to shift the focus to populism.

He took every opportunity to contrast the working-class people of the neighborhoods who formed the backbone of his support with the downtown business titans and blue-blooded reformers who were backing Kennelly. "There are worse bosses than bosses in politics," Daley declared. "They are the bosses of big business and big influence." These "big interests" were using Kennelly's candidacy, Daley contended, "to retain control of the mayor's office." Fixing on a theme he would use throughout his career, Daley insisted that the important division in the city was not between the machine and reformers, but between Chicago's business elites and its blue-collar neighborhoods. "What we must do is have a city not for State Street, not for LaSalle Street, but a city for all Chicago," Daley told an enthusiastic meeting of the Democratic Organization at the Sherman Hotel. "I'm a kid from the stockyards," he reminded a brass-band rally for 3,700 precinct captains. Though Daley headed up the nation's mightiest political machine, he presented himself as a struggling David to Kennelly's Goliath. "I know, and so do you, that they have control of the communications — of radio and of television," Daley complained.

Daley's supporters took every opportunity to contrast Kennelly's patrician ways with the modest background of their own candidate. "Kennelly ain't lived with people," one Daley campaign lieutenant argued in typically homespun fashion. "He picks a fancy apartment, an elevator to take him up away from the people, and when the elevator brings him down his car is waiting. But Richard Daley lives in a bungalow, walks to church, sees his neighbors, and understands people." The Daley campaign also realized the uses to which the candidate's large Irish family could be put. "Those seven kids of his don't hurt," one Daley strategist noted. "I was the one that told him to get their pictures in his ads." Daley increased his working-class appeal by picking up the endorsement of the city's major unions, which all had long-standing ties to the machine. The Chicago Federation of Labor, led by an old friend, endorsed Daley on January 4. A few days later, the state Congress of Industrial Organizations fell into line as well.[61]

On the tricky issue of race, Daley carefully appealed to both sides. The vote in the black submachine wards was simply too large for a machine candidate to ignore. Fortunately for Daley, Dawson had already come out against Kennelly because of his stand on the jitneys and policy wheels, and Daley made private assurances to Dawson that he would not interfere in these spheres. Daley also spoke warmly of Dawson personally. In his attacks on the machine, Kennelly often singled out Dawson as a symbol of everything that was wrong with the Morrison Hotel crowd. "The congressman is a political boss," Kennelly said in a January 30 speech. "I can understand why Dawson passed the word that he couldn't stand for Kennelly. I haven't been interested in building up his power. Without power to dispense privilege, protection and patronage to preferred people, bossism has no stock in trade." Daley came to Dawson's defense — particularly before all-black audiences. On the eve of the election, Daley traveled to the Grand Ballroom in the 6th Ward — the latest territorial addition to Dawson's growing submachine empire — and stood behind the South Side congressman at a rally of 1,200 submachine workers. "Why should they castigate leaders in the lifestream of politics as bosses?" Daley said, one machine head defending another. "I don't say Bill Dawson is a boss. I say Bill Dawson is a leader of men and women." At the same time that Daley was appealing to blacks on welfare issues and personality politics, he sent signals to white voters that on the overriding racial issue of the day — integration of white neighborhoods — he stood with them. In an address to 7,500 members of the United Packinghouse Workers on February 17, Daley told his overwhelmingly white audience that the police department should "not be used to advance the interests of any one group over another," a coded reference to the role of the police in integrating Trumbull Park.[62]

Heading into the final weeks of the election, Daley trailed Kennelly by a substantial margin, according to the rudimentary opinion polls used at the time. A *Tribune* poll found that nearly 57 percent of the 104 voters who expressed a preference backed Kennelly, against only 33 percent who intended to vote for Daley. Kennelly's camp had also been encouraged by the results of its own straw polls. A car carrying four women poll takers and a male supervisor would pull up to street intersections in bellwether wards, get out, and survey passersby. Kennelly's teams kept their stops brief, because within thirty minutes of arriving at a corner, word would reach the machine, and it would dispatch ringers to artificially boost Daley's numbers. But in their shorter and more random stops, Kennelly was outpolling Daley by better than 2–1. "Every sign from these and other sources shows sentiment for Mayor Kennelly is growing every moment," his campaign manager declared. "No matter where you go, there is no grass roots sentiment at all for the Morrison Hotel candidate." But again, the Kennelly campaign was showing a dangerous naïveté about the way the machine operated. One voter polled by the *Tribune,* a retired accountant walking down Clifton Avenue in the North Side 46th Ward, tried to explain how Chicago politics worked. "This is Joe Gill's ward," the accountant said. "Gill is one of the bosses who decided to dump Kennelly. The people in this ward will be herded to the polls like cattle and they will vote as they are told. It's the same in nearly every other ward."[63]

What mattered, in other words, was not abstract public opinion but actual votes, and the machine had a knack for getting its voters to the polls. Kennelly was pinning his hopes on a large turnout to overcome the machine voters, who would turn out without fail for Daley. As it happened, the election fell on Washington's birthday, when banks and schools were closed, and the Kennelly camp was hoping the holiday would stimulate voting. If turnout was above 900,000, they believed, the mayor would be reelected. In the waning days, the Kennelly campaign concentrated on stimulating turnout, but lacking the machine's precinct captains and foot soldiers, it had to get the message out through television. In a commercial repeated at fifteen-minute intervals the day before the election, Kennelly called on voters to show up at the polls in massive numbers to send a message to the party bosses. And in a final half-hour television appearance broadcast from the Erlanger Theater, Kennelly declared that "every vote counts today to maintain the integrity of local government."[64]

The primary was February 22, and Daley's election-night party was held at the Morrison Hotel. Outside the machine headquarters, a crowd of machine true-believers sang "When Irish Eyes Are Smiling." In the inner sanctum, the machine's leaders, the men responsible for turning out the loyal voters, were all in attendance. Dawson had arrived, bringing word that blacks had turned out in force in the submachine wards. The city's labor titans, who had supplied many of the enlisted men in the machine's election-day army, had also shown up — William A. Lee, the Bakery Drivers Union leader who was president of the Chicago Federation of Labor; William McFetridge of the Flat Janitors Union; and Stephen Bailey of the Plumbers Union. Sargent Shriver, at that time a member of the Chicago Board of Education and head of the Kennedy family's Merchandise Mart, was on hand with his wife, Eunice Kennedy Shriver. When the polls closed for the night, nervous ward committeemen filed into headquarters and reported directly to Daley on the precinct-by-precinct tallies in their wards. It was a ritual Daley would act out time and again, accepting the ward committeemen's proffered numbers and reviewing them silently. If the results pleased him, he would jump up excitedly and pump the ward committeeman's hand. If he was unhappy, there was a good chance Daley would scream at the bearer of bad tidings. Daley was once so upset with a ward's results, according to a machine insider, that he reached over his desk and began shaking the terrified ward committeeman by his necktie.[65]

But this night, Daley was happy. The weather had been good all day, but even the clear skies had not prompted a turnout as high as the Kennelly camp hoped — or the machine feared. In the end, fewer than 750,000 Democrats had cast ballots. As the numbers poured into the Morrison Hotel, it was clear to Daley that he had triumphed. At 9:00 P.M., Kennelly went on television to concede. Fifteen minutes later, a telegram of congratulation arrived from Adamowski. At 9:32, Daley came out from his office to make a victory statement. He thanked everyone in the crowd for their hard work on his behalf, ending his remarks by saying, "I shall conduct myself in the spirit of the prayer of St. Francis of Assisi: 'Lord, make me an instrument of thy peace.' "[66] Daley arrived home at midnight, and his family was still awake. Reporters could hear Sis Daley shout, "Here he is, kids!" Daley hugged six of his seven children — Patricia, the firstborn, was at a Sisters of Mercy novitiate in Des Plaines — and promised he would take them fishing. "Tell your mother not to fix anything for dinner," Daley exclaimed. "We're going to bring home some trout."[67]

In the round of postmortems that followed, the ward-by-ward vote totals showed that Daley's edge had come from just a few wards, and they revealed which constituencies put him in office. Daley and Kennelly ran remarkably evenly in thirty-nine of the city's fifty wards. It was the remaining eleven wards, known as the machine's "Automatic Eleven," that were responsible for Daley's victory. He carried these wards by 98,859 votes, almost his entire 100,064-vote victory margin. The Automatic Eleven voters belonged overwhelmingly to the machine's three key voting blocs: working-class white ethnics, blacks, and the syndicate. Several were old-style machine wards, in which powerful white ward committeemen used the traditional methods to turn out a strong vote for the machine slate. Daley also fared well in the so-called plantation wards, which had turned majority black but remained under white control, and in the city's "skid row." Dawson's submachine of five wards also racked up big margins for Daley. Finally, Daley ran unusually well in the syndicate-dominated 1st Ward.[68]

Daley's totals — in the Automatic Eleven, certainly, but in other wards as well — were likely inflated by vote theft and other improprieties. Days before the election, Kennelly campaign manager Frank Keenan implored thousands of machine precinct captains to play fair. "We know most precinct captains are honest men and women," Keenan wrote in a letter to them. "Don't let anyone order you to do anything in the polling place which could bring punishment and also disgrace to your family." But it was a plea that, in many precincts, was flatly ignored. In the days leading up to the election, envelopes showed up in poorer neighborhoods with a dollar bill and a mimeographed message: "This is your lucky day. Stay lucky with Daley." In some wards, the vote theft was overt. After the primary, the anti-machine *Chicago Tribune* published photographs from election day showing Sidney Lewis, a former bail bondsman with the evocative nickname of "Short Pencil," erasing crosses on ballots marked for Kennelly and replacing them with votes for Daley. Years later, in a Pulitzer Prize–winning series, the *Tribune* would document in vivid detail the many methods by which the machine routinely stole votes — "four-legged voting," in which precinct captains accompanied voters into the voting booths; registering flophouse residents without their knowledge and then voting for them on election day; and, crudest of all, just sending someone into a voting booth and having him pull the Democratic straight-ticket lever again and again. How many of the 100,064 votes that made up Daley's margin of victory were stolen is impossible to say, but some of them certainly were. Kennelly may have been thinking in part of the machine's prodigious ballot-box-stuffing ability when he said on election night, "Unbreakable, just unbreakable, aren't they?"[69]

The Republicans turned to a charismatic Democratic alderman named Robert Merriam to run against Daley in the general election. The thirty-six-year-old Merriam represented the liberal 5th Ward, home to the University of Chicago and the surrounding Hyde Park neighborhood, in the City Council. Merriam, who was known as "the WASP Prince of Chicago," was heir to a Chicago reform dynasty. His father, a well-regarded University of Chicago political science professor named Charles Merriam, had also been a 5th Ward alderman, and had himself run for mayor in 1911. Before embarking on a political career, the younger Merriam had been a World War II army captain and war hero, who had survived the Battle of the Bulge and then went on to write a book about it. In the City Council, he was a leader of a group of reformers known as the "economy bloc" because of their skepticism about the machine's wasteful spending of city dollars. And as chairman of the council's crime committee, he had made a name for himself as a crime-fighter by broadcasting actual corruption and crime cases on his television show *Spotlight on Chicago*. The handsome and youthful Merriam spoke articulately about the problems facing Chicago. He was, one Washington columnist declared excitedly, "the type who has been upsetting tawdry, tired machines all over the country."[70]

Merriam was not the unanimous choice of Chicago Republicans. Many of the city's ward committeemen were not enthusiastic about giving their nomination to an unreconstructed Democrat. But Governor William Stratton, who was eager to breathe some life into the moribund Chicago Republican organization, prevailed upon them to give Merriam the nomination and use him to expand the party's base. "The whole idea was to have a fusion ticket of independent Democrats, independents, and what there was of the Republican Party, which wasn't very much," Merriam said later. The crusty *Chicago Tribune* was not pleased with the Merriam candidacy. The leading conservative paper in America at the time, the *Tribune* regularly railed against watered-down Eisenhower Republicanism and the "socialistic" United Nations. It endorsed Merriam over Daley because it despised the Democratic machine even more than it hated

Republican impostors. But Merriam had endorsed both Stevenson and Douglas in their last races, and he was "the darling of the Independent Voters of Illinois, the organized left wing of the Democratic Party," the paper editorialized. "Merriam's marriage to the Republican Party is obviously and shamelessly a marriage of convenience."[71]

The mayoral election was shaping up as a contest between two men who, by all external appearances, could hardly have been more different. Merriam had style and sophistication, while Daley exuded working-class Bridgeport. Daley was a fifty-three-year-old father of seven who had spent decades of his life plodding his way up the ranks of the machine. A short and pudgy man, he had a face that drooped into a vast expanse of hanging flesh. "He would be doomed in the cosmetology of today's politics: those jowls, that heavy-set look," David Halberstam would write in a profile years later. "He doesn't look like a modern municipal leader, a cost-accounting specialist; he looks, yes, exactly like a big city boss." And Daley spoke in the heavy accent of ethnic Chicago, sprinkling his sentences with "dis's" and "dat's." He spoke awkwardly and at times incomprehensibly. According to one observer, he alternated between "a controlled mumble for TV and an excited gabble for political rallies." And throughout his career, his words had a way of coming out in a tangle. When he opened a bicycle path in Odgen Park, a year into his mayoralty, he referred to a bicycle-built-for-two as a "tantrum bike," and expressed concern for the park's "walking pedestrians." The same year, at an atomic energy exhibit at the Museum of Science and Industry, he would declare it "amazing what they will be able to do once they get the atom harassed." He would declare to reporters, "I resent the insinuendos," offer information "for the enlightenment and edification and hallucination of the alderman," and implore his audience to "reach higher and higher platitudes." And in a moment of despair toward the end of his career, he would exclaim, "They have vilified me, they have crucified me, yes, they have even criticized me."[72]

Daley was especially unprepossessing when contrasted with the captivating young Robert Merriam. Merriam may have been polished, but he also looked, as one political observer put it, "like a South Side Chicago image of an Ivy Leaguer." His distinguished manner seemed to put him above the workaday Chicagoans whose votes he was seeking. "You know what the party workers say?" Merriam complained after the election. "They say to each other, 'Have you ever seen this Merriam take a drink? Does he ever drink? I mean, have you ever actually seen him take a drink?'" And Merriam's high-minded reform politics might appeal to the blue bloods who lived near the Lake, but they left many working-class voters cold. Supporters of Boston's legendary Mayor James Michael Curley used to tell the story of the Beacon Hill lady who went door-to-door in working-class South Boston campaigning for a reformer for school committee. One Irish housewife listened to her pitch politely, and then asked, "But doesn't he have a sister who works for the schools or who has something to do with the school system?" The Boston Brahmin lady immediately protested: "I assure you, madam," she said, "he is not the kind of man who would ever use his position to advance the interests of his sister." The Irish housewife replied, "Well, if the son-of-a-bitch won't help his own sister, why should I vote for him?" Merriam's upper-crust idealism was not for everyone.[73]

Merriam's charisma and articulateness did little for him in the campaign. In 1955, television was just beginning to come into its own as a political force. The 1954 Army-McCarthy hearings, which revealed Senator Joseph McCarthy as a bully and tyrant before an entire nation, had powerfully demonstrated the potential the new medium held to influence public affairs. But Adlai Stevenson, an engaging orator, still lost the next year's presidential race to the less articulate Dwight Eisenhower. Election campaigns were still largely won or lost through retail politics. This was particularly true of machine candidates, who generally prevailed not because of their personal qualifications or charisma but because of the strength of the organization backing them. George Washington Plunkitt, a leader in New York's legendary Tammany Hall organization and the foremost philosopher of machine politics, noted in his primer *How to Become a Statesman* that organization candidates who "cram their heads with all sorts of college rot" are wasting their time if the machine is doing its job properly. In choosing the machine candidate, a voter was supporting a whole political system — the ward office that got his street repaved, the ward committeeman who got his child out of a scrape with the law, the patronage system that provided him or a relative with a job. For all of this to continue, the machine candidate had to win. Daniel Rostenkowski, who would rise to be an influential congressman as a result of Daley's patronage, recalls that when his wife saw Adamowski on television, he impressed her so much more than Daley that she asked her husband if he was sure he was backing the right man. "I said, 'LaVerne, it's just bread and butter.'"[74]

Daley made the most of his party affiliation. He never tired of reminding voters that he was the Democrat and Merriam the Republican — not bothering to explain that Merriam had jumped parties because of his frustration with the machine's lock on his party. He taunted his opponent for not being a loyal member of either political party. Merriam was trying to convince Democrats he was not a Republican, and Republicans he was not really a Democrat, Daley said in one debate. "I can't think of anything more difficult than trying to mate an elephant with a donkey."[75]

But Merriam's best chance of winning was, in fact, trying to accomplish a mating of that kind. He appealed to supporters of Kennelly and Adamowski to cross party lines, arguing that he was the rightful heir to their anti-machine campaigns. If he were elected, Merriam promised, he would reappoint Kennelly's Civil Service Commission chairman, who had been targeted by the machine. Merriam had some successes in winning over his fellow Democrats. The Independent Voters of Illinois, the city's most powerful reform organization, abandoned its usual Democratic loyalties to endorse Merriam. But what really would have given Merriam's campaign the aura of Democratic-Republican fusion was an endorsement from either of Daley's Democratic primary opponents, and in this endeavor he failed. Kennelly remained neutral. Adamowski, for all his warnings of the dire consequences that would befall Chicago if Daley won, told Merriam that as a lifelong Democrat he could not endorse a Republican. "The next year," Merriam noted later, "he ran as a Republican for state's attorney."[76]

Issues, in the conventional sense, played only a minor role in the campaign. Daley's positions ran heavily to platitudes. He was against crime, favored hiring more policemen, and strongly supported "beat walking." Daley also wanted government to operate more efficiently. And, in what would become one of his trademarks, he made insistent but vague promises about doing more for the city's neighborhoods. "The neighborhoods are the backbone of the city," Daley told one local crowd. "Revitalizing and protecting them is the first and main job of an administration centered on the people of Chicago." Merriam, by contrast, actually offered creative solutions to many problems confronting the city. To improve transportation, for example, he called for tearing down the ugly and noisy elevated tracks in the Loop and replacing them with a subway system, and for offering transfers between the commuter rail lines and the city bus system.[77]

As he had in the primary, Daley pursued a two-track approach to the racial question. He continued to embrace Dawson and the sub-machine, and campaigned heavily in the Black Belt. Daley, who had grown up close to blacks and attended high school in a black neighborhood, threw himself into Bronzeville in a way that more patrician whites like Kennelly would not. "One of my first experiences in politics was on the South Side at an infamous nightclub at 55th and State," recalls Ira Dawson, William Dawson's nephew. "I watched Daley parade down through that packed, smoked-filled nightclub — it was like the Cotton Club in Harlem — and being very accessible." Daley managed to present himself to the black community as someone who supported them in their struggle for equal rights. In a front-page editorial entitled "Elect Daley Mayor," the *Chicago Defender* declared that "[o]n the vital issues facing Chicago," including civil rights, Daley had "taken a firm and laudable stand." But the truth was, Daley's stand was not especially laudable, and it certainly was not firm. When whites were present, Daley made every effort to dodge direct questions about integration. At a March 28 meeting of the City Club of Chicago, he was asked where public housing should be located. Daley spoke in favor of public housing, but he would not address the most vexing question about it. "Let's not be arguing about where it's located," Daley responded. Through the machine's back channels to the ethnic neighborhoods, Daley got out word that white voters could count on him to hold the line on integration. The militantly anti-integration South Deering Improvement Association, which was leading the battle against blacks moving into Trumbull Park, endorsed Daley for mayor. The group sent out sound trucks on primary day announcing that it had struck a secret deal with Daley, and urged its followers to vote for him. In the days after the election, the *South Deering Bulletin* declared confidently that

Daley would be good for the cause because he lived in a neighborhood "very much like South Deering" and he had stood up for "preservation of neighborhoods." The machine also employed more blatant racial appeals, but it made them quietly. It circulated letters in the Bungalow Belt — the working-class white neighborhoods on the Southwest and Northwest sides — from a made-up group called the "American Negro Civic Association" praising Merriam for his steadfast support for open housing. The machine also spread rumors in these same neighborhoods that Merriam's wife — whose French ancestry made her exotic by Bungalow Belt standards — was black. While they were at it, they also stirred up Catholic voters by circulating copies of Merriam's divorce papers. In a television appearance for Daley, Near North Side alderman Thomas Keane spoke movingly of Daley's family — "that enchantingly adorable mother . . . and those seven children kneeling at the side of their bed at night in family prayer" — and emphasized that "Daley has seven children and they are all his own." It was a reminder that Merriam had divorced, remarried, and was raising two children born to his wife during her first marriage.[78]

Daley sought, as he had in the primary, to fashion his campaign into a populist struggle. He once again made the rounds of the ward luncheons and neighborhood meetings, and he drew on the machine's grassroots contacts to stage a series of "family-to-family" meetings in private homes. Without the benefit of the machine's connections, Merriam's forays into working-class Chicago often left him in front of unreceptive, or at best indifferent, audiences. In one of the low points, Merriam arrived at a South Side revival meeting just as a woman writhing with religious ecstasy was being carted out. "Say what you got to say," the preacher told Merriam. "Do it in five minutes and git out of here." The candidate did as he was told.[79]

Daley also used his organized labor support to reach out to everyday Chicagoans. He was warmly received in the city's union halls. On March 4, an enthusiastic crowd of four thousand members of the AFL International Brotherhood of Electrical Workers heard Daley introduced as "the man who can do us the most good." Several weeks later, he promised a meeting of twelve hundred transit workers that if elected he would appoint a "labor union man" as a member of the Chicago Transit Authority board. In fact, Daley promised, he would appoint labor representatives to city boards in every area — including schools, parks, and health. "I have found union leaders want to serve not only for their unions but for all the people," he said. "That is the kind of leadership we need." Daley brought his father, Michael, with him to a rally of the Sheet Metal Workers Union, of which the elder Daley had been a member for half a century. "Give Dick a vote," Michael Daley implored his union brothers. "We've never had a member or a member's son elected to such a high office." Daley also paid a pre-election visit to the stockyards, mounting a horse and reminiscing for a crowd of 500 about his days as a stockyard cowboy.[80]

Merriam, like Kennelly and Adamowski before him, painted a dark picture of the kind of city Chicago would be under Daley. This was an election, Merriam argued, that would determine whether the city would fall hostage to the "arrogant Morrison Hotel bosses" and their brand of machine politics. "Their transparent and nefarious manipulations," he said, proved "that the Democratic party cannot be trusted to govern the city in the interests of all the people." Merriam also tried to tie Daley to the syndicate. Kennelly had been dumped, Merriam charged, to clear the way for a "wide open city" for syndicate gambling and other illegal activities. He cited an article in *Variety* reporting that strip joints were starting to reopen in Chicago in anticipation of a Daley victory. "I've been hearing reports that Democratic precinct captains around town are spreading the word that after the election — if their man becomes mayor — everything is going to go," Merriam declared. "Every syndicate operation is going to open up in Chicago: open for high stake, high pressure gambling, crooked dice games and all the rest."[81]

As in the primary, Daley responded to Merriam's charges of bossism with sentimental pleas that the voters see his innate goodness. "I would not unleash the forces of evil," Daley protested. "It's a lie. I will follow the training my good Irish mother gave me — and Dad. If I am elected, I will embrace mercy, love, charity, and walk humbly with my God." A key to Daley's strategy of deflecting the charges of machine politics was once again securing the endorsement of reform icon Adlai Stevenson. At a Palmer House dinner for the reform-minded "Volunteers for Daley" group, Daley endorsed Stevenson for president in 1956. Daley's logrolling worked. At the dinner, Stevenson called Daley a "four square friend of judicial and tax reform," and later went on to back him against Merriam.[82]

Merriam's warning that Daley would usher in an age of corruption received a boost when the Chicago Bar Association brought charges against Alderman Becker in connection with the zoning-kickback allegations. Daley, who had stuck by Becker when the accusations were first made, decided to act. He forced Becker off the machine ticket and pushed John Marcin, the nominee for city treasurer, up to the city clerk slot. To replace Marcin, Daley chose Morris Sachs, who had run for city clerk on Kennelly's ticket and lost by a mere 21,000 votes — running 79,000 votes ahead of the mayor. Sachs, who started out as a poor immigrant selling clothing from a pack on his back, had risen to success as a clothing retailer and as creator of the popular *Sachs' Amateur Hour* television show. Sachs was a beloved figure in Chicago, known for his folksy ways. "I sold Dick Daley's mother the first pair of long pants for Dick," he used to boast on the campaign trail, to the delight of his audiences. "Without me, where would he be?" It also did not hurt that Sachs was Jewish, which kept the Democratic ticket ethnically balanced after the removal of Becker. The *Tribune* wasted little time in running a cartoon depicting Sachs as a bellboy at the Morrison Hotel, but Sachs remained popular with the voters, and his ebullient personal style quickly overshadowed the Becker scandal. Daley once again relied on the well-disciplined Chicago machine to turn out his voters. As party boss, he sent word out from the Morrison Hotel that every ward committeeman and precinct captain was expected to produce in this election as he never had before. Daley's frenetic campaigning in the ranks of the machine reached its high point on March 28, at a final rally for nearly six thousand precinct workers at the Civic Opera House.[83]

The newspapers were against Daley, and he knew it. The three largest, the *Tribune,* the *Sun-Times,* and the *Daily News,* all endorsed Merriam, which was no surprise given their anti-machine stance. The machine did manage to secure the endorsement of the fourth, the *Herald-American,* for Daley. The newspaper was ailing financially, and the machine reportedly struck a deal that in exchange for a Daley endorsement, its precinct captains would sell subscriptions. More important than endorsements, however, was news coverage, and by this standard the papers — with their heavy coverage of Merriam's charges of voter fraud, and their hounding Becker off the ticket — were also giving aid and comfort to the Merriam camp. Candidates work hard to win over journalists, but Daley, knowing that the Republican-leaning press was not about to go soft on the machine, seemed to delight in spurning them. He was known to give reporters the address of a vacant lot for his next speaking appearance. Daley's view of reporters, one reporter wrote in the *Sun-Times,* was that he "doesn't seem to want them around."[84]

Merriam was concerned, with good reason, that Daley and his supporters would attempt to steal the election. The Democratic Party was in the hands, Merriam charged, of "dictators who may spend a million dollars — over two hundred dollars per precinct — to try to buy the votes they cannot honestly win." Merriam distributed the primary-day photographs of Sidney "Short Pencil" Lewis stealing votes, and backed them up with new evidence. A man named Admiral Le Roy had sworn out an affidavit saying he had personally observed "Short Pencil" wielding his famed pencil. Le Roy had himself been a victim of the machine's brand of dirty politics. He had announced for alderman, challenging the organization, but he withdrew when he was "beaten up and had a gun pulled on him" and told to get out of the race. To further bolster his charges that the machine intended to steal the election, Merriam sent out thirty thousand letters to registered voters in machine strongholds. Nearly three thousand of them came back "unclaimed" or "moved, left no address" — proof, Merriam contended, that the machine had as many as 100,000 ghost voters hidden away on the Chicago voting rolls. Merriam filed a formal complaint with the Election Board. But he knew it would go nowhere because the Election Board chairman, Sidney T. Holzman, was a member in good standing of the machine — Merriam lambasted him as the "chief spokesman for the Morrison Hotel politburo." County judge Otto Kerner, who presided over the Cook County election machinery and had appointed Holzman, was Daley's good friend and Anton Cermak's son-in-law. Merriam produced a photograph of Kerner warmly congratulating Daley on primary night, and asked how Kerner and Holzman could be trusted to keep the machine honest. Holzman responded that Merriam was "following Hitler's tactics which consisted of this — if you tell a lie often enough, people will begin to believe you." Merriam also charged that some precinct captains in the Ida B. Wells Homes housing project were threatening to evict tenants unless they voted for Daley. The CHA stayed out of the matter, and Daley scoffed at the charges. "Democratic precinct captains don't have to use pressure of that sort to get votes," Daley declared.[85]

In the final days of the campaign, Daley made the most of his financial edge over Merriam. The machine had about $1 million to spend in the campaign, more than three times what Merriam had raised. The Daley campaign distributed thousands of dollars in walk-around money, used to pay for election-day operations and get-out-the-vote efforts. Some of the money went directly into the pockets of voters — or in some cases to buy bottles of whiskey that went into the pockets of voters. But the machine also had more subtle ways of translating dollars into votes. "I have heard it said that it costs about 20 thousand dollars to deliver a Ward in Chicago on election day," one machine chronicler has written. "Most of this money is placed in the hands of precinct captains. The precinct captain has his own ideas on how to cut up the money. He talks to a woman who lives in a six-flat,* a woman who is favorable to his cause and well-liked by her neighbors. Will she be willing to help get her friends' vote for the Party? Well, she might. Of course, there will be a few 'expenses' — And that is the cue for the precinct captain to dig into his pocket for a ten-spot or a twenty." The machine added to its other advantages by resorting to a few of its traditional last-minute dirty tricks. In addition to the letters that went out from the nonexistent American Negro Civic Association endorsing Merriam, Republican voters got letters urging a vote for Daley, on letterhead of the fictional Taft-Eisenhower League. Rumors were also circulated that anyone who had voted in the Democratic primary could not vote for Merriam now. "Voters should beware of such poison, which is typical of the dirty methods of the Democratic machine," Republican county chairman Edward Moore warned.[86]

As in the primary, it seemed that the election would turn on the size of the turnout. Merriam implored Chicagoans to vote in large numbers to offset the machine's strength. "There must be an out-

---

* A six-flat is a three-story building, two apartments to a floor.

pouring of citizens April 5," he declared. "If the confident bosses could defeat the wishes of the people as they did Feb. 22, it would be a catastrophe for Chicago." Conventional wisdom held that the machine would produce about 600,000 votes for Daley. If more than 1.2 million Chicagoans showed up at the polls, Merriam believed, he would win. On election day, the early indications were that the turnout was exceeding all predictions. Merriam attended a memorial service for *Chicago Tribune* publisher Colonel Robert McCormick at midday, and as he entered the Fourth Presbyterian Church he heard a city election official predicting that the turnout would reach 1,500,000. "I spent the whole hour, when I should have been thinking about the soul of Colonel McCormick, thinking about who I was going to appoint to my cabinet," Merriam said later.[87]

Daley arrived at the Morrison Hotel at 5:00 P.M., and holed up in the private offices of the Cook County Democratic Central Committee to wait for the returns. With Arvey at his side, he pored over precinct returns as they were called in by ward leaders. As the hours went by, the offices filled up with Daley's machine allies. Adhering to the machine's rigid hierarchy, operatives below the rank of ward committeeman were kept out of the office by a guard posted at the door. The numbers that were pouring in were good, and equally important, turnout was not as robust as the machine had feared earlier in the day. By 8:30 P.M., Daley emerged from a side door and made his way to the hotel's Madison Room for a victory statement. Daley declared to a cluster of television cameras and radio microphones, "I promise no miracles — no bargains — but with unity, cooperation, and teamwork, we will continue to build a better city for ourselves and our children."[88]

Daley won the mayoralty with about 55 percent of the vote, a healthy victory but the narrowest margin in more than a decade. Daley had received 708,222 votes, more than the Merriam forces had counted on, but not an insurmountable number. With a higher turnout, Merriam might have prevailed, but since only 1.3 million votes were cast in the end, that left less than 600,000 for Merriam. The ward-by-ward results were remarkably similar to the primary. Daley and Merriam had run evenly in most of the city. Again, it was the Automatic Eleven that had given Daley his victory — in this case, a margin of 125,179 votes, almost all of Daley's 126,967-vote citywide edge. And once again, the black vote proved critical. Dawson's five wards gave Daley 81,910 votes to 32,547 votes for Merriam — more than a 49,000-vote margin. When other heavily black wards were added in, Daley's margin from predominantly black wards exceeded 103,000. If these black voters had voted Republican rather than Democratic, Daley would almost certainly have lost. The syndicate performed even more impressively. Daley took close to 90 percent of the 1st Ward vote, winning by 18,233 to 2,304. It may have been the mob's work for his election that caused the *Chicago Daily News* to editorialize: "Some of the finest, high-principled men in the Democratic party worked for Daley in the election. So did some of the most notorious rascals in politics anywhere. Both kinds helped to deliver the votes to the winner. Daley knows which is which. We pray he has the strength to govern himself and the city accordingly."[89]

The *Tribune* welcomed the new mayor cautiously. "We congratulate Richard J. Daley," the paper wrote after the election. "We hope, for his sake, as well as Chicago's, that he will do nothing in the coming four years to sully his good name." More prescient assessments came from those who knew Daley better. Charlie Weber, alderman from the 45th Ward on the Northwest Side and a machine loyalist, told reporters on election night: "Let me tell ya, this Daley — he's gonna be one tough sonofabitch." But it was Paddy Bauler of the 43rd Ward, among the last of Chicago's saloon-aldermen, who got off the line for the ages. The 245-pound Bauler danced a little jig and declared that Daley's election meant that "Chicago ain't ready for reform!" Bauler also gave reporters another less quoted, but equally perceptive, assessment. "Keane and them fellas — Jake Arvey, Joe Gill — they think they are gonna run things," Bauler said. "Well, you listen now to what I am sayin': they're gonna run nothing'. They ain't found it out yet, but Daley's the dog with the big nuts, now that we got him elected. You wait and see; that's how it is going to be."[90]

chapter 4

I Am the Mayor
and Don't You Forget It

Paddy Bauler had good reason to dance a jig on election night: Daley's victory had averted the most serious threat to the Chicago machine in decades. Machine politicians had long belittled reformers and their dreams of cleaning up city government. George Washington Plunkitt, the sachem of New York's Tammany Hall, once dismissed reformers as "mornin' glories — looked lovely in the mornin' and withered up in a short time, while the regular machines went on flourishin' forever like fine old oaks." Chicago machine politicians were equally dismissive of their good-government opponents: Bauler described one reformer as "so dumb he probably thinks the forest preserve is some kind of jelly." But by 1955, reformers were showing undeniable success in dismantling Democratic machines across the country. In Boston, another city with a long history of Irish-Catholic machine politics, reformers had seized City Hall in 1951. In New York, Tammany Hall had been badly wounded by the reform mayoralty of Fiorello La Guardia. And in Chicago, as in the rest of the country, a combination of factors — including suburbanization, ethnic assimilation, and the rise of civil service — were cutting sharply into the machine's base. The Cook County Democratic Organization's power had already begun to wane under Mayor Kennelly. If Kennelly had been reelected, or if Merriam had won, the machine might well have faced extinction.[1]

Daley was too politic to join Bauler in publicly celebrating the defeat of political reform. To the contrary, he rushed to reassure the city's voters and editorial writers of his good-government intentions. On election night, Daley called on the state legislature to come up with the money for two thousand new police officers he had pledged during the campaign. It was an indication that he intended to keep his campaign promises, but also a subtle rebuke to those who had labeled him the candidate of the "hoodlum element." Daley also vowed on election night that his administration would keep civil service operating at its "present high standard." He also declared, as he repeatedly had as a candidate, that he would resign as party chairman to "devote all of my time to the mayor's office." In fact, Daley had no intention of preserving civil service or of stepping down as boss, but his election-night pledges had the effect of breaking the bad news about his anti-reform intentions gently.[2]

At his April 22 inauguration, Daley gave a more honest indication of how he intended to operate. Mayoral inaugurations are usually bland ceremonial affairs — a hall filled with friends and political supporters, and an address setting forth lofty goals for improving civic life. Daley had no problem producing the admirers. From the moment the vote totals were in, he had been inundated with congratulatory telegrams and letters from what seemed to be almost everyone he had ever known in his fifty-three years, and many more he did not know at all. His desk at the county clerk's office had quickly been buried under a scrapbook-collection of old names and familiar signatures. "Joe would have been as proud of you as I am," read one telegram, sent by Mae McDonough, widow of Daley's old political patron. Many of these well-wishers were among the capacity crowd of two thousand who jammed into the seats and standing room of the ornate and historic City Council Chambers. Hundreds more mobbed the corridors, or listened to the proceedings through loudspeakers outside on the street. Sis and six of the seven Daley children were proudly seated in the front row, while the remaining daughter watched on television from the Sisters of Mercy novitiate. Daley was sworn in by his old friend Abraham Lincoln Marovitz, who was now a county judge.[3]

What made Daley's inauguration unusual was the bluntness of his address. Dressed simply in a blue suit, blue tie, and white shirt, he began with the usual words of appreciation for Mayor Kennelly, Democrats, Republicans, the City Council, and "all the people of

Chicago." He also delivered his customary warm words about Bridgeport. "I have lived all my life in a neighborhood of Chicago," Daley said. "All that I am I owe to the influences of my family, church, our neighborhood and our city." But as he spoke, Daley's tone became more serious. He told the City Council he had no intention of interfering with their "proper functions." But it would be his duty, he said, to exercise his veto power "against measures which would be harmful to the people." More significant, he said that he would work to implement proposals made by the Chicago Home Rule Commission to strip the City Council of its executive and budgetary functions and transfer them to City Hall. His goal was "to relieve the council of administrative and technical duties . . . and permit the aldermen to devote most of their time to legislation." What Daley was saying to the City Council, in words that disguised his power grab as a favor, was that he had every intention of turning them into a rubber stamp.[4]

True to his word, Daley went to work to change the balance of power between the mayor and the City Council. A few months before his election, he had arranged for the Chicago Home Rule Commission to recommend shifting responsibility for preparing the city budget from the City Council to the mayor. The commission also called for ending the long-standing requirement that the City Council approve all city contracts over $2,500. When these recommendations became law, Daley could afford to treat the City Council as little more than an advisory body. Equally important, his dual role as mayor and machine boss made the vast majority of the council his political supplicants. With a few words at a slate-making meeting, Daley could end the political careers of most of them. The result was that, except for a few Republicans and independents, the council quickly became a Daley cheering section. In October, Daley submitted three new appointments to the Municipal Tuberculosis Sanitarium Board. After voting 36–11 to suspend its own rules requiring that the nominees be evaluated in committee, the council approved the appointees by voice vote less than an hour after Daley presented it with the names. Daley had taken Chicago's aldermen far from the day when their independent and rapacious ways earned them the nickname "the Gray Wolves." By the time the tuberculosis sanitarium nominees flew through the council, Republicans aldermen were lamenting that Daley had reduced them and their colleagues to mere "puppets." That is how the council would function for the next two decades under Daley. "In the years he was here, we were useful to fill chairs and vote the way we were told to vote," recalls machine alderman Edward Burke. "That was the extent of it."[5]

Daley also went after the City Council's informal powers. The city's fifty aldermen had long had the ability to dispense a wide variety of favors within their wards. A businessman seeking a zoning variance or a driveway permit would ask his alderman to intercede with the appropriate unit of city government to make it happen. One of Daley's first acts in office was to centralize more of this power in City Hall. Under the new rules, all requests for favors of any significant size were channeled to "the fifth floor," the location of the mayor's office in City Hall, and usually to "the Man on Five" — Daley himself. The city council was not happy about the change — some aldermen were charging as much as $20,000 for a driveway permit. But Daley understood the importance of the power to grant these routine favors for a machine politician. "Let me put it in a crude way," Daley's mentor Jake Arvey used to advise young men starting out in politics. "Put people under obligation to you."[6]

Daley spent hours each day seeing visitors who wanted things from him. They moved through his office quickly, often given no more than five minutes to plead their case. Daley's office was spare and his desk was empty, except for a pen or pencil and a small box, about six inches by four inches, with paper in it of slightly smaller size. When supplicants made their pitch, Daley usually absorbed it impassively. "He was not aggressive of speech," says his human relations commissioner, Edward Marciniak. "He listened and asked questions." Meetings often ended with Daley saying, cryptically, "I'll look into it." But Daley operated according to a routine that few of his visitors knew: if the matter was something Daley intended to act on, he generally took a piece of paper out of the box and scribbled a note to himself. "If he doesn't make a note of it, you can forget it," said one Chicago politician. "If he opens his drawer, takes out a pencil and starts making notes and asks a few questions, it's just as good as done."[7]

If it was done, Daley wanted the credit. John Johnson, head of the

Chicago-based black media empire that bears his name, wanted permission to build a private basement parking lot for the new corporate headquarters he was building in the Loop. His plan called for a driveway to be constructed directly on Michigan Avenue, something the city had not permitted in half a century. When Johnson made inquiries, the response was that he had to see Daley personally. The two men had a cordial meeting at City Hall, and the following day an official from the Buildings Department called to say that Johnson's request had been approved. Johnson called Daley to thank him — precisely the result Daley wanted when he wrested this power away from the aldermen. "It was impossible to do business in Chicago at that time without dealing with Mayor Daley," Johnson recalled later. "You couldn't cut a deal with underlings; you had to see him personally. Which meant that you were personally obligated to him."[8]

The inner circle Daley assembled in City Hall was filled with men like him: working-class Irish-Catholics from Bridgeport and similar neighborhoods, with roots in the Democratic machine. A classic academic study, *The Irish and Irish Politicians,* speaks of Irish politicians' tendency toward "clannishness," but Daley press secretary Frank Sullivan put it more simply: Daley's "idea of affirmative action was nine Irishmen and a Swede." The man Daley looked to above all others to help him run the city was his old friend and political ally Tom Keane. Keane shared Daley's conspiratorial approach to machine politics. The two men had spent years plotting together at meetings of the Cook County Democratic Organization, and Mayor Kennelly always suspected Keane had been the main strategist of the machine coup d'état that took the Democratic nomination away from him and gave it to Daley. The *Chicago Daily News* once observed that Keane's rise was evidence of how far a man can go if he has "a little tin in the pot to start with; an I.Q. that goes into the stratosphere; a talent for mischief that would excite the envy of Boss Tweed; and no more scruples than the law requires." The *Daily News* misjudged Keane in one respect: prosecutors would prove, before his career drew to a close, that he had fewer scruples than the law required.[9]

Keane looked like an amiable leprechaun, but his looks were deceiving. He was a tough-talking street politician who had worked his way up the ranks of the 31st Ward Democratic Organization at the same time Daley was rising in the 11th. But Keane's ascent had been eased by the fact that he was heir to an aldermanic seat that had previously been held by his father, an uncle, and his maternal grandfather. Keane shared Daley's talent for acquiring power and using it imperiously. Shortly before Daley's election as mayor, a newspaper matter-of-factly described Keane's ruthless leadership style as chair of the City Council's Committee on Public Safety. On the day a reporter observed him, Keane took up the first item of business, telling the committee secretary that two of the other aldermen on the committee seconded it, though neither had spoken. Keane then declared the motion carried. He did the same thing with six more pending matters, although in each case he was the only one to speak. "Then he put 107 items into one bundle for passage, and 172 more into another for rejection, again without a voice other than his own having been heard," the reporter noted. "Having disposed of this mountain of details in exactly ten minutes, Ald. Keane walked out."[10]

Daley made Keane his City Council floor leader, and it proved to be a good fit. The Chicago City Council was a motley collection of rogues and mercenaries. They were men like Paddy Bauler, the legendary 43rd Ward alderman who was known as the "clown prince" of Chicago. Bauler, who ran a saloon when he was not making city laws, handled ward business and met with constituents over rounds of beers. Bauler once shot a police officer in a barroom altercation. He later explained that the policeman "swore at me and called me a fat Dutch pig." Keane was just the man to keep a chamber full of Paddy Baulers in line. "Keane runs the City Council like a circus ringmaster," a newsman who covered him wrote. "He designates who is to speak on what issue with the flick of a finger." Keane had no trouble beating wayward aldermen into submission, sometimes by shouting "Sit down or I'll knock you down." It was little wonder that under Daley and Keane, the Chicago City Council became a notoriously pliable body — a quintessential rubber stamp. One alderman was famous for doing little but getting out of his seat from time to time to shout: "God bless Mayor Daley!" The Chicago City Council had a reputation for corruption that long pre-dated Keane. As early as 1894, one well-connected lawyer had declared, "There are 68 aldermen in the City Council, and 66 of them can be bought; this I know because I bought them myself." Keane cherished this tradition, and was ever on the lookout for new ways to exploit his legislative office. Like many aldermen, he had real-estate and insurance businesses on the side, and he used them to translate political influence into personal fortune. "You can't view him principally as an alderman," independent alderman Leon Despres once said. "He's in the business of making a living off of politics." Years later, Keane would distill the difference between himself and Daley to a simple choice: Daley had spent his career pursuing power, Keane said, while he had always pursued money.[11]

Daley's leading staff were struck from a similar mold. He named Matthew Danaher, a twenty-eight-year-old Bridgeport neighbor, as his administrative assistant. Danaher had held the same position for Daley in the county clerk's office. One of Danaher's chief duties was maintaining his boss's voluminous patronage records. Fire commissioner Robert Quinn was another classic Daley man. He had grown up in the Back of the Yards neighborhood, and had been a friend for decades. Four days after Daley moved into City Hall, he elevated Quinn from the lower ranks of the department to assistant fire commissioner. Before long, Daley had pushed out longtime fire commissioner Anthony Mullaney to give his old friend the top job. Mullaney started the Daley administration off on a sour note when he stated publicly that Daley had fired him and then lied about it. "That's the type of man he is," Mullaney charged. In time, Daley worked more of his old cronies into top positions. His former law partner, William Lynch, would eventually become general counsel to the Chicago Transit Authority. And when he created the position of commissioner of conservation, Daley named his childhood friend Jeremiah Holland, a retired army brigadier general whose brother had been a politically connected Municipal Court judge. Daley was not deterred by the fact that, in the opinion of the president of the Metropolitan Housing and Planning Council, there was "nothing in the record that demonstrates that he is a qualified expert for this job." Daley eventually appointed Ed Quigley, an Irish ward boss from the West Side's 27th Ward, as sewer commissioner. Quigley readily admitted that he knew almost nothing about sanitation. Asked once if he had ever worked in the sewers, Quigley responded, "No, but many's the time I lifted a lid to see if they were flowing." Daley's top

city officials would soon be tagged with a nickname: "the Irish Ne-
anderthals."[12]

Despite the critical role black voters and the black submachine
played in his election, Daley appointed no blacks to any positions of
consequence. It would be five years before Daley appointed a black
to his cabinet, and that would be as public vehicle license commissioner. Chicago's significant Jewish population, another mainstay of
the city's Democratic Party, was also largely excluded from the upper
ranks of the Daley administration. Though Daley made a point of
selecting Jewish candidates like Becker and Sachs in order to draw
Jewish voters to the machine slate, he had only two Jews on his mayoral staff. One was his press secretary, Earl Bush, and the other was a
secretary held over from the Kennelly administration. Frank Sullivan,
press secretary toward the end of Daley's reign, said he believed
Daley "was not comfortable with blacks and Jews."[13]

Daley was discreet about his racial and ethnic preferences. In an
age when southern politicians openly denigrated blacks, Daley was
careful not to make racially offensive comments in public. This discretion was, if nothing more, smart politics. Unlike in the South,
where few blacks were registered to vote, Chicago's blacks were involved in the political process, and they were a critical part of Daley's
electoral coalition. Behind closed doors, however, it was another
matter. Daley intimates, including those who retain a fondness for
him, have conceded that racism was widespread within Daley's inner
circle. Dr. Eric Oldberg, a suburban doctor who became a friend of
Daley's and president of the Chicago Board of Health, says that one
thing that set him apart from the "rather primitive group that [Daley]
felt comfortable with" was that he did not share its prejudices. "He
would never have had to ask, say, Bob Quinn the Fire Commissioner
or Bill Lee the union fellow, or any of those guys in his circle, what
they thought about something; he knew how they felt," says Oldberg. "It was automatic; it was born and bred in them to think the
same way about everything — including prejudice toward the blacks
and things like that." Frank Sullivan has written that "More than a
few of the members of [Daley's] staff could be described as racists."
And Sullivan tells an odd story of writing a speech for Daley to give
at the dedication of a statue of three Revolutionary War patriots,

George Washington, Gouverneur Morris, and Hayam Solomon. Because Solomon was Jewish, Sullivan wrote a section paying tribute to the contributions made by Jewish-Americans to the nation. When Daley reviewed the remarks, he commented: "Don't you think you have gone a little overboard about the Jews, Frank?"[14]

In the months after Daley's election, Chicago was just beginning to get to know its new mayor. Word spread that Daley would be leaving Bridgeport for a new home more befitting the mayor of America's second-largest city. The Daley family — including Sis, six of the seven children, and Daley's father, Michael — still lived in the simple brick bungalow at 3536 South Lowe Avenue that Daley and Sis had built two decades earlier. It was a modest house, no different from the ones owned by the policemen and government workers who lived on the same block. But those who were saying that Daley was looking to leave Bridgeport did not understand him. When the *Chicago Tribune's* Voice of the People floated the idea of providing mayors with an official residence, Daley said he was not interested. "Perhaps future mayors would like to have a home of this kind to live in and entertain dignitaries," Daley told the newspaper. "I'm very satisfied to live at 3536." Sis Daley also spoke out in defense of Bridgeport. "We have wonderful neighbors," she told the press. "It's true that their houses are very simple on the outside — but the interiors would surprise you. People around here are always remodeling and improving."[15]

Daley was deeply rooted in the Bungalow Belt, the vast expanse of white ethnic neighborhoods that spanned hundreds of blocks on the Southwest and Northwest sides. The Bungalow Belt is, a Chicago writer has observed, "like the South's Bible Belt — as much a state of mind as of geography." Its homes were plain, furnished in a simple working-class style. One visitor to Bridgeport noted that it was a place "of bronzed baby shoes on the parlor mantel, of television sets and undershirts and cans of beer, of corner saloons whose only patrons are 'the boys on the block' and whose windows bear signs such as 'Your husband isn't here.'" Daley fit in perfectly in this world. The Daley homestead was decorated with a large picture of Christ on a living room wall and a statuette of the Virgin and Child on the dining room sideboard. And the Daleys did, in fact, have bronzed baby shoes on the mantel — seven pairs, each engraved with the name of the child who had worn it. There was wall-to-wall turquoise carpeting, a hand-woven rug with the provinces of Ireland, and red-white-and-blue china bearing the Daley family crest, with its motto, "Deo Fidelis et Regi," or "Faithful to God and King." The home had its small luxuries: with an addition in the back, it had been expanded to five bedrooms, and there was a basement rec room with exercise equipment and a piano for the Daley daughters. Outside of family and close friends, though, few people ever got to see the house on South Lowe Avenue. It was, in the words of one member of the Daley inner circle, "the house nobody gets into."[16]

Daley's election as mayor did not change his lifestyle: when he was not governing or engaging in politics, he continued to live much as his Bridgeport neighbors did. "Nobody catches him chatting about literature, music or French cooking," Mike Royko once observed. "He likes White Sox games, fishing and parades." After a rare outing to Chicago's Lyric Opera, Daley is said to have exclaimed happily: "It's just like baseball! You stand and cheer when it's all over!" Daley's one concession to his station in life was his clothing: he dressed himself as extravagantly as an adult as his mother had dressed him as a child. He wore hand-tailored Duro suits, and often made national ten-best-dressed lists. Daley rarely appeared in public in anything less formal than a suit, and almost never removed his jacket.[17]

Daley woke early, and attended morning Mass at Nativity of Our Lord Church. After a quick breakfast at home, he was driven to work by a city policeman in a late-model Cadillac. Daley often got out of the car a few blocks south of the Loop so he could work in a short walk before arriving at City Hall — a gesture to exercise that did little to rein in his fast-growing girth. At lunchtime, he generally made his way over to the Morrison Hotel, where he had a separate office and secretary for his work as machine boss. After returning to City Hall for an afternoon of work, he usually went home for dinner with his family between 6:30 and 7:00 P.M. Daley worked most Saturdays until midafternoon, but spent more time at home on Sundays. On his rare vacations, Daley often went fishing with his father, and on weekends he liked to take his children to Comiskey Park, the "Base-Ball Palace of the World," which was just a few blocks from home.[18]

Sis Daley, for her part, remained every bit the Bridgeport matron. Like many of her neighbors, her life revolved around neighborhood, church, and family. She was active in charity work, preparing flowers for the Altar and Rosary Society at Nativity of Our Lord, and visiting the poor in the parish. She liked to cook, and baked an Irish soda bread twice a week throughout her married life. The secret to making a good soda bread, she once told a neighbor, was to "keep kneading — you get your hostilities and aggression out on the dough." A few weeks into his first term as mayor, on May 15, Daley celebrated his fifty-third birthday with a simple dinner at home. Sis cooked his favorite dish, roast beef, and baked a birthday cake. Sis was interested in her husband's political career and served as a sounding board for his important decisions. But in her public statements, she disclaimed all interest in politics. When she spoke to reporters, which was infrequently, the conversation usually hewed closely to domestic topics. Sis once advised a household-hints columnist that bowls of vinegar are the best air fresheners for stale, smoke-filled rooms. "I suppose if Dick is elected, I will have to be more active," she said on the eve of her husband's election as mayor. But after a year as Chicago's first lady, she reported that her role had remained sharply circumscribed. "I guess you'd say I'm first lady to my children first," she told a reporter. "Making a good, comfortable and happy home for them and Dick still is the thing I like and want to do most."[19]

When Daley socialized outside Bridgeport, it was generally at public appearances that had the impersonal feel of campaign events. Most nights, he attended five or six of these gatherings. His first Sunday in office, Daley ate dinner at home, went out to a dinner at the Morrison Hotel for the Holy Family Villa Retirement Home, and then moved on to the Conrad Hilton for a dinner for Villa Scalabrini, another retirement home. And Daley was a fixture at the life events of people he did not know well. A few weeks into his mayoralty, he attended six weddings in a single day, none for relatives, and the next day he attended two more. He worked the crowd at wakes across the city. Daley's "name is signed in more wake books than any name in the history of Chicago," one associate said. Daley was skilled at making his way through these events. "One thing he learned," says David Stahl, a deputy mayor who often went along with him, "was to work a crowd and keep moving." This frenetic round of appearances came on top of a daily schedule that was filled with ceremonial events: bowling the first ball at Chicago's Tuesday and Thursday Night Classic Bowling League, planting a kiss on six-year-old "Little Miss Peanut" as part of the Kiwanis Peanut Day in Chicago, or being honored with a 50,000-tree forest planted in his name in Israel at a Purim dinner sponsored by the Jewish National Fund. At these appearances, Daley usually offered up a short speech that was more upbeat than insightful. To kick off the first year-round athletic program sponsored by the city, he put on a glove and caught balls thrown by Chicago Cubs pitcher Don Kaiser, and declared that "boys and girls are the citizens of Chicago of tomorrow." Daley also continued to make the rounds of the city's fifty Democratic ward organizations. One such gathering was a tongue-in-cheek graduation ceremony thrown by Alderman Charlie Weber for fifty garbagemen who found their jobs through 45th Ward patronage. The colorful Weber doted on his sanitation workers, whom he referred to as the Knights of Cleanliness. For the ceremony, he distributed white academic gowns and mortarboards to the "graduating" garbagemen. Daley stood on the dais and conferred parchment diplomas, which had summa cum laude notations and five-dollar bills attached. A dinner of turkey and beer was provided. "Don't steal any of them caps and gowns," Weber yelled out to his guests. "I rented 'em. Leave 'em at the door when you go out."[20]

Daley had the kind of social skills that serve a politician well. He had a knack for remembering people; it was said that he could greet half the city's employees by name. David Stahl took his young sons to work one Saturday and introduced them to Daley. Six months later, Daley's secretary called to offer Stahl three tickets to a White Sox game. When Daley showed up, he immediately greeted the Stahl children. "He said, 'Hi Steve, Hi Mike.' Nobody had given him a card. He had an incredible photographic memory." Still, Daley was not a warm man. "You never touched him," says Congressman Daniel Rostenkowski, a friend and political protégé of Daley's. "You wouldn't hug him." Apart from family members, Daley's relationships were largely defined by politics. Many of the people he was closest to were politicians, and Daley was inclined to view them more as rivals than friends. Near North Side alderman Joseph Rostenkowski, Daniel's father, was nominally a friend, but Daley always regarded him warily because of his strong following in Chicago's large Polish community. Daley was able to let his guard down a bit more with younger people. "He never feared me," says Daniel Rostenkowski, who was in his early twenties when he started out with Daley. "I wasn't a threat to him." Daley was a gregarious loner, acquainted with thousands of people but close to almost none. "He's like a post office clerk sorting mail," one Daley associate said. "He keeps men in slots. In a general human sense of trusting somebody, the only person really close to him is his wife." Daley also kept people at arm's length with a fierce temper that rose up without warning. "He was essentially a quiet, soft-spoken person," says David Stahl. "But he had the capacity to get angry and bellow. He did it almost every day of the week." Daley's associates had a gallows humor about his frequent red-faced outbursts. Asked about the best way to approach the mayor they would respond: on tiptoe.[21]

Daley was also suspicious and secretive, in both his private and public lives. He rarely talked about his family or his past. "That was a private world he hung on to," says human relations commissioner Edward Marciniak. Daley was so reticent about even the most basic personal details that when one author set out to write about Daley he found himself unable to verify that he was an only child. "I checked with two people, one a Democratic politician who has known Daley for twenty-five years, and the other, a man who had worked in Daley's office closely with him for a number of years and who had been invited to the weddings of Daley's children," the author wrote. "When asked whether Daley was an only child or whether there were any brothers or sisters, both men replied that they thought [he was an only child] but were not sure." Daley quickly imposed this diffident style on his mayoral administration. He held press conferences almost every day, but he addressed only the topics he chose. City employees were instructed not to answer even simple inquiries from reporters or civic groups without checking with him. Lois Wille, a *Chicago Daily News* reporter who won a Pulitzer Prize for reporting on health care for indigent women, says it was almost impossible to get basic facts on issues like infant mortality out of Daley's City Hall. In one case, she had to arrange a secret rendezvous with a woman doctor at the perfume counter of a department store to get health data that, in any other city, would have been available through the mayoral press office.[22]

Becoming mayor did change Daley in one respect: he quickly came to demand a new level of obeisance from subordinates and friends. Shortly after the 1955 election William Lee, a union official who had provided critical support during the campaign, saw his old friend arriving late for a civic function. "You're late, Richard," Lee said to Daley. "Don't you ever call me 'Richard' in public," Daley replied. "I am the mayor, and don't you ever forget it." Like a rich man who does not like to be reminded of the days before he had money, Daley did not like to be reminded of his more humble origins. South Side alderman Edward Burke recalls a meeting at the LaSalle Hotel where Attorney General William Clark made the mistake of mentioning in his speech that his father was on the City Council when Daley used to get coffee for the aldermen. "He was trying to allude to his long family relationship to the party, but Daley didn't like being reminded he was a gofer," says Burke. "That cast the die for Bill Clark. Daley wouldn't give him the time of day."[23] In this case, Daley's anger did not last. Clark remained a loyal member of the machine, and years later Daley slated him in a losing campaign for the U.S. Senate.

One of Daley's first priorities in office was to rescue political patronage. Despite his campaign rhetoric, he never had any intention of continuing Mayor Kennelly's civil-service reform efforts. The patronage system was simply too critical to the machine's grip on power for Daley to allow it to be undone. Political patronage is often thought of by the uninitiated as a casual practice in which friends hire friends and relatives hire relatives for government jobs. In fact, in a well-run political machine like Chicago's, patronage was anything but casual. Machines held on to power through their ability to trade jobs and other material inducements for political support. Paddy Bauler used to say that reformers could never hope to compete with the machine because their workers simply did not have the incentive to campaign that came with knowing that their livelihoods were at stake. "The type of people you got over there don't need a job as bailiff, so you got to rely on amateurs for your organization," Bauler scoffed at one reform leader. But the supply of patronage positions was limited, and the machine could afford to hand them out only to workers who could be counted on to work hard for it on election day. In his own 43rd Ward, Bauler once boasted, every one of his seventy-six precinct captains had city, state, or county employment. But in exchange, they all turned out their vote on election day.[24]

Patronage workers were chosen carefully, and their value to the machine was constantly reassessed. Daley had individual meetings with each of the fifty ward committeemen to discuss how much patronage his ward would receive for the year. To ready for these meetings, Daley patronage aide Matt Danaher prepared precise tabulations of how each precinct in each of the fifty wards had performed in the last election — more than 3,000 separate vote tallies that Daley personally pored over in making his patronage decisions. Everyone understood there was a "pecking order," recalls Tom Donovan, who followed Danaher as Daley's patronage chief. "Someone who's with the best ward in the city naturally is going to have a better chance of getting key positions than someone who isn't." But there was also room for the machine boss to exercise his discretion, rewarding friends and punishing enemies. "We didn't have a set form," Donovan recalls. "It was something you had a feel for." Ward committeemen with strong connections to Daley, including most of the Irish titans of the machine, tended to do especially well. Daley's political base, the 11th Ward, may have had as many as 2,000 patronage positions, considerably more than it was entitled to based on electoral performance alone. At the other extreme, Frank Keenan, who had defied Daley and the machine by backing Kennelly for mayor, had his patronage cut off entirely.[25]

Despite the inroads made by Kennelly's civil-service crusade, the machine's patronage operation was still vast when Daley took power. Thousands of workers were on the city payroll directly, and many more were on the payroll of specialized government bodies like the Sanitary District, which had their own budgets and taxing authority. Thousands more were placed with machine politicians who controlled large staffs of their own. The president of the Cook County Board of Commissioners at one time employed 3,100, more than half of whom were patronage hires. The clerk of the Circuit Court of Cook County had 1,700 employees, three-fourths patronage workers. In addition to these government jobs, thousands of private-sector positions in Chicago required sponsorship from the Democratic machine. Sears, Roebuck & Co.'s mail-order operations, located in the 24th Ward, used to turn away walk-in applicants who did not come with a letter from alderman Jacob Arvey. All told, the Chicago machine at its height controlled as many as 40,000 patronage jobs. "We had everything that wasn't police or fire or career civil service," recalls Daley patronage chief Tom Donovan. "That gave us a lot of positions to put our people in." Even the worst patronage jobs offered a decent salary, and the best came with some appealing fringe benefits. Some jobs at the Forest Preserve District, a bastion of patronage, included a free house in the forest. Relatively minor supervisory positions often came with city cars. When 29th Ward precinct captain Thomas Fitzsimmons was supervisor of buildings and grounds at the Chicago Tuberculosis and Sanitarium District, he was entitled to a car and driver, although he did not take it. "He didn't believe in calling attention," says his granddaughter, Martha Fitzsimmons.[26]

To get a patronage job, the key was showing up with the right "sponsorship." If the 10th Ward was entitled to six positions with the Sanitation Department, for example, the ward committeeman would send over six men with official "sponsorship letters." Employers kept detailed patronage files, including when an employee was hired, who his sponsor was, and whether a sponsorship letter was on file. William Dawson's correspondence files contain a letter that illustrates how the process worked. "I understand that my friend and office associate, Joseph J. Attwell, Jr., has received the endorsement of the 20th Ward Regular Democratic Organization for the position of trial attorney in your office," Dawson wrote to Cook County state's attorney John Boyle. "I also understand that there are already several appointees in your office from the 20th Ward. Since Mr. Attwell also meets with my approval, I would be happy to have you let your records show that you are charging his position to the Second Ward if that would facilitate his appointment."[27]

Applicants without political sponsorship were usually ineligible for patronage jobs, no matter how qualified they were. There is a classic study of the Chicago machine entitled *We Don't Want Nobody Nobody Sent,* and that was precisely the ethic that prevailed. When Jesse Jackson came to Chicago in 1964 to attend Chicago Theological Seminary, he needed a job. He had a letter of introduction to Daley from North Carolina governor Terry Sanford. Daley met with Jackson, and advised him to work for one of the ward organizations on the South Side. He also offered Jackson a job as toll collector on the Calumet Bridge. Jackson, insulted, turned the job down. "He thought he was going to get something that was more commensurate with his self-concept, if you will," says Jackson's friend Henry Hardy. "You know, he had come out of school as a star athlete, president of the student body, with a letter from the governor — there were other toll collectors, I'm sure, who never had a letter from a governor." Still, there were not many toll collectors who had gotten their job without doing precinct work first.[28]

Workers were generally assigned patronage jobs that corresponded to their place in the machine hierarchy. Precinct captains and assistant captains often became supervisors in the government bureaucracy or minor department heads. Lower-level precinct workers might get jobs as clerical workers, janitors, or street cleaners. Being qualified to do the work was not an important consideration. A high-level Chicago bureaucrat once explained the difference between hiring workers sent by the 29th Ward's Bernie Neistein and those sent by the 26th Ward's Matthew Bieszczat. "Bernie Neistein is reasonable," the bureaucrat said. "If he sends you five guys to put to work, only two are illiterate. But Matt Bieszczat sends you five illiterates and wants you to take them all!" In many cases, little actual work was expected of patronage workers, at least in their nonpolitical jobs. Ed Quigley, who was both Daley's sewer commissioner and ward committeeman for the 27th Ward, was known to be particularly undemanding. "It was the only sewer department in the country where people came to work in white pants, and when they went home they were just as clean," recalls one veteran political reporter. "You didn't have to work hard, and you could often hold down another job."[29]

The patronage system built a political army willing to do battle for the machine in every election. "It gave the mayor a cadre of people who wanted to see him succeed," says Tom Donovan. Patronage workers circulated nominating petitions, put up posters, worked at polling places, or rang doorbells to get their neighbors out to vote. In many departments, any employee who brought a letter from his ward organization could get a paid day off on election day to do political work. Patronage workers were expected to kick back up to 5 percent of their salary to their ward organizations. In some wards, the machine calculated the annual amount and sent workers a schedule of monthly payments. Patronage workers were also expected to attend ward dinner-dances and golf outings and sell tickets to their friends and family, and to buy books of ward-organization raffle tickets to resell. In the 5th Ward, they sold ads in the official program for the annual "Marshall Korshak Night," honoring the ward committeeman; in the 11th Ward, they canvassed to support the annual indoor picnic at the Amphitheatre, in which 12,000 ward residents, most of them children, gathered for a free day of ice cream, soda, Ferris wheels, and merry-go-rounds. Patronage workers were also often pressured to contribute directly to their employers. The summer was a particularly costly time of year for patronage hires. In August 1958, the *Chicago Tribune* noted that four elected officials had already held golf outings, and four more were coming up shortly. "These are the months dreaded by the thousands of temporary workers on the government payrolls," the paper noted. "They are the people expected to make a 'drop' of money for tickets to their ward organizations — either from their paychecks or thru the sale of tickets to others. Workers who fail to meet quotas for ticket sales may find themselves slipping off the payroll."[30]

Patronage employees who did not produce risked losing their jobs. A large number of patronage employees were officially classified as "temporary" workers, who were hired for periods of 60 to 180 days, after which their employment had to be renewed. The temporary worker category was a gaping loophole in Chicago's civil-service system. The law permitted these workers to be hired outside the civil-service guidelines when no competitive examinations had been held — which gave the machine an incentive to see that exams were held as infrequently as possible. In some agencies, like the Park District, more than half of the new employees in a given year would be classified as temporary. Temporary workers who remained in the good graces of the machine could remain on the payroll for twenty-five years or more in their "temporary" capacity. The temporary worker system kept the pressure on patronage workers to fulfill their political responsibilities if they wanted to remain employed. Years later, when the patronage machine was challenged in federal court, workers would come forward with stories of being fired for failing to produce the votes that were expected of them or for not kicking back money to their ward organizations. Ida Barnes, who worked in the traffic ticket collection office of the clerk of the Circuit Court, testified that she lost her job after protesting she could not afford to buy a $50 ticket to a dinner sponsored by the 16th Ward Democratic Organization.[31]

From a purely political standpoint, the patronage system worked. By one estimate, each patronage job produced about ten votes for the machine: the worker's own, the votes of his family and friends, and the votes that his campaign work and financial contributions produced. If the machine in fact controlled 40,000 patronage jobs, it went into every election with a 400,000-vote edge over its opponents. In local races, the impact could be even more dramatic. By one estimate patronage workers could account for as much as 25 percent to 50 percent of the vote in some aldermanic races. James Murray, onetime 18th Ward alderman, recalls that at one point his ward had about three hundred patronage jobs and produced a fairly good vote for the machine. "I remember Matt Danaher said to me, 'Why aren't you as good as the 11th Ward,'" Murray recalls. "I told him, 'We would be if we had the jobs you have in the 11th Ward.'" Daley was a firm believer in the power of patronage. Once, at a meeting of the Cook County Central Committee, a committeeman from suburban Wheeling Township complained that he had more than one hundred precincts but only twelve precinct workers available to cover them on election day. Daley responded that the committeeman should focus on running slates of candidates for office in the villages across his township, with the goal of taking control of the village governments. Once he controlled these local governments, Daley advised, he could hire patronage employees and turn them into political armies.[32]

The patronage system meant more to Daley than just votes. He liked the control it gave him over people. Daley was not comfortable dealing with people who were not under obligation to him. Jerome Torshen, an antitrust lawyer with no ties to the machine, worked closely with Daley on a sensitive litigation project. Torshen was paid for the work, but Daley was uneasy with the fact that when it was over Torshen had no stake in the machine. Torshen recalls that one day he was walking through City Hall and ran into Daley, who greeted him warmly. Mistaking Torshen's specialty of antitrust law for the trust-and-estate work the machine handed out freely to politically connected lawyers, Daley urged Torshen to pick up some legal work from one of his patronage dispensers. "Get some trust work from the city," Daley urged Torshen. "You can start tomorrow."[33]

More fundamentally, Daley simply believed that the patronage system was the way the world should work. A patronage job was a reward for hard work, and for loyalty to the political hierarchy — a secular equivalent to Catholic concepts of getting into heaven through a life of religious duty. To Daley, the innate justice of the patronage system was a given, and should have been obvious even to those who did not rise through the machine. In a phone call with Lyndon Johnson, captured on the White House taping system, Daley can be heard urging the president to appoint his machine ally Edward Hanrahan as a United States attorney. Daley's pitch to the president of the United States sounded like a ward committeeman trying to push a candidate for street sweeper on a wavering streets and sanitation commissioner. "He's a great Democrat," Daley told Johnson. "He ran for Congress. He was defeated. He's a graduate of Notre Dame, of Harvard." After reciting Hanrahan's résumé, Daley delivered what he assumed would be the clincher. "But more than that, Mr. President, let me say with great honor and pride, he's a *precinct captain!*"[34]

Daley wasted little time, once he became mayor, in beginning his war on Kennelly's civil-service reforms. On April 15, just days after the election, Civil Service Commission head Stephen Hurley submitted his resignation, even though he had a year remaining on his contract. Kennelly's reform-minded Civil Service Commission president had done significant damage to the machine's patronage operations by bringing 12,000 political hires under civil-service protection. To replace Hurley, Daley selected his old friend and political ally William Lee. Reformers were outraged by the appointment, because Lee was president of the Chicago Federation of Labor — a position he intended to keep — and actually represented

36,000 of the government workers who would fall under his juris-diction. The Chicago Crime Commission decried Lee's selection as a conflict of interest that was "wrong in principle." Daley cannily framed the reformers' criticism as an attack on organized labor, and defended Lee's selection by pointing out that unions represented "a large segment of our people."[35]

Lee's greatest conflict-of-interest was not his union position, but the fact that he did not believe in the civil-service system he would be in charge of promoting. The Chicago labor movement that Lee came out of was a bastion of favoritism and featherbedding. Its lead-ers were men like "Umbrella" Mike Boyle, onetime head of the plumbers' union, who got his nickname from his practice of hanging up an open umbrella when he went out drinking at his favorite sa-loon, using it to collect political payoffs. Lee set the new tone in the Civil Service Commission with one of his first hires: his own twenty-seven-year-old nephew, Robert E. Lee Jr., who became a labor examiner on his staff. Critics attacked the appointment as undisguised nepotism, but Daley rushed to defend it. Daley declared that he had known the younger Lee and his family for years and that "this man is particularly well equipped for this job." So much, it seemed, for Daley's promise to continue Kennelly's reform policies. Lee's hiring of his relatives did not end with his nephew. Robert E. Lee Sr., father of the new labor examiner, was assigned to work full-time as his brother's bodyguard.[36]

With Hurley out and Lee in, Daley could begin the real work of undoing Kennelly's civil-service reforms. He hired a consultant named Fred Hoehler to consider possible changes in the city's civil-service code. There was, of course, considerable room to improve the civil-service system — the machine was still managing to place tens of thousands of its political workers in patronage jobs. But Hoehler's recommendations were not to extend civil service reform, but to roll it back. Hoehler's report found fault with "the intense rigidity with which civil service has been administered over the last few years." He recommended rewriting the rules to give greater weight to oral examinations and less to written tests. This was exactly the direction Daley wanted civil service to move in, since oral exam-inations were more subjective, and made it easier for employers to give preference to politically connected applicants.[37]

The biggest campaign promise Daley broke on the subject of political reform was his vow to step down as chairman of the Cook County Democratic Organization if he were elected mayor. Daley had made this promise as early as 1953, when Arvey asked him about it, and in the primary and general elections he had made the same public commitment to the voters. But Daley understood better than anyone the political risks he would be taking by keeping his promise. Kennelly had been removed from City Hall because Daley, as head of the machine, had the power to unslate him. If Daley handed over the machine to someone else, they would be able to do the same thing to him at the end of his first term. Daley also understood that, important as the mayoralty was, the position of machine boss carried with it more power. The party boss filled more patronage positions, had more power to punish politicians from the governor down to the lowliest ward committeeman, and controlled more votes in Springfield and Washington than a mayor ever did. "Daley is known as 'Mayor Daley' because 'Mayor' is his prestigious and sonorous title," Leon Despres, a leading anti-machine alderman, would observe on Daley's tenth anniversary as mayor, "but if we used the more powerful title, we would certainly call him 'Party Chairman Daley.'" Once in office, Daley conveniently forgot his promise to step down as machine boss. He would always insist that he tried to offer his resignation, but the Cook County Central Committee had refused it.[38]

The Chicago that Daley inherited in 1955 was in serious decline. The novelist Nelson Algren compared his fading hometown to "a juke box running down in a deserted bar." Chicago's 1950 population of 3,620,962 turned out to be the high-water mark: for the rest of the century, the city would steadily lose inhabitants. Chicago was losing not only people, but jobs, to the fast-growing Cook County suburbs. In the seven years before Daley took over as mayor, the city lost 53,209 manufacturing jobs, while the rest of the county gained 30,000. The city's infrastructure was also in decline: new housing starts had all but ground to a halt, and only one major building had risen downtown in a decade. Even Chicago's once-thriving vice trade, which had serviced generations of farm boys and conventioneers, was sliding into oblivion. "The strip-tease joints are still operating on West Madison and North Clark Streets but with the weary air of sin gone stale," wrote one Chicago journalist. Mid-1950s Chicago, he concluded, had "a surplus of only one thing — ennui." It was in 1955, Daley's first year as mayor, that Chicago suffered the greatest indignity of all: it ceded its status as "hog butcher for the world" when it was surpassed in total receipts from livestock by Omaha, Nebraska.[39]

Among the hardest-hit parts of the city was the downtown business district, better known as the Loop. The Loop had been the center of Chicago's commerce since the 1800s, when the city's vast cable car system, at that time the largest in the world, brought shoppers in from the neighborhoods to State Street, to shop at the mammoth Marshall Field department store. The district got its name from the turnabout, or loop, of cable-car track in front of Marshall Field, which allowed the cars to change directions and head back to the South Side. In time, as the streets became more congested, the cable cars gave way to an elevated railway system that swooped around the perimeter of the downtown commercial district, giving Chicagoans a new and more visible reason to call their downtown the Loop. Chicago's Loop has long been one of the world's most densely concentrated business centers. In 1910, the one-half-mile district contained almost 40 percent of the assessed land value in a 190-square-mile city. And, from its earliest days, the Loop has always had a distinctly rough-and-tumble character. Blue-blooded bankers reported for work next door to pawnshops and honky-tonks. Haute couture was sold in stores that looked out on thrift shops and dancing schools. Many observers were struck by its essential charmlessness. "Buildings are too frequently drab," noted one study that urged an immediate downtown beautification project. "Street furniture is finished in dull grays, black and olive drab. The subway is glum and dreary. The sidewalk paving lacks either color or pattern." A. J. Liebling, who came to know the Loop in his year of exile from Manhattan in the 1940s, dismissed it as "a boundless agglutination of streets, dramshops, and low buildings without any urban character." In the early 1950s, when other cities' downtowns were in the midst of a postwar building boom, the Loop was in the doldrums. From 1947 to 1955, when New York added 10.7 million square feet of new office space, Chicago built less than one million. With growing competition from suburban stores, retail sales in the Loop were plummeting. By 1962, net profits at the five largest downtown department stores were only 30 percent of what they had been in 1948.[40]

Along with the physical decline, Chicago seemed to be in the midst of a citywide crisis of confidence. Chicago had once been the most optimistic of cities, its spirit captured in its motto: "I will." During the 1920s, every day's *Chicago Tribune* carried an injunction to its readers to "Make Chicago the First City of the World," and many Chicagoans believed it was only a matter of time before that lofty goal was achieved. But the city's optimism had been flagging lately. Robert Maynard Hutchins, the legendary University of Chicago chancellor who had done much to build his school into a world-class institution, had resigned and declared on his way out that the city was slipping into insignificance. "Nobody cares about Chicago," Hutchins said bluntly. From his first days in office, Daley set out to revive Chicago's civic spirit. Scarcely a month into his mayoralty, he told *U.S. News & World Report* that despite what appeared to be unstoppable national trends, he intended to "bring people back from the suburbs to our city." And in the tradition of the old *Chicago Tribune* slogan, he boldly predicted that it was only a matter of time before Chicago would eclipse New York in size. Chicago's real problem, Daley insisted, was that it had been hamstrung by years of weak municipal leadership. City government under Kennelly had been "unbelievable," he said — the police and fire departments were in poor shape, and the condition of public buildings was "wretched." But all this was about to change. "I'm dedicated to a program of making this a better city," Daley declared. "I'll go to the people of Chicago whenever I think more money is needed."[41]

And Daley did think more money would be needed. In his first days in office, Daley held a series of closed-door meetings with his budget director, his acting corporation counsel, and the ubiquitous alderman Tom Keane to try to determine how much. At an April 30 conference of city leaders, Daley announced that based on these calculations he would need an additional $35 million for the 1956 budget. Most of the new money, he said, would be used to pay for more policemen and firemen, more street cleaning and playground staffing, and rehabilitation of down-at-the-heels city facilities. Roughly $10 million would be needed just to carry out his campaign promise to hire an additional 2,000 police officers.[42]

There was only one problem with the new spending plans: figuring out how to raise the money. To increase the sales tax, which would have gone a long way toward raising the additional funds, Daley needed the approval of the voters. Referenda of this type were risky — even the machine could not always convince its voters to raise their own taxes. But there was a loophole: Illinois law allowed Chicago mayors to raise the sales tax without a referendum provided the state legislature gave its approval. Instead of risking the vagaries of a citywide vote, Daley could just work on persuading one man — William Stratton, the Republican governor, who could deliver his party's vote in the legislature. Stratton was no ally of the Chicago Democratic machine, and he was not partial to higher taxes, but Daley flew to Springfield to negotiate. After five hours of talks, Daley and Stratton agreed on a package that gave both men something: the city and the state would each be authorized to adopt a half-cent sales tax increase. At the same time, Daley and Stratton agreed on several other common goals, including working toward getting Chicago a world-class exposition center, an expanded airport, and improved highways and mass transit.[43]

Not everyone applauded Daley's shrewd political work in Springfield. Critics of the new sales tax — notably the Illinois Federation of Retail Associations, whose members stood to lose business as a result — complained that Daley and Stratton had improperly taken the question of taxation out of the hands of the voters. Before long, a more sinister charge began to circulate: that Stratton had given Daley the taxing authority he wanted in exchange for a promise that the machine would put up only a token opponent in the next election. Daley angrily denied that he had struck any such deal. The charges came from "a polluted, twisted mind," he said, pausing for breath and then adding that it came from a "vicious, proselyted, deluded mind who sees evil in everything men in public life try to do for people."[44]

Early in his mayoralty, Daley took up a cause he would forever be associated with: improving city services. A few of his policy initiatives were large and cutting edge. In 1956, he directed that Chicago's water be fluoridated, making the city a leader in what was still a controversial area of public health. He also upgraded the health care pro-

vided in city clinics, and allocated city funding for alcoholism treatment, again putting Chicago in the vanguard. But what captured
Daley's imagination were the small things — improved streetlighting
and, most of all, street cleaning. Daley took a personal interest in the
details of municipal housekeeping, and often became directly involved. As he was driven around town in the mayoral limousine, he
often took notes on problems he observed along the way — broken
traffic lights, dirty streets, and potholes. When he arrived at City
Hall, he would direct his staff to fix the problems he had come
across. Daley had a keen eye for potholes: by one estimate, fully half
the city's complaints for pothole repair began in the mayor's office.
Sometimes he took matters into his own hands. Daley once stopped
his car when he saw a man drop a newspaper onto Michigan Avenue.
As the sheets began to scatter to the wind, Daley and his police
bodyguard leaped out and picked up the paper, putting it in the
garbage.[45]

Cleaning up the city became a crusade for Daley. In May 1955, he
returned from his first U.S. Conference of Mayors meeting in New
York and announced a citywide cleanup campaign. By the end of
June, he had purchased forty new street sweepers, raising the total
fleet size to more than one hundred, and Daley vowed that every
street in Chicago would be cleaned at least once a month. His
cleanup drive gained force over the summer, with an initiative to
have businessmen sign pledge cards committing to keep the sidewalks in front of their establishments clean, and to place all their
garbage in covered containers. Daley's Streets and Sanitation commissioner issued a steady flow of statistics charting the drive's
progress. As of August 1, 3,640 shifts had been worked, up from
1,823 in the same period in 1954, and roughly 10,000 tons more
street dirt had been removed than in the same period a year earlier.
Later the same month, Daley spoke to eighty-three community
cochairmen of the city's cleanup campaign, gathered in the City
Council chambers, and outlined plans for improving street cleaning
and garbage removal, including a contest with prizes for blocks with
the best cleanup records.[46]

Daley personally reaped the good publicity that came from the
cleanup campaign. He rode through the Loop in a 1916 Isotta-
Fraschini, heading up an antique car parade. Pulling up the rear were

five city sanitation trucks handing out the first installment of 7,000 new wire garbage baskets Daley had ordered up for immediate distribution around the city. He urged all Chicagoans to "make a special effort over the Labor Day holiday to put waste paper and trash in waste baskets in parks, beaches, and city streets." Daley also inspected a "Cleanerama" display that was touring the city, consisting of eight floats, including a fire truck with signs warning that 25 percent of Chicago's fires began with litter or debris, and a cage showing rats feeding on garbage. Hardly a week went by without a prominent newspaper story featuring the mayor and his war on grime. One day Daley was directing that 2,000 metal signs and 10,000 decals be posted across the city with the message "Keep Chicago Clean." Another day he was addressing 200 members of the Women's Division of the Mayor's Commission for a Cleaner City at the Bismarck Hotel, telling them that housewives were "naturals" to play a major role in cleaning up the city and handing out paper cleanup-drive boutonnieres that they could wear when they went out into the neighborhoods with pledge cards for the merchants to sign.[47]

A tangible symbol of Daley's new attention to city services showed up in the lobby of City Hall on July 18. Chicago's official information booth, technically the Office of Inquiry and Information, was unveiled with great fanfare. Reporters looked on as one Marquard Howe became the first Chicagoan to take advantage of the new service. Howe complained that his neighbor had placed cinder blocks on the parkway near his home, preventing him from parking his car and causing a backup of rainwater onto Howe's lawn. Daley also announced plans for a "City Hall on Wheels," a station wagon that would cruise the streets five days a week, staffed with mayoral aides who would be available to listen to constituents' problems. The City Hall information booth was a Daley favorite, and he marked its one-year anniversary by manning the booth himself and personally answering a citizen's question.[48]

Daley may have had a sincere interest in improved city services. His admirers have always attributed his attention to street cleaning and potholes to his love for Chicago and its inhabitants. Chicago was Daley's "Our Lady of the Lake," a Chicago journalist once wrote, "and he would never stop building shrines and lighting candles for her." Daley's attention to Chicago's streets and sidewalks can be seen as a form of loving ministration. If there was a psychological explanation, though, it is just as likely that his furious efforts to clean and repair were a manifestation of his extraordinarily controlling personality. Chicago was his city, and a litter-strewn sidewalk was as much a challenge to his authority as an insurgent candidate for ward committeeman. Most likely of all, however, is that Daley swept and paved for political reasons. Daley had come into office with a cloud over him: his critics openly predicted that he and his allies would plunder city government for their own gain. "The attitude was that the Daley people were going to get screwdrivers and take the doors off the hinges," recalls Daniel Rostenkowski. To fight this perception, Rostenkowski's father, 32nd Ward alderman Joseph Rostenkowski, offered Daley a word of advice: "Put the money where they can see it." Daley was increasing taxes, but the stream of headlines about city services gave at least the appearance that the money was being used to buy better government.[49]

Improved city services was also good politics in another way: it helped expand the patronage system that had atrophied under Kennelly. Cleaning streets, filling potholes, paving roads, and other aspects of municipal upkeep were all labor-intensive. That meant more municipal jobs to fill with loyal Democrats. The hoopla about streets and garbage pickup also provided cover for Daley as he hired patronage workers in other parts of city government. In 1957, when Daley proposed a city budget that raised spending 15 percent in one year — well above the rate of inflation and the city's population growth — he had a ready answer for those who accused him of padding it with political hires. The new spending was "justified by the record of this administration," he said, "in which we carried on the program of expanding and improving the city's vital services." In fact, much of the new money went to allies of the machine. As much as 90 percent of the city's fast-growing streetlight construction business, for example, was being directed to a single group of politically connected contractors.[50]

Daley also used his control over city services to forge strong bonds with organized labor. He had many personal ties to labor unions: his father had been a labor official, he had briefly been a member of the drivers union, and many of his friends and neighbors in Bridgeport were union men and women. Organized labor was also an integral part of the Democratic machine, and it had played a large role in getting him elected. As mayor, Daley came through generously for the city's labor unions. Shortly after his election, he instituted a new policy that required workers to be paid prevailing wages for all city work. The concept of prevailing wages did not sound extravagant, but as a practical matter, paying prevailing wages to city construction workers, electricians, and other laborers gave them a significant windfall. Nongovernment workers' wages had to be large enough to compensate them for the loss of income between projects, bad-weather days for which they were not paid, and other vagaries that did not affect city workers. "One of the greatest benefits is to be assured full employment," the building industry argued to the City Council. "City workers are practically guaranteed this. Those in private industry are sometimes on the street seeking work." In fact, the salaries produced by Daley's policy were so generous that they could only be viewed as a political payoff from the city's coffers. Daley soon introduced a city budget that, because of the prevailing wage rule, raised the salaries of the city's unionized window washers above the level of starting policemen.[51]

Daley also gave organized labor a large role in running parts of the city government that affected it. He named labor representatives to most of the city and county boards: the Chicago Housing Authority and the Board of Education regularly had at least two advocates for organized labor. Daley generally included on the school board representatives of both the craft unions that formerly made up the American Federation of Labor and the industrial unions that once composed the more radical Congress of Industrial Organizations. Though the two factions had merged in 1953, Daley wanted to keep both happy. The greatest beneficiary of Daley's appointment practices was his good friend William McFetridge, president of the Flat Janitors Union, who was one of the most important behind-the-scenes players in Chicago city government under Daley. "I'm on more committees than anyone else in Chicago," McFetridge liked to boast. The appointments were "part of the quid pro quo" for labor's political support, says Daley's human rights commissioner Edward Marciniak. The labor appointees were fierce defenders of high pay scales, lenient work rules, and featherbedding. When fights developed over building scattered-site public housing, the federal government would be surprised to learn that construction costs in Chicago were, by a considerable margin, the highest in the country.[52]

Daley's attention to city services helped Chicago to develop its reputation as "the city that works." There was some basis for it. Under Daley, Chicago repeatedly won national awards for cleanliness, and there is no denying that thousands of new streetlights went up. But there was much about the city that did not work. The benefits of government were doled out unequally — to those who lived in some parts of the city, and to those with connections to the Democratic machine. Outside the Loop and a few favored wards, upkeep dropped off sharply. "Get off the subway anywhere in the central business area and you won't find a broken city sidewalk," says former Hyde Park alderman Leon Despres. "Get off the subway almost anywhere else, and you will. Between the central business area and the outskirts lie large, almost uninterrupted gray areas of urban dry rot." And a great deal of money was wasted, it would later be revealed, to pay city workers who were hired for political purposes, and who often did no work. "The streets had potholes galore," recalls former Cook County Board president Seymour Simon. "Lights went off. Crime was bad. City workers today are better trained and there is more devotion to jobs."[53]

In June 1955, a delegation of black tenants from Trumbull Park showed up at City Hall to enlist Daley's support. The tenants, who met with Daley and his housing adviser James Downs, brought along a full-page statement calling on Daley to end the violence in their neighborhood "once and for all." Specifically, they wanted more police, more arrests, and an investigation of the South Deering Improvement Association for "conspiracy to incite riot." The visit put Daley in the same bind he had been in during his mayoral campaign. Black voters were too important to the machine for Daley blatantly to support the white segregationists. In his public pronouncements, at least, he had to formally support the right of blacks to live anywhere they wanted in the city. At the same time, he did not actually want to see the white South Side integrated. That, too, would be bad politics. Integration threatened to push white voters out to the suburbs, diminishing an important part of the machine's political base. Open housing would also allow blacks to move out of the traditional black wards, and away from the careful supervision of William Dawson's precinct captains. It would cut the black submachine's vote significantly. "Dawson didn't want [black voters] dispersed," CHA chairman Charlie Swibel said years later. "Many of the [black] aldermen didn't want them dispersed." Politics aside, Daley had his own reasons for opposing integration. The idea that blacks should be allowed to force their way into white neighborhoods that did not want them violated everything he believed in. "He grew up in Bridgeport," says Edward Marciniak. Daley's attitude was "if you grew up in a place, why do you want to come into mine?" Marciniak says. "It wasn't that you can't, or shouldn't, but why? Why would you want to do that?" Then, of course, there was the fact that Daley himself still lived in Bridgeport. "The mayor certainly wanted to keep the black community contained, particularly because his own neighborhood was so close to the ones where blacks were expanding," says Anthony Downs, James Downs's son, and a Daley housing adviser in his own right.[54]

Daley's response to the Trumbull Park delegation was to equivocate. He had learned from the mayoral election that South Side whites did not mind if he met with black leaders and offered vague expressions of sympathy. And that was precisely what he did. Daley assured the visitors that he was concerned about the unrest in their neighborhood, and that he would tolerate "no violence against any citizen because of race." He would not, however, commit to any of the specific courses of action the delegation was advocating. Calling the Trumbull Park situation an "inherited mess," Daley asked them to be patient. "I've been in office six weeks," he said. "Give us a chance." Daley then employed what would become a favorite tactic: buying time by setting up a distinguished committee. He named Chicago Bar Association president Augustine Bowe to head up the twenty-three-member group. The membership of the committee, which included *Chicago Defender* publisher John Sengstacke, was impressive, and Daley said all the right things, urging the members to conduct their inquiry "with broad and human sympathy." But Trumbull Park blacks and their supporters recognized the committee as a stalling device. In August, when Daley had still done nothing, an interracial group of religious and civic leaders came forward calling on him to provide leadership "in this hour of crisis for our city." In

October 1955, five thousand NAACP protesters converged on City Hall, accusing Daley of letting down Chicago's black community with his inaction on Trumbull Park. Two picket lines circled City Hall and marched around it in opposite directions. One demonstrator held a sign reading "Mr. Mayor: Trumbull Park — Chicago's Little Mississippi." Two years of "conferences and discussions with various city officials of the present and preceding administrations have produced promises, but no fruitful action," charged Willoughby Abner, a United Auto Workers Union official and leader of the Chicago branch of the NAACP. "The time for action is now, the time for pleading is past."[55]

It soon became clear, however, that Daley had no intention of taking action in Trumbull Park. The same week as the NAACP protest, Daley visited the neighborhood for a groundbreaking ceremony for a parsonage and recreation room for the South Deering Methodist Church. It would have been an ideal occasion for Daley to talk to neighborhood whites about racial equality and tolerance, but he instead stuck closely to theological topics. "The history of our nation is in many ways directly connected with our religious principles," Daley told the crowd. "The laws of our land, the constitutions of the United States and the state of Illinois, are based on the great truths and moral principles of Christianity." He made glancing reference to the need to "protect the rights of all our citizens," but no one who heard it would have mistaken it for a strong endorsement of integration. More significant than what Daley said was what he did not. Hours before he arrived at the church, Mrs. Clara Page, a black resident of Trumbull Park, had been attacked while attending services across the street. The scene at Saint Kevin's Catholic Church had been ugly, with a white parishioner yelling at Page, "Why did you come to our church? Go back to your kind." Other worshippers joined in, until police had to escort Page and another woman to safety in a squad car. As it turned out, Page had been assaulted several other times since she moved into Trumbull Park a year earlier. In one attack, twenty women threw rocks at her, another woman, and their four children. Daley never mentioned Mrs. Page in his speech at the church across the street.[56]

It did not take long for white residents of Trumbull Park to realize their faith in Daley in the last election had been justified. The South

Deering Improvement Association proclaimed happily, a few months into his mayoralty, that City Hall was at last "starting to see the light . . . and . . . South Deering's side of this fight against forced integration and mongrelization." Supporters of integration, who had been equally convinced during the campaign that Daley was on their side, were bitterly disappointed. The Catholic Interracial Council, many of whose members had backed Daley, complained that now that he was mayor they "were not able to get through" to City Hall.[57]

Though the Loop was in serious decline, it had a powerful ally on its side: Chicago's business establishment. The Chicago area was home to fifty-four companies in the *Fortune* 500, and many of these were based in and around State Street. These Loop businessmen had considerable clout. When John Gunther was in Chicago in the 1940s researching his classic book *Inside U.S.A.*, he asked a leading citizen who ran the city. The answer came back: "State Street and the Irish." Along with its corporate headquarters, the Loop was home to hotels like the Palmer House, department stores like Marshall Field, and banks like the First National Bank of Chicago. Most of these businesses were firmly anchored in the Loop. In the case of the retailers, there was still no other location, certainly not in the still-fledgling suburbs, that could duplicate the customer traffic. The city's major hotels were inextricably linked to their grand downtown buildings. And Chicago's banks, because of antiquated rules against branch banking, had little choice but to keep their operations centered downtown. As long as they were stuck in the Loop, these institutions were all committed to improving it.[58]

As downtown businessmen considered how to turn around the Loop, they concluded that its biggest problem was that it was in danger of becoming what developer Arthur Rubloff called, in a speech to the city's Building Managers Association, "The Central Business District Slum." The Loop was hardly a model of racial integration at the time. Well into the 1950s, many Loop businesses still did not employ blacks; as late as 1958, the First National Bank was still not hiring black tellers. But Loop businessmen feared what the future might bring. The central business district bordered on ghettos to the south and west, and the Frances Cabrini Homes — later Cabrini-Green —

and other housing projects were located nearby. The biggest concern was the Black Belt, which had spread to within blocks of the Loop, due South along State Street. Chicago's black population was soaring at the time — rising from 14 percent of the city's population to 23 percent during the 1950s — and these new black arrivals threatened to push the Black Belt further north into the Loop. Already, the street traffic downtown was becoming increasingly black, and after sunset whites were scarce. The fears of Chicago's business establishment, as historian Arnold Hirsch has observed, were precisely the same as those of whites in working-class neighborhoods on the periphery of the ghetto: each was afraid of being engulfed in a tidal wave of poor blacks. "Unless something drastic is done, you will write off State Street in fifteen years," one Realtor told a University of Chicago researcher. "And the minority groups will take over and then, no matter what the white people do, it can never be brought back, no matter what is done. And the whole goddam town will go to hell."[59]

To the downtown business establishment, the logical solution to the problem was urban renewal. The Housing Act of 1949, which allocated millions of federal dollars to localities to buy and reclaim slum properties, is often credited with starting the national urban renewal movement. But by 1949, urban renewal was already well under way in Chicago. The city's showcase project involved the Illinois Institute of Technology on the Near South Side. When IIT was built in the 1890s as the Armour Institute of Technology, the neighborhood was affluent, but it eventually fell on hard times. By the mid-1940s, the school found itself on the "wrong" side of Wentworth Avenue and the Illinois Central Railroad tracks, surrounded by slums. IIT had trouble finding middle-class housing for students and staff, there was little room for expansion, and fear of crime was hurting the school's reputation. "It eventually became clear," IIT president Henry Heald said later, "that we really had only two choices — to run away from the blight or to stand and fight." Adopting the rallying cry "Stand and Fight," Heald campaigned to upgrade the area around the institute. Heald's masterstroke was appealing to Chicago's business leaders by convincing them that the battle IIT was fighting would soon be their own battle: the urban blight assailing his school would, he argued, soon spread to the rest of the city. Before long, some of Chicago's most prominent citizens had signed on to help IIT reclaim its neighborhood.[60]

Heading up the IIT campaign were three of the city's most influential businessmen: Holman Pettibone, president of Chicago Title & Trust Company; Milton Mumford, vice president of Marshall Field & Company; and Ferd Kramer, president of the Draper & Kramer real estate firm. All three men were members of the Metropolitan Housing and Planning Council, a group of prominent Chicagoans dedicated to fighting slums. Urban renewal, they soon realized, was not easy. IIT would need to assemble parcels of land, raise money to buy the land, and develop mechanisms for relocating displaced residents. Pettibone, an influential Republican, lobbied Governor Dwight Green in July 1946 for help in enacting state urban renewal legislation. When Kennelly took office in 1947, Democratic business leaders lobbied him as well. The result was the passage of the Redevelopment and Relocation Acts of 1947. This landmark state legislation gave Illinois cities the power to condemn slum land by eminent domain, which solved the problem of assembling land parcels, and kept costs down by prohibiting owners from charging extortionate prices. The new law also established a Chicago Land Clearance Commission, which was vested with the power to acquire property and convey it to private developers. To liberals, the CLCC seemed like a deliberate attempt to keep urban renewal out of the hands of Elizabeth Wood and the CHA. If these powers had been given to the CHA instead of the CLCC, Wood could have required any new housing built on condemned sites to be racially integrated.[61]

With these broad new urban renewal powers now in place, IIT and its allies looked for a developer who would be willing to build on the condemned land. Pettibone and Mumford convinced New York Life Insurance Company to invest in apartment buildings near the IIT campus. After the Land Clearance Commission razed 100 acres of slums, New York Life built Lake Meadows apartments, a middle-class complex of 2,000 units of housing in ten apartment buildings, which cover only 9 percent of the land.[62] The new development was racially integrated, and Pettibone would later call it "Chicago's outstanding demonstration that whites and non-whites can live comfortably as neighbors, not only in the same neighborhood but in the same apartment building." Still, the project substantially increased the white population of the area. With rents that were from 300 percent to 600 percent of what had been charged previously, Lake Meadows also changed the economic profile of the area from poor to middle-class. A second institution in the area, Michael Reese Hospital, undertook a similar urban renewal project, which produced Prairie Shores, another middle-income housing complex. Prairie Shores' developers worked to attract white tenants by giving priority to the largely white hospital staff, rather than area residents, and holding a special advance open house for hospital employees. Prairie Shores started out with 80 percent white occupancy. When they were complete, Lake Meadows and Prairie Shores were hailed as resounding triumphs for urban renewal. *Fortune* magazine credited them with creating "an island of decency" amid "the South Side's oceanic slums."[63]

The Loop businessmen had IIT and Michael Reese in mind when they set out to upgrade their own neighborhood. The key to each of these projects was having a strong institution guiding the urban renewal, and the downtown business community decided to create one of its own. The Chicago Central Area Committee was founded in 1956, shortly after Daley's election and with his active cooperation. The CAC grew out of the State Street Council, an association of businesses located on and near the Loop's leading thoroughfare. The CAC's membership was a Who's Who of Chicago's wealthy and powerful. Its chairman was Pettibone, of Chicago Title and Trust Company, and its treasurer was the president of Harris Trust and Savings Bank, one of a handful of big downtown banks. The group's board included the heads of Illinois Central Railroad, Marshall Field & Company, and United Air Lines. The CAC saw itself as a physician working to heal the Loop's urban ills. "The strength of each city will always be marked by the strength and vigor of its central area — the heart of a whole region," the group declared in an early statement of purpose. The CAC developed an ambitious agenda of attracting more corporate headquarters to the Loop, improving traffic and parking, and beautifying the downtown area. But its core mission was doing what IIT and Reese had done: remove blight from the target area, making it wealthier and whiter in the process. "The

central area is not a slum, but it has some disgraceful areas," Pettibone said shortly after the CAC's founding. "The only thing to do is
to tear them down."[64]

The businessmen of the CAC found a strong ally in their new
mayor. Daley's rallying cry in the 1955 campaign had been that he
would rule not for "State Street" but for "all of Chicago." But when
the election was over, Daley proved all too eager to focus on the
problems of State Street. His interest in upgrading the Loop was
in part sincere. He shared the CAC's belief that the well-being of
the city depended in large part on the strength of its business district. Daley also viewed downtown as Chicago's showcase, and
was offended to see dilapidated buildings and blight there. James
McDonough, the commissioner of streets and sanitation, recalled
driving with Daley down State Street years later and ending up in
front of a jumble of run-down old buildings. Daley was so upset by
the sight that he forgot which commissioner he had with him. "I
want those buildings down, they're a disgrace," Daley barked at Mc-
Donough. Back at his office, McDonough had to call Daley's commissioner of buildings and admit that, in the face of the mayor's
anger, he had stepped outside his jurisdiction and agreed to tear
down the buildings. But Daley also had political reasons for throwing
himself behind urban renewal. The business leaders who had come
together to form the CAC were the most powerful men in Chicago.
They were overwhelmingly Republican, and had given large
amounts of money to Kennelly, Merriam, and most other reformers
who challenged the machine. Urban renewal was Daley's opportunity to reach out to these powerful Republicans and win them over
to his side before the next election.[65]

The Democratic mayor and the Republican business community
quickly forged a strong alliance around the issue of downtown redevelopment. Daley met with the CAC shortly after it was formed and
listened to its pitch that he create a new Department of Planning to
bring development squarely under the control of City Hall. The existing bureaucratic structure, which put development in the hands of
the thirty-four-member Chicago Plan Commission, struck the businessmen as too unwieldy. Following the CAC's recommendation,
Daley housing adviser James Downs drafted a plan for cutting the
Chicago Plan Commission's membership to fifteen and relegating it

to a merely advisory capacity. Daley also drew up plans for a new Department of Planning, just as the CAC suggested. He introduced the proposals to the City Council in March 1956, and they were passed without discussion. Daley also changed the membership of the Chicago Plan Commission. In the past, most had been public officials, but Daley decided that henceforth the majority would be "lay citizens." The shift to citizen control had a populist ring to it, but the people Daley appointed to the commission were anything but common folk. They were men like Charles Murphy, partner in the leading architectural firm of Naess & Murphy, whom he named as chairman, and Clair Roddewig, president of the Chicago & Eastern Illinois Railroad. The Chicago Plan Commission would be using its diminished authority to speak out forcefully for urban renewal and development. But the real driving force in the city's redevelopment would be Ira Bach, Daley's first city planning commissioner. One of his first major assignments would be to work closely with the CAC to draw up a plan for transforming Chicago's downtown.[66]

By December of 1955, Daley was well into his preparations for the following year's elections. Those included the 1956 presidential campaign, as well as races for governor, U.S. senator, and many lower offices. As machine boss, it fell to Daley to assemble the slate-making committee to choose the machine's candidates. Daley's approach to selecting committees was simple: he liked to give the appearance of inclusion and democracy, while appointing members who would rubber-stamp the choices he made. Later in his career as mayor, Daley appointed a committee to fill a government position, but at the same time he named the members, he was slipping a note to one of them telling him who should be chosen. To chair the 1956 slate-making committee, Daley named Joe Gill, who had headed up the mayoral slate-making committee a year earlier. Barnet Hodes, another appointee, was also a reliable vote. Daley also named William Dawson, as representative of the black submachine, and 1st Ward alderman John D'Arco, who could speak for the syndicate. Frank Keenan, the county assessor and ward committeeman from the 49th Ward on the Far North Side, would normally have had a slot on the committee by virtue of his powerful political office, but Daley was freezing him out of the machine as punishment for backing Kennelly in the primary. Daley met with his slate-making committee on January 5, 1956, to talk about possible candidates. When he emerged, he told reporters that he favored an open primary, meaning the machine would not make any endorsements. It was an old Daley ruse, trying to play down the importance of the machine, and to hide the strings it attached to the arms and legs of its candidates every year. But no one was fooled. When reporters asked Gill if the machine would endorse candidates in the primary, he responded: "What's the name of this committee?" It would be choosing a slate — Daley's slate.[67]

During slate-making, a parade of candidates filed into the Morrison Hotel to seek Daley's backing. He was impossible to read during these presentations. "I used to see fellows walk into Daley's office," recalled Michael Howlett, who was elected state auditor and Illinois secretary of state with the machine's backing. "They'd walk out thinking that they had his support, when all he had said to them was something like, 'You'd be a good candidate and if you were a candidate we could support you. Go out and see what kind of support you can get.' To the uninitiated, that sounded like Daley was for them, when all he was saying was that if they went out and could show him they could line up a lot of support, why, then he would like to talk with them about getting on the ticket." This time out, the slate-making committee was deluged with candidates. Cook County Board president Dan Ryan, county treasurer Herbert Paschen, sheriff Joseph Lohman, and state's attorney John Gutknecht were all seeking the machine's backing for governor. City treasurer Morris Sachs also showed up to express interest in the position, but he told the committee he intended to run with or without the machine's endorsement.[68]

The slate-making committee ended up selecting Paschen for governor. It was a dubious choice, and one that revived the rumors of a year earlier that Daley had made a deal with Stratton to throw the gubernatorial race. Benjamin Adamowski, Daley's former friend and mayoral opponent, sent out feelers to the slate-making committee seeking its support for state's attorney. It was a lost cause. After his harsh words about the machine in the last election, there was no chance Daley would entrust him with such a sensitive post, which carried with it the power to investigate and prosecute Chicago politicians. The slate-makers renominated the incumbent state's attorney, Gutknecht, who had close ties to the machine. Adamowski also approached the Republicans, and ended up getting their endorsement for state's attorney. His break with the Democratic Party would have profound implications for Cook County politics.[69]

As the April primary drew near, Daley rallied the troops to the machine slate. At a March 6 meeting of party leaders, the ever-supportive Adlai Stevenson declared the Chicago machine to be "an inspiration to the rest of the country." On April 5, the machine held its only mass meeting of the primary campaign. Two thousand ward committeemen, precinct captains, ward heelers, and patronage workers crowded into the Morrison Hotel's Terrace Room to hear speeches from the machine's endorsed candidates. The speeches shared a common theme: fulsome praise for the machine's leader. "If I can do as well for Illinois as Mayor Daley has done for Chicago, I'll go down in history as one of the greatest governors," Paschen declared. When they were not complimenting Daley, the candidates were ingratiating themselves with the machine's all-important foot soldiers. The success of the slate, the machine candidate for the Senate told the packed house, "depends on the untiring efforts you precinct captains put in your work."[70]

Paschen and most of the machine slate coasted to victory in the statewide primary on April 10, but Daley suffered a setback closer to home. The machine had lost in its drive to unseat Keenan, Kennelly's former campaign manager, from his position as ward committeeman. Daley had refused to recognize Keenan as ward committeeman in the year since the mayoral election. But now that he had been re-elected, Daley announced that Keenan would be "welcomed back in the fold" and invited to the machine's "formal and informal meetings." This time, it was Keenan who refused to make peace. He wrote an open letter to Daley on April 23 declaring that he would work to elect Adamowski as state's attorney. Keenan had good reason to dislike the incumbent, Gutknecht, who lived in his ward and had been active in the machine's drive to oust him as ward committeeman. But Daley was livid at Keenan's continuing insurrection. "I'd like to ask if he has submitted this question in a democratic fashion to his organization — the party workers and voters of the 49th Ward," Daley responded. And why, Daley wanted to know, did Keenan not "make his statement before the April 10 primary"? The rift with Keenan was a real loss to Daley and the machine. As county assessor, Keenan assessed and collected personal property taxes — a power that could be and often was used to reward political supporters and punish opponents. The machine lost this power when Keenan broke away. But the rift with Keenan posed an even greater threat. If he could get a sworn enemy of the machine like Adamowski elected state's attorney, the damage could be substantial.[71]

Young Richard Daley as an altar boy at Nativity of Our Lord Church, where he also attended grade school. (*Chicago Tribune*)

Daley, second row from the top, third from the right, with his fellow members of the Hamburg Athletic Association. (*Chicago Tribune*)

Daley and Eleanor Guilfoyle during their courtship in 1929. (*Chicago Tribune*)

Daley carves pumpkins at home in 1951 with his children (from left, Eleanor, Richard, Patricia, John, William, Michael, and Mary Carol). (*Chicago Tribune*)

Harkening back to his days working in the stockyards, Daley begins a 1955 campaign rally on horseback. (*Chicago Tribune*)

Workers in Daley campaign headquarters celebrate his victory over Alderman Robert Merriam. (*Chicago Tribune*)

The morning after his election as mayor, Daley attended Mass and posed for cameras at home on South Lowe Avenue. (*Chicago Tribune*)

Elizabeth Wood, seated at her desk, during her tenure as the first director of the Chicago Housing Authority. (*Chicago Tribune*)

Daley made the city's cleanliness a priority, organizing clean-up campaigns and anti-litter parades. (*Chicago Tribune*)

Days before the 1959 election, Daley receives a boost from Senator Paul Douglas and former governor Adlai Stevenson, two of the state's most respected liberals. (*Chicago Tribune*)

Daley shows a model of his 1958 plan to rebuild downtown to Cook County Board President Daniel Ryan and Governor William Stratton. (*Chicago Tribune*)

Daley uses an ax to start demolition of the first building to be torn down in the Hyde Park–Kenwood urban renewal project. (*Chicago Tribune*)

Daley congratulates James Weston, whose family was the first to move into the Robert Taylor Homes housing project. (Chicago Historical Society)

Daley, at far left, campaigns with Senator John F. Kennedy, at Meigs Field in 1960. (*Chicago Tribune*)

Congressman William Dawson, leader of the black submachine, listens to Mayor Daley during a City Hall budget meeting. (*Chicago Tribune*)

CHAPTER 5

Public Aid Penitentiary

When Daley took office, Chicago had a backlog of public housing waiting to be built. Of the 40,000 units the federal government had approved for the city, fewer than 15,000 had been built or were under construction. Daley was eager to start reaping the benefits of federal public housing. He appreciated the fact that it drew millions of dollars of federal money into Chicago, boosting the economy and creating jobs for Daley's supporters in organized labor. The federal money also meant more contracts for Daley and the machine to allocate to political supporters. Daley wanted to build every public housing unit the federal government was willing to pay for. What he had to decide was how to build the units — and where to place them.[1]

Daley's first decision was to continue with several projects already in various stages of construction. Most were high-rises, and all served to reinforce the city's existing racial lines. The Near West Side site for Henry Horner Homes, which would eventually become one of the city's most infamous projects, had been acquired in 1953; the project itself would open for occupancy in 1957. Work was already under way on Stateway Gardens, a project with 1,684 apartments, which was being built inside the South Side Black Belt; it would open for occupancy in 1958. Shortly after Daley's election, on May 12, 1955, the City Council approved several new projects. Brooks Homes Extension, with 449 apartments, was to be located in a 98 percent black neighborhood that already had three massive public housing projects. The Council also approved an addition of 736 apartments to Henry Horner Homes, located in an area that was already 99 percent black, and Washington Park Homes, 1,445 apartments to be built on scattered sites in the Black Belt.[2]

It was a year into his mayoralty, on May 9, 1956, that Daley obtained City Council approval for the first two public housing projects that were truly his own. Plans for the Robert Taylor Homes and the Clarence Darrow Homes left no doubt that the Daley era of public housing would be marked by densely packed high-rise towers that vigorously reinforced the city's racial boundaries. Robert Taylor was a collection of high-rise towers on a scale that had never been seen in Chicago before — or anywhere else, for that matter. Its 4,415 apartments would make it the largest public housing development in the world. Robert Taylor was designed as twenty-eight nearly identical sixteen-story buildings, clustered together in U-shaped groups of three on a ninety-five-acre strip of land in the heart of the South Side ghetto. The architectural style was classic early-1960s housing project: ugly red and yellow brick exteriors, and fenced-in external galleries. The project had a sprawling institutional feel that a federal commission would later compare to "filing cabinets" for the poor. The second project the City Council approved that day, Clarence Darrow, was smaller but similar in approach. The 479-apartment high-rise was to be located squarely in the middle of the Black Belt ghetto, built hard up against the 2,303 units of the Ida B. Wells Homes and the Ida B. Wells Extension.[3]

It was no secret that Daley's new projects would be almost entirely black. The year before Robert Taylor opened, the *Chicago Daily News* explained in a headline that its "Location Assures It'll Be Segregated." It was also clear that the living environment would be a detrimental one for children. "Except for a few churches, virtually every existing institution, every line of familiar and personal stability, and every semblance of formal and informal organization was cleared out and had to be started again," a Chicago Urban League report found. "It was like going into the wilderness. Those pioneers chosen to go had little means, came in large numbers, and were treated like outcasts." The project's problems were exacerbated by an almost total lack of social planning. The CHA spent years on the engineering details, but gave little thought to the human problems that would come from concentrating thousands of impoverished families in such an unnatural environment. In fact, Robert Taylor's demographics were a formula for disaster. The CHA planned to cram almost 1,000 poor people into each of the project's twenty-eight high-rises. The CHA had also expressly planned to make Robert Taylor a destination for many of the city's largest poor families. Almost 80 percent of the units were built with three or four rooms and most included an extra-large room that could sleep three or four children. Since many of the poor black families who would be moving in were headed by single mothers, it was almost inevitable that Robert Taylor would become a child-dominated world. If fact, when it opened 20,000 of its initial 27,000 tenants were under twenty-one. Making matters worse, the CHA all but abandoned Elizabeth Wood's practice of investigating the backgrounds and qualifications of prospective tenants. By the time the last Robert Taylor buildings were filled, there was almost no screening at all. The buildings that had the least tenant screening, at the southern extreme of the project, ended up having some of the worst problems with delinquency and crime.[4]

Daley's decision to build his first projects as high-rise towers in the ghetto underscored another advantage of public housing: it gave him power to control the demographics of the city. In the post–Elizabeth Wood era, there were no limitations on using public housing to maintain the city's racial separation. High-rises were an effective mechanism for keeping blacks, who were threatening to outgrow the Black Belt, inside the borders of the existing ghetto. That helped solve two of the machine's pressing political objectives. It protected the white ethnic neighborhoods from an influx of black residents, and it locked black voters into the traditional black wards where the submachine could keep them voting the straight machine ticket. High-rises were an especially convenient way for the machine to house its black voters. Residents of the projects were easily available to precinct captains, who could reap hundreds of votes simply working their way down a single elevator bank. It was easier than pounding the pavement and knocking on tenement doors. Public housing also gave the machine an extra level of control over residents: precinct captains often convinced them that they owed their apartments to the machine, and that they would lose them — or, at the least, never get them repaired — if they failed to vote for the machine slate on election day.

In later years, Daley's defenders would argue that the social cost of building public housing as dense high-rises was unknown at the time. Even progressives such as Elizabeth Wood, they claimed, championed high-rises, modeled on the work of the Swiss-born architect LeCorbusier, who advocated tall buildings spread out on large plots of land, to give urban developments the feel of a suburb. "People in the CHA, including Elizabeth Wood, got into a love match with LeCorbusier — vertical neighborhoods in the sky, green space all around," says Edward Marciniak. Wood did believe in building housing projects that were substantial enough that they would not become "islands in a wilderness of slums beaten down by smoke, noise, and fumes." But Wood and her fellow progressives never favored the kind of enormous housing projects that emerged in the Daley years — densely concentrated towers that looked as if they were designed for the purpose of warehousing human beings. Most of her projects were low-rises, like Jane Addams Homes, thirty-two buildings that were mostly three or four stories tall. Even later projects remained relatively low to the ground, like Dearborn Homes, a collection of six- to nine-story buildings. "What Elizabeth wanted was small, well-built complexes where people would feel a sense of community," says James Fuerst, her director of research at the CHA.[5]

The truth was, Daley had received many advance warnings that building projects like Robert Taylor were socially destructive. Housing experts had been talking for years about the danger of concentrating poor people in densely populated public housing projects. In 1949, at a conference organized by the *Chicago Defender*'s Public Service Bureau and attended by CHA board chairman Robert Taylor, the issue was confronted directly. "A public housing project which takes over or dominates a whole residential area . . . has the possibility of being segregated on two counts: (1) on a racial basis, and (2) on a low income basis," South Side Planning Board director Wilford Winholtz warned. "Either basis of segregation can be as bad as the other."[6] Samuel Freifeld of the Chicago chapter of the Anti-Defamation League of B'nai Brith advised a year later that "[i]nterracial housing is brotherhood spelled out in terms of bricks, mortar and people living together as neighbors in a community." And in 1954, Elizabeth Wood delivered a similar message in her final address before being pushed out at the CHA. Two years later, the Welfare Council of Metropolitan Chicago's Advisory Committee to the CHA also issued a direct warning about concentrating public housing in the "Negro ghetto." Many of these warnings were made to Daley and his housing staff directly. When Daley presented his first plans for public housing, Ferd Kramer, a prominent developer, predicted that the "most obvious effect" of the proposed sites was "to create further concentrations of high density . . . segregated housing on the Central South Side." In a letter to one of Daley's housing aides, Kramer wrote that "We hope you will work for a program scattering small public housing developments throughout the city, instead of great colonies of racially, socially, and politically segregated housing."[7]

Daley said at the time that he was aware of the serious problems with high-rise public housing, but he insisted that he had no real alternative. The fault, he argued, lay with federal caps on construction costs. Local housing authorities were prohibited from spending more than $17,500 per unit, and the CHA's cost estimates for low-rise housing came it at $22,000 per apartment. Daley went to Washington to testify for more generous spending guidelines, telling the Senate Housing Subcommittee that Chicago "cannot put up four-bedroom units for $17,500" except in high-rise towers. The trouble with Daley's argument was that at that very moment, architect Bertrand Goldberg and developer Arthur Rubloff were building a complex of three-bedroom row houses on the South Side that sold for $12,900 each, including the cost of the land and the developer's profit. Their design won the 1959 award for excellence from the American Institute of Architects and the Association of Commerce and Industry.[8]

There were, to be sure, extra costs associated with public housing. The Public Housing Administration required that buildings be constructed to last fifty years, and it insisted that even one-story garages have caisson foundations. But many of the forces pushing the CHA's building costs up were of more dubious origins. Robert Taylor cost 22 percent more than comparable construction in New York, the most expensive housing market in the nation. The federal government suspected the CHA was involved in some kind of impropriety. "Perhaps the strongest reason that Chicago does not get good prices is that it does not get strong competition in bidding," said the Public Housing Authority's regional director. Another factor inflating the cost of public housing in Chicago was the city's policy of keeping it segregated. Daley would build new projects only in the existing black neighborhoods, and land costs there were high because of the shortage of available sites and the need to clear the land of occupants and businesses. As much as $2,000 of the cost of each public housing unit went to land cost, far more than in most cities.[9]

The Robert Taylor project was notable not only for its massive size and troubling design, but also for where Daley had decided to locate it: the State Street Corridor. The twenty-eight high-rise towers that made up the project lay directly south of three other large public projects that already lined State Street — the 797-unit Harold Ickes Homes, the 800-unit Dearborn Homes, and the 1,684-unit Stateway Gardens. Adding Robert Taylor extended this long strip of public housing along State Street by another two miles, and more than doubled the number of public housing units in it. It was the densest concentration of public housing in the nation.

On June 4, less than a month after the City Council approved Robert Taylor, Daley announced a dramatic new addition to the State Street Corridor: the Dan Ryan Expressway. The new highway was to be part of an elaborate network of superhighways radiating out of the Loop. Illinois politicians had dreamed for years of building this kind of highway system, but it was only in the mid-1950s, with the advent of programs like the $25 billion Federal-Aid Highway Act of 1956, that the dream started to become a reality. Work on the east-west Congress Expressway (later the Eisenhower) had started shortly before Daley took office. But he was the driving force behind the highways that followed: the Northwest (later renamed the Kennedy), the Southwest (later called the Stevenson), and the Dan Ryan. The Dan Ryan Expressway — named for the president of the Cook County board, who was a champion of the highway system — was intended to serve as a south route out of the Loop. The original plans for the Dan Ryan called for it to cross the Chicago River almost directly north of Lowe Avenue, Daley's own street, and then to jag east several blocks, at which point it would turn again and proceed south. But when the final plans were announced, the Dan Ryan had been "realigned" several blocks eastward so it would instead head south along Wentworth Avenue. It was a less direct route, and it required the road to make two sharp curves in a short space, but the new route turned the Dan Ryan into a classic racial barrier between the black and white South Sides.[10]

In its new location, the Dan Ryan reinforced the South Side's oldest racial dividing line. Wentworth Avenue was the boundary that Daley's Hamburg Athletic Club had defended in his youth and that Langston Hughes had been beaten up for crossing. Although Wentworth Avenue was a well-established dividing line, it was not necessarily a stable one. The population of the old Black Belt was growing rapidly, and Daley was adding to that growth by locating public housing for tens of thousands of additional poor blacks along State Street. Residents of neighborhoods like Bridgeport worried that the black population explosion just blocks away would push the ghetto past Wentworth Avenue and into their midst. Just when the construction of Robert Taylor Homes made those fears seem justified, the city announced plans to reinforce Wentworth Avenue with the Dan Ryan. It was to be one of the widest highways in the world, with a "dual-dual" design consisting of seven lanes in each direction, four high-speed through traffic and three slower-moving lanes. It was the most formidable impediment short of an actual wall that the city could have built to separate the white South Side from the Black Belt.[11]

Years later, sociologists studying long-term unemployment and welfare dependence among blacks on the South Side would conclude that a large part of the problem was "spatial mismatch"— that these would-be workers simply were not located in physical proximity to jobs.[12] But the distance between the Black Belt and the world of work in downtown Chicago was psychological as well as physical. Researchers who interviewed South Side blacks who grew up in places like the State Street Corridor would find that a strikingly large percentage of them had never been to the Loop, and many had never journeyed outside their own neighborhoods. The result was that public housing projects like the Robert Taylor Homes served, in the words of one longtime tenant, as a "public aid penitentiary."[13] That social pathology would follow was all but inevitable. "Concentrating poverty concentrates things that correlate with poverty," notes sociologist Douglas Massey. "People adapt to a hostile and violent environment by becoming hostile and violent."[14]

Once in City Hall, Daley began to come through for one of his biggest supporters: organized crime. In June 1956, he disbanded the Chicago Police Department intelligence unit known as "Scotland Yard." A favorite of Mayor Kennelly's, it had spent several years bugging, infiltrating, and otherwise investigating the syndicate. "It was staffed with some of the best and most honest policemen in the history of Chicago," says an FBI senior agent. Scotland Yard's chief investigator reportedly had five filing cabinets of intelligence on six hundred syndicate leaders and thousands of lower-level mobsters. Police commissioner Timothy O'Connor gave little explanation when he ordered Scotland Yard to cease operations and padlocked its offices. Chicago Crime Commission director Virgil Peterson declared afterward that "the police department is back where it was ten years ago as far as hoodlums are concerned." The syndicate toasted the good news. "Chicago hoodlums and their pals celebrated around a champagne fountain at the plush River Forest home of Mobster Tony Accardo," *Time* magazine reported at the time. "The Accardo soiree, an annual affair, had a different spirit this year. Where once his guests had slipped their black limousines into a hidden parking lot on the Accardo property, they now made an open show of their attendance, and the Big Boss's gardens rang with fresh and ominous joy. Inevitably, the bookie joints unfurled in the Chicago Loop last week like so many Fourth of July flags, ... [and] raked in a take every dollar as good as the rackets produced in Capone's heyday. All this confirmed the Crime Commission's long-held fear that the town would be opened up shortly after last year's election."[15]

Daley never explained the closing of Scotland Yard. But the syndicate was a member of the Democratic machine, controlling the heavily Italian 1st Ward, which contained much of downtown Chicago, including the Loop. The syndicate also had considerable influence in the 28th Ward on the West Side. The 1st Ward's alderman and ward committeeman, John D'Arco, was a well-known front man for Accardo and Sam Giancana. And many of the 1st Ward Democratic Organization's patronage jobs went to notorious Mafia foot soldiers. "Mad" Sam DeStefano, a syndicate "juice man," had a 1st Ward no-show job with the Department of Streets and Sanitation. "No one who knew him could ever imagine Sam sweeping the sidewalks or shoveling snow, but they paid him handsomely for it," says an FBI senior agent. The 1st Ward Democratic Organization had less need for the golf outings and fund-raising luncheons that kept other ward organizations operating. It used mob pressure to collect an estimated $3,000 a month from each of the bars and strip clubs along South State Street.[16]

Daley also owed a more personal debt to the syndicate. There are some who say it was responsible for giving Daley his start in politics. Alderman Edward Burke figures that Daley won his first important machine position, 11th Ward committeeman, because syndicate-connected Italians from the north end of the ward dumped "Babe" Connelly and backed him. "They were sick of the old man," says Burke. "He was probably taking too big a slice of the gambling and whatever." At the very least, the syndicate delivered its precincts strongly for Daley in his citywide campaigns. In the 1955 mayoral primary, Daley beat Kennelly in the syndicate-controlled 1st Ward by 13,275 to 1,961 and carried the syndicate's 28th Ward handily. The syndicate also appears to have given Daley substantial financial help in his campaigns. FBI files indicate that Daley's key connection to organized crime was Thomas Munizzo, a childhood friend from the 11th Ward. "Munizzo reportedly collected vast sums of money from the hoodlum element for the Daley mayoralty campaign," the FBI's files state. Once Daley was elected, Munizzo was "considered the contact man . . . between the hoodlums and the mayor's office for favors . . . with respect to gambling or the crime Syndicate."[17]

Daley's critics had warned all along that he was the candidate of the "hoodlum element." On the eve of the general election, the *Chicago Tribune* advised that "[i]f Mr. Daley is elected, the political and social morals of the badlands are going, if not to dominate City Hall, then surely to have a powerful influence on its decisions." The *Tribune* was not far from wrong. Daley's practice was to let the machine's various constituent groups have input on the decisions that affected them — Polish leaders would help select the Polish candidate on the machine slate, and labor unions would give advice on labor policy. In many ways, Daley treated the syndicate as just one more machine constituency that was able to help make calls on matters of interest to organized crime. Syndicate leaders were apparently able, under Daley, to replace an honest police captain from the district that covered the 1st Ward with a corrupt one. According to an FBI report, when the honest captain stepped down, a Chicago mobster named Murray "The Camel" Humphreys contacted D'Arco and asked him to use his influence with City Hall to get the syndicate's man the job. "D'Arco then contacted Mayor Daley and advised him that he wanted this captain to command his district," said the FBI report. "The appointment was then announced by Commissioner O'Connor." Paul McGrath, a veteran Chicago newspaperman, says it was well known that Daley had an assistant whose job it was to field requests from the syndicate, and if necessary intervene with the police commissioner's office.[18] The FBI believed that Daley was cooperating with Chicago organized crime, and that Munizzo was not his only conduit to the syndicate leaders. John Scanlon, a good friend of Daley and his former law partner, William Lynch, acted as a "go-between" for the syndicate and city government, according to FBI files.[19]

Daley aided the syndicate and syndicate-backed business on other occasions. Ward committeeman John D'Arco co-owned an insurance company called Anco., Inc. with other 1st Ward Democratic leaders, including Benjamin "Buddy" Jacobson, who had been linked to a number of syndicate bosses. Major hotels, nightclubs, and department stores in the Loop found it was easier to get city licenses and permits if they insured with Anco. Businesses that declined to use Anco had city inspectors show up shortly after the refusal looking for code violations. But when the Chicago Crime Commission included Anco on a list of thirty-one "hoodlum-tainted" businesses, Daley rose to D'Arco's defense, saying the commission's charges were all based on "hearsay." Daley never publicly expressed any discomfort about a relationship that the *Chicago Daily News* referred to as "the crime-politics alliance." One former board member of the Building Service Council recalls that he asked Daley how he managed to be so tolerant of the syndicate. "Well, it's there, and you know you can't get rid of it, so you have to live with it," Daley said. "But never let it become so strong that it dominates you." And the syndicate was generally pleased with the treatment it received from Daley. "This mayor has been good to us," the FBI overheard Humphreys saying to D'Arco in 1960 in a wiretapped conversation. "And we've been good to him," D'Arco responded. "One hand washes the other."[20]

The Democrats held their 1956 National Convention in August in Chicago's International Amphitheatre. Daley attracted some national media attention as host mayor. On August 5, a week before the convention started, he appeared on the popular television show *What's My Line?* Daley was introduced to the blindfolded panelists as someone who was "salaried," and after fifteen questions journalist Dorothy Kilgallen correctly identified his "line" as mayor of Chicago. Daley, who was usually cagey about whom he was backing, went into the convention committed to Adlai Stevenson, Illinois's native son and a good friend of the machine. Stevenson had beaten Estes Kefauver in the primaries — capped by a nearly two-to-one victory in California — and on August 1 Kefauver withdrew in favor of Stevenson. That left New York's Governor Averell Harriman as Stevenson's main opposition. Daley did his best to shore up support for Stevenson. After the Texas governor, Allan Shivers, came out against him, Daley responded that Stevenson would win the nomination "by acclamation." And when former president Truman caused a small furor by making positive comments about Averell Harriman, Daley rushed to bring the momentum back to Stevenson. "Mr. Stevenson is the titular head of the Democratic Party and the greatest statesman of our era," Daley said. "I am hopeful and confident he will win the Democratic nomination in 1956 and then go on to become the next president of the United States." Jake Arvey did his part by insisting that newspaper reports of Truman's comments must have been "garbled." Eleanor Roosevelt, an ardent Stevenson supporter, suggested to reporters that Stevenson was better qualified to be president than Truman had been when he succeeded her husband, Franklin D. Roosevelt. By the start of the convention it was clear that the nomination was Stevenson's.[21]

The convention had an air of futility about it. The Democrats had briefly gotten excited about their chances when it looked as if President Eisenhower might not seek reelection. The previous September, he had suffered a heart attack after playing golf. In June, after he had already declared that he was running, he was rushed to Walter

Reed Hospital for emergency surgery for an abdominal obstruction. But Eisenhower continued to insist that he was a candidate. Even most Democrats conceded that Stevenson did not have much chance of defeating him. Four years earlier, Stevenson had lost in a landslide, winning only 44 percent of the popular vote and only 89 of 531 votes in the Electoral College. As a popular incumbent in a time of peace and prosperity, Eisenhower would likely run even more strongly this time. But winning the White House was not Daley's highest priority. As always, he evaluated the candidates based on what kind of coattails they would provide to the machine's slate. As a native son and former governor, Stevenson was the strongest candidate for the machine to have at the top of its ticket. It also counted, of course, that Stevenson had been a loyal friend of the machine over the years. When the time came for the roll call, Stevenson won with 905½ votes to Harriman's 210, and 80 for Senate Majority Leader Lyndon B. Johnson of Texas.

After winning the nomination, Stevenson defied convention and put the selection of his vice president up to the delegates. Tradition held that the nominee chooses his own running mate, and Daley would have preferred it that way. He did not like alienating candidates for vice president by telling them he could not support them. In his eagerness to please all sides, Daley came up with an ingenious solution. Asked what he thought about Governor A. B. "Happy" Chandler of Kentucky as a candidate for vice president, Daley told reporters that in light of the many strong candidates it might be a good idea to elect more than one vice president. He did, in fact, have his eye on one particular candidate. The real race was between Senator Estes Kefauver of Tennessee and thirty-eight-year-old Senator John F. Kennedy of Massachusetts. Daley was on good terms with Kennedy's father, Joseph P. Kennedy, who owned Chicago's enormous Merchandise Mart, reportedly the largest commercial establishment in the world. Perhaps more important, if the Irish-Catholic Kennedy were on the ticket, he could be expected to draw large numbers of votes to the machine slate. Not least, Daley and the machine had not forgotten the damage Kefauver's crime investigation committee had done to them in 1950. Daley delivered most of the Illinois delegation to Kennedy, except for a few downstaters who broke ranks to back Kefauver. Kennedy came within ten votes on the first roll call, but Kefauver won in the end.[22]

The real intrigue at the convention concerned the Illinois state ticket. Reporters got wind of a suspicious "flower fund" in the office of county treasurer Paschen, the Democrats' candidate for governor. Flower funds, also known as employee welfare funds, were used to pay for flowers for wakes and funerals, and similar expenses. But for some reason, banks holding county deposits had contributed more than $29,000 to Paschen's fund, and Paschen had in turn used some of the money to advance his political career. Federal and county grand juries were now investigating the matter. Democrats, fearing he would drag down the whole ticket, urged him to withdraw, but Paschen refused. When news broke of another $4,000 contingency fund that Paschen had failed to account for, it was over. Daley had decided to dump Paschen, and word of the ouster quickly spread through the convention floor. When reporters asked Daley about the rumors, Daley confirmed them, although he had not bothered to tell Paschen, who was sitting just three seats away from him in the Illinois delegation. When the press moved on to Paschen, he insisted he was still on the ticket. Told by reporters about Daley's comments, Paschen went over and confronted the mayor. "Dick, what the hell is there to this thing the reporters are saying?" he said incredulously. Daley, looking straight ahead and expressing little emotion, responded: "What did you expect?" Daley's handling of Paschen was cold-blooded, and fully in character. "With Daley, you know, it was always Daley who came first," said former Illinois secretary of state Michael Howlett. "The other guy always came in third with Daley, no matter who the other guy was."[23]

When the convention ended, Daley met with the machine leadership to review a list of twenty possible candidates to replace Paschen at the top of the ticket. Daley chose Chicago Superior Court judge Richard Austin, once again employing the old machine tactic of selecting a good-government candidate to ward off a damaging corruption scandal. The selection of the relatively obscure Austin revived rumors that swirled when Paschen was selected — that Daley was quietly throwing the election to Stratton. Daley flew to Springfield for a meeting of downstate Democratic leaders on October 9 and was confronted by published reports that Austin was "a candidate set up to be knocked down." Banging on the table for emphasis as water glasses went flying, a red-faced Daley denied the charges and lashed out at those who had made them. "I defy anyone to point to any betrayal in the history of the Cook County Democratic Organization," he shouted. If the machine was setting Austin up for a fall, he seemed oblivious. At appearances before machine audiences, he pledged his undying loyalty. "I want all of you to see me with your problems, patronage or otherwise, after the election," Austin invited. "I will be an organization governor."[24]

The 1956 election was Daley's first presidential campaign as boss and mayor, and Daley pushed the ward organizations to come through as they never had before. At a September 20 strategy meeting at the Morrison Hotel, he directed the ward committeemen and precinct captains to conduct a house-to-house canvass to register voters, and he ordered that 750,000 registration folders be distributed across the city. Daley also organized a series of weekly luncheon rallies for precinct captains at the Morrison, so they could meet the machine candidates they would be promoting to their neighbors. On October 11, state's attorney candidate Gutknecht was the featured candidate, with Austin following a week later. Daley also worked to draw organized labor even more closely into the machine's operations. He held a secret meeting at Chicago's Machinists Hall at which William Lee — his Civil-Service Commission chairman, who was also president of the Chicago Federation of Labor — urged the two hundred union leaders in attendance to "kick in" money to the machine. The highest priority, Lee said, was defeating reformer Adamowski in his campaign for state's attorney. Daley had already advised the ward organizations that they could count on having a large number of rank-and-file union members available to help out on election day. Daley's many favors for organized labor since he took office were paying off. But his most elaborate preparations were for a legendary event — the Chicago machine's pre-election torchlight parade. Organizers were predicting a turnout of 500,000 people, and representatives of all fifty ward organizations, labor unions, and ethnic associations participated in the planning. This year's march, Daley said, would be nothing less than "the greatest spectacle in the history of America." Plans called for 1,000 men with torches and sparklers to march a two-mile stretch of Madison Street from Grant Park to Chicago Stadium. Lending an air of spectacle, there would be flatbed trucks with trapeze artists and circus performers driving by at eight-minute intervals.[25]

The 1956 general election was a disaster for Illinois Democrats. Eisenhower defeated native son Adlai Stevenson handily, in Illinois and nationwide. Stratton was reelected as governor, and Republican junior senator Everett Dirksen was returned to office. If Daley had in fact struck a deal to go easy on Stratton, it was not obvious from the results on election night. Stratton won by only about 50,000 votes, running well behind both Eisenhower and Dirksen. Worst of all, Adamowski won his race for state's attorney. Daley was publicly upbeat, but some Democrats blamed him for the losses. They contended that his new policy of shifting patronage to City Hall had sapped the strength of the ward organizations, and they argued that Daley's heavy-handed leadership of the party had hurt with voters. Steven Mitchell, a lawyer who had been passed over by the machine for the gubernatorial nomination, charged after the election that Daley's "one-man rule" was to blame for the rout. "A small circle or group dominates the party, including the selection of candidates and the development of issues," Mitchell charged. "This is not healthy in a democratic system." Mitchell called on Daley to resign as chairman of the Cook County Democratic Organization, saying it was a "full time job" when done right.[26]

Daley had no intention of heeding calls that he step down as boss. "I offered my resignation when I was elected mayor last year and it was not accepted," he said. "Since then I have led my party to what I think is a good program." But Daley also knew that party leaders who lost elections did not stay in power long. He had seen Mayor Kelly relieved of his leadership of the machine after the disastrous 1946 election, and he had seen Arvey pushed out of power after the Democratic defeats of 1950. To avoid sharing their fate, Daley set to work building up the machine's strength. One of his first priorities was increasing Democratic influence in the Chicago suburbs. In the November election, Chicago's share of the Cook County vote had fallen significantly, and Eisenhower had run especially strongly in the suburbs. In January 1957, Daley appointed eight suburban Democrats to a new committee to consider ways for the party to compete for suburban voters. Daley also went to work purging his most entrenched machine foe. In a post-election gesture of reconciliation, city assessor Frank Keenan invited pro-Daley Democrats in the 49th Ward to his annual Christmas dinner. But Daley forbade his precinct captains from attending. Then, in one of his last official acts, outgoing state's attorney John Gutknecht indicted Keenan for improperly exempting several properties from taxation. Since it was the kind of charge that could have been brought against almost any Chicago politician at the time, it seemed clear that the indictment was political, and it was widely rumored that Daley was behind it. Daley indignantly denounced these reports as "a falsehood, a fabrication, and a lie," but he did admit that he would be happy if Keenan left the Democratic Party. In the end, the tax-evasion charges stuck, Keenan was forced to step down as county assessor, and he went to prison. Daley got the Cook County Board to name John F. McGuane, an old friend and fellow 11th Ward Irishman, to fill the position. Robert Merriam said later that even if the charges against Keenan had some merit, his downfall was largely due to his falling out with Daley. "There was no longer any desire to protect him on the part of the organization," Merriam said. "They play a very hard game."[27]

By the start of 1957, Daley was well at work on his plans for promoting urban renewal and downtown development. Effective January 1, Ira Bach became the city's new commissioner of housing. The next day, Daley announced that he had retained a prominent New York marine engineering firm to study Chicago's port facilities and recommend improvements. At a 120th birthday luncheon for the city in early March, Daley said he expected Chicago would see more than $1 billion in public and private investment over the next five years, and that the influx of funds would make Chicago a "new city." Later the same month, fate intervened to create one more redevelopment project for the city. On March 21, a fire in City Hall in the early evening destroyed the City Council's ornate chambers. Daley borrowed a pair of boots from a telephone company employee at the scene and waded through the water-filled hallways himself to survey the damage. He announced that no important documents had been destroyed, and that the building would reopen for business the following morning. Daley was hailed as a hero for leading four scrubwomen to safety, but he modestly insisted that the real heroes were four women telephone operators who continued to work on the tenth floor throughout the blaze.[28]

Daley was always on the lookout for more money to develop the city. He quickly emerged as a leading advocate for the nation's cities, primarily because he was constantly asking Congress and the president to increase appropriations for programs that benefited Chicago. In April 1957, Daley traveled to Washington to testify before a Senate committee in favor of one such program, a federal slum clearance and community redevelopment initiative that faced funding cutbacks. Daley also tried to raised more money locally, putting a $113 million bond initiative on the June ballot. The bond measure was the occasion for Daley's first public screaming tirade of his mayoralty. When Republican City Council members criticized the proposal as wasteful, a red-faced Daley banged the rostrum repeatedly and exploded at his critics. In the weeks leading up to the election, critics continued to charge that the bonds were not needed and would lead to large tax increases, but they passed.[29]

The most important changes on the development front were occurring at the Chicago Housing Authority. Daley was in the process of pushing out the current leadership and installing his own team. In July 1957, the CHA announced that William Kean was resigning as executive director for "personal reasons." But the truth was, Kean's departure came after bitter feuding with the CHA board, particularly with an outspoken young board member named Charles Swibel. Swibel got his start sweeping floors for Isaac Marks, one of Chicago's biggest slumlords, and in 1954, Daley appointed the twenty-nine-year-old Swibel to the CHA board. Swibel's background was an odd one for someone who would be responsible for guiding Chicago's public housing policies. As president of Marks & Co., he had operated two hotels on skid row, both of which refused to rent rooms to blacks, in violation of Illinois state law, into the 1960s. Swibel owed his seat on the board to Flat Janitors Union president William McFetridge, who felt he could count on Swibel to promote labor's interests. Swibel was well known as an operator — one critic described him as "a do-fer. As in 'What can I do fer you?'" The newspapers just called him "Flophouse Charlie." Kean's run-ins with Swibel and a few other members of the CHA board stemmed in large part from the fact that, like Elizabeth Wood before him, he wanted to run a "clean" agency — one that refused to take on patronage workers, and that held its employees to high standards of performance. The final showdown between Kean and the board came over whether Kean would be allowed to hire and fire CHA employees without the board's approval. In public, Daley assumed the role of peacemaker, even taking credit at one point for talking the embattled Kean out of resigning. But Daley never used his influence with his appointees to the CHA board to stop them from pushing Kean out.[30]

The fact was, the CHA was a bastion of patronage and featherbedding — and neither Kean nor Elizabeth Wood had been able to stop it. The following March, the Public Housing Administration issued a scathing report detailing waste and corruption in the CHA. PHA investigators found that overstaffing, make-work assignments for unionized workers, and inefficient administration at the CHA wasted $1 million a year. The agency's overstaffed and "sluggish" force of glaziers, the report found, installed only 6.5 panes of glass per day per glazier, compared to 18 panes a day by glaziers in Detroit.[31] When new refrigerators were installed in public housing, CHA work rules required an electrician to be present "because of the need for plugging in the cord and starting the motor." Wood had wanted to reform the agency's operations, but she quickly realized the unions and their allies in the machine would not allow it. "That was something Elizabeth just couldn't touch," says former Wood aide James Fuerst. "She just said, 'Look, it's bigger than us.'" When the PHA's report came out, Daley expressed concern. "These are serious charges and I want to know what the facts are," Daley declared at his morning press conference. "I plan to meet with everyone to see if we can't work out solutions for correcting these alleged abuses." Of course, if Daley really wanted to learn more, he would have had little trouble: it was his own appointees to the CHA board that were responsible for much of the corruption.[32]

Kean's departure allowed Daley to select his own CHA executive director. He appointed city welfare commissioner Alvin Rose, who promised from the start to be more accommodating to political pressure than Kean had been. To some observers, it appeared that Swibel was now in charge of the CHA — and that the weak-willed Rose was only there to do the slumlord's bidding. Rose was a "tired, frightened bureaucrat who was terrorized by Swibel," says a *Chicago Daily News* reporter. "He would take you aside and say, 'That man [Swibel] is a devil.'" One of the first areas in which the CHA changed direction was race. Kean had never been an integrationist. He had been brought in to end the Elizabeth Wood era at the CHA, and he had done so. But he was also not an arch-segregationist and under him the CHA continued to investigate potential public housing sites throughout the city, and to recommend some sites "even though they felt the City Council would not approve them."[33]

With Daley's team in charge, a new segregationist era dawned at the CHA. At a January 17, 1958, meeting at the City Club of Chicago, a man from a white neighborhood on the North Side asked why his neighborhood was not getting any housing projects. Rose explained that if a housing project were built in his area, there would be no way of guaranteeing that blacks would not move into it. A former director of the CHA who was in the audience recalled Rose's response as "startling." It "was like saying to the gentleman from Uptown, 'Do you really want a project out here, because if we put a project out here some Negroes are going to move into Uptown?'" The difference between the Kean era and the Rose era was subtle but unmistakable: under Kean, political pressure was allowed to block the agency's attempts at integration; under Rose, there would no longer be any attempts to integrate. The new CHA regime made it even easier for white aldermen to block housing projects that were being considered for their wards. Rose personally contacted every alderman in the city to ask about locating 3,000 units of housing that had come available. If any alderman objected to a proposed project in his ward, Rose said, "it ha[d] no chance of getting through."[34]

During the summer of 1957, Daley faced the most serious patronage scandal of his mayoralty. It was an open secret that since he took over City Hall Daley had been aggressively increasing the number of patronage workers, and pushing out employees who lacked the correct political sponsorship. Robert J. Nolan, who had served the city as an assistant corporation counsel for sixteen years, was fired from his job handling condemnation work for the city. Nolan's offense was to have come to the city's law department from the 19th Ward organization, which had backed Kennelly in the mayoral primary. Nolan went without a fight. "I was going to leave, but this is hurrying it up a bit," he said on his way out. The Civil Service Commission's annual report revealed that the city now employed 6,175 temporary workers, the category most often filled by patronage hires — an increase of 47 percent in the past year. Daley attributed the increase to a "step-up" in city services.[35]

In June, a whistleblower came forward to tell a different story. Dr. Seymour Scher, the Civil Service Commission's personnel examiner, wrote an open letter to Daley declaring that the commission under its new leadership had become a "farce." Scher, who had accepted an out-of-state teaching position and had nothing to lose, disclosed that there had been a sharp decline in the number of civil-service exams given since Daley became mayor. Civil-service procedures called for the commission to post lists of employees who had passed their exams, and these lists had also fallen dramatically — from 216 in 1954, Kennelly's last year in office, to 90 in 1956. When the lists were posted now, they often went up late, after many eligible employees had already given up and taken other jobs. Scher also revealed that the city had been rapidly creating new job titles — 300 in 1957 alone, for a total of 1,700, when he estimated that 400 titles would have been sufficient. New job titles were an effective way around civil service: when a new title was created, there were by definition no applicants available who had passed a civil-service exam for it. The machine was therefore free to fill these slots with anyone it wanted. "It seems the organization asked, 'How many jobs are we going to give our boys this year?'" Scher said. Patronage positions had increased almost 75 percent, he estimated, during Daley's first two years in office. Scher's charges received wide press attention. Republicans in the City Council tried to launch committee investigations, but both times the Democrats defeated their motions. Civic groups called on Daley to appoint a blue-ribbon panel to consider the charges. But Daley curtly dismissed Scher's diagnosis. "Dr. Scher's statement indicates lack of ability to know what is going on," Daley said. "I should appreciate his recommendations and his assistance in making Chicago's civil service the best in the country." Fred Hoehler, Daley's civil service adviser, was more blunt. Scher, he said, was a "cynic" who "does not believe there is any honesty in government." Neither Daley nor Hoehler provided any evidence to refute Scher's charges.[36]

Other controversies followed in quick succession. Daley's 1957 budget included $14 million in pay raises, and members of the City Council's "economy bloc"— the twelve Republicans and one independent critical of Daley's spending practices — detected a pattern to who got them. Among the largest percentage raises were a 15 percent salary hike for Joseph McDonough, an administrative assistant in the city purchasing department who was the son of Daley's old 11th Ward patron. Another generous increase went to an electric light and power inspector who was the brother of 27th Ward alderman Sain, and a 5th Ward precinct captain. Alderman Freeman of the 48th Ward complained that Daley had pushed the pay increases through after the finance committee had completed its hearings, and that they were "90 percent political." After the salary scandal came a dust-up with the new state's attorney. Benjamin Adamowski found his position a perfect perch from which to attack Daley — and he lost no time in lobbing potshots in the direction of his old foe. Adamowski thrust himself into a minor dispute over taxicab licenses — Daley and two aldermen disagreed on the number of war veteran licenses that should be issued — and threatened to convene a grand jury to investigate. The state's attorney's office did launch an investigation of whether the $279,244 the city paid to clean the exterior of the City Hall–County Building was excessive. Daley denied it was, pointing out that it was cleaned at night, and made from a kind of stone that was difficult to clean. *Life* magazine then weighed in with an article saying that Chicago "probably has the worst police department of any sizable city." Daley sent off an angry letter to the editor, calling the article an "unwarranted slur," and saying that although the reporter had "easy access to all of the facts" he had chosen to resort to "wild generalizations."[37]

Throughout the fall, Daley continued to promote his wide-ranging agenda for the city. He invited Queen Elizabeth II to visit Chicago in July 1959 for the formal opening of the Saint Lawrence Seaway, which would make Chicago one of the world's leading seaports. Daley also returned to Washington to tell a Senate committee that Chicago would need an additional $100 million for slum clearance over the next ten years. And he urged the Eisenhower administration

to release another $200 million in slum-clearance money appropri-
ated by Congress but not yet allocated. When he returned to
Chicago, Daley announced that he would meet with his corporation
counsel, John Melaniphy, to discuss a recent U.S. Supreme Court
ruling overturning Chicago's ban on the showing of the French
movie *The Game of Love*. Daley had no patience with the Court's
emerging free-expression jurisprudence, which seemed to him to be
about protecting trash. "I thought the trend throughout the country
was to suppress obscene literature and indecent pictures," Daley declared. "Everyone agrees something must be done to protect our
children from obscenity and filth."[38]

In the summer of 1957, Chicago was swept by a new round of racial
violence. The Black Belt was spreading west and south, and as blacks
moved into white neighborhoods, interracial conflict followed.
Many of the clashes started when newly arrived blacks insisted on
using local parks and beaches. In one South Side neighborhood in
late July, more than six thousand whites attacked one hundred blacks
picnicking in a park that had been exclusively used by whites. The
battle raged on for two days, and five hundred police were needed to
restore order. The same month, hostilities reignited in Trumbull
Park, which had been relatively peaceful for two years. The black
residents who remained in the projects were becoming more as-
sertive about their right to use streets and stores in the neighborhood, and the *South Deering Bulletin* was continuing to fan the flames
of white resistance. A mob of almost one hundred descended on the
apartment of one of the most outspoken black families living in
Trumbull Park, breaking furniture, turning on the gas jets in the
kitchen, and setting fires. Within four months, nine of the thirty
black families living in Trumbull Park moved out.[39]

As the racial violence heated up, Daley looked the other way. In
August, an interracial group of sixty-seven prominent South Side
residents charged him with failing to act during "this hour of crisis
in our city." Daley's "official laxity," the group argued, "had permitted hoodlum elements to outstrip our city's law enforcement procedures." At a national meeting of the Urban League in September,
Edwin Berry, executive director of the Chicago Urban League, de-

clared that Chicago was the most segregated major city in America and that in the city "a Negro dare not step outside the environs of his race." Daley responded to the charges only obliquely, saying that Chicago was not "as bad as some people say it is."[40]

In fact, Daley had a plan for addressing Chicago's growing racial violence: clamping down on civil rights activism in the black community. The leading instigator of civil rights protests in the city was the Chicago chapter of the NAACP. The chapter had not always been so outspoken — for years, it was led by a succession of "legal moderates," who believed all racial progress would come in the courts. But beginning in late 1953, the chapter came under the leadership of Willoughby Abner, who started out as chairman of the executive committee and was then elected chapter president. Abner developed an aggressive agenda for civil rights in Chicago, calling for increased employment opportunities for blacks, an end to overcrowding and double shifts in black schools, and improved police protection in racially tense neighborhoods on the South Side. Abner, an official with the United Auto Workers, believed in demonstrations rather than litigation. He had been the driving force behind the 1955 march outside City Hall to protest Daley's failure to act decisively on Trumbull Park. Abner also rallied Chicago blacks behind the civil rights struggle then unfolding in the South. He championed, in particular, the case of Emmett Till, the fourteen-year-old Chicagoan lynched in Mississippi in 1955. In June 1957, more than seven thousand NAACP members and sympathizers turned out at the Coliseum to hear the Reverend Ralph Abernathy describe his work with Martin Luther King Jr., organizing the Montgomery bus boycott in Alabama. Abner's newly energized NAACP was attracting unprecedented levels of support in the black community. A single Freedom Day dinner, featuring Jackie Robinson as a guest speaker, brought in $25,000, allowing the organization to increase its staff. After his first year as chapter president, Abner was reelected with near-unanimous support.[41]

Abner was outspoken in his opposition to Daley's surrogates in the black community — Dawson and the black submachine. Abner argued that the submachine represented nothing more than black subservience to an oppressive white power structure. In a scathing

"Open Letter to Congressman William Dawson," sent out on NAACP letterhead on August 29, 1956, Abner painted a devastating portrait of Dawson as a traitor to his race. Chicago's only black congressman had remained "thunderously silent," the letter charged, when Emmett Till — his own constituent — was lynched. Nor did Dawson take action when civil rights worker Gus Courts was shot, and Lamar Smith and the Reverend George W. Lee were killed, fighting in Mississippi for black voting rights. The letter recounted that when the NAACP asked if he had introduced any civil rights legislation in the latest congressional session, Dawson replied that he had not and would not. And Dawson was the only Chicago-area congressman, Abner wrote, who voted against the Powell Amendment, which would have withheld federal funds from states and school districts that openly defied *Brown v. Board of Education*. When Dawson got a position on the platform committee of the 1956 Democratic National Convention, he had had yet another chance to come through for his fellow blacks. "Perhaps now at last we would see the fruits of 'working behind the scenes'— a strong, forthright honest plank on civil rights," Abner wrote. "Perhaps now, the inexpli[c]able would become clear. But, alas, our hopes were drowned in a sea of meaningless platitudes, outright evasions and surrender to the Confederacy." Dawson played a critical behind-the-scenes role at the convention, working against a minority report backed by the NAACP, the Americans for Democratic Action, and UAW President Walter Reuther calling for a tougher civil rights plank. The letter concluded by urging Dawson to reconsider his loyalty to "a political philosophy that puts party above all else."[42]

Dawson was publicly dismissive of Abner and his newly radicalized NAACP chapter. "What are they going to do, come into my district and beat me?" Dawson asked. But privately, he was plotting political retribution. The Chicago chapter was scheduled to hold its election of officers on December 17, 1957. Precisely thirty days before the election, the submachine took out memberships for between four hundred and six hundred of its precinct captains and patronage workers. It was the last day that an applicant could join and be eligible to vote, which meant that when Abner and his supporters learned that the chapter's membership rolls had been flooded, it was too late to respond in kind. On the appointed night, the sub-machine's troops turned out in force. A parade of Dawson and Daley loyalists rose to denounce Abner. One of the denouncers was Building Services Union president James H. Kemp, who served with Daley ally William Lee on the executive committee of the Chicago Federation of Labor. In the end, the chapter's members voted to replace Abner with Theodore Jones, an executive with the Supreme Liberty Life Insurance Company who could be counted on to take a more moderate course. Dawson never denied that he played a role in ousting Abner and his fellow civil rights activists. "I'm not interested in controlling the NAACP or its policy making body," Dawson later told historian Dempsey Travis. "However, I do want to see the 'right man' as president."[43]

The 1957 NAACP elections would forever be remembered as the machine's "political takeover" of the branch. "The invaders of the NAACP were elected to make certain that no one in the newly elected NAACP hierarchy or their successors would ever rock Daley's political boat," Congressman Charles Hayes said later. The change in philosophy could be felt immediately. In a victory statement in the *Chicago Defender,* Jones vowed to "take an inventory of the programs and projects in which the branch was committed." Among the first to go were the chapter's challenges to Daley over Trumbull Park and public housing integration. Daley quickly threw his support behind the politically neutered NAACP chapter. He declared a citywide "NAACP Tag Day" in May 1958, and urged Chicagoans to buy NAACP tags that volunteers were selling on street corners. Jones tried to develop a nonmachine base within the NAACP chapter, but his efforts met with only modest success. When the time came for him to run for reelection, he had to bring out the machine foot soldiers once again. "He called us about a week before the election," one black politician recalled later. "He must have woke up and saw that the people he had counted on weren't going to deliver as they had promised. His supporters were supposed to deliver 150 or 200 votes each. But it was closer to 50 or 75 each. . . . So we sent in some people from our wards. If it hadn't been for the organization, I think he would have lost the ball in the weeds."[44]

In February 1958, the University of Chicago unveiled an urban renewal plan that would change the face of one of Chicago's most prominent neighborhoods. Hyde Park was an independent township until it was absorbed by the city in 1889, a year before the founding of the University of Chicago. The area underwent a surge of building in the 1890s, when ground was broken on many of the university's Gothic halls, and numerous elegant apartment buildings and single-family homes were constructed. Before long, Hyde Park was home to some of the city's finest examples of Chicago School architecture, and at least one world-famous building: Frank Lloyd Wright's Prairie School Frederick C. Robie House. The neighborhood's character began to change in the 1940s when poor blacks began to move in. Many of the new arrivals were fleeing the overcrowded Black Belt, which was itself being flooded by migrants from the South. Between 1940 and 1950, Hyde Park's black population more than tripled.[45] During the early 1950s, the black influx continued, and many whites began to move out. In 1956, the population of the greater Hyde Park–Kenwood neighborhood was more than one-third black.[46]

By the late 1940s, University of Chicago administrators and some neighborhood residents worried openly that Hyde Park was on its way to becoming a slum. In response, local residents formed the Hyde Park–Kenwood Community Conference in 1949. Three years later, the University founded the South East Chicago Commission. Both organizations had the goal of preventing the area from going into decline. The community conference supported the idea of an integrated community, but sought to preserve the neighborhood's "high standards." The SECC was more concerned about maintaining a large white presence, and seeing that as much of the black population as possible was middle class. The SECC's stand was far from the first time the university allied itself with attempts to keep blacks out of Hyde Park. In the 1930s and 1940s, the school had actively promoted the use of restrictive covenants to keep houses in the neighborhood occupied by whites. When the *Chicago Defender* objected to the policy in 1937, university president Robert Maynard Hutchins responded that the covenants were legal and that Hyde Park residents had the "right to invoke and defend them." By 1957, that was no longer true, since the Supreme Court had declared restrictive covenants unenforceable in 1948. The university's new goal was, at least publicly, the more modest one of neighborhood "conservation." But in their private communications, top administrators were less circumspect. The high-income housing the SECC was seeking to bring to Hyde Park was, Chancellor Kimpton declared, "an effective screening tool" and a way of "cutting down [the] number of Negroes" living in the area.[47]

Daley's support for Hyde Park urban renewal dated back to before he was mayor. After Daley got the Democratic nomination in 1955, Kimpton went to meet with him and sound him out on the question. Daley readily committed himself to helping the university in its efforts to shore up Hyde Park. His support was, of course, in large part political. Daley, the rough-hewn son of Bridgeport, was eager to ingratiate himself with the administrators, trustees, faculty, and alumni of the city's premier educational institution. In the 1955 general election, many of these university constituencies would back Daley's opponent, Robert Merriam, who was both Hyde Park's alderman and the son of a University of Chicago professor. But in later years, Daley would win surprising levels of support from the university community. Daley also supported Hyde Park renewal to bolster an important city institution. University administrators were predicting disaster if they were not successful in defending the neighborhood. In fact, reports were circulating that the university was considering relocating to the suburbs. It was a remote possibility, given the school's enormous investment in its physical plant, but it was not a risk Daley was prepared to take. A more likely prospect was that the university might go into decline as students and faculty were increasingly put off by the neighborhood. Daley evaluated these concerns, of course, as a resident of Bridgeport, who himself lived only blocks away from the rapidly expanding South Side ghetto.[48]

Hyde Park urban renewal was under way even before Daley became mayor, and it proceeded through a number of loosely coordinated projects. But the capstone of the urban renewal effort was the University of Chicago's Final Plan, released on February 1958. The plan was the brainchild of Julian Levi, the executive director of the SECC and the university's shrewd point man on urban renewal. A lawyer and the son of a rabbi, Levi had grown up in Hyde Park and attended both college and law school at the University of Chicago. Levi was a tenacious advocate for his cause, equal parts missionary and streetfighter. To an academic audience, he could make the intellectual case for urban renewal. In meetings with opponents, he could scream and intimidate to get his way. And out in the community, he was skilled at throwing around the university's money to achieve his goals. Levi's Final Plan, which covered a large stretch of land between 47th Street and 59th Street, was a blueprint for reversing the social transformation that had occurred in Hyde Park over the past two decades. It called for demolishing about 20 percent of the neighborhood's buildings, spread out over an 855-acre urban renewal area. In the name of removing "blight" and creating a "compatible neighborhood" for the university, the plan proposed destroying almost twenty thousand homes in Hyde Park.[49]

Supporters of the neighborhood's poorest residents mobilized in opposition. A focal point of the debate was how much public housing to include in the urban renewal area. Liberals argued that the blight was dilapidated housing, not the poor people who lived in it. Building public housing would upgrade the housing stock, while allowing current residents to remain in the neighborhood. But the university was adamantly against public housing. Levi denounced it as "something harmful to the neighborhood which the people did not want anyway." One of the leading opponents of the university on this point was the Hyde Park chapter of the NAACP. Members of the group denounced the urban renewal plan as segregationist, and called for significant amounts of both public and middle-class housing to be added. They also demanded greater protections for the residents who would end up losing their homes and having to relocate. The Hyde Park chapter began its campaign by lobbying local aldermen to work for modifications in the Final Plan. It was at this point that the NAACP's newly installed pro-machine administration stepped in. On September 6, 1958, Theodore Jones — who had been elected president of the Chicago chapter a year earlier — ordered the Hyde Park chapter and two other local units to close. Jones declared that they had been shut down because they acted "without complete sanction of the parent branch" on a variety of issues, not because of differences over Hyde Park urban renewal. The branch closings were bitterly opposed in Hyde Park, and by some members of the NAACP's citywide board. Beatrice Hughes Steele, treasurer of the Chicago chapter, called Jones's action "a destruction of the grass-roots heart of the branch." After the closing of the Hyde Park chapter, black opposition to Hyde Park urban renewal was effectively quashed.[50]

The Catholic Archdiocese gave qualified support to opponents of the Final Plan. The Church did not dispute the need for urban renewal, but it argued for the construction of at least some low-income housing in Hyde Park, and for greater assistance for people whose homes would be destroyed. "I was not opposed to the plan as such," one archdiocese official explained later. "I wanted the University of Chicago to have protection, but I wanted the people to have protection, too. They couldn't just ride roughshod over 20,000 people." The archdiocese also expressed concern that so much money would be poured into the area surrounding the university — more than $30 million in federal and local urban renewal funds — that little would be left for other Chicago neighborhoods. The Church's stand in favor of the victims of urban renewal may have been motivated at least in part by self-interest. Priests and parishioners in the working-class white neighborhoods surrounding Hyde Park were complaining loudly that thousands of poor blacks pushed out by urban renewal might end up moving into their parishes. In this conflict between the Church and the university, Daley, who attended Mass every day, had no problem siding with the university. Julian Levi recalled discussing the archdiocese's opposition to the Final Plan with the mayor. "He said, 'I go to mass, but I accept no intrusion on public responsibilities.'"

Daley pushed the university's urban-renewal plan through the City Council, and secured the federal and local money needed to implement it. Thousands of units of slum housing were razed in Hyde Park — the *New York Times* declared at the height of the project that the "areas near the university resemble German cities just after World War II." Throughout the neighborhood, substandard buildings and blight were replaced by new housing or open space. When urban renewal was complete, the new Hyde Park that emerged was more attractive, more sparsley populated, wealthier, and whiter. From 1960

to 1970, the neighborhood's population declined more than 26 percent. The people who were being pushed out of Hyde Park were
just the ones the university was concerned about: the poor, and
blacks. During the 1960s, average income in the neighborhood
soared 70 percent, and the black population fell 40 percent.

Daley's urban renewal plan gave the university the kind of neighborhood it wanted, but the transformation came at a cost. The poor,
black residents who had found their way to Hyde Park, one of the
city's few integrated neighborhoods, were once again pushed back
into the ghetto. No doubt many of them ended up, as historian
Arnold Hirsch has suggested, in the new housing projects that were
going up along the State Street Corridor and elsewhere. Advocates
for the poor had hoped that some of the substandard buildings in
Hyde Park would be replaced with public housing, so poor people
could remain in the neighborhood, but the university succeeded in
blocking almost all of the proposed units. In the end only thirty-four
public housing apartments were built, and twenty-two of them were
reserved for elderly tenants. Hyde Park urban renewal also erected
racial barriers between the neighborhood's middle-class residents and
the black neighborhoods surrounding it. Perhaps the starkest example was the University Apartments, two extremely long mid-rises
that stretched down the middle of 55th Street. The buildings, which
stand between the university campus and ghetto neighborhoods to
the north, were designed as "barrier-type" buildings, Alderman
Despres observed, designed to separate racial groups.[51]

On March 4, 1958, Daley presided at the dedication of newly restored City Council chambers, a little less than a year after they had
been damaged by fire. The following month, the City Council experienced a more substantive change. Alderman Tom Keane ascended,
with Daley's backing, to chair the Finance Committee, the most
powerful on the council. Keane was already Daley's floor leader, and
the combination of the two posts made him the most influential alderman in Chicago history. Around the same time, Daley was reelected to another two-year term as chairman of the Cook County
Democratic Central Committee. In his acceptance speech, Daley
called the machine precinct captains "the strength of our party." No

one was more important in a Democracy, Daley said, than "those who translate issues and problems for the electorate."[52]

As his new term as party boss began, Daley was in the process of quietly eviscerating Dawson and the black submachine. Dawson had been one of Daley's most consistent supporters. He had backed Daley for party boss against the Wagner–Duffy faction, and he had schemed with Daley to remove Kennelly from City Hall. At election time, Dawson had always delivered overwhelming majorities for the machine slate. And Dawson had always given Daley cover on race, serving as the black face of the Democratic machine and putting down civil rights uprisings in the black community. Daley's objection to Dawson was not how he exercised power, but how much power he had. As head of the black submachine, Dawson was in a unique position. Unlike other ward committeemen, his influence extended into several wards, and these wards were of considerable importance to the machine. This meant that if Dawson wanted to make things difficult for the machine, he could. Dawson had never given Daley trouble, but Daley had seen how the wily black boss had helped to force Kennelly out of office. With the city's black population soaring, Dawson's power was also rising. Ignoring Dawson's years of personal loyalty, Daley decided to act before it was too late.

The first public sign that Daley was out to undermine Dawson came when 24th Ward alderman Sidney Deutsch died. The once-Jewish 24th Ward had by 1958 become one of the city's leading "plantation wards," so called because they were majority black, but ruled over by white leaders. In the past, Dawson would have been allowed to name the new alderman, extending the reach of the black submachine into yet another ward. But breaking with tradition, Daley decided to install his own man. In the same year, Daley intervened in a dispute in another of Dawson's wards in a way that demonstrated that the old submachine boss had lost his ability to keep the machine out of his turf. As it happened, the clash came over an issue Daley and Dawson agreed on: civil rights. Alderman Claude Holman, of the black 4th Ward, had agreed to cosponsor an open-occupancy bill with independent 5th Ward alderman Leon Despres. Dawson, who naturally opposed the bill, told Holman to back down, and when he refused, Dawson asked the machine to

strip Holman of his patronage. It was the traditional machine response to this kind of act of insubordination, but Daley refused to do
it. Dawson's inability to bring down retribution on Holman sent a
clear message to other members of the black submachine that they
no longer needed to fear their onetime leader.[53]

It did not take long for Dawson's ward committeemen to switch
their allegiance to City Hall. "They began to splinter off," says Dawson's nephew, Ira Dawson. "Everyone vied for power from [Daley] in
order to keep themselves in power." The aldermen who once reported to Dawson now saw themselves as working directly for Daley.
Holman, who had been edging toward the civil rights cause, swung
violently back and became Daley's chief spokesman against open-
housing and fair-employment bills in the City Council. Holman's
blustery opposition to civil rights was far less subtle than Dawson's
behind-the-scenes scheming. "Anything I suggested, Holman would
find a way of twisting it and showing that it really wasn't for freedom, or if it was a good measure, he'd get up and say that my motives were bad," says Despres. "Holman had no inhibitions. He
would flatter Mayor Daley and tell the mayor publicly in the city
council that he was the greatest mayor, in the glare of the cameras
and radio microphones. I remember once he said, 'You are the greatest mayor in history, greatest mayor in the world and in outer space,
too.'"[54]

The once-mighty black submachine was no more. But Daley did
not destroy Dawson entirely. He allowed his old ally to keep his seat
in Congress, and to stay on as boss of the 2nd Ward. Daley also let
Dawson continue to hold himself out as the leading black in the
Chicago machine, an arrangement that suited Dawson's ego and
Daley's political needs. "Whenever a Negro delegation approaches
Mayor Daley with a community problem," the *Chicago Defender*
complained, "they are usually told: 'See Bill Dawson, he'll take care
of it.'" Dawson made some minor attempts to regain his lost standing. In 1959, he tried to form a black-Polish alliance to challenge
Daley. But the truth was, even if the Poles wanted to ally themselves
with Chicago's blacks — and they did not — Dawson could no
longer deliver the black community. His days as a boss were over.
"What Mayor Daley had created — the most powerful black politician in the country," historian William Grimshaw has observed,

"Mayor Daley destroyed, and for the same reason: to advance his own political interest." With the civil rights movement gaining force both at home and nationally, Daley's newfound control over Chicago's black political leadership — from the ward organizations to the local NAACP — would have important implications in the racial struggles to come.[55]

Make No Little Plans

In August of 1958, Daley unveiled a sweeping plan for redeveloping downtown Chicago. Daley's proposal was in the bold tradition of the Plan of Chicago, the blueprint for redesigning Chicago that Daniel Burnham prepared for the Merchants' Club in 1909. "Make no little plans," Burnham, a prominent architect and principal designer of the 1893 Columbian Exposition, advised. "They have no magic to stir men's blood." Burnham's plan had been anything but little. He called for more extensive use of Lake Michigan, including expanded lakefront recreational areas, and the construction of a series of offshore islands. Anticipating the great highways that would one day come, Burnham called for the city to build a major east-west artery stretching out from the lake, and he urged construction of a civic center. The plan advocated a system of broad boulevards, modeled on Paris, Budapest, and Geneva, to ease traffic through the city. But its true genius lay in its vision of the city as a single organism that combined industry and commerce with residential neighborhoods and recreational outlets. Burnham's Plan of Chicago of 1909 was greeted with enormous enthusiasm. A popularized version of the plan became a bestseller, and in textbook form it became required reading for eighth-graders across the city. Like most Chicagoans of his era, Daley read the book as a student. This compendium of bold ideas for refashioning Chicago was, he once said, his favorite book.[1]

Daley invoked Burnham's plan, and quoted his injunction to

"make no little plans," when he presented his own development plan for the central area of Chicago. At the unveiling, Daley stood before an enormous scale model showing how downtown would look after twenty-two years and $1.5 billion in renovations. The models spread out in his office were, Daley declared, "the future of Chicago." In the limited part of the city that it addressed, Daley's plan was every bit as sweeping as Burnham's. It called for erecting several government building complexes downtown, including a new civil court building on Washington Street, a new government mall stretching from City Hall to State Street, and a new federal court building on the site of an existing federal building on the Dearborn-Clark-Adams-Jackson block. It also proposed consolidating railroad stations and using the land under railroad tracks south of the Loop as the site of a new Chicago campus for the University of Illinois. And it sketched out a variety of other ambitious undertakings, including a consolidated transportation center combining access to railroads, buses, and airport terminals and limousines, and construction of new housing for 50,000 families in the downtown area. Some of its suggestions, including expanded access to Lake Michigan beaches and construction of two new islands in the shallow water south of 23rd Street, were drawn straight from Burnham.[2]

The new plan was, as a formal matter, the city's. It had been drawn up under the direction of the commissioner of city planning, Ira Bach. The true guiding force, however, was the business community and the Central Area Committee. The CAC was listed prominently as a consultant on the plan, along with some of its individual leaders, like Clair Roddewig, and its influence was apparent on every page. The first topic addressed by the plan was "traffic flow," a cause close to the hearts of downtown businessmen. Leading city planners of the day, such as Jane Jacobs, were writing eloquently about the importance of pedestrian traffic and street life to the vibrancy of large cities. Daley's plan, however, was focused on automobiles. Downtown businesses were worried that their best customers were increasingly driving to new stores in the suburbs, leaving them with a poorer clientele who arrived downtown by mass transit or on foot. "The people [the downtown businesses] needed were not the low-income whites and Negroes who lived closest to the Loop," one contemporary study noted, "but people with purchasing power to support the great stores, banks, and entertainment places that were the heart of Chicago." The Daley plan contained elaborate super-highways designed to whisk shoppers in from the neighborhoods and the suburbs, and parking lots and new "pedestrian conveyance systems" that would ease their path to downtown stores. The plan called for some residential building, but it too was geared toward the needs of business. Downtown business leaders had long been clamoring for construction of luxury high-rise apartments in and around the Loop. Their hope was that upscale housing would raise the economic status of the area and improve downtown retailing, since the "[p]eople who could afford to live in them would be a good customer base for downtown stores." The plan followed the business community's lead, placing a "special emphasis" on "the needs of the middle income groups who wish to live in areas close to the heart of the City."[3]

Nowhere did the visions of the CAC and the drafters of the plan align more closely than on the matter of defending the borders of the business district. The Chicago central area, broadly defined, is surrounded by water on three sides. The curving Chicago River cuts it off from adjoining neighborhoods to the north and west, and Lake Michigan lies to the east. But there were no natural barriers between the Loop and the expanding ghettos and public housing projects of the South Side. Downtown businessmen at the time were "really concerned about what would happen south of the downtown area," observes a modern-day Central Area Committee president. Of greatest interest to them was a large stretch of land just south of the Loop that contained a combination of railroad tracks and vacant and underutilized railroad property. In time, the tracks would be consolidated and a decision would have to be made about the disposition of the land. Downtown businessmen were concerned that it would be used for public housing, or that it would naturally be filled by the fast-expanding South Side Black Belt. They were relying on Daley to find a use for the land that prevented the ghetto from coming right up their front door.[4]

Daley's plan addressed these concerns about the Loop's southern flank directly. In its projections for the future, the plan anticipated that the Loop would expand in three directions — east, west, and north, all of which led toward white neighborhoods. The one direction it did not see the Loop expanding was south, toward the Black Belt, even though that was precisely the area where the underused railroad properties lay. Instead, the plan proposed using the land to the south of the Loop to build a new Chicago campus of the University of Illinois. The plan stated candidly that this campus would "act as an anchor to contain further southward expansion." The remaining open land between the Black Belt and the Loop was designated in the plan as a "residential re-use area," meaning that new — primarily middle-class — housing would be built, and it too would act as a buffer. To those of a conspiratorial mind-set, the plan seemed expressly designed to keep the central area white, and to physically cut it off from black Chicago. Certainly those rumors spread through the black community, which like black communities across the country harbored suspicions of various white "master plans" for using urban renewal and other development policies to shift greater control to whites. But in the case of Daley's 1958 plan, at least some of those suspicions had a basis in fact. The plan, of course, never addressed these racial issues head-on. In fact, one of Daley's housing consultants recalls that when development documents were drafted in City Hall, "the mayor didn't want any mention of race." Nevertheless, the 1958 plan must be seen now as an important step in a long-evolving process of making Chicago America's most racially segregated large city.[5]

The business community, not surprisingly, was delighted with Daley's 1958 development plan. The *Chicago Sun-Times,* owned by the downtown department store company Marshall Field, greeted it with breathless headlines, including "Let's Dream a Dream of Chicago: What City Would Be Like If All Plans Work Out." What the *Sun-Times* did not dwell on was that, unlike the plan of 1909, Daley's was almost single-mindedly focused on the downtown business district. Where Burnham had looked at Chicago as an organic whole, Daley's planners proceeded as if downtown were the only part of the city whose future mattered. Despite the plan's claim of giving "to all the people the best there is of urban living," the recreation, beautification, new housing, and other improvements it called for were exclusively located in and around the central business district. The only improvement it offered to most of the city's residential neighborhoods was a highway that would move cars more rapidly through them on the way to shopping in the Loop.[6]

It was a particularly unfortunate time for Daley to forget his oft-repeated campaign promise to put Chicago's neighborhoods first. By the late 1950s, many neighborhoods on the South and West sides were in the midst of a severe downward spiral. Continued black migration from the South was rapidly expanding the borders of the Black Belt — during the 1950s, three and a half blocks turned from white to black every week. The Black Belt, once confined to a north-south strip on the South Side, was moving out along two axes — further south into neighborhoods like Kenwood and Wood-lawn that lay just below the existing ghetto, and west into neighbor-hoods like Lawndale and Garfield Park.[7] Racial change in these areas came in the worst possible way. The city's entrenched opposition to fair housing, which prevailed everywhere from the Real Estate Board to City Hall, made it all but impossible for integrated neigh-borhoods to emerge. The real estate industry was actively working against integration, subsidizing neighborhood groups that were orga-nizing against it, and lobbying against fair housing laws. At the same time, individual real estate agents used a variety of tactics to keep blacks from moving into white neighborhoods. One study from the time found that 56 percent of Realtors flatly refused to rent or sell blacks homes in white neighborhoods, and another 24 percent em-ployed such dodges as saying a house was not available when it was. As a result, white homeowners who lived near the ghetto were con-vinced that if a single black family moved onto their block, the whole neighborhood would soon be black.[8]

It was a climate that caused many stable working-class neighbor-hoods to transform into slums. An unscrupulous variety of real estate agent known as the "panic peddler" arose to speed the process along. They practiced "block busting," going door-to-door in white neigh-borhoods on the fringes of the ghetto, warning that an "invasion" of blacks was imminent, and offering the opportunity to get out on "generous" terms while their homes still had some value. Panic ped-dlers posted prominent "sold" signs to scare neighbors into thinking that the block was changing, and spread false rumors about blacks buying nearby homes or crime rates rising. Many employed spies in vulnerable neighborhoods, who helped them locate whites who were getting nervous and might be persuaded to sell. The panic ped-dlers then turned around and sold the houses at inflated prices to middle-class blacks who had few alternatives, or divided them into overcrowded apartments and rented them out at exorbitant rates. The institutions that could have anchored integrated neighborhoods, including churches, were often the first to stir up racial fears. "The Niggers have taken over Corpus Christi Church, Holy Angels and St. Ann's and they are now trying to take over this church; but if it's left to me, they will not," Pastor F. J. Quinn reportedly preached at Saint Ambrose Church in racially changing Hyde Park.[9]

Instead of healthy integrated neighborhoods, the South and West sides ended up with a single black ghetto that engulfed communities in its path. "Much like a monstrous giant, this expansion continually reaches out for the blocks that are located on the periphery of the al-ready existing Negro ghettos," the Chicago Urban League observed. This had not been how neighborhood transformations had occurred in the past, when it was whites who were moving in. Neighbor-hoods like Bridgeport managed to be a patchwork quilt of different white ethnic groups. But when blacks arrived, old white ethnic neighborhoods were swept away almost overnight. On the West Side, North Lawndale and East Garfield Park changed quickly from tidy, white working-class enclaves to black ghettos. Predominantly Jewish North Lawndale, for example, went from 13 percent black in 1950 to 90 percent black in 1960. The loss of old neighborhoods was often painful for the white groups who were displaced. Resi-dents lost friends and neighbors they had known for decades, and left behind beloved churches, synagogues, and schools.[10]

The harm done to newly arrived blacks was equally severe. Blacks who made their way out of the ghetto had no chance to live in a stable, middle-class neighborhood. The white areas they moved into almost immediately became slums themselves. Homes that a single white family had lived in were often sliced up into two or three cramped apartments or "kitchenettes" for black tenants. The over-crowding was frequently extreme. A building at 3323 Calumet Av-enue, which started out housing eight families, was reconfigured to house fifty-four. Landlords often reduced or eliminated maintenance services to the property after blacks moved in, not because the rent collected was less, but because it was now slum property. One study of the Chicago housing market found that although the median rent paid by blacks and whites was identical, blacks lived in units that were on average smaller and more dilapidated. North Lawndale is a classic case of neighborhood decline. As whites moved out, businesses left with them. In the late 1960s, when the neighborhood was overwhelmingly black, International Harvester closed a plant that employed 14,000 people. Later, the world headquarters of Sears, Roebuck left for the Loop, pulling out 10,000 jobs. From 1960 to 1970, North Lawndale lost about 75 percent of its businesses. By the mid-1980s, the neighborhood had become a slum. It had just one supermarket and one bank for its 66,000 residents, but it had forty-eight lottery agents and ninety-nine liquor stores and bars.[11]

Preventing neighborhoods like this from being destroyed would not have been easy, but there were a few neighborhood activists at the time who were meeting with some success. On the South Side, the Organization for the Southwest Community worked to stabilize endangered neighborhoods that stood about a mile "behind the line" of the advancing black population. OSC staff tore down illegal "sold" signs put up by panic peddlers, and held public burnings to protest real-estate scare tactics. The group confronted city inspectors, challenging their failure to enforce building codes and their inaction in the face of illegal conversions of single-family homes. The OSC's community organizers also worked directly with white residents on the Southwest Side, persuading them that they did not need to flee their neighborhood just because blacks were beginning to move in. One of the OSC's most innovative programs was a cooperative arrangement with local banks to provide mortgages with 10 percent down payments, rather than the customary 20 percent to 30 percent. The idea was to stabilize neighborhoods by keeping white families, particularly families affiliated with local Catholic churches, from moving to the suburbs. In the first nine months, the program arranged for eighty-three mortgages. The OSC's approach was far from perfect. To some, the emphasis on stabilizing neighborhoods by obtaining loans for white homeowners seemed anti-integrationist. And by the late 1960s, much of the area that the OSC worked was black, rather than racially integrated. The attempts to stabilize middle-class neighborhoods on the Southwest Side were, in the end, simply "too little and too late."[12]

But the OSC and other groups like it showed what Daley and city government could have tried if they had a more sophisticated approach to the racial change confronting Chicago. With his strong ties to the city banking establishment, Daley could have built a home-ownership program far larger than the one cobbled together by the OSC. The city had far greater resources at its disposal to mediate between white residents and new black arrivals. And Daley could have aggressively worked to enforce housing codes and anti-blockbusting laws. But the truth was, Daley had no interest in working for integrated neighborhoods. And from a political standpoint, segregated white ethnic and black wards were still the mainstay of the machine's support. Daley refused to face the issue of racial transition head-on. A housing consultant to Daley prepared a report early on that predicted that Chicago would become majority black by 1975, and that many white neighborhoods near the existing Black Belt, including Bridgeport, would become black. Daley reacted by burying the report. Nicholas von Hoffman, then a young reporter for the *Chicago Daily News,* gained access to it and printed its conclusions. Daley "had a conniption," the consultant recalled. "This was the first time a city report mentioned race in the history of the city since Daley." Donald O'Toole, a South Side banker, once tried to talk to Daley about the OSC and the progress it was making on racial issues. "I suppose our faces were this far apart," O'Toole says. "And I was explaining, 'Dick, I don't think that you really understand what this organization is doing. The way it is put together is a fascinating thing.' I was very enthusiastic about it, very worked up over it. And we continued to be just that far apart. And when I reached the end of my pearl of an oration, he said, 'Don, when did your dear old dad die? God rest his soul.'"[13]

In mid–October 1958, Daley announced a reduction in the number of mass precinct-captain luncheons that would be held at the Morrison Hotel before the November elections. There would be only two this year, with 1,200 of the machine faithful at each, rather than the usual four. The cutback was widely regarded as a sign of machine confidence that it would do well in the upcoming elections, in which only countywide and local offices were at stake. Daley spent a good deal of time trying to reach out to the fast-growing, and

largely Republican, suburban Chicago. "[T]he suburbs supposedly are
the place for the opposition party," he told an audience of 1,200 at a
five-dollars-a-plate dinner at the Tam O'Shanter Country Club in
Niles. "But that's no longer the case. The balance of power there is
swinging to the Democrats." The Republicans, for their part, circulated "S.O.S" lapel buttons, urging suburban voters to "save our suburbs from the Morrison Hotel gang." Vice President Richard Nixon
campaigned in Chicago a week before the election, declaring that
the Democrats had "run out of gas," and that "if we can keep going
at our recent rate, a lot of people who have been predicting a
Democratic landslide are going to have red faces next week."[14]
Despite Nixon's optimism, the 1958 elections were a sweep for the
Democrats. The machine scored a key victory in the county assessor
race, which a Democratic ward committeeman won by 372,000
votes. This post was a critical one for Daley and the machine, since it
set the value on properties for tax purposes. Property owners could
often be induced to make generous contributions to the machine
in exchange for low tax assessments, an arrangement that explained
the office's nickname: "the party's banker." But the biggest winner
was Otto Kerner, who was elected county judge by 545,000 votes,
including a 6,500-vote victory in the Cook County suburbs. At
slate-making time two years later, Daley would remember how
strongly Kerner had run both in and outside the city.[15]

Daley had been working to build a Chicago campus of the University of Illinois long before it made an appearance in his 1958 plan. In
1945, as a state senator, he sponsored one of the first bills in the legislature promoting the cause. When Governor Stratton paid a courtesy
call to Daley's fifth-floor office to examine the 1958 redevelopment
models, Daley told him that the Chicago campus was one of his
highest priorities. There were political reasons for Daley to favor it.
As a branch of the state university system, it would bring more state
money to Chicago, making available more contracts and jobs for the
machine to hand out to its friends. The 1958 plan had revealed how
the campus could work as an economic and racial buffer for the
downtown business district. And attracting a low-tuition state school
for the sons and daughters of Chicagoans would certainly be an accomplishment that would resonate well with the voters when Daley

ran for reelection. But Daley also seemed to be motivated by a genuine belief that Chicago needed and deserved the campus. As someone who had worked his way out of the working class through college and years of night law school, Daley understood the importance of education. The university's main Champaign–Urbana campus was hundreds of miles south of the city, and many poor and working-class Chicagoans were being deprived of higher education because of the difficulty and expense of traveling downstate to receive it.[16]

But making the University of Illinois at Chicago a reality would not be easy. The first stumbling block was that Daley did not have a site to offer. The 1958 plan called for building it on land that was then occupied by railroad tracks south of the Loop, but those tracks were still in use and it was not clear that the railroads that owned them wanted to give them up. Daley proposed that five railroad passenger terminals spread out across the South Side be combined into a single Union Station, which would free up 160 acres of land south of the Congress Expressway, more than enough for the new campus. But the railroads were not enthusiastic about incurring the substantial costs of consolidation. Daley also faced skepticism from the University of Illinois trustees. Many worried that without the flow of Cook County students, the main campus at Champaign–Urbana would, as one local state senator put it, "return to the great prairie that it once was."[17]

Then, as support grew for building a four-year campus in the Chicago area, many of the trustees inclined toward a suburban location. The suburbs offered cheaper land and more of it, nearby suburban living for the school's faculty, and faster population growth in the surrounding area. The trustees had actually voted in favor of a site in the western suburbs called Miller Meadows. But it was owned by the Forest Preserve District, and the university needed the Cook County Board to approve the transfer. Daley attended meetings between the Cook County Board president and the university trustees, at which his demeanor was described as "Buddha-like." Although Daley never stated his views publicly, the Cook County Board turned down the Miller Meadows proposal, quite possibly under threat that Daley would not reslate any board member who voted for it. Even with this setback, the trustees remained committed to a suburban location for the new campus. "No available site within the city limits of Chicago will meet criteria of [the] Board and long range objectives," one trustee insisted. "A skyscraper university would be expensive to build and to operate, [it would take] many years to acquire a site through slum clearance — [and it would be] costly in funds and time."[18]

Downtown business leaders were one key constituency backing Daley in his quest for a campus in or near the Loop. In early 1957, the Central Area Committee sent a high-powered delegation to meet with the chairman of the University's Physical Plant Planning Committee. The group, which included top-rank executives from Marshall Field, Illinois Bell, and Chicago Title and Trust, proposed several sites in and around the Loop, including Daley's South Loop railroad site. Daley's representative underscored that the mayor strongly favored a site within the city limits, and pushed in particular for the railroad site. Prospects for a Chicago campus seemed to improve greatly after the November 1958 election, in which Democrats defeated three Republican members of the university board, including the board chairman. When the changeover occurred the following March, the board would have a 6–3 Democratic majority. Before it left office, however, the lame-duck board selected Riverside Golf Club, a suburban location not far from Miller Meadows. In doing so, the board ignored a last-minute plea from Daley, who urged that the vote be put off until more information was available on alternative sites. Daley responded to the adverse vote by scheduling a meeting with the full board of trustees in February and asking them to delay their decision until April 15, by which time the city would have completed a feasibility study on the railroad site. Not incidentally, by that time the Democrats would have taken control of the board. As an incentive for delay, Daley told the board that the city stood "anxious, ready and willing" to pay the extra costs associated with building the campus in the city. "If the Riverside site costs 2 million dollars and a Chicago site costs 4 million," Daley assured them, "we'll pay the difference." The board agreed to put off a final decision until April 15, 1959.[19]

In addition to Daley's Loop railroad site, the university was now considering two other locations in the city: Meigs Field, a commuter airport jutting into Lake Michigan southeast of the Loop, and Garfield

Park, a residential area four miles west of State Street. Daley and the CAC opposed the new sites, neither of which would advance their goal of creating an economic anchor and a racial buffer for the Loop. Daley rejected the Meigs Field site out of hand, arguing that transportation to it would be difficult. In May 1959, the trustees voted to make Garfield Park their choice for the new campus. The truth was, Garfield Park was in many ways an ideal site. It was a working-class neighborhood, filled with factory workers and civil servants whose children were precisely the kind of students the campus was intended to serve. The community also badly needed the economic uplift that a major university campus would bring. The Garfield Park–Austin neighborhood was, in the late 1950s, in economic and racial transition. Middle-class whites had been moving out, and they were being replaced by poor blacks squeezed out of the South Side. Placing the university campus in the neighborhood would have anchored it, and perhaps prevented it from becoming an all-black ghetto. The community understood this and, unlike most other areas the university was considering, Garfield Park was eager to be selected. Homeowners groups, elected officials, and the community newspaper all came out in favor of locating the campus in Garfield Park.[20]

The main opposition to the Garfield Park location came from downtown businesses, which still wanted the campus located near the Loop. These industry leaders had far more resources at their disposal than the working-class residents of Garfield Park. Working through their two development arms, the Central Area Committee and the Metropolitan Housing and Planning Council, the Loop businessmen lobbied against Garfield Park and in favor of a Loop site. The *Sun-Times,* with its ties to the downtown department store Marshall Field, also promoted a location near the Loop. Individual business leaders lobbied elected officials directly. On December 7, 1959, eighteen civic and business groups urged Daley and Stratton to put the campus in the railroad site. Daley still favored the Loop location, and he had an opportunity to bring his considerable influence to bear. Though the university had already selected the Garfield Park location, there was an obstacle. The campus would be built in part on land owned by the Park District, which had not yet agreed to sell it. The most prominent member of the Park District board was

Daley's old friend Jake Arvey. While the issue of Park District land remained unresolved, downtown businessmen formed the Joint Action Committee of Civic Organizations to push for the railroad site. JACCO threatened to sue if the Park District board transferred any land in Garfield Park to the university, arguing that portions of the land had been deeded to the Park District on the condition that it remain as a park. The Illinois state legislature passed legislation clearing the way for the Park District to transfer the land, but it was becoming increasingly clear that this would not happen. In the end, the university withdrew its plans to site the campus in Garfield Park.[21]

Although Daley and the Loop businessmen had succeeded in defeating yet another alternative site, they were still not able to secure the railroad site that was their first choice. The railroad companies were now asking for $140 million for the land and for a new terminal, far more than Daley was prepared to pay. And Daley and the companies could not reach an agreement on a consolidated railroad terminal. With negotiations over the railroad site at an impasse, another possibility emerged: a fifty-five-acre urban renewal site in the Near West Side Harrison-Halsted neighborhood. The Harrison-Halsted site was a few blocks west of the Loop, and just south of the Congress Expressway. It was close enough to serve as the kind of "anchor" for the Loop that downtown business leaders were looking for. And it would also serve as a racial barrier — not between the Loop and the South Side ghetto, but between the Loop and another nearby concentration of poor blacks. The Harrison-Halsted site was just a few blocks east of one of the largest concentrations of public housing in the city — the 1,027 units of the Jane Addams Houses, the forty buildings and 1,200 units of the Grace Abbott Homes, and the 834 units of the Robert Brooks Homes. These projects, originally built for white occupancy, were already well on their way to becoming overwhelmingly black. And the neighborhood in which they were located was, according to one contemporaneous account, "probably the most depressed area in the City." The Harrison-Halsted site was already owned by the city, so it could be delivered to the university quickly. An added advantage was that, since it was a designated urban redevelopment site, much of the cost of acquiring the land could be charged to the federal government under the Urban Renewal Act.[22]

Daley formally proposed the Harrison–Halsted site to the university trustees at a September 27, 1960, meeting. It was, he said, the option that would "get the University into Chicago as fast as possible." As it happened, the Garfield Park site was on a slower track because a Cook County Circuit Court judge who owed his seat on the bench to the Democratic machine had recently struck down as unconstitutional the new state law approving the transfer of Garfield Park park land to the university. That decision would later be reversed by the Illinois Supreme Court, but it succeeded in casting doubt over the Garfield Park site at a crucial point. Daley's first choice, the railroad site, was still out of reach, since the railroads showed no signs of coming to terms with the city on transfer of the land. But he had orchestrated the process in a way that made the selection of his other choice, Harrison–Halsted, increasingly inevitable. Daley's presentation to the trustees was well received, and they voted in favor of the Harrison–Halsted campus.[23]

The Harrison–Halsted community, unlike Garfield Park, was bitterly opposed to having a University of Illinois campus built in their midst. Where Garfield Park residents had seen the school as a lifeline, Harrison–Halsted residents saw it as a bulldozer that would raze block after block of their vibrant neighborhood. Harrison–Halsted was an old-fashioned, working-class urban community. It was part of the heavily Italian 1st Ward, which sent the syndicate's favorite alderman, John D'Arco, to the City Council. But the neighborhood was an ethnic mix, including Italians, Greeks, blacks, and Mexicans. Harrison–Halsted was also home to Hull House, the famous settlement house that Jane Addams established in 1889 to serve Chicago's poor. Plans for the new campus would require Hull House to be moved or destroyed. Also threatened was the Holy Guardian Angel Church and its adjoining parochial school, beloved neighborhood institutions that had just relocated in 1959 when their original building was demolished to build the Dan Ryan Expressway.[24]

A grassroots movement, largely made up of neighborhood women, formed to save Harrison–Halsted from the bulldozers. A housewife named Florence Scala, who had been active on the New West Side Planning Board, showed up at a February 13, 1961, meeting at Holy Guardian Angel out of curiosity, and was reluctantly drafted to lead the cause. A week later, she presided over a meeting of more than five hundred neighborhood residents at Hull House. Since the local elected officials had decided to sell out the community to Daley and the machine, the residents decided, they would have to take matters into their own hands. A new organization, the Harrison-Halsted Community Group, was formed, and Scala became its leader. The group took their battle for their homes and neighborhood to any political body that would hear them out. The University of Illinois Board of Trustees, the Federal Housing and Home Finance Agency, the state legislature, the Illinois Housing Board, the Planning and Housing Committee of the City Council, and the full City Council all turned down Scala and her followers and endorsed the Harrison-Halsted site. They also appealed to elected officials for help, but Senator Paul Douglas, Adlai Stevenson, and Bill Dawson all refused to take the community's side against Daley.[25]

Turned down by the power structure, neighborhood residents moved on to direct action. On March 20, one thousand supporters of the Harrison-Halsted Community Group followed Scala on a march from Saint Francis of Assisi Church to Hull House to appeal for their neighborhood to be spared. The demonstrators, most of them women from the area, held signs with messages like "Daley Is a Dictator — He Won't Get Any More Democratic Votes from Us." As the City Council's vote on the proposed site drew near, someone tossed a dummy into the street outside Daley's home. It included a mark that looked like a bullet hole, and a sign that read: "This is Mayor Daley of the future." But Daley was not deterred. "No one is going to threaten me as mayor of Chicago," he said. "If I had been there, I would have taken care of them. . . . I don't fear death either." Daley loudly proclaimed that he would "tak[e] care of the situation" himself, and quietly doubled the police guard outside his home.[26]

When the time came for the City Council to vote, Daley appeared personally to speak in support of a bill to designate 155 acres of Harrison-Halsted as the site of the new campus. It was "unfortunate that in the selection of sites for public improvement some must suffer," Daley told a standing-room-only crowd of four hundred. But he insisted that the debate over the location had overshadowed "the most important issue, that is to give the young people of Chicago and Cook County an accessible university." Daley invoked the spirit of Jane Addams — whose Hull House was being threatened by bulldozers — and promised that the campus's new School of Social Work would be named for her. It was Alderman D'Arco, however, who won cheers from the crowd when he protested that the Harrison-Halsted site had been "picked in desperation and was the choice of no one." The City Council followed Daley's lead and voted in favor of the site.[27]

When the voting was over, two hundred members of the Harrison-Halsted Community Group marched to Daley's office. When they got inside, they pounded on desks, threw things, and railed bitterly against Daley and the City Council. "The rich always take away from the poor!" one woman shouted. Another threatened, "The first surveyor is going to get it in the head with a crowbar; putting us out on the streets. What do you think we are, animals?" Daley, refusing to confront a group made up largely of mothers fighting to protect their homes, slipped out a side door and left them to his director of special events. The demonstrators agreed to leave after they were promised a meeting with Daley the next day. At that meeting, Daley explained that the responsibility for selecting Harrison-Halsted lay with the university trustees — the same group Daley had spent years talking out of the suburban and Garfield Park sites that they preferred. "This has been misrepresented and twisted as though the city had selected the site," Daley told the women.[28]

Plans for construction were proceeding rapidly. Daley's urban renewal commissioner announced that the city had been awarded $26.2 million in federal funds to acquire and clear 105.8 acres for the campus. Groundbreaking for the first of thirteen new buildings was scheduled for the fall. Scala announced that the Harrison-Halsted Community Group was filing federal and state lawsuits to block construction, and on August 15, 1962, the group appealed to Daley to stop further condemnation of their neighborhood until their appeals were ruled on. But Daley would not be deterred. "I never heard him second-guess himself," said his son William. "You make a decision, you don't second-guess yourself or look back. He did not wring his hands."[29]

The Harrison-Halsted Community Group continued its protests, but defeat seemed increasingly inevitable. One day in October, Scala and some of her followers confronted Daley at a sit-in in his office, and made another appeal for residents to be allowed to stay in their homes until their legal appeals could be ruled on. "What is going to happen to these people?" Scala asked of her neighbors. But to Daley, it all came down to politics. "Why don't you take care of your candidate?" he asked Scala, implying that Richard Ogilvie, the Republican candidate for Cook County sheriff, was behind the protests. "You can't even talk to the man," Scala said afterward. "You start to ask him a question and he keeps talking." The following day, Daley announced that the families who lived in the area where the first construction was to occur would have to move out immediately, before their appeals were exhausted. The other residents could remain through the appeal process. The impact of the evictions on neighborhood residents was devastating. "I walked around with Florence Scala at the time when they were clearing people out," says one reporter. "A lot of the people had lived in that neighborhood their whole lives, the old Italian people. A lot of them died — they just couldn't make the move."[30]

In the end, Daley's plans for the University of Illinois–Chicago destroyed two neighborhoods. The toll inflicted by the new campus was obvious in Harrison-Halsted, which lost as many as 14,000 residents and 630 businesses. But Garfield Park, which Daley deprived of the campus, was the second victim. The neighborhood's decline, which was already under way, picked up speed after the decision was made to build the university elsewhere. Middle-class residents put their homes up for sale and, in the familiar cycle, poor blacks moved in. Within years, lower-middle-class Garfield Park had become one of Chicago's worst slums. In 1965, West Garfield Park would become famous as the site of an unfortunate fatality caused by an out-of-control fire truck, which prompted massive riots among the neighborhood's alienated slum-dwellers. The seeds for that unrest were planted when Daley prevented the University of Illinois trustees from building the campus there. The Loop's gain was, undeniably, Garfield Park's loss.[31]

The new University of Illinois campus had just the economic and racial impact on the Harrison-Halsted neighborhood that Loop business leaders had hoped for. Before the arrival of the campus, it was one of the few racially integrated neighborhoods in the city. In 1960, 3,500 blacks lived in the neighborhood, about 15 percent of the population. Some lived in the Jane Addams Houses, but many more did not. A decade later, after the campus was completed, the black population had fallen to 2,900. But the biggest change was that almost all of them now lived in the Jane Addams Houses census tracts. With the campus standing between Jane Addams and the Loop, virtually all of the blacks who lived in this neighborhood abutting the Loop were now separated from downtown by an enormous physical barrier. The neighborhood also underwent an economic transformation. From 1961 to 1965, the cost of land in the area doubled, and from 1965 to 1971 it doubled again. The result of siting the campus in Harrison-Halsted was that a neighborhood that was once becoming more racially diverse was transformed into a far whiter "island of higher incomes and land values."[32]

The other large institution Daley had long hoped to bring to Chicago was a modern airport. The idea for a new Chicago airport dated back as early as 1944, when the Chicago Plan Commission called for the development of "an airport which will make Chicago the center of aviation." The need for a world-class airport was undeniable. Chicago had, by the 1940s, established itself as the regional aviation hub for the entire Midwest. By the end of the decade, Chicago was the first city in the country to average more than one thousand plane movements a day, twice as many as New York City. Chicago Municipal Airport, now Midway Airport on the Southwest Side, would not be able to keep up with the city's air traffic much longer.[33]

Although the need was clear, efforts to get a new airport built continually stalled. In March 1946, the U.S. Air Force donated 1,080 acres of land and a small hangar to the city, which would have made an ideal site, but no one could agree on how to fund construction and operation of the airport itself. At the time, New York's La Guardia Field was running deficits of $1 million a year, and Chicago's airports had also been money-losers. Mayor Kelly tried to arrange a combination of federal and state funds and usage fees from the airline industry, but the airlines balked. They refused to switch flights over to the new airport if its fees were any greater than at Municipal. The City Council authorized the purchase of additional land, bringing the site up to 7,000 acres, but when Mayor Kelly left office the question of how to build and operate the airport remained at an impasse. The domestic airlines flying into the city organized themselves into a bargaining committee, called the Chicago Airlines Top Committee, composed of one executive from each airline. In March 1949, the airlines notified the city that they were interested in a new airport, but they did not say how much they would be willing to pay. Mayor Kennelly signed an ordinance on June 28, 1949, naming the proposed new airport O'Hare Field, after a World War II aviation hero. There was some limited construction on the O'Hare site in the early 1950s, but it was hamstrung by lack of financing. The federal Civil Aeronautics Board allocated $1.8 million, the state contributed $1.17 million, and the federal government came up with another $1.6 million for construction of an 8,000-foot runway. But the overall problem of financing O'Hare was far from settled, and until it was the airlines were refusing to shift any flights to it.[34]

As soon as Daley became mayor in 1955, he began working to end the impasse over the funding of O'Hare. In his first weeks in office, he sent telegrams to top executives of each airline inviting them to meet with him in Chicago, bypassing the intransigent Chicago Airlines Top Committee. Daley had no trouble convincing them that air traffic at Midway was excessive, and that some of it would need to shift to O'Hare. The hard part was bringing the airlines around on finances, the subject that had tripped up previous mayors. Daley hammered away at the airlines, arguing that they were not doing their part. He "made us feel cheap about some of the things," United Airlines president William Patterson said later. In the end, the airlines agreed to assume the cost of operating O'Hare, in a sixty-seven-page document that committed both sides for the next fifteen years. "It is the only contract of its kind," Daley declared, "where a city has operations costs completely guaranteed on a major airport." With financing firmly in place, an air show was held at O'Hare on October 29, 1955, to mark the airport's official opening. It was, at 6,393 acres, the largest airfield in the nation, more than 1,000 acres larger than New York's Idlewild Field, later renamed John F. Kennedy Airport. Regular commercial flights began the next day.[35]

Despite his breakthroughs on financing and securing airline traffic, Daley's work on O'Hare was far from done. The airport was located outside Chicago's corporate limits. That meant that even though the city owned the land, technically it might not even be a Chicago airport. The city's lawyers had advised Daley that, among other problems, there could be legal disputes over Chicago's police powers on the site. Daley proposed in February 1956, to annex five miles of Route 72, also known as Higgins Road, to connect the airport to the city. The nearby suburbs opposed this "O'Hare Corridor," and two of them announced their own plans for annexing parts of Higgins Road. Daley responded by inviting the suburban officials to a meeting in City Hall. If the suburbs agreed to his annexation plans, he told them, he would promise not to annex any additional land near the airport that could get in the way of their own plans to expand. "Chicago is not interested in interfering with plans of other communities in any way," he assured them. The suburbs agreed to Daley's terms, and two weeks later the Chicago City Council voted 48–0 to annex O'Hare Field and connect it to Chicago through Higgins Road. But it did not take long for Daley to renege on his part of the bargain. In March, Schiller Park voted to annex part of a county forest preserve that lay between Chicago and the airport — precisely the land Daley promised not to interfere with. At Daley's behest, the City Council voted to annex most of the remainder of the forest preserve for Chicago.[36]

Even though O'Hare was now formally connected to Chicago, transportation between the airport and downtown remained a problem. There was no direct highway link, and some wags had taken to dubbing O'Hare "the only airport in the world accessible only by air." The Northwest Expressway, later renamed the Kennedy, was supposed to provide a direct highway connection. It had been envisioned thirty-three years earlier in a report of the Chicago Plan Commission, but it had been bogged down in the same kind of delays as the airport it was supposed to connect to. Before Daley was elected mayor, a cash-strapped Cook County had agreed to hand over part of the expressway to the state's toll highway system. When Daley took office, he immediately set out to reverse that decision. He was opposed, on principle, to charging a toll for the trip to the airport, but he also had other objections. Toll roads were barred by state law from including median strips for mass transportation, and they were ineligible for federal highway funds — and Daley wanted his expressway to have both. Daley worked out an agreement with the Toll Commission and the Cook County Board to make the expressway toll-free. By the time it was completed on November 5, 1960, federal funds paid for 90 percent of the road's $300 million construction cost.[37] A decade later, as Daley had hoped, a rapid transit line was opened in the median strip.

Daley wanted to expand O'Hare, but he was looking for a way to do it without saddling the city with costs. Daley's agreement with the airlines left them with the obligation to pay for the airport, and he called for a new round of negotiations. The talks began in the office of the commissioner of public works, but when the airlines and the city could not agree, they shifted to the mayor's office. The two sides met every ten to fourteen days for a period of about three months, but each side had nonnegotiable demands the other side would not agree to. Just when the deadlock seemed unresolvable, Daley got up from his chair, looked around the room, and announced that the city would waive all of its remaining conditions if the airlines did the same. The airlines met for ten minutes outside, and when they returned a United Airlines lawyer announced that the airlines accepted. The airlines agreed to a revenue bond issue for construction of new jet facilities, to be paid off by airport revenue, but guaranteed by the airlines in case the revenues fell short. This pact achieved Daley's goal of getting the airport completed without taxpayer dollars. With the funding settled, Daley announced new plans for expansion and renovation of O'Hare. They were more ambitious than the airlines wanted — the costs were being estimated at $120 million — but in the end they agreed to put up a forty-year bond. O'Hare's status as the world's first self-sustaining airport was preserved.[38]

O'Hare's passenger service buildings were completed in the summer of 1961, and Daley took a tour of them on August 29. The new buildings were "magnificent . . . showplaces of which Chicago justly will be proud," he declared. "No one could fail to be impressed when he stands at the passenger service level and looks for 750 feet past scores of ticket counters and entrances, framed in the wonderful glass walls," Daley said. "And this, remember, is repeated in two buildings." On January 15, 1962, the new O'Hare terminal complex was dedicated. Daley was part of a contingent of two hundred VIP visitors who were given a tour of the new facility, examining ticket counters, passenger waiting areas, and luggage weighing stations. To some critics it was all too much. One newspaper calculated that the longest distance between transfers, if the passenger made no missteps, was 4,200 feet — or four-fifths of a mile. In 1962, O'Hare became the world's busiest airport.

O'Hare stands as one of Daley's most impressive legacies, but it was not immune from the machine's usual rules for doing business. The critical $120 million bond issue that allowed final construction to go forward was awarded to a syndicate of five banking houses through a process of "negotiation" rather than competitive bidding. While the City Council was rubber-stamping the deal Daley had worked out with these politically connected banks, the city comptroller claimed that competitive bidding would have been impossible in this situation. Also without competitive bidding, Norman Drug Stores was awarded a ten-year contract to operate the airport's two drugstores. Critics said that the contracts shortchanged the city, but Daley defended the decision. "Our interest was to protect the public," he said. "While we could have obtained a higher percentage, perhaps, we might not have got the quality operation we do have out there."[39]

Worse revelations were yet to come. When the airport opened for business, it turned out that the right to sell flight insurance at the airport had been awarded exclusively to a single company, Airport Sales Corp., whose corporate parent had retained Tom Keane for the previous eight years. Another company, Tele-Trip, came forward to reveal that it had substantially underbid Airport Sales — proposing to charge $3.75 rather than $5 per $150,000 in passenger insurance. When the company submitted its bid to Daley's aviation commissioner, it said, the bid was ignored. It also came out that another company that had hired Keane, New York–based Malan Construction, had been awarded $35 million in work at O'Hare. Among the projects given to Malan was a $5.4 million airplane hangar, a decision reportedly made over the protests of the city's public works commissioner and the airport architects. In the 1963 mayoral election, Republican Benjamin Adamowski would charge that Daley personally waived almost $1 million in penalties against Malan for failing to complete parts of the airport on time. The airport was being run, Adamowski charged, as "a private concession for Tom Keane."[40]

*   *   *

On December 11, 1958, more than one thousand of the Cook County Democratic loyalists gathered in the Morrison Hotel for a luncheon to launch Daley's reelection campaign. It was a classic machine affair. A live orchestra played "When Irish Eyes Are Smiling" and other standards. The speaker's table was festooned with a large banner proclaiming the Daley motto, "Good Government Is Good Politics," and blown-up photographs showed the major civic projects begun during Daley's first term. Speakers waited patiently for their turn to step up to the podium and shower praise on the mayor. The city clerk and the city treasurer were particularly enthusiastic: just moments before the luncheon started Daley, in his capacity as machine boss, had notified them that they had been reslated for office. When it was Daley's turn to address the crowd, he ticked off a long list of achievements from his first term: increasing the number of police and firemen; doubling the number of three-wheel police motorcycles; quadrupling the number of street cleaners; and installing new lights on 75 percent of the city's streets, part of his campaign to make Chicago "the best lighted major city in the nation." It was dry stuff, but Daley was preaching to the converted — and, in many cases, to the city-employed. The machine faithful burst into sustained applause as Daley proclaimed, "I am grateful for your confidence."[41]

The official Republican party line was that there was a chance Daley could be defeated for reelection. "I can think of four or five good candidates," Governor Stratton said. "Whether they will run is another matter." The truth was, Daley had strong support that crossed party lines. He began, of course, with a solid Democratic base in the machine, and organized labor was firmly in his camp. William Lee, president of the Chicago Federation of Labor, announced an hour after Daley's kickoff lunch that the mayor had the CFL's endorsement — even though the Republicans had not yet settled on a candidate. The newspaper editorial pages that had been wary of Daley four years earlier were now much more warmly inclined. The *Chicago Sun-Times* — owned by Marshall Field and Company, which had a strong interest in Loop redevelopment — led the cheerleading. "In the three and a half years that he has been in the City Hall, Dick Daley has been one of the best mayors in

Chicago's history," the paper declared on the day Daley announced for reelection. "Coming from us, that is quite a compliment, for we opposed him in the 1955 Democratic mayoral election."[42]

Although Daley was riding high at home, he was about to suffer an embarrassing setback at the state level. His longtime downstate Democratic antagonist, Paul Powell, was running for Speaker, now that the Democrats had retaken control of the Illinois House. Word spread that Daley was traveling to Springfield to make a personal appeal for his own candidate for Speaker, a Chicagoan who had the backing of Cook County's fifty-four House members. Normally, that would have been enough to give Daley's candidate the speakership, but Powell cut a deal with the House Republicans. The combined votes of Republicans and downstate Democrats were enough to elect Powell. Stung by the defeat, Daley tried to retaliate by taking away Powell's power to appoint House committees. Daley's scheme, which would have created a Cook County–dominated Committee on Committees, was soundly defeated. It was such a naked power grab, and so divorced of principle, that even thirteen Cook County Democrats mustered the courage to break with Daley on this vote. Daley's loss was a reminder of just how quickly his powers dissipated outside the Chicago city limits. He was at times able to get his way at the state level, as his tax deal with Governor Stratton in 1955 demonstrated. But without the advantage of the machine's near-monolithic control of the political process, as he enjoyed in Chicago, Daley had to use more subtle maneuvering than he did in his blunt assault on Powell.[43]

The Republicans eventually drafted Timothy Sheehan, the son of a Republican precinct captain on the Near West Side, to run against Daley. Sheehan took the obvious route in his campaign, trying to paint Daley as the leader of a corrupt and power-hungry political machine. Making the most of Daley's failed attempt to put his own candidate in as House Speaker, Sheehan charged that Daley was "angry because he was thwarted in his evident wish to run the Illinois Legislature as he runs the Chicago City Council." Sheehan also asserted that vice and drugs were thriving on the South Side because they operated under the protection of Daley and the machine. "There seems to be a positive correlation and connection between those areas which have suffered a breakdown of law and order and Democratic Party success," Sheehan said. Sheehan even attempted to make public housing an issue, charging that Daley's construction plans would result in "skyscraper slums." However valid the criticism, it was not an attack that would win Sheehan many votes. The constituencies he needed to reach — white ethnics, business leaders, and wealthy people — did not oppose building public housing as skyscraper slums. And most black voters, who might have been more inclined to agree with the objection, were too deeply tied to the Democratic Party and the machine to consider backing the Republican Sheehan.[44]

The main difference between Daley's 1959 campaign and his first run, four years earlier, was his newfound support in the business community. Chicago's business leaders had a long history of opposing the Democratic machine. It was, in part, simple political partisanship. Leading businessmen in Chicago, as in most of the country, were heavily Republican. Their interest in low taxes also put them at odds with the machine, which thrived on padding payrolls and handing out sweetheart contracts. And there were social and ethnic factors at work. Chicago's business elite was overwhelmingly comprised of wealthy WASPS from the suburbs, who saw themselves as having little in common with the machine's working-class Catholics, Jews, poor blacks, and recent immigrants. Given the choice, Daley and Tom Keane were not the sort of people most of them would want to run their city.

But in his first term in office, Daley had skillfully won the Republican business establishment over to his side. The most important factor was his vigorous promotion of downtown interests. Daley's 1958 redevelopment plan, which had been all but drafted by the Central Area Committee, made clear to downtown businessmen that the Loop was his highest priority. The business community also appreciated his other improvements: his success in getting O'Hare built, his promotion of highways and parking lots, and his perpetual drive to clean up the commercial district. Daley had also endeared himself to businessmen with his willingness to extend favors and bend rules. "Daley has made it easier to do business in Chicago than almost anywhere else in the country," one national commentator noted. "In the Windy City a favored entrepreneur who makes the right connection with a higher-up in the machine — say an Alderman Keane — finds little difficulty in getting permits, zoning changes, favorable tax decisions from the assessor's office, and bank financing." But Daley's appeal to Chicago's corporate titans was more than just the sum of these pragmatic considerations. He flattered the city's business leaders by soliciting their advice on important issues facing the city, and by appointing them to countless Clean-Up Chicago commissions and committees to welcome visiting dignitaries. And although much of the city's business elite was uncomfortable with Daley's humble origins, many of these upper-class WASP businessmen got a perverse thrill from their relationships with the rough-hewn mayor. Continental Bank president John Perkins recalled once standing on a receiving line with Daley to meet the cardinal. "I said, 'Nice to see you,'" Perkins recalls, "and he whispered, 'Your Excellency.'" To some of these Evanston and Winnetka suburban family men, Daley was a romantic figure. "The man really knows how to use a good sock in the jaw," white-shoe advertising executive Fairfax Cone once said admiringly of Daley. "As these men endorse the machine," *Commonweal* magazine once observed, "they also indulge their own machismo."[45]

The degree of Daley's success with the business establishment became clear when he announced for reelection. On February 12, a bipartisan group of businessmen and labor bosses held a joint press conference at the Palmer House to endorse him and laud not only his "progressive program, but also his major accomplishment in making Chicago a better place in which to live and work." The presence of Daley's old labor cronies was to be expected, but the turnout from the ranks of the city's old-line business leaders was impressive. Among the cochairmen of the committee were William Patterson, president of United Air Lines and a friend from the O'Hare negotiations; Clair Roddewig, president of the Association of Western Railways and a prime mover behind the Central Area Committee; and Fairfax Cone, chairman of the executive committee of the advertising firm Foote, Cone & Belding. Sheehan, who should have been able to count on strong support from the business establishment, ended up with almost none. The defection of the business community was particularly obvious in the area of fund-raising. Sheehan was able to raise little more than the $130,000, making his the most underfunded mayoral campaign since the Great Depression.[46]

In his public appearances, Daley enumerated the long list of civic improvements he had brought to Chicago during his first term. Outside of the spotlight, however, he spent most of his time in quiet meetings with Democratic Party operatives designed to ensure a strong turnout of machine voters. He made a personal appeal to all fifty Democratic ward committeemen at the Morrison Hotel, starting on January 28 with a meeting for wards 1 through 25. He also presided over the traditional preelection luncheons for precinct captains in the Morrison Hotel. Daley was "the best mayor Chicago ever had," Senator Douglas told the party workers at one luncheon.[47] Tom Keane implored the crowd to work to elect good machine aldermen rather than "carping critics." At another precinct captain luncheon, Keane told the crowd that it would be a "sad affair" if Daley got only a normal-sized victory on April 7. "It lies in the hands of the Democratic workers to bring about the victory we deserve — the greatest ever seen in this area." On that occasion, Dan Ryan was on hand to play bad cop to Keane's good cop. Precincts that had brought in only fifty or seventy-five votes in the virtually uncontested February 24 primary elections had not been punished, he said, but those that fell short this time might not be so lucky. The machine held its traditional torchlight parade through Bridgeport on March 9, about a month before the election, ending with a rally at the Lithuanian Auditorium. Of the thousand people in the audience, the master of ceremonies — Daley's park commissioner — introduced more than one hundred by name, including Jake Arvey and Dan Ryan. Daley did much of his campaigning in the city's fifty Democratic ward offices. On March 16, he paid visits to the 40th, 45th, and 49th wards on the North Side, talking to ward heelers and listening to neighborhood problems. Ward organization functionaries greeted Daley, who got his own start ringing doorbells in the 11th Ward, with the special warmth they reserved for one of their own. At a dinner of the North Side, lakefront 44th Ward, at the Belmont Hotel, 330 Democratic party operatives serenaded Daley with a little song of their own composition. To the tune of "The Sidewalks of New York," played on a handy piano, they sang: "Here's to Mayor Daley / He's so tried and true / That's what everyone will say / Next Tuesday, too / You're the greatest leader in the things you do / To a man, the 44th is all for you."[48]

In the great tradition of Anton Cermak's "house for all peoples," Daley also made the rounds of the city's many ethnic organizations. He was an honored guest at a dinner for 2,000 hosted by the Italian American Committee at the Sherman Hotel. In a gesture Cermak would have appreciated, the band played "McNamara's Band" when Daley arrived, and "O Sole Mio" as he left. He was departing, as it happened, for a dinner being given by a Greek Democratic organization. Daley, of course, needed no help in winning over Chicago's large Irish community. The Saint Patrick's Day parade on March 17 functioned as another Daley campaign event. Holding a blackthorn cane and sporting a green fedora, Daley led fifty thousand marchers down State Street. The parade included thirty bands, sixty-eight marching groups, floats with leprechauns and Saint Patrick's Day queens, and a healthy outpouring of Daley campaign posters. When the parade ended, Daley attended an Irish Fellowship Club dinner for 1,200 at the Palmer House.[49]

Sheehan could make little headway against this Daley juggernaut. Out on the campaign trail, he tried gamely to convince the voters that Daley's administration was corrupt. At an appearance before the 49th Ward Republican organization, Sheehan charged that Daley and the machine were protecting the South Side policy wheels. To back up his accusations, Sheehan produced tickets from eight different policy wheels that one of his campaign workers had purchased in a single day. "Mayor Daley and Police Commissioner Timothy O'Connor, with 10,600 policemen, are unable to uncover even one policy wheel," he said. "The reason is that the gambling interests are helping to keep the Democratic city administration in power." Sheehan also attacked Daley in an address to the Business and Professional Women's Club for leading a "ruthless" assault on Kennelly's civil service system. "We in the practical end of politics can cite many instances in the past two elections where civil service employees have been out working actively, violating the spirit and law of the civil service system," he said. Sheehan's charges of bossism and corruption were, of course, entirely on the mark. It is one of the great ironies of Daley's career that in this election, and in several others, he managed to enlist strong support from reform Democrats. Stevenson and Douglas played an important role in Daley's outreach to anti-machine Democrats: they had their own political reasons for keeping on good terms with the machine, and many of their supporters followed them into the Daley camp. Daley benefited from the fact that the reform wing of the Democratic Party was comprised of liberal Democrats, who would sooner vote for him than for a Republican like Sheehan. Daley also did a good job of mouthing reform campaign rhetoric to anti-machine audiences, just as he sounded like a friend of the black community when speaking to black audiences. As in his 1955 campaign, a "Volunteers for Daley" committee formed to raise money and generate support for Daley among reform Democrats. At a dinner for 1,000 at the Sherman Hotel on April 2, Daley told the audience that he had been wrongly accused of being a "machine politician" when he ran four years earlier. "I was tried, I was convicted, and I was sentenced, without a chance to say what I had done."[50]

By the time election day came around, there was little suspense about how things would turn out. In the end, Daley won an overwhelming victory, 778,612 to 311,940, carrying every ward except the Far Northwest Side 41st, Sheehan's home ward. Daley's 71 percent of the vote was a near record, falling just short of the 76 percent that Mayor Kelly won in his 1935 landslide. Sheehan blamed his loss on "the power of an entrenched machine." In his victory statement, Daley thanked the voters and promised that "As mayor of Chicago, I shall embrace charity, love, mercy, and walk humbly with my God."[51]

Two for You, Three for Me

The wave of goodwill that swept Daley into his second term as mayor did not last long. State's attorney Benjamin Adamowski, ever on the lookout for scandals that could be traced to Daley and the machine, found a good one a month after the election. On May 7, he asked a grand jury to hand up indictments in connection with a $500,000-a-year ticket-fixing scandal in Chicago Traffic Court. That the court was fixing tickets was the worst-kept secret in Chicago, but Adamowski's investigation had the potential to tie the practice directly to the Democratic machine. Daley's response to Adamowski's legal assault was to direct his commissioner of investigation, Irwin Cohen, to look into the charges. Cohen was an odd creation. Shortly after taking office, Daley had arranged for one of his allies on the City Council to introduce an ordinance giving the mayor authority for investigating all allegations of wrongdoing. Daley's carefully conceived plan called for an investigator who would serve at the pleasure of the mayor, and who was prohibited from revealing any information he collected to anyone but the mayor. Before taking the job, Cohen had distinguished himself by heading up a City Council crime committee that failed to find any link between criminal activity in the city and politics. The commissioner of investigation's office allowed Daley to take control of impending scandals, pushing other official bodies and the press to the side. As Cohen noted when he was appointed, his agency had been "set up exclusively for the benefit of the mayor." But Daley's critics also understood exactly what

Cohen's office was up to. One Republican had objected a year earlier when Daley shunted another potentially embarrassing case from the City Council to his commissioner of investigation. "One of the chief functions of a legislative body is investigation of charges against public employees," he complained. "This is being by-passed in favor of a secret investigation that will be revealed only to the mayor." Cohen's probe of the Traffic Court would allow Daley to say he was taking the charges seriously, with no risk that anything would come from it.[1]

Adamowski would be far more difficult to control. Daley publicly charged that his old nemesis was on a "fishing expedition," but the trouble was, the fishing was getting good. Three deputy clerks of the court and one bailiff were soon arrested on corruption charges, and the scandal was reaching ever closer to the Democratic machine. The fact was, it would be hard to have a scandal in Traffic Court without involving the machine since it had hundreds of Democratic patronage workers on its payroll. But Adamowski's real target was Daley himself, and he was quick to lay the blame for the scandal at the steps of City Hall. If the mayor had required his comptroller to conduct the required audits of Traffic Court records, Adamowski charged, the misconduct would have been caught. Daley "better start complying with the law," Adamowski declared, "or he may turn out to be the biggest fish we're angling for."[2]

It is difficult to believe that Daley did not know firsthand that patronage workers in Traffic Court were fixing tickets. It had been a thoroughly ingrained practice of the Democratic machine for years. Daley's old patron Jake Arvey once admitted that when he was an alderman "to fix a parking ticket . . . was the pattern." And many Chicagoans had more recent stories of ticket fixing, including one newspaper reporter who said that when he started out there was someone on staff who routinely fixed all of the reporters' traffic tickets. Daley had only one response when the machine's corruption was dragged out into the open in a way that was too credible to ignore. He ostentatiously embraced reform, and turned to men with unassailable reputations to vouch for his integrity. On May 28, with Adamowski still working to expand his investigation, Daley announced that he had hired the directors of Northwestern University's Transportation Center and its Traffic Institute to investigate ticketing procedures in Traffic Court and to recommend reforms. Their inquiry would not concern itself with such mundane matters as which particular Traffic Court employees might have violated the law. It would be not an "investigation of people, but an investigation of a system."[3]

It was a welcome relief from scandal when the queen of England showed up. Daley relished any opportunity to entertain dignitaries, but when Queen Elizabeth II and her husband, Prince Philip, accepted his invitation to join President Eisenhower for the opening of the Saint Lawrence Seaway on June 29, 1959, Daley realized it would be a great moment in Chicago history. It would be the first time a reigning British monarch had ever visited Chicago, and Daley took great pains to choreograph every detail of the visit. On the appointed day, more than a million people lined the shores of Lake Michigan to greet the queen and prince as they arrived on the royal yacht *Britannia,* accompanied by seven warships and five hundred smaller vessels, including two Chinese junks. Daley presented the queen with a box of recordings by the Chicago Symphony Orchestra and the prince with two polo mallets, and he hosted a lavish dinner for the royal couple, complete with gold tablecloths, gold service, and 50,000 roses. In remarks that were perhaps more informal than his royal company was accustomed to, Daley invited them to "come again and bring the children." The queen's visit created a media frenzy that more than met Daley's expectations. The *Sun-Times* alone put the story on its front page, and promised additional stories and pictures on pages 3, 4, 5, 6, 7, 8, 9, 10, 11, 12, 13, 14, 15, 16, 18, 19, 22, 24, and 25, prompting *Time* magazine to snipe that the paper had single-handedly confirmed Chicago's reputation as the Windy City. The queen's visit was one of the highlights of Daley's years in office; his associates say it was an important turning point for him in coming to appreciate the stature that came with his office. Daley might have started out as a precinct captain knocking on doors in the 11th Ward, and he might have still lived in a simple bungalow in Bridgeport. But he had invited the queen of England to come to Chicago as his guest, and she had come.[4]

In another sign that he was moving up in the world, Daley was elevated from vice president to president of the U.S. Conference of Mayors in July. It ushered in an era in which Daley would be seen as one of the nation's leading voices on urban affairs. At home in Chicago, Daley continued to push for downtown redevelopment. In August, he held a press conference at City Hall to unveil plans for a $20 million Hartford Fire Insurance Company building. Daley praised the company for its decision to build in the city, and hailed the building as "another gem for the crown of our new Wacker Drive," a street that had been steadily upgrading since its el was torn down in 1948. Daley had also put together another bond issue for urban development to be voted on in the November election. This time, he was asking the voters to approve a total of $66 million in new borrowing, including a $25 million bond for more streetlights, $15 million for sewer improvements, $15 million for bridges, grade separations, and viaducts, and several smaller bonds. The entire package of bonds was approved by the voters, and after the election Daley said he had directed city officials to proceed "full speed ahead" in spending the money. The easy approval of new construction money only whetted Daley's appetite for more. In a speech to the Better Business Bureau's annual meeting days after the bonds passed, he unveiled plans for an additional $751 million in capital improvement spending over the next five years. The money would be used, he said, to build more expressways, bridges, lighting, government buildings, and downtown parking.[5]

The bad news for Daley was that the city employee scandals were growing. His attempt to pass the Traffic Court scandal off to city investigator Cohen did not end the matter. Adamowski was able to score political points by loudly attacking the "Cohen Rug Company" — where, Adamowski said, Daley sent things to be swept under the rug. The *Chicago Tribune* had also begun to uncover some unsavory employees on the city payroll. An asphalt foreman in the Department of Streets and Sanitation was revealed to be on probation for looting cars in the Midway Airport parking lot. A paving supervisor was found to be working a full eight-hour shift as a trucking company supervisor. It also turned out that he was a juice man for the syndicate who had been arrested twelve times for robbery; on one occasion he had been shot by police while resisting arrest. Another employee collected gambling money in the Loop for the syndicate. It looked as if the syndicate, which had helped put Daley in office, was using its share of patronage positions to keep some of its own staff on the city payroll. Daley lashed out at the newspapers that were making what he considered to be baseless charges. "If we take the attitude that because a man made a mistake 25 or 30 years ago, that he shouldn't be employed, then where are we going?" he said. Daley then added, "If I took that attitude then I wouldn't be in government!" He never elaborated on what lurked in his past that would have made him ineligible for government service.[6]

In December, Governor Stratton announced his intention to run for a third term in 1960. It was generally agreed that a strong Democrat would have a good chance of defeating him. Stratton had barely won reelection in 1956, despite a Republican landslide that year. And 1960 was already looking like a Democratic year — in the 1958 midterm elections, the Democrats had won twelve Senate seats from the Republicans, and forty-eight House seats. Daley's name began to circulate as a possible gubernatorial candidate. As usual, he kept his own counsel, and always dodged the question when he was asked if he was considering running. "What do you think?" he said to one reporter who asked him directly. When he was told that he would have a tough race against Stratton, Daley responded, "Could be, could be."[7] But if Daley was not saying yes, he also was not making any effort to dampen the speculation. There is no doubt that if Daley had wanted his party's nomination for governor, he could have had it. In the end, though, Daley took himself out of the running, without explaining why. If he had run, it would have been a hard-fought race, and Daley's close association with Chicago and the Democratic machine would have hurt him with voters in the suburbs and downstate. The risk-averse Daley might simply have been unwilling to give up the powerful position to which he had just been reelected for the mere chance of becoming governor. Daniel Rostenkowski believes that Daley enjoyed being considered for governor, but that he was not interested in moving beyond his twin posts of mayor and machine boss. Daley's son William says his father's resistance was due to his commitment to running ethnically balanced tickets — and his concern about John F. Kennedy's presidential candidacy. William Daley says his father talked it over with Kennedy. "Kennedy said,

'Why don't you run for governor?'" William Daley says. "He said, 'If we have two Catholics — one running for president and one for governor — only one is going to win, and it's not going to be you.'"[8]

Daley began the presidential campaign year by declaring on January 3, 1960, that John F. Kennedy was "highly qualified to lead our nation." Even though he had hastened to add that there were also "other highly qualified Democrat[s]," Daley's words were strong encouragement to Kennedy, who had just announced his intention to run.[9] Daley had long-standing ties to the Kennedy family. Joseph Kennedy, the candidate's father, owned Merchandise Mart, the massive retailing space on the north bank of the Chicago River, and had been cultivating Daley for years. "Joe Kennedy first approached him in the forties or thirties when he was in the legislature," says William Daley. And Kennedy's brother-in-law Sargent Shriver was chairman of the Chicago Board of Education. Daley was probably genuinely excited by the possibility that a fellow Irish-Catholic might be elected president of the United States — the ultimate rebuke to generations of WASPs who had looked down on and mistreated his long-suffering people. But like most members of the machine, Daley never let idealism interfere with the pragmatic concern of holding on to power. "A lot of these guys, their political horizons extend all the way to end of the ward," a Chicago reformer once said, in describing the thinking of men like Daley. "They don't care what's going on in the state or the country. They don't care whether a bill passes or fails. They want the jobs. They want to run their wards. They don't care who is president or senator. How many jobs has a senator got?" What Daley probably liked best about Kennedy was that with his youth and charm, and his ethnic and religious bond to many Cook County voters, he looked like the candidate with the best chance of sweeping the entire machine slate into office with him.[10]

Now that he had taken himself out of the running, Daley needed a candidate for governor. County judge Otto Kerner had made an impression two years earlier, when he had run strongly, and even carried the Cook County suburbs. Equally important, Kerner was that rare breed, a Protestant with strong ties to the Chicago machine. If Kennedy were at the top of the ticket, Kerner would provide the ethnic balance necessary to hold on to the Protestant vote. When the slate-making committee convened at the Morrison Hotel in early January, Kerner was officially slated for governor. For clerk of the Municipal Court, Daley tapped Joseph McDonough, son of his old 11th Ward patron. It was an obscure position, but one that was vitally important to the machine because of the number of patronage positions it controlled. Daley could trust McDonough. The other critical race was state's attorney. Daley's old nemesis, Benjamin Adamowski, had been the top Cook County prosecutor for the past four years, and he had been using the position as a battering ram against Daley and the machine. If he was reelected, it would mean four more years of allegations and investigations — and the odds were good that he would use the office as a platform to run for mayor against Daley in 1963. It is an indication of just how seriously Daley took the race that he reached outside the ranks of the machine to select a candidate of unimpeachable qualifications and reputation. Daniel Ward, dean of DePaul University Law School, was this year's Paul Douglas or Adlai Stevenson — the machine candidate designed to make voters forget what they didn't like about the machine. Adamowski saw just what Daley was up to in selecting Ward, and at every opportunity he told voters that his real opponent was not Ward, but Daley and the machine. In the course of the campaign, he actually challenged Daley — not Ward — to debate him. "Daley should quit sitting back being the Edgar Bergen of the Democratic organization, with his Charley McCarthys out there in front making the statements coming out of his mouth," Adamowski said.[11]

There is no good time for a mayor to be hit with a massive police scandal, but the timing of the Summerdale scandal was particularly unfortunate. Just as Daley was gearing up for a big election year, Chicagoans learned that their policemen were engaged in the ultimate betrayal of their positions. Corruption in the Chicago police department was certainly nothing new. One history of the Chicago police starts out by noting that "scandal, disgrace, and rampant political corruption characterized the administration of the Chicago Police Department for 100 years." In fact, most Chicagoans looked on police corruption as a bit of odd local color. As columnist Mike Royko once observed, "The Chicago River is polluted, the factories belch smoke, the Cubs are the North Side team, the Sox are the South Side team, George Halas owns the Bears, and the cops are crooked — so what else is new?" Chicagoans learned before they were old enough to drive that the way to beat a speeding ticket was to wrap their driver's license in a five- or a ten-dollar bill when they handed it to the patrolman. Comedian Mort Sahl once observed that the question of whether it was to be five dollars or ten made Chicago's highways the last outpost of collective bargaining in America. Nor was it any great secret that the syndicate, policy wheel operators, drug dealers, and pimps had all worked out their accommodations with the police department — often with Democratic ward committeemen and precinct captains acting as intermediaries. Daley knew these facts of life in Chicago better than most: many of his Bridgeport neighbors, and members of both his family and Sis's, were on the police force. Daley likely shared the prevailing view in Bridgeport that a modest level of payoffs was part of what Chicago police recruits bargained for when they signed on, and that many policemen needed the money to support large families. In fact, Daley had been elected in large part because of his willingness to tolerate flawed law enforcement. Dawson and the black submachine had pushed Mayor Kennelly out of City Hall for ignoring the Chicago tradition of keeping the heat off politically protected policy wheels and illegal jitney cabs.[12]

Even to Chicagoans raised on police corruption, the news that broke in January 1960 came as a shock. Richard Morrison, a twenty-three-year-old burglar in police custody and awaiting trial, revealed that he had been helped in his criminal exploits by twelve officers from the Summerdale police district on the city's North Side. Morrison, whom the newspapers quickly dubbed the "babbling burglar," delivered up a seventy-seven-page confession in which he recounted how for a period of almost two years his police accomplices had helped him steal from local shops, using squad cars to take the goods to be fenced. Incredible charges, but they seemed to be confirmed when investigators raided the policemen's homes and found four truckloads of stolen merchandise. Daley had been on vacation in Florida when the scandal broke, but he came back early to pronounce it "the most shocking and disgraceful incident in the history of the Chicago Police Department." The newspapers eagerly pointed out that crime statistics from the Summerdale district indicated that burglaries in the area where the police burglary ring operated were up 48 percent in the first nine months of the year. Daley acted quickly to contain the political damage. He met with police commissioner O'Connor, who announced that he was taking personal charge of the investigation. O'Connor began questioning 130 policemen from the Summerdale district, and Daley assured the public that "every police officer — every other person who is in any way involved in these crimes and betrayal of the public trust — will be investigated and brought before the civil service board and prosecuted in the courts if the facts so warrant."[13]

The real danger posed by the Summerdale scandal was not the burglary ring itself, though that was plenty embarrassing. It was that the investigation threatened to open the lid on how policing and politics had mixed during Daley's five years as mayor. Reports of other police malfeasance quickly surfaced. Another police robbery ring was uncovered in the North Damen Avenue station. And in another case that received lavish press attention, two burglars in Joliet Prison for stealing $1 million in furs and jewels said that they had bribed policemen with payments of up to $1,000 in an attempt to beat the charges. They reported that they gave one $1,000 bribe to a detective who helped disguise the suspect's hairdo and gave him horn-rimmed glasses so a witness would not recognize him at a police lineup. Most damaging of all were allegations that Daley had personally imposed machine politics on the police department. Jack Muller, an outspoken detective who prided himself on his political independence, charged that Daley was "completely responsible for the scandal which is bringing shame to Chicago's police department." The truth was, he said, that O'Connor was "a commissioner in name only." Daley promoted men up the police hierarchy whom O'Connor did not want elevated, Muller said, and prevented O'Connor from disciplining officers who had "political clout." Muller also invoked Daley's dismantling of the Scotland Yard division after his election. Sheriff Joseph Lohman, a onetime Daley protégé, also came forward to accuse Daley and the machine of intruding themselves on his office. Lohman asserted that Daley had asked him to appoint a ward committeeman from the 18th Ward as a chief deputy in the sheriff's office. Lohman had refused to go along. "This man was working in the Department of Sewers," he said, and "he was not qualified to do police work." Lohman warned that the

Chicago Police Department had to be "freed from clout and the captains' aunties," Chicago slang for a politician who protects a policeman. The Republicans lost no time in putting the scandal to partisan advantage. Governor Stratton held a press conference in his Chicago office, across the street from City Hall, and threatened to step in and take over the Chicago Police Department unless Daley "stops laughing and cleans up the mess himself— quickly." To underscore the Republican theme that the machine and city government were overly intertwined, Stratton demanded that Daley step down as party chairman to devote himself more fully to addressing the police crisis.[14]

The Summerdale charges were dangerous because they played into people's worst fears about Daley. When he first ran for mayor, his critics had attacked him as the candidate of the "hoodlum element," and it now appeared that they were right. The scandal also threatened to make a mockery of Daley's frequently repeated claims that he had improved city services. It would not matter how many garbage cans or streetlights he added if most Chicagoans believed that their local police were in league with criminals. The more he became the focus of the scandal, the more irate Daley became. At a press conference, he turned on a photographer who was trying to take his picture. "Let's not have this sort of thing while I'm talking," he shouted. "I'll not have the mayor's office turned into a circus or hippodrome." In a rant directed at the entire City Hall press corps, Daley yelled, "There are even crooked reporters, and I can spit on some of them right here!"[15]

One reason Daley was so tense was that Adamowski appeared to have gained the upper hand in the scandal. Daley had tried to put the matter in Irwin Cohen's hands, but Adamowski responded that he would charge both Daley and Cohen with obstruction of justice if Cohen didn't "stop sticking his nose into this investigation." Daley realized it was time for more dramatic action. As the then police commissioner, Tim O'Connor, put it, "Somebody has to be the sucker and it could be me." In fact, Daley was soon announcing at a press conference that O'Connor had resigned because of gall bladder problems. And Daley was careful to lay the blame for the troubles at O'Connor's feet. "Tim was always telling me how he went home at night and watched TV instead of running around getting into trouble," Daley said. "I should have asked him why he wasn't running around checking on his policemen at night instead of sitting home watching TV." Daley appointed an acting commissioner, and a search committee to look for a permanent replacement. Once again, he employed his favorite damage-control tactic: drafting someone of unquestioned integrity, ideally an academic, to make it go away. Daley's choice to head up his search committee was Orlando W. Wilson, dean of the criminology school at the University of California, and author of *Police Administration,* a leading criminology textbook. Daley also named his old crony William McFetridge, vice president of the Chicago Federation of Labor, to the committee to keep an eye on Wilson.[16]

The Wilson committee met in executive session for twenty-eight days at the University Club. It considered ninety candidates for commissioner, and interviewed fifty-three. It was an indication of just how bad things were in the department that when the committee asked the twenty-four current members that it interviewed what percentage of Chicago police they believed were dishonest, the estimates ran well over 50 percent. While the committee went about its work, Daley reported that he was getting a "tremendous amount" of mail, and that the letters were running 6–1 in his favor. But when reporters asked to see them, press secretary Earl Bush refused, saying they were "letters to the mayor and aren't meant for publication." On February 22, the committee settled on its choice for Chicago's next police commissioner. "We suddenly realized on Sunday night that the best qualified man for the job was the chairman of our committee," said Franklin Kreml, vice chairman of the committee. The idea had been McFetridge's, and it was clear he was acting for Daley.[17]

Wilson was a brilliant choice. A native of Veblen, South Dakota, he was described by the *New York Times* in an admiring profile as "lean, hard-boiled, soft-talking [and] scholarly-appearing." Wilson had a distinguished academic record, but he had also served as a patrolman on the Berkeley police force, and as police chief of Wichita, Kansas, where the mayor had called him "too damned efficient." As an outsider to Chicago, he could not easily be attacked as a machine hack or a defender of the status quo. Governor Stratton took a break from his criticism of Daley long enough to declare that Wilson "has a good reputation and should be given an opportunity to do a good job." Adamowski was more skeptical. He told a luncheon of Republican women that "Daley is holding this respected man up as a facade while they try to sweep the whole mess under the rug." If the department were ever run honestly, he charged, it would mean the "virtual destruction of the Democratic political machine." Adamowski tried unsuccessfully to block Wilson's appointment on procedural grounds. The thin-skinned Daley was becoming testy under the constant criticism. In Springfield to oppose a bill to reform the Chicago Police Department, Daley lashed out at a Republican legislator from Aurora, Illinois, who asked if there was any corruption in the department that had not yet come to light. "I assume if you look closely enough you'll find dishonest policemen in Aurora," Daley retorted. Then, drawing on his own service in the Illinois legislature, he added acerbically, "I can't attest to the honesty in this room."[18]

Before the Summerdale scandal was over, eight Chicago policemen were sent to jail. Hundreds more officers submitted to lie-detector tests, and those who refused were suspended. When he arrived on the scene, Wilson shook up the Chicago Police Department staff, and soon the Summerdale scandal receded from the headlines. Unfortunately for Daley, it was quickly replaced by a new scandal over "loafing" city workers. The city was forced to suspend forty-four employees from the Bureau of Electricity for putting in for bogus overtime work. Making matters worse, the fraudulent overtime reports were all prepared by a timekeeper with syndicate ties, who had once run a large West Side betting parlor. The newspapers had caught the man weeks earlier running his grocery and meat market when he was supposed to be installing traffic lights near Midway Airport. The newspapers were also reporting that city asphalt crews routinely idled on the job sites or at nearby taverns for the last hour or two of their shifts, claiming they could not get asphalt delivered late in the day. The articles were accompanied by photographs of sewer gangs idling and napping at their work sites. Reporters investigating one foreman found that on three separate workdays he was hanging out in a North Side tavern shooting pool and drinking beer when he was supposed to be supervising a fifteen-man Water Department gang. They also discovered that he was operating a $3 million oil and gas business on city time. Daley responded that the foreman in question was a good worker, and that every time the city checked up on him he had been on the job. The complaints against him came from his competitors in the oil business, Daley insisted. In a concession to the criticism, though, Daley said that in the future the sewer foreman would not be permitted to use a city worker as a chauffeur for his air-conditioned Cadillac.[19]

With the start of the 1960 Democratic National Convention drawing near, Daley was still formally uncommitted in the presidential race. When former president Harry Truman passed through Chicago on April 6, he and Daley met for a friendly breakfast at the Blackstone Hotel and talked politics. Both men agreed that the recent Wisconsin primary results looked good for the Democrats since Nixon, running unopposed, had polled fewer votes than either Kennedy or Humphrey. Daley also highlighted the fact that Kennedy's religion had proved to be a nonissue, despite predictions that the nation was not yet ready to elect a Catholic president. "The people were voting for the man," Daley said. Although Daley seemed to be in the Kennedy camp, there were still other candidates to be reckoned with. The word was out that Illinois native son Adlai Stevenson was contemplating a third run for the presidency. There would be pressure on Daley to stick with his longtime ally, although the consensus among Chicago politicians was that if Stevenson ran again he would lose and pull the machine ticket down with him. At the same time, downstate Democrats were urging Daley to support Missouri senator Stuart Symington. Symington was popular in the agricultural regions of southern Illinois that bordered on his home state, but it seemed unlikely that he would help the Democratic ticket much in Chicago. At a press conference in Daley's office, a reporter noticed a copy of a book about Symington, entitled *Portrait of a Man with a Mission,* lying on Daley's desk. The reporter picked it up and asked if it had any political significance. Daley just laughed and answered, "Take it with you." On May 11, Daley declared that Kennedy's victory in the West Virginia primary — a heavily Protestant state in which Kennedy's Catholicism had been expected to be an issue — was "another indication that Democratic primary voters had spoken in an emphatic manner." It proved, Daley said, that people "vote for the individual and not for his religion or his geographical qualifications." But Daley continued to stop short of an endorsement. "We'll caucus in California and discuss the qualifications of the various candidates," he said. "That will be the time for a declaration by me — but I repeat, no one can watch the series of primary victories without being impressed."[20]

On July 7, Daley and his family boarded a private car attached to the end of the Sante Fe Chief for the trip to Los Angeles. Their route to California was punctuated by signs along the tracks proclaiming good wishes from various Chicago politicians. "I'll never forget . . . seeing these signs," William Daley recalled. A welcoming party that included county assessor P. J. "Parky" Cullerton, Alderman Vito Marzullo, and Congressman Daniel Rostenkowski was on hand to greet the Daleys at Union Railroad Station Sunday morning, the day before the convention opened, but the Daleys snuck out a side door to attend 9 A.M. Mass at the Old Mission Church. Daley's welcoming party eventually caught up with him at the Hayward Hotel and greeted him with a band playing "Chicago, That Toddlin' Town."[21] The fawning continued when Daley settled in at the hotel. He controlled fifty of Illinois's sixty-nine delegates and he was in a good position to swing most of the remaining downstate votes his way — and he had still not made an endorsement. This made Daley the preeminent kingmaker at the convention, and he was subject to lobbying from all camps.[22]

Stevenson had not formally announced, but he made it clear he would be willing to run again. His supporters were hoping they could stop Kennedy from winning on the first ballot, and then they would try to generate a Stevenson draft from the convention floor. Eleanor Roosevelt and Carl Sandburg both made personal appeals to Daley for their friend Stevenson. When Mrs. Roosevelt called to ask for a meeting, Daley traveled to Pasadena, some twenty miles away, to hear her out. But when she was done, Daley told her he could not back Stevenson. Daley's explanation was that the previous spring he had visited Stevenson at his Libertyville, Illinois, home to sound him out about running for president again. Daley said he told Stevenson that if he planned to, he should enter the primaries to show that he still had support, but that Stevenson responded that he had no plans to run. Now, Daley said, he and other onetime supporters had already made other commitments. In fact, Daley was already firmly in the Kennedy camp, and he had been busily twisting arms in the Illinois delegation. Daley worked on Jacob Arvey, who had been supporting Symington, by indicating that he might not reslate his old mentor as Democratic national committeeman unless he backed Kennedy. It was not long before Arvey was urging his fellow Illinois delegates to fall in line behind Kennedy and Daley, saying, "Let's give our chairman the authority to be a dominant force at the convention." The Illinois delegation caucused in secret, and Daley emerged to announce its vote: 59½ for Kennedy, 6½ for Symington, and 2 for Stevenson.

It was a crushing blow to Stevenson. With so little support from his own home state, he had no prospect of putting together a majority of delegates nationally. When he got word of how Illinois had voted, Stevenson tried to make a personal appeal to Daley to reconsider, but Daley dodged his old political patron's phone calls. Stevenson finally convinced Arvey to act as his intermediary and get Daley to call back. When they spoke, Stevenson drew on their long political friendship, which dated back to 1948, when he gave Daley an important career boost by appointing him state revenue director. Stevenson had, of course, also played a key role in Daley's election as mayor in 1955. Stevenson made a spirited argument on his own behalf, reminding Daley that he had been the first Illinoisan since Abraham Lincoln to run for president, and promising that if he won the nomination he would campaign vigorously against Nixon. But Daley bluntly told Stevenson that his arguments were not getting him anywhere, since he had no support in his home state's delegation. In fact, Daley told his old boss, he had not had any support in the delegation four years earlier, and he, Daley, had had to bring the delegates around. As for the lopsidedness of the vote this time, Daley told Stevenson: "You're lucky to have the two votes you've got."[23]

But days later, it was Daley who was being coolly rebuffed. After Kennedy won the nomination, he invited Daley and a few other key backers to his suite at the Biltmore Hotel to discuss his choice of running mates. Daley was, of course, hoping to persuade Kennedy to select a vice presidential nominee who would boost the machine's statewide slate in Illinois. That made him a Symington supporter, since the Missouri candidate could help the Democratic ticket downstate, precisely the region where Kennedy would be weakest.

Daley was least enthusiastic about Lyndon Johnson, who would do less for the ticket downstate and who, as a white southerner, might turn off some of the machine's black voters. Daley told Kennedy that having Johnson on the ticket would make it harder to carry Illinois. When that failed, Daley brought up how much he had done to help Kennedy secure the nomination. Kennedy, who wanted Johnson because of the help he could give the ticket in Texas and the Deep South, reportedly responded to Daley: "Not you nor anybody else nominated us. We did it ourselves." In the *Chicago Tribune*'s telling of the story, Daley had "smoke coming out of his ears" after the encounter.[24]

When he got back to Chicago, Daley traveled to Springfield to stir up enthusiasm for the ticket among downstate Democrats, and to test the political waters outside the borders of Cook County. Daley learned that Kerner was running strongly downstate, but Kennedy seemed to be in trouble. One downstate Democrat was predicting that Nixon would carry Illinois by 200,000 votes. Daley attended four seminars with congressional and legislative candidates where he instructed them on the importance of good organizational work. As election day approached, the statewide races began to hit a fever pitch. The usually restrained Governor Stratton launched a broadside against Kerner and his supporters in Chicago. "We are up against the slimiest, dirtiest machine in the history of Illinois," Stratton declared. "If my opponent is elected, Dick Daley will dictate his every action and every single piece of legislation." Daley fired back: "The people on two occasions have demonstrated what they think of Daley as mayor. There were 70% voting in favor of my record at the 1959 city election."[25]

The state's attorney race between Adamowski and Ward was also turning ugly. Adamowski continued to dredge up new scandals involving City Hall and the machine — and to pick fights with Daley. He had a grand jury investigating charges that city workers were accepting "gratuities" for helping a trucking company cheat the city and county by short-weighting loads of construction supplies. Daley said the allegations were politically motivated and demanded "in the interest of fair play, in the interest of good government, and in the interest of the good name of Chicago" that Adamowski turn over the names of the city employees to him. Adamowski refused, saying that it was just another attempt by Daley to derail an investigation of machine wrongdoing. When Adamowski was not fighting with Daley, he was taking swings at his actual opponent. One debate between Adamowski and Ward at the West Suburban Bar Association was "less a debate than a match under Marquis of Queensberry Rules," according to one reporter who covered it. "The antagonists refused point-blank to shake hands before they came out swinging. And in the swinging they rid themselves of gloves in favor of the old-fashioned bare-knuckle assault." Even when Adamowski was debating Ward, he continued to focus on the threat to Chicago posed by Daley and the machine. "In Cook County there is an organization that has its tentacles in every office and many businesses with the single exception of the state's attorney's office," he warned. Daley, for his part, told a Ward fund-raiser at the Sherman Hotel that Adamowski was a "sadly inadequate person" who was trying to "soft-pedal and cover up his own failures."[26]

The Kennedy-Nixon race in Illinois was not as bare-knuckled, but it was still attracting considerable attention. With Eisenhower's eight years as president drawing to a close, one era of America was ending and another was dawning. The choice between the young and suave Massachusetts senator and Eisenhower's two-term vice president presented two very different directions for the nation. That Kennedy would be the first Roman Catholic to occupy the White House added to the controversy. In some parts of the country, including large swaths of downstate Illinois, fears that the pope would run the country under Kennedy was generating strong support for Nixon. In other regions, like Cook County, the prospect of a Catholic president was filling voters with excitement and pride. Presidential elections in Illinois generally broke down into a battle between Catholic-black-Jewish-immigrant-Democratic Chicago against Protestant-white-Republican downstate. But this year, Kennedy's Catholicism made the traditional schism more pronounced than ever. Going into the election, straw polls indicated that the outcome was very much in doubt. On Chicago's final registration day about 200,000 new voters added their names to the voting rolls. Combined with 40,000 additional registrations that had been collected in the weeks before, it was the largest number of new registrations in Chicago since 1944. Voter enthusiasm was, Daley declared, the highest it had been since that year, which marked Franklin Delano Roosevelt's last run for the presidency. Much of the enthusiasm was clearly being generated by the presidential race, but the machine's highest priority was the Adamowski-Ward contest. Word from the Morrison Hotel was that nothing — not even electing Kennedy — was as important as taking back the state's attorney's office. "State's Attorney Adamowski is right," the *Daily News* declared. "City Hall is out to get him. Many Democratic precinct captains, under urging from the ward committeemen, are reported writing off Kennedy as far as many voters are concerned if they'll only vote for Adamowski's opponent."[27]

Sargent Shriver had resigned from his position as chairman of the Chicago Board of Education to run his brother-in-law's Illinois campaign. But there was no question that Kennedy's real Illinois campaign chairman was Daley. Daley had definite ideas about how to run a statewide race in Illinois. Kennedy's national staff wanted him to make some early appearances in Chicago, but Daley had Kennedy start out by making an early swing through downstate, where he could try to steal away some Nixon votes. Next, Daley had Kennedy campaign in the Cook County suburbs, also Republican territory, joined by gubernatorial candidate Kerner and Senator Douglas, who was running for reelection. Daley wanted Kennedy to make an appearance in Chicago, but not yet. His plan was to unleash Kennedy on the city in the waning hours, in the tradition of Harry Truman, whose appearance at a rally in Chicago late in the 1948 campaign was credited with helping him capture Illinois and the White House. In the meantime, Daley continued to fire up the machine for the battle of its life. On October 28, he gathered in the faithful for a massive Chicago-style luncheon-for-thousands at the Sherman Hotel. Tables stretched out of the ornate ballroom and into the mezzanine to accommodate a crowd that was said to be the largest in the history of the hotel. Hundreds of others who had been unable to purchase tickets forced their way in, either to bask in the glory of the Cook County Democratic Organization at the height of its powers or simply to make sure that their ward committeeman noted their attendance.[28]

As election day drew near, rumors began to spread through the city that Daley and the machine were preparing to steal the election. The *Chicago Daily News* investigated the city's election operations and found that the stage was set for election fraud. Of the 180 jobs at the Board of Election Commissioners, the paper found, all but four were held by Democrats. Most of these workers, who were responsible for ensuring the integrity of the election process, had been hired on the recommendation of machine politicians, and the paper detailed which sponsors were responsible for particular employees. The *Daily News* also printed a series of articles calling attention to thousands of ineligible names on the Chicago voter rolls, an issue that would take on greater significance after the voting was done. Also before election day, Republicans and nonpartisan civic groups began to question the integrity of the process. Adamowski charged that city workers aligned with the machine were threatening homeowners who put his campaign posters up in their windows. City workers were also tearing his posters down from telephone poles, he charged. Adamowski conceded that there was a city ordinance prohibiting the placing of campaign posters on telephone poles. "But what amazes me," Adamowski said, "is that the city workers with their rakes and shovels tore down only the Republican posters."[29]

On October 27, David Brill, chairman of an organization calling itself the Committee for Honest Elections, asked Daley to meet with him to discuss preventing fraud in the upcoming election. Daley insisted that there was no reason to worry, and charged Brill's organization with acting irresponsibly in making the charges. But Brill said that canvassers from the Committee for Honest Elections had already turned up evidence of potential fraud, and he challenged Daley's description of his organization's efforts. "If calling the election commissioners' attention to registration from vacant lots, barber shops, and vacated buildings is an 'irresponsibility' then that word has lost its usual meaning," he said. Brill got his meeting with Daley the next day. "I'm not here to create acrimony," Brill assured Daley. All he wanted was City Hall's help in purging unqualified voters from the rolls. Daley reacted angrily, as he often did when his interests were threatened, and accused Brill of being politically motivated. "Everyone knows you're a Republican," Daley said. "Why don't you admit it." Daley denied Brill's request for credentials for inspectors from the Committee for Honest Elections to observe polling places on election day.[30]

Kennedy finally made his long-awaited appearance in Chicago on Friday night, November 4, when he was the guest of honor at the machine's torchlight parade. The parade was a remarkable Chicago event, a means of reaching hundreds of thousands of voters in an age when live campaigning had not yet been displaced by television. In addition to whipping up enthusiasm for Democratic candidates among the electorate, the parade fired up the party faithful to work hard in the final days leading up to the election. Every ward organization, elected official, and patronage worker was under intense pressure to generate a large turnout. The night before the parade, ward offices across the city were filled with party workers calling patronage workers and friends of the organization to remind them to show up. The notices sent out by machine leaders left no doubt that participation was mandatory, and attendance would be taken. "You must be present at 4654 Cottage Grove, Democratic Headquarters, at 4:30 P.M. Friday," Alderman Claude Holman wrote to members of the 4th Ward Organization. "I personally will receive you aboard the bus." The parade began at Michigan Avenue and West Madison, and proceeded west toward Chicago Stadium. It was a raucous event, filled with band music, floats, and glimmering torches, which gave the march an almost primeval feel. Leading the way were Daley and the charismatic young candidate for president. City officials were no doubt overstating when they estimated that more than 1,000,000 people watched or participated, but Kennedy and the machine together did produce a massive turnout. At the Chicago Stadium rally, a capacity crowd of 28,000 watched a lineup of 110 entertainers, including Gene Kelly, Joey Bishop, Vic Damone, and Myrna Loy, and listened as Daley promised that Kennedy would win Chicago by half a million votes.[31]

Election day, November 8, was cold and windy in Chicago. Daley and Sis voted, as they always did, at the firehouse at 35th and Lowe, half a block from their home. After stopping in at the 11th Ward offices, Daley went to City Hall to wait out the election returns. The uninviting weather did nothing to dampen voter turnout across the city. An extraordinary 89.3 percent of eligible voters in Chicago were reported to have cast ballots, compared to a national turnout of less than 65 percent. Throughout the day, news reports from Illinois and around the nation indicated that the presidential race was incredibly close. As the first returns began to come in, Chet Huntley declared on NBC, "It looks like we have a cliff-hanger." As the night wore on, it appeared that the presidential race would turn on the results in four states where the lead had been seesawing all night: California, Michigan, Minnesota, and Illinois. But Daley hastened to assure Kennedy that when all the votes were tabulated he would emerge victorious in Illinois. According to Theodore White's *The Making of the President 1960,* Daley called Robert Kennedy at around 1:00 A.M. to tell him that Illinois would go Democratic because "Daley knew which of *his* precincts were out and which of *theirs* were out." Daley later called Kennedy friend and campaign staffer Kenneth O'Donnell and told him to reassure the senator that even though his lead appeared to be dwindling as the downstate vote came in, he would nevertheless carry Illinois. "We're trying to hold back our returns," O'Donnell quotes Daley as telling him. "Every time we announce two hundred more votes for Kennedy in Chicago, they come up out of nowhere downstate with another three hundred votes for Nixon."[32]

When the election-night canvass was complete, Kennedy had carried Illinois and won the race. Kennedy had won the popular vote nationally by a razor-thin 49.7 percent to 49.6 percent margin, but nowhere was the vote closer than in Illinois. He had won the state by a mere 8,858 votes out of 4,657,394 cast, powered by a remarkable 456,312-vote edge in Chicago. Kennedy's Chicago vote total resulted from unprecedented margins in some of the key machine wards. The Automatic Eleven gave Kennedy a 168,611-vote edge, 35 percent more than Daley had squeezed out of them in his own election in 1955. Dawson's five wards produced an 81,554 margin for Kennedy, 49,363 votes more than Daley had won there in 1955, an election in which Dawson had worked hard to pull out every last voter he could. The vote totals in individual wards were also striking — Kennedy took Daley's 11th Ward and Vito Marzullo's 25th by 14,000 votes each. In Illinois and Cook County, it was a clean sweep for the machine: Otto Kerner unseated Stratton from the governorship by a wide margin, Senator Paul Douglas was easily reelected, and most satisfying of all, Ward ousted Adamowski from the state's attorney's office by 25,000 votes. Daley's triumph was complete, and for the first time since he took over the machine his influence would extend to the White House. Within days of the election, he was in the flattering position of having to deny a flurry of rumors that he would be leaving Chicago for a position with the Kennedy administration.[33]

The only discordant note for Daley was the fact that Kennedy's paper-thin win in Illinois was quickly becoming, as Mike Royko put it, "a subject of debate, as well as lawsuits and fist fights." Republicans and good-government groups had, of course, been saying for months that the machine was gearing up to steal the election. On election night, as the Illinois returns came in, the Republicans believed their fears were being borne out. It appeared that the machine was engaging in an old tactic: waiting to report the tallies from their reliable precincts until they could tell how many votes they needed to win. "The Democrats are holding back about two hundred Cook County precincts, waiting to see what the count is downstate," Nixon campaign chairman Leonard Hall said at 2:30 A.M., according to Nixon's *Six Crises*. "We are trying to get them to throw them in but they refuse to do so. Unless they do, they will be able to count us out, no matter what happens downstate." Nixon saw a Daley-Kennedy conspiracy at work, but Adamowski was just as convinced that he was the true target of Daley's vote manipulations. On election night, Adamowski said later, he could see from the odd fits and starts of the vote reports that the machine was stealing the state's attorney race. When the first returns came in, he said, he turned to his wife and said, "'I will win on the basis of these returns.'" But for the next few hours, Adamowski says, returns came in for every office except state's attorney. At 11:00, the returns started to come in again for his race, and this time they were weighted heavily against him. "[W]ithin a matter of five or ten minutes I leaned over to my wife," Adamowski related later. "I said, 'Well, you might as well get prepared. I'm going to lose by between 25,000 and 40,000.'"[34]

Machine sympathizers have generally responded in two ways to charges that Daley intentionally held back election results in 1960 either to elect Kennedy or to defeat Adamowski. Some, like Daley biographer Len O'Connor, have argued that no votes were withheld on election night. In fact, O'Connor argues, Daley actually rushed votes out in order to intimidate downstate politicians and let them know that the Democrats were running so strongly it would be pointless for them to try to manipulate the results. The problem with O'Connor's argument is that it conflicts with how most observers recall votes coming in on election night, and with O'Donnell's account of what Daley told him on election night. The other explanation commonly offered is that Daley did hold back votes, but that he did it not to steal the election, but to prevent Republicans from stealing it downstate. In Eugene Kennedy's account, Daley was simply waiting for a few untrustworthy downstate counties to report their results. "He reported the withheld votes because now it was too late for additional returns to come in from downstate," Kennedy writes approvingly. "He had outwaited them."[35]

The question of whether Daley had stuffed ballot boxes for Kennedy was of more than merely academic interest. The results in the Electoral College were not as close as they had been in the popular vote, but Nixon would have won if he had carried two states where the election results were suspect and the margins of victory were narrow: Illinois and Texas. The Democrats had carried Texas, the home of Kennedy's politically resourceful vice presidential running mate, but by a mere 46,000 votes. The question for the Republicans was whether to undertake the difficult, and incendiary, task of trying to overturn the results of a presidential race by alleging fraud. Working against them was the fact that the Texas Republican state chairman was saying that even if Lyndon Johnson's political cronies had somehow stolen the state for the Democrats in his home region of East Texas, it was pointless to try to challenge it now. Texas Republicans knew, as the *New York Times* put it, that "they can't out-count Lyndon Johnson." After giving serious thought to throwing his weight behind a formal challenge to the presidential results, Nixon decided against it. "The Vice-President ran the race and accepts the decision of the voters," his press secretary Herbert G. Klein announced on November 11. "The decision made on Tuesday stands."[36]

The Republican National Committee did not give up as easily. It announced that it was sending representatives into eight states, including Illinois and Texas, to investigate the election returns. A series of newspaper articles by Earl Mazo, a journalist and Nixon biographer, made the case that there had been widespread fraud around the country, but particularly in Texas and Chicago. The Mazo articles, which were picked up in the *Washington Post* and the *New York Herald Tribune,* gave new weight to the Republican charges. Senator Thurston Morton of Kentucky, chairman of the RNC, paid a visit to Chicago in December and announced that he was forming the National Recount and Fair Elections Committee. Leading Republicans were also beginning to speak out. Barry Goldwater declared that Chicago had "the rottenest election machinery in the United States." In Illinois, Republicans were also complaining about how the election had turned out. Adamowski, the loudest of the in-state critics, charged that Daley had stolen 100,000 Democratic votes in ten machine-dominated Chicago wards and had become "the most powerful political boss in America through a rigged election contest."[37]

Daley reacted forcefully to the Republican accusations. "The people of Chicago are just as honorable and honest as any section of the state," he insisted, and the Republicans had offered up nothing more than "Hitler type" propaganda in support of their allegations. The Democrats welcomed a statewide recount and would even help pay for one, he told reporters. What it would show, he said, was that the voting irregularities were at least as widespread in Republican strongholds downstate as they were in Chicago. "In certain counties, the results are so fantastically, overwhelmingly Republican that there might have been error in their eagerness," Daley said confidently. "You look at some of those downstate counties and it's just as fantastic as some of those precincts they're pointing at in Chicago." Daley detected a nefarious anti-Kennedy conspiracy behind the vote-fraud charges. "It's a joint effort by Republican conservatives in the north and Dixiecrats in the south to prevent the man elected by the people from becoming President of the United States," he insisted.[38]

There were several recanvasses and recounts of the Chicago voting, at the urging of the Republicans. A reexamination of so-called D&O ballots, those that had been marked "defective" or "objected to," and defective voting machines, showed a moderate but unmistakable pattern of errors in favor of the Democrat in both the presidential and state's attorney races. A recount of ballots cast in the 906 Cook County precincts that still used paper ballots revealed an even clearer pattern of mistakes working in favor of the machine slate. The Democrat-dominated Board of Election Commissioners and the Republican vote counters disagreed over how to interpret various kinds of disputed ballots, and the two groups ended up with widely differing tallies. The discrepancy was not surprising, given that the Board of Election Commissioners included in its ranks a chairman who had long machine ties, Daley's corporation counsel, and a newly elected county judge whom Daley had personally slated for his judgeship. Despite its bias in favor of the machine, even the Board of Election Commissioners conceded when the recanvass ended December 9 that Nixon had gained 943 votes in the process and Adamowski had picked up 6,186. The Republicans contended that the recanvass had produced an additional 4,500 votes for Nixon, and 13,000 for Adamowski. In some precincts, the errors were large and fairly suspicious. In the 57th precinct of the 31st Ward — which just happened to be Tom Keane's home turf — the first tally gave Kennedy 323 votes and Nixon 78, but the recanvass found that Kennedy had only 237 votes and Nixon actually had 162. In the same precinct, Ward's victory margin plunged by two-thirds in the recount. If the Republican count was correct, this canvass of less than one-third of the Cook County precincts, looking at only one particular kind of voting irregularity, had erased more than half of both Kennedy's and Ward's margins of victory.[39]

Although these initial recounts suggested serious flaws in the reported election results, the Republican challenges to the election went nowhere. A Republican national committeewoman filed a suit in Cook County Circuit Court. The case was assigned to Judge Thomas Kluczynski, a machine loyalist who less than a year later would be appointed to the Federal District Court on Daley's recommendation. Not surprisingly, on December 13, Kluczynski summarily dismissed the Republicans' case. Taking another tack, the Republicans tried to convince the State Electoral Board not to certify Illinois's electoral votes for Kennedy. The Republicans presented written evidence and called witnesses to support their fraud claim. Daley personally delivered the Democratic response. The election had been "more closely supervised than any in recent years," he insisted. "We in Chicago are no better or no worse than the rest of the State," Daley told the board. "They could allege fraud about results

in Grundy County, Moline, they could allege the same thing in Du-
Page County, and that has been alleged, but I say to you people who
allege fraud, come up with the evidence." The board rejected the
Republican appeal. It did not affirmatively decide that the election
had been clean or that the Democratic ticket actually had won more
votes. It simply decided that the Republicans had not put forth
enough solid evidence of fraud to justify the extraordinary step of
setting aside a presidential election in the state. Illinois's votes were
duly cast for Kennedy when the electors met in Springfield on December 19, 1960.[40]

If Daley and the machine did steal the election for Kennedy, it
would not, by itself, have changed the outcome. Kennedy ended up
prevailing in the Electoral College 303–219 (with fifteen votes cast
by independent "Dixiecrat" voters from the Deep South for Senator
Harry Byrd of Virginia), a wide enough margin that he would have
been elected even if Illinois had gone Republican. But Daley and the
machine could not have known that on election night, when the
presidential race looked like a dead heat. If they were stealing votes
for Kennedy on election night, it meant that they were willing to
steal the White House as casually as they would have stolen an aldermanic seat. In his memoirs, Nixon explains why he decided not to
contest the Illinois results. He was concerned that a challenge to the
legitimacy of a presidential race would have hurt the nation's standing in the world, he says. Perhaps more sincere was the other reason
he gave: his concern that if he did contest the result "[c]harges of
'sore loser' would follow me through history and remove any possibility of a further political career." Although he did not participate in
the challenge to the Illinois result, Nixon seemed to believe he had
been robbed by the Democratic machine. A vivid but electorally in-
accurate comment by Pat Nixon about the head of the Chicago
Board of Elections probably expressed Nixon's own views: "If it
weren't for an evil, cigar-smoking man in Chicago, Sidney T. Holzman, my husband would have been President of the United States."[41]

Was the election stolen? There have always been those in Chicago
who have sworn it was. Curtis Foster was a bodyguard for West Side
alderman Benjamin Lewis and president of the 24th Ward Organization. The once heavily Jewish 24th Ward was by 1960 poor and

black, and it was precisely the kind of loyal machine ward where vote theft was reported to be routine. In the Kennedy-Nixon election, it produced some of the most eye-catching returns for the Democratic ticket. Kennedy carried it by 24,211 to 2,131 — getting almost 92 percent of the vote — and Ward bested Adamowski by 23,440 to 2,190.[42] Andre Foster recalls sitting in his father's polling place in a barbershop on Roosevelt Road that night when someone came to the door after the polls had closed. "Some guy knocked on the door and said, 'We need thirty more votes,'" recalls Foster. "I heard him say it." And, says Foster, "If they gave him an order to get thirty more votes, they gave a lot of people the order." Precinct captains often stole votes for the machine, according to Foster, and they certainly did on November 8, 1960. If the precinct captain then fabricated the required number of votes, depending on how he did it, it might well not have been detected in the minimal recanvasses conducted afterward, checking paper ballots against the number of votes on tally sheets.[43]

The 1960 election would certainly not have been the first in which a political machine stole votes on a massive scale. For as long as there have been machines in America, there have been creative methods of making the votes work out right on election night. In the pivotal 1886 New York City mayoral election, Tammany Hall kept control of City Hall by simply throwing out votes cast for United Labor Party candidate Henry George. For days after the election, uncounted ballots for George could be seen floating down the Hudson River. Chicago politicians have historically been as resourceful in this regard as any. In Chicago's very first mayoral election, the winning Democratic candidate was accused of stealing the election — by an indignant Whig Party. In the 1880s, about half of the city's polling places were located in saloons, where Democratic votes could easily be bought off in exchange for a "liquid reward." And in 1935, more than one hundred election officials were sentenced to jail for fraud.[44] Finley Peter Dunne, the Chicago journalist who spoke through his fictional alter ego saloonkeeper–philosopher Mr. Dooley, recalled his own days as a precinct captain in the 6th Ward: "I mind th' time whin we r-rolled ip twinty-siven hundred dimocratic votes in this wan precinct an' th' only wans that voted was th' judges iv election an' th' captains." Traditional machine methods included casting ballots for noncitizens, copying signatures of drunks off flophouse registration books, and, of course, voting the dead. In the Chicago vernacular, voter fraud fell into two categories: "running up the count," and "leveling the count." Leveling the count occurred after the polls closed. After tallying the votes, election judges would reduce the votes for Republican and independent candidates to some predetermined level, and shift those votes into the Democratic column. Running up the count occurred in many ways, limited only by the ingenuity of individual precinct captains and machine workers. "It was the easiest thing in the world to do in the old machine," says Andre Foster, who helped his precinct captain father work the 24th Ward. "My father did it and I did it."[45]

Just how Chicago vote theft worked — and how commonly it occurred — was laid bare in 1972 by a *Chicago Tribune* investigative series that won the paper a Pulitzer Prize. Machine functionaries knew that if they did not produce the vote totals Daley expected from them they were likely to be "vised," or removed from office. As one article in the series explained in a headline, "Vote Stealing Boils Down to Precinct Chief Survival." Precinct captains were under pressure to run up the count however they could — ghost voting, bribing voters with groceries or whiskey, getting machine partisans to vote "early and often," or literally stuffing the ballot box. Given that the machine controlled the Chicago Board of Elections, which was supposed to protect against this kind of malfeasance, there was little to stand in the way. To report its 1972 series, the *Tribune* sent reporters and investigators from a Chicago good-government group to observe polling places firsthand on election day. The worst suspicions of the machine's critics were confirmed, and Daley's repeated denials were convincingly refuted.[46]

Voting fraud began on registration day. Daley regularly preached about the critical importance of registering voters. A good machine precinct captain went door-to-door to every home in his district to make sure that every eligible adult was registered, and whenever possible registered as a Democrat. But the machine often took this registration process a step further. It turned out that precinct captains made it a practice of stopping by skid row hotels and copying names out of the registration books. These skid row denizens, many of whom were alcoholics, transients, or mentally unstable, were not likely to vote on their own, so the machine could simply vote a straight Democratic ticket on their behalf. As part of his reporting, Bill Recktenwald, a *Tribune* reporter who worked on the vote fraud series, moved into transient hotels and flophouses that charged $7.25 a week for tiny "cubicle rooms." He registered under false names like Henry David Thoreau, Jay Gatsby, and James Joyce. One of the hotels he moved into was the McCoy Hotel, owned at the time by Charles Swibel, chairman of the board of the Chicago Housing Authority, and a close political ally of Daley's. The hotel was located in the ward in which Edward Quigley, Daley's sewer commissioner and a pillar of the machine, was ward committeeman. Recktenwald watched as precinct workers arrived at the hotel to sign up new voters. "It didn't take long to see that something was wrong, because no one was there in front of the desk when they were registering people," he recalls. When he checked the registration rolls, he saw that he had been among those involuntarily signed up to vote. "James Joyce became a registered voter at the McCoy Hotel."[47]

One reason vote theft was so easy was the imbalance between the two parties in Chicago. Every ward theoretically had both Democratic and Republican ward organizations, each headed by its own ward committeeman. But in many wards the Republican leadership was weak, or had cut a deal with the Democratic machine. In the 36th Ward, Peter J. Miller was Republican ward committeeman and a member of the Illinois House of Representatives. But at the same time, Miller held a Democratic patronage job as paymaster of the Chicago Sanitary District, and regularly voted with the Democrats in the legislature on issues of importance to Daley. Many Republican ward organizations did not even have precinct captains. When Charles Percy ran for governor against machine Democrat Otto Kerner in 1964, Percy demanded that Chicago's Republican ward committeemen produce lists of their precinct captains. It turned out that 1,500 to 2,000 of the city's precincts did not have Republican precinct captains.[48]

In his defense of the 1960 results to the State Election Board, Daley emphasized that 25,000 election judges had been present in the precincts on election day to oversee the voting. It was true that, according to state law, both Republican and Democratic election judges were to be present at every polling place. But as Daley well knew, in many Chicago wards the Democratic ward bosses selected both the Democratic and Republican judges. Despite what the election law said, it was not uncommon for all five judges in a precinct to be Democrats. In one ward, the *Tribune* found a mother and daughter, both Democrats, who had been recruited to serve as judges by their Democratic precinct captain. In one election, Mrs. Alla Reeves served as a Democratic judge while her daughter Beverly served as a Republican. The next year, they switched. Actual Republican judges were often turned away by the Democratic machine when they showed up at polling places. In 1972, the machine-dominated Board of Elections declined to appoint 474 Republican judges, claiming their applications had never been received.[49]

Even when Republican election judges were present, the machine could usually intimidate them into doing nothing even when they saw the election law being broken. Election judges were nominally in charge of the voting on election day, but as a practical matter the Democratic precinct captains were in control. Election judges had the legal right to order a police officer to stop voter fraud, and even to make an arrest. But as a practical matter, it was not likely that a Chicago policeman would take a Republican's side against a Democratic machine operative. On the other hand, Republican election judges knew that if they behaved, they would receive not only the official stipend of $25, but a little something extra from the Democratic precinct captain — and they would be allowed to share in the breakfast, lunch, and dinner provided by the precinct captain for his workers, rather than fend for themselves. Judges who did try to exert their authority were easily intimidated by the captain and his staff. In cases where Republican judges raised objections, Democratic captains were known to "fire" them — and remove their names from pay vouchers. In a hotly contested 1966 election, twenty-five-year-old James Hutchinson showed up at a South Side polling place as a Republican poll watcher. When he asked to inspect the voting records, he was arrested. He was kept in custody in a room in Chicago City Hall until the polls were closed, although he was never charged with any crime. One election judge reported that after she and a colleague asked too many questions at a 24th Ward polling place, three gang members showed up and asked, "What does it take to get you guys out of here, a death threat?" The gang members, who were seen talking to an assistant precinct captain, said they had been sent by "the organization." Before they left, they told the judges, "You better be out of here by the time we come back." It was not an idle threat. Poll watchers who interfered with the machine's work were often roughed up. A University of Illinois student who tried to stop fraud as a poll watcher at the 14th precinct of the 24th Ward in 1972 testified before the state legislature that he had his life threatened, and then was beaten up by two Democratic workers as a Chicago policeman looked on. Wesley Spraggins, director of a West Side insurgent political group, told the same committee that while trying to keep the machine honest, his members were beaten up and received death threats, and had bricks thrown through their windows. His own dog, he said, had been poisoned.[50]

With no one to keep it honest, the machine's election-day offenses were anything but subtle. Most common was so-called four-legged voting, in which a ward heeler literally walked into the machine with the voter to make sure he voted a straight Democratic ticket. It was useful for those whose infirmity or poor command of written English made them unreliable voters. But it also ensured that people whose votes the machine had bought by one means or another kept their side of the bargain. Precinct workers sometimes hovered outside the booth and intervened when a voter took more than about thirty seconds, a sign he might be splitting his vote, rather than pulling a single lever to vote the straight Democratic ticket. Ghost voters were another mainstay of machine politics — voters who were dead, had moved out of the district, or perhaps never existed at all. Before the 1972 election, the *Tribune* sent out a mailing to 5,495 voters listed on the registration rolls but not in the phone book. More than 10 percent were returned by the Post Office because the recipient was dead, had moved, or was unknown. Of these, sixty-two were found to be registered from vacant lots or empty buildings, even in a new supplemental list that was prepared one week before the election. No list is perfect, and part of the problem might have been that the process of purging names when voters died or moved was flawed. But the *Tribune* found no shortage of evidence that the machine was actually casting ballots for many of these ghost voters. Fred Tims, an elderly man with a heart condition who was too ill to vote, said that a scrawl written in the precinct binder in the 5th precinct of the 24th Ward when his vote was cast was definitely not his. In the 11th precinct of the same ward, the *Tribune* found four voters named "Mitchell" whose names, according to a handwriting expert, were all forged by the same person.[51] In the 23rd precinct of the 25th Ward, Elizabeth Roland, nominally a Republican judge, tried to vote although she was not listed in the precinct binder. A poll watcher from a nonpartisan civic group challenged her attempt to vote, pointing out that it would have violated the election law. But when the poll watcher stepped away to make a phone call, Roland voted, giving as her address 2117 W. Roosevelt Road, a nonexistent address.[52]

The election law stated that only election judges could handle election materials and tally votes. But it was most often the Democratic precinct captain and his assistants who had control over the ballot box. As a result, in precincts that still used paper ballots, machine workers could simply add and erase pencil marks until the tally turned out right, as "Short Pencil" Lewis was alleged to have done back in 1955 when Daley was first elected. Votes could be stolen just as easily with voting machines. One nonpartisan poll watcher showed up at the 51st precinct of the 24th Ward to observe the voting in the 1972 election. When he arrived at the polling place, a barbershop on Pulaski Avenue, a half hour before the polls opened, he was not allowed in. He watched through a window, however, as precinct captain Walter Simmons and five election judges jumpstarted the democratic process. "We looked into the polling place and saw the [judges] and Mr. Simmons voting repeatedly," the watcher reported. "Simmons voted five or six times, and each of the [election judges did the] same thing two or three times." Before the polls officially opened, the machine slate was twenty votes ahead. In one 21st Ward precinct, a reporter watched as a Democratic judge voted three times on paper ballots, and three times in the voting machine. And Recktenwald watched one man stand in a voting machine and vote seventy times. When Recktenwald asked what he was doing, the man said he was testing it. The Democratic machine also transported voters by van from one polling place to another, and had them vote each time they got out. "You could register to vote in twelve different precincts," says Andre Foster. "There was no way to check it, and that's what we did."[53]

Adamowski continued challenging the outcome of the election even after Kennedy took office in January 1961, but the machine's brand of vote theft was difficult to detect through recanvassing. The Cook County Circuit Court, a machine stronghold, was also imposing heavy expenses on Adamowski for the labor-intensive process of hand-checking ballots. Before long, he gave up the challenge. "Under the guise of expediting the case, the court took the recount out of the hands of my attorneys and proceeded to burden me with every conceivable expense," he said after Ward's election was certified. "It was justice by bankruptcy." As it turned out, that was not the end of it. A final inquiry was conducted by a special prosecutor, Morris J. Wexler, who was appointed to act in place of state's attorney Ward, who was deemed to have a conflict. Wexler investigated vote theft for several months, tracking down specific allegations of miscounts, vote buying, and other improprieties. His report, released April 13, 1961, confirmed that something had been amiss in the election. He found that in precincts with "major mistakes" in both the presidential and state's attorney tabulations, when both were in favor of the same party — suggesting possible malfeasance — a statistically improbable 7 of 7 favored the Democratic candidates.[54] He also found a variety of other troubling practices, like a voting machine in one precinct that was set up so party workers could see how voters were voting. But ultimately, Wexler's findings were inconclusive. In a public statement, Wexler estimated that Adamowski might have been illegally deprived of as many as 10,000 votes — more than Kennedy's statewide victory margin.[55]

Wexler stunned Chicago by deciding to bring criminal charges against 650 election officials for their part in the alleged fraud. The machine maneuvered to get the case assigned to a Democratic judge from East Saint Louis who was an old friend of Democratic county clerk Edward Barrett. Judge John Marshall Karns's pro-defense rulings over the course of the prosecution eviscerated Wexler's case. In the end, all of the defendants had their charges dismissed. The machine's critics were appalled. The Republican *Chicago Tribune* fumed that Judge Karns had "never allowed the prosecution to present" its case, or to vindicate "the legal right of citizens to have their votes counted and not stolen." With this setback, the attempts to learn the truth about the 1960 election were almost concluded. Charges of vote theft in the election surfaced one last, idiosyncratic time, in another criminal case. In the spring of 1962, a precinct captain and two precinct workers from the 28th Ward were prosecuted after an election judge confessed to her priest that she had witnessed vote tampering in her precinct on election night. Several election judges cooperated with the government and testified that ballots had been changed. The FBI supported the prosecution with the results of their examination of the ballots in question. Faced with this compelling evidence, the three defendants changed their pleas to guilty. On March 6, 1962, the men were sentenced to short jail terms.[56]

Daley, true to form, tried to respond to the accusations of corruption by appealing to a respected institution to lend him some of its moral stature. He appealed to three University of Chicago professors, all Democrats, to prepare a report on the charges of vote fraud. One of the study's authors had been appointed by Daley to the board of the Chicago Regional Port Authority. The professors made no real attempt to undertake an independent investigation of whether fraud had occurred. Instead, they conceded, they proceeded by attempting to "examine evidence put forward by Republican leaders and the Chicago newspapers to support the charges which they made." They also relied heavily on information provided to them by Daley press secretary Earl Bush. Based on this very limited inquiry, they concluded in their forty-eight-page report that the accusations that "wholesale election fraud was perpetrated in Chicago were baseless and unsubstantiated." Daley and the machine also continued to insist that Republicans had stolen votes in Kankakee, LaSalle, and other downstate counties, and that this vote theft in Nixon's favor was not being investigated.

Still, despite the machine's best efforts, neither Daley nor Kennedy would easily shake the suspicion that Illinois had been stolen for the Democrats. A joke was making the rounds in Washington that had President Kennedy, Dean Rusk, and Daley in a lifeboat that had only enough food for one. The three men had to decide which two would jump overboard. Kennedy said that he was too important. Rusk said that he was too important. And Daley said the only democratic thing to do was to vote. Daley won the vote, 8–2. At the spring 1961 Gridiron Club roast, attended by President Kennedy, the

Washington press corps put on a humorous skit about the presidential election. Washington reporters impersonated Cook County poll watchers and sang, to the tune of "Tea for Two":

> Two for you, and three for me
> And here's a few; they all are free
> And counting fast, I see they're all cast for Jack.[57]

Beware of the Press, Mayor

Mayor Daley was given exalted treatment at the Kennedy inauguration. He and Sis were invited to join the Kennedys in the presidential box. At the main ball, the new president made a point of walking out of his box and stopping by Daley's table, saying he just wanted to "visit." Kennedy also invited the Daleys to the White House the following morning. When they arrived for their 10:15 appointment, they were the first visitors to the Kennedy White House other than a former occupant of the residence, Harry Truman. Daley said later that his visit was "strictly social," but word quickly spread that Kennedy had offered to appoint him anything from commerce secretary to postmaster general. Rumors of a cabinet appointment are, of course, far easier to come by than an actual appointment. Around the same time, William Dawson's name began to be mentioned as a candidate for postmaster general. When the elderly congressman's name made it into the papers, it was arranged that he would be offered the position with the understanding that he would turn it down. Even if Kennedy had made Daley a real offer, it is unlikely he would have accepted. "He always wanted to be considered," says Daniel Rostenkowski, "but when shove came to push he wasn't going to take it." Chicago City Hall, not Washington, was the center of Daley's world. Years later, when machine loyalists briefly sported "Daley for President" buttons at the 1968 Democratic National Convention, it was understood that he would not be interested in that job. "The mayor doesn't want to be president," the joke went. "He just wants to stay here and send one of his guys down there to the White House."[1]

Daley's highest priority, when he returned to Chicago, was once again working on his plans for urban renewal and new construction. In April, he unveiled an ambitious new five-year capital improvement program that included more than 1,200 projects at a cost of $2.1 billion. Daley budgeted $179 million for new expressways, $145 million for new public housing sites, $83 million for new bridges, viaducts, and grade separations, and other large sums for street improvements, streetlighting, airports, and sewers. He hoped that with a new Democratic administration more federal money for cities would be forthcoming, and he tried to help the process along, traveling to Washington to testify for a Kennedy-backed housing bill that would increase federal spending by $3.2 billion over the next ten years. With the proper funding, Daley told the congressional committee, Chicago's slums could be eliminated in that time period. But even with more funds from Washington, Daley understood that much of the money he wanted would have to be raised locally. One of his ideas for increasing municipal revenue was to raise the city sales tax by 0.5 percent. To get authority for the tax increase, he had to go to the state legislature, just as he had after his election in 1955. This time, the governor was the machine's own man, Otto Kerner, and he immediately endorsed the tax hike.[2] Daley worked to build a coalition of supporters that extended beyond the Chicago city limits, but he always had trouble working with politicians he could not control. He emerged from a dinner with mayors and village presidents and announced that the group had unanimously voted to support his sales tax bill. But one member of the group, the village president of Mount Prospect, disputed Daley's account, saying that in fact between one-third and one-half of those present had not raised their hands when Daley asked for their support. Even with Governor Kerner's support, Daley's tax bill failed in the Illinois legislature. The Democratic-controlled House passed it, despite Republican sniping that it was an "attempt to bail out a corrupt administration in Chicago." But the bill — which was quickly dubbed the "Daley double," because it would double Chicago's share of the sales tax — was voted down in the Republican-controlled Senate in a party-line vote.[3]

Without the authority to raise sales taxes, Daley was forced to fall back on trying to raise property taxes. His 1962 budget called for a nearly 11 percent property tax hike. But that route also proved problematic. Daley's critics pointed out that taxes had been rising steeply since he took office, up 14 percent in the last year alone. And they argued that he should not be given more tax money until the machine stopped raiding the city's coffers for political purposes. A citizens' committee appointed by Daley recommended that the city stop the use of temporary employees, because those positions were so frequently used for political patronage. Daley accepted some of the committee's minor proposals, but not that one. James Worthy, president of the Republican Citizens League of Illinois, accused the machine of defending municipal waste. "The loafing city gangs of so-called workers, exposed time after time by the newspapers, are all immune to punishment because of powerful political sponsorship," he charged. Daley's response was an ad hominem attack on the suburbanite Worthy. "Does Mr. Worthy live in Chicago?" Daley asked. Daley's talk of higher property taxes eventually prompted a grassroots uprising. More than one hundred civic leaders from the South and Southwest Side met in Marquette Park to plan a march on City Hall.[4]

The big showdown over Daley's property-tax proposal came late in 1961, when the City Council had to vote on Daley's 1962 budget. George Hermann, vice president of the Republican Citizens League of Illinois, came to the City Council to testify against the budget. Daley and Keane had seen a written version of Hermann's remarks in advance, and Keane had pointedly introduced Hermann as a resident of suburban Winnetka who had come to "deliver a political diatribe in behalf of a political party." Hermann responded that he owned a business in Chicago and paid city taxes. In his testimony, Hermann called the budget "strong arm robbery." Daley was trying to stock the city payroll, Hermann charged, with patronage workers, including "bookmakers and juice men, subsidized by Chicago taxpayers as courtesy to the Democratic political organization." As Hermann left the chamber, a red-faced Keane shouted out questions about the budget of Winnetka after him. When Hermann's appearance was over, Daley collapsed in his chair and gulped from a glass of water, as the Democratic aldermen gave him a standing ovation. To the surprise of no one, the City Council adopted Daley's budget 40–3.[5]

The other big issue confronting Daley at the start of the new decade was race. Black Chicagoans had been watching the civil rights drama unfolding in the Deep South, many with extra interest because they were born down South or had family there. For years, Chicago's black community had been largely quiescent. There had been a few isolated demonstrations in the 1940s, including the White City Roller Rink protests of 1946. In the 1950s, Willoughby Abner organized the NAACP's Chicago chapter into an activist organization promoting the cause of racial integration. But it was really after the southern sit-in movement got its start at a lunch counter in Greensboro, North Carolina, that a modern civil rights movement began to emerge in Chicago. The Chicago chapter of CORE and the Youth Chapter of the NAACP organized scattered pickets of Woolworth stores, in solidarity with the southern lunch counter protests. And in the summer of 1961, blacks and whites on the South Side organized "wade-ins" to protest the racial segregation that still prevailed at the beaches along Lake Michigan. But the first major flash point of Chicago's civil rights movement was the public schools.

The Supreme Court's 1954 decision in *Brown v. Board of Education* had drawn the nation's attention to the problem of racial segregation in southern schools. What was less well known was that many of the large northern school systems were almost as segregated, by practice if not by law. A 1958 NAACP study had found that 91 percent of Chicago's elementary schools were segregated, which it defined as being either 90 percent black and Puerto Rican or 90 percent white. Chicago's schools turned out to be as unequal as they were separate. As the city's black population grew, black school enrollment had also been increasing rapidly. From 1953 to 1963, overall Chicago school enrollment jumped from 375,000 to more than 520,000, and much of that growth had occurred in black neighborhoods. The NAACP report found that the average black elementary school had almost twice as many students as the average white elementary school. The city had built some additional school buildings to handle the enrollment increases, but not enough.[6]

School superintendent Benjamin Willis's response to the overcrowding in black schools was to require their students to attend class in double-shifts, the first group in the morning and the second in the afternoon. The educational consequences of attending school in shifts were significant: for double-shift students, the school day ended as early as noon. Some white schools were also on double-shift, but more than 80 percent of all double-shift students in the city were black. Willis's other solution to the overcrowding problem was expanding the use of mobile classrooms, which were quickly dubbed "Willis Wagons." What made the situation particularly troubling for many in the black community was that while black students were going to school in shifts and trailers, there were vacancies in many of the city's white schools. Prodded by the *Chicago Defender* and civil rights groups, many black parents applied to the Board of Education to transfer their children to underutilized white schools. As part of this campaign, called "Operation Transfer," CORE sent the Board of Education a seven-page list of schools that were reported to contain empty classrooms, and urged that black students be admitted to them. The Board of Education refused the transfers.[7]

Protests against the school system began quietly at the grassroots level. The movement started in middle-class neighborhoods along the expanding borders of the Black Belt. In September 1961, parents from the South Side neighborhood of Chatham whose children were denied transfers to white schools filed a lawsuit. A few months later, mothers staged a protest at an overcrowded school in another black neighborhood when their children were transferred to a distant black school, bypassing a closer, underused white school. But the most heated rhetoric about schools was coming out of one of the city's poorest neighborhoods. The Woodlawn Organization, a community group founded by radical organizer Saul Alinsky, was encouraging poor parents to protest about the conditions in the neighborhood and teaching them how to bring their concerns to the attention of the city. TWO quickly became a driving force in the school movement. Led by the Reverend Arthur Brazier, the group organized a massive protest at an October 1961 public hearing at the Board of Education. The following month, TWO began holding "death watches" at Board of Education meetings, with several members in the back dressed in black as an arresting form of protest. School activists also started holding teach-ins across the city to educate more citizens about the problems in the Chicago school system and what should be done. In February 1962, the Chatham–Avalon Park Community Council sponsored a conference called "Segregation in the Chicago Public Schools." A month later, the Chicago Urban League held a citywide conference on "quality and equality" in the schools.[8]

Around the same time, an influential interracial group of teachers, Teachers for Integrated Schools, was forming. One of TFIS's first projects was producing a short pamphlet called "Hearts and Minds," which made a personal appeal to Mayor Daley to do something about the overcrowding, segregation, and educational shortcomings of the city's public schools. On May 17, 1962, the eighth anniversary of *Brown v. Board of Education,* teachers affiliated with TFIS fanned out across the Loop at the end of the workday to hand out "Hearts and Minds" and urge Chicagoans to take a stand in favor of integrating and upgrading the public schools. These teacher-activists distributed some 65,000 copies of "Hearts and Minds" in downtown Chicago, an extraordinary event for that still politically restrained era, but there were no news stories about it the following day. "The most curious thing about the pamphleteering was that nobody mentioned it," recalls college professor Meyer Weinberg, who helped found TFIS. "No newspaper, not even the *Defender,* and none of the local news shows." Shortly after the demonstration, Weinberg ran into an old classmate who was working at the *Chicago Daily News* and asked why they had not covered it. "He said, 'Don't you know they refer to this as "nigger news," and nobody [wants] to get into trouble by printing . . . it. . . .'"[9]

In April 1962, a new coalition formed in Chicago that would become the driving force for the city's civil rights movement. The Coordinating Council of Community Organizations (CCCO) was a citywide organization that included representatives of both large national organizations such as the NAACP and the Urban League and local groups such as Teachers for Integrated Schools and The Woodlawn Organization. The CCCO immediately threw itself into the battle over schools, and made one of its first causes the nominations Daley was about to make to the Chicago Board of Education. There were two vacancies on the board, and Daley's all-white nominating commission had just sent him a list of candidates, all of whom were white and none of whom had a record of concern about matters of race. The CCCO met with Daley to express its unhappiness with the candidates. Daley went ahead and chose two of the white nominees, though he later invited a black group, the Cook County Physicians Association, to send a representative to the nominating commission.[10] Meanwhile, protests against Willis Wagons were gaining force. They made a good target for the protesters because they were a concrete enemy for a movement that largely concerned itself with abstractions. During protests in May and June, Reverend Brazier and other leaders emphasized that Willis Wagons were "a means of maintaining segregation." The U.S. Civil Rights Commission issued a report late in the year that found that, just as the black community was charging, there was enough extra space available in white schools to alleviate the overcrowding, but the school system had failed to use it. The Board of Education had most likely "impeded rather than promoted integration," the report concluded.[11]

Throughout these early school protests, Daley kept a low profile. He had no reason to get involved. He did not believe in school integration philosophically, and he realized it would not help him politically. Like open housing, school integration threatened to destabilize the working-class white neighborhoods that were the heart of the machine's electoral base. But at the same time, Daley realized he had little to gain by coming out forcefully against school integration. He was in a different position from the southern politicians who were fulminating against integration and vowing "massive resistance." Because blacks in the South were systematically denied the right to vote, white politicians there did not need to worry about offending black voters. But in Chicago blacks did vote, and their votes went overwhelmingly to Daley and the machine. There was no need to jeopardize this support needlessly by appearing insensitive on the subject of black education. Daley claimed he was staying out of the school controversy because of a philosophical commitment to keeping politics out of the school system. It was a position that sounded admirably reformist, but his philosophy was more likely rooted in some advice Mayor Kelley had given him years ago: "Avoid the public schools. They'll kill you."[12]

Looking forward to the 1962 spring primary election season, Daley had some details to take care of. The district lines for the city's fifty wards had been redrawn since the last election, the first redistricting since 1947. Daley instructed the ward committeemen that they were responsible for establishing precinct captains and ward operations in their new territories, but that under no circumstances were any precinct captains to lose their patronage jobs simply because redistricting had pushed them into another ward. Daley also had to fill the ward committeeman position for the 24th Ward, which had been vacant since Sidney Deutsch, the legendary Jewish ward boss, died. Daley chose Benjamin Lewis, who was already the alderman, thereby giving that black ward its first black ward committeeman. Lewis had proven his loyalty to the machine in the City Council, and the bad blood between him and Dawson meant there was little danger of Lewis bringing the 24th Ward back into Dawson's weakened black submachine. "Lewis became Daley's 'house boy' and took great pride in attacking Dawson publicly on signal," notes historian Dempsey Travis. "He constantly bragged about the fact that none of his precinct captains were 'Dawson men' and that his telephone line ran directly to the fifth floor in City Hall and not to Dawson's headquarters at 34th and Indiana Avenue." Daley also elevated Seymour Simon, a Keane ally, from 40th Ward alderman to president of the Cook County Board of Commissioners. To some machine-watchers, it appeared that Daley was promoting Simon to head the Jewish faction of the machine in order to further diminish the role of his one-time friend Arvey.[13]

Daley's most pressing concern going into the election was selecting a U.S. Senate candidate to challenge Republican incumbent Everett Dirksen. At a testimonial dinner in May, Daley had virtually endorsed Illinois House Speaker Paul Powell for the nomination. Daley may have been carried away by the moment, but back in the sober environment of City Hall it would have occurred to him that downstater Powell would do little to help the machine ticket win in Cook County. Word had it that Daley was trying to persuade Stevenson to give up his job as United Nations ambassador to make the run, but Stevenson refused. Daley next turned to Sidney Yates, a Chicago congressman. Yates would have a hard time winning the race, because his candidacy violated the Illinois tradition of reserving one of the two Senate seats for a downstater. "You are not going to beat Dirksen starting out by dropping at least 50,000 to 75,000 downstate votes," a Democratic leader from Madison County warned the slating committee. "The practice of sharing the two Senate seats is more than a tradition — it's a rule of politics." The warning proved to be on the mark, but Daley was not all that concerned about sending another Democrat to the U.S. Senate. He was looking for a candidate who would help the machine win its races in Cook County and hold on to the thousands of patronage positions that came with those offices. If that meant nominating a candidate like Yates who was unlikely to put together enough votes statewide to win his own race, Daley considered it a small price to pay.[14]

Daley was still looking for new ways to raise money for his ambitious spending projects. He put together a $66 million package of six bond initiatives, including a $22.5 million bond for urban renewal, $22.5 million for sewers, and $7 million for garbage disposal and streetlighting. Daley's plan was to put the bonds up for a vote in the upcoming April election. It was a favorite technique to put new spending initiatives on the ballot in low-turnout elections that the machine could win by delivering its faithful voters to the polls. Republican alderman Sperling charged Daley with playing politics and urged that the bonds be put on the November general election ballot, when more people would be voting. Daley offered the unconvincing response that if the bonds were on the ballot in November "some would attempt to make partisan politics out of what is strictly a municipal government question." Daley campaigned hard for his bonds. The week before the election, in good machine fashion, he invited almost a thousand ward committeemen and precinct captains to a Morrison Hotel lunch and implored them to get their people to vote yes. But when the votes were in, all six individual bond issues on the ballot had been defeated by margins of almost 3–2. The urban-renewal bond had lost by the largest margin of the six. Daley's strategy of putting the bonds up for vote in an off-election had been thwarted: turnout was an unusually high 44 percent. The results, which *Time* magazine called a "tax-time tantrum," were widely interpreted as a taxpayer rebellion against the city's fast-rising property taxes. The Republicans argued that the vote had also been a referendum on the integrity of Daley and the machine. But there also appeared to be a racial element lurking in the returns. The bonds had been labeled in some quarters as an urban-renewal initiative, and to many white Chicagoans, urban renewal was becoming synonymous with uprooting blacks from the ghetto and potentially dispersing them into white neighborhoods.[15]

When a seventeen-year-old Girl Scout, Ann Graham, visited City Hall in May to serve as mayor for the day, Daley had some simple advice for her: "Beware of the press, Mayor." It was wisdom Daley had come by the hard way. The *Chicago Tribune* had just been awarded a Pulitzer Prize for an exposé of corruption in the Sanitary District. When an alderman had introduced a resolution in the City Council to congratulate the reporter who won, a furious Daley had ordered it buried in committee. Throughout the spring and summer of 1962, the exposés kept coming. In June, the Better Government Association released a report on loafing in the city's patronage-heavy Forestry Division that it said was costing taxpayers "millions a year." BGA investigators had taken motion pictures and still photos of forestry crews sleeping, sunbathing, and wasting time during the workday. They also caught forestry workers going into taverns and drinking during the workday. One worker actually went behind the bar to serve a BGA investigator a drink. A forestry truck was observed delivering lumber to a private home, and another was driven to Gary, Indiana. Confronted with this seemingly incontrovertible evidence of municipal waste, Daley responded angrily that the BGA was "lock, stock and barrel an arm of the Republican Party." At a City Hall press conference, he reminded reporters that cutting down a tree is hard work, and asked the press corps if any of them had ever cut down a tree.[16] Daley insisted that it was wrong for the BGA to "blacken all city employees by use of a report dealing with 15 people," but by the end of June he grudgingly announced that four forestry workers had been suspended for periods ranging up to twenty-nine days. The BGA director responded that the suspensions were a "very fine start," but that his group's investigation indicated that the Forestry Division could cut its staff by one-third without appreciably affecting its work.[17]

Increasingly, Daley's critics tried to tie the use of patronage employees to the city's soaring tax rates. Since Daley took office seven years earlier, property taxes had climbed 86 percent. Daly bristled when the subject of tax increases came up. At one press conference, he lectured the City Hall press corps that the cost of newspapers had doubled in the past ten years, while the cost of government had not. But the *Chicago Tribune* did the math and then pointed out in its news pages the next day that while its price had increased from five cents to seven cents in the past decade, the operating budget of the city had actually soared 114 percent.[18]

The attacks over municipal waste and high taxes were beginning to take their toll on Daley. Reports were even circulating that he was losing favor to Tom Keane, the second most influential force in the Democratic machine. Keane had demanded that Daley let him name either the next Cook County board president or the next tax assessor, *Chicago Tribune* political columnist George Tagge reported, and Daley ended up slating Keane's protégé, Seymour Simon, for Cook County board president. As Tagge saw it, Daley gave in because, after losing on the spring bond issues, he was becoming more risk-averse when it came to slating. Daley realized it would look bad if he turned Keane down and then his own candidates went on to lose. Daley also did something odd in the way he slated the seventeen Superior Court judge candidates for the November 1962 elections. He stole away six Republican candidates who had lost in the April judicial elections and put them on his own "good government" ticket. Republican leaders were outraged by Daley's effrontery, but once again some political observers interpreted it as sign of weakness or at least risk-aversion. Rather than load up the ticket with a full slate of machine loyalists, Daley was willing to give up some of the judgeships in the hope of luring Republican and independent voters.[19] Daley also forced the Sanitary District — which had been the subject of both a Pulitzer Prize–winning exposé and a federal grand jury investigation — to clean up its operations. A blue-ribbon panel had selected a reform candidate, Vinton Bacon of Tacoma, Washington, as the next superintendent, but the Sanitary District trustees balked. The trustees said it was because they wanted to be given three candidates to choose from, but it seemed that they just were not ready for reform. In the middle of the meeting to consider a new superintendent, the president of the board of trustees got up to take a phone call and returned to say that he was now backing Bacon. It was widely suspected that it was Daley on the other end, although he later insisted that the choice had always been the trustees' to make.[20]

There were still more signs of trouble for the machine in the upcoming election. When William Dawson got up at a party rally to introduce senatorial candidate Yates to machine workers, he put in an embarrassing performance, repeating a few sentences over and over until a state representative led him off the stage. And the issue of machine voting improprieties loomed again when Adamowski declared that he had come into possession of devices that could be used to prevent voters from casting a ballot for certain candidates on a voting machine. He said he had gotten them from a well-connected political worker, and he charged that they had been widely used in poor wards in the 1960 elections. Daley's response to the wave of bad news was to focus on energizing the machine to work its hardest for the Democratic slate. At the annual 11th Ward family circus at the International Amphitheatre, in his own neighborhood of Bridgeport, Daley mingled with the precinct captains and told them that the Democratic Party was "one family." Daley also organized a traditional pre-election luncheon for one thousand at the Morrison Hotel's Terrace Casino, where precinct workers could hear in person from the full Democratic slate, from Yates on down to the three candidates for Sanitary District trustee. As a final election ploy, Daley filed his 1963 budget early, so voters could see it before the election. The new budget called for cutting spending by $44 million compared to the previous year, and it contained a $7 million property-tax cut. Republican alderman Sperling attacked it as "a self-serving political document designed to mislead the people," but it clearly demonstrated that Daley understood the voters' sour mood about rising taxes.[21]

The 1962 elections turned out fairly well for Daley. Yates did lose to Dirksen, in large part because of the drubbing he received downstate, but the loss was of little consequence to the machine. Within Cook County, the Democrats swept all but one of the major offices. On closer inspection, however, the returns contained some troubling signs for the machine. The Democratic candidate for assessor won, but his margin of victory was less than half of what it had been in the 1958 Democratic landslide four years earlier. The machine's candidate for Cook County board president won by only 150,000, compared to 446,000 four years earlier. Daley himself was up for reelection in six months, and this erosion of support for the machine was an indication of the trouble Daley himself would encounter.[22]

*   *   *

Architectural Forum devoted its entire May 1962 issue to the boom times in Chicago. The city had been transformed, the magazine declared, since Daley took over. Most notably, "that most glamorous structure, the office building, is sprouting again, in the Loop and on its fringes." Technically speaking, the Loop revival began slightly before Daley became mayor. The Prudential Building, the first new Loop skyscraper since the 1930s, opened in 1955, the year of Daley's election, but ground had been broken for it three years earlier. Still, there was no denying that the pace of downtown development had picked up considerably during the Daley years. Since the Prudential went up, another 3 million square feet of office space had been built in the Loop. The Inland Steel Building opened in 1957, part of a wave that would go on for decades, culminating in the Sears Tower, the world's tallest building, in 1974. With the new boom in downtown construction, the city's downtown business district began to expand beyond its traditional boundaries. On June 20, 1963, Daley presided over groundbreaking ceremonies for the $30 million, thirty-five-story Equitable Life Assurance Society Building. The Equitable Building, located on the northern bank of the Chicago River, was part of a northward migration of the business district that would in time turn North Michigan Avenue into an impressive array of upscale office buildings and luxury stores. In 1965, Gateway Center I opened, marking an important step in the Loop's drive westward, onto the western bank of the curving Chicago River. And in the late 1960s, an underdeveloped eighty-three-acre parcel east of Michigan Avenue was developed as the sprawling mixed-use Illinois Center, pushing the downtown business district eastward. The hodgepodge of buildings, including the Mies van der Rohe steel-and-glass skyscrapers at One and Two Illinois Center, anchored a previously underdeveloped area tucked between the Chicago River and the north end of Grant Park.[23]

In addition to the boom in office construction, the Loop also saw a dramatic increase in government buildings. Daley used his influence with Washington to see that Chicago got more than its share of federal construction dollars. Starting in the late 1950s, work began on a new complex of Mies van der Rohe federal buildings for the east Loop: the thirty-story Everett McKinley Dirksen federal court building; the forty-two-story John C. Kluczynski Building; and a one-story U.S. Post Office, Loop Station. These three buildings, all of which face a central plaza, form what is perhaps the most imposing federal complex in any downtown outside Washington, D.C. Daley could also claim substantial credit for construction of McCormick Place, the world's largest exposition hall, which opened South of the Loop on the shores of Lake Michigan in 1960. McCormick Place, named after the late *Chicago Tribune* publisher Colonel Robert McCormick, arose out of negotiations Daley had with Governor Stratton. They agreed on a bipartisan bill, passed by the legislature in June 1957, to create a public authority that was authorized to issue bonds to finance its construction. The location was controversial: some Chicagoans were troubled that it violated Burnham's dictum that the lakefront should remain "forever open, clear and free." But from a commercial standpoint McCormick Place, with its 300,000 square feet of exhibition space, was a great success, putting Chicago in a far better position than it had been to lure conventions and trade shows.[24]

Along with the corporate and government construction, Daley's plan for Loop construction emphasized using residential buildings to redevelop the Loop. Downtown business leaders were eager to see new housing go up to attract upper-income — and, there was no denying it, white — residents to the central business district. The business community believed that if pedestrian traffic in the Loop became too black, a "tipping point" would be reached, and whites would cease to shop there. "I'll tell you what's wrong with the Loop," developer Arthur Rubloff told the *Chicago Daily News*. "It's people's conception of it. And the conception they have about it is one word — black. B-L-A-C-K. Black. We have a racial problem we haven't been able to solve. The ghetto areas have nothing but rotten slum buildings, nothing at all, and businessmen are afraid to move in, so the blacks come downtown for stores and restaurants." The Central Area Committee saw luxury apartment buildings as the solution. It was an idea as old as the 1958 plan, and by the early 1960s it finally started coming to pass. The most dramatic example was the $36 million Marina City, twin sixty-story corncob-shaped residential and office towers. Marina City was an upscale world on the banks of the Chicago River, with restaurants, built-in parking lots, movie theaters, a health club, and its own 700-boat marina. The complex's 900

apartments, an immediate hit with the public, were fully rented before the buildings opened in 1965. As it happened, Marina City was
put together by two men who were extremely close to Daley: janitors union president William McFetridge and CHA board chairman
Charles Swibel. Swibel managed to obtain an option on the river-
front property at well below market value, and McFetridge pulled
together money from the Janitors International Union and several
locals to underwrite initial work on the project. Swibel then made
the rounds of Chicago and New York banks to put together the rest
of the financing. Swibel ended up doing very well as a result of
his role in Marina City. His management company was awarded a
lucrative contract to run the complex. And later, when the buildings' apartments were converted to condominiums, Swibel would
make more than $6 million by legally buying up apartments at in-
sider prices and flipping them.[25]

In transforming a dying downtown into one of the nation's most
dynamic, Daley benefited from fortunate timing. "It was the best of
times for being mayor," notes Continental Bank president John
Perkins, who worked with Daley on downtown development. "I
don't mean to debunk the mayor or anything, [but] postwar prosperity was really starting to move Chicago." Still, Daley should get credit
for a good part of the turnaround. His 1958 plan laid the groundwork for many of the downtown improvements that followed. And
Daley made things easier for projects that fit in with his plans for
downtown. Developers' first step was often to meet with a department head like Lewis Hill, Daley's commissioner of urban renewal.
"If you got a good reception Hill would probably say, 'Let me talk to
the mayor about it,'" says Daley aide Edward Marciniak. "Then there
might be a meeting with the mayor. The mayor liked this because his
job was not to say no, but to say yes." Once the mayor was on a developer's side, says mayoral aide Tom Donovan, he "could move
through the bureaucracy." Projects with Daley's approval proceeded
on a special track. Daley waived zoning requirements, extended
water and sewer lines, and built and closed streets in order to see that
buildings he wanted were built. Daley's critics conceded that much
good was being done downtown, but they were concerned that
Loop development was being overemphasized. "You have to say that
a cardinal point of his policy, perhaps *the* cardinal point, has been the

subsidy and encouragement of the central area — the Loop and the Near North Side," said Independent alderman Leon Despres. "They have been nourished, caressed, assisted, encouraged and dealt with in every way to produce the maximum development." City Hall was not doing anything for Chicago's declining residential neighborhoods, which also needed help to stave off decline. The problem, critics said, was that Daley answered only to power: the Central Area Committee had it, and the residents of poor and working-class neighborhoods did not.[26]

Even before Daley announced for reelection in 1963, major endorsements started to pour in. Chicago's business community was not only backing Daley, it was lobbying him to make sure he would run for a third term. Fairfax Cone of the advertising firm Foote, Cone & Belding, who had been a mainstay of Daley's previous non-partisan business committees, announced that he would organize another Non-Partisan Committee to Re-Elect Mayor Daley. Within days, a long list of business leaders, including many of the same ones who backed him in 1959, had publicly come out for Daley. At the same time, organized labor remained firmly in Daley's camp. On December 4, 1962, the Chicago Federation of Labor once again backed Daley, in a resolution introduced by Daley's friend and civil service commissioner, William Lee. As these influential forces lined up behind Daley, he professed to be uncertain about whether to seek reelection. "Running for a third term is something you don't make your mind up about overnight," he said. Daley's indecision did not last long. On December 14, 1962, he finally made his intentions known to a closed meeting of Democratic ward committeemen, who gave him their unanimous support.[27]

The campaign started out on a sour note for Daley. Even before the Republicans had a candidate, they had their first issue. Charges about the machine's links to the syndicate, which had plagued Daley since his first race for mayor, resurfaced just days after his announcement. John D'Arco, the 1st Ward alderman, was stepping down in favor of state senator Anthony De Tolve. The word on the street was that syndicate boss Sam Giancana had personally ordered the change after meeting with his fellow mobsters in a Loop hotel. "I'm shocked at the arrogance of the Syndicate in attempting to move their man into the city council," Republican alderman John Hoellen declared. "Doesn't Mayor Daley have courage enough to run the Syndicate out of Chicago . . . ? What unseen power holds the mayor back?" Daley challenged the accusers to come up with more support for their allegations. "Is there any proof or evidence of this?" Daley asked. "Is relationship with anyone the basis for condemnation?" At the same time, he said there was nothing he could do about what was occurring in the 1st Ward. "I do not interfere with any campaign for alderman in any ward," Daley said. "I have been told by Mrs. D'Arco that he has refused to run because of his health." His defense was patently false, of course, since he had frequently forced out officeholders who crossed him or threatened his power.[28]

Things only got worse for Daley when the Republicans settled on their candidate, his old antagonist Benjamin Adamowski. Adamowski was a proven vote-getter, who had carried Chicago when he was elected state's attorney in 1956. He had narrowly lost his position in 1960, but he still attributed that defeat to the vote theft by the machine. As a Polish-American, Adamowski also began with a built-in base among the city's 600,000-strong Polish community, a critical part of the machine's white ethnic base. Most important, Adamowski was smart and articulate, and his past investigations — including the Traffic Court and Summerdale police scandals — had done real damage to the machine's reputation. During the election, Adamowski would have fresh scandals to exploit. The Sanitary District was being buffeted by charges of kickbacks, bribes, and fraudulent civil-service examination results. And reminiscent of Summerdale, the Chicago Fire Department was being accused of looting fire victims' homes. A fire victim named John Nesbitt, who worked as a public information director for the National Safety Council, charged that his home and another in his building had been robbed by a fireman who responded to a fire call. Daley responded that Nesbitt was on a witch-hunt, and he demanded that he take a lie detector test.[29] Adamowski was also fortunate to be running at a time when the voters were unhappy with the city's high spending, as they had demonstrated by voting down Daley's $66 million in bonds a year earlier. He made clear from the outset that he would challenge Daley on taxes and question how much of the money raised was going to machine patronage and waste. "We'll talk about his record — and the cost of it all to the taxpayers," Adamowski promised. "I think the big issue is the size of the tax bills."[30]

Daley began 1963 with the kind of show of strength that only the Democratic machine could exhibit. On January 2, he filed a sixteen-foot-high stack of nominating petitions containing 750,000 names. Daley kicked off his campaign by emphasizing his work redeveloping the city and improving municipal services. His reform of the police department was already translating into reduced crime rates, he said, and he boasted that Chicago had won awards in 1959 and 1961 as the cleanest big city in America. During the campaign, Daley also announced that he had received a telegram from the National Clean-Up, Paint-Up, Fix-Up Bureau in Washington stating that Chicago was also designated the cleanest large city for 1962. The Chicago newspapers helped Daley out by picking up on his themes, and they generally gave him high marks. And *Time* magazine put Daley on its cover shortly before the election, with his preternaturally jowly face set off against a bright Chicago skyline, and the headline "Clouter with Conscience." Inside, *Time* included photos of the city's new skyscrapers, O'Hare International Airport, and an autographed photograph of President Kennedy welcoming the Daley clan to the White House. Chicago was in the midst of reinventing itself — a "new facade is rising in steel and zeal" — the magazine cheered, and it gave credit for the transformation to the city's singular mayor. "Daley's stubborn resolve to rebuild his city has given Chicago a new stature," the article said. "Making things happen is Daley's passion." The magazine's brief mention of Adamowski dismissed him as a former state's attorney who "distinguished himself by never successfully prosecuting a major case."[31]

Adamowski ran a spirited campaign that challenged Daley's upbeat picture of Chicago government. He refused to concede that city services had improved since Daley took office. The Chicago Fire Department, when it was not looting homes, was letting fire deaths soar 150 percent in the last year, Adamowski charged. He also blamed Daley's fire department for one of the worst tragedies in Chicago history, the infamous 1958 fire at Our Lady of Angels School, in which ninety students and three nuns perished. Adamowski also questioned how much progress had been made at the police department since the Summerdale scandal. The Chicago police had recently allowed the "babbling burglar" himself, Richard Morrison, to be ambushed and shot while leaving the Criminal Court Building after testifying in a Summerdale-related matter. Adamowski also hammered away at Daley, as promised, on waste and high taxes. His charge that Daley routinely overpaid municipal workers was buttressed by a new study that found that the city was paying $3.34 a square foot for cleaning and maintenance, compared to an average of 55.2 cents in thirty-nine Loop offices studied.[32] Republican state legislators also helped Adamowski by introducing a bill to put a tax ceiling on Chicago's general expenditure fund. Daley was adamantly opposed to it, and he was forced once again to publicly oppose a measure he had helped defeat in 1957, 1959, and 1961 — and thereby associate himself in the voters' mind with high taxes. With Daley positioning himself as the candidate of business and big labor, Adamowski tried to present himself as the people's candidate. "I hear State Street is against me, the bankers are against me, and the labor leaders are against me," he declared, in remarks that sounded uncannily like Daley's in 1955. "State Street doesn't make Chicago big, it's the other way around. I'll take Western Avenue, Nagle Avenue, Ashland Avenue, and Milwaukee Avenue, where the little people reside. I'll take the bank depositors over the bankers any day. That goes for the little people in labor, too."[33]

Even while Daley was in the midst of his usual election-time denials that he was a machine boss, he was quietly pulling strings in the upcoming aldermanic races. In the racially changing 21st Ward on the Southwest Side, the white ward committeeman had the necessary support from the ward's precinct captains in his race for alderman, but Daley decided he would have to step aside in favor of a black candidate. At the same time, in the 17th Ward on the Far South Side, which had become 80 percent black, Daley refused to let the white incumbent be removed. And at a closed-door slating meeting at the Morrison Hotel with top ward committeemen — including Dawson, Keane, Parky Cullerton, and Joseph Gill — Daley beat down a challenge to another white alderman. Keane urged Daley to dump independent alderman Leon Despres, his biggest irritant in the City Council. Dawson, who was eager to put his own man in as 5th Ward alderman, joined Keane's appeal. But Daley instructed the 5th Ward Organization to back Despres, because he did not want to alienate the liberal independent voters of Illinois, who backed Despres and whose support he wanted in the mayoral election. As word of Daley's dictates leaked out, Adamowski said they were further proof that "we do not have one-party rule, we have one-man rule."[34]

In the aldermanic election, the machine- and Independent-backed Despres overwhelmingly defeated Dawson's candidate. But the big news came two days later, when newly reelected alderman Benjamin Lewis was found in his West Side 24th Ward office handcuffed to a chair and shot three times in the head. Lewis was in the process of easing white precinct captains out of the ward, and he had been talking about keeping a larger share of the ward's gambling money for himself. The killing had the look of a syndicate hit, but no one was ever arrested. The Lewis killing was embarrassing for Daley and the machine, and it caused a rapid volley of charges and countercharges over which of the two mayoral candidates was more corrupt. Lewis's death was only the latest "chapter in the sordid history of the Chicago Democratic machine," Adamowski declared. "Now we are apparently at the beginning of an era of violence and bloodshed." Daley mobilized his supporters to attack Adamowski's integrity. Daniel Ward charged that when he took office as state's attorney he discovered that Adamowski had failed to account for $833,984 in discretionary funds. Adamowski responded that he had destroyed the relevant records to protect informants who had helped him to investigate corruption in city government and other scandals. And he threw the charges back at Daley, asking for documentation on the forty-three city contingency funds under the mayor's control. Daley promised to divulge his contingency fund spending, but he never did. Through it all, Daley continued to insist that he was not a machine politician. A reporter visiting from Brazil told him, "You have quite a reputation in Brazil as the last of the city bosses." Daley responded, "No, I'm the first new leader."[35]

Adamowski tried to appeal to white ethnic voters by coming out against open housing. Politically, it was not a difficult choice for him. Daley and the machine had a virtual lock on the black vote, and Adamowski would be unlikely to pick up many black votes even if he took a pro–civil rights stand. But he had a chance of making significant inroads into the machine's white ethnic base by strongly opposing integration. Adamowski's stand put Daley in a difficult position. Daley had no intention of supporting open housing, both because he opposed it and because he did not want to lose support in the Bungalow Belt. But he was constrained, as Adamowski was not, by the need to avoid offending black voters. He needed blacks both to support him and to turn out enthusiastically. Daley's solution was to duck the issue. Asked at a City Hall press conference if he supported open housing, Daley said, "Everyone knows my record on adequate housing for all people." When the reporter pressed him again, Daley simply responded: "You know my record."[36]

As always, Daley's electoral strategy relied on energizing the machine faithful. He pulled out all of the usual tricks, including a torchlight parade, and a luncheon for 1,400 precinct captains and other machine functionaries at the Morrison Hotel, where he was lauded by Governor Kerner and Senator Paul Douglas. He also pulled out some new ones, like another rally downtown with an elephant wearing a banner reading, "I am voting for Dick Daley too." Just as he appealed to both sides on race, Daley played both sides of the organized crime issue. He received enthusiastic applause at a meeting of the syndicate-dominated 1st Ward organization when he boasted of his proven record of putting convicted criminals on the city payroll. "I've been criticized for doing this," he told the standing-room-only crowd, "but I'll make no apologies. I'll always stand alongside the man with a criminal record if I think he deserves another chance."[37]

This time around, Daley was able to call in a better class of political debt. On March 25, barely a week before voters went to the polls, Daley decided that it was time for another O'Hare dedication now that the airport's circular restaurant was complete. President Kennedy agreed to attend, and Daley's campaign made the most of it. Crowds up to five deep lined the seventeen-mile route between O'Hare and the downtown Conrad Hilton Hotel, where Daley presided over a "civic luncheon." Cynics in the press grumbled that the ceremony "may make O'Hare the most dedicated airport in the nation." But Daley was able to bask in Kennedy's well-timed declaration that O'Hare "could be classed as one of the wonders of the modern world," and that it stood as "a tribute to Mayor Daley who kept these interests and resources together, working together, until the job was done."[38]

When the votes were counted on April 2, Daley won 679,497 to 540,705. Daley's 56 percent of the vote was a sharp drop-off from the 71 percent he had taken four years earlier, and less than he had predicted going into the election. It was also the first time that his vote total had fallen under 700,000. The ward-by-ward mayoral election returns revealed the source of the machine's difficulties. Daley had run strongly among black voters, taking 81 percent of their votes. But his support among white voters had actually slipped to 49 percent. In part, it was due to ethnic voting. Adamowski had run strongly among his fellow Poles, most of whom usually voted a straight machine ticket. But Daley had also suffered significant fall-offs in wards like Tom Keane's 31st, where his vote total was about half what it had been four years earlier. In the 1st Ward, where he was hurt by his University of Illinois stand as well as tensions with the syndicate, his vote fell about 40 percent.[39]

Now that Daley was no longer the candidate of white Chicago, he faced a stark choice. He could have decided to govern in the New Deal tradition of the Kelly-Arvey wing of the Democratic Party. Like Kelly, he could have tried to govern as a racial progressive, and then worked to keep enough moderate white voters behind him to stay in office. It would have been a difficult path — Kelly had failed to make it work. But Daley would have had four years to navigate the issues of open occupancy and public housing and chart a compromise-filled political course that kept the Democrats in power and promoted the civil rights of his most loyal voting block. Chicago might have become an entirely different city if he had proceeded along that path. But instead, Daley decided to make a strong appeal to the white "backlash" voters in the Bungalow Belt who had begun to desert him in the 1962 bond referendum and the 1963 mayoral election. He would come out more directly against open housing and equal rights for blacks, so there would be no confusion among white voters about where he stood. He intended to hold on to as much of his black support as he could, but he would do that not by his stand on the issues, but through patronage and the work of the black ward organizations. Alderman Despres, Daley's foremost foe in the City Council, drafted a memo setting out what he took to be Daley's cynical approach to racial politics. "While controlling the votes of Negro Chicagoans through partisan patronage and the national attraction of the Democratic label, make all necessary concessions to white segregationists by maintaining the pattern of racial housing segregation, school segregation, and social segregation," Despres wrote. But he added a warning: "Since a pattern of housing and school segregation guarantees a growing ghetto and a declining city, the segregation policy which wins each election hastens a tragic explosion."[40]

In early July, NAACP delegates descended on Chicago for the organization's national convention. The summer of 1963 had already been an upsetting one for the civil rights movement. The NAACP's Mississippi field secretary, Medgar Evers, had been shot dead by a white supremacist outside his Jackson, Mississippi, home. The local police had shown little interest in cracking the case, but they did arrest 160 mourners for marching silently in Evers's memory. In Tuscaloosa, Alabama, Governor George Wallace had made his famous stand in the schoolhouse door to stop black students from enrolling at the University of Alabama. And in Birmingham, public safety director Eugene "Bull" Connor had greeted nonviolent protesters with snarling police dogs and high-pressure fire hoses. Chicago blacks followed all the ugly details in the pages of the *Chicago Defender,* whose headlines lately had been a steady drumbeat of "New Miss[issippi] Violence: Club-Swinging Jackson Cops Attack Evers Murder Protest March" and "Birmingham Still on the Edge of Racial Blow-Up!"[41]

As difficult as events were down South, the NAACP delegates were also aware of the problems blacks faced in their host city — the slums, the segregated schools, the high-rise housing projects. Daley delivered an opening address to the convention that scrupulously avoided taking on any of these controversial issues. Instead, he declared that there were "no ghettos in Chicago." He meant the remark to be uplifting, a statement of his high regard for all of the city's neighborhoods. But Dr. Lucien Holman, the Joliet, Illinois, dentist who headed the statewide chapter of the NAACP, snapped at a startled Daley, "We've had enough of this sort of foolishness." And then Holman launched into a spirited rebuttal. "Everybody knows there are ghettos here. . . . And we've got more segregated schools than you've got in Alabama, Mississippi and Louisiana combined." Still, when it was over, members of the black submachine and other black allies rushed to assure Daley that they understood what he meant. It seemed to be an isolated incident.[42]

The highlight of the convention was a July 4 "Emancipation Day" parade through the Loop. Daley agreed to lead a procession of 50,000 civil rights marchers through downtown. The parade, whose slogan was "Free in '63," was a cost-free way for Daley to make a gesture to the black community, since its focus was on the South. No homeowner in the Bungalow Belt would much care if Daley took a stand against conditions in Mississippi and Alabama. Daley marched in front of a car carrying Medgar Evers's young widow, Myrlie, and smiled as spectators along the route rang "freedom bells" and shouted "Jim Crow must go." Daley and the other marchers finished their hour-long trek at Grant Park, a stretch of green wedged between downtown and Lake Michigan. The parade's organizers asked him to make a few remarks to the large crowd now gathered around the park's bandshell. Daley had not expected the invitation, but he readily agreed. He was soon spouting his usual brand of painfully bland expressions of civil goodwill. "May I say that we are happy to welcome this convention and the delegates to our city," he began. But as Daley spoke, a crowd of between one hundred and two hundred protesters began to march toward the speaker's platform. If he saw them, he ignored the disruption and plunged ahead. "We are glad you have come to see us and we hope you come to see us again and again."[43]

The hecklers picked up their pace, and they were fast winning converts. The air began to fill with shouts of "Daley must go!" and "Down with ghettos!"— a reference to his recent comment about there being no ghettos in Chicago. Daley forged ahead, but the hecklers would not give up. One woman turned her back to the speaker's platform and bowed her head. She seemed, at first glance, to be embarrassed by the crowd's behavior. But she turned out to be a city worker who was trying to join the booing without being seen by her Democratic precinct captain. Bishop Stephen G. Spottswood, chairman of the NAACP national board of directors, stepped down from the speaker's platform and tried to quiet the protesters, but their yelling only grew louder. The more the hecklers shouted, the more flustered Daley became. After fifteen minutes of boos and catcalls, he angrily stormed off the stage.[44]

Moments after Daley left, the Reverend Joseph H. Jackson took the podium. Jackson was minister of the South Side's 15,000-member Olivet Baptist Church and president of the National Baptist Convention, whose 5 million members and 30,000 affiliated churches made it the nation's largest black organization. Jackson was an outspoken opponent of the civil rights movement, who had most recently angered activists by coming out against the proposed March on Washington that Martin Luther King Jr. was to lead. The previous Sunday, protesters had picketed outside Jackson's church during services. The moment Jackson was called on to speak, a deafening roar arose from the crowd. For fifteen minutes, the audience booed and yelled "Uncle Tom must go!" When a group of fifty demonstrators circled him and shouted "Kill him! Kill him!" the embattled minister had to be escorted from the park by police. Daley also fled the scene and, after wading through the crowd, located his limousine. Asked by a reporter what had gone wrong, Daley replied curtly that the protest must have been planned by the Republicans.[45]

In fact, the July 4 heckling indicated just how quickly race relations were changing in Chicago. When the NAACP convention held its closing session at the Morrison Hotel on July 6, it was clear that Daley still retained significant support in the black community. The delegates adopted a resolution thanking him for his cooperation. But another version, which pointedly expressed appreciation only to unnamed "municipal authorities," got about one-third of the vote. A few days later, after the NAACP delegates had left town, an interracial group from the Chicago chapter of the Congress of Racial Equality held a sit-in at the Board of Education to protest segregation in the public schools. The protesters occupied a conference room for eight days, until the police finally removed them. The situation was "bordering on anarchy," said the president of the Board of Education. Board business was being interrupted, and the protesters had broken the door between the conference room where they were holding the sit-in and the president's office. Daley supported the police, who arrested and carried off seven men and three girls, saying, "We can't let anybody physically take over city offices." But the protesters were only getting started. On July 22, CORE held a one-hour demonstration in a hallway outside Daley's office. In a brief meeting, the protest leaders asked Daley to mediate the school crisis. Daley responded that the Board of Education was an independent body, and insisted he could not possibly intervene. It was, of course, merely an excuse. Daley was intimately involved in the schools and meddled with them when it suited his purposes. Clair Roddewig, school board president during the early years of the crisis, would later say that he spoke to the mayor "almost daily about school matters."[46]

The next civil rights battle was waged in the City Council. The 1963 aldermanic elections had produced Charles Chew, a civil rights leader unlike any Chicago had ever seen. Chew had run as an independent in the racially changing 17th Ward on the Far South Side. He won by persuading middle-class black voters to reject the white machine candidate and the machine's "plantation politics." When he got to the City Council, he was the only black alderman who did not need to follow Daley's edicts on civil rights. On July 1, he joined Alderman Despres in sponsoring an open-housing bill. As usual, the six black machine alderman — the so-called silent six — led the opposition. Judiciary Committee chairman Claude Holman, one of the "silent six," got the bill tabled until August 22. When the Despres-Chew bill came up again, Daley was ready with an open-housing bill of his own. Daley's bill, which he had arranged to have sponsored by a biracial coalition of aldermen, was a pale imitation of the Despres-Chew proposal. The Daley bill required only that real estate brokers not engage in unfair practices. Rather than stressing "fair housing," it used the term only twice, both times in the preamble. It was, as critics pointed out vociferously, a "subterfuge" designed to co-opt the open housing movement by making it look as if the City Council had acted.[47]

In normal circumstances, Daley would have had no trouble getting his bill passed. He controlled a large majority on the council, and it was an elemental rule that officeholders slated by Daley — whether for Sanitary District board or U.S. Senate or alderman — gave him their vote when he asked for it. The machine was not subtle about sending out instructions to its legislators, which was just as well, since many were not particularly bright. "They put out a so-called idiot sheet every day during the [state] legislative session," former suburban Democratic commiteeman Lynn Williams recalled. "A mimeographed sheet is sent around to the Chicago delegations — House Bill 2351, dog muzzles, yes; House Bill 2500, change judiciary, no; House Bill 2961, divorce, no. There's no secret about it. You can go to the desk and see them sitting there with this sheet." Daley sent the word out to the City Council to vote for his fair housing ordinance. That should have ended the matter, but most of the white aldermen were afraid to vote even for the machine's toothless bill. James Murray, who ended up sponsoring the bill, initially told Daley he was worried. "I said, 'Why me? — My community is up in arms,'" Murray recalls. "He said I was [president pro tem of the City Council] and the city needed the ordinance." Keane and Murray met in Daley's office the day of the City Council vote, and Daley called each alderman personally to tell them they were expected to back the bill. At the council, the vote was delayed eighty minutes while Daley and Keane threatened to deny patronage to aldermen who broke with the machine. In the end, the bill passed 30–16, the most defections Daley had ever suffered in the City Council.[48]

As the summer wore on, the civil rights movement gained momentum. On July 21, pickets marched outside the Olivet Baptist Church in opposition to Reverend Jackson and school board member Mrs. Wendell Green, two of the leading anti–civil rights figures in the black community. Green, a machine loyalist, was possibly the most anti-integrationist member of the board. The protesters carried signs reading "Birds of a feather flock together — Green, Jackson, and Jim Crow," and "Mrs. Green, enemy of our children." At the same time, whites were continuing their own protests. When two black families moved into apartments, there were three days of clashes at 56th and Morgan streets on the Southwest Side, and Daley had to plead for "law and order to prevail everywhere." When civil rights protesters demonstrated outside the president of the Board of Education's home, Daley lashed out at the media. "Without publicity, the demonstrators would stop tomorrow," he said. Taking a leaf from the book of governors and sheriffs across the South, Daley also began to blame outside agitators for the unrest. "They come from all over town, and some from out of town," says Daley. "I see that some of them are from out of state, one is from Nassau County, N.Y., and another from Green Bay, Wisconsin." Chicago's racial difficulties were starting to become national news. A page-one story in the *New York Times* on August 26 concluded that "the situation seems potentially more explosive than in most Southern communities."[49]

The school protesters were coming to realize that they had an ideal villain in their midst: School Superintendent Benjamin Willis. Willis had gotten his start as the principal of a four-room schoolhouse in rural Maryland, and worked his way up through the state's racially segregated educational system. After a stint as superintendent of schools in Buffalo, New York, he came to Chicago. Willis's admirers considered him a skilled administrator, who championed teacher salary increases, smaller class sizes, and rigorous graduation requirements. But to his critics, both black and white, Willis was uncommunicative and arrogant. The president of the Chicago PTA, at the end of her two-year term, complained that Willis had not met with her or her delegate assembly once. "We have asked, but Dr. Willis has not found time for us," she said. Even the Board of Education found him to be imperious. Willis had "contempt for the judgment of any board member who has the temerity to disagree with him," one member said in 1966 as he stepped down from the board. Willis also shared Daley's secretive nature. He instructed his staff to refuse requests for information about double-shifts, empty classrooms, and other basic facts about the public schools. Many blacks had a more specific problem with Willis: they were convinced that his views on race were the ones he had absorbed early in his career in the Jim Crow school system in Maryland. "There are certain people who stand out from all others and epitomize evil, wrongness, or just plain bigotry," says Ira Dawson. "Willis was a bigot who said, 'You don't exist' to the black community."[50] Civil rights activists who met with Willis said his inability to reach out to blacks was almost visceral. "He couldn't say the word 'Negro,'" said TFIS activist Meyer Weinberg. "He said 'them' or 'they,' or he would point a certain direction with his chin." Willis seemed like the closest thing Chicago had to the epic civil rights enemies of the South. He was, the *Chicago*

Defender declared, "the Gov. Wallace of Chicago standing in the doorway of an equal education for all Negro kids in this city."[51]

Daley, however, was hearing none of it. Rose Simpson, chairman of the Parents Council for Integrated Schools, met with Daley in August and urged him to remove Willis. He "is not concerned about Negro education and he fosters segregation in the schools," she said. Daley responded curtly that Willis was doing a fine job and that he continued to support him. It was Willis's contentiousness, not Daley's lack of support, that got him in trouble. In the fall, Willis took several white high schools off a list to receive student transfers under a new school board plan. It seemed clear that he had done it to stop those schools from being integrated. The school board ordered him to restore the schools to the list, and they backed it up with a court order. Willis responded by announcing on October 4 that he was stepping down. If Willis's resignation was a tactical ploy to rally whites behind him, it worked. White community groups like the Southwest Council of Civic Organizations and the Property Owners Coordinating Committee threatened a march on City Hall unless Willis was convinced to stay on. Twenty-three of Chicago's top business leaders wired the Board of Education to register the business community's strong support for Willis. The machine's allies in the black community also stepped forward to defend the man others were branding an enemy of black schoolchildren. The attacks on Willis were "mass hysteria," the Reverend J. H. Jackson said, and it would be tragic if they were allowed to bring down a man of his "professional caliber." Daley had, of course, previously told black parents that he could not intervene in educational matters. But now that Willis was threatening to leave, Daley had no qualms about publicly rushing to his defense. "I think it's pretty much hoped by everyone that he comes back," Daley said in a television interview. Within days, a school board committee had prevailed upon Willis to rescind his resignation.[52]

Outraged that Willis was back, civil rights leaders announced a boycott of the public schools. Support for the boycott grew rapidly, with thousands of black parents promising to keep their children out of school on the appointed day. It was a sign of just how strong the pro-boycott sentiment was in the black wards that Daley, in a break with tradition, freed members of the black machine to support it if they wanted. He was not going soft on civil rights, historian Dempsey Travis notes. He just wanted his black allies "to run as fast as hell and catch up with the majority of their constituents." With this clearance from the Morrison Hotel, Dawson's 2nd Ward Organization and several of the "silent six" black aldermen issued statements expressing their support for the boycott. On October 22, the day of the boycott, the response from black parents and children was overwhelming. About 225,000 students stayed out of school, far more than even the organizers expected. Activists set up "freedom schools" in churches, meeting halls, and community rooms, providing alternative instruction. They offered an improvised curriculum of civil rights songs and lessons on freedom and equality. In one exercise, black children were asked to analyze the word "equal" from a variety of perspectives, starting with arithmetic and moving on to current events. The idea, they were taught, was that equality meant not being the same, but being worth the same. At the same time, about ten thousand demonstrators marched on City Hall and the Board of Education. Despite the success of the boycott, activists were still having trouble translating their protests into new educational policy. Weeks of meetings between the CCCO and school officials ended in deadlock. Frustrated by the lack of progress, the CCCO called a second boycott for the following February.[53]

One month after the first school boycott, on November 22, 1963, Daley was having lunch with aides at the machine offices at the Morrison Hotel. His secretary, Mary Mullen, arrived with news that President Kennedy had been shot in Dallas and was near death. Daley burst into tears and then dictated a statement before heading home for the rest of the day. "I cannot express my deep grief and sorrow over the tragic death of President John F. Kennedy," Daley said. "He was a great President — a great leader." Daley's friend William Lee called Kennedy's death "the most terrible moment in our history." The following day, Daley led a memorial service in the City Council chambers. Speaking from a rostrum decorated with a large picture of the slain president, American and Chicago flags, and white chrysanthemums, Daley declared that Kennedy "lived and died in accordance with his own words, 'And so, my fellow Americans: "Ask not what your country will do for you. Ask what you can do for your country." ' " At the end, Daley added, "I have lost a great friend." One week later, the City Council voted unanimously to rename the Northwest Expressway in Kennedy's honor.[54]

The whole nation was stunned and saddened, but Daley had reason to feel Kennedy's death more than most. The two men had remained close since the 1960 election, and just a few months earlier Daley had stopped by the White House while he was in Washington to testify before Congress. He had said at the time that he had no urgent business but that he "just dropped in to say hello." Their relationship was no doubt driven to a large extent by political calculation on both sides, but Kennedy had at least been a reliable political ally, whether it meant approving an urban renewal grant Daley wanted or putting in an appearance the week before Daley's closest mayoral election. Just a few months earlier, Kennedy had nominated Daley's old friend Abraham Lincoln Marovitz to a Federal District Court judgeship at Daley's urging. Daley's relationship with Lyndon Johnson was not as warm. The new president likely knew that Daley had pushed Kennedy at the 1960 convention to keep him off the ticket. Johnson and Daley did not share an ethnic bond, and Johnson did not have the ties to Chicago that the Kennedys did through the Merchandise Mart. Still, the 1964 election was coming up, and Johnson was a shrewd enough politician to understand Daley's importance. He called Daley shortly after he was sworn in, and kept calling, writing, and visiting. And Daley was one of only four guests invited to sit with Johnson's wife and daughters during his first speech to a joint session of Congress. Daley and Johnson would in time become close, particularly over their common interest in Johnson's Great Society initiatives. Daley was able to deliver the votes of the Chicago congressional delegation for the social programs Johnson wanted passed. Johnson, in turn, "was very much into doing programs [that brought] money to cities, trying to solve problems in cities," says William Daley. In the end, he says, his father had "a different, but in some ways a better relationship" with Johnson than he had with Kennedy.[55]

Daley's difficult year ended with a round of criticism over his latest municipal budget. The $532 million he was proposing to spend in 1964 was a record, and taxes would once again have to be raised. Daley's critics charged, as usual, that the money would be used to fund the machine's patronage operations. The Civic Federation, a nonpartisan taxpayers' organization, examined Daley's 1964 budget and concluded that it was riddled with wasteful spending. Among its findings was that the city was routinely paying exorbitant wages to employees who did clerical work. The city was also paying 28 percent more than the going rate for carpenters when, according to the Building Employers Association, because of the advantages of working for the city it should have been paying 20 percent less. According to another study, the number of temporary workers — most of them patronage hires — had now tripled since Daley took over from Kennelly. Two of Daley's leading critics on the City Council issued a joint statement charging that it was "almost impossible to overstate the loss" to the city from employing the 8,493 temporary workers now on the payroll. Daley once again argued that the spending was needed to deliver the high level of municipal services Chicago enjoyed. But a new study cast doubt on Daley's constant assertions about the quality of city services. The National Board of Fire Underwriters issued its national evaluations of fire-preparedness. The group gave Chicago 1,235 deficiency points for shortcomings in fire protection, giving the city a rank of 3 on a scale from 1 to 5. No city had a 1 rating, but seven large cities received 2's, ranking them ahead of Chicago. The insurance industry used the NBFU's ratings to calculate risk, which meant that Chicagoans had to pay higher premiums as a result of the city's mediocre standing. Despite the charges of waste and patronage, Daley's 1964 budget sailed through the machine-controlled City Council in early December. One critic warned, however, that "Mr. Daley's policies are driving homeowners out of the city and destroying neighborhoods."[56]

Daley began the year's first cabinet meeting by declaring that "our aim in 1964 is to give the best service in the most economical manner." But he was soon hit with yet another study documenting the large number of patronage employees being supported by Chicago taxpayers. The Better Government Association charged that more than twenty thousand — or almost 30 percent — of the employees of Chicago's six main local government units were outside civil service, and that the vast majority of these were patronage hires. Many more patronage workers were tucked away in state government, the

Chicago Transit Authority, the Chicago Housing Authority, and other payrolls the machine had access to. The BGA charged that Daley's Civil Service Commission was contributing to the problem by conducting few civil-service examinations, making it easier to make non-civil-service patronage hires. In the previous year, exams were held for only forty-four of the city's 1,656 job titles. The BGA also found other instances of corruption, including a widespread practice in the Sanitation Department of supervisors taking bribes to let their crews work overtime, for which crew members were paid time-and-a-half on Saturday and double-time on Sunday. Days later, the State, County, and Municipal Employees Union joined in, charging that Daley was ignoring a list it had compiled of two thousand workers who were being overpaid as a result of phony job titles. Victor Gotbaum, district director of the union, said patronage workers were routinely being promoted to jobs that should have gone to the civil-service workers he represented. Daley responded, as usual, that the attacks on him were partisan. He charged that the BGA was "an arm of the Republican Party," despite the fact that it had a bipartisan board of directors and had previously endorsed him for mayor.[57]

The new year brought Daley no relief on the school front. He was asked at an early January press conference whether he still supported Willis. With a second school boycott looming, he sounded less than enthusiastic. "I have great confidence in the entire membership of the school board," he responded. If Daley wanted to weaken Willis's position, he would soon have the chance. There were two vacancies coming up on the school board, and Daley was about to fill them. The CCCO sent a twenty-member delegation to urge Daley to select members who would work for integration — one of whom they hoped would be black. Daley heard his visitors out but, true to form, told them he could not commit himself "to any positive course." Before long, the single black member of the nominating committee broke the news to the civil rights activists that Daley was unlikely to appoint the sort of members they were hoping for. "The Southwest Side is more active and influential than we are," he told them. In fact, Daley was not about to yield any ground to the integrationist forces. Dr. Eric Oldberg, the politically moderate suburban doctor who chaired the nominating committee, said that he and other moderates had been urging Daley not to continue to appoint pro-Willis board members. "I told him, 'Goddamn it, Dick, it won't work — maintaining a school board that is polarized.' . . . But he was obdurate; he bluntly told me that nobody was going to tell him who he could appoint, to the school board or anything else." Daley ended up appointing two whites with no known civil rights sympathies: Cyrus Hall Adams, a downtown merchant, and Mrs. Lydon Wild, a South Shore socialite and friend of the Daley family.[58]

With planning for the second school boycott now under way, Daley took back the freedom he had previously given black machine members. He now expected them to support Willis strongly, and to work actively against the civil rights sentiment sweeping through the black wards. In the City Council, the only black member of the City Council school committee fell into line and voted in favor of the nomination of Cyrus Adams and Wild, even as liberal white alderman Leon Despres voted against them. And black machine politicians formed a new group called the Assembly to End Prejudice, Injustice, and Poverty that, despite its name, opposed the CCCO and the school movement. "We hope the school boycott fails, and we're working hard toward that end," the group's president, South Side 20th Ward alderman Kenneth Campbell, said at a February 4 press conference. The black machine sent precinct workers door-to-door in the same wards the CCCO was trying to organize, warning parents that the boycott was an "ineffective weapon" that "harms children." Machine canvassers carried leaflets to be signed and returned by parents, saying: "Your children need all the education they can get. Let nobody fool you into believing that another school boycott can do any good." Daley denied, not very convincingly, that he had any involvement in the formation of the Assembly to End Prejudice, Injustice, and Poverty. "They sent me a copy of the programs and objectives," he insisted. "That's all I know about it." But civil rights activists were not convinced. "Captain Richard J. Daley has cracked the whip," said Rose Simpson, whose recent meeting with the mayor had gone so badly, "and his plantation overseers jumped in line."[59]

When February 25 came, about 125,000 students stayed away from school, an impressive showing in absolute terms, but a sharp fall-off from the first boycott. The black machine's new campaign had made itself felt. In a march on City Hall coinciding with the boycott, demonstrators carried placards reading "The polls are next — watch out Daley," and "If we don't get rid of Daley, we'll have boycotts daily." The protesters also carried a mock coffin bearing the names of Dawson, Willis, and the six black aldermen from the submachine who opposed the boycott. The message the civil rights protesters and the parents of the 125,000 school children were trying to send was lost on Daley. "I don't think civil rights is a political issue," he said. "It is not a political issue, just as education and unemployment are not."[60]

Civil rights activists had long maintained that the Chicago schools were highly segregated, and on March 31, 1964, they received official confirmation. University of Chicago professor Philip Hauser had been commissioned, as part of the settlement of a federal discrimination lawsuit, to study the racial situation in the Chicago school system. Hauser's report struck a conciliatory tone, noting that the problem of school segregation was not "unique to Chicago." Still, it found that 84 percent of the black pupils in Chicago attended schools that were at least 90 percent black, and that 86 percent of white students were in schools that were at least 90 percent white. The Hauser Report faulted the Board of Education for not moving "earlier and more rapidly . . . to resolve the problem of school integration." As debate raged over the report, Daley had the chance to fill three more vacancies on the Board of Education.[61]

The most controversial issue Daley faced was whether to reappoint Mrs. Wendell Green to another five-year term. The elderly Green, who had risen out of the black submachine, remained the greatest apologist for Willis and the school system on the question of race. "I don't know what integration means," she told the City Council when she testified seeking reappointment. "There is no segregation in Chicago schools." Edwin Berry of the Chicago Urban League spoke for most of the school movement when he warned Daley that "[r]eappointment of Mrs. Green would be a monumental tragedy." Dr. Oldberg tried to talk Daley into appointing her to a vacant two-year term, rather than the full five years. "Dick, she's going to be over eighty," Oldberg argued. "Since there's been such a ruckus, give her the short term." "Fine, Doc," Daley replied. But in the end, he reappointed Green to a five-year term. In a surprising act of political independence, 6th Ward alderman Robert Miller broke with his fellow members of the "silent six" and voted against Green in committee. He changed his position by the time her nomination reached the floor, but by then it was too late to restore his standing with the machine. In his usual punitive fashion, Daley withdrew the machine's support in the next election, and Miller lost to an independent candidate. "Daley wouldn't forgive him for going against his wishes," challenger A. A. "Sammy" Rayner said afterward. "I really won by default."[62]

President Johnson traveled to Chicago in April 1964 to address a machine fund-raiser, where he declared his commitment to build "a Great Society of the highest order." The crowd of six thousand loyal Democrats greeted Johnson's declaration with raucous applause. "If you could make a graph of this administration, perhaps this would be a sort of peak," Lady Bird Johnson wrote in her diary. The Great Society was Johnson's plan for extending the progressive ideals of the New Deal through programs like the War on Poverty and Medicare. The War on Poverty was actually a holdover from the Kennedy administration. The late president had asked his aides in the fall of 1963 to develop a program that would extend the nation's growing prosperity to those who were being left behind. After Kennedy's death, Johnson picked up the torch and instructed his staff to "[g]ive it the highest priority." Johnson, who started out in humble circumstances in rural East Texas, had strong personal feelings about fighting poverty. One of his proudest accomplishments was his early work bringing electricity to rural Texas. "Electricity changed those people's lives, made things easier, brought light into the darkness," he recalled to an aide who was helping to develop the Great Society. Johnson also saw his anti-poverty campaign as an integral part of the drive for racial justice. As the battle against Jim Crow was being won in the South, blacks would still need economic assistance to bring them up to the status of whites. Johnson was committed, he said in his first State of the Union address, to using his office on behalf of those who "live on the outskirts of hope — some because of their poverty, and some because of their color, and all too many because of both."[63]

Johnson guided a series of Great Society initiatives through Congress in 1964 and 1965. He established the Department of Housing and Urban Development to take on the problems of the nation's large cities, and allocated $900 million to fight rural poverty in Appalachia. And he persuaded Congress to support his Medicare program, signing it into law in Independence, Missouri, with eighty-one-year-old Harry Truman at his side. It was the Economic Opportunity Act, however, that laid the groundwork for the War on Poverty. The new law created an Office of Economic Opportunity, which Johnson put under the leadership of Sargent Shriver, director of the Peace Corps and brother-in-law of President Kennedy. The choice of Shriver was an indication that Johnson intended the agency and its anti-poverty mission to play an important role in his administration. Shriver was a tireless worker and a bureaucratic warrior who, as the Peace Corps' first director, had turned a start-up program into one of the defining undertakings of the Kennedy era. Daley and Shriver had strong ties, going back to Shriver's time in Chicago as manager of the Kennedy family's Merchandise Mart, and as a member of the Chicago School Board.[64]

The architects of the War on Poverty intended for it to take a bold new approach to the nation's ills. It was aimed, Johnson declared, "at the causes, not just the consequences of poverty." The OEO included eight major programs designed to take on distinct aspects of economic disadvantage. Head Start focused on improving early childhood education for 1.3 million low-income pre-schoolers. The Job Corps was designed to provide job-training opportunities for underprivileged youth. And Volunteers in Service to America, or VISTA, was established as a domestic version of the Peace Corps. Conservatives complained that the War on Poverty was undermining the free market by creating unnecessary government programs and entitlements. Republicans began sporting buttons proclaiming, "I'm fighting poverty, I work." But for the most part, Johnson's efforts to reach out to the nation's most disadvantaged citizens were well received in the early days. "This is the best thing this administration's done," Johnson told Shriver. "I've got more comments and more popularity on the poverty thing than anything else."[65]

The most innovative of all the new anti-poverty initiatives was the $1 billion Community Action Program (CAP). Traditional welfare programs placed bureaucrats and social workers in downtown office buildings and put them in charge of dispensing checks to needy people who lived far away. CAP called for moving welfare programs out of downtown and into the neighborhoods where poor people lived. The most innovative piece of the CAP model was its "maximum feasible participation" rule. The Equal Opportunity Act required that local programs be "developed, conducted, and administered with the maximum feasible participation of residents of the areas and members of the groups served." Buried in this dense statutory language was a truly radical notion. Poverty programs were to be run by neighborhood-based organizations that were "broadly representative of the community." If the mandate was followed faithfully, it would empower poor people to run their own programs for the first time, and give them millions of dollars in federal money to distribute in their communities. Robert Kennedy, testifying in favor of the act, hailed its departure from the traditional model of anti-poverty efforts that "plan programs for the poor, not with them." Richard Boone, a key framer of the OEO legislation, said it was intended as an end-run around city halls and welfare bureaucracies that did not have the interests of the poor at heart. Advocates for the poor believed CAP had the potential to completely change the national landscape. Shriver called it "the boldest of OEO's inventions," and predicted that its grassroots network of neighborhood offices would become "the business corporation of the new social revolution." Michael Harrington, author of the influential anti-poverty manifesto *The Other America,* declared that the Equal Opportunity Act could end up doing as much to organize the poor as the Wagner Act had done to organize workers thirty years earlier.[66]

Daley did not share this enthusiasm for the War on Poverty or CAP. He was not, by temperament, a believer in welfare programs. His upbringing in Bridgeport had taught him that life was a struggle, and that people caught up in hard times should look to themselves first. "Look, Sister," Daley once said to a nun who complained to him about the problems of Chicago's ghetto residents. "You and I come from the same background. We know how tough it was. But we picked ourselves up by our bootstraps." Nor did Daley believe in the increasingly fashionable talk about "welfare rights," and what poor people were owed by the government. "In his heart of hearts," one Daley associate said, "I think he would like to grab these people by their lapels, shake them, and say, 'Get to Work!'" But there was one thing Daley liked very much about the War on Poverty — it promised to send millions of dollars of federal money to Chicago. Daley was one of a contingent of big-city mayors, including New York's John Lindsay, Los Angeles's Sam Yorty, and Detroit's Jerome Cavanaugh, who went to Washington for a private briefing on the program. Daley, who could track a federal dollar better than anyone, overcame his philosophical objections and declared after a two-hour meeting with Housing and Urban Development secretary Robert Weaver that the new anti-poverty initiative was a "bold, imaginative enterprise."[67]

Daley was more than willing to take the federal money, but he was determined not to let Chicago's CAP operate under maximum feasible participation. The whole idea of letting poor people manage poverty programs, which the Johnson administration was so excited about, struck Daley as absurd. "It would be like telling the fellow who cleans up to be the city editor of a newspaper," Daley declared. Daley also immediately grasped the serious political implications of maximum feasible participation. Policymakers in Washington saw it mainly as a way to sidestep the "board ladies and bureaucrats" who controlled poverty programs. Daley, who looked at everything through the lens of machine politics, understood that it would take money, patronage jobs, and ultimately power away from City Hall and the machine and hand them over to neighborhood activists. Daley had seen it all before. The idea of maximum feasible participation had been borrowed from a Kennedy administration juvenile delinquency program. Daley had watched that program channel money to the machine's opponents in the neighborhoods. Ultimately, he shut the program down, sending millions of dollars back to Washington, and then established a new city-funded program that operated under his close supervision. To avoid being put in this position again, Daley went to Washington to testify against including a maximum feasible participation requirement in the CAP statute. The nation's mayors believed, he told the House Committee on Education and Labor, that "any project of this kind, in order to succeed, must be administered by the duly constituted elected officials of the areas."[68]

Daley lost this early skirmish in the war. Maximum feasible participation remained in the law. But the language of the act remained imprecise enough that a local government that wanted to evade it had considerable leeway. The act did not specify how many poor people had to participate, or what kind of decision making they had to be part of. Daley's approach to implementing CAP, which was quickly dubbed the Chicago Concept, was to keep control over the money and the important decisions in City Hall. "It is a mistake for mayors to let go of control of their programs to private groups and individuals," he insisted. "Local government has responsibilities it should not give up." He established the Chicago Committee on Urban Opportunity to oversee CAP, naming himself as chairman and Clair Roddewig, the firmly pro-Willis president of the Board of Education, as vice chairman. The ninety-member CCUO board that Daley named had only seven residents of poor neighborhoods — a level of participation that seemed suspiciously less than the "maximum feasible." The vast majority of the board were machine loyalists, city bureaucrats, friends from the business community, and other people Daley could rely on to see things his way — including five black aldermen who voted with the machine on civil rights issues. One poverty activist charged that the CCUO board selected by Daley "reads like a fund-raising list of the Democratic party."[69]

To serve as executive director of the CCUO, Daley selected Dr. Deton Brooks, a former research director with the Cook County Department of Public Aid. Brooks, who was black, had close ties to Daley and the machine. While heading up the CCUO, he served as cochairman of the reelection campaign of machine congressman Roman Pucinski — despite protests from Republicans that his dual roles violated the Hatch Act's prohibition on federal employees working in political campaigns. Brooks was responsible for setting up the network of local CAP organizations. He named directors for the twelve neighborhood service centers, who in turn chose local residents to serve on neighborhood advisory councils. This was the grassroots network that the War on Poverty theoreticians hoped would become the engine for reinventing anti-poverty programs nationwide. Under Brooks and Daley, of course, the network turned into an adjunct of the Democratic machine. As a gesture to maximum feasible participation, the CCUO designated one thousand poor people as salaried "community representatives," but the vast majority of them were selected by the Democratic ward organizations. To be part of the network, one critic charged, "your precinct captain and ward committeeman must recommend you." Daley was unapologetic about the machine's involvement in CAP. "What's wrong with a Democratic committeeman sending a capable man or woman when the test is on the person's qualifications and not who sends him?" he asked. "It's only a question of putting a force of the best men and women possible together." In some cities, poor people were allowed to vote for members of local anti-poverty boards, but Daley insisted that Chicago's representatives be appointed. It was, of course, another way in which Daley ensured that the machine dominated CAP at the local level. But Daley insisted he could not envision anyone wanting to participate in an election of this kind. "Would you want to come and vote and be forever known as poor?" he asked.[70]

In April 1964, the Daleys left for a three-week European tour, with Police Superintendent Wilson, Alderman Marzullo, and city director of special events Colonel Jack Reilly among those in tow. If Daley's trip was designed to give him an air of worldliness — even, perhaps, to put him in the running to be named as Johnson's running mate in 1964 — his mundane observations about the world capitals undercut the intended effect. On his first visit to Paris, in the shadow of Notre Dame and the Louvre, Daley exclaimed, "It's marvelous the way they're trying to have a clean city." After an audience with Queen Elizabeth II at Buckingham Palace, he observed: "We all have the same problems, especially traffic." The Daleys visited Berlin, Vienna, Copenhagen, Stockholm, Lourdes, and Dublin, and had a private audience with Pope Paul VI. The highlight of the trip was a visit to Daley's ancestral home of Dungarvan, in County Waterford, Ireland, where he was greeted by five thousand townspeople who wished him *cead mile failte,* Gaelic for 100,000 welcomes. Daley learned from the locals that his maternal grandfather, a well-known wrestler known as Big Diamuid O'Duinn, had been the town tug-of-war champion. In County Clare, Mrs. Frances Condell, the mayor of Limerick, told Daley that the O'Daleys were well-known poets in the area. She told Daley that one of his ancestors, Donough More O'Dalaigh, was the official poet of Bunratty Castle, where the Daleys ate a medieval dinner.[71] Daley's welcome when he returned to Chicago was less gracious: the newspapers were once again full of corruption scandals. This time, the newspapers had discovered that city employees were making large amounts of money renting trucks to the city at inflated prices. It also turned out that the Forestry Division was buying all of its flowers, at inflated prices, from a single company owned by a Forestry Division employee.[72]

In August, at the Democratic National Convention in Atlantic City, the Democrats were torn by one of the most searing disputes in the party's history. The Mississippi Freedom Democratic Party, a biracial civil rights coalition, petitioned to be seated in place of the all-white "regular" Mississippi delegation, arguing that a segregated state delegation should have no place in the National Democratic Party. Fannie Lou Hamer, the last of twenty children born to share-croppers, gave powerful testimony about the beatings and abuse she had suffered in her struggles to organize blacks to vote. Hamer's tele-vised testimony before the credentials committee riveted the nation until President Johnson — who was worried that Hamer's appeal would divide the party — hastily scheduled a press conference to preempt her. Daley had the Illinois delegation adopt a resolution favoring the seating of the all-white Mississippi delegation, which was headed by Lieutenant Governor Paul Johnson — who had once joked that NAACP stood for "niggers, alligators, apes, coons, and possums." As usual, Daley had his black machine followers take the lead in this anti–civil rights cause. The resolution backing the white Mississippians was sponsored by Alderman Kenneth Campbell, one of the "silent six," and aldermen Claude Holman, Ralph Metcalfe, and William Harvey all spoke out in favor of rejecting Fannie Lou Hamer's heartfelt plea.[73] The convention eventually adopted com-promise, brokered by Hubert Humphrey, which permitted two members of the MFDP to be seated as part of the Mississippi delegation.[74]

On September 12, in the midst of the national election campaign, the Chicago Commission on Human Relations received a report that a white group had purchased a two-flat at 3309 S. Lowe in Bridgeport, just three blocks from Daley's home, with the intention of renting it to a black family. The purchasers included John Walsh, a high school teacher and former president of Teachers for Integrated

Schools. Rumors quickly spread through Bridgeport that the house had been sold to a black family. Within a day, there was a small fire in the house. Within a week, excrement had been thrown into a vestibule. On September 19, Walsh wrote to Daley to say that he planned to rent the home to a black student from the nearby Illinois Institute of Technology and his dental-technician wife. "Since these young people are moving into a basically fine community, I'm sure that you will encourage all of your neighbors to make their new neighbors feel welcome in Bridgeport," Walsh wrote. Faced by the community's hostile reception, Walsh's black couple backed out, but he found two young men — a twenty-one-year-old student and a nineteen-year-old mail clerk — to take their place. On October 3, a Saturday evening, white youths gathered at the house and shouted, "Two, four, six, eight. We don't want to integrate." Over the next few days, larger crowds arrived and threw rocks and bricks through the windows.[75]

With the election only weeks away, Daley was in his usual bind over race. He could not afford to alienate Democratic voters in the black wards by endorsing housing segregation. At the same time, he did not want to lose white ethnics by supporting integration of the Bungalow Belt. The battle for 3309 South Lowe, of course, had an added layer of complexity because it literally hit close to home — compromising the racial boundary that the Hamburg Athletic Club of his youth had defended by force. Asked at a press conference about the clashes occurring down the street from his house, Daley declared, "Every person has the constitutional right to live wherever he wishes." Human relations commissioner Edward Marciniak also insisted that the city was concerned about "protecting the rights of all people to live as good neighbors wherever they choose." But while Daley championed open housing publicly, it was segregation that prevailed. The black men's belongings were removed from the house without their consent, and a real estate agent rented it without Walsh's knowledge to two whites, who proceeded to hold an open house for their neighbors. Walsh sued to evict the white tenants from his property, but the judge ruled in favor of the white tenants. Walsh took satisfaction in having shown that Daley did not really support open housing. "I proved that Daley was guilty of passive hypocrisy,"

Walsh said later. "He could have prevented all the trouble . . . [but] Daley didn't lift a finger."[76]

President Johnson and Republican Barry Goldwater were now engaged in a heated — but, according to the polls, not especially close — presidential election. The Chicago machine, which had done disappointingly in the 1963 mayoral election, was gearing up for a massive effort on behalf of Johnson and the entire Democratic ticket. On September 14, five thousand precinct workers poured into the Medinah Temple for a pre-election rally. Dawson set off a five-minute frenzy of applause and cheering by shouting, "Dick Daley is the greatest political brain in the United States of America!" and "We have the most powerful political organization in the nation!" The Republicans were also preparing for the election, in their case by having volunteer canvassers examine the Chicago voting rolls as part of Operation Double Check. The party filed complaints against four thousand questionable voters, including the usual assortment of Democrats registered from vacant lots and psychiatric hospitals. The canvassers turned up one voter named Benjamin Franklin registered from a store at 4640 South Cottage Grove Avenue, though the store owner said no one lived there. Daley dismissed the canvass as "an effort to make political capital of a worn-out issue." The machine held a traditional torchlight parade for Johnson on the eve of the election, with three thousand torches spread out at ten-foot intervals. Daley had ordered each of the city's fifty ward organizations to turn out five thousand people, though one reporter on the scene said "it did not appear they had succeeded" and that some of those who showed up "looked like troops waiting to be dismissed." Johnson, however, did not seem disappointed when he entered Chicago Stadium to the strains of the Democratic theme song, "Happy Days Are Here Again," and was greeted by a capacity crowd. "Mayor Daley," Johnson declared, "is the greatest politician in the country." On election night, Johnson won Illinois by almost 900,000 votes, carrying Governor Kerner and the whole Democratic ticket in with him. The voting returns underscored the importance to the machine of handling the race issue correctly. One reason for the size of the Democrats' margin of victory was the extraordinary growth in the state's black vote. As a result of continued migration from the South, more than one million blacks now lived in Chicago. There were now some 500,000 blacks registered in Illinois, an increase of 300,000 in eight years.[77]

After the election, Daley delivered his 1965 municipal budget. This budget was more modest than the ones that had sparked battles with the economy bloc in recent years. It did not seek pay increases for most city workers and, in response to newspaper stories critical of the cost of operating City Hall, it called for cutting the number of maintenance and operation workers there by more than 25 percent. Daley said he expected the new budget would lead to a reduction in property taxes. Also in response to recent criticism, Daley announced that the city had given 35,000 civil service tests in 1964, triple the rate in 1963. In another sign that Daley was shaking off some of the bad headlines of the last few years, the National Board of Fire Under-writers finally upgraded Chicago from 3 to 2, making it one of only eight cities to get that rating. On November 21, Daley's second daughter, Mary Carol, married Robert Vanecko at Nativity of Our Lord Church. Joseph McKeon, a neighbor and longtime friend of the family, drove the bride in a limousine for the one-and-a-half-block trip to church. "She wanted me to do it because I drove her father and mother on their wedding day," he said.[78] Governor Kerner, Lieutenant Governor Samuel Shapiro, and other elected of-ficials attended. The Daley family received a two-foot-high stack of telegrams, including one from President Johnson.[79]

In late November, the machine moved its headquarters from the Morrison Hotel to the Sherman Hotel across the street from City Hall. The Morrison, the machine's home for the last thirty-five years, was being torn down to make room for the First National Bank of Chicago building. A few weeks later, Daley scheduled a meeting in his office with the city's Committee on Organized Crime Legislation. The committee, which was headed by an associate dean at Northwestern University Law School, recommended making cer-tain kinds of gambling a felony. A bill drafted by the committee that provided for prison sentences for bookmaking and policy games was signed into law a few months later by Governor Kerner. Coming after Daley's decision to locate the University of Illinois campus in the 1st Ward — which had led to a large piece of the syndicate's home neighborhood being torn down — the latest round of legislation seemed to signal that Daley was finally making his break with organized crime. Daley's turning against the syndicate appeared to be largely political. He had gladly used it to help him get to City Hall, but now that he no longer needed it he had to worry — as he had with Dawson — that it might at some point use its power against him. The syndicate was also proving increasingly embarrassing to the machine, with round after round of newspaper stories revealing that it had placed gambling operators and juice men in patronage jobs. The syndicate was well aware that its relations with the mayor's office had grown chillier. The FBI was picking up that "the criminal element" in Chicago had begun to express dissatisfaction with Daley and "felt it should have more control over him since it helped him attain the position." Daley's FBI file reports on a conversation between an unnamed political figure and syndicate leader Sam Giancana. The political figure complained that Daley would not listen when he tried to prevent a particular nominee from being slated for Cook County sheriff. He "claimed that Daley was the most powerful political figure in Chicago history and he bemoaned the fact that prominent Chicago Ward politicians were no longer able to influence the Mayor," the FBI report says.[80]

We're Going to Have a
Movement in Chicago

Daley left for Washington on January 17, 1965, to attend President Johnson's inauguration. In the pecking order of inauguration VIPs, Daley ranked near the top: the Daleys were invited to sit on the platform during the swearing-in ceremony, and to sit in the presidential box during the Inaugural Ball. At a party at the Shoreham Hotel, Daley was chosen to introduce the new president, and Johnson exclaimed: "This looks like a real Dick Daley crowd here, all enthusiastic, all happy, and all Democrats." When Daley returned to Chicago, however, the mood was less festive. Willis's contract was due to expire on August 31, and the battle was already under way over whether it would be renewed. Professor Philip Hauser, a respected voice on education issues, had joined the anti-Willis camp, declaring that "in light of recent developments and the animosity of a large part of the population toward him, it would be unreasonable for him to stay on." Willis's defenders were equally committed, and it seemed clear that Daley was quietly in their camp. *Chicago Sun-Times* columnist John Drieske had predicted in late December that Willis would end up keeping his job if he wanted it because Daley had selected him and the mayor was "not one to admit he was ever wrong in anything."[1]

In the spring, with the time drawing nearer for a decision over Willis's fate, both sides were actively mobilizing. There were the usual anti-Willis protests, including a Good Friday march on City Hall organized by a new group called Clergy for Quality and Equality in Our Public Schools. But now Willis's white supporters were also speaking out. A citywide group of mothers organized a Tribute to Dr. Benjamin Willis Committee. The committee's president conceded that it was all white, but added that "we welcome any Negroes who wish to support Dr. Willis." White PTAs, property owners' organizations on the South and West sides, and business leaders also weighed in, and more than 100,000 pro-Willis leaflets entitled "The Chicago Public Schools and Benjamin C. Willis" were distributed throughout the city. Political observers handicapping the school board's politics were saying that it was deeply divided: four for Willis, three against, and three in the middle. The swing votes — Wild, Adams, and Louise Malis — were all recent Daley appointees. Cyrus Adams was typical of this group. He favored integration in theory, but he was convinced it always ended up badly because white parents simply took their children out of the public schools. The more he saw of actual attempts to integrate public schools, he told a meeting of the Citizens' School Committee, the more convinced he became that the best course was simply to work on "preserving such integration as existed."[2]

In April 1965, the city took a break from its civil rights turmoil to mark Daley's tenth anniversary as mayor. The City Council held a ninety-minute tribute to "The Daley Decade." Even by the extravagant standards of the City Council, this ceremony set new records for mayoral flattery. Keane lauded Daley for building new highways, completing O'Hare Airport, and luring the University of Illinois–Chicago campus. Claude Holman breathlessly told Daley that "the city has a rendezvous with destiny," and that "you are the north star that leads us." But it was Casimir "Casey" Laskowski, the alderman-mortician from the Northwest Side 35th Ward, whose encomiums reached the highest level. "I hate to speak of this and make a comparison, but once on this earth there walked a man named Jesus Christ," Laskowski said.[3]

In mid-May, it appeared that Willis was finally on the brink of dismissal. The *Chicago Sun-Times* declared in a banner headline, "Board Refuses Willis Contract." The word leaking out of the school board was that the board had voted in a secret session not to renew his contract. These reports of Willis's demise turned out to be premature. His supporters on the board managed to stall the resolution for two weeks, and in the interim both sides launched heavy lobbying campaigns. At a Witness Against Willis rally on the South Side, University of Chicago professors Hauser and Alvin Pitcher called for Willis's ouster. But on May 22, at the Edgewater Beach Hotel, 1,100 people gathered for a dinner honoring Willis. Machine congressman Roman Pucinski declared that "[t]he children of this city have had a rare experience from his profound wisdom and experience." During this tense time, rumors were rampant that Daley was secretly working to keep Willis in office. He was overheard by a reporter telling his newly appointed school board members that he hoped they would "be able to sit down and work this thing out." When the two-week cooling-off period ended, a compromise was reached that allowed Willis to remain in office another sixteen months, until he turned sixty-five. The three votes that changed came from Daley's recent appointees — Wild, Adams, and Malis.[4]

Willis's opponents were outraged, and they called another school boycott for June 10 and 11. The city's political and business establishment once again lined up against the boycott. The Board of Education went to court and got an injunction prohibiting the CCCO and the NAACP from leading the boycott. The *Sun-Times* advised organizers to negotiate instead, asking "Of What Avail a Boycott?" And Daley urged parents to send their children to school. "It is only through education that we will have the type of society we want," he said. Despite the opposition, on the appointed days 100,000 students stayed away from classes. CCCO head Al Raby, barred by the court order from working on the boycott, led several hundred protesters on a march on City Hall. No one was arrested, but Daley vowed that there would be no more protests. The next day, when the marchers returned, the police arrested more than 250 of them. Daley had limited patience with political demonstrations. He believed that the political process was the appropriate way of making decisions and allocating benefits. The leaders elected by the black wards were the machine politicians who were supporting him and opposing the school boycotts. If civil rights activists wanted their views to prevail, Daley believed, they should present themselves to the voters and win in an election. "Who is this man Raby?" Daley asked after the march on City Hall. "He doesn't represent the people of Chicago." Daley also believed in authority, as he was taught to in his traditional Irish-

Catholic upbringing in Bridgeport, and he was offended by the tactics of the Al Rabys of the world. "I come from a people who had no say in their government and so they came to this country," Daley told an annual meeting of the South Shore Commission days after Raby's City Hall march. "When they elected an official here, they had respect for him. But people today have forgotten this. Unless we have free men and women who uphold order and the law and have respect for the public officials they elect, then we have anarchy and conflict."[5]

Daley also blamed the media for the protests. "Consider the millions that are spent by commercial enterprises to get their messages before the readers and viewers of the mass media," Daley told a graduating class at the Illinois Institute of Technology. "Then consider a lone picket marching around one public building and the publicity he gets. Would all these pickets be willing to march if they didn't get their pictures on television? Would they stay if the reporters and television cameramen were to leave?" Daley found new villains to blame over the next few weeks. Some of the money for the anti-Willis protests might well be coming from Republicans, he charged at a press conference. And he announced that police files showed that many of the participants in the civil rights marches were Communists. "You know, these people take part in any disturbing thing they can," Daley said. Raby responded by accusing Daley of engaging in "witch-hunting." On June 28, school protest leaders met with Daley and the school board to try to work out their differences. Daley opened the meeting with a plea for negotiations "around the table, in the true American way, and not in the streets."[6] The civil rights activists brought a nine-point list of demands, including immediate removal of Willis and adoption of a plan for integrating the Chicago school system. But it soon became clear Daley did not intend to offer much, and Raby called the two-hour session "fruitless." The following day, Daley and the civil rights activists met with the school board. After Daley urged "cooperation," one CCCO member responded, "We stand ready to cooperate . . . if the board will give us anything to cooperate with." The meetings ended in stalemate, and with the CCCO vowing to take its case against the school system to the federal government.[7]

Down South, the civil rights movement had begun to enter a new phase in the spring of 1965. It had been an arduous struggle, but it was finally being won. Popular opinion had steadily shifted in favor of King and his followers. In 1963, *Time* had named King its "Man of the Year." In December 1964, he had received the Nobel Peace Prize. And in early 1965, the Selma-to-Montgomery voting rights marches — which brought televised images of Alabama state troopers beating marchers into living rooms across the country — had solidified national support for the cause. With the passage of the Civil Rights Act of 1964 and the Voting Rights Act of 1965, Congress had put the country firmly on the side of civil rights. There was still important work to be done implementing these new laws. Many schools and public accommodations needed to be integrated, and millions of blacks would have to be registered to vote. But the legal system of Jim Crow had gone down to defeat.[8]

These successes had brought division in the ranks of the civil rights movement. Prominent members of the Southern Christian Leadership Conference leadership were urging King to declare victory in the South and bring the movement up to the big cities in the North. The debate was about ideology as much as geography. The problems of the urban centers in the North were mainly poverty and ghetto living conditions, not legal discrimination, so taking the civil rights movement north would mean reorienting it toward a greater focus on economic issues. James Bevel, an SCLC staff member with family ties to Chicago, was the most outspoken proponent of heading north. "Chicago is not that different from the South," he argued. "Black Chicago *is* Mississippi moved north a few hundred miles." But other influential activists argued that the SCLC should maintain its focus on the South. Bayard Rustin, the architect of the August 1963 March on Washington and one of the SCLC's most respected strategists, maintained that the organization's work in the South was not yet done. "SCLC's special mission is to transform the eleven southern states," Rustin argued. "There won't be any real change in American politics and in the American social situation until that is done." Andrew Young agreed, arguing that even with good laws on the books, the Justice Department could not be trusted to bring the lawsuits and apply the pressure that would be needed to dismantle the Jim Crow system. Young also worried that the move north was beyond the group's limited resources. The SCLC was operating with a staff of only about one hundred and an annual budget of less than

$1 million. "We're just kidding ourselves if we say we can do Chicago and maintain the same presence in the South," he insisted.[9]

The real obstacle to bringing the movement north was the different kind of civil rights problems it would confront. In the South blacks were subordinated by law, and King and the SCLC succeeded in arguing that this kind of official discrimination had no place in America. But in the North, the laws were for the most part racially neutral. Discrimination against blacks was often a product of informal policies, like racial steering or racial preferences in employment; the actors were generally private, such as Realtors or union apprenticeship programs; and much of the harm done to blacks was a result of the overall economic and social conditions that prevailed in the ghetto. This kind of de facto discrimination was inherently more difficult to fight than the de jure discrimination that existed in the South. Rustin and others in the movement were convinced that an attempt to cure the racial ills of the North would end in failure. While the SCLC was debating how to proceed, Bevel began to talk openly about the need for a northern civil rights movement. At a fund-raiser at Northwestern University, in the Chicago suburbs, Bevel promised that when the Alabama voting rights campaign concluded, the SCLC would begin a drive to "break up ghetto life" in the North. "[T]he non-violent movement in a few days, in a few weeks, in a few years will call on Chicago to address itself on the racist attitude that is denying Negroes the right to live in adequate housing," Bevel said. "We're going to have a movement in Chicago."[10]

By the spring of 1965, critics' worst fears about the State Street Corridor had been confirmed. In the three years since the first family moved in, Robert Taylor Homes had spiraled downward. In an April 1965 series on the project, the *Chicago Daily News* reported that its residents were "grappling with violence and vandalism, fear and suspicion, teen-age terror and adult chaos, rage, and resentment." Garbage, beer bottles, and TV sets were thrown out of windows and over porch railings so frequently that maintenance workers routinely wore hard hats. Assaults were so common in the stairwells that county welfare workers were under orders not to use the stairs. With few sports facilities or social centers available, many young people passed time by loitering outside the buildings, getting drunk, and shooting off guns. "We live stacked on top of one another with no elbow room," one mother of five told the *Daily News.* "Danger is all around. There is little privacy or peace and no quiet. And all the world looks on us as project rats." The paper led one article in the series by quoting a seventeen-year-old boy standing on a twelfth-floor gallery in one of the project's high-rises. "They ought to tear this whole place down and start all over," he said.[11]

While most impartial observers concluded early on that Robert Taylor was a model for disaster, Daley continued to defend it, even after the devastating *Daily News* series. The project was better than the "firetraps" and slum housing that had previously existed on the site, he insisted. Daley did not address the idea that after $70 million worth of government housing had been erected on the site, the standard of evaluating it should be higher than whether it was better than the tenement housing it had replaced. Daley, once again, blamed the media for stirring up trouble. Residents were being "castigated as living in ghettos," he said, and were being "made to feel ashamed" of where they live. It did not help Daley's credibility on the subject of poor people's housing that just a few months later the chairman of the CHA, Charles Swibel, was cited for numerous code violations in the skid-row hotels under his management. Daley was also quick to defend Swibel, whom he praised as "one of our most outstanding citizens."[12]

Daley was not only defending the projects that had already gone up in the State Street Corridor — he was actively building new ones there. His latest plan was to build the Raymond Hilliard Center, a 710-unit public housing project, at the north end of State Street. Daley had received ample warning that it was the wrong place to construct still more public housing. In October 1964, when the Hilliard Center was still in the planning stages, the Metropolitan Housing and Planning Council issued an urgent warning to Daley not to proceed. The proposed project would just add "more monolithic, high-rise buildings" to the "four-mile wall" along State Street, the council said. Monsignor John Egan, a respected pastor who was deeply involved in racial issues, brought his own objections directly to Swibel. "I appeared before him," says Egan. "I repeated — they're high-rise slums." But Daley ignored the warnings and went ahead with his plan. "I lost because I don't think the mayor of Chicago and the business community gave one damn," says Egan. Hilliard was, at least in design, a departure from the Robert Taylor model. The architect was Bertrand Goldberg Associates, designer of the innovative Marina City luxury complex. Hilliard Center's two buildings for families were made out of reinforced concrete and built in an arc shape, giving them an unusual look for a housing project. The two buildings in the project set aside for elderly tenants were cylindrical, and even more distinctive looking. In the beginning, some whites moved into Hilliard Center, but before long its family units were entirely black.[13]

Hilliard Center was the final installment in the State Street Corridor. When it was completed in 1966, this strip of land one-quarter mile wide and four miles long was home to almost 40,000 poor black tenants. The five massive projects lined up along State Street — 710-unit Hilliard, 797-unit Harold Ickes Homes, 800-unit Dearborn Homes, 1,684-unit Stateway Gardens, and 4,415-unit Robert Taylor — took up thirty-four consecutive blocks, except for a stretch between 30th and 35th streets where the campus of the Illinois Institute of Technology is located. To the east lay the old Black Belt ghetto stretching out to Lake Michigan; to the west was the Dan Ryan Expressway, with its fourteen lanes of automobile traffic and commuter rail lines. "Most white Chicagoans thought the idea was splendid," notes Chicago journalist Bill Gleason. "When lawyers, certified public accountants, stock and bond salesmen and politicians gazed from the windows of Rock Island commuter trains that brought them to the Loop from Morgan Park, Beverly Hills and Brainerd, they saw the progress of the construction of those highrises for the poor and were assured that 'the Negroes are being kept in their place.'"[14]

At the same time Daley was extending the State Street Corridor to the north and south, the CHA was actively keeping blacks out of public housing projects in the white parts of the city. In the mid-1960s, although blacks made up a large part of the public-housing waiting list, projects in white parts of the city remained almost completely white. At Trumbull Park, there were still only 27 blacks among the 435 families. At Lathrop Homes, located four miles north of the Loop, the 900 families included only 30 blacks, and at Lawndale Gardens, blacks were only 4 out of 125 families. At Bridgeport Homes, the housing project in Daley's backyard, there were no blacks at all. It therefore came as no great surprise when, in late 1966, a former CHA supervisor revealed that the housing authority had been intentionally handing out apartments on the basis of race in order to keep the projects racially segregated. In a sworn statement in a race discrimination suit against the CHA filed by the American Civil Liberties Union, Tamaara Tabb, the agency's former supervisor of tenant selection, revealed that the housing authority kept separate waiting lists for white and black applicants — white families were called "A" and black families "B." The CHA staff kept apartments in Trumbull Park, Lathrop Homes, Lawndale Gardens, and Bridgeport Homes vacant until a white applicant was available, rather than rent it to blacks on the waiting list. For a black family to be moved into a white project, Tabb said, there had to be "specific prior clearance of the executive director or his designee." The agency's experience was that if it took long enough to act, blacks on the waiting list would eventually accept an apartment in one of the city's black projects.[15]

On July 4, 1965, Al Raby filed a complaint with the U.S. Office of Education charging the Chicago Board of Education with operating a segregated and unequal public school system. The CCCO formally requested that the federal government cut off all federal aid to the Chicago schools until the illegal conditions were corrected. In a second filing later in the month, the CCCO set out in detail its claims that the school system had drawn its district lines to keep the schools segregated, and that black schools were systematically shortchanged by the system. These practices were all intentional, the CCCO argued. "After all, it takes some real know-how to segregate a big-city school system," said Meyer Weinberg. "You have to adopt elaborate rules and processes to make it work."[16]

The CCCO's complaint was a bombshell. The modern round of civil rights laws had been passed by Congress to address the de jure racial discrimination that still prevailed in the South. The states of the Old Confederacy had laws on the books, and years of entrenched tradition, that expressly established separate schools for white children and black children. Federal education officials fully expected to be asked to use statutes such as Title VI of the Civil Rights Act of 1964, which barred discrimination on the basis of race in federally funded activities, to force those states to dismantle their dual school systems. What they did not foresee was that, along with complaints from the South, they would receive challenges to the school systems of Chicago, Boston, and Chester, Pennsylvania.[17] The U.S. Office of Education was not even certain that statutes like Title VI applied to the de facto discrimination that existed in the North. When the CCCO's complaint came in, staff members were not certain how to proceed.[18]

The stakes for the CCCO's complaint were high. In past years, a federal funding cutoff would have meant little, since school systems were mainly financed by states and localities. In April 1965, however, President Johnson and Congress signed the Elementary and Secondary Education Act, appropriating $1.3 billion in aid to the nation's schools. The law was touted as benefiting education for poor children, and in fact it did provide more than $1 billion in new money for disadvantaged students. But a major reason for the new funding was to give President Johnson leverage to convince southern school systems to comply with the integration provisions of the Civil Rights Act of 1964. To get the new federal money, states had to be certified as meeting the integration requirements of the act for the start of the 1965–66 school year. The new funding law put enormous power in the hands of the U.S. commissioner of education, Francis Keppel, to prod southern schools to desegregate — and to do it more quickly than the Supreme Court, with its relatively undemanding "all deliberate speed" standard, was requiring. Keppel warned the seventeen southern and border states that they risked losing a total of $867 million in federal funds if they did not take specific steps to desegregate their schools, including integrating four out of twelve grades by the start of the new school year. Alabama stood to lose $54 million if it failed to comply, and Georgia would lose $64 million. What no one close to Daley considered at the time was that if the cutoff were applied to Chicago, it would lose $32 million.[19]

After the Office of Education examined the CCCO's complaint about the Chicago schools, Keppel declared it "unquestionably . . . the most detailed" one his department had ever received. One of the most compelling examples in the complaint concerned the schools in and around the Altgeld Gardens housing project on the Far South Side. Altgeld had been built during World War II as housing for black workers in nearby war industry plants. At the time, the sparsely populated area already had an all-white elementary school called Riverdale. Its graduates fed into nearby Fenger High School, which was more than 95 percent white. When Altgeld Gardens was built, three elementary schools and one high school, Carver High School, were included on the site. The school board issued a directive that no children from the Altgeld housing project would be assigned to Riverdale, even though it was only five blocks away. And even though Riverdale was only a few blocks from Carver High School — the new school built on the grounds of Altgeld, whose enrollment was 99 percent black — and a full three miles from Fenger, Riverdale students would continue to be assigned to Fenger after they graduated. The school system worked out this arrangement by adopting the fiction that Riverdale was actually a "branch" of another virtually all-white school, located four miles away, that fed its graduates to Fenger. The few white families who lived right next to Altgeld were taken care of through a second fiction. The area near the project was declared to be a "neutral zone," whose residents could choose to attend any of the schools in the area, not necessarily the closest one. As it worked out, the white families chose to send their children to white schools. There was no way to explain the school board's elaborate efforts except as an intentional attempt to keep white students from having to attend school with blacks. These race-based assignment rules applied even when they forced black children to attend badly overcrowded schools, and to attend in double-shifts. In 1964, average class sizes at the four schools in the housing project were 32.7 and higher, while average class size at Riverdale was less than 17.[20]

The CCCO complaint also presented the Office of Education with the case of Orr High School. Orr was created in 1962 as a white "unit" of black West Side Marshall High School. It was housed not at Marshall, but inside the building of white Orr Elementary School. At first, Orr shared a principal with Marshall, but in 1964 it was given one of its own. The attendance zone for Orr High School was drawn so its feeder schools included the three white elementary schools in the area. The attendance zone for Marshall was drawn to include the black schools. Marshall ended up being severely overcrowded, and Orr significantly underutilized, but the school system did not alter the assignment patterns. The CCCO complaint also included twenty "cases for further study." Among these were two schools in the racially changing North Lawndale neighborhood, all-white Hammond and all-black Pope. Hammond seemed to be underused — part of its building was demolished — while the overcrowded Pope operated on double-shifts for six years. The CCCO argued that Chicago's school system was as unequal as it was segregated. The complaint marshaled an array of statistics showing that the more white a school was, the better off it seemed to be. White elementary schools in Chicago had an average of 29.7 pupils per classroom, while integrated and all-black elementary schools had averages of 34.0 and 34.4 respectively. White schools had 12 percent noncertificated teachers, while integrated schools had 23 percent and black schools had 27 percent. And in white schools, when a teacher was absent a substitute was sent to cover the class 80 percent of the time, while in black schools, substitutes covered classes with absent teachers only 41 percent of the time. The complaint also raised questions about the Washburne Trade School, operated jointly by the school system and the city's trade unions. Washburne was the only school in Chicago that prepared students for apprenticeships in the city's trades. Though the city school system was majority black, Washburne's enrollment was 97 percent white.[21]

Martin Luther King and the SCLC were still trying to decide whether to bring their movement north. On July 23, King came to Chicago to lay the groundwork for a possible campaign there. Ironically, one of the factors that was drawing King to Chicago was Daley. King was impressed by how much power Daley had, and he was convinced that Daley's absolute control over the city could ultimately work to the movement's advantage. "King decided to come to Chicago because . . . Chicago was unique in that there was one man, one source of power," says the Reverend Arthur Brazier, of The Woodlawn Organization. "This wasn't the case in New York or any other city. He thought if Daley could be persuaded of the rightness of open housing and integrated schools that things could be done." Earl Bush, Daley's press secretary, agrees that Daley's role was a critical factor in bringing King to town. "King considered Daley to be in complete control of Chicago, which in a way he was," says

Bush. "King thought that if Daley would go before a microphone and say, 'Let there be no more discrimination,' there wouldn't be."[22]

Daley dispatched Ed Marciniak, executive director of the Commission on Human Relations, to greet King personally on his arrival. It was Marciniak's introduction to a role he would play repeatedly over the next year. "My job," he says, "was to never let it grow into . . . confrontation." The warm welcome belied Daley's true feelings about King and his tactics. Daley was bitterly opposed to the civil rights movement's insistence on working outside the existing political structure. In his machine-politics view of the world, blacks elected aldermen and ward committeemen to represent them, and Chicago blacks had never elected King and his followers to anything. "Daley felt there were good black people and bad black people," says Edward Holmgren, a former CHA official under Elizabeth Wood who went on to become executive director of the Leadership Council for Metropolitan Open Communities. "The good black people were people like Bill Dawson and the Silent Six." King also insisted on carrying out his campaign in a language Daley did not speak. To Daley, politics was a process of negotiation. A ward committeeman who delivered 20,000 votes on election day was entitled to a certain number of patronage jobs, and to a say in where a fire station was placed in his ward. Anyone who wanted city policy to change had to show where his support was coming from, and why he had the kind of clout that made him worth listening to. King's appeals were not to politics, but to a sense of right, and his tools were not votes, but slogans, marches, and publicity. "King didn't think, 'I have thirty units of power so I get thirty units of results,'" says veteran Chicago reporter Paul McGrath. "He was operating in a whole different way."[23]

Nor did Daley agree with the substance of King's message. It was one thing in Montgomery, Alabama, to say that blacks should not be forced by law to ride in the back of a public bus. But Chicago did not have legally enforced racial segregaion. To King, Chicago was the "most segregated city in the North," but to Daley it was simply a "city of neighborhoods." What King viewed as Jim Crow–like segregation, Daley saw as the natural instinct of free people to stick with their own kind. Daley also believed that King was asking the government to do things for blacks that they should be doing for themselves. Of course blacks did not want to live in slums — just as Irish immigrants, if given a choice, would not have wanted to live in shacks along the banks of the Chicago River. The Irish worked hard, digging canals and slaughtering livestock, until they could move into better jobs and better neighborhoods. Daley did not see why King's followers could not work hard and pursue their own path to the American dream. "Why don't blacks act like the Jews, the Poles, the Irish, and the Italians — he was constantly frustrated by that question," recalls former Daley aide Richard Wade.[24]

Daley's opposition to King was also rooted in simple politics. King's prescription for Chicago would have freed blacks to move out of the ghetto and into white neighborhoods. If King succeeded in integrating Chicago, it would change the demographic layout of the city to the detriment of the machine. Blacks would move out of the traditional black wards, where ward committeemen and precinct captains had for years been turning them out consistently for the machine's candidates. And when blacks moved in, whites would flee their neighborhoods for the suburbs, cutting into another important part of the machine base. Just as troubling, the civil rights movement challenged the machine's careful racial balancing act. The machine held on to black votes by giving the black community patronage jobs rather than civil rights, and it held on to the white vote by assuring the Bungalow Belt that it would not be integrated. If integration became a real possibility, the machine would be challenged from the left in black wards, by independent candidates promising to fight hard for integration. And in the white wards, white backlash candidates would run to the machine's right, promising to be more outspoken in opposition to open housing. Even King's visit had set off warning signals among white voters, who were watching to see how Daley handled it. "Daley's main job as political leader was to keep the lid on blacks," says independent alderman Leon Despres. "He was terrified when Martin Luther King Jr. came to Chicago."[25]

There was also something more visceral about Daley's reaction to King's arrival. Chicago was Daley's city, and he did not understand what King and his followers were doing there. "It was like if you came home and found a burglar in your living room," said McGrath. Like many southern politicians before him, Daley was irate that out-of-town agitators — even ones led by a Nobel Peace Prize recipient — had arrived to stir up trouble and make demands. "Daley was very dogmatic," says CHA chairman Charles Swibel. "He felt that no one was going to come into his city . . . and disrupt it." This direct challenge to his control over Chicago bothered Daley to the point of making him physically ill. Before King's Chicago Campaign was over, Dan Rostenkowski would suggest to presidential aide Lawrence O'Brien that the White House find an assignment that would take his friend Daley "out of the country for a week or two." Rostenkowski was "most concerned," he told O'Brien, about the toll the civil rights campaign in Chicago was having "on the mayor personally."[26]

Unlike the governors and sheriffs King squared off with in the South, Daley was shrewd enough to keep his emotions in check. King had a productive visit in Chicago, meeting with community groups, preaching at two churches, and speaking to a crowd of 15,000 in suburban Winnetka. On July 26, King addressed an even larger gathering at Buckingham Fountain in Grant Park, and then led a march on City Hall. Standing outside City Hall, King offered a prayer for the "nonwhite citizens of this city, who have walked for years through the darkness of racial segregation and a nagging sense of nobodyness." After King returned home, Daley showered him with kind words. His "position against poverty and discrimination, for which he was awarded the Nobel Peace Prize," was one that "all right-thinking Americans should support," Daley said. The two men had minor differences, Daley acknowledged, but "there can be no disagreement that we must root out poverty, rid the community of slums, eliminate discrimination and segregation wherever they may exist, and improve the quality of education." Daley sounded like a committed civil rights activist. No wonder that before King's Chicago Campaign concluded, he and his followers would compare their encounter with Daley to "punching a pillow."[27]

Meanwhile, by the summer of 1965, Chicago's home-grown civil rights marches were no longer generating much attention. Dick Gregory, the comedian and civil rights activist, had led more than forty marches from Buckingham Fountain to City Hall, and they were all starting to look the same. Civil rights activists were trying to come up with more innovative approaches. At a July 24 CORE march on City Hall to protest slum housing, the fifty demonstrators came armed with dead rats. One female protester placed a dead rat on the desk of a receptionist for one of Daley's aides. The marchers carried signs with slogans like "Mayor Daley, would you want a rat for a roommate?" The next day, Chicago civil rights activists added a new twist by following Daley outside the borders of Illinois. When he arrived in Detroit for a meeting of mayors, they arranged for pickets to be on hand to welcome him. "Mayor Daley, won't you please go home?" asked one of the signs.[28]

Another variation, introduced by Gregory, was a series of evening marches into Bridgeport. These demonstrations drew heightened media attention because of the drama of blacks descending on Daley's home. And they had the added advantage of highlighting the fact that Chicago's mayor lived in a neighborhood that was not integrated. The marchers were under orders to behave themselves, walking two-by-two, keeping on the sidewalk, and remaining silent. The sight of blacks in the heart of Bridgeport was unsettling to many neighborhood residents, but they also made an effort to restrain themselves. A few whites held signs reading "We know and love our Mayor" and "Daley is for Democracy, pickets are for publicity," and some shouted "Go back to the zoo!" But Daley had 11th Ward precinct workers circulate through the neighborhood telling residents not to get drawn into any confrontations. "The one overwhelming impression you get is this," journalist Lois Wille wrote in *The Nation*. "Here are two teams of superbly disciplined, fiercely determined combatants. Neither is going to yield — ever."[29]

The tense peace in Bridgeport did not hold. A minor riot broke out on August 2, 1965, when two thousand whites threw eggs, tomatoes, and rocks at the civil rights marchers. The police told the black protesters that their presence was creating a dangerous situation, and ordered them to leave. When most decided to remain, sixty-five were arrested, including Gregory. In a letter to NAACP Legal Defense Fund counsel Jack Greenberg requesting legal help, Al Raby described the scene. "Large 'Ku Klux Klan' signs were prominently displayed in several places," Raby wrote. " 'Wallace for President' signs were numerous, and a group of sub-teens, mostly girls, sang, 'I wish I were an Alabama trooper. Yes, that is what I would truly like to be, I wish I were an Alabama trooper, Cuz then I could kill niggers legally.' The police, however, arrested *us,* the silent demonstrators, stating publicly that they were arresting 'the cause of the riot,' not the rioters." Daley stayed in his home throughout the confrontation, and later lashed out at the marchers for coming to Bridgeport. "People in their homes have a right to privacy," he said. "I don't think it helps their cause to be marching in residential areas. I think they are surely trying to create tension."[30]

The fight over Chicago's anti-poverty programs was starting to heat up. The War on Poverty was being attacked on both sides: Daley and his fellow mayors charged that it was being used to undermine elected city government, while poverty activists contended that city governments had hijacked programs that were intended to be run by poor people. Chicago's CAP was operating, its critics said, with maximum feasible participation of the Democratic machine. At the central office, Deton Brooks and his staff carefully screened funding applications to make sure that no anti-poverty money found its way to the machine's enemies. And at the community level, the advisory councils were firmly in the grip of machine loyalists The Woodlawn Organization protested that only seven of its nominees had been selected for the twenty-five-member Woodlawn advisory council — not enough to have any real impact on its decisions. Daley responded by raising the number of TWO members to twenty-one, but at the same time increasing the council's total membership to seventy-five, maintaining machine control. In making its funding decisions, the Woodlawn advisory council steered clear of projects that might possibly stir up trouble. It rejected a $500,000 program by the Interreligious Council on Urban Affairs to develop leaders in West Side neighborhoods, but accepted another proposal for choir singing. The Woodlawn Organization tried an end-run around the machine by submitting two proposals — for a medical center and for a day-care center — directly to the OEO, but both were rejected. The overall result of the Chicago Concept, its critics charged, was that poor people were shut out of the decision-making process. "The poor are being pushed out of planning poverty programs by men who drive Cadillacs, eat three-inch steaks and sip champagne at their luncheon meetings," one minister complained.[31]

The allegations that Daley's Chicago Concept was violating the CAP guidelines were heard in Washington. In January 1965, the OEO notified Brooks that Chicago's CAP was in danger of having its funding cut off. As it turned out, Chicago kept its funding but Robert D. Shackford, the acting head of the OEO's midwestern office who lodged the complaint, lost his job. His post was later filled by Theodore Jones, the same black machine politician Daley and Dawson had installed as president of the Chicago branch of the NAACP in 1956, replacing the activist Willoughby Abner. Though it seemed obvious that Daley had forced Shackford out and dictated Jones's appointment, Shriver dismissed the charges as "rumormongering." Daley was one of "hundreds of people" who had been consulted before Jones's selection, Shriver conceded, "but under no stretch of the imagination did Daley suggest him or force such an appointment." A year later, Governor Kerner rewarded Jones for his work at the OEO by appointing him state revenue director. In April 1965, the House Committee on Education and Labor's subcommittee on the War on Poverty held hearings at which critics were given a national forum to lash out against Daley's management of CAP. "In Chicago, there is no war against poverty," TWO president Lynward Stevenson fumed. "There is only more of the ancient, galling war against the poor." Stevenson attacked Chicago's CAP for shutting out neighborhood organizations. "We have asked Deton Brooks for funds for a day care center and for a medical center, but he cannot talk sense," he said. "He speaks the meaningless sociological drivel designed not to lift people but to keep them dependent." But for Stevenson, the real villain was Daley, whom he called "a plantation boss who thinks he knows what's right for the slaves."[32]

Daley had his own concerns about CAP. He worried that poor people's advocates would find a way to gain access to the program's funding, and use it to hurt the machine. And he believed that the OEO was too sympathetic to these insurgent forces. As the Shackford firing showed, Daley's political connections allowed him to have his way with the program. When necessary, he was willing to take his complaints directly to the president. "What in the hell are you people doing?" Johnson aide Bill Moyers recalls Daley asking. "Does the President know he's putting *money* in the hands of subversives? To poor people that aren't a part of the organization? Didn't the President know they'd take that money to bring him down?" Johnson, who did not want to risk losing Daley's support over the issue of community participation in CAP, would regularly take his side over the OEO. "We had problems with Daley on *everything,*" says CAP director of operations Frederick Hayes, "and he always went to the White House, and always won." Other mayors had more trouble fighting off the federal bureaucrats. Philadelphia mayor James Tate tried to create a city department to run the War on Poverty, but when he asked for $13 million in federal funds, Sargent Shriver turned him down until the city established an independent anti-poverty organization. Shriver was also openly feuding with Los Angeles mayor Sam Yorty over that city's failure to establish a program that sufficiently included the poor. The OEO said the city's Youth Opportunities Board failed to meet federal guidelines because it did not represent all of the city's constituencies. Yet despite its obvious domination by City Hall and the machine, Shriver hailed Chicago's CAP as "the model CAP in the country."[33]

Daley eventually became the leader of a group of big-city mayors who shared his concerns about the uses to which CAP was being put. In New York, Mayor Wagner was at war with Harlem congressman Adam Clayton Powell over control of New York's anti-poverty funds, which Powell charged were being used for "fiestas of political patronage." In Los Angeles, Mayor Yorty was risking $22 million in federal funds by refusing to appoint representatives of the poor to his board, insisting that it would be wrong to allow nonelected private citizens to make decisions about spending public money. In San Francisco, Mayor John Shelley also refused to allow representatives of the poor, asking, "What if they elect a Communist or a criminal?" And Syracuse's Republican mayor William Walsh charged that anti-poverty money in his city was going to political activists who seemed intent on removing him from office. "These people go into a housing project and talk about setting up a 'democratic organization' — small 'd' — but it sounds just the same as Democratic — big 'd,'" Walsh complained.[34]

Daley and the other mayors insisted that more control over the program be given to city government. The mayors made it clear that unless CAP yielded to them, they would withdraw their political support. Daley warned that the "irresponsible, scurrilous charges" being lodged by organizations like TWO threatened the very survival of the War on Poverty. Congressman Roman Pucinski, following his boss's lead, warned that as a result of the "fantastic power struggle going on all over America" for control of CAP, "the poverty program has never been in graver danger." At a June 1965 meeting of the U.S. Conference of Mayors in Saint Louis, Daley was chosen to chair a new War on Poverty Committee. The mayors were prepared to adopt a resolution accusing federal anti-poverty programs of "fostering class struggle" against city government, and urging the OEO to work through city halls in administering CAP projects. But they agreed that rather than embarrass the president by doing so, they would work with the administration to change its anti-poverty policy. Later in the month, Daley and a group of his fellow mayors had a productive meeting on the subject with Vice President Hubert Humphrey. "It was agreed that the success of the program depends on very extensive leadership by local government and that's what they are going to get," said Conference of Mayors executive director John J. Gunther. "The local government is to be the principal organizer at the local level." The Johnson administration, true to its word, began to exert pressure on the OEO to address the mayors' concerns. A front-page article in the *New York Times* on November 5, 1965, reported that the Budget Bureau, the fiscal arm of the White House, had informed the OEO that in its view maximum feasible participation "means primarily using the poor to carry out the program, not to design it." Reports leaking out of the OEO also indicated that controversial programs would no longer be permitted to bypass city government and appeal for funds directly to Washington.[35]

In another sign of warming relations between the OEO and the nations' mayors, Shriver went to Chicago on December 6 for a Daley-sponsored conference on the War on Poverty. Daley used the conference to promote his idea of having politicians control anti-poverty efforts. "What's wrong . . . if the politician is conducting his office in a proper manner with integrity and with honor?" Daley asked. In his remarks, Shriver echoed Daley's views by praising the positive role "the establishment" was playing in the War on Poverty. "Let's not prejudge the establishment," Shriver said. "The establishment is not a bunch of guys in black hats against good guys in white hats." Shriver was warmly received inside the hall. But the two hundred demonstrators gathered outside, holding placards with slogans like "The war on poverty is a big fraud," were less impressed. And The Woodlawn Organization was circulating an eleven-page "black paper" attacking the War on Poverty as a war against the poor. "We are sick unto despair of having rich whites and their carefully chosen black flunkies tell us what our problems are, make decisions for us, and set our children's future," the black paper declared. Shriver's new stand on maximum feasible participation seemed to reflect the current thinking of the Johnson administration, but some critics also suspected a more personal motivation. Shriver reportedly wanted to run for governor or senator from Illinois, and his new views on CAP seemed like a blatant appeal for Daley's support.[36]

What was being lost in the rush to capitulate to Daley was the fact that his CAP continued to flout federal law. There was still, as Republican congressman Charles Goodell insisted, an "almost total lack of involvement of the poor in the Chicago program." There was also evidence that much of the money was not making its way to poor people: a study of Chicago's Head Start program found that more than 27 percent of the enrolled children came from families with incomes above the legal limit, including some "very affluent" children. Federal investigators had also determined that more than 70 percent of all anti-poverty funds spent in the city was going to pay salaries of anti-poverty workers, which seemed to support critics' charges that money for poor people was being used for patronage. A bipartisan delegation headed by New York Democrat Hugh Carey came to Chicago on February 16, 1965, to investigate Chicago's anti-poverty programs firsthand. But no one had made Daley comply with the law so far, and it seemed unlikely a few critics in Congress would have any more success.[37]

Martin Luther King, who was by now leaning strongly toward bringing his movement north to Chicago, had his mind made up for him one sweltering summer night in Los Angeles. On August 11, 1965, a California highway patrolman pulled over a black man for what should have been a routine driving-while-intoxicated stop. But Watts, a northern-style ghetto set down among the palm trees of Southern California, responded by erupting in rioting. As false rumors spread — among them, that the officers had attacked a pregnant woman with a billy club — a crowd showed up at the scene and began throwing rocks at the police. A mob of 2,000 was soon roaming the area, vandalizing cars, looting stores, and assaulting strangers.

It grew to 5,000, many armed with guns and Molotov cocktails, and spread out over a 150-block area. Arsonists set hundreds of fires, and snipers shot at the 14,000 National Guardsmen who had been called in to put down the disturbance. After six days of rioting, the death toll stood at 34, with another 898 injured, and more than 4,000 arrested. Economic losses were estimated at $45 million.[38]

The Watts riots stunned the nation. The sheer fury that had been unleashed was unprecedented. Only the Detroit race riots of 1943 had produced as many fatalities, and they had resulted in far less physical damage. King traveled to Watts just as the unrest was ending, and when he toured the riot-scarred neighborhood he was deeply affected by what he saw. It was not lost on King and his followers that the uprising had occurred not in the South, where black anger was expected, but in a big-city ghetto. The depth and breadth of the anger that set off the rioting struck him as a powerful argument for extending the civil rights movement to the rest of the country, and trying to improve the condition of blacks in places like Watts. Having come around to the view that he and his followers had mistakenly "neglected the cities of the North," King now added his powerful voice to those who were pushing for SCLC to choose a northern site for its next major campaign.[39]

The SCLC considered several large cities, including New York, for its historic journey north. But there were many compelling reasons for choosing Chicago. In terms of racial segregation, it was as bad as any major city, north or south. In 1959, the U.S. Commission on Civil Rights had called Chicago "the most residentially segregated large city in the nation." The racial separation that the Jim Crow system preserved by law, Chicago had simply achieved through other means: racial steering by real estate brokers; racially restrictive covenants on house sales; and the ever-present threat of violence if established racial boundaries were crossed. Blacks were no more welcome in working-class white neighborhoods on the South Side of Chicago than they were in white neighborhoods in Alabama. To King, Chicago was "the Birmingham of the North," and he said that if the civil rights movement could "break the system in Chicago, it can be broken anywhere in the country."[40]

The SCLC staff was also impressed by Chicago's indigenous civil rights activists. The CCCO was the largest local civil rights network in any northern city. And it had already scored some notable successes, with its two school boycotts and the anti-Willis campaign, which had succeeded in getting the superintendent of schools to resign, if only briefly. Chicago's civil rights community had received King warmly on his last visit, which had not been the case in every city he stopped in. On the same trip, King and the SCLC had been greeted warily by black leaders in other cities. In New York, Adam Clayton Powell, the influential Harlem congressman, had been critical of King and publicly warned him against bringing the movement to New York. The head of the Philadelphia chapter of the NAACP, Cecil Moore, had also warned King away, protesting loudly that his visit would only serve to help the white power structure to diminish "my stature in the Negro community" and pit blacks against blacks. Chicago's civil rights leadership, by contrast, had been actively campaigning for the SCLC to come to town. The SCLC had learned hard lessons in the South about the importance of working closely with the local leadership, and the CCCO seemed to offer the best new allies for what would be a difficult campaign.[41]

A decision was reached, but it was not unanimous. Some SCLC activists were skeptical about the movement's chances of succeeding in the north, and they did not agree that Chicago was hospitable terrain. At a meeting in Atlanta, Rustin and SCLC staffer Tom Kahn tried to persuade King he was underestimating the difficulty of prevailing in Chicago — and underestimating Daley. "King had this naive faith that he could do in Chicago what he had done in the South, that he could reach down and inspire them, and so forth," says Kahn. "And Bayard kept saying, 'You don't know what you are talking about. You don't know what Chicago is like. . . . You're going to get wiped out.'"[42]

The day after the rioting began in Watts, Chicago had its own ghetto uprising. On August 12, 1965, a speeding hook-and-ladder truck lost control on its way out of a fire station, knocking over a stop sign, and a young woman in the West Garfield Park neighborhood was killed. West Garfield Park had deteriorated considerably since Daley stopped the University of Illinois from locating its Chicago campus in the area. In just five years, it had changed from being 84 percent white and solidly middle-class to 85 percent black and desperately poor. The fire station involved in the accident was staffed entirely by whites, and civil rights protesters had been picketing outside it for weeks, protesting its employment policies. Neighborhood residents, prodded by rumors and leaflets alleging that a "drunken white fireman" had caused the fatal accident, began to riot and did not stop for the next four nights. Roving bands of neighborhood residents threw rocks and bricks at white pedestrians and drivers, and a white plainclothes policeman was beaten up.[43]

At a City Hall press conference, Police Superintendent Wilson, flanked by Daley, warned that unless West Side residents did "all in their power" to assist the police, the situation was in danger of becoming as bad as Watts. When the violence finally ended, there were 80 injuries and 169 arrests. Together with Watts, the rioting was a sign of the growing level of desperation in black ghettos across the country. And like Watts, it showed the chasm of mistrust that had developed between poor blacks and the largely white police and fire departments that worked in their neighborhoods. Raby and other black leaders regarded the riots as a warning of serious social problems that had to be addressed before more violence occurred. But Daley viewed the unrest in less complicated terms. "It was a question of lawlessness and hooliganism," he said.[44] Raby asked for a meeting to discuss the situation, and Daley agreed. But rather than engaging in the substantive discussion Raby was hoping for, Daley had various city officials explain how much was already being done for the black community. "This was not the meeting I had requested," Raby said bitterly. The riots did succeed in getting the first black firefighters assigned to the West Garfield Park station. "We have been trying to integrate that firehouse for 10 years, " said National Urban League executive director Edwin Berry, "and with a killing and a riot they integrated it in two minutes." Six weeks after the riot, 40 of the city's 132 firehouses were racially integrated. But of the 4,446 uniformed firemen only 209, or at least minimally less than 5 percent, were black.[45]

In response to the CCCO complaint about the school system, the U.S. Department of Health, Education and Welfare sent a team of investigators to Chicago. It was a chance for Willis to respond to the

civil rights group's charges, but he refused to cooperate. Even before
the CCCO complaint, Willis had a history of defying federal requests for education information. He would not let Chicago schoolchildren take achievement tests given nationally in connection with a
U.S. Office of Education survey mandated by the Civil Rights Act.
And he would not meet with a Northwestern University professor
working on a federal report, even though he came with a letter of
introduction from Office of Education commissioner Keppel. After
four months, the professor finally got a phone call. "It consisted of a
denunciation of my mission and myself," the professor wrote later.
"He refused at that time to discuss any matter of substance, but indicated that I could call for an appointment this week." He was never
given an appointment, and was not allowed to see published reports
prepared by Willis's staff. Even with the city's federal education aid at
risk, Willis remained defiant. He refused to provide the Office of
Education investigators with attendance data to evaluate the claims of
segregation. He would have to consult with the Illinois congressional
delegation first, he said, and if he did respond "the answer might
well be two months in coming — if that soon." The Office of Education was also hearing that Willis intended to use the new federal
education money, which was earmarked for economically disadvantaged students, for middle-class white districts — and to build more
Willis Wagons. Keppel took these reports seriously because they
went to "the fundamental purposes" of the earmarked federal aid,
"which was to put money behind the poor kids." Willis, it seemed,
was all but daring the federal government to rule against Chicago on
the CCCO complaint.[46]

On October 1, 1965, Keppel did just that. In letters to Willis and
to the state superintendent of public instruction, he declared that the
Chicago school system was in "probable non-compliance" with
Title VI of the Civil Rights Act of 1964. He said he believed the
matter could be investigated quickly, if Willis's department cooperated, but that it would have to be "satisfactorily resolved before any
new commitments are made of funds." Keppel had put millions of
dollars in federal education aid to a major Democratic city, presided
over by the nation's most powerful mayor, in jeopardy. That was, as
Keppel recalls, "when everything happened." Daley was irate that the
federal government had taken the side of a ragtag group of civil

rights activists against Chicago's mayor and school board. Keppel's irresponsible action had "done irreparable damage," Daley seethed, "to the whole concept of federal aid to education." A furious Willis sent Keppel a telegram asking "What is 'probable non-compliance'" and "When will you let us know?" The Chicago congressional delegation immediately applied pressure to get Keppel's order reversed. Representative Pucinski demanded an investigation by the General Accounting Office, and vowed that "Congress won't appropriate another nickel for education programs" unless the federal government backed down. Illinois Democrats also threatened that William Dawson's House Government Operations Committee would begin an investigation of Keppel.[47]

But the key to resolving the standoff between the Office of Education and the Chicago school system was Daley's relationship with President Johnson. Johnson had treated Daley with great deference since becoming president. "I'm a Dick Daley man," he had said in a phone call after the 1964 elections. "I always have a warm spot for you." Daley returned the good feeling, saying, "My wife said that never did we meet a finer couple than you and Mrs. Johnson." There may have been some real affection between these two men. Lady Bird Johnson wrote in an April 21, 1964, diary entry that Daley was "one of her husband's 'favorite people,'" and went on to describe Daley as "a very arch type of political boss, ruddy-faced, emanating efficiency and friendliness." But Johnson also had clear political reasons for cultivating Daley. He was still planning on running for reelection in 1968, and would want Daley's help in winning Illinois. And Johnson had grown to appreciate Daley's control over the machine's sizable congressional delegation. "Daley was critical to the success of the Great Society," former Johnson domestic adviser Joseph Califano recalled. "A call to Daley was all that was needed to deliver the fourteen votes of the Illinois Democratic delegation. Johnson and others of us had made many calls to the Mayor and Daley had always come through."[48]

Daley insisted on taking the matter to the president directly. Johnson was in New York on October 3, to sign an immigration bill at the Statue of Liberty, and then to visit with the pope. Daley rushed to New York, and waited for the president in Ambassador Arthur Goldberg's apartment at the Waldorf Towers. When Johnson arrived,

Daley was seething. He "was so mad," Keppel said later, that he was "just sputtering." Johnson said later that Daley was so unrelenting in his arguments that the money be restored that the meeting between the president and the pope was delayed by ten minutes. Johnson assured Daley he would look into the matter as soon as he returned to Washington. The next day, the president called in HEW secretary John W. Gardner and Keppel and "gave them unstinted hell."[49] Gardner sent undersecretary Wilber Cohen to Chicago to investigate. Cohen found that Daley was deeply offended with how the federal government had proceeded. "You're taking away the funds from me without ever having consulting me," Cohen recalls Daley protesting. "You never told me about the issue; you never consulted me or asked me what my views are; you never tried to get me to resolve it; all you do is send a telegram and I read it in the newspapers."[50]

After meeting with Daley, Cohen sat down with school board president Frank Whiston. The CCCO tried to arrange its own meeting with Cohen, but they were unable to do so. The CCCO leadership realized at that point that Cohen's mission was not to investigate the school situation further, but to work out a political accommodation with Daley. On his way back to Washington, Cohen held a press conference at the airport to announce that he and Whiston had reached an agreement. The Chicago school system would appoint a five-member committee to review complaints about school boundaries and other matters, and it promised to take steps to address segregation at Washburne Trade School. And the federal funding would be restored. Whiston said that Daley had been "very interested" in the negotiations, and called as soon as his meeting with Cohen ended. The CCCO activists were crushed. The release of the funds was the result of a "shameless display of naked political power exhibited by Mayor Daley," Raby said. They had no faith in the agreement worked out between Cohen and Whiston. "They were going to investigate themselves," says Weinberg. "That sounded just horrible to us." Daley loyalists agreed that the commitments the school system made to Cohen were a sham, and they were overjoyed. "These concessions are meaningless," Pucinski exclaimed. "They're just a face-saving device for Keppel. This is an abject surrender."[51]

But Daley's revenge was not complete. After the funding was restored, Keppel was quietly removed to a position where he could do no further harm. He was given the new title of assistant secretary for education at HEW, and his position of U.S. commissioner of education was given to a man who would make a point of staying out of Daley's way. "I was hopeless, I was replaced very soon," Keppell recalled later. "Oh, they made me an assistant secretary for some reason — I've forgotten — and I just stayed on . . . and spent most of my time trying to keep out of the way of my successor. . . . In effect, I was fired." By April 1966, Keppel's service in the federal government was over. Daley's maneuvers had a lasting impact on how the federal government would evaluate racial discrimination in the North. The Johnson administration issued new regulations requiring proof of discrimination — and requiring federal officials to first attempt to elicit voluntary compliance — before education funds could be withheld. The agreement between Cohen and the Chicago school board was a "black day in the catalogues of mankind's eternal freedom struggle," Adam Clayton Powell declared. The "integrity of the 1964 Civil Rights Act was gutted by the most barbaric exercise of tawdry ward politics." But Daley had scored points with his white constituents — the very voters that had abandoned him in the 1963 election. Liberal columnist Joseph Kraft lamented that Daley's "tactic of blocking civil rights moves in order to court favor with anti-Negro white[s] . . . has won out again."[52]

By the fall of 1965, word spread that King and the Southern Christian Leadership Conference would in fact be coming to Chicago that winter for a prolonged stay. Daley said he would be happy to meet with King whenever he wanted. "No one has to march to see the mayor of Chicago," Daley said jauntily. "The door is always open and I'm here 10 to 12 hours a day." And Daley insisted that he shared King's agenda. "I'm always happy to have help and assistance in resolving difficult problems of housing, education, and poverty," Daley said. "I would like to show Dr. King some of our fine installations." At the same time, Daley began mobilizing black machine politicians to undermine King's efforts in Chicago. Alderman Ralph Metcalfe announced plans for a community action program designed to provide an alternative to King's Chicago Campaign. Organizers of the new group, called the Chicago Conference to Fulfill These Rights,

Inc., included three more black aldermen, four black judges, and other black elected officials, lawyers, and religious leaders with ties to the machine. Metcalfe declared that King was not "objective" because he had not talked with Daley, and that in any case he was not needed in Chicago. "This is no hick town," Metcalfe said. "We have adequate leadership here." Al Raby called the formation of the group a "tragedy."[53]

With all the headlines about civil rights, it was hard to get excited about yet another scandal in Chicago Traffic Court. But the newspapers were now reporting that drivers were routinely permitted to substantially underpay their tickets when they were marked with the initial "D," for "Democrat," and the number of a ward organization. In some cases, the payments were as low as fifty cents on a ten-dollar ticket. The charges were not hard to believe, particularly with the Traffic Court operating under the supervision of Joseph McDonough. McDonough, the clerk of the Circuit Court, was a longtime Daley protégé, and the son of Daley's own 11th Ward mentor, Alderman Joseph McDonough. Daley was quick to brand the scandal as another Republican plot. "The 'D' written on the tickets by the investigators could stand for 'doctor' and might mean 'dog' and it might mean a lot of other things," the mayor said. His old friend McDonough was, he insisted, doing an "outstanding job."[54]

In late November, concerns about corruption were raised once again when Daley submitted his 1966 city budget. Republicans charged that the $545 million budget was inflated with patronage and waste. And they charged that Daley now oversaw a "shadow budget" for poverty programs, urban renewal projects, air pollution control, and airports, all of which received federal funding. Daley had been using these new budget lines, they said, to transfer current city welfare bureaucrats into higher-paying jobs in federal poverty programs. This, in turn, opened up more patronage jobs that could be filled on the city payroll. The new Daley budget called for a property tax increase of between 8 and 10 percent, well above the rate of inflation. Critics charged that the steep increases in taxes since Daley took office were destroying the city. The president of the Chicago Real Estate Board said that apartment buildings in the city had lost 15 percent of their value as a result of higher real estate taxes. John Hoellen, the Republican alderman, declared that the city's neighborhoods were "rotting away," that stores were boarded up, and that 276 industrial plants had left Chicago in the past ten years. "When we look at the tax bills," he said, "we know why."[55]

King flew north in October to attend a retreat to work out the details of the Chicago Campaign. The three-day conference, at a camp in Williams Bay, Wisconsin, brought together about one hundred activists from SCLC and CCCO. On one level, it was a get-acquainted session, designed to foster camaraderie and trust among two distinct, and in many ways very different, organizations. One CCCO member who was there recalls that Andrew Young had a guitar and went around making up songs about each of the participants. But the expressed purpose of the retreat was to develop a joint strategy for what would become the Chicago Freedom Movement. The two groups were working on a plan that would "broaden our interest — not just schools but housing, political emasculation, poverty, welfare jobs," Raby said. To achieve these goals, "protest demonstrations will be heightened." King told reporters that the focus of the movement would be the city's racial problems, not its political system or its leaders. "I don't consider Mayor Daley as an enemy," he said. King, who expressed an interest in "eventually" meeting with the mayor, said that he understood that Daley would not react with the kind of violent outbursts that had helped the SCLC gain sympathy in the past. "The movement in Chicago will be different from that in the South," he said. "There will be fewer overt acts to aid us here . . . naive targets such as the Jim Clarks and George Wallaces will be harder to find and use as symbols." Still, hope for the new effort ran high. "Chicago will be like a test tube," one King aide declared. "The whole world will be waiting to see what happens here."[56]

After King headed back south, Bevel and other organizers set about planning the details of the Chicago Campaign. They established a headquarters at the Warren Avenue Congregational Church in the West Side ghetto, and worked with local activists to plan neighborhood kickoff rallies that were held across the South and West sides between October 20 and November 4, 1965. Jesse Jackson, then a young SCLC staffer, organized the city's Baptist ministers to support the upcoming campaign, and other activists were working with the city's gangs, some holding weekend workshops designed to direct gang members toward nonviolent political protest. Bevel led an effort to draft a written outline that would set out the overall themes of the campaign. The drafters concluded that although the civil rights movement had prevailed in the South by choosing narrow goals, like integrating a bus system or desegregating a lunch counter, the Chicago Campaign would have to pursue a broader agenda. "The Chicago problem is simply a matter of economic exploitation," the document said. "Every condition exists simply because someone profits by its existence. This economic exploitation is crystallized in the SLUM," which the outline called "a system of internal colonialism."[57]

King returned to Chicago on January 5, 1966, for two days of meetings at the Sahara Inn between SCLC representatives and local black leaders that formally kicked off the campaign. When King emerged, he explained why he had come to Chicago. The city's slums were "the prototype of those chiefly responsible for the Northern urban race problem," he said, and he and the SCLC had been invited in by the forty-five local civil rights groups that comprised the CCCO. "Our objective will be to bring about the unconditional surrender of forces dedicated to the creation and maintenance of slums," King declared. "The Chicago Freedom Movement will press the power structure to find imaginative programs to overcome the problem." The group adopted Bevel's draft outline, which came to be known as the "Chicago Plan," and it explained to the press in more detail how the campaign would proceed. King said the SCLC would be increasing its staff in the city to several dozen. And he announced that when he returned to the city, he would be moving into a "West Side apartment that will symbolize the 'Slum Lordism' that I hope to smash."[58]

CHAPTER 10

All of Us Are Trying to Eliminate Slums

In selecting a tenement for King to move into, the Chicago Freedom Movement made a deliberate choice to put him on the West Side rather than the South Side. Chicago's South Side, home to more than 400,000 blacks, was the traditional center of the city's black life. It was the Chicago's historic "Bronzeville," home to great black institutions like the *Chicago Defender* and thriving black businesses, insurance companies, and funeral homes. The West Side was a newer ghetto of roughly 250,000 blacks, many of them recent arrivals from the rural South. Though living conditions in the South Side ghetto were bad, they were far worse on the West Side. West Side blacks were poorer, job opportunities were fewer, youth gangs were more active, and more of the residents lived in the kind of dilapidated, below-code apartments the anti-slum campaign was targeting. West Side blacks were also likely to be easier to organize. Many South Side blacks were more conservative, with strong ties to old-line black churches and the black submachine, two of the forces in the black community most skeptical of the civil rights cause. The West Side had fewer community institutions, and those tended to be the kind of grassroots organizations that backed the CCCO. And not least, West Side blacks were on the whole more culturally similar to the SCLC staff. More of them had been born in the Deep South, and many of them shared the worldview of the church-inspired southern civil rights movement. "We had a lot of experience dealing with black Mississippians," Bernard Lafayette would say later, "and here they were transported north."[1]

But if parts of Chicago reminded them of home, King and the SCLC staff quickly realized just how different this sprawling urban metropolis was from the South. It was far larger than the other cities they had organized campaigns in before — 10 times as large as Birmingham, and 100 times as large as Selma. Ralph Abernathy recalls how astonished he was the first time Jesse Jackson took him on a driving tour of Chicago. "As we drove through the South Side, where a large segment of the black population lived, we kept waiting for the slum tenements to give way to warehouses, vacant lots, and then country stores and open fields where cows were grazing," he recalls. "Instead we saw more slum blocks. And more. And more. We had a feeling that if we drove much farther south we were going to see the Gulf of Mexico. 'That's nothing,' said Jesse. 'Wait till you see the West Side.'" And to southerners used to a region where almost everyone fell into the simple category of "black" or "white," Chicago was a confusing array of Irish, Poles, Jews, Lithuanians, and other ethnic groups.[2]

Another thing the SCLC was unprepared for when it arrived in Chicago was the opposition it would face from significant parts of the black community. "Chicago was the first city that we ever went to as members of the SCLC staff where the black ministers and black politicians told us to go back where we came from," says Dorothy Tillman, then a young SCLC staff member from Alabama. "Dr. King would frequently say to me, 'You ain't never seen no Negroes like this, have you Dorothy?' I would reply, 'No, Reverend.' He said, 'Boy if we could crack these Chicago Negroes we can crack anything.'" Some Chicago blacks professed to be as offended as Daley that outsiders were coming and telling them what to do. "Dr. King can move into Alabama and say, 'This is it,'" said the Reverend W. H. Nichols, a West Side minister, "but here in Chicago each man stands on his own two feet." To some on the SCLC staff, the black opposition seemed to be rooted in years of oppression by whites. "The Negroes of Chicago have a greater feeling of powerlessness than I've ever seen," says SCLC staff member Hosea Williams. "They don't participate in the governmental process because they are beaten down psychologically. We are used to working with people who want to be free." But the truth was, much of the opposition came not because Chicago blacks were powerless, but because they had more power than blacks in the rural South. Daley, who needed black votes in a way that southern politicians did not, had handed out elected offices, patronage jobs, and money in the black community, and had singled out a few Dawsons and Metcalfes to represent blacks on a citywide level. These black leaders, and their armies of patronage workers, had a personal stake in the status quo, in a way that few blacks in Selma or Birmingham did.[3]

One of the most prominent of the machine's black allies was the Reverend Joseph H. Jackson, the Olivet Baptist Church pastor who had been booed off the stage with Daley at the NAACP's July 4, 1963, rally in Grant Park. "When the white establishment wanted to find out what was going on," says civil rights activist John McDermott, "they consulted J.H." Jackson, who had been a strong supporter of Willis, bitterly opposed the Chicago Freedom Movement. He was particularly outspoken in his attacks against King, whom he viewed as a rival, accusing him of waging a "militant campaign against his own denomination and his own race." Jackson never relented in his views of the Nobel Prize–winning civil rights leader. After King's assassination, Jackson moved the front entrance of his church from South Park Way to a side street so its official address would not bear the boulevard's new name, Martin Luther King Jr. Drive. King and the SCLC were not prepared for these anti–civil rights black ministers, but they were also disappointed to see how reluctant even ostensibly sympathetic black clergy were to stand up for civil rights. "Many ministers who were with us had to back off because they didn't want their buildings to be condemned or given citations for electrical work, faulty plumbing, or fire code violations," says the Reverend Clay Evans of the Fellowship Missionary Baptist Church. Mattie Hopkins of the Episcopal Society for Cultural and Racial Unity, who had worked with King in Selma and Montgomery, says she never saw King as depressed as he was after meeting with a group of black ministers in Chicago. The ministers told King that they supported him, but could not speak out from their pulpits because they had already come under pressure from mortgage holders, city building inspectors, and others with ties to the Democratic machine. "He got his first real picture of the way Daley ran this town," Hopkins says. The SCLC located its headquarters in the Warren Avenue Congregational Church, which had a white minister, because they could not find a black minister who would give the group space. The other religious group the SCLC was not prepared for was the Chicago-based Nation of Islam, which did not share the Chicago Freedom Movement's goal of racial integration. "If anything they were more zealous in support of segregation than Mayor Daley, since the mayor paid lip service to racial tolerance and the Muslims were black supremacists," says Abernathy. "They would probably have joined us if we had proposed killing all the white people, but they certainly didn't want to listen to anyone preach the gospel of brotherly love."[4]

As political theater, the decision to move King into a tenement apartment was a masterstroke. The *Chicago Defender* was delighted with the plan, declaring that "[w]hile there he will eat, sleep, and absorb the full meaning of what it is to call a hovel 'home.'" The Freedom Movement's initial efforts to secure an apartment for him failed, as landlords declined to rent when they learned who the tenant would be. But eventually, organizers found a four-room, third-floor walk-up apartment at 1550 South Hamlin Avenue in the West Side's Lawndale neighborhood — often called "Slumdale" — and rented it in the name of an SCLC staff member. The $90-a-month apartment was to house King and his wife, Coretta, although the couple planned to make weekly trips to Atlanta so King could conduct Sunday services at Ebenezer Baptist Church. An adjoining apartment was rented for the Reverend Ralph Abernathy, the SCLC vice president. Furniture was brought in from a secondhand furniture dealer. When King moved in on January 26, 1966, more than three hundred people were on hand to greet him and Coretta. The apartment was not nearly as bad as most slum apartments in the area, and when the landlord realized who would be moving in he sent work crews out to improve it. "[T]he entire place had been painted, repapered, and redecorated," Abernathy says. "It didn't look like an apartment in *House Beautiful,* but it was clean and bright — probably the best looking quarters within fifty blocks of that location." The joke in Chicago civil rights circles was that the best way to end the slums would be to have King move from apartment to apartment and watch each one get fixed up. Still, even after white paint had been thrown on the living room walls, and yellow and gray paint slapped on in the other rooms, the apartment was undeniably a tenement. The building that housed it was still in poor shape, with a strong smell of urine wafting through the stairwells, impervious to all efforts to clean it out with disinfectant. "There were no lights in the hall, and only one dim light at the head of the stairs," Coretta Scott King said after spending one night in the apartment. "There was not even a lock on the door. I had never seen anything like it." And the neighborhood was tough enough to cause many of the new southern transplants to fear for their lives. "I was truly frightened that some junkie was going to knife me for twenty dollars," says Young. "When walking up those four dark, creaky flights of stairs at night, my heart would pound and wouldn't slow for some time after I was within our apartment with the door securely bolted." In a matter of days, King saw the effect of the environment on his own children. "Their tempers flared and they sometimes reverted to almost infantile behavior," he wrote later. The South Hamlin Avenue tenement apartment was "just too hot, too crowded, too devoid of forms of recreation." Life in Lawndale, King said, "was about to produce an emotional explosion in my own family."[5]

The new tenants were not particularly conscientious about tenement-living. King often stayed at a friend's more inviting home, and Abernathy, after spending a night or two on South Hamlin, checked into a hotel in a black part of town. But they spent enough time in Lawndale to get an education in northern ghetto life. King used the apartment to hold educational sessions and strategy meetings. He invited activists to talk with him about conditions across the city and ideas for action, and let each of his guests give a presentation on his area of expertise. "After each one talked, King said something to relate it to what had come before," says Meyer Weinberg, who was there as an education expert. "You could see how brilliant he was, how he was putting it all together tactically." King and other SCLC staff ventured out on neighborhood tours, which let them witness Chicago slum life up close. On one walking tour, Raby took King to a twelve-unit apartment building, originally built as a six-flat, where two families shared a bathroom that had been burned out in a fire and was no longer fit to be used. "We are here in Chicago," King told the residents, "to say to ourselves and to the Negro commu-

nity that we can do something about our condition if we organize a
union to end slums." Another time, King and Abernathy toured a
building not far from their own that was without heat, hot water,
and electricity, and where mothers said they had to keep a candle-
light vigil through the night to protect their children from "rats as
large as cats." Louise Mitchell, a mother of ten children including a
ten-week-old baby, showed the visitors her run-down third-floor
apartment, where boards and bottles were used to plug up large holes
in the walls. Another tenant pointed to an area behind his kitchen
stove and told King, "That's where I usually catch all of the rats."
King and Abernathy asked the tenants if they had considered holding a rent strike.[6]

Another aspect of northern life that was unfamiliar to the SCLC
staff was Chicago's gang culture. Atlanta and Montgomery had nothing like the Blackstone Rangers, the Vice Lords, and the Cobras,
which had divided up poor neighborhoods on the South and West
sides. James Bevel had been working with gang members, and the
Freedom Movement leaders hoped they could be brought into the
movement. In his first night at the South Hamlin Avenue apartment,
King met with six members of the Vice Lords, who stopped by to
"meet the leader." On his tours of the neighborhood, King always
made a point of engaging gang members. He listened to the young
men's complaints about the bleakness of ghetto life, and their constant run-ins with other gangs, white mobsters, and abusive Chicago
police. The answer, King told them, was not arming themselves with
switchblades and handguns, but joining in nonviolent struggle to
change the conditions they were living in. "Power in Chicago," King
told them, "means getting the largest political machine in the nation
to say yes when it wants to say no."[7]

Rather than accept the role of villain in King's drama about the
Chicago slums, Daley decided to begin his own campaign against
substandard living conditions in the ghetto. Coming back from an
eight-day vacation with Sis and four of the children to the Florida
Keys and Puerto Rico, Daley declared at the San Juan airport that
there were "no slums" in Chicago, only "bad housing." In a January 26, 1966, taped television appearance, he predicted that all of the
city's blighted buildings would be eliminated in the next two years.[8]

Daley insisted that he was working as hard as anyone to improve conditions in Chicago's poorest neighborhoods. "All of us, like Dr. King, are trying to eliminate slums," he said. "Elimination of slums is the No. 1 program of this administration, and we feel we have done more in this field than any other city." Daley argued that federal and state government also had to be part of the solution, and he traveled to Washington on February 3 to lobby President Johnson for a proposed $2.3 billion nationwide anti-slum program. When he returned to Chicago, he held a joint city-county press conference on February 10, 1966, at which he committed "the full power and resources of the city to be used in an unlimited way to erase the slum blight." Daley's timetable was speeding up: now he said his goal was to wipe out all slum housing in the city by 1967.[9]

Daley's office gave him some advantages over the civil rights protesters when it came to waging a war on slums. King could try to organize tenants to withhold rent, but Daley could engage in a rent strike of his own, since the county welfare department paid for private housing for many poor families. To drive the point home, he held a joint press conference with the Cook County public aid director, who threatened to withhold monthly rent payments for 1,600 welfare recipients unless their landlords cured building code violations immediately. "I believe we now have in sight the complete wiping out of slums in Chicago," the public aid director declared. "Slums have been winning the battle up to now, but this changes the tide." Daley also announced a new drive to inspect living conditions in slum buildings. The city had assigned as many as fifty housing consultants and aides to conduct the inspections, Daley said, and the city's legal office was considering putting various slum buildings across the city into receivership by the Chicago Dwellings Association, a quasi-public agency, which could collect rent and then arrange for repairs to be made. To show he was serious, Daley made public a list of eight specific landlords who had been ordered to make repairs, most of whom, he said, "have been in and out of court."[10]

It was obvious that his anti-slum campaign was an effort to co-opt King and the SCLC, but Daley denied it. "We have been doing much code enforcement and placing many buildings in receivership long before Dr. King arrived in Chicago," he said. If the city seemed to be stepping up its efforts, it was only because new laws were now available for use against landlords, Daley said. But the Republican sponsor of a law making it a felony for landlords to violate the building code, state senator Arthur Swanson, said Daley had never bothered to use his substantial legal authority to take on slum conditions until King arrived in town. "It does little good for legislators to act on vital public needs if elected officials will not make efficient use of the new laws," Swanson complained. Now that Daley had adopted the anti-slum cause, he pursued it aggressively. On March 1, he announced an ambitious new program of door-to-door inspections for code violations in 15,000 buildings in three poor West Side neighborhoods including, as it happened, the one King now lived in. At the same time, Daley was sending emissaries out on a more surreptitious mission: going to community leaders in the neighborhoods the Chicago Freedom Movement was trying to organize and buying them off with offers of city money for their programs. "[A]s fast as they would organize a neighborhood," recalls Andrew Young, "the Daley forces would come in and offer a preacher a contract for subsidized day care in his church."[11]

The biggest blunder southern officials had made in dealing with the civil rights movement was their angry and poorly planned use of law enforcement. When Alabama state troopers beat up voting rights marchers, it had been a public relations disaster, and when Birmingham police arrested King, he wrote *Letter from a Birmingham Jail*. Daley was resolved not to turn the Chicago Freedom Movement leadership into martyrs. Police Superintendent O. W. Wilson invited King and his wife, Coretta, for a personal tour of the Chicago Police Department. In an informal meeting between King and top police officials, a warmly complimentary Wilson told the civil rights leader that he understood that King had some Irish ancestors. Daley proudly told reporters that King's visit with the Chicago Police Department was the first meeting of its kind anywhere in the country. Though King never asked for a police guard, Daley arranged for him to have full-time protection every time he came to the city. But Daley's hospitality had its limits. When Alderman Leon Despres introduced a resolution inviting King to address the City Council, Daley's floor manager, Tom Keane, immediately shouted out "subcommittee," sending the resolution to oblivion.[12]

King received a more sincere welcome from Chicago's Catholic Archdiocese. On February 2, King and Chicago Archbishop John Cody met for an hour at Cody's North Side mansion to discuss the Chicago Freedom Movement. The Catholic Church in Chicago had a mixed record on civil rights, particularly at the parish level. In some parts of the Bungalow Belt, Catholic priests were known to share the anti-integrationist feelings of their flocks, and many worried that racial transition would rob their parishes of their white bases. Cody's predecessor, Albert Meyer, had spoken out on racial matters, testifying before the U.S. Civil Rights Commission and ordering parish priests to give at least three sermons a year on improving race relations. Cody had come to Chicago in August 1965 from New Orleans, where he had overseen the desegregation of the city's parochial school system in the face of stiff opposition from white Catholics. In the controversy that followed, three segregationists were excommunicated, and Cody was bitterly attacked for promoting integration so forcefully. King was pleased by his meeting with Cody, declaring afterward that it had been "a very friendly and I might say fruitful discussion."[13]

On February 23, King and his followers took the bold step of seizing control of a tenement. The building, located just blocks from King's apartment at 1550 South Hamlin, lacked heat, and the Chicago Freedom Movement had learned that there was a sick baby living in it. King, Raby, and other members of the SCLC and CCCO dressed in work clothes and personally began cleaning it up. The Chicago Freedom Movement declared that it had assumed trusteeship over the building, and that henceforth rent collected from the tenants would be paid into a fund that would be used to make needed repairs. Asked about the lawfulness of the action, King appealed to a higher law. "I won't say that this is illegal, but I would call it superlegal," he said. "The moral question is far more important than the legal one." The "superlegal" seizure of 1321 South Homan would have been a natural point for Daley's policy of tolerance to end. Many Chicagoans believed that by seizing a privately owned building the civil rights movement had crossed the line from political protest to lawlessness. James Parson, a respected black judge and chairman of the National Conference on Religion and Race, called the seizure "theft" and "a revolutionary tactic." But Daley, sticking to his script of agreeable accommodation, said, "The situation at 1321 South Homan is a matter between the lawful owner and those who attempt to assume ownership. We all recognize that what is being done is good for our city — the improvement of housing and living conditions."[14] Far from defending the landlord at 1321 South Homan, Daley filed his own suit in Chicago Municipal Court the next day charging that the building had twenty-three code violations. What happened next was a powerful illustration of the difficulty of transporting the civil rights movement north. King's staff had failed to research the ownership of 1321 South Homan. After they took trusteeship, they found out that the cruel landlord they had cast in their morality tale was a sickly octogenarian who was only too happy to let the civil rights activists have the building. "I think King is right," the old man declared. "I think his intentions are right, and in his place I'd do the same thing." The Chicago Freedom Movement's selection of 1321 had unwittingly supported the argument of some of its opponents: that slum conditions were a product of complicated economic forces, and that it was too simplistic to put all the blame on landlords.[15]

In early March, Al Raby announced that the CCCO was starting to build a political organization that would take on Daley and the machine if the Chicago Freedom Movement's demands were not met. Raby said that the CCCO's efforts to improve black schools had failed because they had been organized on a "civic" rather than a "political" basis. "Instead of organizing wards, amorphous political groups were formed," said Raby. "The Democratic party could thus justifiably predict that Negro defection would not reach the danger point." With the help of the SCLC, Raby said, "cohesive organizations are now being formed in the ghetto communities that can become politically active if necessary." Turning the CCCO into a political organization would not be easy. It was a coalition of disparate groups, some of which were prohibited by their charters from engaging in partisan political activity. But the biggest obstacle to Raby's plan was King's reluctance to use civil rights to organize a political movement. Throughout his career, King had always worked outside the political system, hoping to draw people of all political persuasions to the cause of civil rights. He still had not given up hope that Daley could eventually become an ally of the Chicago

Freedom Movement. Still, Raby was not alone in seeking to shift the movement toward electoral politics. Dick Gregory, the comedian and protest leader, had already announced plans to challenge Daley for mayor in 1967. It was unlikely Gregory would win, but a strong third-party candidacy could conceivably take enough black votes away from the machine to put a Republican in City Hall.[16]

On March 10, Daley held a slate-making meeting at the Sherman Hotel to select the machine's candidates for the 1966 elections. Daley's primary interest was in the political assassination of a wayward officeholder. Seymour Simon, the bright and ambitious president of the Cook County Board, had been placed on the board as a protégé of Thomas Keane. He was widely regarded as a rising star on the Chicago political scene, and the talk was that he would run for mayor if Daley stepped down in 1967, or perhaps for governor. But first, he had to be renominated as Cook County board president. The first indication that there might be trouble was on the day before the 1966 slate-making meeting, when Daley called Simon and told him, "Seymour, be humble when you go before the slate-makers. Some of them say you are arrogant. So take my advice and be humble." Simon took the advice as an indication that Daley was on his side. But when Simon showed up before the slating committee, an enemy of his, Irwin "Izzy" Horwitz, was there. Horwitz was not a member of the Central Committee, from which members of the slate-making committee were usually drawn, but he came with the proxy of the 24th Ward committeeman. When the proceedings began, Horwitz launched into a bitter attack on his foe, and Simon was denied renomination.[17]

The abrasive Simon was brought down by a number of missteps, including a feud with another member of the board who was close to Daley. But the critical factor was that Keane, his onetime patron, now wanted him out of the presidency and off the board. Simon would later explain that their falling-out had come about one day when Keane showed up in Simon's office and asked him to reverse a decision of the county zoning board. A developer friend of Keane's had applied to turn a piece of land into a garbage dump. The board had sided with neighborhood residents, who were bitterly opposed to the plan.[18] Simon later explained that he was against the landfill both because of the neighborhood opposition, and because the commander of a nearby naval air station had said that seagulls attracted to the dump would pose a danger to his aircraft. When Simon refused to support the developer's plan, he said, his friendship with Keane was over. Keane was apparently mad enough to go to Daley and demand that Simon be removed from the board in the next election. After he was dumped, the newspapers were filled with headlines like "Simon Names Old Pal Keane as Ax Man in His Party Execution" and "Simon Dumped by a Dump?" When word of Simon's unslating got out, the machine nomination for Cook County board president was hardly worth having. Simon's replacement, postmaster Harry Semrow, lost badly to his Republican opponent. Although Daley lost the position, he was able to send a clear message to everyone in the machine about the cost of independence. "People in the organization realized that if he could knock me out, he could knock them out if they didn't toe the line," says Simon.[19]

On March 12, the Chicago Freedom Movement held a major fund-raiser at the International Amphitheatre. Organizers, who had been planning the event for months, sold 12,000 tickets and lured some of the leading black stars of the day, including Sidney Poitier, Harry Belafonte, Dick Gregory, and Mahalia Jackson. "Never before in the history of the civil rights movement has an action campaign been launched in such splendor," King told the enthusiastic crowd. "Never has a community responded more splendidly to the call for support than you have in Chicago." The rally demonstrated the broadest support yet in the black community for the Chicago Campaign, and brought in a much-needed $80,000. But a few days later, Daley had his own effusive public gathering that demonstrated how popular he remained with other segments of the city. On March 17, Daley presided over the city's massive Saint Patrick's Day parade. As was his custom, Daley personally led the throng of 70,000 marchers down State Street, while a crowd of 350,000 cheered from the sidelines. The parade was the usual exuberant mix: the Shannon Rovers Bagpipe Kilty band, Daley's favorite, played a medley of Gaelic airs; the University of Notre Dame's marching band played "McNamara's Band"; and a float with thirty members of the Illinois Toll Highway Commission sang "Hello, Dolly." An array of machine politicians, ranging from Senator Paul Douglas to local precinct captains, jammed the reviewing stand on Madison Street. Ireland's secretary of commerce and industry, who had flown in for the festivities, declared that "Chicago was more Irish than Ireland — I cannot say the isle has anything to compare with this."[20]

In mid-March, Daley held an open meeting at City Hall to report on his administration's progress in improving conditions in the ghetto. Deton Brooks, head of the Chicago Committee on Urban Opportunity, announced that the city was operating seven urban progress centers with a staff of 928, and had already conducted visits to 96,761 poor families. Kenneth Plummer, director of information for the City Board of Health, reported that a federally funded rodent-control program had found that 85 percent of housing in poor neighborhoods was rodent-infested, with an estimated ten rats for every citizen. The city had already visited 4,461 buildings, Plummer reported, to fill 27,301 rat holes, and an estimated 1,675,941 rats had been killed. Daley outlined four major goals for the future: improvements in education; increased employment opportunities; better access to health care; and elimination of slums by December 31, 1967. Daley continued his publicity campaign by holding a joint press conference on March 18 with John Boyle, chief judge of the Cook County Circuit Court, to announce that the city's Housing Court was being expanded from four to six full-time judges, to handle the extra work being created by the new door-to-door inspections on the West Side, and the city's other anti-slum initiatives. "Mayor Daley has made an all-out effort to eliminate slums and blight and the courts will cooperate 100 per cent," Judge Boyle told reporters. Daley's image as a slum-buster, which he was working so hard to burnish, was set back two weeks later when it was revealed that building code violations had been found in two buildings run by Marks & Co., the real estate firm headed by Charles Swibel, Daley's Chicago Housing Authority chairman. City buildings inspectors discovered twenty-eight code violations, and evidence that apartments in the buildings had been unlawfully converted to smaller units. Daley asked for a report on the charges, saying, "I'm sure the law should be applied equally and strongly to everyone, and that will be the case here."[21]

While the Chicago Freedom Movement focused on its anti-slum

campaign, SCLC staff member Jesse Jackson pursued a different tack. Jackson was heading up Operation Breadbasket, an economic self-help initiative that was being tried in a number of cities across the country. Operation Breadbasket took its name from boycotts of Atlanta bread companies in 1962, and its inspiration from the selective buying campaigns of Reverend Leon Sullivan in Philadelphia. Its goal was to convince white-owned businesses working in and near black neighborhoods to hire more blacks and make greater investments in the black community. Operation Breadbasket's strategy combined moral appeals, negotiations, and threats of boycotts. It focused its efforts on businesses that sold directly to the public, and which were therefore particularly vulnerable to consumer boycotts. Operation Breadbasket started its work in Chicago in February 1966, and in its first months scored some impressive victories. Hawthorne-Melody Farms, a Chicago dairy whose workforce was more than 90 percent white, agreed to hire an additional 55 blacks. Hi-Lo grocery stores agreed, after ten days of picketing, to hire an additional 183 blacks. And after fourteen weeks of protests, A&P committed itself to hire 970 blacks in its Chicago stores, and to hire a black firm to collect its garbage. Operation Breadbasket also negotiated increased work for the city's black exterminators. "We have a monopoly on rats in the ghetto, and we're gonna have a monopoly on killing 'em," Jackson said. Some civil rights activists dismissed Operation Breadbasket's work as less than significant — one commentator, writing in *The Nation,* dubbed it "Operation Drop-in-the-Bucket." But it was attracting enough attention that Daley decided to unveil a similar program of his own. Daley's version was called Operation Lite — an acronym for Leaders Information on Training and Employment — and it was aptly named. Daley's version was, in every sense, an Operation Breadbasket light. It recruited 160 businessmen, clergy, and social service professionals to distribute job information folders. As part of the program, Daley and John Gray, the city's merit employment chairman, announced that ministers and volunteers would make 800 calls to businessmen and others in a position to counsel blacks about job opportunities. They also planned to distribute a directory of job training and placement opportunities. Operation Lite did little for Chicago's disadvantaged, but it succeeded in its real purpose: making it appear that Daley was concerned about black employment opportunities.[22]

Daley invited King to join him at a summit with Chicago clergy to discuss the city's efforts to combat slums. The invitation was yet another illustration of how different the civil rights struggle was in Chicago than it had been in the South — Governor George Wallace of Alabama and Selma mayor Joe Smitherman had not looked to King for advice on how to govern. But Daley was shrewd enough to try to have his first meeting with King occur at a meeting of clergymen, so it would seem less like a showdown between the civil rights movement and City Hall, and more like a group inquiry into how to work toward change. King turned down Daley's invitation to the clergy summit, pleading a "long standing prior engagement" in Texas. But the summit went forward, and many of the city's leading clergymen did attend, including Archbishop Cody, Episcopal Bishop Gerald Francis Burrill, and the omnipresent Reverend Joseph H. Jackson. Daley discussed his work combating poverty and racial discrimination, and delivered updates on the city's progress. And he asked the clergymen to return for a second summit the following week, bringing along recommendations for how the city should proceed. King did come to this second meeting, on March 25, making it the first time the two men had met since the civil rights leader had arrived in Chicago. King listened attentively as city officials reeled off what the Daley administration was doing on a variety of fronts, and outlined areas where help was needed. Police Superintendent O. W. Wilson said there were more than 100,000 unauthorized firearms in the city, and asked the clergymen to encourage their parishioners to turn them in to the police. Fire Commissioner Robert J. Quinn told the audience that accumulated garbage was the biggest cause of fires, and asked for help in reducing the amount of refuse in their neighborhoods. Charles Swibel, chairman of the CHA board, said his agency planned to build an additional six thousand units in the next two years, and then asked the clergymen to deliver messages from their pulpits on the importance of cleanliness and being good neighbors. But the greatest drama in the three-hour meeting came when King and Daley engaged in a thirty-minute colloquy about the city's problems. King told the meeting that Chicago "has a long way to go," and described some of the problems he had seen firsthand since arriving in the city.[23] Daley responded that "these problems were created thousands of miles away from here in Georgia, Mississippi, and Alabama. This deprivation of education can't be laid to the people of Chicago. They had nothing to do with it." After the closed-door meeting ended, King and Daley spoke about each other in respectful terms. "I believe the mayor is concerned in his search for answers . . ." King said. And Daley pronounced King "a religious leader who feels intently the causes he espouses." The next day King settled an important question when he told a reporter, "I'm not leading any campaign against Mayor Daley. I'm leading a campaign against slums." Without King's support, the prospect of a strong black independent mayoral campaign diminished considerably.[24]

Daley continued his high-profile work as a champion of Chicago's slum residents. The same day as the clergy summit, he spoke to the opening session of the First International Conference on Freedom of Residence at the Conrad Hilton Hotel. Daley told an audience of labor, religious, and civil rights leaders that "opportunity for freedom of residence for everyone can only be achieved if thousands of people become greatly concerned." On March 27, he convened a meeting of one hundred business leaders in the City Council chambers and urged them to increase job opportunities for minorities. John D. deButts, president of Illinois Bell Telephone, reported that through the work of the Chicago Association of Commerce 312 companies had agreed not to discriminate in employment and had pledged to work for equal opportunity in hiring and agreed to offer in-house skills training for employees who needed it. The following day, Daley announced that he was stepping up the city's war on rats, promising that an additional $250,000 would be spent to treat all 20,427 blocks of alleys in the city over the next two months.[25]

Daley was finding it increasingly hard to keep his real feelings about the civil rights movement in check. Even as he spoke about his commitment to improving slum housing, he began to argue that the Chicago Freedom Movement was overstating the extent of the problem. "Look at 35th and State Street," he said, referring to a once-run-down area that had been razed to build public housing. "I lived there and went to school there. It was one of the worst areas in the city, but what do you see now?" In fact, most people still thought it looked pretty bad. In private, Daley was even less restrained in his attack on King and his followers. At a closed-door meeting of the Cook County Democratic Central Committee in mid-April, Daley told machine leaders that King and his followers were simply trying to "grab" power. "We have no need to apologize to the civil rights leaders who have come to Chicago to tell us what to do," Daley said. "We'll match our integrity against their independence."[26]

The spring of 1966 was not all run-ins over slums and civil rights. Daley's work in building up the city was increasingly being recognized, and was bringing him accolades. The National Clean-Up, Paint-Up, Fix-Up Bureau honored Chicago as the cleanest large city in the nation at a luncheon at the Bismarck Hotel. It was the fifth time in seven years that Chicago had taken the prize. The Loop, in particular, was thriving. The clearest illustration of downtown Chicago's impressive upswing was the rapid transformation of North Michigan Avenue. North Michigan, the upscale retailing strip jutting out of the northeast corner of the Loop, had undergone one of the most dramatic transformations of any part of the Chicago landscape. It had begun life as narrow and dowdy Pine Street. Burnham's 1909 plan called for widening it into a grand European-style boulevard, and that process began in 1920, with the building of the Michigan Avenue Bridge across the Chicago River. In the next few years, several architecturally significant buildings went up along the avenue, including the Tribune Tower and the Wrigley Building. In 1947, developer Arthur Rubloff dubbed North Michigan the "Magnificent Mile," but it was at that point still wishful thinking. It was only during the mid-1960s that it was truly beginning to approach magnificence. In 1965, the thirty-five-story Equitable Building opened, adjacent to the Tribune Tower, and in the next few years the march of development continued northward up the avenue. A decade later, the avenue would be capped off by Water Tower Place, a sixty-two-story hotel and condominium that included eight floors of luxury stores, contained in the nation's first vertical shopping mall. In time, Michigan Avenue would become so overrun with swank stores and high-rent office towers that one critic would lament that it had become "alas, the Manhattanized Mile."[27]

Chicago's was not the only American downtown to boom in the

post-war years, but it was one of the few in the northern Rust Belt whose fortunes were rising. What prevented Chicago from going the way of Cleveland and Buffalo? Much of the credit lies with Daley's aggressive program for downtown redevelopment. Beginning with the 1958 plan, Daley declared his intention to put the full power of his office behind Loop redevelopment. And he did a masterful job of keeping all of the key constituencies in place. His strong working relationships with the city's business leaders kept them invested in the city, and helped persuade them to build and expand in the Loop. His close ties to the city's major unions were a key factor in the years of labor peace that prevailed in the city. And his influence in Washington and Springfield brought in millions of dollars to fund urban renewal projects that benefited the central business district. Edward Logelin, vice president of U.S. Steel and chairman of the Chicago Plan Commission, said the renaissance of Chicago's downtown was in large part due to Daley's ability to bring together "the best of labor, politics, religion, education, and business."[28]

Another critical factor in Chicago's downtown development was the way in which Daley professionalized the city's planning and development bureaucracy. The Department of City Planning that he formed in 1957 with twenty-four employees had grown to eighty-four by 1964, and its budget had soared from $149,500 to $914,500. Daley also assembled an unusually talented group of workers, who would come to be known as the "whiz kids," to fill these positions. Hired on the basis of ability rather than patronage, they were highly qualified — most had trained as engineers — and committed to the nuts-and-bolts work of improving the city. "It was a very well-educated, professional group of people," recalls David Stahl, who started with Daley at age thirty-two and would eventually become a deputy mayor. "That group could have run any company in the United States of that size." Typical of the whiz kids was John Duba, forty-three, whom Daley appointed in June 1965 to head the city's new Department of Development and Planning. Duba, who taught at the Illinois Institute of Technology before joining city government, was a hands-on technocrat.[29] When he supervised the construction of the Kennedy Expressway, he often walked its entire length to check on progress. "It really wasn't so bad," Duba said. "It would take only about three hours and it was the way to get to see the problems and what could be done about them." Duba's deputy, Louis Westmore, had been head of the Department of City Planning and Landscape Architecture at the University of Illinois.[30] Daley also named Lewis Hill, thirty-nine, an engineer with degrees from the Illinois Institute of Technology and the University of Minnesota, as commissioner of the Department of Urban Renewal. Brooklyn-born Milton Pikarsky, Daley's commissioner of public works, was also an engineer. Although Daley cared enough about development issues to make merit appointment to these positions, the whiz kids worked alongside many city workers who were still hired the old-fashioned way. John J. Gunther, executive director of the U.S. Conference of Mayors, recalls attending a budget meeting of Daley's and being impressed with the caliber of his planning staff. "As we were going over to the Sherman Hotel for lunch I asked him where the hell is all this patronage I keep hearing about, because I had met his people and they were very able," Gunther recalls. "We got off the elevator and were walking across the lobby and there was an old fella there that was showing you which elevator to get on, and another old fella running the elevator. Daley said, 'That's the patronage.'"[31]

Daley held a press conference on March 31 to announce plans for a new bond issue. He had been stung badly by the defeat of the 1962 bonds, and this time he was leaving nothing to chance. He had an all-star lineup of civic leaders on hand to speak out in favor of the additional debt for the city, including Continental Illinois National Bank chairman David Kennedy and Chicago Federation of Labor president William Lee. The $200 million package of bonds covered an assortment of new projects, from rapid-rail lines on the Kennedy and Dan Ryan expressways to more mundane undertakings like $45 to $100 million for sewer modernization. To avoid the racial backlash that had hurt the 1962 bonds in white wards, Daley had decided not to use the words "urban renewal" anywhere in the text of the initiative this time. After the initial press conference, Daley continued to round up endorsements. The Civic Federation, a good-government watchdog that had backed only one of the 1962 bond issues, this time endorsed the whole package. And in a flourish of bipartisanship, Daley even won the support of Republican state treasurer William Scott.[32] It was a measure of just how important the bonds were to Daley that he testified for them before the City Council Fi-

nance Committee, a first in his eleven years in office, and took questions for an hour. Daley promised, in his testimony, that the bonds
would not raise taxes, but his critics in the economy bloc remained
skeptical. "This familiar promise was expressed with each package of
bond issues since 1955, and each package that passed brought an increase," Alderman Despres argued. "The only bond issues that ever
failed to increase taxes were the 1962 bond issues, which were defeated."[33]

In early April 1966, the General Services Administration announced that construction of the forty-five-story federal office building that Daley had worked so hard to bring to the Loop was being
delayed indefinitely. The decision appeared to be an economy measure by the regional GSA chief, coming as it did after President
Johnson made an appeal to cut federal spending wherever possible.
Daley was outraged by the move, and made it clear that he would
not tolerate a delay. "We want that building," he declared. "We are
going to urge the federal government to go ahead immediately with
the construction." In a lower-key repeat of the showdown with
Francis Keppel over school funding, Daley made a direct appeal to
Washington, and the GSA quickly backed down. Within two days
the agency said that its announced "indefinite delay" had been a misunderstanding. The agency said it would be seeking bids for construction of the foundation of the $45.5 million project in June.[34]

On May 2, Daley presided over the dedication of the Civic Center, a major component of his restoration of the Loop. Daley had
been laying the groundwork for a new complex to house state and
local governments as far back as his 1958 plan, and he had done a
brilliant job of making it a reality. The Civic Center was constructed
by the Public Building Commission, a public authority that Daley
had created in 1956. The PBC was invested with sweeping powers to
condemn property through eminent domain, and to issue revenue
bonds to finance its projects without going to the voters with a referendum or going to Springfield. It was Chicago's version of the public authorities Robert Moses was quietly using in New York to fund
and build projects without approval from the voters or the political
branches. "He used the Public Building Commission to achieve
things he might not have achieved if he had gone to the legislature,"
says former Chicago Plan Commission chairman Miles Berger. "If

you have the bonds, you can build whatever you want to build." Daley himself was chairman of the PBC, and his planning commissioner Ira Bach was secretary. Daley used his position with the PBC to oversee every aspect of the project, from the financing to the choice of architects. The $87-million glass-and-steel Civic Center, which would later be renamed the Richard J. Daley Center, substantially improved the facilities available to local government. It provided 111 courtrooms and eight hearing rooms for the Cook County Circuit Court, as well as space for the Illinois Appellate Court, the Illinois Supreme Court, the state's attorney, the sheriff, and other government personnel. A vibrant city block, filled with stores and restaurants, was bulldozed to make room for the Civic Center and a large open-air plaza surrounding it. But most critics, including the authors of the American Institute of Architect's *Guide to Chicago,* found that the trade-off was well worth it. "[S]omething wonderful was gained; the plaza has become Chicago's forum," the *Guide* concluded. "As the locus of activities as diverse as concerts, farmers' markets, and peace rallies, the Daley Center fulfills a civic purpose consistent with its architectural dignity."[35]

Although the war on slums had been grabbing the headlines since King came to town, the battle over the schools had still not been resolved. On March 21, Daley announced his new appointments to the School Board Nominating Commission. In a concession to the black community, he added a representative of the Chicago Urban League, declaring that "the commission should be a cross-section of our city." But at the same time, he also added a representative of the Teamsters Joint Council, who could be counted on to cancel out the Urban League's vote on any sensitive racial issues. On March 31, Daley held a third closed-door meeting with the city's clergy to discuss racial matters. King, who was on a European fund-raising tour, did not attend. Daley pronounced the session "amicable, friendly and highly informative," but Chicago Freedom Movement representatives were disappointed that Board of Education chairman Whiston, who was supposed to attend to discuss the school situation, did not show up.[36]

The school controversy heated up again when Willis, who was scheduled to retire on December 23, his sixty-fifth birthday, announced plans to push his departure date up to August 31. The Chicago Freedom Movement was overjoyed. Willis's departure would remove "a major stumbling block [to] quality integrated education in Chicago," Raby declared. A committee of the school board had been actively looking for a successor. By late April, they had interviewed six candidates, and Daley said that a decision on a successor was imminent. When Willis left office, the board hired James Redmond, superintendent of the Syosset, New York, schools, who had a reputation as a racial progressive when he served as New Orleans school superintendent in the 1950s. That Daley was willing to go along with the selection of a racial moderate at this point was not surprising. By the end of his career, Willis had become a polarizing figure, who had only helped the Chicago Freedom Movement to win converts in the black community. Redmond would fit in well with Daley's current policy of co-opting the civil rights movement by appearing to share its concerns. At the same time, Daley's control over the Chicago school board would ensure that Redmond would not take any steps extreme enough to scare voters in the white wards. And Daley was not ceding any power on the school board to the black community. Three positions on the school board had recently become vacant. Although his nominating committee forwarded two blacks among its seven nominees, Daley passed over the two black women — one of whom was a Yale graduate, doctor's wife, and mother of three — to choose three white men. The departure of Willis did not appear to have made much difference. "Mayor Daley has tightened his grip of direct political control over the schools," one critic observed a few years into Redmond's term as superintendent. "The school board, with the pretense of independence, performs a puppet show for public consumption. Redmond does what he is told."[37]

King and the Chicago Freedom Movement were continuing their efforts to reach out to Chicago's youth gangs. On May 9, movement staff screened a documentary on the Watts uprising for about four hundred Blackstone Rangers. The civil rights activists were trying to demonstrate the futility of violence, but the screening would later be seen by some whites as an attempt to encourage young blacks to riot. Two days later, King himself spoke to a meeting of gang members, urging them to turn away from violence and toward voter registration and other civil rights work. These efforts to bring gang members into the movement suffered a setback on May 13, when fighting and gunfire broke out at an SCLC meeting at a South Side YMCA to which both the Blackstone Rangers and their rivals, the East Side Disciples, were invited. Some fissures were emerging in the Chicago Freedom Movement, particularly around the issue of nonviolence. Moderate members of the movement, including organizations such as the Chicago Catholic Interracial Council, worried that the campaign was becoming more accepting of violence and "spreading hate." But King insisted that the Chicago Freedom Movement's commitment to nonviolence was as strong as ever. "Chicago will have a long hot summer, but not a summer of racial violence," King said. "Rather it will be a long hot summer of peaceful non-violence."[38]

The long hot summer erupted earlier than expected, and in an unexpected quarter. While all of Chicago wondered whether blacks would rise up, on June 10 it was the city's small Puerto Rican enclave on the Near Northwest Side that broke out in rioting. Chicago's Puerto Ricans were as poor and discriminated against as blacks, but because of their small numbers and the language barrier, they were even more marginalized. Daley "manages to attend many wakes in his part of town," Mike Royko wrote. "But when the Puerto Ricans invited him to a banquet last week — their biggest social event of the year, except for the riot — he couldn't make it." But the Puerto Rican community's invisibility ended when a police officer shot and killed twenty-one-year-old Arceilis Cruz while he allegedly tried to pull out a revolver. More than a thousand neighborhood residents, many of them women, threw bricks and bottles at the hundred policemen sent to restore order. The crowd set fire to police cars, pulled fire hoses away from firemen trying to put them out, and looted stores along Division Street, the neighborhood's main shopping area. The unrest continued for two days, and before it was over several dozen were injured. King cautioned that the Near Northwest Side riots reflected the broad disaffection that prevailed in all of the city's poor neighborhoods, but Daley blamed them on instigation by "outsiders."[39]

In 1966, the national civil rights movement was entering a new and more difficult era. What civil rights theoretician Bayard Rustin called its "classical" period of destroying the "legal foundations of racism in America" had drawn to a close. What would follow was uncertain. To a growing number of activists, the answer was "black power," a militant strain that promoted nationalism and was skeptical of the role of whites in the movement. On May 14, the Student Nonviolent Coordinating Committee held a watershed election at its annual meeting in a camp outside Nashville. Stokely Carmichael, a charismatic Black Power champion, was elected chairman over moderate John Lewis by a single vote. Carmichael and his followers mocked the integrationist ideals and Gandhian tactics of King and his followers. "To ask Negroes to get in the Democratic Party," Carmichael declared acerbically, "is like asking Jews to join the Nazi Party." Under the new regime, SNCC stopped using integrated field work teams. The organization would "not fire any of our white organizers, but if they want to organize, they can organize white people," Carmichael said. "Negroes will organize Negroes." Many whites, believing they were not welcome, resigned from the organization. In June, Carmichael delivered a speech in Greenwood, Mississippi, that has been credited with bringing the integrationist era of the movement to a close. Forget the goal of "freedom," he told a large crowd gathered in a schoolyard. "What we gonna start saying now is Black Power."[40]

The rising tide of black nationalism was in evidence from July 1 to July 4, when the Congress of Racial Equality (CORE) held its national convention in Baltimore. The traditionally integrationist and interracial group invited Black Muslims and other black nationalists to share the platform for the first time in its history. The NAACP, the National Urban League, and the SCLC all boycotted the meeting. King, who had been expected to speak, announced on the first day of the convention that his "duties as a pastor in Atlanta" prevented him from attending. Giving the keynote address, Carmichael declared that "[t]his is not a movement being run by the liberal white establishment or by Uncle Toms." Other speakers attacked the black middle class as "handkerchief heads" and "Dr. Thomases," and moderate ministers like King as "chicken-eating preachers." Although CORE had been 50 percent white only five years earlier, few whites attended the Baltimore meeting. One of the few who did, a nun, complained to the press that "[t]his is the Congress for

Racial Superiority." On July 5, white author Lillian Smith, author of the haunting novel *Strange Fruit,* resigned from CORE's advisory committee. "CORE has been infiltrated by adventurers and by nihilists, black nationalists and plain old-fashioned haters, who have finally taken over," she said. From July 5 to July 9, the NAACP held its own national convention in Los Angeles, where delegates distanced themselves from the Black Power movement. Vice President Hubert Humphrey told fifteen hundred delegates on July 6, "We must reject calls for racism whether they come from a throat that is white or one that is black." The convention passed a resolution stating that the NAACP would not cooperate with civil rights groups that were headed in a more radical direction. "In view of the sharp differences," said assistant executive director John Morsell, "unified action just seems unlikely."[41]

The Chicago Freedom Movement was itself at a crossroads. It was nowhere near adopting the rallying cry of Black Power. The Chicago movement had always been resolutely interracial, and its guiding force remained King, the nation's leading voice for integration and racial cooperation. And at a time when Carmichael and his followers were rejecting campaigns aimed at mere "freedom," the goals of the Chicago Freedom Movement — such as integrated education in regular classrooms — remained strikingly mainstream. But Chicago's black community was feeling the radical tides that were sweeping across the country, and King worried that Daley's intransigence could force the movement in a more radical direction. "[H]e fails to understand that if gains are not made and made in a hurry through responsible civil rights organizations, it will open the door to militant groups to gain a foothold," King told the *New York Times.* The more immediate issue confronting the Chicago Freedom Movement, though, was the need for a new issue to rally around. Willis's departure had been a great victory, but it had also removed the single best organizing tool Chicago activists had ever had. It was hard to keep up the demonstrations and school boycotts when a racially moderate new superintendent was just taking office. The inclination among most fair-minded people was to give him time to make improvements first. At the same time, Daley had been doing a brilliant job of stealing away the issue of slums. The power of the anti-slum cause had receded since Daley began holding almost daily press conferences announcing stepped-up code enforcement, tenements put in receivership, and sweeping new anti-rat campaigns. King and the other members of the Chicago Freedom Movement debated how to proceed, and at a steering committee in late June 1966 decided to focus the movement on a new issue — open housing.[42]

Racial discrimination in housing had theoretically been illegal in Chicago since the City Council passed the Fair Housing Ordinance of 1963, but the reality was that blacks remained trapped in a few ghetto neighborhoods. When they tried to move to other parts of the city, they found that real estate brokers steered them back to the ghetto. Landlords in white neighborhoods generally would not rent to blacks, and white homeowners would not sell to them. The rigid color bar in Chicago not only prevented blacks from living where they wanted, it also kept them in overpriced, low-quality apartments. A study of the Chicago housing market by the American Friends Service Committee found that white and black families in the city on average paid the same amount in rent, $78 a month, even though white families' incomes were 50 percent higher. But whites got more value for their rent money, because they had more neighborhoods to choose among. The report found that black families lived in an average of only 3.35 rooms, compared to 3.95 for whites. "Negroes pay the same for slums that whites pay for good conditions," the AFSC concluded. "The role of supply and demand will always hold true and Negroes will continue to pay a color tax for housing until the entire housing market is open."[43]

Open housing was also a cause that made good strategic sense. It carried some of the same moral force as the anti–Jim Crow battles in the South. Assigning blame for slums was difficult, and remedies often involved complicated interventions in how people used and maintained private property. But the principle that a family should be able to live anywhere it could afford to was clear-cut, and comported with the most fundamental American ideals. Open housing also seemed a worthy goal because if it could be achieved, many other benefits would follow. If blacks moved into middle-class white neighborhoods, their housing conditions would improve, their children's schools would become better, and they would have greater access to jobs. Housing discrimination also seemed easier to solve than some of the movement's other targets. There were limits to how much city government could do about joblessness and poverty, or even bringing the housing in poor neighborhoods up to code. But the mayor could end discrimination by enacting a single ordinance, and the city had the power to take away the licenses of real estate brokers who failed to obey it.[44]

Not least among its virtues, an open-housing focus paved the way for the Chigaco Freedom Movement to begin a direct-action phase. By taking the movement directly into white neighborhoods, it had a more confrontational feel, which was satisfying to those who believed that the movement was too accommodationist. It also promised to trigger the kind of dramatic clashes between civil rights demonstrators and white resisters that had been critical to success in the South. "Nonviolent direct action seeks to create such a crisis and establish such creative tension that a community that has constantly refused to negotiate is forced to confront the issue," King wrote in *Letter from a Birmingham Jail*. "It seeks so to dramatize the issue that it can no longer be ignored." If the Chicago Freedom Movement started to march into working-class white neighborhoods, it might end up with its own version of Selma — Alabama's Bloody Sunday — ugly racial violence that played badly on television. Open housing was probably the best option the Chicago Freedom Movement had, but King was becoming increasingly pessimistic about his chances of prevailing. Daley's response so far had been "to play tricks with us — to say he's going to end slums but not do any concrete things," King complained to the *New York Times* in July. "He's just trying to stay ahead of us just enough to take the steam out of the movement."[45]

The Chicago Freedom Movement's big event of the summer of 1966 was a rally at Soldier Field on Sunday, July 10. Daley worked hard to steal the rally's thunder. On July 8, he announced publicly that he and King would be conferring the following Monday, as King had requested, "to discuss the many problems affecting our city." The day before the Soldier Field rally, Daley told reporters that in the previous eighteen months, 9,226 buildings with 102,847 units had been brought into full or partial code compliance. The Chicago Dwelling Association had been named receiver of 151 buildings, and fines imposed by the Housing Court were running at more than twice the rate of the previous year. And 332,000 rooms had been inspected in the city's rodent control program, and 140,000 rat holes were closed. It was, Daley declared "the most massive and comprehensive rodent eradication program ever undertaken in this country."[46]

The rally's organizers had hoped to attract 100,000 people, but they fell short. Whether it was due to Daley's efforts at dampening enthusiasm, lukewarm support for King and the movement, or the day's scorching high-90s temperatures, the crowd that showed up in Soldier Field was somewhere between the city's estimate of 23,000 and the 60,000 rally organizers claimed. The organizers did do an impressive job of attracting performers, ranging from gospel legend Mahalia Jackson to folk singers Peter, Paul, and Mary to a young Stevie Wonder. "Mahalia Jackson sang that day as if the heavens were coming down on Soldier Field," recalls a community organizer from the West Side. "You can't explain that feeling, but you knew then that things are going to change, it must change. You felt that God was with us." Archbishop Cody, who was unable to attend, sent a greeting that was read to the audience. The Black Power movement was not officially part of the program, but they showed up anyway, revealing a growing schism in the black community. About two hundred young people, some members of the Blackstone Rangers youth gang, marched on the field carrying a banner reading "Black Power," and signs saying "We Shall Overcome," with a drawing of a machine gun.[47]

King arrived in a white Cadillac to a hero's welcome. When the thunderous applause died down and the standing ovation ended, he launched into a powerful oration about the hard struggle that lay ahead. "We will be sadly mistaken if we think freedom is some lavish dish that the federal government and the white man will pass out on a silver platter while the Negro merely furnishes the appetite," King said. "Freedom is never voluntarily granted by the oppressor. It must be demanded by the oppressed." King called for an end to the slums, and said that black Chicagoans must be willing "to fill up the jails of Chicago, if necessary" to make it happen. He also launched into the movement's newest cause, an open housing campaign that would free blacks to live anywhere they wanted. "We are tired of having to pay a median rent of $97.00 a month in Lawndale for four rooms, while whites in South Deering pay $73.00 a month for five rooms," King declared. Although he had insisted since he first arrived in Chicago that his enemy was the slums and not individual elected officials, King's Soldier Field address contained his most pointed challenges yet to Daley and the Democratic machine. "This day, we must decide to register every Negro in Chicago of voting age before the [1967] municipal election," he said. "This day, we must decide that our votes will determine who will be the mayor of Chicago next year. . . . [W]e must make it clear that we will purge Chicago of every politician, whether he be Negro or white, who feels that he owns the Negro vote rather than earns the Negro vote."[48]

The rally ended with King leading a march from the stadium to City Hall to present Daley with a list of demands. A crowd estimated at anywhere from 5,000 to 38,000 followed King, whose aides had by now dubbed him the Pied Piper of Hamlin Avenue, and watched as he affixed the movement's demands to the LaSalle Street door of City Hall. King was harking back to his namesake Martin Luther, who began the Protestant Reformation by nailing his ninety-five theses on the door of Castle Church in Wittenberg, Germany, in 1517, though on this occasion King used cellophane tape. A crowd of demonstrators filled State Street from curb to curb and stretching back for blocks. They sang civil rights songs, chanted "Daley Must Go!" and held up banners with slogans like "End Modern Slavery — Destroy Daley Machine." The document King attached to City Hall included what it billed as "14 basic goals aimed at making Chicago a racially open city." Some of the items were addressed to the business community, like demands that real estate brokers show listings on a nondiscriminatory basis, and that companies conduct racial head counts and integrate their workforces. Others were aimed at City Hall: that the CHA improve conditions in public housing and increase the supply of scattered-site housing, and that the city create a citizen's review board for police brutality and misconduct. One demand was addressed directly to the machine: that it require precinct captains to be residents of their precincts, which would end the practice of absentee white captains remaining in charge of West Side precincts that had long since turned black. Jack Reilly, Daley's special events director, removed the demands after King and Raby taped them up, and said he would deliver them to Daley.[49]

The day after the rally and the march on City Hall, Daley met with King and ten members of the Chicago Freedom Movement. He heard his visitors out with his usual impassive demeanor. Then, reading from a forty-page memo, he launched into a recitation of the "massive programs" he had overseen to improve the lot of the city's poor blacks. "What would you have us do that we haven't done?" he asked.[50] Daley refused to get drawn into a discussion of the specific demands King had posted on the door of City Hall. Police superintendent Wilson rejected the demand for a civil complaint review board of the kind New York City had recently introduced, declaring that it would interfere with the department's efforts to reform itself. But with that single exception, Daley was as careful not to reject any of King's demands as he was not to accept them. "The Freedom Movement wanted to get a no out of the mayor on each of the demands and he refused . . . . he'd say, 'Well, we could look at it from this perspective, and maybe we could do something over here,'" one civil rights observer noted. Daley argued that the problems the Chicago Freedom Movement was taking on were complicated ones, and that the city would need time to work on them. But King insisted that continued delay was unacceptable. "We cannot wait," King said in his closing statement. "Young people are not going to wait."[51]

King was more frustrated than ever. When he emerged from the three-hour meeting, he told reporters gathered outside that Daley simply failed to grasp "the depth and dimensions of the problem" facing the city. "We are demanding these things, not requesting them," King said, because the "seething desperation" among the city's blacks was "inviting social disaster." In the face of Daley's resistance, King said, the movement had no choice but to "escalate" its efforts and engage in "many more marches." Daley, for his part, came away from the meeting indignant that King was using their impasse for publicity purposes. A furious Daley, so irate that he stumbled over his words, insisted to reporters that the problems they were discussing "cannot be resolved overnight." There was a need for "massive action," Daley conceded. "We will continue it. I am not proud of the slums. No one is. We will expand our programs."[52] But Daley insisted that King was deliberately making the city look bad for his own political purposes. Chicago had "the best record of any city in the country," Daley said, and even King "admitted himself they have the same problems in Atlanta." Asked about King's promise in his Soldier Field address to begin a direct-action campaign that would "fill up the jails of Chicago, if necessary," Daley was firm. "There is no reason for violation of the law," he said. "This will not be tolerated as long as I am mayor."[53]

The peace in Chicago was shattered the following day. The city was going through a massive heat wave on July 12, with temperatures lodged above 90 degrees for the fifth consecutive day. To preserve the city's water pressure, fire commissioner Robert Quinn ordered that the city's fire hydrants be kept closed. Two police officers, called to the Near West Side to rescue an ice cream truck caught in a hole in the street, noticed some black teenagers on Roosevelt Road cooling themselves in the water of a fire hydrant. Open hydrants were illegal, but they were also an entrenched Chicago tradition. They were one of the few ways for poor people, and particularly poor blacks, to cool off in the summer heat. There were four Chicago Park District swimming pools within walking distance of this Near West Side neighborhood, but three of them were restricted to whites. When the police turned off this open hydrant, it struck many as yet another abuse at the hands of city government, and it was inevitably fraught with racial implications. "The seething anger over the fire hydrants on the near west side was a mental throwback for older blacks who remembered vividly their inability to eat hamburgers in white restaurants in Chicago," civil rights historian Dempsey Travis has written. Neighborhood resident Donald Henry defiantly reopened the hydrant, and the police took him into custody. As he was being led away, Henry made an appeal to the crowd forming around him. "You are not going to let these policemen arrest me," Henry implored. "Why don't you do something about it?"[54]

The crowd began to resist, and clashes broke out between the police and neighborhood residents. The police called for backup, and thirty squad cars appeared on the scene. Five or six youths were beaten with police clubs, and police began manhandling members of the crowd. The issue quickly shifted from fire hydrants to police brutality, and before long guerrilla-style warfare broke out between residents and police over a several-mile area. At the Liberty Shopping Center on Racine Avenue, most of the windows in the eight stores were smashed. King and other civil rights activists hurried to the area and tried to calm the rioters. At a late-night mass meeting at the West Side's Shiloh Baptist Church, King pleaded with the community to reject violence. But much of the audience, believing that the principles of nonviolence had already been breached by the actions of the police, walked out in the middle of King's presentation and headed back onto the streets. By the end of the first night of rioting, ten people were injured, twenty-four were arrested, blocks of store windows were smashed, and some of the stores were looted. On Wednesday morning, King called the incident a "riot," and put the blame for it on the brutal actions of the police. Daley, seeking to minimize the events of the previous evening, refused to call it a riot, referring to it instead as a "juvenile incident." The area where the uprising had occurred was quiet throughout the day on Wednesday, but violence broke out again that evening. Rioting spread to new neighborhoods, stores were firebombed and looted, and snipers were shooting down from rooftops. Firemen sent to put out burning stores were stoned. Hundreds of police working until past midnight were needed to put down the rioting. Eleven people, including six police, were injured.[55]

Daley met with key staff members on Thursday to plan a response. He told the group — which included police superintendent Wilson, fire commissioner Quinn, human relations commissioner Marciniak, and Chicago Housing Authority head Charles Swibel — that he would call in the National Guard if necessary to restore calm. Wilson argued that the real problem was that a few agitators in the community were using charges of police brutality to stir up the mob. The violence that followed on Thursday was the worst yet. Rioting spread into the West Side neighborhoods of Lawndale and East and West Garfield Park. Thousands of young blacks roamed the streets looting stores, throwing bricks and Molotov cocktails, and attacking passenger cars seemingly at random. Some black-owned businesses put signs in their windows saying "Soul Brother" or "Blood Brother" to discourage looters from attacking. The police and snipers engaged in furious gunfighting across the West Side. At one point, police identified rounds of gunfire coming from a tenth-floor apartment in the Henry Horner Homes. They turned floodlights on the apartment and sprayed it with bullets. In the end, two blacks were killed, including a twenty-eight-year-old man who police said had been looting, and a pregnant fourteen-year-old girl who was caught in crossfire. Many more people were injured by gunfire, including six policemen. Daley placed police on twelve-hour shifts, and deployed 900 officers in the affected area. He sealed the region off from the rest of the city, and declared that Chicago's curfew for youth under seventeen would be strictly enforced. By Friday morning, Daley had asked Governor Otto Kerner to mobilize the National Guard.[56]

Daley blamed the Chicago Campaign for the outbreak of violence. "[Y]ou cannot charge it to Martin Luther King directly," he told a press conference. "But surely some of the people that came in here have been talking for the last year of violence, and showing pictures and instructing people in how to conduct violence. They're on his staff and they're responsible. . . ." The "showing pictures" seemed to refer to the film of the Watts rioting that civil rights activists had shown to youth on the West Side. Daley also insisted there were "certain elements" working in the city "training, actually training" young people how to engage in violence. "[W]ho makes a Molotov cocktail?" he asked. "Someone has to train the youngsters." Daley claimed he had "tapes and documentation" proving the involvement of King's followers, but he would not make them public or further elaborate on his charges. Police superintendent Wilson argued that the police brutality was the fault of the rioters. "Brutality grows out of arrest incidents where a person resists an officer," Wilson said. "But some people think they can resist arrest." The machine's black allies echoed Daley's charges. "I believe our young people are not vicious enough to attack a whole city," the Reverend J. H. Jackson told a press conference. "Some other forces are using these people."[57]

King was indignant about Daley's accusations. "It is very unfortunate that the mayor . . . could perpetuate such an impression," King said. "My staff has preached nonviolence. We have not veered away from that at any point." The films of Watts that had upset Daley so much were shown "to demonstrate the negative effects of the riots," King said. The truth was that the civil rights activists had played a critical role in defusing the violence, King insisted, by traveling across the riot-torn neighborhoods and pleading with rioters to desist. "If we [had not been] on the scene," King told a reporter, "it would have been worse than Watts." The real cause of the riots, ac-

cording to King, was Daley's poor record of dealing with "the problems we face in the Negro community," and the latest round of
rioting was a wake-up call. If Daley continued to resist the reasonable demands of the civil rights movement, King warned, Chicago
was headed toward "social disaster."[58]

While the two men were publicly trading charges, King was trying
to schedule a meeting with Daley at City Hall. When he was unable
to secure an appointment, a contingent from the Chicago Freedom
Movement simply showed up. Daley was out, but King and his group
settled in and waited for the mayor to return. While they waited,
Archbishop Cody and six other clergymen showed up, also seeking
to talk with Daley about the unrest. When he returned to his office,
Daley sat down and talked to his visitors. Face-to-face, Daley was
more accommodating toward King than he had been in his comments to reporters. "Doctor," Daley said to King, who was seated
just to his right, "you know you are not responsible for these unfortunate happenings." After an hour and a half of discussion, Daley announced that the group had agreed to take a number of steps,
including directing precinct workers in the riot area to encourage
residents to stay home, appointing a citizens committee to advise
City Hall on relations between police and the community, and
building more swimming pools in the affected areas. Daley's course
of action struck King and his followers as paltry — King said they
failed to meet the "basic needs" of Chicago's ghetto residents. Civil
rights leaders had called on Daley to put more swimming pools in
poor neighborhoods, but when he agreed to build them, the plan
was easily mocked. Columnist Mike Royko scoffed that City Hall
was on a campaign "to make Chicago's blacks the wettest in the
country." Daley's more substantive reforms also struck the Chicago
Freedom Movement as unimportant. His citizens committee on police relations was merely advisory, and fell short of the independent
civilian complaint review board that activists were seeking. Still, King
called Daley's proposals a "step in the right direction," and said he
would be "going back to the people saying some positive things are
being done, that changes are being made."[59]

The unrest on the West Side was now over. More than 2,000
members of the National Guard, armed with rifles and bayonets,

were patrolling on foot and in jeeps, while another 2,200 were on reserve at five armories spread out across the city. The Park District had purchased ten portable swimming pools, and on July 17 installed the first one at a playground near where the fire hydrant riots had begun. A day later, when the streets were still quiet, Major General Francis P. Kane, commander of the 33rd National Guard Infantry Division, withdrew his men. The final toll from the fire hydrant riots stood at two dead, more than eighty injuries, and more than five hundred arrests. Property damage was estimated at more than $2 million, and many commercial streets in the affected areas were devastated. Roosevelt Avenue, by one account, "looked like a tornado had churned through."[60]

Each side drew its own lessons from the rioting. To Daley, the uprisings were getting too much attention, and were detracting from the many things that were going right in the city. "I would like to see demonstrations by the thousands of Chicagoans who have obtained jobs, returned to school, and worked together as tenants and landlords as a result of anti-poverty programs on the federal, state, and local levels," Daley told a convention of the United Beauty School Owners and Teachers at the Palmer House. But King and his followers continued to insist that unless something was done, worse violence would follow. The Freedom Movement staff set out to work with young people in the ghetto and convince them to adopt a policy of nonviolence. They held a five-hour meeting at King's apartment on July 16 with leaders of the major West Side gangs, who by the end of the session agreed to renounce violence. "This puts us over the hump," Andrew Young declared. "This was a real breakthrough." The movement staff promised one leader of the Roman Saints, who had what one staff member called "almost a religious conversion to non-violence," that he would be given a chance to meet with Daley personally to express his views. But the Freedom Movement staff had failed to check with City Hall first, and when they tried to set up the meeting they soon learned that Daley favored a tougher approach. "They live in a fantasy world," one Daley staff member said. "They expect to walk into the Mayor's office and say they're responsible for those killings, for shooting policemen, for looting stores and throwing Molotov cocktails and then make a planned pitch that society made them that way. Why, the first thing we'd do is throw them in the jug."[61]

The Chicago Freedom Movement opened a new chapter when it began leading a series of peaceful open-housing marches into the working-class white neighborhoods of Gage Park, Chicago Lawn, and Marquette Park. These Southwest Side neighborhoods were located near the black ghetto, and had housing stock that was within the financial reach of the city's growing black middle class. But according to the 1960 census, only seven of the 100,000 residents of the Gage Park–Chicago Lawn–Marquette Park area were nonwhite. Blacks who tried to buy or rent in the area quickly encountered a white wall of resistance, starting at neighborhood real estate offices. The Freedom Movement had been sending testers into Gage Park, and had already documented 121 cases of racial discrimination. The marches began uneventfully. On Saturday, July 16, an integrated group of 120 demonstrators marched from an "action center" in the black neighborhood of Englewood into nearby Marquette Park for a picnic. The next day, 200 marchers held a prayer vigil near a Catholic church in Gage Park, where they were taunted by neighborhood white youths. To ensure that there was no confusion about what was at stake, a protest leader declared that the marchers "had come to take a look at the community because this is where they plan to send their children to school and to live."[62]

The peace finally gave out on July 29, when protesters held an all-night vigil at F. H. Halvorsen Realty in Gage Park. The Freedom Movement had selected Halvorsen because, according to recent testing, it repeatedly discriminated against black applicants. Movement staff had also done research into the various white neighborhoods and "determined that this was the area that we were going to [get the] greatest resistance," says civil rights activist Gloria Palmer. "And the researchers and analysts were correct — we almost got destroyed." Not long after the open-housing protesters arrived at Halvorsen, white counter demonstrators showed up and the atmosphere turned tense. "The police protecting [the protesters] were getting more edgy," recalls the Freedom Movement's press officer. "Jesse Jackson and Jim Bevel made an agreement to get the crowd out in paddy wagons." The protesters left under police guard but, worried that their departure would be seen as a giving in, a crowd of about 250 movement demonstrators returned the next day to continue the vigil. Once again, they were met by a hostile white crowd that pelted them with rocks and bottles. This time, the marchers were forced to turn back even before they reached Halvorsen. Fortunately, the protesters could always escape from the white mobs by running over the racial dividing line and back into the ghetto. "The really stunning thing about Chicago segregation was that there was this war going on — rocks being thrown, bottles — but as soon as we got to the color line," says activist Don Rose, "it was just peace."[63]

A larger crowd of demonstrators returned on Sunday, July 31. This time, 500 neighborhood residents met them, hurling cherry bombs, rocks, and bottles. It was the meanest crowd yet. When Sister Mary Angelica, a first-grade teacher marching with the open-housing demonstrators, was hit in the head and fell to the ground, the counterdemonstrators cheered and shouted, "We've got another one!" Others yelled "White power!" "Polish power!" and "Burn them like Jews!" Before it was over the white mob, which had grown to 4,000, injured more than 50 people, including a Catholic priest, burned a dozen of the protesters' cars, overturned a dozen more, and pushed two into a lagoon. "I'd never seen whites like these in the South," says Dorothy Tillman, who left Alabama to join the Chicago Freedom Movement. The Gage Park counterdemonstrators were "up in trees like monkeys throwing bricks and bottles and stuff," Tillman says. "I mean racism, you could almost cut it." To make clear that they were not singling out any one part of the city, the open-housing demonstrators next shifted their focus to the Northwest Side. The reception they received in the Belmont-Cragin neighborhood, though hostile, was more subdued than what they had seen on the Southwest Side.[64]

Daley finally entered the fray on August 2, when he met with political, community, and religious leaders from Gage Park and adjoining Chicago Lawn. The white residents of these neighborhoods had assumed Daley would come to their aid, but he had been remarkably silent. Making matters worse, the police on the scene were widely seen as taking the side of the civil rights demonstrators, since they generally tried to prevent the white mobs from attacking. The community leaders who met with Daley represented some of the most conservative organizations in Gage Park and Chicago Lawn, including the infamous homeowners' associations, whose primary interest was in stopping integration. They wanted to hear specific plans from Daley for how demonstrators would be kept out of their neighborhoods. But Daley spoke only about the need for all sides to observe the law. "We are in agreement that this is a reflection on the city and that recognizing law and order is necessary," Daley said afterward. "I appeal to all people in all communities to cooperate with the Police Department." The white residents felt Daley had betrayed them. "[T]he Mayor's only answer was 'They have a right to march,'" one complained afterward.[65]

In fact, Daley was just as eager as the white neighborhood delegations to see the marches stop. But he understood that issuing an order, or having the police stop them forcibly, would only advance the protesters' cause. What Daley wanted to do was negotiate. He approached the Chicago Freedom Movement through CHA board chairman Charles Swibel. Swibel argued that since King had "gotten in over his head and needed a 'victory,'" the movement and the city would both benefit by working out some kind of deal. Swibel was a canny negotiator, and he opened with a lowball offer. The city would install elevator guards in public housing, establish a committee to investigate integration issues, and build or restore about 400 units of housing. In exchange, Swibel asked King to issue a statement lauding Daley's "wise leadership" and promising his "cooperation to Mayor Daley in implementing the positive programs the city has underway." When King rejected Swibel's offer, Daley and Swibel announced they would implement the improvements anyway. Next, Daley dispatched a delegation of black machine politicians to negotiate with King and Raby. The aldermen and state legislators, who met with the civil rights leaders for three hours, said they shared many of the movement's goals, including tougher open-housing legislation, stricter building standards, more bank loans for blacks, and a racial head count of employees. These were strange words, certainly, coming from men who regularly opposed civil rights measures in the City Council. But the machine delegation insisted that the city and the Freedom Movement should be able to work out some kind of agreement. As it happened, this attempt to begin negotiating with King and his followers was well timed. After seven months in

Chicago, King had grown increasingly discouraged, and was looking for a way of ending his campaign gracefully. "He told us they just couldn't go any further, but they had to have some kind of victory so they could withdraw without loss of prestige and that they wanted our help in achieving that," said Alderman Despres, the one white elected official present. "King was really announcing a surrender, and they worked out a formula for King to leave town." The gathering ended with Metcalfe, the leading black machine alderman, putting his arm around King's shoulder.[66] The whole scene made Despres "very sad," he said later. "Metcalfe could hardly conceal his pleasure with the thought that King was ready to leave town."[67]

While both sides worked toward some process for entering into negotiations, the marches continued, and the violence in the neighborhoods grew worse. On August 5, Raby and gospel singer Mahalia Jackson led more than five hundred demonstrators — the biggest contingent yet — back to Marquette Park. White residents had been gathering for hours in the park, a grassy expanse with a golf course and a lagoon. The crowd waved Confederate flags and held banners supporting Alabama governor George Wallace for president, and a few wore Nazi helmets. When the civil rights marchers began to arrive in the late afternoon, the white counterdemonstrators called out, "Two, four, six, eight, we don't want to integrate," and yelled, "We want Martin Luther Coon" and "Kill those niggers." A gray-haired woman shouted, "God, I hate niggers and nigger-lovers." Other whites screamed out "nigger-loving cops" at the police who were trying to keep the two sides apart. "About ten thousand screaming people showed up to harass, curse, and throw debris on us," Andrew Young recalled. "Bottles were flying and cherry bombs were going off. We felt like we were walking through a war zone."[68]

King arrived by car and joined the demonstration. While he was marching, he was struck above the right ear by a rock "as big as [a] fist." The nation's foremost advocate of nonviolent protest fell to the ground. "When we saw Dr. King go down in that line I didn't realize that I could be so mad at the world," said civil rights activist Nancy Jefferson. "I think everybody in that line wanted to kill everybody that was on the other side of the line." King got up and continued marching. As the marchers continued to make their way toward Halvorsen Realty, another heckler threw a knife at King. It missed him and hit a young white man in the neck. Members of the crowd yelled, "Kill him, kill him," as King walked by. Demonstrators held up signs with such slogans as "Reds, race mixers, queers, junkies, winos, muggers, rapists . . . you are all persona non grata here," and "King would look good with a knife in his back." King escaped without further harm, but the scene only got more tense. As the marchers prepared to board buses, a crowd of about 2,500 whites threw bottles, smashed bus windows, and clashed with the police. White women ran down the street with bags of sugar, which they poured into the gasoline tanks of protesters' cars. Other cars were set on fire. A mob descended on Father George Clements, a black Catholic priest, and police had to escort him to safety. Even after the marchers left, the clashes between the white mob and almost 1,000 police went on for another five hours. In the end, forty-four people were arrested, and thirty-one were injured enough to require hospitalization. "I've been in many demonstrations all across the south, but I can say that I have never seen — even in Mississippi and Alabama — mobs as hostile and hate-filled as I've seen in Chicago," King said afterward. "I think the people from Mississippi ought to come to Chicago to learn how to hate."[69]

With the open-housing campaign under way, Chicago blacks were starting to resist the CHA's plans to build more public housing in the ghetto. On July 6, the City Council voted down a ten-story building the CHA proposed to build in Woodlawn — one of twelve new sites the CHA had submitted — after an outpouring of neighborhood opposition. The Reverend Arthur Brazier, chairman of The Woodlawn Organization, testified against the building, saying it would overcrowd the neighborhood. Mrs. Tarlease Bell, one of more than one hundred Woodlawn residents who showed up to oppose it, told the City Council that "high-rise housing is a monument to segregation." A few weeks later, residents of Kenwood-Oakland, another ghetto on the South Side, turned out for a hearing at CHA headquarters to oppose plans to build more public housing in their neighborhood. A pastor from Kenwood United Church of Chicago charged that the CHA was "intensifying the ghetto." Swibel, however, continued to defend the CHA's plans. "I am taken aback that you seem to object to the poor and say they ought to live elsewhere," said Swibel, who himself lived in suburban Winnetka. "Everybody wants public housing to be somewhere else. I wish you would join us in making public housing so good that it will be accepted everywhere."[70]

Meanwhile, the clashes between open-housing marchers and angry neighborhood mobs showed no signs of letting up. Two days after the latest confrontation at Marquette Park, 1,100 demonstrators, 500 police, and 5,000 white residents faced off on the streets of the Belmont-Cragin neighborhood on the Northwest Side. Business and civic leaders from the Chicago Lawn neighborhood asked Daley to join them in petitioning the U.S. attorney general, Nicholas Katzenbach, to investigate Communist infiltration of the civil rights movement. The *Chicago Tribune* called on the black community to shake off King and his fellow civil rights agitators. "Why not a great petition, or a huge rally, to signify to King and his imported troublemakers that Chicago Negroes want an end to this campaign to stir up the antipathy of white people and want to give the races a chance to live in harmony?" the Republican paper asked. But harmony was not what the city seemed to be moving toward.[71]

Jesse Jackson had been talking for some time about leading a march into the all-white suburb of Cicero. Cicero was so hostile to integration — and its response to civil rights marchers was likely to be so violent — that Jackson's talk struck most observers as an idle threat. But at an August 8 rally, Jackson announced that he would lead a march into Cicero in the next few days. "We expect violence," Jackson said, "but it wouldn't be any more violent than the demonstrations last week." In fact, such a march was likely to be incendiary. Cicero, population 70,000, was perhaps the largest municipality in the country without a single black resident. A working-class town made up predominantly of Poles, Italians, and Bohemians living in simple brick bungalows, Cicero had cemented its reputation for racial hatred in 1951, when black bus driver Harvey E. Clark Jr. rented an apartment there. A crowd of 5,000 whites surrounded the building and threw bricks, rocks, and bottles through the windows. Members of the white mob eventually got inside the building, smashing stoves and refrigerators, and burning Clark's furniture. After Governor Adlai Stevenson called in the National Guard to restore order, and Clark left town, there were no further attempts to integrate Cicero.

Only a few months before Jackson's announcement, a black teenager named Jerome Huey had been killed by white teenagers when he went to Cicero looking for a job. When a network TV reporter said Cicero had a reputation for hating Negroes "deserved or not," one native scoffed. "The people of Cicero would be the first to say that the reputation was deserved," he insisted.[72]

On August 9, the day after Jackson's ominous announcement, Daley called on both sides to stop marching and start negotiating. Archbishop Cody echoed Daley's appeal, saying a moratorium on marches was needed to "avert serious injury to many persons and even the loss of life." Daley lobbied influential Chicagoans to support his efforts to bring a halt to the marches. On August 11, he sat down with seventeen of the city's top labor leaders, including his old friends William McFetridge and William Lee, at a meeting called by United Auto Workers midwestern regional director Robert Johnston. The Freedom Movement's "demonstrations on the streets" were the city's "number one problem," Daley said. Daley's proposal for ending them was to convene a summit meeting at which all the necessary parties could hammer out an agreement on open housing. He directed his Commission on Human Relations to begin laying the groundwork. The commission would have been the logical choice to host the summit, but Daley was intent on not being put in the position of negotiating against the Chicago Freedom Movement. He preferred to frame the summit as a meeting between the Freedom Movement on one side, and the Chicago real estate industry on the other. Daley asked the Chicago Conference on Religion and Race, a respected group with known civil rights sympathies, to convene the summit. It was a clever arrangement, and one that, human relations commissioner Marciniak noted, "took the focus" off Daley.[73]

The Freedom Movement was divided about whether to attend Daley's summit. Many of the younger, more militant members distrusted Daley and favored continuing to engage in direct action. They noted that the civil rights movement had tried negotiating with him in the past, and it had always gone badly. Daley always had his mind made up going in, and simply used the meeting for publicity purposes. That was, in fact, Daley's record in dealing with the movement. Meyer Weinberg recalls the time he and other CCCO representatives met with the mayor to discuss Willis and conditions in black schools. The CCCO delegation made their case with passion, but it elicited almost no response from Daley. "He was very bored with us," Weinberg recalls. "He just seemed like he couldn't wait to go home. We went away just feeling terrible." But King and the movement's more moderate leaders wanted to participate in the summit. King argued his position with what seemed to be an almost naive belief in the possibility that Daley could be converted to the cause. Daley "is no bigot," he told other members of the Freedom Movement, but he "is about my son's age in understanding the race problem." The decisive factor, though, was that the Chicago Campaign was stalled, and the movement was eager for any kind of victory, even a negotiated one. "The most significant event of this year is the spread of the Negro revolution from the sprawling plantations of Mississippi and Alabama to the desolate slums and ghettos of the North," King said in his report to the annual meeting of the SCLC in Jackson, Mississippi, on August 10. Chicago was the "test case," King declared, for whether the civil rights movement could succeed in the North. Daley's summit seemed to offer at least a chance that the northern civil rights movement would not end in total failure. After considerable debate, the Chicago Freedom Movement agreed to negotiate.[74]

CHAPTER 11

The Outcome Was Bitterly Disappointing

In the days leading up to Daley's housing summit, the Chicago Freedom Movement continued taking its fight to the streets. On August 12, the same day the Chicago Conference on Religion and Race sent out formal invitations, James Bevel led 600 protesters on a march to a high school on the Southwest Side. Two days later, Bevel, Jackson, and Raby led simultaneous marches on Bogan, Gage Park, and the Northwest Side. And on August 16, the day before the summit started, civil rights protesters held another round of demonstrations. There were vigils in Jefferson Park on the Northwest Side, and pickets at City Hall, the Chicago Housing Authority, and the Cook County Department of Public Aid. The Chicago Freedom Movement was sending a clear message that although they were willing to negotiate, they intended to keep up the "creative tension" until a satisfactory agreement was reached. The movement also embarked on a pre-summit campaign of real estate–agent testing. As expected, blacks were lied to about the availability of housing in white neighborhoods and turned away. King and Raby collected enough evidence to file seventy-four discrimination complaints against sixteen real estate brokers. Equally important, the testing gave them fresh evidence going into the summit that the problem of housing discrimination was real, and that the city's Fair Housing Ordinance of 1963 was not being enforced.[1]

The leaders of the Chicago Freedom Movement, stretched thin by the need to keep their campaign of direct action going, found little time to plan for the upcoming negotiations. The night before the summit began, they quickly cobbled together a set of proposed reforms. True to his character, Daley plotted his course of action more carefully. He assembled a team of experts who would be able to go head-to-head with the civil rights delegation on any subject they were likely to raise. Edward Marciniak and Ely Aaron, executive director and chairman, respectively, of the city's Human Relations Commission, would be on hand at the summit to speak to the overall racial situation in the city. And Daley called on city administrators such as Charles Livermore, executive director of the city's Commission on Youth Welfare, and Charles Swibel of the CHA, to be prepared to discuss their areas of expertise. Daley wanted Swibel at the summit for more than just his knowledge of housing. He was, in an odd way, Daley's ambassador to parts of the city's progressive community. Swibel, who was a slumlord by trade and ran the much-criticized public housing authority, was no great liberal. But he had managed to cultivate ties with some leading civil rights activists, including Chicago Urban League executive director Edwin Berry. Berry hosted many parties, and Swibel showed up frequently, usually the only person in attendance who was not part of Chicago's progressive community. Berry was likely to be a key player on the Freedom Movement side of the table. He was well regarded in civil rights circles, and had a good relationship with King, whom he helped to convince to come to Chicago. There was a chance that the most difficult issues at the summit could be resolved between Swibel and his friend Berry.[2]

To prepare for the negotiations, Daley and his team drew up an eleven-point proposal for resolving the conflict. Daley's approach, as it had been with the 1963 open-housing ordinance he drafted, was to blame the lack of fair housing in Chicago on the real estate industry rather than city government. Once again, it was a formulation that made Realtors and the civil rights movement the combatants, and avoided placing Daley in a showdown with King. As Daley envisioned the summit, he would act as a mediator between the two parties to the conflict: King and his followers on one side and the Chicago Real Estate Board on the other. It was a clever strategy, and once the summit began the civil rights contingent would become convinced that Daley had always viewed the summit in purely tactical terms. "It never seemed to me that Daley was trying to figure out how to deal with the broader race and housing problems in Chicago," says John McKnight, who attended the summit as a U.S. Civil Rights Commission observer. "It was about stopping the marches, which were tearing at the heart of the Democratic Party."[3]

The summit began at 10:00 A.M. on Wednesday, August 17, in a parish meeting hall of the Episcopal Cathedral of Saint James. Almost seventy men gathered around three tables shaped in a U configuration. The room was hot and stuffy, cooled only by a single floor fan.[4] After sending out the invitations, the Chicago Conference on Religion and Race had decided that it did not want to preside, so its members would be free to speak out in support of the Chicago Freedom Movement. The gavel passed to Ben Heineman, chairman of the board of Chicago North Western Railway. Heineman was sympathetic to open housing, and had presided in June at a White House conference on civil rights for President Johnson. But he was above all a member of the city's business establishment and a friend of Daley's. Flanking him at the center table were some of the city's most important religious leaders, among them Archbishop Cody and Robert Marx, a prominent rabbi. Daley sat on the left-hand branch of the U, with some of the city's leading business and political figures. Thomas Ayers, president of Commonwealth Edison and head of the Chicago Association of Commerce and Industry, represented downtown business. Two of the city's leading bankers came, David Kennedy, president of the Commerce Club, and Chicago Mortgage Association president Clark Stayman. The Chicago Real Estate Board, whose role would be critical, was represented by its board president, Ross Beatty, and past board president Arthur Mohl. On the right-hand branch of the U was the Chicago Freedom Movement delegation. It was led by King, recently back from a trip south, and Raby, and included James Bevel, Jesse Jackson, Andrew Young, and Arthur Brazier of The Woodlawn Organization.[5]

It had been agreed that King would speak first, followed by Daley, and that King would then issue the Freedom Movement's demands. But Heineman let Daley start off. His opening remarks were characteristically vague. "We have to do something to resolve the problems of the past few weeks," Daley said by way of introduction. When King's turn came, he delivered a more lofty oration, describing

Chicago in the same terms he had used in the past to depict the South. Chicago's problem, according to King, was one of "dualism." It had "a dual school system, a dual economy, a dual housing market," King said, "and we seek to transform this duality into a oneness." Raby followed, and assumed the bad-cop role he would maintain throughout the summit. "I am very pessimistic about the negotiations today because my experience with negotiating has indicated that our success has always been very limited," he said. The only reason the summit was occurring, Raby contended, was because of the open-housing marches. "We will not end the marches with a verbal commitment," Raby said.[6]

Despite the agreement that King would be allowed to present the Freedom Movement's demands first, Heineman called on Aaron to present Daley's eleven-point proposal. The city's position was that the real estate industry would have to take firmer steps to ensure that it was not discriminating in the sale and rental of housing, and that the civil rights movement had to promise to halt its marches into the neighborhoods. If Daley's plan had been to deflect attention from the city by pitting these two groups against each other, it worked. The Real Estate Board, both in Chicago and nationally, strongly opposed government-imposed fair-housing policies. The Chicago Real Estate Board had lobbied against state and city fair-housing laws, and it had filed a lawsuit challenging the Chicago fair housing ordinance. Real estate agents saw open housing as bad for business, but with the whole housing summit focused on them, it was not a good time to make a full-blown philosophical argument against it. Instead, they argued that open-housing mandates directed at real-estate agents were impractical. Realtors were mere agents of the sellers and landlords they represented, the Chicago Real Estate Board's Mohl said, and these were the people the civil rights movement needed to focus on. "We need a cooperative venture here, not bullying, but a program to sell people in the neighborhoods on the idea that the world won't end if a Negro moves in," he argued. King had little sympathy for the Real Estate Board's predicament. "All over the South I heard the same thing we've just heard from Mr. Mohl from restaurant owners and hotel owners," said King. "They said that they were just the agents, that they were just responding to the people's unwillingness to eat with Negroes in the same restaurant or stay with Negroes in the same hotel. But we got a comprehensive civil rights bill and the so-called agents then provided service to everybody and nothing happened and the same thing can happen here." The civil rights delegates were no happier than the Real Estate Board with what Daley's presentation called for. They did not want to agree to give up their right to march until they could be assured that they would get what they wanted at the summit. At this early juncture, that was not looking likely. Daley's proposal fell far short of what the movement was hoping for with regard to open housing, and King reminded Daley that the movement had demands "in the areas of education and employment and you are hearing here only our demands in the area of housing."[7]

The Chicago Freedom Movement finally got its turn to lay out its position. The movement's nine-point proposal focused on Daley and the city, not the Realtors. It called for the city to step up enforcement of fair-housing laws, through a program of real estate–office testing and filing complaints against violators. The civil rights delegates also wanted a commitment that the CHA would stop building high-rises in the ghetto, and a promise that urban-renewal programs would in the future be used to decrease segregation. When King asked Daley if he would agree to the demands aimed at the city, he quickly said he would. Once again, King's efforts to engage Daley in combat were defeated by the mayor's unwillingness to disagree. The movement delegates would have little choice but to aim most of their fire at the parties at the table who continued to resist. Not long after Daley agreed to King's demands, Swibel began to chip away at the terms. It would be hard, he said, for the CHA to agree to a total moratorium on high-rises in the ghetto, since the agency intended to build some high-rises for the elderly, and might not be able to get land elsewhere. Rather than suggest that an exception be made for elderly housing, Swibel instead substantially restated the public housing demand, saying that he was agreeing "that we will build non-ghetto low-rises as much as feasible." For good measure, Swibel also asked the civil rights movement delegates to have the American Civil Liberties Union's recently filed *Gautreaux* lawsuit, which challenged racial discrimination by the CHA, withdrawn.

Marciniak made one of Daley's favorite points: that the open-housing problem was a "metropolitan" one, and that the Chicago

Freedom Movement needed to spend more time working on opening up the suburbs. It was true that the suburbs were every bit as exclusionary as the city's white ethnic neighborhoods, and that opening them up would give Chicago blacks a broader range of choices about where to live. The problem was, there was little civil rights activists could do to open the white suburban ring. The Freedom Movement had leverage with Daley because it posed a two-pronged threat to the Democratic machine's hold on power. Its activism in black neighborhoods had the potential to radicalize black voters and drive them away from the machine. And its rallies in ethnic neighborhoods threatened to push the machine's white base to move to the suburbs. It was in Daley's interest to reach a compromise with the movement before it started to erode his hold on power. But the Freedom Movement had nothing to threaten the Republican suburbs with. It also had few legal weapons at its disposal, since the Illinois legislature had refused to pass an open-housing law that applied to the suburbs, and suburban governments were not about to pass their own civil rights laws. Daley may have been right that Chicago was being singled out, but as a practical matter the Freedom Movement had little choice.[8]

The original plan was for the summit to last no more than two hours, but Daley told Heineman he wanted to work through to an agreement. Heineman went along. "We're going to stay here," he told the crowded parish meeting room. "I have no plans to recess except for lunch." At this point, Thomas Ayers gave the first indication of where the business community stood. "I think we support all the points in the proposals of the Chicago Freedom Movement," he said, following Daley's lead and further isolating the Realtors. It was now virtually everyone in the room against the real estate industry. "The key problem, the core problem, is that Realtors refuse to serve Negroes in their offices," Bevel said. "And that must change." The Real Estate Board representatives in the room insisted that they could not speak for all Chicago real estate agents. But King tried to lift the real estate delegates to a higher moral plane. "I appeal to the rightness of our position and to your decency," he told them. "I see nothing in this world more dangerous than Negro cities ringed with white suburbs. Look at it in terms of grappling with righteousness. People will adjust to changes but the leadership has got to say that the time for change has come. The problem is not the people in Gage Park. The problem is that their leaders and institutions have taught them to be what they are."[9]

Daley had been sitting back for some time now — in a pose one participant described as "Buddha-like" — watching contentedly as the Freedom Movement focused its discontent on the real estate industry. When Raby suggested that the meeting be adjourned, Daley spoke up to urge that the proceedings continue. What was needed, he said, was for the Real Estate Board to "get on the phone to their members and do something about these demands now." Daley's comments came as a surprise, and they put considerable pressure on the real estate representatives to modify their uncompromising position. One member of the real estate contingent tried to stall for time, saying, "We cannot possibly deal on the phone — we cannot possibly work out a resolution to these things today." But Daley's allies in the room followed his lead. In the guise of "summarizing" what had transpired, Heineman told the Real Estate Board that "the monkey, gentlemen, is right on your back, and whether you see it as fair or not, everyone sees that the monkey is there." The question now, Heineman told them, was "how are you going to deal with the demands placed on you?" Swibel had been acting throughout the negotiations, according to one participant, as "the chief cheerleader for Mayor Daley," and at this point he launched into an impromptu pep rally. "We need a victory for Mayor Daley, a victory for the City of Chicago." At the mention of a victory for Daley, a groan went up from the Freedom Movement side of the room.[10]

The decision was made to break off the summit until 4:00 P.M., to give the real estate representatives time to talk with their board. During the break, King and the Freedom Movement had lunch at the Catholic Interracial Council, and negotiated further over whether to agree to a moratorium on marches. The consensus was that they should accept a moratorium only in exchange for significant concessions on open housing. Daley telephoned Real Estate Board chairman Ross Beatty during the break and made it clear he expected the board to change its stand. "In the interest of the city of Chicago, you cannot come back here this afternoon with a negative answer," Daley told him. The pressure worked, and Beatty announced that his organization was modifying its position. The Real Estate Board made a

The Daley family on South Lowe Avenue, around the dining room table in 1963. Children, from left: Mary Carol, Michael, William, John, Eleanor, Patricia, and Richard Jr. (*Chicago Tribune*)

Daley faces the cameras with the Reverend Martin Luther King Jr. as King brings his movement north to Chicago in 1963. (*Chicago Tribune*)

President Lyndon B. Johnson and Daley talk at a McCormick Place dinner in 1964. (*Chicago Tribune*)

About fourteen members of the Congress for Racial Equality (CORE) protest over school segregation outside Daley's home; they are outnumbered by more than one hundred of Daley's sign-carrying neighbors. (*Chicago Tribune*)

From the roof of the Civic Center in 1966, Daley looks out on the Chicago skyline, which has developed dramatically in his three terms in office. (*Chicago Tribune*)

Daley discusses civil rights with religious leaders, including King (second from right), in his office in 1966. (*Chicago Tribune*)

Daley, flanked by Lord Mayor Thomas Tierney (left) of Galway, Ireland, and an array of Irish politicians, marches through the Loop on St. Patrick's Day, 1968. (*Chicago Tribune*)

Following the assassination of Martin Luther King, Chicago's West Side erupts in riot. (*Chicago Tribune*)

A furious Mayor Daley demands to be heard on the floor of the 1968 Democratic National Convention. (*Chicago Tribune*)

Surrounded by supporters, Daley yells as Senator Abraham Ribicoff denounces the Chicago police. Daley insists that he was merely calling Ribicoff a "faker" but many observers believe they heard an obscenity. (*Chicago Tribune*)

National Guardsmen beat up anti-war protesters who refuse to move from Michigan Avenue after they have been gassed. (*Chicago Tribune*)

After the convention and considerable criticism of Daley in the national media, 11th Ward supporters greeted the mayor at his home. (*Chicago Tribune*)

Days before the 1971 election, precinct captains and machine loyalists gather at the Sherman House for a luncheon honoring Daley. (*Chicago Tribune*)

City Council Floor Leader Thomas Keane wanders over and talks with Daley in 1972 while a non-machine alderman is speaking. (*Chicago Tribune*)

About 25,000 Chicagoans come to pay their last respects to Mayor Daley in 1976 at the Nativity of Our Lord Church in Bridgeport. (*Chicago Tribune*)

general commitment to freedom of choice in housing as the right of every citizen, and promised to withdraw its opposition to state-level open occupancy legislation. It also agreed that the board would remind its members of their duty to obey the Chicago fair housing ordinance. At the same time, the board warned that further marches would "harden bigotry and slow down progress," and that "if demonstrations do not terminate promptly, we may lose control of our membership, and be unable to fulfill the commitments we have here undertaken."[11]

The board's new position was an improvement over its earlier intransigence, but it was unclear how much of an improvement. To some observers, it appeared to be a "complete reversal" and "the most significant result" of the summit. But it was obvious that the board's concessions had been carefully crafted. Withdrawing opposition to a state open housing law, for example, was an empty gesture. Even if the Chicago Real Estate Board went along, the Illinois Association of Real Estate Boards would ensure that these bills did not become law. Some of the other positions were drawn so fine that they were hard to follow. "We've heard your statement," Raby told Beatty, but "we're not sure what you're saying." After some time spent trying to determine exactly what the board was offering, Bevel said that the real issue was not complicated. "The question is whether Negroes are going to be served at your office tomorrow morning," he told the Realtors. Several speakers said that concern was already addressed in the city's existing fair-housing ordinance, but Bevel kept pressing for concrete changes. "Gentlemen, in Memphis, in 1960, we had a series of marches to try to open up the restaurants, and finally, we had a meeting like this and what was agreed was not that they were going to pass a law or anything like that," Bevel said, now standing up. "The power structure said that they were going to see to it that we could eat in Memphis and one week later we went out and we ate and we have been eating in Memphis ever since. Now that's what we want here today. I want to re-emphasize that we need Negroes to be served in real estate offices. And you people here can see that will happen."[12]

To some on the civil rights side, the Chicago Real Estate Board's new position was still inadequate. King had whispered, "This is nothing" when Beatty finished talking. Perhaps sensing that it had been a mistake to let Daley get out of the negotiations early simply because he had said yes to everything, Raby tried to pull Daley back in from the sidelines. "Now, I want to know when the mayor will see that an ordinance is enacted to require that all real estate dealers post in their windows the open-occupancy law and a statement of policy on nondiscrimination," Raby demanded. But Daley had no interest in being drawn back in. "I said already this morning that I would do that," Daley responded testily, "and I keep my word." Daley once again underscored the need for a regional solution. What was needed was a fair-housing law that covered the whole metropolitan area, he said, and such a law would have to be passed at the state level. "The Democrats have always supported a state open-occupancy law," he said, again trying to shift the focus away from himself. "The Republicans have fought it." Edwin Berry, branding the Realtors' offer "totally unacceptable," also pressed Daley to be part of the solution. "I want to ask Mayor Daley, if the Chicago Real Estate Board can't do something about our demands, can you?" Daley made a vague statement about how the city would "act as an agency through the Human Relations Commission" and again shifted the focus to the Real Estate Board. "I think they've done a lot," Daley said. "It shows a real change that they've come in here indicating that they will no longer oppose open occupancy." In light of the concessions from the Realtors, Daley insisted that it was now time for the Chicago Freedom Movement to settle. "We have agreed to virtually all the points here and everyone says that they are going to move ahead," he said. "Now let's not quibble over words; the intent is the important thing. We're here in good faith and the city is asking for your help." Heineman again lined up with Daley in pushing the Freedom Movement toward an agreement. "Bill, now you said the statement is worthless," Heineman said to Berry, whom he knew well. "But isn't point three, the willingness of the board to stop opposing the state open-occupancy law, a significant change?" Under continuing pressure from Heineman, Berry began to back down. "Well, on fourth reading I would have to concede that the third statement is something." Yes, Heineman said, "It is a concession."[13]

The talk turned next to whether to institute a moratorium on open-housing marches. Heineman expressed his view that since the negotiators appeared to be "well on our way to realization" of an agreement acceptable to all sides," it would be appropriate for the demonstrations to "cease until we see if these agreements are working out." But the Freedom Movement was less certain about how much progress had really been made. "I don't think we're nearly so clear on all of these things as Mr. Heineman thinks," Raby said. Andrew Young spoke of the critical importance of desegregating the city, which he believed was getting lost in all the talk about stopping the marches. The violence surrounding the open-housing marches had prompted this summit, Young argued, but everyday life in the ghetto was more violent than the marches. "It is more dangerous in Lawndale with those jammed-up, neurotic, psychotic Negroes than it is in Gage Park," Young said. "To white people who don't face the violence which is created by the degradation of the ghetto, this violence that you see in Gage Park may seem like a terrible thing. But I live in Lawndale and it is safer for me in Gage Park than it is in Lawndale. For the Negro in the ghetto, violence is the rule. So, when you say, cease these demonstrations, you're saying to us, go back to a place where there is more violence than where you see violence taking place outside the ghetto." It was an eloquent statement, but Daley missed its point. "Did I hear you say that we are going to have more violence in this city?" he asked. No, Young said, he was just saying that the ghetto was inherently a breeding ground for violence. "The city didn't create this frustration, or this situation," Daley said. "We want to try to do what you say."[14]

The discussion was threatening to move away from open housing to the larger, and far more complicated, issue of general conditions in the ghetto. Raby asked whether the Cook County Department of Public Aid would place the families in its charge in housing outside of poor, black neighborhoods. And he wanted to talk about the CHA's policy of building high-rises in the ghetto. Heineman tried to steer the negotiations back to the question of open housing, saying, "We understood that your proposals were on these two pages." But Young insisted that the real issue was "a plan to implement what is on these two pages." Swibel said the marches should be stopped immediately, for a period of twelve months, a suggestion that elicited groans from across the table. Charles Hayes, a black representative of the Packinghouse Workers Union, warned that empty promises were not enough, and that the civil rights negotiators had to have something concrete to take back to black people outside the closed doors of the summit. "I think that you need to be a Negro to really understand what the situation is here," Hayes said. "[W]e can't go out after these negotiations and tell the guy on the street that what we got was an agreement from the Chicago Real Estate Board that they philosophically agree with open occupancy. The people want to hear what we're going to do for them now. If I as a union negotiator ever came back to my men and said, 'I got the company to agree that philosophically they were in support of seniority,' I'd be laughed out of court."[15]

The summit broke for a fifteen-minute recess, at Raby's request, so the Freedom Movement could discuss how to proceed. The civil rights delegates were well aware, Ralph Abernathy says, of Daley's habit of "mak[ing] vague promises about an unspecified future, while refusing to be pinned down about any specific goals and timetables." None of them favored a moratorium based on what had been offered so far. "In your mind the question may be a moratorium," Raby told the summit after the recess, "but we would have to say that we would have a moratorium on demonstrations if we had a moratorium on housing segregation." Under questioning from Heineman, Raby said the demonstrations would continue. At this, Daley leaped up:

> I thought we were meeting to see if we couldn't, if there couldn't be a halt to what is happening in our neighborhoods because of the use of all the police and the crime rate rising throughout our city," he said. "I repeat, as far as the city is concerned, we are prepared to do what is asked for. I appeal to you to understand that we are trying. I ask you why you picked Chicago? I make no apologies for our city. In the name of all our citizens I ask for a moratorium and that we set up a committee.

It was classic Daley vagueness, a style one summit participant described as "many words, but they have so little content, they're so general, that you are not sure that anything has been said when [he] is done." Raby tried once more to move the discussion to specific remedies. "[L]et me give you an example," Raby said. "Is the mayor going to ask for the legislation to require brokers to post the ordinance in their windows? Will he ask for that legislation next Tuesday and will he get it? Will that actually be implemented?" But Daley responded that the Freedom Movement first had to show the City Council it was doing something. It was the first time Daley had expressly made a halt in the marches a quid pro quo for progress on fair housing. Raby was irate. "If I come before the Mayor of Chicago some day, I hope I can come . . . with what is just and that he will implement it because it is right rather than trading it politically for a moratorium." Heineman jumped to Daley's defense. "In a cooler moment, I think you'll realize that the Mayor cannot help but want fewer demonstrations, he's concerned about the safety of the people. And the Mayor is accustomed to having his word taken."[16]

With Raby and Daley at loggerheads, the prospects for a summit agreement were beginning to look grim. It was King who broke the tension by delivering a moving, but ultimately conciliatory, explanation of why Raby and the others were so reluctant to give in on the moratorium issue. "This has been a constructive and creative beginning," King said. And if Daley was tired of demonstrations, he should realize that the Chicago Freedom Movement was equally tired of demonstrating. But the marches were necessary, King contended, in order to change conditions. "Now, gentlemen, you know we don't have much," King said. "We don't have much money. We don't really have much education, and we don't have political power. We have only our bodies and you are asking us to give up the one thing that we have when you say, 'Don't march.' We want to be visible. We are not trying to overthrow you; we are trying to get in." By the time King was done, the tension in the room had broken considerably.[17]

Young suggested that a working committee be appointed to consider the kind of specific measures that Raby and the other members of the Freedom Movement were demanding. Heineman, who had been pushing the two sides to keep talking, agreed. He named a committee that included representatives from the Freedom Movement, the Chicago Real Estate Board, business, labor, and City Hall. Heineman directed them to return after a nine-day recess with "proposals designed to provide an open city." Before the summit could adjourn, an issue had to be resolved: What would be said to the reporters massed outside about the day's progress? Heineman hoped to say something about the marches. If he could not announce a moratorium on the protests, he at least wanted to say that "the movement would proceed with great restraint" and with "the overall interests of the city" in mind. Swibel pressed the issue further, trying one last time to extract an agreement that there would be no marches at all, but Raby snapped, "[T]hat question has already been answered." Eventually, Daley stood up and said, "I think everybody should be allowed to say anything they want to, that it be made clear this is a continuing meeting, and that this has been a beginning." It was almost 9:00 P.M. when the summit participants filed out of the meeting room.[18]

Both King and Daley were skeptical after the first day of the summit meeting. King was not convinced that the Real Estate Board would be willing or able to deliver on its promise to change its members' ways. The following day, he announced plans for a sweeping new program of racial testing. The Chicago Freedom Movement was going to send 250 testers to 100 realty firms on the Northwest and Southwest sides to see if anything had changed as a result of the summit. "The real estate people indicated in our meeting on Wednesday that they wanted to do something about open housing in Chicago," King told an overflow crowd of 1,000 at the Greater Mount Hope Baptist Church. "We want to see if they are serious. Some people have high blood pressure when it comes to words and anemia when it comes to action." The Freedom Movement also resolved the moratorium issue by announcing that it was resuming its open-housing marches. In a public utterance clearly designed to get under Daley's skin, Bevel declared, "We will demonstrate in the communities, until every white person out there joins the Republican Party."[19]

Daley, for his part, was also unhappy with how things were going with the summit. He was angry that King and Raby had still not agreed to a march moratorium, which he regarded as an affront to his control over the city. He was also furious at the damage the Freedom Movement was doing to the machine's political base. The white neighborhoods that King and Raby were targeting with the latest round of marches had already started drifting toward the Republicans in the 1963 elections. And ward committeemen and precinct captains were reporting that the civil rights activity since then had done even more damage to the machine. "We lose white votes every time there's an outburst like this," one precinct captain complained after a march came to his neighborhood. At the same time, the civil rights movement was tearing loyal black voters away from the black machine. Every successful open-housing march increased the standing of the Al Rabys of the black community, and hurt the Dawsons and the Metcalfes. Daley had agreed to the summit to get a moratorium on marches, and now he had no confidence he would get one from the negotiations.[20]

Tired of waiting for the civil rights movement to agree to a moratorium, Daley decided to go to court. On August 19, 1966, city lawyers showed up in Cook County Circuit Court Chancery Division seeking a court order stopping the fair-housing marches. Daley was in friendly territory when he went into the county court system. Most of the judges had made it to the bench by performing years of service for the machine, and Daley had slated many of them. Daley did not hesitate to tell judges how to rule in the cases before them. Senator Paul Simon recalls visiting Daley at City Hall and hearing him ask a judge, in a telephone call, to rule in favor of a party in a pending case. Weeks later, Simon saw a newspaper article reporting that the judge had done as Daley asked. Daley was known to punish judges who ruled against him, just as he retaliated against officeholders who failed to toe the machine line. Daley had approached one judge, Daniel Covelli, early in his career, about a case. Daley asked Covelli if he was not inclined to rule the machine's way to give the case up to a judge who would. Covelli refused to give up the case and ended up ruling against the machine. Daley unslated him in the next election.[21]

The march moratorium case went more smoothly. Cases filed in the Chancery Court went to Chief Justice Cornelius J. Harrington for assignment. Harrington was a product of the same world as Daley. He was a director of Catholic Charities, vice president of the Catholic Lawyers Guild, a trustee of DePaul University, and a member of the Knights of Columbus. As a young soldier, he vowed that if he survived World War I he would go to church every day, which he did for the next fifty years of his life. He graduated from Daley's alma mater, DePaul University's law school. Most important, he was strongly aligned with the machine. Cornelius was a "political animal," recalls Jerome Torshen, a lawyer with close ties to Tom Keane, and a frequent litigant before the Chancery Division. "In order to have that position you had to be extremely tied in, and they had to be able to rely on you in cases like that." Harrington decided to assign the march moratorium case to himself. Daley's lawyers told Harrington the marchers were a threat to the "order, peace, and quiet, health, safety, morals, and welfare of the city." The Freedom Movement would have responded that it was the white counterdemonstrators who posed the real threat, but they never got a chance to make the argument. Hours after Daley's motion was filed, before Raby and the others could even be located, Harrington granted the injunction. Depriving the Chicago Campaign of their constitutional right to demonstrate without even allowing them to state their case was an outrageous way for the court to proceed, but it prompted little reaction from the Chicago press or white Chicago.[22]

Daley's lawyers chose not to ask for a complete prohibition on open-housing marches, which would have been hard to defend constitutionally. Instead, Harrington's injunction imposed onerous conditions on future marches. There could be no more than one civil rights march a day within the city limits. No more than 500 marchers could participate. Marches had to be held during daylight hours, but not during rush hours, which the order defined as 7:30 A.M. to 9:00 A.M. and 4:30 P.M. to 6:00 P.M. And written notice of the time and route had to be given to Police Superintendent Wilson twenty-four hours in advance. "The Negroes assert the right to full-fledged participation in society," city corporation counsel Raymond Simon said after the injunction was issued. "We must make sure there is a society to participate in." After Harrington issued the order, Daley requested ten minutes of evening television time on the city's three main stations to explain why it was necessary. "There is no desire on anyone's part to interfere with these orderly civil rights demonstrations," Daley said. The real issue, he insisted, was that the marches "diverted too many police who were needed in other parts of the city particularly at those areas where there are the most families — the most children."[23]

When King and the rest of the Freedom Movement learned that Daley had gone to court to achieve what he had not been able to win from them at the bargaining table, they felt betrayed. "The city's move is unjust, illegal, and unconstitutional," King told reporters at the Greater Mount Hope Baptist Church. "I deem it a very bad act of faith on the part of the city in view of the fact that we are negotiating." It was particularly galling to King and his followers that Daley had gotten a court order that even Governor George Wallace of Alabama, at the height of the Selma voting rights campaign, had been unable to obtain. Wallace had tried to stop King's planned march from Selma to the state capital in Montgomery. He had argued, much like Daley, that King's voting rights campaign in Selma had already disrupted "the normal function of government." But U.S. District Court judge Frank Johnson ruled that Wallace's attempt to stop the march was a violation of the demonstrators' First Amendment rights. The burden was on the state to "preserve peace and order," Johnson ruled. Days later, 25,000 supporters of black voting rights marched to Montgomery and demonstrated outside the Alabama State Capitol. The streets of Alabama, it turned out, were freer for civil rights demonstrations than the streets of Chicago. The City Council, not surprisingly, sided with Daley. A resolution introduced by Alderman Keane, and adopted 45–1, lauded him for his handling of the marches and his decision to obtain an injunction. All seven black aldermen voted for the resolution, with Metcalfe declaring that "people of good intent should realize we lose our gains through actions such as Watts and several things that have happened here." Another black alderman called King "a great man whose intentions are right, but who is surrounded by a lot of people who are not right." Alderman Despres cast the single negative vote, but his dissent was not allowed to spoil the sentiment. Keane declared that he could not remember "any such unanimity in commendation" in his forty years in political life.[24]

The day Judge Harrington issued his injunction, the summit subcommittee was holding its first meeting. Some of the Freedom Movement delegates expressed unhappiness with the mayor's action, but no one suggested ending the discussions. "The issue is still justice in housing," Raby said. Outside the negotiation room, Jesse Jackson and some others argued for defying the court order, but King urged a more temperate response. He did not see what would be accomplished by violating the injunction, and he worried the movement would lose its moral high ground if it broke the law. King argued

that the civil rights forces could make their point just as effectively by
organizing marches that fell within the limits set out by the court.
On Sunday, August 21, a group of demonstrators did just that. King
personally participated in a march on the far Southeast Side, while
others led marches in Chicago Heights and Evergreen Park, two
nearby suburbs that, because they were outside the city limits, were
not covered by the injunction. American Nazi Party leader George
Lincoln Rockwell chose the same Sunday to come to Marquette
Park and deliver an anti-integration diatribe from a swastika-
bedecked stage. Representatives of the National States Rights Party
and the Ku Klux Klan also showed up to preach white resistance.
There was a troubling symbolism to the fact that King's followers had
been pushed out to the suburbs while Nazis were happily holding
forth in Marquette Park. The following day, at his first press conference in two weeks, Daley announced that he had received thousands
of phone calls, letters, and telegrams supporting the city's decision to
obtain an injunction. He was asked if he would declare the American Nazi Party and the Ku Klux Klan unwelcome in Chicago. "We
don't want any people who come into our city for the purpose of
agitation regardless of who they are," Daley responded. "This includes the list you mentioned and a lot more who have been spreading words of discord and inciting violence and everything else in our
city." It seemed that he was putting King and his followers in the
same category as the Nazis and the KKK. When a reporter asked,
"Do you include some civil rights leaders in that?" Daley turned
toward his private office and shouted back, "You can answer that."[25]

With tensions already running high, as black and white Chicagoans
waited to see how the housing summit would turn out, King announced plans for a march on Cicero on August 28. "Not only are
we going to walk in Cicero," King declared, "we're going to work
in Cicero, and we're going to live in Cicero." There was no telling
how much blood would be shed. If King's goal was to generate a little fear about what would happen if the summit negotiations ended
badly, it worked. Cook County sheriff Richard Ogilvie, a Republican who wanted to be governor, promptly called for the National
Guard to be on hand at the march, and lamented that "marching in
Cicero comes awfully close to a suicidal act." Jesse Jackson said that if
an agreement was reached at the summit, it was possible the Cicero

march would be called off. But if no agreement were reached he warned that there would be further "escalation" of the protests.[26]

Meanwhile, the summit subcommittee was still meeting, trying to reach a settlement. The group had begun its work on Friday, August 19, two days after the initial summit meeting, and it had met for long days of negotiations on the following Monday, Wednesday, and Thursday. The discussion started with the Freedom Movement's nine demands, but Raby and the other civil rights delegates were hoping to expand on them. The nine demands centered on open housing, but the Chicago Freedom Movement saw its mission as including education, employment, and living conditions in the slums. When Raby and the other delegates tried to bring up these broader topics, Marciniak and subcommittee chair Ayers complained they were negotiating in bad faith. The Freedom Movement delegates were also interested in adding specifics about how the nine demands would be enforced. The subcommittee agreed to establish a supervisory body to monitor implementation, but the precise structure and powers of the body were left vague. On the whole, the settlement that was emerging was far less than the Freedom Movement delegates wanted. But they were coming around to the idea of accepting it. There were reports that Daley and Swibel were playing a major behind-the-scenes role, arguing to Berry that the deal was good, and that it was the best the Freedom Movement was likely to get. Daley may also have spoken to Senator Paul Douglas, and gotten him to call Berry — a friend and Hyde Park neighbor — to put more pressure on him to promote acceptance of the settlement. "Berry was a great guy, but he was a realistic, pragmatic person," says McKnight. "I guess the ultimate decision was what Bill thought was the best they could do."[27]

The final agreement that the subcommittee arrived at had ten provisions, most of them drawn from the Chicago Freedom Movement's initial proposal. The provisions seemed to address the movement's core concerns. The city would promise to do more to enforce the 1963 open-housing ordinance, and Daley would agree to work for state open-housing legislation over the next year. The Chicago Housing Authority would seek out scattered sites for future public housing, and would limit new buildings to no more than eight stories. The Department of Urban Renewal and banks that offered mortgages would ensure that the mortgages did not encourage segregation. And the Chicago Real Estate Board would drop its opposition to fair housing and encourage its members to obey the law. Still, the language remained aspirational and unspecified, and the agreement lacked significant mechanisms for enforcement. Still, it did not address any of the issues beyond housing that many in the Freedom Movement hoped it would. "Our starting point became their ending point," one negotiator said ruefully.[28]

On Friday, August 26, the full housing summit reassembled in the Palmer House Hotel. The meeting opened with a prayer and then, at Heineman's request, Ayers read the subcommittee's report. When he was done, Heineman turned to Daley and asked for his reaction. The report proved, Daley said, that "[w]hen men of good faith sit down and talk they can solve problems." Without waiting for anyone else to comment, he called for a vote on the subcommittee's recommendation. "Just a minute here," Raby called out. The report still lacked specific timetables for when white neighborhoods and suburbs would be integrated, he protested, and it did not answer Bevel's critical question: "When do we foresee the time when a Negro can go into a real estate office in Chicago and be served?" As Raby said the words "in Chicago," Daley broke in and added "and in the suburbs," reiterating Marciniak's earlier point about public housing being a "metropolitan problem." But no one addressed the substance of Raby's objections. Archbishop Cody, Episcopal Bishop Montgomery, and some of the other delegates spoke in general terms about their commitment to ensuring open housing. And Beatty promised the Realtors would do all they could, although the more he talked the more he appeared to be reverting to his old position that it would be difficult for the beleaguered Realtor — who is "usually a small businessman in a small office" — to live up to the conditions being placed on him. The more the Real Estate Board representatives seemed to be backing off from the agreement, the more visibly nervous Daley became. The Freedom Movement also appeared to be wavering. Raby started talking about making any vote "an indication of sentiment" and not "binding." Heineman responded that he would have thought the Freedom Movement would want the agreement to be unanimous and binding. Raby asked for one last recess for the movement delegates to caucus.[29]

King spoke for the group when they returned. He was still unhappy about the injunction, which he regarded as "unjust and unconstitutional." And he was troubled that the newly created monitoring body was not better defined, and that there was no answer to Bevel's question about whether blacks would now be served when they showed up at real estate offices. "[W]e are very concerned about implementation," King said. "Maybe we are oversensitive, but there have been so many promises that haven't materialized, that this is a great thing in our minds." Daley struck a conciliatory tone in response. "I want you to know that I was raised in a workingman's community in a workingman's home," Daley said. "My father was a union organizer and we did not like injunctions. I know the injustice of injunctions. But I also faced the decision of what to do with three and a half million people." Daley claimed that the city's crime rate was soaring, due to diversion of police to the sites of the marches. And police superintendent Wilson complained that the Freedom Movement was not giving him the advance notice about march times and routes that he needed. "The course I took was the only one I could take," Daley said. Ultimately, he assured King, the injunction was about to become a moot point. "[I]f this agreement is made and everybody keeps to it, you will have no worry about the injunction because you won't need to march." When King continued to object, Heineman brokered a peace between the two men. Would the city be willing to sit down with the Freedom Movement to negotiate modifications that would allow them broader demonstration rights? "The city will sit down and talk over anything with anybody," Daley responded. "Speaking specifically, we can amend our injunction, I know, as a lawyer, and we would be glad to sit down and discuss [it]." When the vote was taken, it was unanimous in favor of accepting the subcommittee's recommendations.[30]

The summit ended with King standing up and speaking about his hopes and fears about Chicago's future. "We read in the scripture, 'Come, let us sit down and reason together,' and everyone here has met the scriptural mandate," King said. "We seek only to make possible a city where men can live as brothers. I know this has been said many times today, but I want to reiterate again, that we must make this agreement work. Our people's hopes have been shattered too many times, and an additional disillusionment will only spell catastrophe." In their public statements outside the summit, the parties all tried to be upbeat. Daley called it a "great day" for Chicago, and promised that "we will go ahead to eliminate slums, provide better schools, and more jobs in our city." Heineman concurred, saying that "the city of Chicago, through all elements of society represented here, the city government, the freedom movement, religious leaders, business, and labor took a giant step forward." Even King put aside his private reservations to declare that "never before have such far-reaching and creative commitments been made and programs adopted and pledged to achieve open housing in a community."[31]

The reaction of the rest of Chicago was less enthusiastic. White working-class residents of the Bungalow Belt, accepting the open-housing language of the agreement at face value, were convinced Daley had handed their neighborhoods over to blacks. The Kilbourn Organization, a community group on the Northwest Side, voted to go down to City Hall for a meeting with Daley to protest the agreement. "The races spoke, religion spoke, but who spoke for the tax-payers of Chicago?" one member asked. "We demand an equal voice and equal rights for the people who pay for these promises." In all, twelve neighborhood organizations notified Daley they would be arriving at City Hall the following Monday to register their objections to the summit agreement. Daley never responded to their requests for a meeting. On Monday, a small group of demonstrators gathered at the LaSalle Street entrance to City Hall carrying signs saying "Daley Sold Out Chicago," and "The Summit Another Munich." A member of the Kilbourn Organization tried to get in to the mayor's office, but he was told Daley was not in. When the housing chair-man of the Clearing Civic League, representing the Far Southwest Side neighborhood of Clearing was turned away, she asked bitterly: "Who had the right to give our city away, as the mayor did?"[32]

Black activists were just as convinced it was their side that had been betrayed. Chester Robinson, leader of the West Side Organiza-tion, charged the negotiators with "selling out Negro interests" in exchange for "empty promises." And the head of Chicago's CORE chapter, Robert Lucas, denounced the settlement as "nothing but another promise on a piece of paper." When King spoke about the summit to an open-housing rally, SNCC was there circulating a leaflet urging the crowd to "WAKE UP" and oppose the agreement.

"King says we should celebrate a 'significant victory' tonight because he got some concessions from the city," the flyer said. "These concessions were just more empty promises from Daley, a man who has lied and lied to the black man in this city for years. Many people are calling it a sellout. . . ." Critics of the agreement charged that it was just another example of King yielding too readily to government authority — one biographer has called this tendency on King's part the "Selma bridge syndrome," after his willingness to delay the 1965 Selma-to-Montgomery march in response to federal pressure. Some Freedom Movement activists believed he had simply found the Chicago Campaign too difficult, and had decided to give up. King never explicitly said this to the movement's rank and file, but some of them suspected it when he and Raby failed to report back to the CCCO's regular Saturday morning meetings during the summit. They seemed to be saying that there was little left to talk about. Despite the criticism, King continued to defend the summit agreement. Preaching back at his father's Ebenezer Baptist Church in Atlanta, King declared it to be perhaps the most "far-reaching victory that has ever come about in a Northern community on the whole question of open housing." But it was weak praise, since the North had few other open-housing victories, and this one had absorbed eight months of the movement's time and effort.[33]

As part of the summit agreement, King had pledged to call off the planned march on Cicero, but some civil rights activists broke rank and announced they would press forward. "We respect Dr. King and leaders of the Chicago Freedom Movement," Chester Robinson declared. But he maintained that "too little was secured to call off the Cicero march." Robinson wanted to stick to the original August 28 date, but King managed to get it put off a week, and he was hoping to get it canceled entirely. "Martin understood that a march in Cicero was more effective as a threat than as a reality," Young says. "He wanted to continue to hold out the march . . . as leverage over implementation of the agreement." On September 1, King and Young met with Robinson and tried to talk him into abandoning the Cicero march. In exchange for King's agreement to promote The Woodlawn Organization's public housing and welfare reform agenda, Robinson agreed to cancel his plans. Some members of the black community saw a conspiracy at work in the cancellation, and suspected Daley was behind it. When King spoke at a rally at Liberty Baptist Church on the South Side, SNCC activists handed out leaflets saying "Daley blew the whistle and King stopped the marches."[34]

There were still activists in the Freedom Movement who wanted a march on Cicero, and Chicago CORE leader Robert Lucas said he would lead one. On September 4, Lucas paraded into Cicero with a ragtag, largely black contingent of about two hundred protesters. Despite the low turnout, the march had its moments of drama. Hundreds of Cicero residents lined the march route shouting insults, and one major fight broke out. But the thousands of police and National Guardsmen were largely able to keep the peace. A few days later, Lucas announced plans to march on an all-white South Side neighborhood. Daley was enraged that after the summit agreement had put an end to Freedom Movement marches, a rogue element was still marching. The open-housing marches were continuing only because the media were covering them, Daley charged. "All these people are looking for is publicity." By now, Daley was through negotiating. He put an end to Lucas's plans by having him jailed for failing to pay fines for civil disobedience that he committed a year earlier.[35]

In late September, the Metropolitan Chicago Leadership Council for Open Housing was formed to implement the summit agreement. Daley attended the Palmer House press conference where James Cook, president of Illinois Bell Telephone, was named president of the new organization. "We're fortunate indeed to have such a fine man to head up such an important council," Daley declared. "Chicago is leading the way for the entire nation." That was not an opinion widely shared among supporters of open housing. Cook's organization faced some significant obstacles, including the fact that it had no office, no staff, and no budget. The financial problems were solved when Chicago's corporate leaders responded to Cook's solicitations for contributions. And within a month, Cook persuaded Edward Holmgren, Elizabeth Wood's venerable onetime assistant, to serve as executive director. The Leadership Council went on to become an influential force for open housing in Chicago and the suburbs. It organized conferences, disseminated information, and filed hundreds of lawsuits challenging housing segregation, including two that went up to the U.S. Supreme Court. "I say the freedom movement won because we got the Leadership Council . . . out of it," says

Marciniak. "We have the business community and other civic leaders espousing fair housing, so they were on our side." Well-meaning as the Leadership Council was, there were limits to how much change a single advocacy organization could bring about. The real test of the summit agreement, as Bevel insisted all along, was whether it was enforced and whether it changed the lives of Chicago's black citizens.[36]

Daley's advisers already knew for certain what the leaders of the Freedom Movement only suspected: that Daley had no intention of keeping the promises he made at the summit. He could not say it outright, since he needed the civil rights marches to stop and for King to go home, but this was always Daley's plan. "I remember my father saying he was at a meeting with Martin Luther King, talking about King marching through the South Side," says Anthony Downs, son of James Downs, Daley's top housing adviser. "My father came home and said, 'I could just see the mayor decide at that moment how he was going to handle King, that he was going to lie to him. I could just see the moment in which he decided the only way he could get rid of the guy was to tell him a whole lot of lies.'" Daley made some gestures, in addition to creating the Leadership Council, that suggested he was committed to reform. William Robinson, former treasurer of the CCCO, was named to head the Cook County Public Aid Department. It was an important job, and one the civil rights community cared about deeply, but Robinson would not have the power to integrate the white neighborhoods Daley was concerned about protecting. Despite all of the talk at the summit, the city was less than aggressive about suspending the licenses of Realtors who continued to discriminate. The changes at the Chicago Housing Authority were largely cosmetic. The agency did not start assigning black families to white projects, or otherwise try to integrate its existing housing stock. When it opened two new elderly projects in white neighborhoods in the months after the summit, it did not assign a single black tenant to either one. Swibel did announce, with great pride, the installation of $18,000 in new door locks, and plans to send 500 housing project children to one week of summer camp.[37]

With King gone from Chicago and the marches over, Daley's attention shifted back to downtown. In September, he proposed a major urban-renewal project for a 156-acre area adjacent to the University of Illinois campus on the New West Side. It would be the biggest slum-clearance project yet, surpassing the 100 acres razed to build the Lake Meadows development. Daley wanted to add about 50 additional acres to the campus, and use the remainder of the cleared land for commercial purposes. Perhaps as a lingering response to the Freedom Movement and the housing summit, Daley also announced that the city and the University of Chicago were jointly seeking a federal grant to build a social service center to serve the Woodlawn neighborhood. The center, which would be operated by the university's School of Social Service Administration, was badly needed in Woodlawn, and it would connect the university to a neighboring community upon which it had turned its back. But Daley's support for the project cost him little. It was aimed at improving living conditions in the ghetto, not at helping ghetto residents to move out. The university would take responsibility for running it, and the federal government would be paying the bills.[38]

In the fall of 1966, with the Chicago Freedom Movement only an unpleasant memory, Daley was worried about the November elections. The stakes for the machine were high. Senator Paul Douglas, the Hyde Park liberal who had stood by Daley over the years, was facing a tough challenge from Republican Charles Percy. The boyishly appealing Percy had come within 179,000 votes of defeating Kerner for governor in 1964, even as Goldwater was losing Illinois by almost 900,000. This time he did not have the burden of running with Goldwater at the top of the ticket, and he was waging an aggressive campaign that portrayed the seventy-four-year-old Douglas as a relic from another age. Daley also had a full slate of statewide and Cook County candidates to worry about, and a delegation of Chicago congressmen who were taking heat from their constituents over civil rights. According to the polls, the civil rights issue was actually hurting Democrats with both black and white voters. In working-class white wards, voters blamed the Democrats for appeasing the Freedom Movement at the housing summit and for being too soft on open-housing demonstrators. In Cicero, which deeply resented becoming a backdrop for the open-housing marchers, polls showed Douglas's support down by as much as 30 percent from 1954 and 1960. At the same time, civil rights activists were urging black voters to abandon the machine's candidates to protest that more was not being done. "It is a myth that the Negro is in any way indebted

to or obligated to vote for the Democratic party," James Bevel proclaimed."[39]

The Republicans were eager to exploit the trouble civil rights was
causing the Democrats. Percy formed an alliance with David Reed, a
twenty-five-year-old "independent Republican" who was challenging Congressman Dawson. Percy, who sponsored six "Reed-Percy"
campaign headquarters in Dawson's district, hoped to benefit from
Reed's message that "for too long the people of the First District
have lived on Mayor Daley's Plantation." The polls showed that
Douglas was in trouble, but Daley remained optimistic in his public
pronouncements. "We still have work to do and we're going to do
it," he said. Daley, who was predicting Douglas would win by
200,000 votes, said the press was wrong when it said "white backlash" would be a significant factor in the voting. "I hate to think that
anyone would cast a ballot on the basis of hate," he said. To minimize
defections on both sides of the color line, Daley tried to frame the
election as being about anything but race. "It is the Democratic Party
that has given the people Medicare and expanded social security;
federal aid to schools, including expanded opportunities for attending college; the minimum wage and increases in minimum wage;
and measures to rebuild cities that provide decent housing, end air
and water pollution, and improve transportation," he wrote in a pre-
election statement in the *Chicago Tribune*. Daley reached out to the
machine's white ethnic base with unusual vigor this time. In a four-
day period, he marched with 250,000 Poles in the Pulaski Day parade and 300,000 Italians in the Columbus Day parade. Daley also
brought Douglas around to the Plumbers Hall, and urged the 4,000
union leaders and members in the audience to get the labor vote out
on election day. "We are not on the ropes," Daley said. "But we have
to get the people out to vote." Daley hoped Johnson would come to
Chicago for an election-eve rally, but the president pleaded health
problems and did not attend. Still, the machine held a lunchtime pre-
election parade through the Loop, complete with bands, one hundred floats, and a telegram from Johnson. It was, Daley declared
"another great day for a great city."[40]

Daley's public good cheer masked his worries that the machine
ticket would lose badly. He called in the ward committeemen from
all fifty wards and gave them an unusually tough talk about coming

through on election day, threatening sanctions for those who failed to deliver. Hundreds of precinct captains and patronage workers were also called down to machine headquarters and admonished to redouble their efforts. The machine also resorted to another of its traditional tactics: dirty tricks. Percy leaflets began to appear in working-class white neighborhoods with pictures of the candidate with blacks and declarations of his support for open housing. Percy threatened to file a complaint with the largely ineffective Fair Campaign Practices Committee, but the machine insisted it did not know who was behind the leafleting. Daley had one more clever idea for finessing the race issue. On the eve of the election, he announced that King had come to Chicago for the first time since the housing summit to urge blacks not to vote Democratic. He also complained that Bevel had urged blacks to abandon the Democratic Party. Daley's charges about King were untrue. King had actually been coming to Chicago almost weekly since the summit ended, and had scrupulously avoided taking any partisan political stands. But it was clear what Daley was up to: he was telling white voters not to worry that the Democratic Party had become the party of civil rights. Speaking from Atlanta, King called Daley's accusations that he had come out against the Democratic ticket "totally unfounded" but "shrewd and timely . . . for his purposes."[41]

In the end, Daley's shrewd tactics were not enough. Douglas carried Chicago by only 184,000 votes, and lost Illinois by 400,000. The news was not much better in the Cook County races. Sheriff Richard Ogilvie was elected president of the Cook County Board, the first time a Republican had won the office in decades, robbing the machine of 18,000 patronage jobs. Republicans were also elected county treasurer and sheriff. County assessor P. J. "Parky" Cullerton and county clerk Edward Barrett were among the few Democrats to survive the Republican sweep. It was the Republicans' best off-year election performance since 1950. One of the few bright spots was that thirty-six-year-old Adlai Stevenson III, Daley's handpicked candidate for state treasurer, won his race. Daley also managed to return all of his incumbent congressmen, but the margins in some of the races were uncomfortably close.[42]

It was, all things considered, a disastrous election for the Democrats. The results were particularly ominous for Daley, who would be running for election the following year. Douglas had won only 57 percent of the vote in Chicago, and ward-by-ward tallies showed that the Republicans had indeed made deep inroads throughout the Bungalow Belt. Congressman Pucinski, whose district had been the site of open-housing demonstrations over the summer, was reelected by only 4,700 votes. Two years earlier, he had won by 31,000. "I've been the guy who was claiming there was no backlash," Pucinski said afterward, "but I'm the first to admit now I was dead wrong." Just as troubling, the Democratic vote had fallen sharply in the black wards, where it seemed that many voters had simply decided to stay home. Daley tried to put the result in the best possible light. "The city of Chicago went overwhelmingly for every Democratic candidate," he said on election night. "I think the good people of Chicago are still Democratic." But Percy, in a burst of victory-night enthusiasm, hailed the "Republican resurgence" and predicted that Daley would be defeated if he ran for reelection.[43]

With the election safely over, the truth about the housing summit agreement came out. Keane, the number-two man in city government and Daley's co-negotiator at the summit, declared on the floor of the City Council that there was no open-housing agreement. "There were only certain suggestions put down and goals to be sought," he said during finance committee hearings on the city's 1967 budget. When word of Keane's statement reached King, he was outraged. "Hundreds of thousands of Chicago citizens live in slums today awaiting the severities of winter," King said. "Last summer they were given the hope that their hardship would come to an end, that the slums could be eliminated, and that decent homes would be made available to all families in all neighborhoods. Any attempt to destroy that hope is an act of cruelty and a betrayal of trust." King insisted Daley now had an obligation to speak out. "[B]ecause Mr. Keane so often seems disposed to speak for the entire city government, I think that Mayor Daley himself should clarify his own position," King said. "After all, the mayor praised the open housing agreement when it was reached last August."[44]

Daley did take a stand, but not the one the Chicago Freedom Movement had in mind. He agreed with Keane that the housing summit had produced no enforceable agreement, although he did concede that there was a "gentleman's agreement under a moral banner" to address the concerns that were raised there. Once again, Daley was engaging in shrewd racial politics. By backing up Keane, he was sending a clear signal to the white wards that they did not need to worry that the summit agreement would cause their neighborhoods to be integrated. At the same time, his talk of a "gentlemen's agreement" and a "moral banner" offered blacks just enough that they could probably be convinced to continue to vote for the machine. Civil rights leaders were not impressed by Daley's carefully parsed expressions of support. In December, Raby complained publicly that nothing had changed since August 26, the day the agreement was reached. That would become a common refrain in the days ahead.

In the end, there were many reasons the Chicago Freedom Movement failed where the southern civil rights movement had succeeded. Chicago was certainly more difficult terrain. It was harder to fight complex social ills like slum conditions than to challenge the segregated buses and closed voter rolls blacks faced in the South. But much of the credit for defeating the Chicago Campaign — and for taking the steam out of the civil rights movement as it tried to move north — belongs to Daley. His response to King and his followers was shrewd: he co-opted their goals; he dispatched black leaders like Dawson and the Reverend J. H. Jackson to speak out against them; and he refused to allow them to cast him as the villain in the drama. The housing summit was Daley's masterstroke, a way of ending the protests and driving the movement out of town in exchange for vague and unenforceable commitments. "[L]ike Herod, Richard Daley was a fox, too smart for us, too smart for the press, . . . too smart for his own good, and for the good of Chicago," Ralph Abernathy would write in his memoirs. "Did we make a mistake in taking his word and leaving Chicago with our signed agreement and our high hopes? I believe we did the right thing, even though the outcome was bitterly disappointing."[45]

The Chicago Campaign was nominally about open housing and slums, but it was also about something larger: a battle between two very different visions of what kind of city Chicago should be. The Freedom Movement's goal was what it called an "open city," in which residents would be free to live wherever they wanted without regard to race. When it came to development, the civil rights activists wanted the emphasis to be on improving living conditions in the city's worst neighborhoods. At the same time, Daley was working to build a wealthier and more powerful Chicago, anchored by a revitalized Loop. Racial integration was not necessarily inconsistent with Daley's vision, but he saw it as a threat because it had the potential to drive middle-class whites to the suburbs, and to discourage businesses from investing in and locating downtown. The defeat of the Freedom Movement was a victory for Daley's city of stable, middle-class, white ethnic neighborhoods, and a booming downtown. With King and his followers out of the way, Daley could return to his work in building his city.

Shoot to Kill

In late 1966, Daley was hard at work planning his reelection campaign. As usual, his allies weighed in early. On December 6, the Chicago Federation of Labor, headed by his friend William Lee, endorsed Daley, pronouncing him "the greatest mayor in American history." Two days later, the machine slate-makers drafted him to run again. On December 29, Daley formally announced that he would seek an unprecedented fourth term. Adamowski wanted the Republican nomination again, but Cook County Board president Richard Ogilvie and the rest of the Republican leadership were against it. The party leaders were looking for a candidate in the mold of John Lindsay, the dashing Republican-Liberal elected mayor of New York in 1965. They made overtures to a young, charismatic bank executive, but when he turned them down, they offered the nomination to 23rd Ward Republican committeeman John Waner. Waner, a wealthy heating and air-conditioning contractor, did not have much in common with New York's WASP prince. The son of Polish immigrants, Waner — who was born Jan Ludwig Wojanarski — did not learn English until the age of nine. But Waner was a fresh face, he could make an ethnic appeal to the city's large Polish population, and he had the resources to finance his own campaign.[1]

The same day Daley announced that he was seeking reelection, Alderman James Murray announced he was not. Murray, who had served in the City Council since 1954, was convinced he could not win again. Murray's 18th Ward on the Southwest Side had become a hotbed of white-backlash sentiment. His constituents had never forgiven him for sponsoring Daley's 1963 open-housing ordinance. The law was political window dressing, Daley's effort to convince black voters that he was on their side when he was not. But even that toothless law was too much fair housing for 18th Ward whites. And this year, passions on the issue of race were running higher than ever: one Bungalow Belt alderman was campaigning as Casimir "I voted against the fair-housing ordinance" Laskowski. Murray says he knew he was in trouble when he went to a civic association meeting in the ward to discuss mundane neighborhood improvements. "A guy got up and said, 'This guy would be a great alderman if he wasn't such a nigger lover,'" Murray recalls.[2]

Daley unveiled a new master plan for the city to coincide with his reelection campaign. The $6 billion plan, which had been in development for five years, was the first comprehensive plan for Chicago since Burnham's in 1909. It called for clearing 1,850 acres of slums, building 35,000 new units of public housing, adding 50 more acres to the University of Illinois at Chicago campus, and building a controversial Crosstown Expressway. Unlike Daley's 1958 plan, this one contemplated development outside the Loop. It called for the city to draw up sixteen distinct development plans for neighborhoods across the city. At the time of the announcement, though, only two of those plans had yet been drafted, for the University of Illinois area and the Near West Side — both, as it happened, neighborhoods on the fringes of the Loop. Daley's 1967 plan demonstrated how much the racial climate in Chicago had changed since 1958. In the four years since his near-defeat by Adamowski, Daley had been sending clear messages to white voters that he would protect them from black encroachment. That sensibility was reflected throughout the 1967 plan. Where the 1958 plan had spoken in code language about removing "blight" from the central area and moving in more affluent families, the 1967 plan boldly stated its racial intentions on its first page. The city wanted to have a "diverse, harmonious population," the drafters wrote. But it was also seeking to make the changes necessary to "reduce future losses of white families."[3]

Daley kicked off his campaign with a flourish. On January 4, he appeared in person at the city clerk's office wheeling a handcart with nominating petitions stacked ten feet high. According to his aides, the pile contained the signatures of 500,000 Chicagoans. Waner, who was at the clerk's office at the same time, had only 11,000 signatures. It was more than enough to qualify, but the discrepancy was daunting. Waner said Daley had benefited from the tens of thousands of patronage workers and their families who were pressured to sign and carry the machine's petitions. In the privacy of the voting booth, he insisted, they would vote Republican. In the end, Dick Gregory did not even try to get his name placed on the ballot. The word in political circles was that this was just as well — that no matter how many signatures he had submitted, Daley would have made sure that the machine-dominated board did not certify him to run for mayor.[4]

Once again, Daley had to engage in a difficult racial balancing act. In his public comments on civil rights, he tried to appeal to white and black voters at the same time, which often left him speaking in meaningless platitudes. "There are some who say that we have gone too far with our community improvement programs, while there are others who say we have gone too slow," Daley said in a speech kicking off his campaign. "There are some who say that we have done too much for minority groups, while there are those who say we have not done enough. It is important that we keep pace with the times." In fact, Daley had good reason to worry about his standing with both groups. For all of his success in defeating King and the civil rights movement, it was not clear how white ethnic voters were feeling about him or the machine. If James Murray was now widely hated in the 18th Ward, Daley himself might not be much more popular. At the same time, Daley had to worry about defections in the black wards. The most recent sign of trouble was that King had returned to Chicago on December 2 to announce that he would be sending sixteen civil rights activists to town to staff a "massive" new drive to register black voters. King insisted that the drive was non-partisan. "We do not endorse candidates," he said. "We feel the people will be intelligent enough to vote for the right candidates when they know the issues." Still, the machine, which once had a lock on black voters, was nervous enough that Daley refused to help with the drive. When civil rights activist Hosea Williams asked city officials to set up neighborhood registration centers, he was turned down. "They said it would be too expensive," said Williams. "They wouldn't even give us what we got in Birmingham!"[5]

Daley was counting on the black machine to keep its voters in line, and most of Daley's black supporters seemed eager to do their part. On January 7, twenty-two black clergymen wearing Daley campaign buttons stopped by City Hall to endorse Daley. The Reverend Clarence Cob, pastor of the First Church of Deliverance, said many blacks were confused about Daley's record, and that he and his colleagues would educate them. The truth was, despite the civil rights insurgency of the past year, there was still a lot of life left in the old black submachine. A key factor in its staying power was its knack for co-opting anti-machine candidates. In the 29th Ward, an undertaker named Robert Biggs had almost defeated the machine candidate in 1963. Ward committeeman Bernard Neistein made Biggs the machine candidate in 1967, and Biggs was elected as a pro-machine alderman. Charles Chew, who had been elected 17th Ward alderman in 1963 and then state senator on an anti-machine platform, had come around to the view that his future would be brighter if he made peace with the machine. Chew was now a supporter of Daley and a critic of the Freedom Movement — and he drove around the ghetto in a white Rolls-Royce.[6]

On January 16, McCormick Place was destroyed by fire in the middle of a National Housewares Manufacturers Association exhibition. The roof of the main exhibition center, which was as large as six football fields, collapsed. It was unclear how such a new building could have burned so easily, and why it was built with no sprinkler system or fire walls. Daley said that the most important thing was to ensure that the facility, which he credited with making Chicago "the convention capital of the United States," was rebuilt as quickly as possible. Within a day, he gathered the chairman, the general manager, and virtually the entire board of the Metropolitan Fair and Exposition Authority, at City Hall to announce plans to build a new McCormick Place twice as large as the old one. Daley kept up his flurry of pre-election development work, personally presenting the city's proposal for fifteen miles of transit lines along the Kennedy and Ryan expressways to the Chicago Plan Commission, which immediately approved them. Daley also announced some well-timed federal grants. Almost $1.3 million in federal funds had come through for the social services center that the city and the University of Chicago had been planning for Woodlawn. And HUD approved

$15.5 million for five urban renewal projects, including the one Daley had been planning near the University of Illinois campus.[7]

As they did every four years, downtown business leaders came together to form a Non-Partisan Committee to Re-Elect Mayor Daley. The business leaders had the usual reasons for supporting him. Some wanted him to keep up his urban renewal efforts in the Loop, and others wanted help with development projects of their own. Committee cochairman C. Virgil Martin was president of the company that held the lucrative restaurant concession at O'Hare. The city's business titans made large contributions to Daley's campaign, but the machine was also skilled at extracting money from small contributors who wanted specific favors, ranging from lowered tax assessments to the kind of minor perks the machine specialized in. "There are lots of goofs out there," Waner said later. "Here's a guy that is maybe cum laude from some college and has a very successful business, but he is obsessed with the idea that he has got to have a three-letter license number, which is a very simple thing for a politician to do. He sends him a three-letter license number, then someone will come around and say, 'So and so is running for office. Would you care to make a little contribution?' He takes out a checkbook and sends a few thousand dollars."[8]

The machine's dominance left Waner with few places to raise money for his own campaign. When he tried to put together his own committee of businessmen, he found that even die-hard Republicans had already committed themselves to Daley. He held a $100-a-plate fund-raising dinner, the kind of event Republican candidates were usually able to pack with wealthy contributors, and it lost money. Waner did manage to convince one prominent Republican, John T. Pirie Jr., chairman of a downtown department store, to raise funds for him. But shortly after Pirie signed on he backed out, hailing Daley for his "truly remarkable achievements." Waner commented bitterly that Daley's camp "probably told him they'd tear up the sidewalk in front of his store." In the end, Waner's total campaign budget was about $175,000, much of it his own money. John Lindsay, the man whose candidacy the Republicans were using as a model, had spent $3 million to be elected in New York two years earlier.[9]

Some of Waner's supporters were urging him to make a bid for

white-backlash voters, but he ran a campaign that was more pro–
civil rights than Daley's. Waner hammered away at Daley for being
"more interested in maintaining plantation politics in public housing" than in solving the problems of those who lived there. At the
same time, he was not prepared to write off his Republican base by
backing open housing. Waner argued that other issues, such as jobs
and urban renewal policies, were ultimately of greater importance
to the black community. "Since 1960, the city has displaced over
50,000 people, and after the new buildings went up, no one could
afford to move back into the new neighborhood," he said. "There
was no attempt made to provide decent low-cost homes for rent or
for purchase." Democrats preferred to have blacks trapped in public housing, Waner charged, "because it enables the Democratic precinct captain to corral votes for the machine."[10]

As he always did, Daley got to work energizing the machine to
turn out a large vote. The second important stage in the campaign,
after the filing of petitions, was the February 28 primary. Daley called a secret meeting of the machine inner circle — including
county assessor Parky Cullerton, city clerk John Marcin, 5th Ward
committeeman and city treasurer candidate Marshall Korshak, 29th
Ward state senator Bernard Neistein, and Democratic state chairman James Ronan — and told them he wanted to win with 400,000
votes, up from the 396,473 he received four years earlier. When the
votes were counted, the machine more than met this benchmark,
pulling out 420,000 votes for him, far ahead of the 72,000 Waner attracted in the Republican primary. Daley could also take comfort in
the fact that he outpolled Marcin and Marshall Korshak. Waner tried
to put a positive spin on the results. "With 50,000 employees and
their families, Mayor Daley can produce 400,000 votes at will in a
primary," he said. "But when the voters turn out and don't have to
reveal their party, they will defeat the last big city machine in the
country, April 4."[11]

After the primary, Daley gathered his ward committeemen for a
meeting at party headquarters at the Sherman House Hotel. He
informed the ward committeemen who had not produced 8,000
votes — their one-fiftieth share of his 400,000-vote goal — that they
had to do better in the general election. On March 14, Daley announced that the federal government had approved almost $46 mil-

lion in federal grants for his planned transit lines along the Dan Ryan and Kennedy expressways. The timing was obviously political — yet another favor Daley managed to extract from the Johnson administration — but Daley denied it. "It is a customary program for a dynamic city," he said. "It had nothing to do with the election." Daley also had city employees working overtime to clean up the city before the election. Sanitation workers were putting in six-day weeks filling potholes, and Bureau of Electricity employees were working nine-hour days, six days a week rushing to finish installation of lighting in all 2,300 alleys in Chicago.[12]

Martin Luther King ended up helping Daley's reelection campaign in a backhanded way. King was in Chicago March 24 to speak to an anti–Vietnam War rally at Liberty Baptist Church. Asked about housing, he lamented the city's "failure to live up to last summer's open-housing agreement." After reviewing a report prepared by the Chicago Freedom Movement's evaluation committee, King said it might be necessary to hold even bigger open-housing marches over the upcoming summer. Daley immediately struck back, charging King with making "political" statements designed to hurt him in the election. No matter what King said, Daley promised, he would not permit civil rights marchers to disrupt the city. It was the second year in a row Daley attacked King on the eve of an election, and Republicans were convinced it was a bald attempt to win the white backlash vote. In fact, Daley had spent the last four years using the race issue to appeal to white voters. In 1963, he was a politician with a strong black base, whose urban-renewal programs appeared to be destabilizing the city's black community — and, the fear was, driving them into white neighborhoods. By 1967, he had a strong record of racial resistance: standing up for Willis; forcing the federal government to release the school funding Francis Keppel had withheld; going to court to enjoin civil rights marches in white neighborhoods; moving blacks into housing projects in the ghetto and keeping them out of white projects; and presiding over the housing summit that ended the Chicago Freedom Movement and sent King home to Atlanta. Daley's political realignment seemed to be working. Polls showed him running far more strongly in the Bungalow Belt than he had against Adamowski four years earlier. The *Chicago Tribune* reported that its interviews with voters showed that those who had been "grumbling about Daley's concessions to Negroes" were now backing him because "they decided Daley was a seasoned veteran of such problems."[13]

Daley won in a landslide, taking 73 percent of the vote and winning all fifty wards. His 792,238 votes surpassed his previous record of 778,612 votes in 1959. Dick Gregory, who in the end ran as a write-in candidate, took less than 1 percent of the vote. The polls that detected the white ethnic neighborhoods shifting back toward Daley turned out to be correct. In 1963, his support in nonreform white wards had fallen to 44 percent; this time, he took 69 percent of the vote in these same wards. In the race against Adamowski, Daley had won 66 percent of the vote in Tom Keane's 31st Ward, a weak performance in one of the machine's strongest wards; this time he took almost 84 percent. It was a testament to Daley's skill in handling the race issue — and to the hold the machine still had on black voters — that his support in the black wards had eroded only slightly in four years, from 84.1 percent to 83.8 percent. Daley defeated Waner in the heavily black West Side 24th Ward 15,336 to 918, with 351 write-in votes cast for Dick Gregory, compared to 17,429 to 968 against Adamowski in 1963. There is no single answer to the intriguing question of why Daley, who had spent the last year at loggerheads with Martin Luther King Jr., fared so well among black voters. In part, it was due to his careful expressions of support for equal opportunity and improving conditions in the slums, even while he co-opted the Freedom Movement's attempts to take on those issues. It helped, certainly, that the Republican Waner was not a particularly appealing candidate for black voters, and that Gregory was not officially listed on the ballot. But Daley's success in the black wards was at least in part a quiet rebuke to the Chicago Freedom Movement, and a reminder of the power of a political spoils system to deliver the votes of the poor. The goals of the Freedom Movement did not always speak to the immediate needs of poor blacks. Many did not aspire to move into hostile all-white neighborhoods, or to put their children onto buses to attend schools in white neighborhoods. Daley's precinct captains, in contrast, offered things that did make a difference in their daily lives: help in getting welfare and public housing; assistance in navigating a confusing government bureaucracy; and, most of all, patronage jobs. Daley had relied on machine politics to overcome idealism among black voters, and the election returns showed that, at least this time, his strategy had worked.[14]

On election night, Daley promised that he would continue his hard line on disruptions of the peace. "No one is going to take the law into his own hands," he said in his victory statement at Democratic headquarters in the Sherman House. "There will be law and order in this city as long as I am mayor." The following day, he expanded on his pledge. "There will be no demonstrations that close off traffic or interfere with people's rights," he said. "We won't prohibit demonstrations and marches, but we say they cannot conflict with your rights as a private citizen. If you are driving home or on a bus, no one has the right to hold you up." Daley also promised that there would be more development in the next four years than in the previous four. Among his plans were replacing the elevated tracks that circle the Loop with a subway, and building a third Chicago airport on a man-made island in the middle of Lake Michigan. On May 9, President Johnson and the Democratic leadership in Congress honored Daley as Democrat of the Year for 1967. The award gave Daley a national platform to speak out about his encounters with political demonstrators, and the importance of standing up to them firmly. "I believe in civil rights, but with law and order in our streets, and not with disorder," Daley said. "Today we have many faint hearts in our party."[15]

The War on Poverty — and particularly Chicago's self-styled version of it — remained as controversial as ever. On May 18, a Senate subcommittee came to town to investigate the Chicago program once again. New York's liberal Republican senator Jacob Javits repeated the standard line about machine domination of the Chicago program. When his questioning of Daley failed to produce any damaging admissions, Javits moved on to Deton Brooks, challenging him about his work in the reelection campaign of Roman Pucinski while he was director of the Chicago anti-poverty program. Javits had brought along a memorandum that quoted Brooks as saying, when asked about his political work for the machine, "I'll do what I darn please." When the hearing ended, Javits expressed his suspicions that Daley had hijacked the program. "It is not easy to find proof, but there is a heavy overtone that it is being politically run," he said. "I'm not persuaded that the Chicago system gives the poor representation on community boards." But the Democratic senators on the committee — including New York's Robert Kennedy and chairman Joseph Clark of Pennsylvania — came to Daley's defense. Chicago's program was no worse, they said, than programs in many other cities.[16] Civil rights activists also continued to speak out against the way the War on Poverty was being run both in Chicago and nationally. Chester Robinson, director of the West Side Organization, charged that War on Poverty programs were still failing to address the greatest forms of deprivation in poor people's lives. "What good does it do a poor person if the Great Society takes his child for a tour of the art museum?" Robinson asked. "The child still has to come back to the same rat-infested, overcrowded, underheated slum tenement, go back down to the same overcrowded, understaffed slum school and bear the same burden of his father's inability to get a good-paying job."[17]

But by the spring of 1967, more of the criticism of the War on Poverty was coming from conservatives. The growing Black Power movement had by now reached new heights of militancy. Stokely Carmichael resigned as chairman of SNCC in May to travel to Cuba and Vietnam. He left behind a successor, H. Rap Brown, who was even more confrontational. "If you give me a gun I might just shoot Lady Bird," Brown declared. The violent rhetoric coming out of the black liberation movement was contributing to a phenomenon that the national media had seemingly fallen in love with: white backlash. Some of the backlash was aimed at CAP, which was increasingly identified in the minds of white America with radical black politics. In Houston, the mayor accused anti-poverty program employees of contributing to racial unrest that culminated in a gun battle at Texas Southern University, the state's largest historically black college. In Alabama, Governor Wallace charged that $500,000 in grants to programs in Wilcox and Lowndes counties amounted to funding the Black Panthers, which began as a black political party in Lowndes County. Even in Chicago, where Daley and Brooks were keeping a close eye on CAP, there were charges that War on Poverty money was being diverted to fund civil rights protests. Washington handed critics a new argument for opposing the program when The Woodlawn Organization was given a $927,000 grant to hire gang members to provide job training to other gang members. The money went directly from Washington to TWO, bypassing the local Daley-controlled board, the CCUO. By the end of the year, it would come out that eight of the staff hired by TWO had been charged with or convicted of serious crimes, including a twenty-one-year-old "center chief" who had been charged with murdering a thirteen-year-old boy.[18] "This is the only program not included under the jurisdiction of the city of Chicago," Daley fumed when the staff's brushes with the criminal justice system came to light. "People say we should have participation by outside agencies and we are for this," he said. "But we feel it has to be under some direction." Daley eventually convinced the OEO to cut off funding to the group.[19]

On June 5, the Leadership Council for Metropolitan Open Communities held a luncheon for 1,300 at the Hilton Hotel to kick off Project: Good Neighbor. Daley told the crowd that the one-week project had the potential to "do much to erase prejudices which long ago should have been thrust aside." Other speakers talked about the importance of open housing. And Robert Ingersoll, board chairman of Borg-Warner Corporation and chairman of the project, urged everyone in attendance to sign a "Good Neighbor Declaration." But the event had a hollow feeling, since Daley and the others did not seem to be taking many practical steps to advance the cause of open housing. In late April, six progressive aldermen had introduced an amendment to strengthen the city's open-housing law. They proposed to extend the law, which applied only to brokers, to cover all sellers and renters of housing, including owners of single-family homes. The machine did not back the measure, and Daley's corporation counsel, Ray Simon, weighed in with his opinion that the city did not have the authority to pass such a law. Meanwhile, Daley's development plans for the city were proceeding impressively. On July 12, he announced that McCormick Place would be rebuilt in no more than eighteen months. It was a quick schedule, he conceded, for such a mammoth project, but "with crews working 24 hours a day if necessary, it can be done," he said. "Where there is a will there is always a way." The following day, Daley stood at the corner of Dearborn and Madison to preside over the cornerstone ceremony for the First National Bank of Chicago Building.[20]

This municipal tranquillity was soon threatened, when a rash of urban rioting swept the nation. It started on July 12 in Newark, New Jersey, with an altercation between a black cabdriver and two policemen. A day later, protesters clashed with the Newark police and began looting stores. Then, the unrest escalated. Rioters and looters seized control of roughly half of Newark's twenty-four square miles. Snipers took positions on rooftops, and arsonists set buildings on fire across the city. It took five days, 1,400 Newark police, and 300 New Jersey police to restore the peace. Before it was over, twenty-seven people were dead, and there was $10 million in property damage. Days later, rioting began in Detroit, and the devastation was even worse. Large sections of the city were set on fire, forty-three people were killed, and a staggering 7,000 people were arrested. To restore the order in Detroit, 4,700 army paratroopers and 5,000 National Guardsmen had to be called in to back up the local police. When the rioting ended in one city, it began in another — Milwaukee; New Haven, Connecticut; Wilmington, Delaware; and Flint, Michigan.[21]

Daley was adamant that Chicago would not go the way of Newark or Detroit. He called a press conference on July 27 and delivered a grim-faced warning that rioting would not be tolerated. The National Guard was on alert, he said, and it would be on the streets in an hour with live ammunition. "As long as I am mayor of Chicago, law and order will prevail," Daley insisted. When a reporter pointed out that King had warned that Chicago had the kind of problems that had led to riots in other cities, Daley lashed out at the man he had once gone to great lengths to embrace. "We don't need him to tell us what to do," Daley said of King. "He has been asked to join in our constructive programs and he has refused. He only comes here for one purpose — or to any other city he has visited — and that is to cause trouble." The next day, Daley addressed an enthusiastic audience at the 49th annual Illinois American Legion at the Palmer House and repeated the promise he made at the press conference: "Law and order must prevail; it will prevail." In fact, this time law and order did prevail. In the summer of 1967, when more than 128 American cities erupted in rioting, Chicago somehow escaped unscathed.[22]

Daley's admirers were happy to give him the credit. It was his tough talk, many of them said, that let potential rioters know they would be dealt with swiftly and harshly. Others said it was the anti-poverty money Daley had attracted to the city. "Chicago is in on every conceivable program the Federal Government has to offer," one reporter noted. Some attributed the absence of rioting to the Democratic machine, which reached into every block of the ghetto, and made even the city's poorest blacks feel they had some stake in the system. "The trained and loyal members of the Democrats' campaign army are armed with the promise of food and favors," said Joseph Meeks, president of the Illinois Retail Merchants Association. "They will be effective in influencing almost anyone who has a modicum of reason." But rioting, and the absence of rioting, is not so easily explained. Less than a year later, the machine would still be handing out food and favors, and Daley would be talking even tougher. But the response in Chicago's ghettos would be very different.[23]

Every headline about a city erupting in looting and arson drove another nail into the coffin of CAP. The program's defenders argued that the unrest only illustrated more vividly that the nation's urban poor were desperately in need of intervention, but that was not the majority view. The uprisings "not only raised the question whether the poor should be 'rewarded' after engaging in violence," *New York Times* columnist Tom Wicker observed, "it also brought wild but unsubstantiated charges that O.E.O. employees had helped foment the riots." The War on Poverty was rapidly losing the support of the two groups that dominated the Democratic majority in Congress: urban liberals from the North, and rural conservatives from the South. Southern Democrats increasingly identified Washington's anti-poverty programs with black militancy and voter registration drives that threatened the white power structure in some regions. Northern Democrats had also become convinced that federal anti-poverty money was being used to fund political protests and acts of insurrection, like a Cleveland demonstration in which angry poor people marched on City Hall and dropped rats on the steps. Even many urban liberals were finally coming around to Daley's long-held view that a poverty program not under the control of the political establishment was worse than none at all.[24]

The reform being proposed was an amendment to the Economic Act of 1967 that would reshape the entire CAP program along the lines of Daley's Chicago Concept. It was a measure Congressman

Pucinski, Daley's point man on the issue, had been promoting for some time, but the actual amendment was introduced by House Committee on Education and Labor chair Edith Green (D–Oregon). Republican congressman Charles Goodell attacked the proposed modification as a "bosses and boll weevil amendment," a joint effort by machine politicians from the North and legislators from the rural South to take control over the federal poverty program. It soon became clear, however, that CAP was not going to be reauthorized without it. Green's amendment passed, finally closing the chapter on the contentious idea of "maximum feasible participation." A few months later, Shriver left the War on Poverty to become ambassador to France. In the end, Daley was the victor in the War on Poverty. His Chicago Concept, once attacked as illegal and corrupt, was now law nationwide.[25]

On August 15, 1967, Daley unveiled a new rust-colored Picasso sculpture to stand in front of the Civic Center. The 162-ton statue, which would come to be known simply as the Chicago Picasso, had already endured weeks of abuse. Amateur art critics were comparing Picasso's abstract creation to everything from a dodo bird to a giant cheese slicer. The *Chicago Daily News* had called it Chicago's "greatest conversation piece since Mrs. O'Leary's lantern." The *Chicago Tribune,* seemingly straining to find the right words, hailed the sculpture's "off-beat attractiveness — not the attractiveness of a marble nymph in a glade but of a great monumental something which turned aside questions and pulled the mind in a strange direction." Chicago poet Gwendolyn Brooks composed a poem that she read at the unveiling. It captured Chicago's awkward relationship with its new masterpiece: "Art hurts," Brooks declared. "Art urges voyages — and it is easier to stay at home, the nice beer ready." Republican alderman John Hoellen, happy to have found another issue on which to bait Daley, introduced a resolution in the city council to send the sculpture back to France and replace it with a likeness of Cubs first baseman Ernie Banks. (City Hall was not amused. Told that Hoellen was objecting that no one knew what the statue was, Tom Keane responded: "It's a baboon, and its name is John Hoellen.") Daley, with his ingrained Bridgeport sensibility, did not care for the artwork he was unveiling. "He was disturbed," recalls his

speechwriter Earl Bush. "He said, 'Picasso's art is not what's appreciated.' I said, 'Look, it doesn't matter that you like it or not. Picasso
brings credibility, no matter how grotesque it is.'" Daley appreciated
the credibility and went ahead with the unveiling, even though his
heart was with the demonstrators who were gathered at the scene
holding signs reading "Give It Back," and "Colossal Boo Boo."[26]

Over Labor Day weekend, 2,000 delegates representing 200 leftist
organizations gathered at the Palmer House in Chicago for a convention of the National Conference for New Politics. The chaos that
ensued was one of the clearest indications yet that the Black Power
movement was tearing the left apart. When Martin Luther King gave
the keynote address, black militants drowned him out with chants of
"Kill whitey." Black delegates, who were only 10 percent to 15 percent of the convention, demanded and were given 50 percent of the
votes on all resolutions. The delegates then went on to adopt a series
of radical resolutions, including a condemnation of Israel's Six Day
War as an "imperialist Zionist war" in the Middle East, which many
Jewish delegates viewed as anti-Semitic, and an injunction to do
work among white Americans to humanize their "savage and beast-
like" character. The disastrous gathering deepened a divide that already existed on the left between Vietnam War–focused whites and
civil rights– and Black Power–focused blacks. "We are a movement
of people with radically different needs," white radical Rennie Davis
said afterward. "A super-coalition makes no sense."[27]

That fall, Daley traveled to Washington to attend a $500-a-plate
dinner for the Democratic National Committee. Daley and his congressional stalwarts Dan Rostenkowski and John Kluczynski listened
politely as Johnson told a black-tie audience of thousands that he
would not back down over Vietnam. By now, popular opinion was
turning against "Johnson's War." The number of dead and injured
Americans had been growing at an alarming rate — from 2,500 in
1965 to 33,000 in 1966, to 80,000 so far in 1967 — and the United
States seemed no closer to winning. Liberal media had been fulminating against the war for years, but now moderate-to-conservative
publications like the *Richmond Times-Dispatch,* the *Los Angeles Times,*
and *Time* magazine were beginning to express doubt or outright opposition. On September 20, the *Christian Science Monitor* had reported
that of 205 congressmen interviewed, 43 said they had recently

dropped their support for Johnson's policies. Daley had been silent on the great issue that was tearing the nation apart. "He was very much domestic in focus," says his son William Daley. "His focus was never international in anything except promoting Chicago."[28]

Though he would later go down in history as one of the great enemies of the anti-war movement, Daley did not in fact support the Vietnam War. In the early years, he paid little attention to the far-off hostilities. "He probably thought, like most Americans in 1961 and 1963, that it was no big deal," says William Daley. He grew to like the war less as young men, particularly young Chicagoans from neighborhoods like Bridgeport, started coming back with horrible injuries or in pine boxes. Daley's son John had gone to grammar school with a young man who went off to serve. "His mother came pounding on the door one night," William Daley recalls. "The poor kid ended up stepping on a mine. He survived and had hundreds of operations, and died a few years later." With the casualties mounting, and America accomplishing so little, Daley began to form more definite views. An important consideration for Daley, of course, was the effect that the war could have on the Chicago Democratic machine. Like the civil rights movement, the Vietnam War had become a deeply divisive issue that threatened to drive a wedge through the machine's electorate. Independent anti-war candidates might begin to make inroads among some machine voters, just as pro–civil rights candidates had begun to. Before the 1966 elections, Johnson aide Lawrence O'Brien went on a trip around the country. "There was a conversation I had with Mayor Daley, initiated by him, where he expressed great concern about Vietnam," says O'Brien. "He said this was a growing disaster and this was going to be devastating to the Democratic party. I sent the President a memo, 'If Richard Daley has become concerned about Vietnam, you've got to realize that it is not some passing cloud.'" Daley had an opportunity that same year, 1966, to tell Johnson personally how he felt about the war. Daley was at the White House lobbying for federal aid for various Chicago projects. As he began to leave, Johnson stopped him. "Listen, Dick, I've got a lot of trouble over there in Vietnam," the president said. "What do you think about it?" Daley thought for a moment and answered. "Well, Mr. President, when you've got a losing hand in poker you just throw in your cards," he said. "But what about American prestige?" Johnson asked. "You put your prestige in your back pocket and walk away."[29]

Daley's opposition to the Vietnam War may have been largely political. But he also had a more personal reason to feel that it was time for the hostilities to end. In May 1967, one of Bridgeport's most beloved young men enlisted and was killed in Vietnam. Joseph Mc-Keon was a star — one of the few Bridgeporters or De La Salle graduates to attend Harvard — and a friend of Michael Daley's. "We used to socialize with him," recalls Alderman Edward Burke. "There was nothing in his background that would have ever indicated he wanted to be a Marine and go to Vietnam." McKeon's parents were friendly with Daley, and owned a funeral home that was a neighborhood institution. "He was the neighborhood's bright guy," says William Daley. "He goes into the Marine Corps, had a great future ahead of him and he's there three weeks and boom." The loss of young McKeon hit Bridgeport hard, and considerably dampened the neighborhood's enthusiasm for the war.[30]

Daley did not have Vietnam on his mind the night of the October 1967 Democratic Party fund-raiser. He had gone to Washington for a specific reason: to make a pitch to host the upcoming Democratic convention. Chicago had not hosted a Democratic convention since 1956, when Stevenson was nominated. Daley had a dozen years of building and redevelopment he wanted to share with the world, and the national media glare of a major political convention was one of the best ways to do it. He also saw a Chicago convention as a means of boosting the machine ticket in the November election. The Democrats were likely to have a tough fight for governor on their hands, whether Otto Kerner ran for a third time or not, and the excitement of a convention in Chicago could make the difference in a close race. National Democrats were also contemplating a Texas location, since President Johnson was still considered likely to run for reelection. But intraparty fighting in the state, as well as the long shadow of Kennedy's assassination in Dallas, made Texas an unlikely choice. The television networks wanted the Democrats to join the Republicans in Miami Beach, since it would reduce their costs of covering the conventions. But Daley buttonholed Johnson and made the argument that he found worked best with presidents. Johnson might lose Illinois and its twenty-six electoral votes, he warned, if the convention were held anywhere but Chicago.[31]

On October 8, the day after Daley's appearance at the black-tie dinner, Chicago was selected to host the convention. New Jersey attorney general David Wilentz, chairman of the site selection committee, declared that the committee was favorably impressed by Chicago's central geographic location and its experience in holding conventions. But DNC chairman John Bailey said the financial incentives Chicago offered had played an important role in the final decision. The proposal put together by Daley and his business allies had been generous: $750,000 in cash and another $150,000 worth of services. Daley had accentuated Chicago's positives through an aggressive marketing campaign. He mailed "A New Platform for Chicago," a paean to the city's many fine points, to members of the site selection committee, and had it printed in the *Chicago Daily News* and the *Sun-Times*. Daley made his own personal pitch through his statements to the media. "It has great hotel facilities," Daley said of Chicago. "It has great newspaper and TV facilities. And it's in a good time zone for viewing on TV."[32] Daley also promised that Johnson's vote in Chicago would exceed the 65 percent he got in 1964, and that law and order would prevail during convention week. "No thousands will come to our city and take over our streets, our city, and our convention," he said.[33]

The Democrats certainly were not coming to Chicago for its convention infrastructure. The McCormick Place fire had robbed the city of its best convention site. What Daley had to offer was the International Amphitheatre in the stockyard district, just a few blocks from his home. The Amphitheatre was built in 1934, after a massive fire destroyed an eight-block section of the stockyard district and razed the area's exposition hall. It was a rush job: the exhibition hall had burned down in May, and contractors had a new one in place for the annual livestock show in December. The building that went up was far more modest than the old McCormick Place. The International Amphitheatre had been the site of the 1956 Democratic and 1960 Republican conventions, and of a 1964 Beatles concert. But it was also a popular site for cattle shows and rodeos. Two mountains of manure, seventy feet wide and ten feet high, were just a few blocks away. The Democrats would later decide, after assessing the situation more closely before the start of the convention, that speakers who appeared at the podium should be sprayed first with bug repellent.[34]

Daley called the selection of Chicago a "great honor," but not an unexpected one, since Chicago was the "number one convention city." Reporters asked if Daley had gotten the convention because of his promise to keep control over events inside and outside the Amphitheatre. "Let someone else say it," Daley said. "We talk about our location, our accommodations, our great newspapers and radio and TV stations. We talk of our experience in handling conventions." But in fact, others were saying that Daley had won over Johnson by his promise to keep order. The unrest in Newark, Detroit, and other cities over the summer had raised fears that the convention would be held in the middle of another long, hot, and riot-filled summer. Chicago, on the other hand, had remained peaceful all summer. Johnson also had to be worried about disruptions aimed at him. The peace movement was gaining force across the country, especially on college campuses, and it was likely that thousands of anti-war demonstrators would make an appearance wherever the Democratic convention was held. "Daley and Johnson are close politically," Cook County Republican chairman Timothy Sheehan reasoned in explaining the choice of Chicago. "And the Democratic organization is well-versed in controlling crowds. They'll make sure that no strange outsiders . . . pack the gallery. They'll pack them themselves."[35]

Daley assured the Democratic Party and the nation that Chicago would provide a peaceful and hospitable setting for the convention. "Our people realize that we are working in a positive direction to solve their problems," he said. But 1967 ended on an ominous note. In the last few days of December, two aldermen were attacked and a charity worker was killed. Independent 5th Ward alderman Leon Despres was shot twice in the leg while walking home from his office, and 14th Ward alderman Joseph Burke foiled burglars in his home. Mary Virginia Tunney, a forty-two-year-old bookkeeper for Goodwill Industries, was found shot to death on the sidewalk outside her South Side apartment building. Daley vowed to put five thousand more police on the street if necessary. "There is no excuse for violence anywhere," he said.[36]

*　　*　　*

As the Democratic primaries began, it was clear that President Johnson was in trouble. Four years earlier, when he won the White
House in a landslide, a second term seemed almost inevitable. But
the Vietnam War had changed everything. In early 1968, Johnson's
chances of being reelected were looking increasingly remote. The
Tet Offensive in late January had driven even more Americans into
the anti-war camp. The Viet Cong's bloody assault on South Vietnam, waged by some 60,000 troops, was the most persuasive evidence yet that, despite the optimistic assessments emanating from
Washington, the Vietnam quagmire was nowhere near an end. In the
six weeks after the start of the Tet Offensive, Johnson's approval ratings sank from 48 percent to 36 percent, and approval of his handling of Vietnam plunged from 40 percent to 26 percent. Anti-war
activists had transformed themselves into a political force — the
"Dump Johnson" movement — that initially coalesced around Minnesota senator Eugene McCarthy. But with McCarthy's once
quixotic-seeming anti-war candidacy gaining strength, Robert
Kennedy was considering launching his own anti-war candidacy.
Kennedy had early support from California Assembly Speaker Jesse
Unruh. To become a candidate, Kennedy said, he would need to be
urged to run by "one more politician of the national stature of
Unruh." It was widely interpreted as a direct appeal for Daley's support.[37]

But Daley was not rushing to jump on board. He was still a Johnson loyalist, and was uncomfortable with the idea of McCarthy and
Kennedy seeking to depose an incumbent Democratic president.
Daley was also close to organized labor, an important component of
the machine, and would not lightly break with the major unions,
which had started out in Johnson's camp and then, after he withdrew, moved on to Vice President Hubert Humphrey. Daley also had
specific reservations about Kennedy. He had not shown himself to be
an organization man so far in his political career. Daley had been put
off during the 1960 presidential election when, after the Chicago
machine came through for John Kennedy and helped him win the
Democratic nomination, Bobby showed up in Illinois to set up a
campaign organization for his brother, independent of the machine.
Nor could Daley rely on Bobby's political instincts. As attorney general, he had been unduly eager to investigate corruption and take on

organized crime. As a candidate, he seemed too sympathetic toward black militants. With someone like Johnson or Humphrey, Daley knew exactly what he was getting. Bobby Kennedy was complex and constantly evolving, two qualities Daley did not particularly admire in a politician.[38]

Still torn about whether to run, Kennedy came to Chicago for a breakfast meeting with Daley on February 8. The more Kennedy talked about his differences with President Johnson over the Vietnam War, the more his candidacy appeared to Daley to be just another variant of the municipal conflicts that ended up in his office on a regular basis. Daley, ever the believer in working out compromises among competing constituencies, then presented Kennedy with a truly bizarre proposal. Rather than go through the divisiveness of a primary challenge to a sitting president, Kennedy should get Johnson to agree to submit the future of the Vietnam War to binding arbitration. It must have seemed odd to Kennedy that his presidential candidacy, viewed by his supporters as a moral crusade, was being reduced to the level of a truckers' strike. But Kennedy promised to think it over, and Daley said he would mention arbitration to President Johnson, which he did by telephone not long afterward.[39]

With Daley still resolutely on the sidelines, Kennedy announced his candidacy on March 16. He continued to see Daley's support as critical, and Daley received a steady stream of phone calls from the Kennedy camp lobbying him to come around. In late March, *New York Daily News* columnist Jimmy Breslin asked Kennedy where Daley stood in the race. "He's been very nice to me and doesn't like the war," Kennedy said. "You see, there are so many dead starting to come back it bothers him." But at the same time, Kennedy said, Daley was a party loyalist, which pulled him toward Johnson. When Breslin asked where he stood if Daley endorsed him, Kennedy responded, "Daley means the ballgame." These were flattering words, but Daley liked to make his slating decisions behind closed doors, not in the newspapers. He remained cool toward Kennedy's candidacy. Asked about Kennedy's "ballgame" comment, Daley responded: "He means I'm a great White Sox fan." Daley spoke with Johnson by phone in March, and Johnson asked what chance he had of carrying Chicago if he ran again. "Well, Mr. President, there are good years and bad years and I don't think this will be a good year for the national ticket in Chicago," Daley said. "But I'm backing you all the way, Mr. President. It doesn't matter that you can't win here."[40]

Not long after he delivered his gloomy assessment of Johnson's prospects, Daley got a phone call from White House aide Marvin Watson. The March 31 call, which Daley took at home on a private line upstairs, was to give him advance word that Johnson was withdrawing from the race. When he came down and joined his family in the den, they saw Johnson on television announcing that he was not seeking reelection. Daley's was the first call Johnson accepted at the Executive Mansion. Daley called to offer to draft Johnson at the convention if he wanted to be drafted, but Johnson said he did not. Johnson told Daley he was flying to Chicago the next morning to give a speech to the National Association of Broadcasters. Daley met Johnson at the airport, with Rostenkowski and Chicago's new U.S. attorney in tow. Daley spent the day, including the ride back to the airport, trying to persuade Johnson to reconsider his decision. With Daley now truly uncommitted in the presidential race, he had no shortage of suitors. Johnson made a pitch for Humphrey. Daley also began talking with mayors Joseph Barr of Pittsburgh, James Tate of Philadelphia, and Jerome Cavanaugh of Detroit about sitting on the sidelines rather than rushing to endorse a presidential candidate. It appeared to be an attempt to slow the momentum that was building around Robert Kennedy's candidacy.[41]

On March 2, 1968, the National Advisory Commission on Civil Disorders — widely known as the Kerner Commission — issued its report on the riots of the summer of 1967. President Johnson had appointed a blue-ribbon panel on July 27, 1967, with Democratic governor Otto Kerner as chairman and liberal Republican New York City mayor John Lindsay as vice chairman, to investigate the causes of the riots and to explore "the conditions that breed despair and violence." Johnson's commission was moderate in composition — he was criticized for not appointing more progressive voices like Martin Luther King, Tom Hayden, or even Stokely Carmichael — but its report was far from restrained. The Kerner Commission's arresting conclusion was that the urban unrest had been caused by the fact that "Our nation is moving toward two societies, one black, one white — separate and unequal." The commission's dense report backed up that assertion with a wealth of detail, and called for a substantial new round of social programs to address ghetto conditions. The commission found that there was a great need for additional public housing, but that it was critical that the State Street Corridor model be abandoned once and for all. "[W]e believe that the emphasis of the program should be changed from the traditional publicly-built, slum-based high-rise project to smaller units on scattered sites," it said. "Where traditional high-rise projects are constructed, facilities for social services should be included in the design, and a broad range of such services provided for tenants." Johnson declared the commission's work a "good report by good men of good will," but he also complained that "they always print that we don't do enough. They don't print what we do." He showed no interest in following up on its extensive policy recommendations.[42]

Daley was at home eating with his sons John and Bill on Thursday, April 4, 1968, when his aide Jack Reilly called to say that Martin Luther King had been shot by a sniper on the balcony of a motel in Memphis. Daley ordered the flags at City Hall lowered to half staff. Now that King was dead, Daley spoke of him as a fallen comrade. "Chicago joins in mourning the tragic death of the Rev. Martin Luther King Jr.," Daley said in a prepared statement. "Dr. King was a dedicated and courageous American who commanded the respect of the people of the world." Jesse Jackson, who was still heading up Operation Breadbasket in Chicago, was among those who would not let Daley off so easily. "The blood is on the chest and hands of those that would not have welcomed him here yesterday," Jackson said.[43]

President Johnson appeared on television and appealed for calm and order. "I ask every American to reject the blind violence that has struck down Dr. King, who lived by nonviolence," Johnson implored. Nevertheless, black America erupted in a spasm of sorrow and rage. In the wake of King's assassination, 168 cities and towns were struck by rioting, arson, and looting. The national statistics were staggering: before it was over, there were 2,600 fires, and 21,270 injuries. This time, it was Washington, D.C., that got the worst of it. Arsonists set 711 fires, including some just blocks from the White House. Black Power leaders took advantage of the situation to incite the sort of violent actions that it would have pained

King to watch. "Go home and get your guns," Stokely Carmichael advised young people. "When the white man comes, he is coming to kill you." It was, of course, a minority view in the black community. But the press was filled with Black Power rhetoric and vivid accounts of the violence. Whatever force of man or nature had prevented Chicago from becoming embroiled in the 1967 riots did not work this time. By mid-morning on Friday, the day after King's murder, black students were walking out of class, and by the afternoon schools in black neighborhoods had emptied. Young people gathered in Garfield Park, where speakers exhorted them to direct their frustration toward local businesses. The disorder began with smashed store windows and looting; arson and sniper attacks came soon afterward. By 2:00 P.M., Daley asked Acting Governor Samuel Shapiro, who was filling in for Governor Kerner, to send in the National Guard. Daley addressed the city on radio and television at 4:20 P.M. "Stand up tonight and protect the city," he urged. "I ask this very sincerely, very personally. Let's show the United States and the world what Chicago's citizens are made of."[44]

Shapiro sent 600 National Guardsmen while Daley dispatched the entire Chicago fire department, and the borrowed departments of eight suburbs, to put out the fires that were engulfing black neighborhoods. Daley spent Friday night at City Hall, with a radio tuned to police calls and a television set broadcasting the spreading unrest. He went to the Sherman House for a seventy-five-minute break, to eat and take a short nap, and then returned to City Hall. Power lines on the West Side were now dead, leaving much of that part of the city in darkness, and giving encouragement and cover to the looters. As the looting entered its second day, 1,500 more National Guardsmen were deployed on the Chicago streets. On Saturday afternoon, Daley imposed a curfew from 7:00 P.M. to 6:00 A.M. for all youth under twenty-one. He directed James Conlisk, the police commissioner who had taken over when O. W. Wilson retired a year earlier, to ban liquor sales in areas where there was "serious disorder." With military deployments guarding every intersection on the West Side, Saturday night was quieter but far from tranquil. Molotov cocktails were still being tossed, buildings were being torched, and firemen were being shot at by snipers. Troops patrolled the West and Near Northwest sides in jeeps. After two nights of rioting, black neighborhoods lay in ruins and at least eleven people were dead. Stores along West Madison Street, a modest boulevard of small shops with simple apartments in the upper floors, were charred for a twenty-eight-block stretch. By early Saturday, 300 people had been arrested for looting and scores were jammed into the lockup at police head-quarters at 11th and State streets. Thousands were homeless. In many parts of the city, power and phone lines were dead.[45]

The following morning, Palm Sunday, Daley and fire commis-sioner Robert Quinn spent forty-five minutes surveying the West Side by helicopter. They hovered over the smoldering wreckage of buildings on West Madison and saw devastation spreading down two miles south to Roosevelt Road. Daley was visibly shaken when he exited the helicopter. "It was a shocking and tragic picture of the city," he said afterward. "I never believed that this would happen here. I hope it will not happen again." After the tour, Daley returned to City Hall, where he met with school superintendent James Red-mond, health commissioner Samuel Adelman, and streets and sanita-tion commissioner James Fitzpatrick. On Monday, April 8, Daley appointed a committee to investigate the riot and named federal judge Richard Austin to head it.[46]

That same day, Daley attempted to explain the devastation that had struck the city. He had looked haggard and depressed since the riots broke out, and his unrehearsed comments turned into a bizarre rant. Thrashing around to make sense of the disorder, Daley insisted that the riots had been caused by the violent conditions that pre-vailed in Chicago's public schools. "The conditions of April 5 in the schools were indescribable," he said. "The beating of girls, the slash-ing of teachers and the general turmoil and the payoffs and the ex-tortions. We have to face up to this situation with discipline. Principals tell us what's happening and they are told to forget it."[47] School superintendent James Redmond expressed puzzlement the next day over the charges leveled by Daley. "I do not know of any beatings of girls," Redmond said. Nor could he understand Daley's reference to April 5. He knew of no incident in which a teacher had been slashed that day — the only school day during the riots — and he was not aware of anyone giving principals instructions to "forget it." But Redmond nevertheless launched an investigation. "We are concerned and we are reviewing all activities which led up to Friday," he said. Daley's anger over the rioting seemed to have pushed him over the edge.[48]

Daley's reaction to the rioting became more coherent, but no less inflammatory, as the days passed. The police bore some of the blame as well, he said on April 15, because of the restraint they showed. "I have conferred with the Superintendent of Police this morning and I gave him the following instructions," Daley said, "which I thought were instructions on the night of the fifth that were not carried out: I said to him very emphatically and very definitely that [he should issue an order] immediately and under his signature to shoot to kill any arsonist or anyone with a Molotov cocktail in his hand in Chicago because they're potential murderers, and to issue a police order to shoot to maim or cripple any arsonists and looters — arsonists to kill and looters to maim and detain." Daley said he had thought these instructions would not even need to be conveyed. "I assumed any superintendent would issue instructions to shoot arsonists on sight and to maim the looters, but I found out this morning this wasn't so and therefore gave him specific instructions," he said.[49]

Many cities had been torn by rioting in the wake of King's assassination, but Daley was alone in advocating that his citizens be fatally shot. In New York, Mayor John Lindsay had responded to riots in Harlem by walking the streets of black neighborhoods, doing call-in shows, and assuring blacks that he empathized with their frustration. "I think I understand," Lindsay said. "I understand the temptation to strike back." Daley's "shoot to kill" comments set off an impassioned debate. His supporters rushed to back him up. "I don't know why we are disturbed about the mayor's statements," Alderman Keane said. "Instead of criticizing actions of police, I feel it's time to use brass knuckles and get down to telling those committing crimes to stop." But U.S. attorney general Ramsey Clark called Daley's statements a "dangerous escalation" of racial violence. Independent aldermen also took issue with Daley. A. A. "Sammy" Rayner charged that Daley was "apparently going to great lengths to save the Democratic national convention." Even Wilson Frost, one of the machine's heretofore silent black aldermen, called Daley's comments inflammatory. In the face of the criticism, Daley backpedaled. He called a press conference the day afterward and insisted: "There wasn't any shoot-to-kill order."[50]

The Daley camp also began to resort to one of its favorite tactics: blaming the press. Earl Bush, Daley's press secretary, had an ingenious explanation for why the whole "shoot-to-kill" controversy was reporters' fault. "They should have printed what he meant not what he said," Bush insisted. Daley also lashed out at reporters. "They said that I gave orders to shoot down children," Daley complained. "I said to the superintendent, if a man has a Molotov cocktail in his hand and throws it into a building with children and women up above, he should be shot right there and if I was there I would shoot him. Everybody knows it was twisted around and they said Daley gave orders to shoot children. That wasn't true." It was not what Daley had said originally, but Daley's policy on the use of force was getting better in the retelling. His own investigative committee would later note that Illinois General Order 67-14 actually prohibited the police from using the kind of "deadly force" Daley had called for. But Daley found ultimate vindication by having Jack Reilly announce that he had been getting letters of support for his policy from all fifty states, and that the mail was supporting his position by 15 to 1.[51]

After calm was restored, Daley lifted the curfew and, playing to his strengths, assembled a package of state and federal aid to rebuild the West Side. His analysis of what set off the riots never went any deeper than his wild stories about the school system and his flailing at the police for exercising too much restraint. The truth was, of course, more complicated. One of the most notable aspects of the riots was that they were concentrated on the West Side. The West Side was the newer of Chicago's two ghettos, comprised of neighborhoods that had been white not long ago. Compared to the South Side, it had fewer community organizations, less-established churches, and fewer black-run businesses and institutions. Its residents were also different from blacks on the South Side. More of them had personally made the Great Migration from the rural South. They were more likely to be poor and undereducated, to have loose ties to the city, and to still be experiencing the disappointment of the gap between what they expected when they moved north to Chicago and what they found there. Another large group of West Side residents were uprooted migrants from closer by. West Side neighborhoods were home to many blacks forcibly displaced by Daley's urban-renewal programs — a Chicago Urban League report called them "dumping grounds for relocated families." In a 1958 series on urban renewal, the *Chicago Daily News* compared "Chicago's DP"— for the most part poor blacks pushed out by urban renewal — to European "displaced persons" uprooted by world war. Chicago's DPs were "made homeless not by war or communism or disaster but by wreckers," the *Daily News* reported, and were "refugees of the relocation that inevitably accompanies redevelopment. They are people, angry, indifferent, resentful, resigned." It was the kind of alienation, the Chicago Urban League's report concluded, that made an area a likely site for civil unrest.[52]

Not long after the race riots ended, a new group arrived on the scene to challenge Daley's control over the city. The Chicago Peace Council, gearing up for the Democratic National Convention, organized 6,000 anti-war protesters to march from Grant Park to Civic Center Plaza on April 27. Stung by Daley's rebuke that they had been insufficiently forceful during the April riots, the police were intent this time on preserving order at all costs. The marchers were moving peacefully along their route, straggling a bit more than police expected, when the trouble started. At the march's midway point, policemen in riot gear tried to disperse them, yelling, "Move, move, get out of the Loop, move, move, get out of the Loop." In minutes, the police began attacking. They clubbed some demonstrators and pushed others into the Civic Center fountain. Shoppers and other bystanders who happened upon the scene were also beaten. The police arrested more than sixty demonstrators. Clark Kissinger, coordinator of the march, complained that "by making a non-violent protest impossible, they made a violent one inevitable."[53]

A citizens panel, headed by Dr. Edward J. Sparling, president emeritus of Roosevelt University, was appointed to investigate. The Sparling Commission issued a sixty-two-page report, entitled "Dissent and Disorder," on August 1 that placed full blame on the police. Their treatment of the protesters, it found, had been "inept as well as hostile." The commission also rejected the notion that the clashes were the work of rogue officers. "The evidence seemed to indicate it could not have happened without the collaboration of the Mayor's office and the Superintendent of Police and his lieutenants," Sparling said at a press conference announcing the commission's findings.

Monsignor John Egan, pastor of Presentation Catholic Church, agreed: "Supt. Conlisk was present, saw what happened, and allowed [the police] to continue to operate in that manner." Years later, a former Chicago policeman was quoted saying: "Each one of us was told that we had to make an arrest. I couldn't believe it. There was nobody bad there."[54]

The April 27 clash could have saved Chicago from the violence and ignominy that were to come in August. The Sparling Commission put the entire city on notice that the Chicago police had a propensity for attacking peaceful protesters and innocent bystanders. If Daley had used the Sparling report to rein in his police and to train them in appropriate methods of dealing with demonstrators, convention week would have gone differently, and much less blood would have been shed. Instead, Daley denounced the report as "not true," and placed the blame for the clashes squarely on "the constant efforts of [the peace marchers] to confront the Police Department." To Daley, it was the marchers' missteps — including small deviations like failing to march in twos on the sidewalk — that made the violence inevitable. "The Police Department is always being attacked on marches such as this one," he complained. "The police didn't cause the problem. They only tried to enforce the law."[55]

Preserving Disorder

W hat's happening to our society?" Daley asked ruefully. He had just gotten word that Robert Kennedy had been assassinated in Los Angeles, at the Ambassador Hotel on the night of the June 4, 1968, California primary. "This was a shocking and stunning incident," Daley told the City Hall press corps the following day, "and it proves again there is great hatred, violence and bitterness in all the things that are happening in our country." The previous two months, between the assassinations of Martin Luther King and Bobby Kennedy, had dramatically illustrated Daley's point. In addition to the rioting that swept through the nation's cities, university campuses were in turmoil. There were massive demonstrations, student strikes, and bitter face-offs between undergraduates and administrators. The most widely noted of these showdowns occurred at Columbia University, where students seized buildings to protest plans to build a university gymnasium in Morningside Park, which was primarily used by blacks. There was no pretense of civility: before the occupation, student leader Mark Rudd sent a letter to university president Grayson Kirk that ended with a quote from black radical LeRoi Jones: "Up against the wall, motherfucker, this is a stick-up." Then the students, under the battle cry "Gym Crow Must Go," occupied Kirk's office, drinking his sherry and smoking his cigars. After eight days of negotiating, university officials called the police, who beat and kicked students and threw some down concrete stairwells, before arresting 692.[1]

Many of the same student anti-war groups that had taken over campus buildings that spring would be coming to Chicago for the Democratic National Convention. The planning had been under way for months — anti-war leaders David Dellinger and Rennie Davis talked about a convention protest as early as October 1967, during a march on the Pentagon. In January 1968, twenty-five anti-war organizers met in a New York apartment to hammer out strategy. To the anti-war movement, the Democratic convention was a tempting target. As the party of Lyndon Johnson, the Democrats seemed to be an appropriate focus of the movement's rage over the Vietnam War. Chicago was also the culmination of Eugene Mc-Carthy's anti-war campaign: it was on the convention floor that his supporters would make their final stand. And to a movement that was media savvy, if not media obsessed, the sheer number of television cameras and reporters who would be on hand made the convention almost irresistible.

Another key factor attracting the protesters to Chicago was Daley himself. Nothing rallies a political movement like an appealing enemy, and Daley seemed to be the perfect embodiment of the establishment that the anti-war movement was fighting. Though Daley did not actually favor Johnson's Vietnam policies, his unwillingness to break with the president over the war put him on the wrong side of the issue they cared about most passionately. As boss of a machine that thrived on patronage, corruption, and vote theft, he stood for everything they disdained about the old political order. And Daley's authoritarianism was the antithesis of the libertarian spirit that animated the anti-war movement. To young people who believed in all-night political debates and free-wheeling "be-ins," Daley's penchant for telling his followers how to vote and punishing them when they stepped out of line seemed antiquated and oppressive. Just as important, Daley was sixty-six at the time of the convention, which seemed ancient to a movement whose rallying cry was "Never trust anyone over thirty."

Rennie Davis, field director of the National Mobilization Committee to End the War — commonly known as MOBE — was calling for a "massive confrontation" between anti-war demonstrators and Democratic leaders at the convention. But much of the press attention focused on the more whimsical Youth International Party, or

Yippies, who were making outlandish claims about what they would do when they got to Chicago. The Yippies called themselves "revolutionary artists" and boasted that, in the words of founder Abbie Hoffman, "our concept of revolution is that it's fun." They talked gleefully about dispatching an elite group of 230 sexy male Yippies to seduce the delegates' wives, daughters, and girlfriends. And they promised to drop LSD into the Chicago water supply to "turn on" the entire city. The Yippies said they would disguise themselves as chefs and drug the delegates' food, and paint their cars to look like taxis and drive delegates to Wisconsin. Abbie Hoffman said he was plotting to pull down Hubert Humphrey's pants on the podium. Much of it was ludicrous stuff, but Hoffman and fellow Yippie Jerry Rubin reveled in the humorless reaction they got from Daley and the stodgy Chicago newspapers. When Hoffman goofily told city negotiators he would call off all his plans for a payment of $100,000, an indignant *Chicago Tribune* reported: "Yippies Demand Cash from City."[2]

Daley was hard at work on his own convention plans. He had taken personal charge of the preparations, and was spending a half-million dollars to get Chicago into shape. He created a Cook County version of a Potemkin Village by erecting a "redwood forest" of wooden fences to obscure the blight that visitors would pass as they traveled by bus from the Loop to the International Amphitheatre.[3] On the expressway leading to the Amphitheatre, workmen painted a new coat of silver on the mud-spattered dividing rail. Streets surrounding the hall — many of them barred to all but VIP traffic — were painted kelly green. No detail was too small to escape Daley's attention. Ten days before the convention was scheduled to begin, he led reporters on a fifteen-minute tour of the International Amphitheatre. He asked Jack Reilly if the silver-blue metal folding chairs for the delegates would be fastened together. Daley enlisted the ward organizations and machine politicians to help put on a good show. "If you have particular points of interest in your wards, arrange for tours of those places," Daley told a luncheon at Democratic headquarters at the Sherman House. Reilly reminded the machine crowd "to impress on the delegates that they are not just visiting Chicago, but Mayor Daley's Chicago."[4]

There were a rash of labor problems on the eve of the convention that complicated preparations. For a time, it looked as if Daley's well-run city was on the brink of falling apart. In early July, a group called Concerned Transit Workers had staged a wildcat strike that snarled public transportation for four days. The dissident organization was now threatening to hold another strike starting on August 25, the day before the convention began. The International Brotherhood of Electrical Workers had been striking against Illinois Bell for over one hundred days, and Daley was running out of time to convince them to put down their picket signs and wire the convention for television service. Chicago was also in the midst of a taxi strike. Daley scrambled to make it all work. He negotiated a temporary arrangement that allowed for 3,200 telephones and 200 teletypes to be installed at the Amphitheatre. He tried his best to win over the taxi drivers by sympathizing with their demand for more money. Prices were rising everywhere, Daley told them. Gesturing to the reporters at a press conference, he added that "I'd like to see you fellows get a pay raise, too." But he was not able to settle the taxi strike. The Democratic National Committee rented buses to transport 5,244 delegates and alternates between the twenty-one hotels where they were housed and the Amphitheatre. And three hundred cars donated by auto manufacturers and driven by young Democrats were made available to transport VIPs.[5]

Daley's most meticulous preparations involved security — turning the convention facilities into what the press dubbed "Fort Daley." A seven-foot-high chain-link fence, topped with more than two thousand feet of barbed wire, appeared suddenly around the International Amphitheatre. Firemen stood by to deter bomb throwers, and a catwalk was built into the convention hall so Secret Service and police could look down on the proceedings below. Manhole covers in the area were sealed with tar. Daley put the city's 11,900 police on twelve-hour shifts, with battle plans, command posts, and mobile tactical forces all carefully plotted out on charts. Five schools were readied to house the thousands of Illinois National Guard who were waiting in reserve. A thousand FBI and Secret Service agents were deployed from Washington, and 7,500 army troops trained in riot control were airlifted from Texas, Oklahoma, and Colorado. Though the Water and Sewers Department dismissed the Yippies' threat to dump LSD into the water supply — they estimated five tons of LSD would be required — Daley deployed police to guard the city's water filtration plants. The measures were, he said, "an ounce of preven-tion."[6] The Chicago police also assembled "Daley dozers," jeeps with barbed wire attached to the front, to clear the streets of demonstra-tors. A "macabre atmosphere pervades the convention" and "Daley's chambered fortress," Russell Baker of the *New York Times* reported.[7]

Daley was also, it would be revealed years later, infiltrating anti-war groups. The Chicago Department of Investigation, Daley's per-sonal investigative body, sent undercover agents to New York to disrupt an anti-war group that was making plans for the convention. The activities were detailed in a thirty-eight-page statement, written by department member John Clarke after the convention and re-leased a decade later in response to a lawsuit. Daley's agents sabotaged the Radical Organizing Committee's plans to charter buses and raise money. "As a result of our activities in New York, instead of 200 busloads of demonstrators coming to Chicago, they ended up with eight carloads, totaling 60 people," Clarke wrote. Other Department of Investigation agents infiltrated peace groups in Los Angeles, San Francisco, and Oakland "in an attempt to sabotage the movement with great success." The department also sent an agent to pose as a volunteer in the MOBE headquarters in Chicago who, when no one was listening, discouraged callers from coming to Chicago for the convention.[8]

The Chicago police were also infiltrating peace groups. The Chicago Police Department's "Red Squad," formally known as the Security Section of the department's Intelligence Division, had about 850 informants spying on groups like the National Lawyers Guild and the League of Women Voters. Red Squad agents also en-gaged in disruptive behavior and worked to set different anti-war groups against each other. In an incident in late 1967, an undercover Chicago police officer who had joined the Chicago Peace Council broke into the group's offices — to which he had obtained a key — stealing money and equipment and spray-painting slogans purporting to come from the Students for a Democratic Society. "The police have a perfect right to spy on private citizens," Daley insisted. "How else are they going to detect possible trouble before it happens?"[9]

Despite the attention the anti-war movement was getting, Daley was at least as concerned about black uprisings during the convention.

Any illusions he once held that Chicago's ghettos were not susceptible to rioting had been put to rest with the chaos after Martin Luther King's assassination. There were also several specific rumors about gang activity that was being planned to coincide with the convention. City officials were worried about the Blackstone Rangers, a large South Side gang, and a militant black group called the Black Turks that had come to Chicago from Cincinnati and Cleveland in August. They had reportedly been holding meetings that included dry runs for guerrilla warfare. The 7,500 soldiers who had been airlifted to Chicago were put through an exercise dubbed "Operation Jackson Park," in which they acted out how to respond to rioting. The Jackson Park of the title is located on the South Side, near poor black neighborhoods like Woodlawn — an indication of where the threat was perceived to be coming from. Daley was particularly worried that blacks would disrupt the convention by firing guns from the housing projects along State Street, which lay just across the Dan Ryan Expressway from the International Amphitheatre. Throughout the convention, he had two police helicopters flying up and down the area, patrolling for snipers.[10]

Daley used carrots as well as sticks to keep the city's black neighborhoods in line. The months leading up to the convention were a time of extraordinary generosity from City Hall. Daley's office arranged for Gale Sayers, the immensely popular Chicago Bears running back, to direct a touch football program in twenty playgrounds and parks across the city. "To be blunt about it, it grew out of the riots following the assassination of Dr. King," concedes Deputy Mayor David Stahl. "We said we've got to do something in the predominantly black part of the city where there was a huge degree of social disorganization."[11] In May, Daley ordered up a $27.5 million program to modernize older public housing buildings and install more social centers. He personally addressed hundreds of public housing residents in the City Council chambers, telling them that the goal was "to upgrade Chicago public housing developments and to improve the quality of life for residents." And Daley ordered housing officials to rush to build sixteen prefabricated houses for low-income tenants, which he wanted ready before the convention began.[12]

Daley also drew on his influence in Washington. In another of Daley's well-timed grants, it was shortly before the convention that the federal government found $500,000 to fund a three-year program to help blacks find housing in the suburbs. Ten days before the convention started, machine congressman John Kluczynski scheduled hearings for the House Small Business Committee at the Stockyard Inn, just blocks from the International Amphitheatre. Daley showed up to testify in favor of building a 77-acre industrial park for the impoverished neighborhoods of East Garfield Park and Lawndale. Daley's concerns about having a peaceful convention also led him to do something he had resisted for years: expand the city's fair housing law. On June 19, Daley proposed a change in the law that would finally extend it beyond brokers to include owners, renters, and other parties to real estate transactions. Daley was determined to get all the credit for the change. Alderman William Cousins, an independent who had tried to introduce a similar bill a year earlier, asked if he could be put down as a cosponsor. "No," Daley's floor leader said bluntly. "We are the sponsors."[13]

Most disingenuous of all, Daley began to wrap himself in the mantle of his old foe Martin Luther King. Daley introduced a City Council resolution to rename South Parkway, a major South Side thoroughfare that ran only through black neighborhoods, in honor of King. He took the occasion to indicate that King, who was talking about returning to Chicago to lead protests shortly before he died, would be delighted by the state of race relations in Chicago if he were only still alive. "He told me Chicago had made more progress than his own Atlanta or other cities," said Daley. "He visited projects on the South Side. He visited hospital developments. And he said, 'Wouldn't it be great if the entire city was like this?'" Daley advised that the important thing for blacks to do now was to let go of their bad feelings. "We could talk of the persecution of the past of the Jews and the Irish," he said. "When I was in Ireland a few years ago, I was told they had no feelings against the English because that was all behind them. That's how it should be here." Independents on the council grumbled about Daley's insincerity — and the fact that the street being dedicated to the integrationist King went through only the black ghetto. (Independent alderman Leon Despres proposed naming a street in the Loop after King — a suggestion that went nowhere.) In the end, the resolution to rename South Parkway for King passed unanimously. A week before the start of the convention, Daley spoke at ceremonies dedicating "Martin Luther King Drive." He invoked King's devotion to nonviolence in a verbal formulation that made it sound as if Daley had the idea first. "I once told him, and he agreed, 'Doctor, we will never do it in conflict and violence.'"[14]

At the same time Daley was rolling out the red carpet for his convention visitors, the city was sending clear signals that it would not welcome those with whose politics and lifestyles it disagreed. "We didn't want the hippies to come," Daley press secretary Earl Bush recalled. In a moment of unusual candor, William McFetridge, Daley's friend and head of the Chicago Park District, remarked that Chicago simply would not make its parks available to unpatriotic groups. In an era when public spaces around the country, from New York's Central Park to San Francisco's Golden Gate Park, were being used by hundreds of thousands of hippies and political protesters, Chicago's approach opened the city up to nationwide criticism. "The host city, under Mayor Daley's tight control, is showing no hospitality to demonstrations of any kind — legal as well as illegal," the *New York Times* objected in an editorial.[15]

Welcome or not, the hippies and Yippies were coming. They began arriving in Chicago on Saturday, August 17, a week before the delegates were to show up. The Yippies had announced plans to hold a Festival of Life, to contrast with the pro–Vietnam War festival of death they expected to be held at the Amphitheatre. They made their central gathering spot Lincoln Park, a 1,185-acre expanse of green along Lake Michigan on the North Side. When the Yippies showed up, the sleepy neighborhood park was transformed into a massive be-in of tie-dyed shirts, meditation, poetry readings, folk songs, and political orations. The Yippies engaged in their trademark brand of street theater. Jerry Rubin and several other members of his Youth International Party were arrested when they took a 125-pound pig named Pigasus, whom they were nominating for president, to a press conference at Civic Center Plaza. When the Chicago police arrested the pig, the Yippies announced that they would instead nominate a sow named Mrs. Pig. Later in the week, Abbie Hoffman would be arrested by Chicago police in the coffee shop of the Lincoln Hotel for having an obscene word written across his forehead.[16]

The peace movement's more serious agenda for convention week was still up in the air. MOBE and the Yippies were still trying to obtain permits for anti-war marches and rallies, but City Hall was dragging its feet. "[I]t was very conciliatory, very 'Yes, you'll get it — the permit is being processed,'" Abbie Hoffman recalled. "When anyone called, they'd say, 'Oh, it's definitely set — we've just met with this commissioner and that one and they assure us it's coming next week.'" Yet the permits never came. Eventually, the 150-member Coalition for an Open Convention filed suit in federal court to force the Chicago Park District to grant a permit for a rally in Soldier Field or Grant Park. Not surprisingly, the case ended up being assigned to U.S. District Court judge William J. Lynch, Daley's former law partner. Lynch ruled that the Park District had the discretion to deny permits whenever it felt that was appropriate to "safeguard public comfort, convenience, and welfare." Even if denying the permits was legal, it was not clear it was good policy. Allard Lowenstein, the anti-war activist and New York congressional candidate whose Coalition for an Open Convention had been denied the right to hold a rally at Soldier Field, warned Daley that by denying the permits the city was "inviting violence." Lowenstein was not alone in arguing that the permit denials were counterproductive. Six organizations, led by the ACLU, asked Daley to avoid trouble by meeting with the "responsible leaders" of the protesters and working out an agreement for demonstrations in the parks. And Judge Hubert Will, one of the few liberal independents on the federal bench in Chicago, told Daley to allow the protesters to demonstrate.[17]

On Thursday, August 22, Daley struck a deal with the anti-war protesters. After negotiating in Judge Lynch's chambers, the city and David Dellinger of the National Mobilization Committee agreed that an anti-war rally would be held the following Wednesday during the convention's third day. But the two sides had trouble agreeing on a location. MOBE wanted to lead a 150,000-strong march on the International Amphitheatre during the convention. Corporation counsel Ray Simon proposed five alternate routes that all led to the band shell in Grant Park. When negotiations between the city officials and

MOBE reached a deadlock, Lynch stepped in. It was clear that his sympathies lay with the city. Lynch sided with Simon on the march routes, holding that a demonstration in the vicinity of the Amphitheatre would interfere with convention security. Dellinger was also seeking an order lifting the park's 11:00 P.M. curfew so demonstrators could camp out on the grounds overnight. Lynch again took the city's side, ruling that it had no obligation to allow the park to be used for sleeping accommodations.[18]

Even before the convention began, Daley's relations with the media were strained. There had been an early round of press reports anticipating that Daley would use his control over the convention to minimize the role of the peace candidates, senators Eugene Mc-Carthy and George McGovern. Daley was incensed, and fulminated against reporters he viewed as irresponsible. "Among the false statements printed and uttered, emanating outside of Chicago, printed in national magazines and certain papers and over radio and TV, was that there was an attempt on my part to prevent some candidates from holding public gatherings," Daley declared in a rambling statement at one pre-convention news conference. "This is a vicious attack on this city and on its mayor." The television stations, for their part, were unhappy with the restrictions Daley was imposing on them. Pleading security concerns, the city refused to allow cameras to be placed in the area outside the Amphitheatre. And police refused to allow television vehicles to park in front of the hotels where convention delegates were staying. In a statement Walter Cronkite read on the *Evening News,* CBS called the ban a "totally unwarranted restriction of free and rapid access to information." CBS correspondent Eric Sevareid added that Chicago "runs the city of Prague a close second right now as the world's least attractive tourist attraction." Daley purported to be unconcerned by the criticism. "Who's Eric Sevareid?" Jack Reilly asked. "The mayor and I have never heard of him." But Daley met with network executives at City Hall on August 24 and agreed to allow their trucks greater access.[19]

With the national press streaming in, Daley tried to project an image of a busy city executive calmly leading a world-class metropolis. John Swearingen, chairman of Standard Oil of Indiana, came to City Hall to announce plans to build a $100 million office building downtown. Daley also found time on August 20 to appear in person at the dedication of the first eight low-cost prefabricated homes being built for Chicago's poor. The new homes were, he said, "symbolic of the spirit of Chicago." He urged his audience to "build, not burn," and to "construct, not riot." But the first violence of the convention came from the Chicago police. On August 22, just four days before the convention opened, Dean Johnson of Sioux Falls, South Dakota, one of the young people who had thronged to Chicago for the excitement, was shot to death by the police. They said they shot him after he fired a .32 caliber revolver at them. Of more concern to Daley, several Blackstone Rangers were arrested after appearing as witnesses in an investigation of an alleged plot to disrupt the convention. Their plan, according to a jailed gang member, was to assassinate Vice President Humphrey and Senator McCarthy, the leading contenders for the nomination. Thomas Foran, the U.S. attorney for Chicago installed by Daley, launched a secret probe of the charges. Evidence of the "plot" was extremely thin. Initially, Foran called the story "completely unverified," but a few days later he ordered a grand jury investigation, citing "new information." Nothing ever came of the inquiries, which seemed designed to justify oppressive levels of convention security. In the days leading up to the convention, Warsaw Pact troops were marching into Czechoslovakia to crush the liberal reforms that had been ushered in by Prague Spring. Daley denounced the invasion as a "dastardly act of suppression of freedom and liberty." To Daley, it was a Cold War lesson in the evils of communism. He failed to see any parallels between how the Soviets had used force to crush liberal young Czechs, and how he was planning to unleash the Chicago police and Daley dozers on liberal young Americans. Asked by a reporter what effect the events in Prague would have on the convention, Daley said, "I think it will affect a lot of doves that are flying around here."[20]

In addition to serving as host of the convention, Daley would also be playing his traditional role of kingmaker. His ability to deliver 118 Illinois delegates made him one of the few individuals who could actually affect the outcome. There was considerable speculation about which way Daley was leaning. It seemed unlikely he would back either McCarthy or McGovern, but he did not seem to be in a rush to endorse Humphrey. Daley was convinced a Democratic ticket headed by Humphrey would lose Illinois badly. He had been talking to politicians from around the country, and they shared his concerns about Humphrey's electability. There were rumors Daley was trying to draft Senator Edward Kennedy of Massachusetts, perhaps working with Jesse Unruh, the California party boss who controlled the lion's share of his state's 174 delegates. Daley had been hatching a plan to draft Kennedy for some time. John Criswell, an aide to President Johnson, was at a press conference Daley held in July about the status of the convention preparations. In a report to Johnson, Criswell recounted: "We were finished and a reporter asked him if he agreed with Bailey that Ted Kennedy would be a help to the ticket. He said he agreed and then, almost under his breath, added, 'I hope the convention drafts him.'"

On the Saturday before the convention began, Daley called Kennedy at Hyannis Port and urged him to run. Daley told Kennedy that the politicians he was speaking with were not enthusiastic about Humphrey. The thing for Kennedy to do, Daley said, was to come out to Chicago for the convention, or at least to make it known that he would accept a draft. The only problem with Daley's plan was that Kennedy did not want to run. He was only thirty-six, a freshman U.S. senator, and he was still grieving for the second of his brothers to be taken by an assassin's bullet. Kennedy told Daley he would not be attending the convention, and that he would not be available for a draft. But if there was any need to get in contact with him, his brother-in-law Stephen Smith, who was a delegate from New York, would be on hand to represent his interests. At the same time as the Kennedy draft rumors were circulating, there were also reports that Daley had not given up hope of convincing President Johnson to accept a draft to run for reelection. Johnson's birthday fell on the second day of the convention, and Daley continued to make birthday plans for the president. He was ready with a Texas-sized birthday cake, and a reservation at the Stockyard Inn, near the Amphitheatre, for a party. Daley had also hidden a cache of signs in the convention hall with the inscriptions "Birthday Greetings" and "We Love You LBJ." But Johnson's mind was made up. He remained in Texas, and on August 24 he assured a college audience that he was "not a candidate for anything except maybe a rocking chair."[21]

On Sunday, August 25, Daley was scheduled to announce his

presidential choice at a 3:00 P.M. meeting of the Illinois delegation in a ballroom at the Sherman House. Humphrey, McCarthy, and McGovern all addressed the delegates, many of whom wore blue-and-white "Daley for President" buttons. Humphrey spoke for thirty-seven minutes. McCarthy and McGovern each spoke for seventeen minutes. Lester Maddox, Georgia's segregationist governor, was sent away the first time he showed up, but when he returned he was allowed to address the delegates. After twenty-five minutes, Daley put an arm around Maddox's shoulder and said: "Governor, I know you'll understand when I tell you our wives have been waiting for us at the reception for some time." There was no great enthusiasm in the room for any of the candidates. Some delegates could be heard grumbling out loud that Humphrey, the front-runner, was a weak candidate. Though Daley had said repeatedly he would announce his decision at this meeting, he had already told Stephen Smith that "the boys might decide to hold off for forty-eight hours." In other words, he was going to put off his decision by two days to allow more time for a groundswell to develop around Edward Kennedy. Bill Daley says that, at least at one point during convention week, his father seemed to be working to draft Kennedy. "When I got home [one night of the convention], I was planning to go out. There were lots of parties. My dad said, 'Why don't you stick around?' I asked 'Why?' He said, 'I think we're going to endorse Teddy Kennedy tomorrow morning.'"[22]

Out on the streets, tensions were rising between protesters and the police. The anti-war movement was by now divided into two separate camps: the Yippies were still up in Lincoln Park on the North Side, while the more political MOBE was using Grant Park, located down the lakeshore closer to the Loop, as a base of operations. On Saturday night, the police had cleared Lincoln Park of demonstrators. The 200 who were ejected formed a line along Clark Street, on the west side of the park, and taunted the police: "Red Rover, Red Rover, Send Daley right over." On Sunday afternoon, August 25 — the last day before the convention started — about 100 anti-war demonstrators marched through downtown chanting "Peace now" and "Dump the Hump." Delegates checking in at the Hilton Hotel, headquarters for out-of-town delegates, were greeted by 800 protesters, more than half of whom had made the two-and-a-half-mile march from Lincoln Park. The first major clash between police and demonstrators occurred later that night in Lincoln Park. The police charged in at 11:00 P.M. and, invoking the rarely enforced curfew, began clearing out the park. The Yippies and other demonstrators who had settled in for the evening were taken by surprise. "I honestly believed that nothing was going to happen in Lincoln Park — that people who stayed in Lincoln Park would be relatively safe," Abbie Hoffman said later. "It was inconceivable to me, up until that Sunday night at six o'clock, when the police first charged into the park, that they were not going to let us sleep in the park that night."[23] For the next three hours, police beat unarmed protesters and reporters until the park was finally empty. During the attacks, two policemen told a reporter that "the word is out to get newsmen." Daley insisted later that journalists had not been singled out, but added: "We ask the men of the news media to follow the instructions of the police as other citizens should." The Sunday night skirmish in Lincoln Park was the first time convention reporters were roughed up, and it helped turn press coverage against Daley. Mike Royko, in a column entitled "Cops Threaten Law and Order," took it upon himself to explain Daley to his national colleagues. "He's been conning people so easily, I'm sorry to say about my fellow Chicagoans, that he thought he could keep it up this week," Royko wrote. "But sorry, Mayor, when your trained musclemen slapped around the nation's press I was listening. They think you are nothing but a less articulate version of Governor George Wallace. That's not much, after 13 years in office."[24]

When the convention began on Monday morning, August 26, Daley still had not made an endorsement. As volunteers handed out white stickers with red letters reading "Draft Ted," rumors swept the convention that Daley had endorsed Kennedy. The "Draft Kennedy" headquarters was being besieged with phone calls indicating that delegates from across the country — New York, Pennsylvania, Alabama — were lining up behind a Kennedy draft. The only trouble was, Kennedy had never agreed to be drafted, and after repeatedly saying he would not allow himself to be nominated, he finally sent a telegram that removed all doubt. With Kennedy out of the running, Daley began looking to Johnson. In response to a question from a reporter, Daley said that he was trying to keep the option open for President Johnson to enter the race. It was telling that Daley was vacillating between President Johnson, the anti-war movement's devil incarnate, and Ted Kennedy, its great hope. The Democratic Party was being split down the middle over Vietnam, the great moral issue of the day. But Daley's concerns were much more practical: finding a candidate who would run strongly in Cook County.[25]

Daley spoke to the convention's opening session Monday night. The Illinois delegation, ignoring the rule against demonstrations on the floor, interrupted the proceedings by holding a small pro-Daley parade in front of the podium, complete with "Daley for President" signs. In his address, Daley made no apologies for bringing the convention to Chicago. "I greet you as Mayor," Daley told the packed Amphitheatre and a national audience watching at home. "But, if I can have a moment of politics, I would say it is an important sign of faith to the American people for this national political convention to be held here — not in some resort center, but in the very heart of a great city where people live and work and raise their families." Daley made a point of clarifying what kind of person he was welcoming and what kind he was not:

> I do not refer to the extremists . . . who seek to destroy instead of to build — to those who would make a mockery of our institutions and values — nor do I refer to those who have been successful in convincing some people that theatrical protest is rational dissent. I speak of those who came conscientiously because they know at this political gathering there is hope and opportunity. I speak of those who came because the instinct that brings them here is right.

Daley insisted, as he always did, that he would be firm with the protesters who were gathered in the parks and on the streets. "As long as I am mayor of this city," he said, "there is going to be law and order in Chicago."[26]

Outside the convention hall, law and order was in fact already breaking down. But it was once again the police who had become lawless. The same night that Daley addressed the convention, the Chicago police got into some skirmishes in Grant Park and engaged in what would later be called a "police riot" in Lincoln Park. Policemen charged through crowds, firing tear gas and swinging clubs and yelling "Kill, Kill, Kill." Some removed their badges and nameplates to avoid being identified. Setting a pattern for the week, the police attacked bystanders as eagerly as demonstrators, and those who did not resist as much as those who did. Once again the police seemed to be singling out news reporters — who were marked with distinctive white armbands — for harsh treatment. One *Chicago Tribune* reporter was told he would have his "head busted" if he did not leave. Twenty reporters ended up with injuries that required hospitalization. "Chicago police are going out of their way to injure newsmen, and prevent them from filming or gathering information on what is going on," *NBC News* commentator Chet Huntley complained. "The news profession in this city is now under assault by the Chicago police." The morning after the clash in Lincoln Park, Police Superintendent Conlisk met with representatives of the four Chicago newspapers, and other media organizations. He promised to launch an investigation of police conduct toward reporters, and announced the formation of a special police unit to protect reporters and photographers. Still, Daley was not particularly impressed by the reporters' complaints about the violence that was directed at them. "We ask their cooperation and help and that they not join in the running and rushing which is part of these disorders," he said. If the police responsible for the violence could be identified, Daley said, "the least that can be expected is a reprimand."[27]

As the convention entered its second day, Daley was still giving no clue about which way he intended to swing the Illinois delegation. He appeared to be stalling for time in the hope that some alternative would emerge to a Humphrey candidacy. After a speech to the Illinois delegation on Tuesday, August 27, he told reporters he did not think Kennedy was likely to run. But it was possible Kennedy in-law Sargent Shriver could be the vice presidential nominee. In a break from national politics, Daley spoke to the Cook County ward committeemen, who had assembled to nominate candidates for eight judicial vacancies. He did not share his thoughts about the presidential race, but these machine functionaries understood their place. "You lead — we'll follow," Cook County clerk Eddie Barrett said. Despite his private worries that his party was about to nominate an unelectable candidate, Humphrey, Daley challenged the "doubting Thomases" and "apostles of despair" who were saying the Democrats were doomed to defeat. "We're going to come out of this convention with the next President of the United States!" he insisted.[28]

Tuesday evening, the convention delegates argued about Vietnam late into the night. After 1:00 A.M., while a contentious battle was looming over whether to add a peace plank to the platform, Daley repeatedly drew a finger across his neck to signal to convention chair Carl Albert to end the proceedings for the evening. That image, of a mean-faced Daley stage-managing the convention from his perch in the Illinois delegation, became one of the most enduring of the convention and of his career. It confirmed the suspicions of anti-war delegates: that despite all the democratic procedures built into the party structure, a single party boss was calling all the shots. As the hall erupted in shouts and catcalls, Albert called on "the great mayor of Chicago" to offer up a motion to adjourn. Daley's motion to recess until noon the next day was adopted by a chorus of "ayes." On the way out, Daley took a swipe at the incivility of the peace activists who had been causing an uproar over the issue of Vietnam. "The convention was not out of order," Daley said. "It was the people in the galleries. They were our guests but they did not act like guests in this building, the home of our party while the convention is going on." The disorder continued on the streets that night. Several peace groups organized an "un-birthday party" at the Coliseum, one block from Michigan Avenue, to mark President Johnson's sixtieth birthday. The police once again clashed with demonstrators in Lincoln Park. This time, the police were more aggressive, and the demonstrators held their ground more firmly. More than sixty protesters received injuries that required medical treatment, and more than one hundred were arrested.[29]

Wednesday, August 28, was the day the delegates would be voting for president, and Daley had promised to announce the Illinois delegation's choice in advance. Kennedy had by now taken himself firmly out of the running for "personal and family reasons." After meeting with the Illinois delegation at the Sherman House on Wednesday morning, Daley informed reporters that "after a long session in the typical spirit of Illinois democracy" the delegation would cast 112 of its 118 convention votes for Humphrey. Daley's machine allies — including William Lee, Matt Danaher, George Dunne, and Dan Rostenkowski — petitioned Humphrey to consider nominating Daley for vice president. Daley had not expressed interest in the job, they said, but they thought he could be convinced. Daley himself was, at least publicly, backing Maine senator Edmund Muskie.[30]

The only permit issued to MOBE, after all the negotiations, was for a rally in Grant Park on Wednesday afternoon. In the hot sun, about 10,000 people assembled in front of the oyster-shaped band shell. As the young people handed out peace buttons and anti-war literature, the Chicago police passed out a stern leaflet from Superintendent Conlisk stating that the demonstrators were limited to holding a stationary rally and that any attempts to conduct a march would subject the participants to arrest. Thirty people were injured when a skirmish broke out between police with nightsticks and protesters throwing debris. Other clashes involved National Guardsmen, who fired tear gas directly into the faces of demonstrators. One assistant U.S attorney told investigators he saw "hundreds of people running, crying, coughing, vomiting, screaming." But the worst fighting that day occurred on Michigan Avenue. The Conrad Hilton Hotel, at Michigan and Balbo, had become a rallying point for demonstrators in nearby Grant Park. Five thousand protesters were gathered outside the hotel, and Daley had called out 800 members of the National Guard to face them down. When Brigadier General Richard Dunn shouted at the demonstrators through a bullhorn, he was drowned out by "This Land Is Your Land" played over a sound system. As the evening wore on, the situation deteriorated. Just before 8:00 P.M., deputy police superintendent James Rochford ordered the crowd to leave the area. Getting no response, the police charged the crowd.[31]

The fighting that followed would later be known as the Battle of Michigan Avenue. In a twenty-minute orgy of violence, police beat up demonstrators and bystanders, fired off tear gas canisters, and shoved people through restaurant windows. Demonstrators were knocked to the ground and then kicked repeatedly. Heads were bloodied by swinging billy clubs. "I was hit for the first time on the head from behind by what must have been a billy club," one secretary who was in the crowd recalled later. "I was then knocked down and while on my hands and knees, I was hit around the shoulders. I got up again, stumbling, and was hit again. . . . After my second fall, I remember being kicked in the back, and I looked up and noticed that many policemen around me had no badges on. The police kept hitting me on the head." She eventually made it to a hospital, "bleeding badly from my head wound," and received twelve stitches. Journalist Shana Alexander observed the scene in an impromptu first aid station on the fifteenth floor of the Hilton, where a surgeon treated bleeding young people as "Happy Days Are Here Again" played in the background on a TV set broadcasting live from the convention. "One boy ha[d] a severed artery in his leg," Alexander recalled later. "He and his girl were in the street, there as spectators, not demonstrators, when the cops shoved people back against the Hilton with such force that a shop window shattered and the boy and girl were pushed backward through the glass. Police leaped in shouting surrealistically, 'Clear the Room! Clear the Room!' and clubbed and Maced the boy as he lay on the floor. The surgeon's wife, a nurse, had found the young couple hiding under a back stairs, terrified the blue [uniformed] police would come again." On another bed Alexander saw a wounded young man wearing a Red Cross armband indicating that he was on the scene as a medic. His head had been beaten in by a police club. "See those stellate-type wounds," the surgeon said as he examined the young medic. "The way the scalp is split like a pumpkin, these are all full-force blows."[32]

The rallying cry on Michigan Avenue that night was "the whole world is watching," and the protesters were not far off. Unlike the earlier melees, this police riot was captured by the television cameras set up outside the Hilton Hotel. The footage was quickly edited and broadcast to a national audience who had gathered around their televisions expecting to see the Democratic Party nominate a presidential candidate. The networks did an ingenious job of cutting back and forth between shots of the bloody police attacks and of a laughing Daley on the convention floor, giving viewers the impression Daley was celebrating the violence. The network switchboards immediately lit up with phone calls, most expressing outrage at the police actions. Daley's supporters would later point to the Wednesday night broadcasts as evidence that the media were out to get Daley. It was part of the national media's "colossal propaganda campaign" against Chicago and its police department, police spokesman Frank Sullivan charged. "The intellectuals of America hate Richard J. Daley because he was elected by the people — unlike Walter Cronkite."[33]

The news from Michigan Avenue was slow to reach the Amphitheatre. The delegates were engaged in their own squabbles until 9:30 P.M., when the television monitors scattered around the hall carried the same television footage the rest of the country was seeing. The riot scenes intensified the divisions in the convention hall. Robert Maytag, chairman of the Colorado delegation, interrupted the proceedings with a point of order and asked, "Is there any rule under which Mayor Daley can be compelled to suspend the police state terror being perpetrated at this minute on kids in front of the Conrad Hilton?" Daley reacted with red-faced anger while his supporters booed Maytag until the chair ruled him out of order. Connecticut senator Abraham Ribicoff took to the podium to nominate George McGovern. Departing from his text, Ribicoff declared, "With George McGovern we wouldn't have Gestapo tactics on the streets in Chicago." There was a moment of silence, as Daley flushed purple before a national television audience, shook his fist, and screamed an epithet toward the stage. To many, it seemed clear that Daley had just called Ribicoff a "fucker," but Daley's defenders would insist that the word he used was "faker." Either way, his fury was evident. Four Daley loyalists — county commissioner George Dunne, Alderman Thomas Keane, Democratic state chairman James Ronan, and Francis Lorenz — jumped up from their seats and gestured for Ribicoff to get off the platform. Looking down at Daley, who was just twenty feet away, Ribicoff said: "How hard it is to accept the truth. How hard it is." Daley tried to look calm, as a tight ring of security officers gathered around to protect him, though the source of the threat was not clear. Daley joked with Dunne, well aware that television cameras were focused on him and that they had already captured him looking irate and possibly profane. Before long, Daley stalked off the floor. He was not there to see 103¾ votes from the Pennsylvania delegation put Humphrey over the top.[34]

After the Battle of Michigan Avenue, the national media became more outspoken in their disgust at the scene in Chicago. "I want to pack my bags and get out of this city," Walter Cronkite declared. Roger Mudd wondered on CBS whether anyone had ever "done so much damage to a great political party" as Daley. But Daley stead-fastly defended law enforcement's handling of the protests. "Our po-lice department is a great police department," he said. "They are all good and decent men and they don't respond with undue vio-lence."[35] The fault, Daley insisted, lay with the hippies, who "aren't the youth of this country."[36] Thursday morning, Daley went on a public relations offensive. At a City Hall press conference, he read a statement and asked for it to be "given the same kind of distribution on press, radio and television as the mob of rioters was given yester-day." The demonstrators were "terrorists" who had come to Chicago determined to "assault, harass, and taunt the police into reacting be-fore television cameras," Daley said. And he charged that the media had "distorted and twisted" the truth about the city and the police. In a departure from his usual practice, this time Daley refused to take questions.[37]

Thursday night, August 29, Daley took his public relations cam-paign to the convention hall. Copies of his press conference state-ment, accompanied by sympathetic newspaper stories, were placed on the buses that took delegates to the Amphitheatre that night. A fresh run of "We Love Mayor Daley" posters, ordered from the printer at 4:00 P.M. and delivered by 8:00 P.M., were plastered around the Amphitheatre. The rafters were packed with enthusiastic machine loyalists — Daley's "Ruly Crowd," in David Halberstam's phrase — who broke into regular shouts of "We Love Daley" throughout the evening. The acrimony of the previous day was replaced by reverent silence when a thirty-two-minute film tribute called *Robert Kennedy Remembered* was shown, and when it ended the delegates rose in uni-son for a five-minute standing ovation. But after the applause ended, the delegates were once again divided. When Carl Albert tried to bring the convention to order, peace delegates — mostly from the New York and California delegations — launched into a rendition of "The Battle Hymn of the Republic." The Illinois and Texas delega-tions, the heart of the party's old guard, made a point of sitting down and waiting for the interruption to end, as the peace delegates continued their demonstration. After almost twenty minutes, an or-ganized contingent from the Illinois delegation marched in from the Amphitheatre's south gallery chanting "We love Daley! We love Daley!" That did not stop the anti-war forces, but Daley then came up with a shrewd ploy that did: he sent Ralph Metcalfe up to the podium to offer an unscheduled tribute to Martin Luther King Jr. The peace delegates had no choice but to stop and listen.[38]

Humphrey selected Maine senator Edmund Muskie as his running mate, and the two men accepted their nominations Thursday night. In his acceptance speech, the new presidential nominee struggled to bring together his bitterly divided party. Humphrey offered something to both Daley and the demonstrators. "We do not want a police state, but we do need a state of law and order," he said. Humphrey, who had a reputation for equivocating on important issues, found that his attempts to please everyone pleased no one. As a sign held by a protester in Grant Park earlier in the week put it: "There are Two Sides to Every Question — Humphrey Endorses Both of Them." But Humphrey's bigger problem was the damage the disastrous events of the last week had done to the Democratic Party. "It seems to me, on the last day of the Democratic convention, the party could fairly be classified as a disaster area," David Brinkley said in an NBC news broadcast at the end of the convention. "Hubert Humphrey, after a long time of yearning for it, has finally won his party's nomination, and in the opinion of a great many people, including a great many of the delegates, there is serious question now about how much the nomination he won is worth."[39]

The police attacks, like the convention itself, were winding down. The police arrested another eighty people on Thursday, and police and National Guardsmen turned away two marches headed toward the International Amphitheatre. There was a brief melee at 18th and Michigan, south of the Loop, where three thousand marchers were routed by three volleys of gas, but the crowd dispersed without resisting. Further up Michigan Avenue, near the Hilton Hotel, more serious trouble was developing. At 4:00 Friday morning, responding to reports that objects were being thrown out the windows onto Michigan Avenue, police got passkeys from hotel management and raided the entire fifteenth floor, which was the headquarters of the McCarthy campaign. Sleeping McCarthy staffers and volunteers — on the Michigan Avenue side and on the opposite side — were roused from their beds and beaten. One staff member who told police they had no authority to do what they were doing was beaten by three policemen. An Irish businessman who came to Chicago as part of an "Irish for McCarthy" contingent recalled that when McCarthy's young supporters were heading out through the hotel hallways, the police began attacking again: "I saw a policeman's club raised high in the air among the McCarthy workers still in the hall," he said. "For a long time it seemed to hang there. Then it was descending in a gleaming arc with rapid and enormous force. I heard it hit a boy's head. It was sharper and louder than a door slamming. Like the sound of the first impact in an auto accident. It was followed by the distinctive *squish* of flesh and skin parting. And the boy had done nothing to provoke this. Then other clubs started to fall and girls began screaming. . . ." Senator McCarthy, who was awoken by his staff, came out and complained to the police about their treatment of his staff. "You can't just come up here and knock heads," he objected. In fact, that is just what the Chicago police had done. The attack on the McCarthy staff did nothing to dampen Daley's enthusiasm for his police. As the week drew to a close, he sent a teletype message to police superintendent Conlisk stating that "The Democratic National Committee and the mayor of Chicago express their heartfelt gratitude to the men and women of the Chicago Police Department for their devotion to duty and a job well done."[40]

When the convention was over, the majority of the national media were caustic in their assessment of Daley's performance. "The blame has to be taken at the top," the *Washington Post* editorialized. "Brutes ought not to be put into police uniforms. Chicago has been disgraced by them — and even more by those responsible for their barbarity." The convention had been a "military nightmare, Richard J. Daley, host," columnist Mary McGrory wrote. "The truth was," Tom Wicker wrote in the *New York Times,* "those were our children in the streets, and the Chicago police beat them up." But Daley's local reviews were more favorable. The conservative *Chicago Tribune* strongly endorsed his law-and-order stand, and had little sympathy for the victims of the violence. In a front-page editorial, the paper denounced the "bearded, dirty, lawless rabble" that used "every sort of provocation against police and National Guardsmen — vile taunts, lye solutions, bricks and rubble." It concluded that "Mayor Daley and the police deserve congratulations rather than criticism."

The *Chicago Daily News,* in an August 31 editorial, said that while Daley bore "a large burden of blame," there was another side of the story. The paper agreed with Daley that radical groups and hard-core dissidents had instigated much of the violence. And they found grim solace in Daley's assessment of the week: what really mattered was that "no one was killed." It was not only the newspapers that took Daley's side — many Chicagoans spoke out in support of Daley, and few dared to question his actions. "Knock on any door. Any cab door. The response is Johnny-One-Note: 'Daley's OK,'" Chicago historian Studs Terkel observed dejectedly after the convention. "And what of THE University, boasting more Nobel Prize winners than any other campus on earth, Doc? Their silence is the silence of the dead."[41]

Daley began his September 9 press conference, his first after the convention, in a jovial mood. But it did not take long for him to explode. A *Chicago Daily News* reporter suggested that when Daley shouted at Ribicoff he had used a "four letter word beginning with mother." Daley shouted: "You're a liar. Don't say that. I never used that kind of language in my life." But Daley would not say what he had shouted at Ribicoff. It was, he said, "immaterial." Matt Danaher, sitting outside the press conference, backed up his boss's story. "I was sitting next to him," Danaher said. "He'd never use a word like the one [the *Daily News* reporter] said. He doesn't talk that way. . . . He's a daily communicant." Daley then summed up the Chicago police philosophy in a quote that his critics would repeat endlessly. "Gentlemen, get this thing straight for once and for all," he said. "The policeman isn't there to create disorder. The policeman is there to preserve disorder."[42]

A few days earlier, Daley's office had published an official report on the convention violence. "Strategy of Confrontation" was an expansion of the points Daley outlined in his Walter Cronkite interview. It made now-familiar arguments about "revolutionaries" who had come to Chicago determined to engage law enforcement in "hostile confrontation," and policemen who did their best to avoid being drawn in. "Strategy of Confrontation" talked archly of information obtained by the Intelligence Division of the Chicago Police Department concerning "schemes to assassinate Senator Eugene

McCarthy, Mayor Richard J. Daley and other political and civic leaders." The report indicated that among the threats to the social order that had occurred in Chicago, unbeknownst to most of America, was a plan to murder a young female supporter of Eugene McCarthy and blame it on the police. Naturally, the police did not want to mention these schemes and rumors at the time "for fear of planting the idea in still other minds." The document also contained an occasionally bizarre list of weapons used by the demonstrators, including items like "aerosol can with contents which act like stink bomb," and "paint." Among the "battle" supplies listed were "revolutionary literature" and "dangerous drugs."[43]

Daley was also involved in a filmed version of "Strategy of Confrontation." His staff worked on producing the video, while he asked the networks for help in "balancing the one-sided portrayal" of the Chicago police during the convention. All three networks turned Daley down. NBC responded with an invitation to discuss the events with a panel of reporters in a special edition of *Meet the Press,* which Daley declined. Within a month, a private film company, working with city employees, had completed *What Trees Do They Plant?* The title was one of Daley's favorite swipes at reformers, who sat back and criticized while men like Daley were getting things done. Daley pursued independent stations, and found 140 in the U.S., Canada, and England who agreed to air it. The film featured footage of police officers describing being attacked by peace protesters, and an assortment of weapons said to have been confiscated from demonstrators, including a flattened beer can and broken park bench slats. The standout in the arsenal was a Louisville Slugger with the words "Cops are Pigs" on one side, and "Love" on the other — though it was unclear where exactly it had come from.[44]

For all the national criticism directed at Daley, his reputation in Chicago did not seem to have suffered. Even before his propaganda efforts, he claimed that mail to City Hall was running 60,000 in support of him and the Chicago police and only 4,000 against. The numbers seemed improbably one-sided, but there were other indications that Daley's stance had been popular with average Chicagoans. Cars around the city began to sport bumper stickers saying "We Support Mayor Daley and His Chicago Police." Jack Mabley, a columnist with Chicago's *American,* had written one of the most disturbing pieces of reportage to come out of the convention. It described a policeman who "went animal when a crippled man couldn't get away fast enough." The policeman, angry that the man hopping along with the help of a stick was not gone, shoved him in the back, hit him with a night stick, and threw him into a lamppost. Mabley got an overwhelming response to his reporting — 80 percent to 85 percent of it supporting Daley and the police. "You can't help that gnawing feeling — can all these people be right and I be wrong?" Mabley said. In mid-September, Daley received praise from an unexpected quarter: Georgia's segregationist governor Lester Maddox announced that he was supporting an independent ticket of George Wallace for president and Daley for vice president.[45]

The November elections did not go well for Daley and the Democrats. Humphrey won Chicago by 370,000 votes, which was not enough to stop Nixon from carrying Illinois by 135,000 votes. Governor Samuel Shapiro, who had moved up to the job when Otto Kerner was named to the federal bench in May, lost to Republican Richard Ogilvie. Though the Democrats lost the governorship, downstate Democrat Paul Simon was elected lieutenant governor. Simon explained his win — the first time the two parties had split the state's top two offices — by saying that he was able to "convey an image of independence" Shapiro had not. But the election was not without its bright spots for the machine. With Ogilvie out as chairman of the Cook County Board, the board — which now had a 10–4 Democratic majority — would certainly choose a machine loyalist as his successor. That would allow Daley to once again take control of Cook County government. And Daley protégé Edward Hanrahan was elected state's attorney, keeping that important prosecutorial position in the machine's hands. Daley had no easy explanation for the Democrats' poor showing statewide — he attributed Humphrey's loss to the fact that "he didn't get enough votes." But he was emphatic that the November elections were only a temporary setback. Asked by a reporter at a press conference if he was worried about Governor-elect Ogilvie's threat to "disassemble the Chicago Democratic machine," Daley responded defiantly: "You try it!"[46]

On December 1, an investigative commission headed up by Daniel Walker, a corporate lawyer and president of the Chicago Crime Commission, released its report on violence at the Democratic convention. Walker's investigation, undertaken at the behest of President Johnson's National Commission on the Causes and Prevention of Violence, sifted through almost 3,437 eyewitness accounts, 180 hours of film, and 20,000 still photographs, and relied on the work of 212 investigators. The Walker Report, also known as *Rights in Conflict,* offered tepid criticism of the protesters but came down hard on the Chicago Police Department. The police were involved in "enough wild club swinging, enough cries of hatred, enough gratuitous beating to make the conclusion inescapable that the individual policemen, and lots of them, committed violent acts far in excess of the requisite force for crowd dispersal or arrest," the report stated. Its famous conclusion was that the Chicago police had engaged in a "police riot." The Walker Report traced the police misbehavior directly to Daley, and his shoot-to-kill comments after the April 1968 unrest. Daley's remarks were "widely reported both in Chicago and throughout the nation," the report noted. "Undoubtedly it had some effect on the attitude of Chicago policemen towards their role in riots and other disorders." The report also criticized the city for not publicly condemning the offending police officers after the convention violence. "If no action is taken against them, the effect can only be to discourage the majority of policemen who acted responsibly, and further weaken the bond between police and community," the commission concluded. Daley, not troubled that this careful study had labeled his police officers rioters, cautioned that the 345-page report "must be read in full." He was gratified, he said, that the Walker Commission had concluded that "the majority of policemen did act responsibly under extremely provocative circumstances."[47]

We Wore Suits and Ties

Daley, who rarely got ill, began 1969 by staying home sick with the flu.[1] His associates noticed that he was starting to slow down, and that he seemed to be losing his edge. There was talk that the travails of 1968 — the West Side riots, the convention clashes, and the excoriation by the national press — had taken a physical and psychological toll on him. Daley's friend Dr. Eric Oldberg, president of the Chicago Board of Health, said the mayor "was on the brink of something serious. . . . He was in very bad shape." It was unfortunate timing, because 1969 was a year in which he would need all the strength he could muster.[2]

On February 10, a federal court ruled against the city in the *Gautreaux* case. The landmark decision confirmed the obvious: that the Chicago Housing Authority had discriminated against blacks for decades in where it located its projects and which tenants it allowed to move in. The case had begun in 1965, when the Illinois affiliate of the ACLU set up a Civil Rights Committee, which investigated the city's public housing policies. Alexander Polikoff, then a lawyer in private practice, agreed to head up a team to investigate the possibilities of litigation. The ACLU filed its class-action suit against the CHA on August 9, 1966, on behalf of Dorothy Gautreaux, a public housing tenant, and other black tenants and applicants. The plaintiffs charged that since 1950, virtually all the sites selected by the CHA to build family housing were "in Negro neighborhoods and within the areas known as the Negro Ghetto" because of the CHA's policy of avoiding placing public housing in white parts of the city. The plaintiffs charged that the CHA's policies violated the Civil Rights Act of 1964, which prohibits racial discrimination in federally funded programs.[3]

The case had been assigned to Judge Richard Austin. It looked at first like another example of an important lawsuit being assigned to a judge who owed a political debt to Daley. Austin and Daley had a long history. Daley had plucked him from obscurity, handing him the Democratic nomination for governor against incumbent William Stratton in 1956. Afterward, Daley was responsible for President Kennedy appointing Austin to the federal bench. But Austin's gratitude may have been tempered by hard feelings over the 1956 gubernatorial race. It was said at the time that Daley had struck a deal with Stratton that in exchange for increasing Chicago's taxing authority, the machine would run a weak campaign against him in the next election. The rumor was that Austin had been "trimmed," or not given the machine's full support. The evidence on this point is mixed, and Austin may simply have lost a very close election because Adlai Stevenson dragged down the whole Democratic ticket that year. But the 1956 election may also have inclined Austin to use the case to pay Daley back.[4]

Austin seemed skeptical about the lawsuit at first. Polikoff recalls that Austin's initial reaction to the plaintiffs' claims was "Where do you want to put 'em? On Lake Shore Drive?" But his views changed after the plaintiffs set out their claims of racial discrimination in painstaking detail. Their case, which unfolded over two and a half years of pleadings and hearings, explained how the CHA had worked with the political establishment to keep public housing out of white wards. Of the thirty-three project sites that had been proposed by the CHA since 1950, the plaintiffs noted, thirty-two were in predominantly black neighborhoods. And since Daley's election as mayor, virtually every new unit of housing built by the CHA had been built in the black ghetto. Of 10,256 family apartments completed or in development, 18 were in the Lincoln Park urban renewal area, 12 were in the Hyde Park urban renewal area, and another 33 were in a white neighborhood with a growing black population. The remaining 10,193 apartments — 99.4 percent of the total — were located in black neighborhoods. The result of these "siting" decisions was that by 1967, outside of the CHA's four white projects, the city's public housing tenants were about 99 percent black. "The pattern of segregation," the plaintiffs charged, "has been nearly perfect."[5]

The plaintiffs' case also featured damaging testimony from the CHA's own employees about the degree to which racial considerations permeated its operations. C. E. Humphrey, executive director of the CHA from 1968 to 1973, gave a view from inside the agency of the cooperation between the CHA and the City Council about racial consideration in site selection. As for tenant selection, Tamaara Tabb, former supervisor of tenant selection for the CHA, testified that the CHA had different policies for whites and blacks. The agency had a firm policy of keeping apartments in Trumbull Park, Bridgeport, and other projects vacant rather than rent them to black families, Tabb said. The CHA kept separate waiting lists for blacks and whites, and the Central Rental Office and the staffs of each of the four white projects were instructed not to rent to "B" families — CHA code for blacks.[6]

In the end, Judge Austin was convinced. "Given the trend of Negro population movement, 99½ per cent of the CHA family units are located in areas which are or soon will be substantially all-Negro," Judge Austin wrote. "It is incredible that this dismal prospect of an all-Negro public housing system in all-Negro areas came about without the persistent application of a deliberate policy to confine public housing to all-Negro or immediately adjacent areas." Judge Austin directed the parties to work out a plan to address the illegal racial discrimination.

Daley's initial reaction was restrained. He was concerned, he said, that placing restrictions on site selection would slow down the building of new housing. "We are facing a difficult situation," Daley said. "We need more housing immediately, but how do we get it?"[7] That was a problem Chicago and other cities were faced with long before the *Gautreaux* decision was handed down. Federal money for large-scale public housing was far below the levels of the 1950s and early 1960s. The CHA's last significant construction had been a modest 1967 project, known simply as "Scattered Sites," consisting of 300 apartments in nineteen low-rise buildings scattered throughout the Black Belt. Daley also argued, as the Daley camp had at the housing summit with King, that the real answer was to come up with a solution that involved the entire Chicago metropolitan area. Experts were saying, Daley noted, "that there also should be public housing in the suburbs as well as Chicago."[8]

When the parties were unable to agree on a plan to implement the court's judgment, on July 1, 1969, Judge Austin issued his own instructions to the CHA. Judge Austin not only ordered the CHA to stop discriminating prospectively, he imposed an affirmative requirement that the CHA redress its past misdeeds by placing a disproportionate number of new units in white neighborhoods. The court divided the city into different racial spheres. It designated the city's minority census tracts — those with 30 percent or more nonwhite population — as a "Limited Public Housing Area." The rest of the city it called the "General Public Housing Area." Judge Austin ordered that the next 700 units of public housing be built in the General Public Housing Area. After that, 75 percent of all units would have to be built in the General Public Housing Area. Housing projects could rise no more than three stories and contain no more than 120 residents, the court ordered, and they could make up no more than 15 percent of the total housing in their census tract.[9]

Judge Austin's July 1 remedial order, with its detailed plans for building housing in white neighborhoods, provoked an angrier response than his earlier ruling that discrimination had taken place. Residents of white neighborhoods lashed out at Judge Austin — it was noted often that he lived in the suburbs, which were neither a "Limited Public Housing Area" nor a "General Public Housing Area." And they flooded elected officials with demands that his orders be resisted. "If I wanted my wife and family to live near blacks, I would have moved closer to Cabrini-Green," one white man wrote his alderman. Congressman Pucinski said the ruling "probably has dealt the death blow to public housing here." The CHA made a few gestures toward accepting the court's decision. It hired a Chicago community relations agency, Community Programs, Inc., to put together a public relations campaign to try to change white perceptions about public housing. The cornerstone of the campaign was an attempt to persuade whites that the "new look" in public housing would fit in well in their neighborhoods.[10]

* * *

While Judge Austin was issuing his first *Gautreaux* ruling, Daley was squaring off with neighborhood activists over the Model Cities Program. Model Cities was a federal anti-poverty program that picked up where the Community Action Program had left off. Its goal was to create demonstration programs — or "models"— of what kind of urban programs could work to alleviate the problems of the ghetto. The architects of the program intended for it to be politically savvier than the ill-fated CAP. It was to be run out of the Department of Housing and Urban Development, rather than the more ideologically driven OEO, and its community participation requirements were considerably less demanding than CAP's "maximum feasible participation." Nixon HUD secretary George Romney said bluntly that "it will be up to the mayors how they spread the money." Finally, a federal guideline Daley could live with. He took full advantage of his new prerogatives.[11]

From the outset, it was clear that Chicago's Model Cities Program would operate along the same lines as the Chicago model developed for CAP. To direct Chicago's Model Cities, Daley had installed Erwin France, a state employment bureaucrat who would soon run for Congress with the machine's backing. The application the city submitted to HUD more than a year earlier was prepared by city agencies that were firmly under Daley's control. Daley did not solicit input from the four neighborhoods — Woodlawn, Lawndale, Grand Boulevard, and Uptown — that he was proposing as Model Cities sites. The Woodlawn Organization objected to Daley's heavy-handed approach and in December 1968 announced that it had submitted its own application. Two months later, Daley and TWO worked out a compromise under which TWO got limited representation on the Model Area Planning Councils that ran Chicago's Model Cities program, and TWO withdrew its application for Model Cities funding. As with the CAP councils, Daley made sure the Model Cities planning councils remained firmly under his control. He appointed half of the members outright, and the ward organizations were able to control most of the remaining elected seats. More than 10 percent of council members held Model Cities jobs — in violation of HUD rules — and many more held government patronage jobs. "This is a perfect example of the way the machine tries to control things," the executive director of the Better Government Association charged. "There are nearly 50 council members in Model Cities and other jobs who probably believe they must go along with the [political] bosses to avoid getting fired."[12]

Daley and the machine siphoned off much of the Model Cities money before it could reach the needy. A 1972 investigation by the *Chicago Tribune* found that almost half of the program's $53 million budget went to administrative expenditures, many of dubious value. France set up a costly central-office bureaucracy, with nine staff members assigned to public relations. Delegates from the four Model Area councils attended a conference at the Conrad Hilton in downtown Chicago, and spent thousands of dollars to stay overnight at the hotel. But the greatest beneficiaries of the program were Daley's machine cronies. The single biggest recipient of Model Cities money was the insurance company founded by Joe Gill, Daley's predecessor as machine boss, which received at least $195,000 in premiums on contracts for which there was no bidding. Another $185,000 in insurance premiums was awarded to a firm that shared an office and telephone switchboard with Gill's firm. Model Cities money was funneled to an array of other machine leaders and Daley allies: $140,000 to the Real Estate Research Corp., headed by Daley housing aide James Downs; $127,000 to Urban Associates, Inc., headed by former city planning commissioner Ira Bach; and $30,000 to Crown Office Supply Co., whose president was Reuben Arvey, brother of former machine boss Jacob Arvey. Model Cities jobs were handed out as machine patronage, to applicants who came with sponsorship letters from their ward committeemen. Despite the Hatch Act's prohibition on federal employees participating in partisan politics, the Chicago Model Cities Program payroll was filled with machine politicians and hangers-on, including Cook County sheriff Richard Elrod's uncle Samuel Elrod, a precinct captain in the 48th Ward; and a rabbi at the temple attended by 46th Ward committeeman and state senator Robert Cherry.[13]

In the end, Daley and the machine had no trouble crushing the idealistic vision behind Model Cities. Much of the money that was not wasted on administrative expenses and sweetheart contracts was simply sent out in the form of checks to poor people, a large number of whom used the money not to improve their neighborhoods but to move out of them. All four Model Cities neighborhoods lost a large percentage of their population during the course of the program.[14]

In the March 1969 aldermanic elections, the machine was facing an increasingly restless electorate. Daley's hard line on the Chicago Freedom Movement and the anti-war demonstrators had restored the machine's traditional hold on the Bungalow Belt wards that had begun to drift away in the 1963 election over civil rights. But the machine was now facing defections in two other areas: the black wards and the liberal lakefront neighborhoods. These weaknesses were evident in the aldermanic elections. On the South Side, there was a hotly contested battle for 2nd Ward alderman. The 2nd Ward, Bill Dawson's longtime political base and home of the State Street Corridor, was one of the machine's "Automatic Eleven." But independent former social worker Fred Hubbard was running a dissident campaign against the machine's candidate, Dawson administrative assistant Lawrence Woods. "We're a sure winner," Dawson declared. "We always are." But Dawson, who was seriously ill back in Washington, could do little for Woods, who turned out to be a lackluster candidate, hampered by a bribery indictment on his record. Hubbard, who campaigned especially energetically in the ward's many housing projects, won by better than 2 to 1. Hubbard's victory was a serious setback for the machine. With black voters making up a growing percentage of the citywide electorate, Daley could not afford to have the black wards break away.[15]

Liberal whites were also growing increasingly disenchanted with the machine. Along the lakefront on the North Side, another reform-versus-machine face-off had developed in Paddy Bauler's redistricted old ward. When the incumbent alderman was appointed judge, a young lawyer named William Singer jumped in to challenge the new machine candidate. Singer was a native of Jake Arvey's West Side, and had grown up in the middle-class South Shore neighborhood. He had not come up through a ward organization, and had an unlikely pedigree for an alderman. He was a graduate of Brandeis and Columbia Law School, and worked for U.S. District Court judge Hubert Will and Senator Paul Douglas. Singer had also worked for Robert Kennedy in his Senate race, and again in his 1968 presidential campaign. After Kennedy's assassination, he had been recruited to run George McGovern's Chicago campaign office.

Singer had the backing of the Independent Precinct Organization, a fledgling anti-machine group. Just so there were no misunderstandings, Singer appeared before the 44th Ward Democratic Organization to tell them he would run with or without their endorsement. Not surprisingly, they did not support him. Understanding Daley's popularity, Singer did not run an anti-Daley campaign, but instead tried to articulate a new vision for the city, arguing that residents of the ward should have an independent voice in City Hall. He emphasized issues like good schools, that cut across machine-versus-reform lines. The result was that he landed in a runoff election with James Gaughan, deputy county controller and a machine stalwart, for the seat. Singer and Gaughan reflected a new fault line that was emerging in Chicago Democratic politics. Singer relied on a campaign army of students and reformers, while Gaughan imported precinct workers from across the city. Singer raised money at coffee klatches in high-rise buildings, and employed such unmachinelike methods as a group of girls called the Singer Singers, who belted out campaign theme songs on street corners. Revealing a dark side of Chicago machine politics, Gaughan and his followers made blatant anti-Jewish appeals to working-class Catholic voters in the non-lakefront end of the district. Singer's campaign was run, one Gaughan campaign worker said, by "a brigade of porcupines whose snout is their most prominent feature." Singer printed up "Porcupine Power" buttons, and had his campaign workers wear them in Jewish parts of the ward. State treasurer Adlai Stevenson III campaigned for Singer. "A few years ago, I wouldn't have thought a grubby aldermanic election could be a great occasion for citizen participation," Stevenson said. "But you have to use the opportunities at hand." The turnout on election day was enormous, and Singer eked out a victory, winning 11,983 of the 23,263 votes cast.[16]

The machine's hold on the city remained secure. Even with Hubbard and Singer joining the City Council, Daley still controlled at least 37 of its 50 seats. But there was no denying the powerful symbolism of both Dawson's and Bauler's old seats falling to reformers. After the election, Daley indignantly denied reports that his machine was in decline — they were, he said, a "hallucination of some segments of the press." Daley may not have admitted the machine's setback publicly, but he did not ignore it. Shortly after Singer was elected, Seymour Simon, who was now a North Side alderman, asserted that county clerk Edward Barrett had fired three of his 40th Ward precinct captains from their county jobs because they had campaigned for Singer. Daley also lashed out at Stevenson for working for Singer, saying outsiders should not get involved in a ward's politics. Daley was angry not only at Stevenson, but at the larger political realities the aldermanic elections had revealed. Daley's handling of the 1968 Democratic convention may have been popular with his core constituency, but it had hurt him and the machine in the city's liberal precincts. And his hard line on civil rights, and pronouncements like "shoot to kill," played well in the Bungalow Belt, but they had alienated other parts of the old machine coalition.

Daley had not yet put the Democratic convention behind him. In March, U.S. attorney Thomas Foran, a machine Democrat put in office by Daley, handed up a series of indictments in connection with the convention week disturbances. In sharp contrast with the Walker Commission findings, Foran's indictments were directed solely at the anti-war demonstrators. The defendants, who would come to be known as the Chicago 8, were a motley assortment. Yippie organizers Abbie Hoffman and Jerry Rubin and MOBE leaders David Dellinger, Rennie Davis, and Tom Hayden were among those indicted. But so was Black Panther Party minister Bobby Seale, who had been in Chicago for less than a day during the convention and had said and done little. Lee Weiner and John Froines were minor protesters, whose connection to the weeks' disturbances was equally tenuous. Foran's indictments were also a legal stretch, the first ever returned under a provision of the Civil Rights Act of 1968 that made it a felony to "travel in interstate commerce . . . . with the intent to incite, promote, encourage, participate in and carry on a riot."[17]

On April 23, 1969, after fourteen years and three days in office, Daley became the longest-serving mayor in Chicago history, beating Mayor Kelly's record. Baskets filled the corridors of his office in City Hall. Daley's favorite Irish band, the Shannon Rovers, played Gaelic tunes as he and Sis came out of his private office to greet the throngs of well-wishers. After the band broke into "Chicago," Daley delivered a short homily. "I've had the blessing of a fine wife and family, and I've tried to do the best I could while I was mayor. None of us is perfect. But as my good mother and dad would say, do the best you can." In a moment of emotion, he added: "I hope that wherever they are Lill and Mike are proud of me." Daley kissed his wife and had tears in his eyes. Richard, John, William, and Patricia joined him in the receiving line.[18]

April also marked the one-year anniversary of Martin Luther King's assassination. On April 3, the day before the anniversary, unrest broke out in the Chicago schools by noon, and before the day was over black neighborhoods had once again broken out in rioting, looting, and sniper fire. Daley cracked down quickly, talking tough and calling out the National Guard. This time, the conflict ended by nightfall. Nor were the anti-war protests entirely over. More than 10,000 demonstrators marched down State Street on April 5 to call for an end to the Vietnam War. The march included some dramatic street theater. Demonstrators ran into a truck called the "war machine" and came out the other end with makeup looking like blood and burns; one group of marchers held an oversized Uncle Sam covered with simulated dead children. The Chicago police along the route were under instructions to show restraint. The protesters were told by march organizers not to taunt police, and not to carry "defensive equipment," such as helmets or gas masks.[19]

The opposition to the machine that had shown surprising strength in the March 1969 aldermanic elections continued to increase throughout 1970. Adlai Stevenson III was becoming a central figure in this reform movement. Like his father, the younger Stevenson had a complex relationship with Daley and the Democratic machine. He had finished first in the statewide at-large election of 177 state legislators in 1964, and two years later bucked the Republican tide and was elected state treasurer with Daley's backing. In 1968, when Governor Kerner was made a federal judge, Stevenson had made a blunt pitch to machine slate-makers for the party's gubernatorial nomination. But Daley had preferred Lieutenant Governor Sam Shapiro, who had worked closely with him on state legislation. Stevenson then expressed interest in challenging Senator Everett Dirksen in

1968, but Daley slated state attorney general William Clark instead. After these rejections, Stevenson began to speak out publicly against Daley, criticizing his handling of protesters during the Democratic convention and later accusing him of maintaining a "feudal" political system of "patronage and fear." An informal group called the Committee on Illinois Government — which included Stevenson, Singer, and Abner Mikva — had begun meeting in Stevenson's Near North Side home. The committee planned an enormous picnic in September 1969, in Libertyville, Illinois, at the Stevenson farm. Organizers invited 15,000 reform-minded people and planned to offer up a manifesto called the Libertyville Proclamation for signatures. A key proviso of the proclamation was that the Democratic Party should "end reliance upon the purchased loyalties of patronage."[20]

Daley decided at the last minute to surprise the reformers by showing up at Libertyville. He arrived in a limousine with Congressman Dan Rostenkowski, Cook County Circuit Court clerk Matt Danaher, and state auditor Michael Howlett. Wearing his usual formal attire of a dark suit and tie, Daley stood out from the 8,000 progressives dressed for a country picnic. He took the stage and delivered a speech aimed shrewdly at his anti-machine audience. Daley spoke of his hard work for Stevenson's father, for Senator Paul Douglas, and for President Kennedy. And he called the Reverend Jesse Jackson and Adlai Stevenson III some of "the great leaders of our day." Before he was finished, Daley almost sounded as if he himself was joining the anti-machine ranks. "[W]e need the participation of people who are dedicated to decency in the government," he said. "And we cannot live in the past. I welcome the modernization of the Democratic Party." Stevenson threw away a prepared speech and spoke graciously of Daley.[21]

During his own speech, Senator George McGovern stopped to announce the news that Senator Everett Dirksen had died. McGovern launched into an impromptu eulogy, and Jesse Jackson led a choir in a rendition of "The Battle Hymn of the Republic" as everyone held hands. But it was Daley who attracted the attention of the seasoned politicians in the crowd. As de facto head of the Democratic Party, Daley would choose the Democrat who would run against the Republican-appointed interim senator who would fill Dirksen's seat. The man Daley decided to nominate was the picnic host. It was a brilliant act of co-optation, removing the leader of the state's fast-growing movement of independent Democrats. "On Daley's part, his performance was a master-stroke," wrote *Chicago Tribune* political editor George Tagge. "He assured himself of relative freedom from liberal harassment as he sets about his reelection plans for spring of '71." Like his father before him, the reform-minded Stevenson turned out to be entirely willing to enter into an alliance with Daley and the Chicago machine in order to get elected. "Stevenson said Daley was a feudal boss," the joke went, "but he didn't say he was a bad feudal boss."[22]

The Chicago 8 trial began in U.S. District Court in Chicago in September 1969. If Daley and Foran were hoping the proceedings would settle the score with the anti-war demonstrators, they were about to be bitterly disappointed. The trial quickly devolved into an absurdist piece of political theater. Chief defense counsel William Kunstler, who shared the Yippies' iconoclastic sensibility, moved for a mistrial because of the way in which the judge read the charges to the jury on the first day. "Your Honor sounded like Orson Welles reciting the Declaration of Independence," Kunstler protested. At various points in the trial, the defendants placed a Vietcong flag over the defense table, read comic books, and showed up in court dressed in judicial robes. When prosecutor Richard Schultz mentioned Abbie Hoffman in his opening statement, Hoffman blew the jurors a kiss.

To the defendants, the proceedings were a chance to put the system on trial. They were helped considerably by the presence of Judge Julius Hoffman, the crusty seventy-four-year-old Eisenhower appointee who was presiding. Hoffman did not even try to appear impartial in considering the arguments of Foran (whom he called "one of the finest prosecutors in the country") and Kunstler (the defendants' "mouthpiece," Hoffman called him). When the American Civil Liberties Union tried to file a friend-of-the-court brief, a common occurrence in federal court, Hoffman snapped, "I'm not running a school for civil rights." The trial reached its nadir when the irascible Hoffman ordered the outspoken Seale to sit in the courtroom gagged and handcuffed to a metal folding chair. The next day, demonstrators descended on the courthouse with "Free Bobby" signs. Seale was later unbound, but he continued to act out, at one point calling Hoffman "a pig and a fascist and a racist." Hoffman eventually sentenced Seale to four years in jail for contempt of court, turning the Chicago 8 into the Chicago 7.

Outside the courtroom, hundreds of members of the radical Weatherman faction of Students for a Democratic Society had descended on Chicago to hold a "days of rage" protest in sympathy with the Chicago 8 defendants. Organized into what they called the New Red Army, Weathermen wearing motorcycle helmets and armed with clubs attacked automobiles, beating up passengers seemingly at random. They hurled rocks through the windows of stores, banks, and government buildings. ("The first rock of the revolution went through a window of the Chicago Historical Society," the *New York Times* observed wryly.) The radicals focused much of their wrath on the Gold Coast along the lakefront, walking down elegant streets shouting "Ho, Ho, Ho Chi Minh," smashing the lobby windows of luxury apartment buildings, and in one case throwing a doorman into a hedge. Chicago police faced off against the Weathermen, wielding clubs and tear gas. The clashes were reminiscent of the convention week violence that was being recounted in federal court, but with a difference: few people believed that the police were overreacting in their response to the New Red Army. Over several days, more than 150 demonstrators were arrested, and three were shot by police. Daley eventually asked Governor Richard Ogilvie to send in the National guard, and 2,600 guardsmen were deployed to keep the peace.[23]

In between the outbursts, the prosecutors tried to make their case against the defendants. Several Chicago police officers testified that they observed the defendants during convention week, including one who claimed to have seen Rubin flip a lit cigarette at a policeman, and another who reported hearing Abbie Hoffman tell a group of demonstrators, "Tomorrow we're going to storm the Hilton." But the defendants put on their own evidence that it was the Chicago police who had caused the violence. Rennie Davis testified that he was struck 30 or 40 times near the Grant Park band shell by police yelling "Kill Davis, Kill Davis." After the beating, he said, "my tie was solid blood." He needed thirteen stitches to close his scalp wounds.[24]

The most eagerly awaited moment of the trial came on January 6,

1970, a blustery below-freezing day, when Daley himself showed up to testify. Many spectators had waited in line all night, camping out in sleeping bags, for a chance to see the defense lawyers try to tear the mayor apart. "You could feel the excitement in the courtroom the way you sense and see bubbles before water boils," a journalist on the scene observed. Daley looked to be in good spirits when he arrived with his entourage, eager to answer any questions the defense had for him. In his questioning, Kunstler tried to show that it was Daley who was the center of a conspiracy surrounding the convention week clashes. Wasn't William McFetridge, the superintendent of the Park District who denied the permits, the same man who nominated him for mayor in 1954? Hoffman sustained the prosecution's objection. Wasn't Judge Lynch, who denied permits to the protesters, Daley's former law partner? Another objection was sustained. And what, Kunstler asked, was Daley's relationship to Foran, the U.S. attorney who had started out as land acquisition counsel for urban renewal projects in the Chicago Corporation Counsel's office? "I think he's one of the greatest attorneys in the United States," Daley responded. Hoffman shielded Daley from most of the defense's line of inquiry, sustaining all seventy of the prosecution's objections. But Daley helped himself by remaining uncharacteristically cool throughout it all, even when Kunstler asked him, "Did you say to Senator Abraham Ribicoff, 'Fuck you, you Jew son of a bitch?'" In the end, Daley had little of substance to add to the case. The defense wanted badly to show that he and his "corrupt" political machine had conspired to crush the demonstrations, but Daley insisted under oath that he had never told anyone to deny permits to the protesters. "I gave Mr. Stahl the same instructions I gave any other department, certainly, to meet with them, to try to cooperate with them, and do everything they could to make sure that they would be given every courtesy and hospitality." Daley also insisted that he had not spoken with Judge Lynch about the permit litigation pending before him. To many observers, Daley's testimony was not credible, but by keeping his cool and sticking to his story, he came off well. At one point, Abbie Hoffman went up to Daley and, gesturing to invisible shotguns on his waist, said, "Why don't we just settle it right here? To hell with this law stuff." Daley simply laughed.[25]

When the trial finally ended, after four and one half months, the jury reached a compromise verdict. It found the defendants not guilty of conspiracy, but five of them — Dellinger, Hoffman, Rubin, Davis, and Hayden — guilty of crossing state lines with the intention of violating the statute. Each was given a five-year jail sentence and a $5,000 fine. Asked if he saw the verdict as a vindication of his actions during the Democratic National Convention, Daley responded tersely: "I look no place for vindication." It was just as well, because in the end the trial gave him none. The Chicago 7's convictions were all later reversed on appeal, in a decision that took Judge Hoffman to task for his "antagonistic" attitude toward the defense. After the trial was over, Hoffman cited the defendants for contempt during the trial and imposed hundreds of years of prison sentences on them for the alleged contempt. These rulings were also set aside on appeal, in another decision sharply critical of Hoffman.[26]

In the spring of 1969, trouble was quietly brewing between blacks and the police on the West Side. City Hall's attitude toward the black neighborhoods changed after the April 1968 riots: Daley and his staff were now always wondering when the next blowup would come. Much of their concern centered on the Black Panthers, who had founded an Illinois branch two months after King's assassination. At the center of the Chicago Black Panther movement was Fred Hampton. Hampton had become a local hero in 1967 when he led a protest in Maywood, a small suburb west of Chicago, against "whites only" swimming pools. Hampton had been president of the Youth Council of the Maywood NAACP until he joined Bobby Rush and several others in founding the local Black Panther group. Black leadership in Chicago, which had shifted from the accommodationist Dawson to the confrontational but peaceful Raby, entered a new phase with Hampton. He ran afoul of the law shortly after the founding of the Panther chapter for being part of a group of black youths who beat and robbed a Good Humor Ice Cream man, stealing his ice cream and distributing it in the ghetto "Robin Hood" style. Hampton, who claimed he was nowhere near the playground in question, told reporters: "I may be a pretty big mother, but I can't eat no seven hundred and ten ice cream bars." Though Hampton was convicted, he and his supporters claimed it was a political frame-up.[27]

The two black groups City Hall feared the most — the Black Pan-

thers and the Blackstone Rangers street gang — were themselves bitter rivals. The Daley administration and the FBI watched their
antagonism play out, hoping they would destroy each other in a
power struggle. Their enmity reached its high water mark when
a Panther was shot by a Ranger on the South Side. Afterward, Blackstone Rangers leader Jeff Fort met with Hampton, Rush, and other
Panthers to talk about merging the two groups. The negotiations
foundered, but an informal truce was arranged. As they had in other
parts of the country, Chicago's Black Panthers had begun to gain
some credibility in the mainstream black community by establishing
a health clinic and free breakfast program. As the free-meal program
expanded throughout the city, feeding hundreds of poor children,
mainly through churches, the Chicago police and the FBI grew
more intent on quashing them.

At 4:45 A.M. on the morning of December 4, 1969, the Chicago
police led a pre-dawn raid on a first-floor apartment at 2337 West
Monroe Street in the West Side ghetto, the home of Black Panther
Fred Hampton. The raiding party, fourteen heavily armed officers
under the direction of state's attorney Edward Hanrahan's office, had
ostensibly come to serve a search warrant for a cache of illegal weapons. But they arrived in the early hours of morning, when all the
lights in the apartment were off, and within moments gunfire broke
out. After eight solid minutes of shooting, two of the nine people
in the apartment were killed — Hampton and fellow Panther Mark
Clark — and another four had gunshot wounds. Two policemen were
also injured, neither seriously. According to the police, they arrived
at the apartment, announced their intention to search the premises,
and were met with gunshots. "There must have been six or seven of
them shooting," one policeman said. "Our men had no choice but to
return the fire." That afternoon, Hanrahan held a news conference at
which he displayed eighteen shotguns, rifles, and pistols, and a thousand rounds of ammunition that he said were confiscated from the
apartment during the raid. He commended the officers for their restraint and bravery under the circumstances.[28]

The Panthers immediately challenged Hanrahan's account, and
pronounced the raid a "planned murder." The occupants of the
apartment who survived the attack insisted that no shots had come
from inside, and that the police had fired without provocation. The

police blundered by failing to seal the apartment for the next thirteen days. This open access allowed Black Panther deputy defense minister Bobby Rush to conduct a tour for reporters in which he pointed to evidence that he said confirmed the Panthers' version of events. "A look at the holes in the walls would show anyone that all the shots were made by persons who entered the apartment and then went from room to room firing in an attempt to kill everyone there," he said.[29]

The Panthers were not alone in questioning the police account of the raid. While Hampton was eulogized before a crowd of more than five thousand, the Illinois Civil Liberties Union, the Afro-American Patrolmen's League, and three independent alderman demanded an investigation. And columnist Mike Royko openly mocked Hanrahan's assertion that the police had "miraculously" avoided injury in the melee. "Indeed, it does appear that miracles occurred," Royko wrote. "The Panthers' bullets must have dissolved in the air before they hit anybody or anything. Either that or the Panthers were shooting in the wrong direction — namely, at themselves." Hanrahan continued to insist that the police had done nothing wrong, and his office produced a twenty-eight-minute reenactment of his version of the raid — in the tradition of Daley's *What Trees Do They Plant?* — that ran on local television. But it was Hanrahan's misfortune that the Nixon administration was now in charge of the U.S. Justice Department, and it was eager to investigate big-city Democratic machines. On January 5, 1970, the Republican U.S. attorney impaneled a grand jury to consider the Black Panther deaths. Rather than allow the Republicans to conduct the only inquiry, Daley had Cook County Circuit Court judge Joseph Power, his onetime law partner, appoint Barnabas Sears, a former president of the Chicago Bar Association, as a special prosecutor to conduct an independent investigation.[30]

The city's 1970 Saint Patrick's Day parade was held three days early, to avoid conflicting with the upcoming primary day. Daley stood on the reviewing stand as 500,000 people thronged to State Street on March 14. The machine's candidates ran strongly in the congressional primary on March 17. In the most important race, Alderman Ralph Metcalfe, the machine's nominee to replace the retiring Bill Dawson, defeated anti-machine candidate Alderman A. A. "Sammy" Rayner. In another important congressional race, on the racially mixed Southwest Side, white machine candidate Morgan Murphy Jr. defeated civil rights activist Gus Savage. But not all of the news for the machine was good. Voter registration figures showed that Chicago was continuing to lose voters: enrollment in the city was 1,552,434, down from 1,656,445 in 1968 and 1,701,088 in 1966. Most of that decline was occurring because of the flight of the machine's base — white ethnic voters — to the suburbs. At the same time, enrollment in the Cook County suburbs had surpassed one million for the first time.[31]

The eighty-member Cook County Democratic Committee re-elected Daley as county chairman on March 31. Daley's machine supporters gave him a standing ovation for several minutes and made their usual efforts to outdo each other in praising the boss. Congressman Rostenkowski, chairman of the state's Democratic congressional delegation, called Daley "the greatest political phenomenon in the country." It was widely agreed that Daley would be running for reelection in 1971. In his remarks to the group, Daley let loose another classic Daleyism. Noting that the Democratic Party needed to have faith in itself, he reflected: "Today the real problem is the future." A few days later, the Chicago Civil Service Commission reported that while the city's population was declining, the number of temporary or patronage employees in the city had risen to a record 15,680, up from only 3,478 when Daley was elected in 1955.[32]

On May 15, 1970, a federal grand jury issued a 249-page report that was highly critical of the Black Panther raid, of the subsequent police department investigations, and of Hanrahan. Although the police had claimed that six or seven Panthers had fired at them, the grand jury found that only one of the 82 to 99 bullets recovered at the scene could be traced to the Panthers' weapons. The grand jury also found evidence of a law enforcement cover-up. The police firearms expert testified that he had initially lied about the results of ballistics tests to keep his job. And the coroner's office had misreported Hampton's wounds in a critical respect. It turned out that Hampton had actually been shot from above while lying in bed, circumstances that were inconsistent with the official account of a tense shoot-out with police. The city's investigation of the incident was "so seriously deficient that it suggests purposeful malfeasance," the grand jury reported. Daley pronounced himself "shocked" by the findings, and said the new report would be "given the most serious consideration."[33]

Two weeks later, Daley declined to reappoint a member of the Chicago school board. Jack Witkowsky had done a "fine job," Daley said, but he had decided to appoint a politically connected lawyer who had worked as an adviser to several elected officials because of his "better understanding of the legislature." It seemed clear that Daley's real motivation was to ensure that board president Frank Whiston would be reelected, foiling an attempt to replace him with the more liberal Warren Bacon. In the end, Bacon withdrew and Daley ally Whiston had no opposition. But Daley's dumping of Witkowsky was just another indication that he had been less than honest, during the Willis crisis, when he repeatedly claimed that he did not meddle in school politics.[34]

The summer of 1970 marked another milestone for the Loop: plans were unveiled to build the world's tallest building, Sears Tower, on South Wacker Drive. Daley's hard work encouraging companies to build in the Loop had been paying off handsomely. The previous year, 1969, had been the most successful yet — eight new buildings opened, adding 4.6 million square feet of office space. Daley had played a critical behind-the-scenes role in many of them. One of the recent gems was the First National Bank Building, a sixty-story granite skyscraper that opened in 1969 on Madison Street, between Dearborn and Clark streets. The bank held title to almost all the land it wanted to build on — everything except a small sliver of land owned by the city. The bank had tried for some time to purchase this remaining piece, but there seemed to be no way to accomplish this until Daley became mayor. When the bank approached him, Daley agreed to sell for just $77,500. "The deal was done quickly, over the phone, directly with the mayor," writes historian Ross Miller. "No committees, no reports, no lengthy deliberations, no glossy plans." The First National Bank Building quickly became a popular addition to Chicago's downtown. The granite skyscraper's design is distinctive — it tapers upward from a broad base — and its enormous sunken plaza along Monroe Street provides much-needed open space in the heart of the Loop.[35]

Daley's work on the Sears Tower called on more of his powers of persuasion. Daley knew that Sears, Roebuck and Company, the world's largest retailer and a Chicago institution, was considering building a massive new world headquarters in the suburbs. He made a personal appeal to the company to instead locate the $100 million building in the city. Sears was willing to consider a location just west of the Loop, but it ran into a problem: the two-block parcel it wanted to build on was divided by Quincy Street, which was owned by the city. Sears's chairman, Gordon Metcalf, met personally with Daley to discuss the situation. Daley believed that giving up a city street that dead-ended in the Chicago River was a small price to pay for having the tallest building in the world. He told Metcalf that there would be no problem. Corporation counsel Raymond Simon drew up a bill to sell the street to Sears at a modest price. The city also ended up assuming the cost of relocating water and sewer lines that lay under the street.[36]

On July 27, Daley and Metcalf held a joint press conference at the Sherman House to announce plans for the new Sears Tower. The massive tower, which would allow Sears to consolidate employees who were scattered in seven locations around the city, would soar 1,454 feet, making it 104 feet taller than the twin towers of New York's World Trade Center. Its 4.4 million square feet of interior space would make it second in capacity only to the Pentagon. "I want to thank Sears for the confidence they are showing in the future in planning and designing the building which will adorn the West Side," Daley told the press conference. In a time when older cities were being abandoned by big business — Detroit, for example, was reeling from Chrysler's decision to build a new 1,700-acre complex in a suburb seventeen miles north of the urban core — Daley was scoring one of Chicago's greatest triumphs.[37]

On the eve of the 1970 general election, Daley was particularly worried about the prospects of two candidates: county assessor candidate P. J. "Parky" Cullerton and state treasurer candidate Alan Dixon. Cullerton was being opposed by Benjamin Adamowski, who was, as usual, running an aggressive anti-machine campaign. Adamowski was charging that Cullerton routinely gave large tax breaks to developers and property owners who contributed to the Democratic machine. At a closed meeting of the Democratic Central Committee at the

Sherman House, Daley told the ward committeemen that electing the entire machine slate was important but that they should work particularly hard for Cullerton and Dixon. Daley was also counting on the magical name of Adlai Stevenson at the top of the ticket to help Democratic candidates statewide.[38]

On election day, November 4, Daley voted in his Bridgeport polling place, taking just under eight seconds to cast his ballot. Asked how he voted, Daley left no doubt that he had pulled the Democratic straight-ticket lever, which registers a vote for the whole Democratic slate at once. "I guess you could tell from the length of time I was in there," he told reporters with a smile. "That's the way I've been voting ever since I began." Stevenson ended up winning his U.S. Senate race by a landslide, taking nearly 60 percent of the vote against the Republican incumbent. Cullerton and Dixon also won handily. Daley waited until after the election to announce that he was submitting yet another record city budget. The new city spending, including raises of up to 10 percent for police and firemen, would require a property tax increase of 18 percent. Republicans noted that in the past ten years, Daley had raised the city's operating budget by 125 percent while the city's population had declined by 8 percent. "It's politics as usual," Republican alderman John Hoellen said. "The budget still has the evil of too much patronage."[39]

In December 1970, Daley ended the speculation that had overtaken the city and announced at a hastily arranged news conference that he would be running for a fifth term. He then went to the Sherman House where the ward committeemen — some sporting buttons reading "Daley is the one in '71"— officially slated him. It was yet another occasion for Daley to bask in the effusive praise of his machine followers. Claude Holman, City Council president pro tem, declared that lauding Daley was "a joy and a pleasure for a black man." Daley responded with his usual assertions that he was "fighting for the cause of the people" and that "no one walks through life alone." In what had become a campaign-time ritual, Daley earnestly declared that he dreamed of "a city in where there are no slums." In a concession to the growing strength of the black vote, the slate-makers named Joseph Bertrand, a black bank president, for city treasurer. He would, if elected, become the first black to hold a major office in city government.[40] To run against Daley, the Republicans nominated lawyer Richard Friedman, a former executive director of the Better Government Association. They were hoping that the reformist Friedman could assemble a coalition of Republicans and independents that would give Daley and the machine a strong challenge.[41]

The year ended with another racially charged fight over the school system. School board president Frank Whiston had died, and the board was evenly divided between supporters of Warren Bacon, a black executive with Inland Steel Company, and United Steelworkers of America executive John Carey. The board members closest to Daley were backing Carey. Blacks and liberals lobbied Daley to use his influence with the board to select the first black president for a school system that was by now 60 percent nonwhite. Bacon's supporters presented Daley with 50,000 petition signatures asking him to back Bacon, and a special appeal signed by such prominent Chicagoans as Professor Philip Hauser of the Hauser Report, developer Philip Klutznick, and Nancy Stevenson, the new senator's wife. But Daley made no commitments to Bacon, and when the vote came, Carey was elected. Bacon and his supporters were especially bitter that the board had decided to take the unprecedented step of voting by secret ballot — an indication, they believed, that the fix was in. "I am an object lesson of the powerlessness of the more than one million black people that reside in this city," Bacon said afterward. "We are the people who have given the majority votes in this city to the Daley administration, and I have never seen the black community more of one mind than it was on this issue, but we lost." A group of thirteen black aldermanic candidates held a press conference to denounce Daley for "his underhanded tactics in causing the defeat" of Bacon.[42]

Almost two years had passed since Judge Austin ordered the CHA to come up with public housing sites in white neighborhoods. The city appeared to be stalling until after the April 1971 mayoral election in order to avoid facing white backlash at the polls. But the plaintiffs continued to press the CHA to come into compliance, and Judge Austin took their side. After losing appeals all the way up to the Supreme Court, the CHA capitulated in early March and released a proposal for 1,746 units of low-rise public housing on 275 scattered sites. The city was formally complying with the law, but Daley declared that the court's order was "detrimental to all of the people of Chicago, and in my opinion these units should not be built." Daley was careful to couch his objections in a way that made it seem that he was not opposed to integration per se. He noted that the Nixon administration was resisting efforts to compel usually Republican suburbs to accept low- and moderate-income housing but at the same time it was "pursuing the exact opposite policy in the cities." It was wrong, Daley contended, for Chicago to have to bear the whole burden of integrated public housing. He also pointed out that Judge Austin's ruling would prevent the building of public housing in black neighborhoods "where this kind of housing is most needed and accepted." It was not just whites who wanted public housing in black areas, Daley said. "Some communities have requested this kind of low rise public housing, but under the court order their requests have been denied."[43]

The reaction to the CHA plan to build in white neighborhoods was immediate. Thomas Sutton, a suburban attorney leading the opposition inside the city, told a meeting of twenty-five homeowner associations that Judge Austin's orders would never be allowed to take effect. "If the construction really starts, we'll take action of some sort, and not letters or petitions," he said. "In the meantime, we'll put pressure on the aldermen to stop it. If they don't, we'll run them out of town on a rail." At the same time, individual neighborhoods were maneuvering to get themselves off the list. Alderman Hoellen, one of only two remaining council Republicans, contended that a site chosen by the CHA in his Northwest Side ward had already been selected by the YMCA for a building expansion, which he viewed as more important to the community. "I think [the CHA] got the ouija board out and tried to strew some of the devil's brew, and where it fell, that's where they put a public housing project," he said. But civil rights advocates supported the CHA proposal and urged that it be implemented quickly. "This is what Chicago has needed for a long time," Hyde Park alderman Despres said. "The city has to bring an end to the pattern of segregation and the ever-growing ghetto so every neighborhood has a chance to survive." A black newspaper columnist asked what happened to Daley's belief in law and order, noting that "Mayor Daley forgot to stress compliance with the law when he so forcefully denounced our federal court's ruling on public housing integration."[44]

Daley was eager to prevent the CHA proposal from injecting racial issues into the upcoming mayoral election. Friedman was already campaigning hard in black and independent wards, and public housing was an important part of his platform. As he had seen in the 1963 mayoral race, open housing questions had the potential to set the machine's black and white constituencies against each other. In his statement about the proposal, Daley strained to argue that the public housing dispute was not racial in nature. "Those who claim that public housing is solely an issue of race ignore the experience of communities, black and white, which have rejected public housing because of economic reasons," he said. "Many communities have and will accept low income families, black and white, where they will not accept public housing." But Friedman argued it was about race, and charged Daley with "race-baiting Chicagoans with the low-income housing question." Friedman tried to make an issue of Daley's attempt to put off the release of the sites until after the election — without himself coming out in favor of integrated public housing. Daley was "the one who picked the 275 low-income housing sites, along with Charlie Swibel, Chicago Housing Authority director, that he is now repudiating," Friedman charged. "He is lying to whites and blacks alike. He's fighting for time until the election is over with and if he wins then he is going to go ahead and okay those sites. He had the list of sites locked up in his desk drawer for over a year, but he didn't have the guts to tell the people in the neighborhoods targeted for the project." Friedman also contended that the federal Model Cities Program was withholding the release of $55 million in federal Model Cities grants for Chicago because the city did not have an acceptable housing plan. Still, Friedman was as eager as Daley to dodge the difficult questions. He said he would have to poll Chicago's citizens, both black and white, before deciding where he stood on the CHA proposal.[45]

Daley used the release of the CHA plan to continue to talk about a position on open housing he had promoted since the 1966 housing summit: that the suburbs should have to accept some of the burden. "Those who occupy public housing, through no fault of their own, require many local governmental services and the cost of providing them should not be borne disproportionately by the taxpayers of Chicago," he said. "The entire metropolitan area must share in the responsibility for providing housing for all income groups." Daley was clearly advocating public housing in the suburbs in an attempt to minimize the amount that ended up being built in Chicago's white neighborhoods. In making his case, however, he used an argument liberals would make years later: that poor blacks would be better off in the suburbs, where economic opportunities were greater. He cited a Harvard University study of Cook County estimating that between 1962 and 1968, 30,000 jobs would have been open to low income workers in the suburbs if housing had been available for them nearby. In fact, Daley was right. The suburbs were a better place for new public housing than white neighborhoods in the city, which were older, poorer, and closer to the ghetto, and therefore more likely to "tip." But the politically powerful Republican suburbs did not want any public housing, and as Daley pointed out, they had an ally in the Nixon administration.

Though he could not stop the federal courts from ordering the list of sites released before the election, Daley could bottle it up in the City Council. As protesters packed the galleries with signs like "Austin belongs in a home," the council voted 33–6 to send the siting proposal to the Rules Committee, which, one editorial page noted at the time, "doubles as a cemetery for legislation Daley doesn't want." The council had no further meetings scheduled before the mayoral election. The liberal Catholic Interracial Council called the City Council's decision to send the proposal to committee a racist act, but Daley was rid of the issue until after the election.[46]

Despite Friedman's energetic attempts to forge an anti-machine coalition, Daley seemed to be gliding to victory. It was an indication of the machine's continued strength that Daley and his running mates submitted 975,000 nominating signatures to get on the ballot — a remarkable two-thirds of all registered voters in the city.[47] Daley continued to emphasize the progress the city had made in new building and infrastructure during his time in office. In early January, he presided over the opening of the new McCormick Place, almost exactly four years after the first one burned down. "This is the 'I Will' spirit of Chicago," Daley said, invoking the city motto. As he did in every election, Daley reached out to the machine's core interest groups — the ward organizations, the ethnic groups, and organized labor. A labor dinner at the new McCormick Place attracted 10,158 union members, each of whom paid $15 to eat filet mignon with Daley. The dinner's sponsors boasted that it was the largest dinner ever held in a single room. Daley made his entrance, walking down a red carpet, preceded by the Shannon Rovers and accompanied by William Lee, president of the Chicago AFL-CIO. As Daley walked through the hall, each row of tables burst into a wave of applause. Lee introduced Daley as "the greatest mayor in the greatest city of America." After a full minute of applause, Daley pledged his support to labor, calling for less welfare and more employment. "It appears to me," he said as he looked out over 125 yards of tables, "that there is no better way to rescue able-bodied, employable but unemployed men from their present eroding idleness, which slowly kills morale and initiative, destroys the spirit and affects the offspring, than to give meaningful work at decent wages."[48]

In this election, like every past one, Daley used Chicago's Saint Patrick's Day parade as his own personal campaign rally. He marched up front with men sporting huge white buttons with a green shamrock and "Daley '71" written on them. The day after the parade, Daley addressed 1,100 precinct captains at the Sherman House, telling them that on April 6 he expected them to help him obtain "the greatest majority ever cast." A sign on the wall read: "Work, Work, Work." It was apparent this time, however, that the usually indefatigable campaigner was starting to slow down. Daley turned most of the actual campaigning over to machine surrogates, not making the rounds of the ward rallies the way he had in his past races. In the final days of the campaign, while Friedman set out on a forty-hour last-minute sprint for votes, Daley confined his activities to one rally held by the Women's Auxiliary of the South Side 6th Ward Regular Democratic Organization.[49]

Within an hour of the polls closing on election night, Daley had enough reports from his ward committeemen to know that he had won the race handily. The sixty-eight-year-old Daley ambled out to the Old Chicago Room of the Sherman House a few hours later to tell the crowd of his victory. Daley's margin was impressive: he had 735,787 votes to Friedman's 318,059, or 70 percent of the vote. He carried forty-eight of the city's fifty wards, losing only two liberal white wards — the 5th Ward, containing University of Chicago–Hyde Park, and the 43rd Ward along the lakefront on the North Side. Once again, he had managed to hold on to the support of both blacks and anti-integrationist whites. Judge Austin's ruling, in the end, probably helped Daley with white voters by reminding them that they needed him in office, because he could be trusted to continue to hold the line on public housing. At the same time, Daley ran relatively well among black voters. Friedman was hurt among blacks by his affiliation with the Republican Party, and by his unwillingness to come out strongly for integration. But he insisted that the machine's grip on the black wards was to blame for his poor showing. "He had the black vote in his hip pocket," Friedman said of Daley. "He gave out morsels — jobs and the like — and precinct captains put out the word that welfare checks would be stopped if voters voted for me. I had a lot of black friends who were beholden to Daley and I did not expect them to support me."[50]

Daley's victory margin was, of course, inflated by the machine's usual vote theft and other irregularities. In the 29th Ward, a black "plantation ward" presided over by white committeeman Bernard Neistein — who lived outside the ward in a lakefront high-rise — Friedman poll watchers and election judges were not allowed into seven voting precincts. When a twenty-seven-year-old Friedman campaign worker showed up in the 29th Precinct of the 29th Ward to install a Republican poll watcher, they were both arrested and charged with disorderly conduct. In the 49th Precinct, Dolores Bosley was allowed to remain but she could not stop Democratic judges from walking into the voting booth with voters and pulling the lever for them. "I kept telling them this was illegal, but they paid no attention to me," she said afterward. In the 5th Precinct, a Democratic worker attacked a *Chicago Daily News* photographer who tried to photograph the voting. And when a *Chicago Sun-Times* reporter with poll-watcher credentials tried to examine a voting machine in the 24th Ward, the Democratic precinct captain shoved him against a wall. When the reporter pointed out that he was allowed by law to check the machine, the precinct captain responded "You don't come out here to get no law" and ejected him from the polling place. An investigation by the attorney general would later reveal that 272 votes had been cast in the precinct, although only 259 voters had requested ballots. Daley would have won without these improprieties, but the machine continued to resort to vote theft even in elections that were not close.[51]

Friedman's attempt to put together an anti-machine majority — cobbled together from reform Democrats, Republicans, and blacks — had failed dismally. Many blacks remained loyal to the machine because they regarded the small favors their precinct captains handed out as better than nothing — which is to say, better than the reformers were offering. Many were also skeptical of white reformers on questions of race. "Chicago blacks are all too familiar with reform candidates," wrote black columnist Vernon Jarrett, who noted that blacks had suffered when Mayor Ed Kelly was ousted in favor of racially insensitive reformer Martin Kennelly. But there were nevertheless signs that the machine's hold on black voters was beginning to erode. Voter turnout was light — the lowest in a mayoral election since 1935. The drop-off in black wards was particularly sharp. In the 2nd Ward, home of the Robert Taylor Homes and the heart of the old Dawson submachine, the Democratic vote plunged 21 percent from the last mayoral election, in 1967. As he had been doing for the last eight years, Daley made up for these lost black votes by picking up more votes in white wards on the Northwest and Southwest sides, where homeowners had decided that Daley was their best hope of keeping public housing out of their neighborhoods. Many of these voters were Republicans who claimed they were casting their first Democratic votes ever for Daley.[52]

In an uncanny bit of timing, it was just after the April mayoral election — when the political risks to the machine were least — that Daley's special state investigation of the Black Panther raid was ready to announce its findings. Sears told reporters he might have a story for them later in the day. But Judge Power, who had oversight of the grand jury, ordered Sears not to say anything, and the announcement was put off. Hanrahan went to the City Council chamber where Daley was presiding, and the two men had a private talk. When a reporter asked about the conversation, Daley insisted Hanrahan had just stopped by to say hello. Asked whether they had discussed the grand jury, Daley scowled and asked, "What grand jury?" Rumors spread that the grand jury had wanted to indict Hanrahan, but that Judge Power had stopped it from doing so. What was clear was that Judge Power had turned against Sears, the special prosecutor he himself had chosen, and had even appointed a "friend of the court" to start investigating the conduct of the special prosecutor. It was hard to avoid the conclusion that a fix was on, and that the machine was stepping in to protect Hanrahan. "Judge Power's excessive activities on Mr. Hanrahan's behalf serve no public purpose other than to remind everyone that both he and Mr. Hanrahan are close friends of Mayor Daley and leading figures in the Democratic machine," the *Chicago Tribune* noted in an editorial. The indictment of Hanrahan that did not come earlier finally came in August. Hanrahan and thirteen other law enforcement officials were charged with conspiring to obstruct justice by engaging in a police cover-up and interfering with the defenses of the seven surviving Panthers who were charged with attempted murder. The Chicago Bar Association suggested Hanrahan take a leave of absence or resign to defend himself, but Hanrahan dug in his heels. Daley once again blamed the bind he found himself in on the press. "We've got to stop this doctrine of guilt by association and accusation without proof," he said. "I hope this thing will be tried on the evidence and not through the news media."[53]

But blaming the media did not get Daley out of his political bind. Hanrahan was now a deeply divisive figure — reviled by many blacks, but still popular in the white ethnic wards. Daley could not afford to lose the state's attorney's office — Adamowski had shown just how effective the position could be for launching a prosecutorial war on the machine. To win the race, Daley would need the votes of both white ethnics and blacks. He initially reslated Hanrahan, hoping that the uproar would die down. But within weeks, under pressure from blacks and white liberals, Daley dumped Hanrahan and slated Raymond Berg, chief judge of Traffic Court. Berg, who was not much involved in politics, was a "blue ribbon" choice, designed to put the controversy over Hanrahan and the Panther raid to rest. But Hanrahan had other ideas: he promptly announced that he was running for reelection anyway. Daley's support for Berg was lukewarm. He allowed most of the machine's white ward committeemen to line up behind Hanrahan, who remained popular with the machine's white ethnic base. Daley's handling of the state's attorney race lost the machine support among black voters: many resented that Hanrahan had been reslated, even briefly, and some suspected Daley was still quietly on his side. The Panther killings, and the machine's response to them, were for some black voters a political turning point. As Bobby Rush explained with only mild overstatement: "The legacy of Fred's murder was that the black community totally and completely broke the chains that bound them to the Democratic Machine."[54]

During the summer of 1971, Daley's behavior seemed to be turning erratic and peculiar. His health and vigor were in decline, and he was becoming more withdrawn. Unlike his early years in office when reporters gathered at his desk for daily press conferences, Daley was now meeting with the City Hall press corps only infrequently. And an uncharacteristic bitterness was creeping into his public statements. When his proposal for a $55 million lakefront stadium drew criticism from environmentalists and others, Daley lashed out. He decried the "polluted and twisted minds" of his critics, and said to reporters covering the story: "It is the nature of guys like yourselves that ruins everything. You great geniuses."[55] In Milwaukee for a meeting of the Conference of Mayors, Daley announced that he intended to nominate Milwaukee mayor Henry Meier for vice president of the United States in 1972. No one was more astonished than Henry Meier, who called the announcement "news to me."[56]

Daley's most bizarre outburst came at a City Council meeting in July. First-term alderman Dick Simpson of the lakefront 44th Ward, a University of Illinois–Chicago political science professor and Singer ally, assailed Daley's naming of Thomas Keane Jr., son of Alderman Tom Keane, to the city's Board of Zoning Appeals. "We must end nepotism," Simpson said. "There has to come a time when we say that city government is open to all the people." Simpson also objected that the younger Keane was an executive with Arthur Rubloff's real estate firm. "Charges will be made that this represents big business and politics," Simpson said. Asked by Daley who would make the charges, Simpson said, "My students." Machine aldermen lined up to defend Keane and Daley from Simpson's charges, and Daley read a treacly poem celebrating the father-son bond. The outcome was never in doubt: the Keane appointment was approved

45–2. Daley was nevertheless livid at being challenged. After stepping down from the podium and turning the gavel over to Alderman Claude Holman, the council's president pro tem, he unleashed a tirade at Simpson. "If you are a teacher, God help the students who are in your class," Daley said. "I hope the halls of all the great educational institutions will stop being places for agitation and hatred against this society. And talk about the young people! With their cynical smiles and their fakery and their polluted minds!" Singer recalls that during the tirade Daley was "purple." Daley's strangely vitriolic outburst was as hard to explain as it was frightening. Dr. Eric Oldberg, Daley's friend and physician, said, "This thing has been bottled up" in Daley since the 1968 Democratic convention.[57]

The increasingly thin-skinned Daley was soon the subject of another attack — the most withering of his career. *Chicago Daily News* columnist Mike Royko had long been one of Daley's fiercest detractors. Royko was a crusading populist who had been taking on Daley since 1964 for all of the usual reasons: that he was wrong on civil rights, too brutal at the Democratic convention, and too mired in corrupt politics. The criticism was not original, but Royko's words mattered in a way that attacks from Lakefront liberals and Republican reformers did not. Royko, the son of a Ukrainian tavern owner and a Polish housewife, was a certified Bungalow Belt white ethnic who spoke directly to the machine's political base. He also had a way of lacing his barbs with caustic humor. In a 1967 column about corruption in Daley's Chicago, Royko suggested changing the motto on the city seal from *Urbs in Horto* (City in a Garden) to *Ubi Est Mea* (Where's Mine). A 1970 column on Chicago's high-rise public housing called Daley's role in kicking off construction at one site "a shovelful of bad thinking."

In the fall of 1970, Royko published *Boss,* a scathing portrait of Daley. The book, which attacked the mayor as "arrogant, crude, conniving, ruthless, suspicious, and intolerant," became an instant bestseller. What hurt the most, though, was that it was being snapped up in working-class white neighborhoods — the machine's political base. Royko reported in his column that Sis Daley had been spotted in a store near the Daley home turning a cardboard advertisement for the book facedown, turning books on the shelves around so the title did not show, and asking the store manager to stop selling the book.

In fact, *Boss* was pulled from the shelves of two hundred Chicago-area stores, but customer demand was so great that most restored it. Daley did not respond to Royko's attack, but Sis delivered a retort that no doubt spoke for both of them. "When there is an odious criticism of the mayor, I always consider the source," she said. "I read the book one evening after we'd retired to bed. Mind you, Royko never talked to any member of the family, so his information is shallow, secondhand, hogwash at best." Sis was not done with Royko. "He is a hater — a man who hates men in government, generally. The book is trash. I advised the mayor it wasn't worth his reading."[58]

Before 1972 ended, another federal investigation presented serious trouble. On December 15, former governor Otto Kerner, now a Federal Appeals Court judge, was indicted for bribery, conspiracy, and tax evasion. He was charged with arranging favorable horse-racing dates for a track in exchange for racetrack stock that he was permitted to buy far below its market value. Kerner was eventually convicted, and sentenced to three years in federal prison.[59] Kerner's indictment had been brought by a zealous young Republican U.S. attorney, James Thompson, who was appointed by Nixon and was working with Nixon attorney general John Mitchell to put the heat on the Democratic machine. If Thompson could bring down a sitting federal judge like Kerner, there would be nothing to stop him from going after Daley's allies in the machine, and even Daley himself. During the Kerner trial, it appeared that Thompson might indeed have been planning to go after Daley next. Thompson had a former Illinois Racing Board chairman testify that Daley had introduced him to Kerner in 1960 and "induced" him to lend $100,000 to Kerner's gubernatorial campaign. Daley insisted that he had done nothing wrong, and pointed out that, unlike Kerner, he had never received any racetrack stock. "I never have and I never will," Daley declared.[60]

The machine lost another federal case a few months later that would prove even more damaging. On April 19, 1971, the United States Supreme Court refused to disturb a Federal Appeals Court ruling that struck down a key component of the machine's patronage operations. The lower court had held that, other than policymakers and other high-level officers, city workers could not be dismissed based on their political affiliation. The suit had been brought by

Michael Shakman, a Hyde Park lawyer who was an independent candidate for delegate to the Illinois 1970 Constitutional Convention. Shakman lost his election to a machine candidate by just 623 votes out of 24,000 cast, and as he noted in his court papers, considerably more than 623 patronage employees lived in the district. Shakman charged that the patronage system was responsible for the fact that every Chicago mayor elected since 1931 had the backing of the Democratic machine, and that the current composition of the City Council was one Republican, three independent Democrats, and forty-six members of the regular Democratic machine. The Shakman case had started out before U.S. District Court Judge Abraham Lincoln Marovitz, through the same purportedly random process that had assigned the 1968 Democratic convention rally case to William Lynch. Marovitz had been friends with Daley since their days serving together in the Illinois legislature in the 1930s, and he maintained that he spoke with Daley by telephone almost every evening. Shakman had asked Marovitz to disqualify himself, but Marovitz refused. "It's an obvious fact of life," he said, "that men in high public positions know each other. I was and am a close friend of Mayor Richard J. Daley." Marovitz had initially dismissed Shakman's case quickly. But on appeal, the U.S. Court of Appeals for the 7th Circuit reversed that decision. Now that the Supreme Court had denied review, Marovitz would be forced to preside over the dismantling of the patronage system.

After more than a year of negotiations, Shakman and the city reached a settlement. The consent decree, which Daley signed in 1972, prohibited the firing of government workers on political grounds. It was a significant blow to the machine: without the threat that they would be fired, patronage workers would not feel the same pressure to deliver on election day. Still, the settlement did not entirely undo the patronage system, since it did not prohibit Daley from hiring government workers on political grounds. Daley was also adept at finding loopholes in any restrictions he agreed to. During the settlement discussions, he offered a resolution declaring it the "official policy" of the party to "condemn and oppose compulsory financial contributions by public employees, contractors or suppliers, to any individual or organization." But he explained to reporters: "This means no dues. But the key word is compulsory. Voluntary contributions can be accepted." It would take a second round of litigation, known as Shakman II, to outlaw the hiring of government workers on political grounds. That decision, which proved far more damaging to the machine, did not come until after Daley's death.[61]

The machine was also seeing erosion on another important front: the black wards that had long been a critical part of its electoral base. When Dawson stepped down in 1970, Daley had handed his congressional seat to Ralph Metcalfe. Metcalfe was a heroic figure in the black community, a onetime track star who had finished second to Jesse Owens in the 1936 Olympics. Metcalfe also had a perfect machine résumé. He began as a protégé of Dawson's, and won election as 3rd Ward alderman in 1955, when Daley was first elected mayor. In the late 1950s, when Daley crushed the Dawson submachine, Metcalfe had switched his loyalty to Daley. Metcalfe had been a member in good standing of Daley's "silent six," the compliant black aldermen who spoke little and uniformly supported him on civil rights issues. And he had negotiated for Daley with King in 1966, encouraging the civil rights leader to moderate his demands. Metcalfe won his congressional seat by running against Alderman A. A. "Sammy" Rayner, an independent who had earlier challenged Dawson for the same seat — on a platform of ending Dawson's "plantation–Uncle Tom politics"— and lost.

In the span of a year, Metcalfe went from being one of the machine's most subservient followers to one of its harshest critics. There were many factors involved in Metcalfe's break with the machine. As a congressman, he had a stronger political base than he had as an alderman, meaning there was less the machine could do to punish him if he went his own way. Metcalfe's political supporters and constituents were also becoming more ambivalent about the machine, and some of them — notably his own son, Ralph — were urging him to sever his ties. But the issue that drove a wedge between Metcalfe and Daley was the police, a source of great bitterness in the black community. As Renault Robinson, executive director of the Afro-American Patrolmen's League, explained: "You were as afraid of the police as you were of burglars and robbers because if you ran into a white police officer, he would rather kick your teeth in than help you." Metcalfe had long remained silent about police misconduct, but he became sensitized to the problem in March 1971 when Dr. Herbert

Odom, a South Side dentist and a friend, was stopped in his Cadillac one night because his license plate light was out. The police ticketed him, and the dentist and the officers got into an argument. Odom was taken away in handcuffs and jailed for several hours. A furious Metcalfe called Police Superintendent Conlisk and asked him to a meeting in the ward. Conlisk would not come.[62]

Then a second black dentist, Daniel Claiborne, ran into trouble with the police. Claiborne had suffered a stroke and was unconscious in his car, but the police assumed he was drunk and took him off to jail rather than getting him medical attention. After this second incident involving another of his leading constituents, Metcalfe stormed into Conlisk's office with a list of demands, including recruitment of more black officers and establishment of a citizens review board. Conlisk refused to meet with Metcalfe, and Daley declined an invitation to a meeting in the ward about police brutality, saying he had set up his own conference on the subject. Daley's refusal to come to his district to discuss the problem was the final straw. When Metcalfe broke with the machine, he broke completely, and quickly became one of its harshest critics. As he put it at a PUSH rally several years later, "It's never too late to be black."[63]

Metcalfe's political conversion was a milestone in Chicago politics. "No one ever broke away until Metcalfe did," independent 5th Ward alderman Leon Despres wrote in a memo discussing how the machine used its black elected officials. Black machine politicians traditionally held their offices as part of an implicit deal. In exchange for their power and perquisites, they had to follow the machine's line on racial issues, from housing segregation to police brutality. Metcalfe, the city's leading black political figure and heir to Congressman Dawson, had now declared that this long-standing arrangement was no longer satisfactory. Daley was furious at the betrayal, and was quick to retaliate against his wayward protégé. The city dispatched building inspectors to Metcalfe's 3rd Ward offices and cited him for code violations. His police guard was taken away, and Daley inflicted the oldest form of machine revenge: Metcalfe was stripped of his patronage, including ten summer Park District jobs he had been getting for decades. Three staff members working in his year-round ward athletic program — a program the machine had been especially proud of in an earlier day — were terminated.[64] Daley's retribution was not merely to even the score, but to send a message. "No alderman dared take Daley on for fear that he would punish them," William Singer said later. "The clearest case was Metcalfe."[65]

The March 1972 primary results held more bad news for Daley. Edward Hanrahan, whom Daley had removed from the ticket, had defeated Daley's choice, Raymond Berg. That meant that the next state's attorney — who had the power to prosecute malfeasance in city government — would be either a renegade Democrat whom Daley had formally dumped from the ticket or a Republican. Making matters worse, Daley's candidate for governor, Lieutenant Governor Paul Simon, had suffered an upset at the hands of Daniel Walker, the Chicago lawyer known for being the author of the Walker Report and popularizing the phrase "police riot." Walker had made his candidacy a referendum on the Chicago machine. "Across the nation the Democratic Party has been opening its doors, reforming its organization, modernizing its rules," Walker had declared. "But not in Illinois. The party here is still controlled by an antiquated machine dedicated to special privilege politics and performing a discredited function: the exchange of jobs for blocs of votes. The voters deserve better."[66]

But Daley's biggest grief arose from the presidential delegate election that was also on the ballot. Lost in the commotion over peace protests and police riots at the 1968 Democratic convention was a significant change in party policy. The delegates had adopted a new set of rules governing the selection of convention delegates. The McGovern Commission, as the Commission on Party Structure and Delegate Selection was known, had traveled around the country soliciting views about the party and its operations. Alderman Despres spoke for many of the witnesses that appeared before the commission when he condemned the local Democratic Party as an "autocratic, authoritarian organization" that "leads to shameful exploitation of the voter." What the McGovern Commission recommended, and the delegates adopted, was a plan to require that at the next convention blacks, women, Spanish-speakers, and people between the ages of eighteen and thirty had to be represented as delegate candidates in proportion to their population in each congressional district. The new rules also required that delegate selection be done in public, with the time and place of the sessions publicized in advance.[67]

Daley argued that the McGovern Rules had no validity under Illinois law. In the March 1972 primary, in which fifty-nine Chicago delegates were to be selected, the slate put up by the machine looked like a cross-section of the inner sanctum of the Sherman House on election night, heavy with older white men like Tom Keane and Matt Danaher. When Chicago's delegation fell short of the party's new equal-representation rules, independent alderman William Singer teamed up with the Reverend Jesse Jackson to question the validity of the slate. They held caucuses throughout the city, and elected their own slate of delegates in informal voice-vote elections, where voting was conducted over the heckling of machine representatives who had infiltrated the meetings. The Daley slate and the Singer-Jackson slate represented two extremes of the cultural chasm that had split the Democratic Party four years earlier. "They laughed at us because we wore suits and ties," said Alderman Edward Vrdolyak, a Daley delegate and one of the lawyers who represented the group before the Credentials Committee. "Some of them weren't even wearing shoes."[68]

Daley filed suit in Circuit Court seeking an injunction to prevent the seating of the Singer-Jackson group. Not surprisingly, given the machine's record in the local courts, Daley prevailed. But the Singer-Jackson group got the case moved to federal court, where they won. As the legal skirmishes continued, the matter moved toward the Convention Credentials Committee in Washington just ten days before the convention was to meet. Daley was confident he would prevail there. Asked if this party organ might rule against him, Daley replied: "You know they wouldn't do that to me." But in a sign of how much the party had changed in just four years, the Credentials Committee voted 71–61 to seat the Singer-Jackson slate, because the Daley slate had not complied with the delegate selection rules. The Daley camp was outraged that delegates duly elected at the ballot box were being replaced by delegates chosen by a handful of people voting in community rooms and church basements. "It is an insult to Chicago voters," said former Chicago Corporation counsel Raymond Simon, who was working for the Daley slate, "to tell them that their spokesmen at the convention are to be the people they voted to defeat at the primary March 21." Daley insisted that it was anti-Democratic. "How can they be told they must have so many delegates who are women, who are black, and who are Spanish-speaking?" he asked. "Where are the rights of the people to elect who they want as delegates?"[69]

The Democratic convention was about to begin in Miami, and rumor had it that Daley had traveled there to make a personal appeal to have his delegates seated. In fact, he had remained at his lake house in Grand Beach, Michigan, venturing out only for brief visits to Notre Dame Roman Catholic Church in Long Beach, Indiana. The Daley delegates settled into the Diplomat Hotel, still hoping a floor fight would lead to the expulsion of the Singer-Jackson contingent. Before the full convention voted, various compromises were floated, including seating both delegations and giving each of the 118 delegates half a vote. McGovern was eager for a compromise, but Daley would not accept phone calls or visits from the McGovern staff. "He needs us more than we need him," one Daley associate said of McGovern. When the full convention voted to seat the Singer-Jackson slate, by 1,486.05 to 1,371.55, Daley was furious. After McGovern got the nomination, Daley broke with tradition and failed to rally around his party's candidate. He did not make his usual congratulatory phone call. Washington senator Henry Jackson quoted Daley as saying the groups that had gotten McGovern the nomination were "destroying the Democratic party."[70]

The fall campaign in Chicago was conducted under a shadow: U.S. attorney James Thompson indicted forty people on September 16 on charges of vote fraud in the 1972 primary. Thompson's investigation, which found that up to 50 percent of the votes cast in some Chicago precincts were fraudulent, arose out of the vote-fraud series the *Chicago Tribune* had published earlier in the year. On the eve of the presidential election, the number of indictments went up to seventy-five. Among those charged were four Democratic precinct captains, fifteen Democratic election judges, and a high-ranking member of the 24th Ward Organization. Most of the defendants had worked in machine strongholds on the South and West sides. In many cases, ballot applications were so crudely forged, Thompson said, that they should have easily been caught by the Chicago Board of Elections. Thompson's office declared that Chicago's whole political system was permeated with fraud and that it could bring more than a thousand indictments "if we had the manpower and time." Before the investigation was over, there would be eighty-three indictments, and sixty-six people would be convicted or would plead guilty.[71]

McGovern and Daley eventually had a meeting — Daley insisted that it be one-on-one — to discuss the presidential race. McGovern sought the advice of his vice presidential running mate, Sargent Shriver, who knew Daley well. Shriver told McGovern not to focus on Vietnam and other policy issues, but instead to try to convince Daley that he was a good man, concerned about his family, about religion, and that he would be a political ally if he were elected. The meeting between McGovern and Daley did not go particularly well — McGovern talked too much about the war — but the two men eventually worked out a chilly alliance. Several Daley allies were named to the Democratic National Committee, and Daley signed on with the McGovern campaign. At a September 12 rally at the corner of State and Madison, Daley introduced McGovern as the "next president of the United States" and urged Chicagoans to support him. Perhaps more significant, earlier in the day Daley had brought McGovern to the Sherman House to meet with the Cook County Democratic Central Committee. "This has been an unusual election," Daley told the committeemen, many of whom had been locked out of the Miami convention by the McGovern forces. "But that's all behind us now," Daley said. "Today we're interested in electing all the ticket." McGovern carried Chicago by 171,928 votes, on his way to losing Illinois and forty-eight other states. McGovern's showing in Chicago was low for a Democratic presidential nominee, but it is hard to know how much of the fault lies with Daley and the machine. McGovern ran weakly across the country, and Nixon's campaign shrewdly targeted the white ethnic voters who made up the core constituency of the Chicago machine. "We delivered Chicago for George McGovern," Daley said afterward, "one of the few big cities which did." In late October, less than two weeks before election day, a judge dismissed all the charges against Hanrahan arising out of the Black Panther raid. But Hanrahan was rejected by Cook County voters, losing ten of the city's fourteen black wards in the process. Hanrahan's defeat left Daley with something he had worked for years to fend off: a Republican state's attorney. And the new governor of Illinois was Dan Walker, who had been elected after a campaign in which he walked 1,200 miles across the state, decrying machine corruption the whole way.[72]

If a Man Can't Put His Arms Around His Sons

Daley began 1973 on a wistful note, returning to Springfield to pass the torch to a new generation. Richard M. Daley, Daley's eldest son, had been elected to fill his old state senate seat the previous fall. Daley, Sis, and a brigade of other family members accompanied thirty-year-old Richie to Springfield on the first day of the legislative session. "I was here this morning 34 years ago," Daley reflected. "It brings back many memories." The passage of time seemed to be sapping Daley of his relentlessly optimistic approach to Chicago's problems. At a February appearance at the University of Chicago, he abandoned his frequently repeated refrain that the end of slum housing in Chicago was imminent. "All of us want to end poverty, to eliminate slums, to provide every child with the best possible education, to have decent housing for every family," he declared. But these would not be easy goals to achieve. "Eliminating slums involves people," Daley explained. "And it's obvious that working out problems of individuals is more taxing and time-consuming than working with the physical environment. . . . In the human situation we have very little control and the problem changes constantly."[1]

Daley also found himself in the middle of a new scandal, one that hit closer to home than any so far. *Chicago Today* reported, in its February 8 edition, that more than $2.9 million in city insurance premiums had been switched to the Evanston insurance firm of Heil & Heil shortly after Daley's son John joined it. These particular premiums had a long political pedigree: Daley had previously given them to Joe Gill, his predecessor as head of the Cook County Democratic Central Committee, as a reward for supporting him for boss. Two months after Gill died, which happened to be just around the time John Daley got his insurance license and signed on with the firm, the premiums ended up with Heil & Heil. David Stahl, who was then city controller, recalls that Daley called him into his office one day while John, who was working as a summer volunteer for a city welfare program, was present. Daley informed Stahl that John had accepted a job with Heil & Heil, and that the city business should follow him. Several months later, a reporter asked Stahl if Daley had been behind the transfer. Stahl did not respond, but raised the matter with Daley. Thinking that Daley had given him permission to tell the truth, Stahl spoke openly about Daley's role in the transfer after the news broke in *Chicago Today*. As it turned out, Stahl had misunderstood what the mayor wanted him to do; he ended up confirming that Daley had ordered the insurance business moved at the same time the mayor was denying it.[2]

More disclosures about Daley's sons followed in the next few days. Next in the limelight were Richard and Michael, both lawyers, who were criticized for benefiting from lucrative court appointments from several Circuit Court judges. In one case, a judge had named Richard Daley and one of his partners as trustees in a class-action suit against Montgomery Ward for which they received fees totaling $150,000. Judge Daniel Covelli, who had appointed the Daleys to eight cases in the past several years, said: "I don't know what the hell is wrong with appointing the Daley boys. I've found them to be the finest gentlemen I've ever met." The day the story broke, a furious Daley made his own views on the subject known at a meeting of the Cook County Democratic Committee. "If I can't help my sons then they can kiss my ass," Daley told his machine colleagues, who listened to this explosion in rapt attention. "I make no apologies to anyone. There are many men in this room whose fathers helped them, and they went on to become fine public officials." Daley then unleashed a line that became famous: "If a man can't put his arms around his sons, then what kind of a world are we living in?"[3]

Every day's newspapers seemed to bring more exposés of favoritism and conflict. Daley's response was, as always, to turn the criticism back on the media. When a reporter asked how much money John

Daley had received in commissions from Heil & Heil, the mayor snapped: "It will be disclosed at the proper time. And it will bring to a head some of the untrue statements and unfair statements made." When asked when the proper time might be, Daley moved for the door and said: "That's the end of this. No comment." More than ever, Daley had begun to see reporters in conspiratorial terms. "Don't cozy up to the press, but be dignified," he admonished a meeting of city officials. "They are trying to destroy me and the Democratic Party. They are not going to destroy me." One reform Daley did institute as a result of the Heil & Heil scandal was pushing out the excessively honest David Stahl. Stahl, one of the "whiz kids," had enjoyed a bright career and a good working relationship with Daley. But he soon left Chicago for a job with a Washington think tank. "This was a difficult time," recalled Stahl. "I was not welcome in his office. He did not shed a lot of tears when I came in to tell him I was resigning and moving to Washington." But larger reforms were elusive. North Side alderman Dick Simpson introduced a resolution that would have required Daley to give account for the "nepotism and conflict of interest" involving his sons. Not surprisingly, the City Council buried it.[4]

James Thompson was less forgiving of official corruption than the Chicago City Council. Thirty-six-year-old James Thompson, a six-foot six-inch native Chicagoan, taught criminal law at Northwestern Law School for five years before Nixon appointed him U.S. attorney on the recommendation of Senator Percy. Thompson had made a strong impression by sending Kerner, a respected former governor and federal judge, off to prison. He followed the Kerner case just a few months later by charging Cook County clerk Edward Barrett with accepting bribes to buy voting machines from a particular manufacturer. Barrett, who had been county clerk since 1955, was closer to Daley than Kerner had been, and he was more important to the machine: his position put him in charge of thousands of patronage jobs. Thompson was clearly looking for more machine targets: he had set up a public corruption unit in cooperation with the Internal Revenue Service called "CRIMP"— for Crime, Racketeering, Influence, Money and Politicians. In fact, it seemed increasingly clear that prosecutors at all levels were interested in the machine. When local police raided fifty-three suspected policy wheel locations around the city, Bernard Carey — the Republican state's attorney who had defeated Ed Hanrahan — said he believed Daley condoned policy wheels and knew that Democratic precinct captains played a large role in the policy racket. Daley dismissed Carey's charges as "political bunk."[5]

Amid the growing tide of scandal, Daley continued to promote downtown development. In May, he attended a ceremony marking the placement of the final 2,000-pound girder on the Sears Tower, which made it the largest tower in the world. Dignitaries at the event listened as a chorus of hard-hat electrical workers sang a song they had written especially for the occasion. It was a proud moment for the city, even though reviews of the Sears Tower itself were mixed: one critic would say its appearance was "not unlike staggered stacks of catalogs." Despite all of the new skyscrapers that had gone up in the Loop in recent years, Chicago's central business district still had work to do to upgrade its image. Daley alluded to the Loop's problems in a backhanded compliment he delivered to the annual meeting of the State Street Council at the Palmer House. "I'm not afraid to come down to the Loop to shop — with or without bodyguards," he told a less-than-amused audience of retailers and businessmen.[6]

The Central Area Committee, still concerned about the state of the Loop, hired the architectural firm Skidmore, Owings & Merrill for $400,000 to draft yet another plan for the city. Their lavishly illustrated 125-page plan, which was released in May 1973, bore the boosterish name Chicago 21, because it was intended to carry the city into the twenty-first century. Chicago 21 laid out a $15 billion blueprint for overhauling downtown Chicago, including new construction and an aggressive campaign to double the central area's population. Among its suggestions were building more family-sized apartments, constructing a playground on the banks of the Chicago River, and developing more mass-transit lines. In time, the plan envisioned an entirely new transit system containing moving sidewalks, gondola cars, and two levels of underground streets to separate cars and trucks from pedestrians. The main thrust of Chicago 21 was finding ways to make Chicago more attractive to middle-income and wealthy residents, who had been fleeing the city for the suburbs in large numbers. The suburban ring around Chicago added a million new residents during the 1960s, climbing from 2.6 million to 3.6 million. During the same period, Chicago's population declined from 3.6 million to 3.3 million. The city was also rapidly becoming blacker and poorer. It had gained 300,000 black residents in the 1960s, for a total of 1.1 million, while it lost 570,000 whites. Chicago began the 1960s with about one in ten residents on government assistance, and ended with nearly one in five.[7]

Community groups, and the public generally, were more sophisticated about the racial implications of urban planning than they had been in the 1950s when the CAC drafted its first downtown development plan. Critics complained that Chicago 21 was a thinly veiled attempt to move racial minorities farther from the Loop. This criticism had by now taken on a multicultural tone: Mexican-Americans joined blacks in arguing that they were being targeted by urban-renewal bulldozers. Residents of the Near Southwest Side Pilsen neighborhood, which had changed from being Czech, German, and Polish to Mexican, contended that the new development plans called for pushing poor Latinos out and replacing them with middle-class whites. "They have good reason to fear," said Douglas Shorieder, vice president of the Chicago chapter of the American Institute of Architects. "Most of the residents of these communities are recent Mexican-American immigrants and low-income blacks who couldn't afford to live in the communities if rents and taxes increase."[8]

Like the 1958 and 1967 plans, Chicago 21 was particularly concerned about the region south of the Loop, between downtown and the Black Belt. The developers were looking to build a large middle-class residential development that would serve as a racial barrier. The hope was that the new development would firm up the southern flank of the Loop, putting an island of middle-class housing between downtown office buildings and businesses and the Black Belt ghetto and public housing projects to the south. It was also intended to change the demographic mix of the residents and clientele of the central business district. Downtown business leaders were looking for more middle-class customers and also, they admitted candidly, a greater percentage of whites. The Loop businessmen were troubled by the current racial mix of downtown after-hours retailing, the *Chicago Tribune* reported in 1972, because "many whites [particularly suburbanites] stay away — not essentially because of prejudice, but uneasiness."[9]

There was a precedent for using a new middle-class housing development as a barrier between affluent areas and the ghetto. In the late 1950s, residents of two wealthy North Side neighborhoods, Lincoln Park and the Gold Coast, were worried the Near North Side ghetto would spread toward them. In Lincoln Park, the fear was that blacks and Hispanics would move north over the traditional racial boundary of North Avenue, known at the time as the area's "Mason-Dixon line." Residents of the Gold Coast along the lakeshore were worried the ghetto would move east toward the lake. Daley declared a swath of poor housing on the Near North Side to be an urban-renewal area, known as the Clark-LaSalle Redevelopment Project, and invited bids for middle-class housing. The Chicago Land Clearance Commission spent $10 million, most of it federal money, to acquire and raze blocks of old buildings on the site. Competition for the land was fierce, with two hundred developers sounding out the commission about development rights. In the end, the rights to a ribbon of land a block wide and almost a half-mile long were awarded to Arthur Rubloff to build a large middle-class housing development. Rubloff's long, thin project, to be called Carl Sandburg Village, was unmistakably designed to insulate Lincoln Park and the Gold Coast. It would also help protect North Michigan Avenue, the burgeoning luxury retailing boulevard to the southeast. "That was Rubloff's argument, that we needed a massive infusion of middle-class housing," recalls Daley's human rights commissioner, Edward Marciniak, "and that we needed to make it large enough so it wouldn't be swamped." David Kennedy, chairman of the Continental Illinois National Bank and Trust Company of Chicago, provided $20 million in funding to start the project off. Carl Sandburg Village, which was developed between 1960 and 1975, worked exactly as planned. The sprawling development contained thousands of units of high-rise apartments and townhouses, occupied by middle-class and overwhelmingly white tenants. Sandburg's strip of middle-class housing separated the Gold Coast from the thousands of public housing tenants in Cabrini-Green a few blocks west. It also formed an anchor for the area south of North Avenue, preventing the black ghetto from spreading north into Lincoln Park.[10]

Chicago 21 proposed to do for the south end of the Loop what Carl Sandburg had done for the north end. By the early 1970s, as a result of declining railroad passenger traffic and the rise of interstate trucking, the railroad land Daley had tried to obtain for the University of Illinois campus was available. A group of downtown businessmen, led by Commonwealth Edison president Thomas Ayers and Continental Illinois National Bank & Trust Co. president John Perkins, united to form a corporation to build a "new town" on the railroad land south of the Loop. Daley and his commissioner of development and planning, Lew Hill, worked closely with the business community on the project. Private funds were used to purchase the land and construct the buildings, but the city agreed to pay to build new streets, schools, and sewers.[11]

Dearborn Park, the "suburb in the city" that resulted, was a great success. Its apartment towers and town houses were soon home to a community of thousands of middle-class professionals, both white and black. It was also successful in its role as a racial barrier: it separated the poor, black population at the north end of the State Street Corridor from downtown Chicago. Dearborn Park's design created what critics called a fortress effect. All of the buildings faced inward, and the project's parks were to be fenced off and limited to residents. The project was also planned with no north-south through streets — only streets running east and west. It appeared that the intention was to keep ghetto residents from driving up from the Black Belt. "We think the general thrust of Chicago 21 is to prevent the poor, the blacks, and brown people living in the inner ring around the Loop from 'taking over' the Loop," the Coalition of Central Area Communities, an organization of low-income residents, charged. But defenders of Dearborn Park say the purpose was more benign. "It was not racism . . . that drove the plan," says Lois Wille, a Chicago journalist who wrote a book about the development, "but an overriding conviction that the project would fail unless prospective residents felt safe living there."[12]

President Nixon flew into Chicago on a cold day in January 1974. Daley met him at O'Hare and escorted him downtown to his appearance before the Executives Club. The Shannon Rovers, the mayor's favorite musical group, greeted Nixon as he walked into the

Conrad Hilton. Daley had never failed to meet a president passing through Chicago, and he was not going to let the fact that Nixon's Justice Department was indicting his colleagues stop him from observing this protocol. But in other ways, Daley was changing his ways. He was becoming less agile and less willing to appear in public in unstructured settings. He was also getting increasingly nervous about security. He had guards posted at the front and rear of his home on South Lowe Avenue, installed new bulletproof windows in his mayoral limousine, and began to have a tail car follow him. Daley also put his office suite, where reporters once roamed and the public was once welcomed, off limits, with three uniformed policemen standing guard. And when he approached City Hall now, his guards used two-way radios to alert police in the lobby, who in turn prepared the elevator, making sure no stranger rode up with him.[13]

Daley's close associates were continuing to get caught up in Thompson's snare. In February 1974, an unlikely member of Daley's inner circle was indicted: Earl Bush, the mayor's bespectacled wordsmith. Bush, a former newspaper reporter, had not worked his way up the ranks of the machine, and did not appear to operate by its loose moral code. But the U.S. attorney's office discovered that he had quietly acquired an ownership interest in Dell Airport Advertising, the company that had held the city contract for advertising since 1962. Bush had recommended to a special city advisory committee that Dell receive the contract, without disclosing his financial stake in the company. Bush, who made $202,000 from Dell between 1963 and 1973, was fired by Daley after the news broke.[14]

Other Thompson indictments came in quick succession. In April, he indicted Tom Keane's law partner, 49th Ward alderman Paul Wigoda, for tax evasion. The charge against Wigoda arose out of a $50,000 payoff he allegedly accepted in return for zoning the ninety-two-acre Edgewater Golf Course in a way that increased its development value. Days later, Matt Danaher, one of Daley's closest allies and a longtime protégé, was indicted. Danaher was a Bridgeporter who had followed closely in Daley's footsteps. His mother had asked Daley to get her son a job in 1948, and the young man started out as Daley's driver. He went on to serve as Daley's administrative assistant, and then as his patronage aide, before being elected alderman in Daley's own 11th Ward. With Daley's backing, Danaher had moved up to clerk of the Cook County Circuit Court. Danaher's indictment stemmed from charges, first reported in the *Chicago Sun-Times,* that he had received more than $300,000 in payoffs from two Chicago builders in exchange for voting for zoning changes to clear the way to build a South Side subdivision. Word also leaked out that Danaher was being investigated by a federal grand jury because he had allegedly failed to pay for a $20,000 remodeling job on his house at 3504 South Lowe, a few doors down from the mayor.[15]

On May 2, Thompson indicted Tom Keane, the second most powerful man in Chicago government. Keane had once famously observed of his days in public life that "Daley wanted power, and I wanted to make money, and we both succeeded." Thompson investigated how Keane made his money, and ended up indicting him on seventeen counts of mail fraud and one count of conspiracy. Keane was charged with using his position in the City Council to purchase 218 parcels of tax-delinquent land going back to 1966 and then reselling it to city agencies like the Department of Urban Renewal and the CHA for a profit of 125 percent. Daley stood by his City Council floor leader. "I've known him for many years," Daley said. "He represents one of the finest families. I know his wife and his children. I'm shocked that anything like this could happen."[16]

Thompson would no doubt have been delighted to move on to Daley himself, but no indictment was forthcoming. His supporters said the reason was simple: no matter what went on around him, Daley was not personally corrupt. Stahl, who ran Daley's $60,000 contingency fund for four years, emphasizes that Daley was above reproach in his own financial dealings. "This was a totally honest man," Stahl insists. "He used it to send Sister so-and-so to Rome on the occasion of her 25th anniversary. He used it to fix the holes in the roof of St. Stanislaw's Catholic Church. It was like a little welfare fund. Not a penny went into his pocket." Daley also wanted City Hall to operate cleanly. Financial impropriety "was not part of the public trust we had," says Stahl. Daley may have presided over a system that was inherently corrupt. Jobs were given out on the basis of political work, not ability to perform, and workers were fired if they did not fulfill their political obligations. Work for the Democratic machine was routinely done on city time, and patronage employees were expected to kick back part of their salaries to their ward organizations. Votes were stolen, and decisions of government bodies on matters like zoning were for sale. But there is no evidence Daley ever gained financially from any of it.[17]

Thompson's indictments were not the only legal troubles facing Daley in early 1974. Reports were circulating that John Daley, twenty-seven, and William Daley, twenty-five had actually failed their 1971 insurance license tests, but that the exams had been altered to provide them with passing scores. Several state officials charged that the exams bore signs of multiple erasures, indicating that they had been tampered with. The Daleys had insisted that John and William knew nothing about the alleged wrongdoing, and that the charges were politically motivated. But the scandal would not go away. In a county grand jury investigation, Gordon Casper, a former state insurance examiner, testified that William Daley did not answer six essay questions on the exam and would have failed it if Robert Wills, another former examiner, had not completed it for him. William Daley's examination allegedly had answers written in two different colors of ink from two pens. Another witness testified that on one of the Daley tests the first 20 of the 120 multiple-choice questions were erased, and that in 19 of those 20 the answer was changed from incorrect to correct. Casper told the grand jury that Wills wrote the answers to the essay questions on William Daley's test paper at the kitchen counter of Casper's Springfield apartment. "Wills told me he was doing it because he wanted to do a favor for [Senate minority leader Cecil] Partee," Casper said. Then Wills spent about twenty minutes working on Daley's paper, Casper testified. Daley would later testify that he could not be certain whether the handwriting on the questionable answers was his or not. "I'm not an expert," he said. "I can't be sure." Casper, who was fired from his job as an insurance examiner, was hired by the Employee Service Division of the State Labor Department. Wills, who also lost his job, got a new job — and a pay raise — as a custodian in the State Archives, which was under the jurisdiction of secretary of state Michael Howlett. Rumor had it that Partee had arranged for Wills's new job, a possibility Partee himself did not entirely dismiss. "Whether I helped Wills get a job as a custodian is a gray area," Partee said. Daley continued to insist that the insurance-test flap was politically motivated.

"The idea apparently is if you can't get at the father, attack the sons," he said.[18]

There were still more charges swirling around the next Daley generation. Around the time the Daley sons were at the center of the insurance-test scandal, the newspapers were also reporting that a North Side home owned by Patricia Daley and her former husband, William Thompson, had not been properly appraised after improvements were made to it. And Daley son-in-law Dr. Robert Vanecko was called to testify before a grand jury investigating charges of vote fraud in the 11th Ward. The inquiry centered on absentee ballots cast on behalf of purportedly sick voters, accompanied by certificates signed by doctors. Some of the voters said they had not seen the doctors and did not vote in the elections in question.[19]

On top of everything else, Daley was now confronted with another police scandal. Police superintendent Conlisk had resigned the previous October after some of his men were convicted in an elaborate, and highly organized, scheme of shaking down tavern owners. The shakedowns reportedly netted more than $500,000 for the police participants. The latest scandal was part of a disturbing pattern of corruption in the department. Over the preceding three years, 86 policemen had been indicted for crimes and 407 fired, or forced to quit, for involvement with drugs and vice, and other improper activities. After Conlisk stepped down, Daley elevated deputy police superintendent James Rochford to take his place. In one of his first acts, Rochford ordered all top-ranking police officers to take lie-detector tests to determine if they had been involved in organized crime or corruption; of the 70 officers taking the test, seven failed entirely and nine failed one or more questions. And the police department had other troubles. In November 1973, the *Chicago Tribune* had reported on numerous cases of police brutality, including a teenager who lost an eye after being struck by a police officer. The series led to the indictment of four members of the force. In February 1974, it was revealed that the proportion of nonwhite police officers, which had never been high, had actually declined in recent years, even though the city's black and Hispanic population had been increasing. The Afro-American Patrolmen's League urged Daley to do something about the racial disparity, and eventually sought help from the federal government. After Daley resisted the efforts of the

Justice Department to address the problem through negotiation, the police department was drawn into multiple federal lawsuits.[20]

The signs that Daley's health was in decline were becoming harder to ignore. He was elected to a twelfth term as chairman of the Cook County Democratic Organization in April. None of the fifty ward and thirty township committeemen present at the La Salle Hotel voted against him, but two liberal suburban committeemen abstained. It was another impressive political victory, but those in attendance reported that Daley appeared "upset and perturbed." In a long, rambling acceptance speech, he went on about how the ousting of his delegates in 1972 had been "disgraceful" and charged that the Singer-Jackson slate of delegates had been selected in "telephone booths." Within days of Keane's indictment, Daley's condition declined more abruptly. He appeared in the City Council chamber on May 6, but after feeling dizzy left hastily for an appointment with his physician, Dr. Thomas Coogan. After a brief examination, Daley entered Presbyterian–Saint Luke's Hospital. City Hall's public relations campaign went into high gear. Dr. Eric Oldberg, president of the Chicago Board of Health and a family friend, announced that Daley was suffering from hypoglycemia. Sis, the seven Daley children, and several of their spouses, converged at the hospital. Reporters suspected that the mayor was in a serious condition, but Daley's new press secretary, Frank Sullivan, denied it. "This is a sign of the affection the kids feel for the mayor," he said by way of explaining the visits. Sullivan stuck by the hypoglycemia story for nearly a week until reporters found out that Daley had, indeed, experienced a mild stroke. The family had held the news so tightly that even Sullivan apparently had not known the truth. The stroke, it was revealed later, involved the left side of his brain and impaired sensory perception and speech. Daley celebrated his seventy-second birthday in the hospital. When he went home, after a ten-day hospital stay, he was greeted by well-wishers holding signs welcoming him back to Bridgeport. Onlookers were kept at a distance so they were unable to discern any impairment. Daley returned to the hospital on June 1 for surgery to unclog a partially blocked carotid artery and then headed to the family home in Grand Beach, Michigan, to recuperate.[21]

For the first time in two decades, Daley did not attend the Cook County Democratic Organization's annual dinner in May 1974.

More than 6,500 of the machine faithful gathered in ten ballrooms at the Conrad Hilton. The guests, who had paid $100 each, initially exchanged rumors about whether Daley would appear. But the question was settled when his son Richard M. Daley rose and delivered a standard speech about "unity and cooperation" in his father's place. Daley's incapacitation prompted a flurry of speculation about whether he would seek a sixth term. In his absence, local politicians conjectured about Daley's future, and their own. Jake Arvey, who had been eased out of influence by Daley, told reporters gathered at a reelection rally for Senator Adlai Stevenson III that Daley would not run again. But the Daley forces refuted the suggestions that the mayor's career was drawing to a close. Apparently with Daley's approval, Jane Byrne — the lace-curtain Irishwoman who had become a recent protégée — called a news conference to decry the "little men of greed" jockeying for power while the mayor recuperated. Byrne, whom Daley had appointed to be the city's first commissioner of the Department of Consumer Sales, Weights, and Measures, condemned such talk as the "ghoulishness of political vultures" and called for it to stop. Daley stayed in near-total seclusion in Grand Beach, Michigan, about ninety minutes from Bridgeport. The Daley home there, fenced in and dotted with "No Trespassing" signs, was obscured from public view. Daley's long absence from City Hall added to speculation that he would not seek reelection. Independent alderman William Singer, who had announced in October of 1973 that he would run for mayor, attracted enthusiasm and press coverage from those who thought he might be able to win if Daley did not run again. Blacks were also getting organized, looking for a candidate to run. The Reverend Jesse Jackson, president of Operation PUSH, announced a voter registration drive. Thompson, the bane of the Democratic machine, was also seen, at least by the media, as a potential Republican contender for City Hall.[22]

Most damaging of all to Daley were charges that undermined his image as being personally honest. On July 11, 1974, the *Chicago Sun-Times,* working with the Better Government Association, published a story titled "$200,000 Nest Egg — Mayor Daley's Secret Firm." The investigation revealed that Daley and his wife were owners of a real estate company, Elard Realty, with assets of more than $200,000. The secret company Elard, an abbreviation for "Eleanor and Richard," had been set up in 1957. In searching property records in Berrien County, Michigan, investigators discovered that in 1965, a year after Daley bought it, the Grand Beach home was transferred to the name of Elard. The property was valued between $70,000 and $80,000. Before long, reporters learned that Elard Realty also held several small plots in Chicago, including the mayor's 11th Ward Democratic headquarters, valued at about $100,000, a cash bank account of about $40,000, and securities valued at $31,000. Daley had always presented himself as a man who never got too rich for Bridgeport. "I'm tremendously wealthy because I have a fine family," he once said. "But financially speaking, I'm not a rich man. My salary is my major source of income." During nearly two decades in office, Daley had only disclosed his finances once, during his reelection race in 1971. Those reports, limited to the years 1966 to 1969, showed that his income was only slightly above his $35,000 salary. But the situation appeared to be more complicated. Daley had at least one other source of income, from his second job as head of the machine. "What some people didn't understand," explained David Stahl, "was that in addition to being paid $35,000 a year for being mayor, he was also paid for being chairman of the Cook County Central Democratic Committee. I don't know what [his salary] was, but that enabled him to live pretty well." Thompson subpoenaed the financial records of Elard Realty, and Daley's spokesman Sullivan refused to comment. He said Daley would answer questions at a news conference when he returned from his recuperation. The BGA added to the intrigue by disclosing that the president of Elard Realty was Peter Shannon, a longtime Daley friend and associate, who had received nearly $500,000 since 1972 for consulting on auditing work for the city. In the end, though, the Elard Realty flap went nowhere. Even the BGA, which called on Daley to explain his ties to the company, never alleged Daley had done anything illegal.[23]

While Daley was in Grand Beach in August, President Gerald Ford appeared in Chicago to address a Veterans of Foreign Wars convention. Daley did not meet with him, the first time in nineteen years Daley had not greeted a visiting president, and it led to more rumors that Daley's health was worse than was being reported. After seventeen weeks away from City Hall, Daley returned the day after Labor Day, and held one of the most heavily attended press conferences of his career. Reporters were given two handouts, one detailing the recent accomplishments of the administration, the other dealing with Elard Realty. The first question put to Daley, who was thinner and more subdued than before his illness, was whether he would run for a sixth term in 1975. "The doctor has said I should not try to work as hard as I did in the past and then see," replied Daley. "We'll try it and give you the answer later." On the subject of Elard Realty, Daley explained that on the urging of lawyers, he and his wife had created the company to safeguard their personal property from lawsuits brought against the city and, by extension, the mayor in his official capacity. There were no illegalities, he insisted. If there were, Thompson's office never found them, or at least did not bring an indictment based on them.[24]

On October 9, Daley appeared in federal court to testify at Earl Bush's trial. In his earlier deposition, he had denied any knowledge of Bush's connection to Dell Advertising. It turned out that Bush had filed a statement with the city clerk indicating his ownership of Dell, but had omitted this detail in the copy he filed with Daley's office. Daley praised Bush, but said he had insisted he leave City Hall when he found out about the arrangement. After his testimony, Daley slowly left the courtroom. He was greeted by reporters who gave him the bad news that Tom Keane had been convicted in his own trial. Daley's bodyguards escorted him down the elevators to an official car that was waiting to take him home to Bridgeport. The next day, Alderman Wigoda was found guilty of income tax evasion and then, three days later, on October 11, Earl Bush was found guilty. After the three convictions were in, Thompson said: "I think it's been an extraordinary week in Chicago." Though Daley was not involved in Keane's enterprises, the conviction of the number two man in his administration left him vulnerable to charges that he tolerated corruption. "Chicagoans have been asked for two decades to wink at the fix and shakedown on grounds that Chicago is the city that works," said Alderman Singer, who was gearing up for his mayoral run. Keane, Wigoda, and Bush were all sentenced to prison. The voters, however, were not inclined to blame Daley, for the scandals, or if they did, they did not regard them as important. The *Chicago Sun-Times* published a poll revealing that 75 percent of city voters still thought Daley was doing a good job.[25]

In early December, Daley traveled to Kansas City for the Democrats' midseason mini-convention. After his embarrassing exclusion from the 1972 convention, the national party had been actively reaching out to Daley. In August 1973, the party selected Chicago as the official kickoff city for its national telethon, a formal gesture indicating that Daley and Chicago were once again in the mainstream of the party. In Kansas City, party chairman Robert Strauss kissed him on the forehead on network television, and presidential hopeful Jimmy Carter hailed Daley as a "tremendous leader" whose stewardship had made Chicago "the best managed and governed city in the nation." Back in Chicago, Daley announced to a luncheon of Chicago ward committeemen and Democratic officeholders that he would run for reelection to a sixth term. For the first time in his career, it was not a forgone conclusion. With his ill health, many politically active Chicagoans were convinced Daley would step down.[26]

Despite all of his political and health troubles, the Republicans once again had a hard time finding a candidate to run against Daley. In the end, the party announced it had selected Alderman John Hoellen, Daley's longtime foe and the lone Republican left on the fifty-member City Council. Hoellen, a reluctant candidate, did not sound especially sanguine about his prospects. "I'm the best available, but not the best," he said. As Christmas neared, on Sunday, December 15, Daley learned that his old friend Danaher had been found dead, of an apparent heart attack, in his room at the Ambassador West Hotel. Danaher, separated from his wife for six months, had been living in the hotel, waiting to go on trial the following month on corruption charges. Daley served as a pallbearer in Danaher's funeral.[27]

Daley began 1975 facing something he had never had seen in his twenty years as mayor: what appeared to be significant opposition in the Democratic primary. All three of his opponents were formidable candidates — hard-driving independent alderman Bill Singer, black state senator Richard Newhouse, and former prosecutor Ed Hanrahan, who was trying to stage a political comeback. Singer had been the first to enter the race, a full sixteen months before the election. Singer made the poor state of the city's 584 public schools a central part of his campaign and vowed to visit every one of them. He blamed Daley for Chicago's loss of 200,000 jobs, and vowed to start bringing jobs back to the city. Singer drew his heaviest support from the city's two most liberal areas, the affluent lakefront and Hyde Park. He had put together a strong grassroots organization of reformers, and had raised about $600,000. Singer also had the endorsement of Congressman Metcalfe, who had disappointed many voters when he decided not to run for mayor himself. "Daley's had 20 years to run this city," Metcalfe said at a South Side appearance with Singer. "My neighborhood looks like it's been hit by a bomb."[28]

Many blacks had hoped Metcalfe would run himself. Chicago's black community had come a long way from the days of Dawson and the "silent six." There was now a small but growing contingent of black independents, including South Side alderman Anna Langford and state senator Charles Chew. Months earlier, Metcalfe had taken some tentative steps toward running for mayor, and had even begun to raise money. When Metcalfe bowed out, Newhouse jumped in. Newhouse's chances were diminished considerably as the black community splintered among three candidates. Newhouse had the endorsement of Jesse Jackson and PUSH. Daley had the support of John Johnson of Johnson Publications and the *Chicago Defender*. And he was still able to call on his traditional Dawson-style supporters. A group of 250 black ministers, the Volunteer Ministers Committee for the Reelection of Mayor Richard J. Daley, called on their followers to turn out for Daley. Urging other ministers to support Daley, Bishop Louis Ford said, "We believe he has the spirit of God, it moves him and revenerates [sic] him daily." Singer had Metcalfe, and many of Metcalfe's followers. Without the support of Chicago's leading black media or its leading black congressman, Newhouse's candidacy would be an uphill struggle. Finally, there was Ed Hanrahan. The black community was united in its hatred of him. Hanrahan had shown in the state's attorney primary in 1972 that he still had a following among whites, although he was defeated two years later in a race for Congress. In the mayor's race, Hanrahan had a chance to appeal directly to the white-backlash vote. Throughout the campaign, Hanrahan attacked Daley for his "arrogance of total political power."[29]

It was clear during the course of the campaign that Daley was by now a shadow of his former self. He had grown increasingly out of touch with the city and with the times he was living in. Singer introduced an initiative at the City Council to provide incentives to businesses to locate in Chicago. "Daley went ballistic," Singer recalls. "Daley shouted at me, 'Alderman, we shouldn't have to pay anyone to come here. This is a wonderful city.'" But the race would not be decided on policy initiatives. Daley refused to appear on the same platform or in the same broadcast studio with his challengers. He limited his public appearances to uncontroversial statements in highly controlled settings. Several days before the primary election, 3,000 elderly voters were taken in city buses to the McCormick Place convention center to receive coffee, cookies, and Daley campaign paraphernalia. As he entered the vast room, the senior citizens sang a variation on "Honey" that went: "Loved you from the start, Daley; bless your little heart, Daley."[30]

The *Chicago Tribune* did not make an endorsement in the primary. The choice presented by the Democratic field, the paper said in an editorial, was "whether to stay about the rudderless galleon with rotting timbers or take to the raging seas in a 17-foot outboard." The editorial was a break from the *Tribune*'s years of support for the mayor. But Daley professed to be unconcerned about the defection. "That's for the *Tribune* to decide." he said. Both Singer and Newhouse expressed delight with the paper's position. "Now, everybody has deserted Richard Daley and has said that he is no longer fit to run the city," Singer said. "That's the most significant factor." In the final days, it was clear that the race had, as a practical matter, narrowed to Daley and Singer. Daley continued to believe in the power of his machine, but he relied more heavily than ever before on television. Singer imported media consultant David Garth, fresh from his successful work on New York governor Hugh Carey's campaign. Daley made Garth himself an issue, and used him to tar the East Coast–educated Singer. Daley warned of "carpetbaggers" with "striped pants and patent leather shoes." The advantages of incumbency extended even to the battle for the airwaves. Daley was able to air, without cost, his traditional half-hour "Mayor's Report," a sort of travelogue starring gleaming Chicago, days before the primary election.[31]

It was only on election day that it became clear how little of this really mattered. Daley won with 58 percent of the vote against

Singer's 29 percent, Newhouse's 8 percent, and Hanrahan's 5 percent. The mayor's surprisingly large victory margin showed that rank-and-file Chicagoans were not particularly concerned by the corruption in City Hall and, in fact, rallied to Daley. "They couldn't throw him out of office," Singer said later. "They couldn't vote against him." The results of the election illustrated that even a popular and well-funded reformer like Bill Singer could not attract the middle-class majorities necessary for a victory. The failures of both Singer and Newhouse also showed how difficult it was to crack the machine's grasp of the black wards. Most notable of all, it showed that Daley had once again managed to hold on to the black wards without making the kind of concessions to blacks that would hurt him — and had hurt him in 1963 — in the white wards. Daley carried all of the South Side and West Side black wards. In over thirty of the city's fifty wards, he received more than 80 percent of the vote.[32]

The general election was a mere formality. John Hoellen was so ambivalent about the race that he insisted on campaigning to retain his City Council seat at the same time. Hoellen, like so many Daley opponents before him, received virtually no support from his fellow Republicans. Daley carried all fifty wards and won the April 1 election with 78 percent of the vote. Hoellen's strategy of running for city council at the same time as he ran for mayor was also a failure. Daley cut off services to the ward, and a machine Democrat took the seat Hoellen had occupied for twenty-eight years. "You can't stop a Sherman tank with a flintlock rifle," Hoellen said philosophically. With Hoellen now out of the City Council, the fifty-member body had no Republicans at all.[33]

Daley was sworn in, for the sixth time, by his old friend Judge Marovitz. The two men looked gray and small in a City Hall crowd that was so big that many had to watch the ceremony on a television at a movie theater across the street. In May, for the first time in twenty years, Daley insisted that his birthday not be celebrated in City Hall. He was thinking less of himself these days and more of the next generation of Daleys. His desire to leave a political legacy to his sons appeared to play a role in his slating decision when John Kluczynski, Daley's own congressman from the Southwest Side, died of a heart attack in January 1975. Since the district was a machine stronghold, Daley's choice would be rubber-stamped in the May special election and head to Washington. Alderman Edward Burke of the 14th Ward, a politician in his thirties, was regarded as the front-runner for the nomination, particularly after Daley asked Burke to perform the very public act of serving as a pallbearer at Kluczynski's funeral. This was generally regarded as a symbol of anointment. "I had visions of myself sailing on the waters of the Potomac," recalled Burke. "As Daley was wont to do, he led me to believe that I was going to be the successor. He had a great way — when you went to him and entered your supplication, he said, 'Oh, you would be a wonderful congressman. Do you think that is the best thing for you and your family?'" Just before the slating, Burke heard that Daley had tapped John Fary, a Polish alderman, for the seat. The specula-tion was that Daley had made this decision to please Polish voters. Burke and others interpreted the decision differently. For Daley, fam-ily came before everything. "There was a sense that he didn't want to commit to making me a congressman and foreclosing the possibility that he could send one of his kids to Congress," Burke said. "It was clear that John Fary was a temporary seat warmer."[34]

Daley was also less able to shape the city than he had been earlier in his mayoralty. Since the mid-1960s, he had been promoting the Crosstown Expressway, a $1 billion road that would go north-south and then east-west to connect to the Dan Ryan Expressway. Daley declared that the Crosstown would be a "New Main Street for Chicago," the first highway that would improve rather than destroy the communities it ran through. The expressway's planners issued press releases contending that it would "add elegance" to the neigh-borhoods it crossed. But even by Daley's own figures, the 6.5-mile east-west stretch alone would displace 1,390 homes, 371 businesses, two schools, and 37 factories that employed 1,134 people. According to some estimates, the entire Crosstown would destroy almost 3,500 homes and displace more than 10,000 people. Residents of the middle- and working-class neighborhoods along the Crosstown's pro-posed routes came out strongly against the expressway, objecting that it would end up destroying their homes and neighborhoods. Blacks objected that planners had chosen to place the east-west segment at 75th Street rather than 59th Street, as was originally being consid-ered, because the new route would destroy black neighborhoods rather than white, Catholic ones. This grassroots opposition was helped considerably when Governor Daniel Walker added his voice in opposition to the Crosstown. The Crosstown would have meant considerable disruption, but not much more than the siting of the University of Illinois campus or Hyde Park urban renewal — both of which Daley had been able to force through despite considerable opposition. It was an indication of Daley's declining power that he could not make his dream of a Crosstown Expressway a reality. "It was the older Daley versus the younger Daley," says William Singer. "The younger Daley would have developed a coalition of good government and young Democrats in favor of the Crosstown. But old Daley was in charge."[35]

By the spring of 1975, word had begun to leak out about the activities of the Red Squad, the Chicago Police Department unit that had been keeping dossiers on an array of civic leaders, politicians, and journalists, particularly liberals and blacks. It turned out that the group had been spying on an incongruous group of people, from Theodore Hesburgh, president of Notre Dame University, television commentator Len O'Connor, and Alexander Polikoff, the lawyer who brought the *Gautreaux* case. Civil rights groups were another significant target. One memo from the Chicago Police Intelligence Division — labeled "Security Analysis Unit (Subversive)"— reported that the Afro-American Patrolmen's League was holding a benefit dinner honoring Hesburgh, Congressman Ralph Metcalfe, and special prosecutor Barnabas Sears. These documents confirmed some liberal and black groups' suspicions that Chicago was just a bit more like a totalitarian police state than most other American cities. Daley responded that the spying was regrettable, but he assured the targets that "if you don't do anything wrong, there's no need to worry."[36]

New information also came out about the shady dealings of CHA chairman Charles Swibel. When Swibel's private Marina City project was in trouble, it turned out, Continental Bank had taken title to the property, took over the development, and hired Swibel's management company for $79,000 a year to run it. Around the same time, Swibel was involved in switching a significant part of the $100 million the CHA handled annually to Continental Bank. Some of these funds were placed in non-interest-bearing accounts that cost taxpayers $44,000 a year. It also turned out that Swibel had switched the CHA's guards contract to Wells Fargo after the company installed and maintained a burglar alarm in his suburban Winnetka home without charging him. And Swibel was charged with directing his staff to admit his friends and relatives into elderly housing ahead of applicants on the waiting list. The Better Government Association, equating Swibel's actions with those of an "out-and-out crook," demanded that Daley remove him. "There is little hope of improving the housing authority if its chairman is more interested in using his office for financial benefit than in providing services for CHA tenants," the group declared.[37]

Daley moved at a slower pace, and lost some public battles, but he continued to use his power to hurt those who crossed him. In an old game of political chess, Daley tried to use reapportionment to increase the congressional seats for the machine and decrease the influence of the Republican suburbs. As part of this scheme, Daley eliminated the seat held by Congressman Abner Mikva, a liberal, Hyde Park independent who had endorsed Bill Singer in the 1975 election. Mikva's South Side district was redrawn to be over 90 percent black, forcing him north to Evanston. Mikva protested that the redistricting was being done as punishment for his differences with Daley. Daley did not disagree, calling Mikva "a partisan narrow-minded bigot who thinks he has a divine right to his congressional seat." Daley also had special plans for Congressman Ralph Metcalfe, who had so dramatically split with the machine. So far, Daley had merely inconvenienced Metcalfe by pulling back some of his patronage jobs. But with the new reapportionment plan, Daley could shave off some precincts and possibly put his seat at risk. Even worse, just as Daley had anointed Metcalfe over Dawson's objections, in December he slated Erwin France, also black and head of Chicago's Model Cities and anti-poverty agencies, to challenge Metcalfe in the March 1976 primary.[38]

As 1976 began, there at last appeared to be a final resolution to the years of litigation over integration of the police department, initiated in 1970 when the Afro-American Patrolmen's League charged the department with discriminating against blacks. In January 1976, Federal District Court Judge Prentice Marshall not only ordered the department to set up remedial racial quotas in its hiring but also reaffirmed the court's impoundment of $95 million in federal revenue-sharing funds until the police department ended its discriminatory practices. The money had been withheld since December 1974 when the city first lost the suit in federal court. Even after the court's 1974 ruling, Daley had continued to insist that the Chicago Police Department was among the most integrated in the country. Marshall disagreed, however, criticizing the city's resistance to the suit and emphasizing that the department was only 17 percent black and Hispanic when those minority groups represented 40 percent of the city.[39]

This order was unacceptable to Daley. Even though resisting the order hurt the city financially, acceding to it would alienate his political base of white city workers and their families. Indeed, one of the linchpins of white ethnic support for the machine was the virtual exclusion of blacks from certain city and county jobs, along with its defense of white ethnic neighborhoods. With the federal funding still impounded, in December Chicago was forced to borrow $55 million from local banks to pay its policemen. To Daley, it was worth it to take a stand against hiring quotas. In defending his actions, Daley spoke out against racial quotas in employment. "The quota system is totally un-American," Daley insisted. "We'll continue to fight this as long as we're around."

Daley sent off a letter to Washington in an attempt to get the impounded bonds released. He suggested that the federal money be made available for the city to spend on a "variety of other purposes, including social services." In the days of Lyndon Johnson, the White House would have jumped when Daley made his appeal. But the Republicans were less solicitous. Once again, failure to elect a Democratic president in 1968 was continuing to haunt him.[40]

The upcoming Illinois Democratic primary election in March was very important to Daley. It was widely viewed as a test of his hold on power — particularly races involving machine enemies like Metcalfe. Daley miscalculated the election disastrously. Drawing on his own popularity, as well as growing voter discontent with Daley's interference, Metcalfe handily beat Daley's congressional candidate, Earl France. Even in his race for committeeman, Metcalfe beat Daley's handpicked candidate, machine alderman Tyrone Kenner. He won

by only eleven votes, but this victory was significant because the machine virtually never lost a committeeman election. Conventional
wisdom held that it was mainly machine voters who bothered with
these party races — but not this time. Metcalfe had even overcome
the machine's ultimate punishment: that it had taken the patronage it
stripped him of and given it to Kenner. The outcome was a humilia-
tion for Daley, who had staked considerable political capital on ousting Metcalfe from office. "The people have spoken. They want to be
free," said Metcalfe. "People did not like the idea of Daley sending a
puppet to destroy another man."[41]

Metcalfe was not the only candidate Daley tried to force out of
office. He also had his sights on defeating the incumbent Democratic
governor, Dan Walker. Walker had ridden the 1972 wave of voter
anti-machine sentiment into office, but he had proven to be an inept
politician. He squabbled with Daley on minor issues and was unable
to deal with state legislators, even Democrats, most of whom were
more loyal to Daley than to him. But the last straw for Daley was a
bill to assist the perpetually financially troubled Chicago public
schools. Walker vetoed the bill, and in the fall of 1975, Daley made a
rare journey to Springfield to generate support for an override. He
stood in the well of the state senate chamber and made an emotional
appeal that so drained him that he immediately had to take a rest afterward. Daley lost on the long-shot override, but after that, relations
between the two men were irreparably damaged.[42]

Daley selected secretary of state Michael Howlett to challenge
Walker in the Democratic primary. Howlett, an affable Irishman, born
and raised on the West Side, had come up through the machine but
was never in Daley's inner circle. Nonetheless, he projected the right
image to Democratic primary voters for Daley's purposes — getting
Walker out of office. And Howlett knew what was required. At a
fund-raising dinner shortly before he announced his candidacy for
governor, Howlett stressed the theme of "loyalty" to the crowd of
3,500 people, repeating the word several times. Howlett was being
touted as "Mr. Clean," so when Republicans charged him with a conflict of interest over his role as a consultant to a steel firm, Daley was
furious. In characteristic style, he attacked the reporters, not the Republican leader who made the charge. "They get a few drinks, and
they get a little high and they write a lot of things that are not true,"

Daley said of the press. On election night, though, the machine prevailed, as it generally did in primary elections. Daley got his revenge
on Walker, as he watched him go down in defeat. The fact that Daley
had badly damaged the Democrats' prospects through this intramural
bloodletting — and made the hated James Thompson's election as
governor all but certain — was apparently of little consequence to
him.[43]

The issue of public housing — which had all but faded from view —
reappeared briefly in April 1976 when part of the *Gautreaux* case was
decided by the United States Supreme Court. Daley had, of course,
long insisted that public housing required a metropolitan solution
that would take in the suburbs as well as the city. The *Gautreaux*
plaintiffs agreed, and filed a separate lawsuit against the federal Department of Housing and Urban Development that sought just such
a metropolitan-area-wide remedy. Judge Austin at first rejected this
claim, but ultimately, on April 20, 1976, the U.S. Supreme Court
held that including the suburbs was appropriate. Daley hailed the decision, repeating his view that "the only way to do something about
housing is on a metropolitan basis." Three months later, HUD and
plaintiffs' lawyer Alexander Polikoff announced a joint plan to move
400 existing CHA tenants and people on the waiting list into private
apartments in integrated settings in Chicago and the suburbs, with
rents subsidized by the federal government. This demonstration program, administered by the Metropolitan Leadership Council for Open
Housing, yielded impressive results. In addition to increasing residential integration, studies of the families involved showed that they had
greater educational and employment success than those who remained behind in the ghetto. The demonstration program proved to
be the lawsuit's greatest legacy. In addition to improving the lives of
many of its participants, it has provided policymakers with strong
empirical evidence that racial and economic integration can make a
difference in the lives of inner-city blacks. Unfortunately, the program had space for only a small fraction of the tenants trapped in
Chicago public housing and desperate to get out. The lives of those
left behind in Daley's State Street Corridor remained as impoverished as ever. One researcher who interviewed blacks on the South
Side found that many were almost completely cut off from the rest

of the city. Many had never been to the Loop, and a surprising number had never even left their own neighborhoods.[44]

On the larger issue of new housing construction, Congressman
Pucinski's prediction — that the *Gautreaux* decision would spell the
end of new public housing in Chicago — turned out to be prophetic.
Gautreaux was not entirely to blame: the federal commitment to
funding public housing declined rapidly in the late 1960s and early
1970s. But with *Gautreaux*'s requirement that new construction
occur in white neighborhoods, the political will at the local level was
all but eviscerated. In the decade after Judge Austin's decision, the
CHA built only 117 units of new public housing. This later construction came in the form of "scattered-site" housing — units
spread across a wide geographical area — rather than the mammoth
projects of earlier days. But even after the court order, most of the
scattered-site housing ended up being built in poor, minority neighborhoods. Almost two-thirds of it was located in just ten wards, nine
of which were overwhelmingly minority. Almost none was built in
wealthy white neighborhoods like Lincoln Park or Beverly, or white
ethnic neighborhoods like Bridgeport.

A 1975 HUD investigation revealed one more part of Chicago
public housing that was segregated: housing for the elderly. Racial
segregation was achieved not by actively directing blacks and whites
to different projects, but by a clever procedure for making assignments. The CHA put the names of applicants for elderly housing on
a master list, and noted their preference for particular buildings. The
CHA permitted applicants to turn down buildings that came open
first, to wait for those they preferred. Because the wait list was substantially longer for the city's predominantly white projects, blacks
on the master list would generally accept one of the predominantly
black buildings when it came open. By the time a vacancy occurred
in a primarily white building, the applicants at the top of the wait list
would be almost exclusively white. HUD found that as a result of
these CHA rules, eleven buildings for the elderly in black neighborhoods on the South and West Sides had fewer than five white tenants. The situation in predominantly white elderly housing was the
reverse: twelve CHA buildings on the North Side, with between 116
and 450 apartments, had fewer than ten black residents each.[45]

*   *   *

Over the years, as the political landscape changed, Daley's blessing became less important to presidential candidates. Nevertheless, in 1976, Daley sought to be the kingmaker as presidential contenders paraded through Illinois. Jimmy Carter, the obscure former Georgia governor, had wooed Daley for years, beginning with personal expressions of concern through the summer of Daley's stroke. Carter even extended an invitation to visit Warm Springs, Georgia, to recuperate. Throughout the primary season, Carter called Daley to give him status reports on the campaign. And when he traveled to Chicago, Carter made a point of visiting Daley, not even minding that on one trip — after he had all but clinched the nomination — Daley was introducing him as "Jim Carter." This massaging aside, Daley was predisposed to Carter, since he remembered that Carter, as governor, had led his Georgia delegation in voting to seat Daley at Miami Beach in 1972.[46]

But on the eve of the March Illinois primary, Daley was still uncommitted. The presidential portion of the Illinois primary was composed of two unrelated parts, the election of delegates pledged to candidates and a nonbinding "beauty contest." Daley put together a slate of delegates pledged to Senator Adlai Stevenson, who had said that he would not run. By keeping these delegates uncommitted, Daley was trying to assure himself a broker's role at the convention. Jimmy Carter played along with Daley, only running Carter-pledged slates in the congressional districts outside the city.[47]

Still, Daley refused to make it easy for Carter. When Kennedy in-law and presidential candidate Sargent Shriver came through Chicago, Daley broke the rules and allowed only Shriver, and no other candidate, to address a meeting of the Cook County Democratic Committee. In the end, Carter shored up his status as front-runner by winning the nonbinding preference primary in Illinois with 48 percent of the vote. Alabama governor George Wallace was the next closest with 28 percent, followed by Shriver with 16 percent. Carter's delegate slates led outside the city, but in Chicago, Daley's Stevenson slates swept to victory.[48]

Daley played coy about his presidential preference for months, but he simply appeared old and out of touch. He did not take to the campaign trail over the summer. Instead, he remained more deeply rooted in Bridgeport, where his influence still seemed to matter.

Daley was elected to his thirteenth full term as chairman of the Cook County and Chicago Democratic parties. He turned seventy-four on May 15, and as he had the year before, remained at home. A contingent of parochial school children, including some of his grand-children, paraded along South Lowe Avenue in his honor.

Finally, on June 8, Daley told reporters at a morning news confer-ence that if Carter won the Ohio primary that day he should get the nomination. Carter "has fought every primary, and if he wins Ohio, he'll walk in under his own power," the mayor declared. The follow-ing day, after Carter's victory in the Buckeye State, Daley went fur-ther than his vague position of the day before. "Carter's victory in Ohio is the ball game," Daley said. "The man has such a strong amount of support throughout the country . . . there's no use in hes-itating now. I'll cast my vote for him and there will be a Carter vic-tory." He declared that he was releasing his slate of eighty-five delegates, technically committed to Stevenson, to Carter. But Daley's action was meaningless. Carter already had enough delegates.[49]

Daley attended the Democratic convention in New York City, where he was once again welcomed back into the party fold. A parade of well-wishers found him in the Illinois delegation, and many of them hastened to assure him that they had voted to seat him and his dele-gates in Miami four years earlier. "If all of these people had voted for me in Miami," he said in a caustic aside to his aide Jane Byrne, "why wasn't I seated?" Daley rebuffed the entreaties of the "Anybody But Carter" movement, which was casting about for some alternative to the frontrunner. Daley's unwillingness to join the anti-Carter cam-paign was no doubt largely pragmatic: it was clear by the time of the convention that Carter would get the nomination, with or without the Illinois delegation. But Daley also professed admiration, sincere or not, for the former Georgia governor. "He's got courage," Daley said. "I admire a man who's got courage. He started out months ago, entered into every contest in every state, and he won 'em and lost 'em, and by God, you have to admire a guy like that."[50]

Daley was not looking to repeat the contentiousness of the 1968 and 1972 conventions. "It's good to have one for a change that's all cut and dried," he said. When two twelve-year-old reporters for *Children's Express* asked him to comment about the violence at the

1968 convention, Daley responded, "Don't believe everything you hear, ha, ha, ha." The young journalists continued to press Daley, but he would not reply. "We've got so many things to do today it's more important than talking about ancient history," he said. Daley was not the biggest dinosaur at the convention: that distinction went to George Wallace. His last-gasp presidential candidacy having fizzled, Wallace gave a limp and almost inaudible speech from the rostrum before being wheeled out to the strains of "Alabamy Bound." But *Time* still referred to Daley as the "woolly mammoth of Democratic legend," saying that "he and everybody else knew the actuarial tables were about to expire on him."[51]

The convention had featured a whole new generation of new-style politicians, and the contrast with Daley was striking. It was made even more apparent that his generation was passing when, in August, his old friend and law partner Judge William Lynch died. The two men had grown apart in their later years. Two close Daley associates — Chicago Health Department head Dr. Eric Oldberg and former secretary of state and gubernatorial candidate Michael Howlett — said that Daley had dropped Lynch before he died. "I guess the Daleys just gave up on Lynch as a lost cause; they recognized now that he was an alcoholic," said Oldberg. "I think you could say that the Daleys decided Lynch had just outlived his usefulness." Howlett said that Daley was "a real cold potato" about Lynch's illness. Although Lynch had moved to Lakeshore Drive, his funeral was held back in Bridgeport. Daley, standing in white gloves outside Nativity of Our Lord Church, blinked tears as the casket passed by.[52]

In November, Daley suffered perhaps his worst general election setback ever. On election night, Carter called Daley to see how things stood. Daley told Carter that he was holding back one thousand Chicago precincts until he heard how things looked downstate. In the end, Daley delivered Chicago by only 425,000 votes — 50,000 votes less than for John Kennedy in 1960. Daley was unable to deliver the state for Carter. Illinois, which had gone with the winner in every presidential election since 1920, went for Ford. The presidential race went down to the wire, but it was evident early in the day that Howlett was doomed. He barely won the city and ended up losing the state to Daley's nemesis, U.S. attorney James Thompson, by over a million votes, the most lopsided gubernatorial victory in Illinois history. Thompson pronounced Mayor Daley a "wounded old lion"— bloodied but dangerous.[53]

The outcomes of the local races confirmed Daley's waning influence. Metcalfe, of course, retained his seat in Congress. Daley also failed to oust state's attorney Bernard Carey. And voters rejected Daley's friend Judge Joseph Power in his bid to be retained on the Circuit Court bench. Power had been criticized during the campaign for his alleged attempts, during the special grand jury investigation, to prevent the indictment of Ed Hanrahan. Power was asked if his relationship with Daley hurt him in his election bid. "It is certainly no insult to be described as a friend of the Mayor," Power replied. "He's a good Mayor and a good man, and I'm proud to be his friend." For the first time in memory, Daley did not appear in City Hall after an election: he went fishing in Florida instead. In the days after the machine's crushing defeat, there was open speculation that his days as a kingmaker had come to an end. The *Chicago Sun-Times,* in an editorial entitled "For Daley: The End Begins," captured the new mood in Chicago's political circles. "This is not a political obituary for Richard J. Daley or his machine," the paper declared. "You can wonder, however, if the organ notes are starting to be heard in the back of the chapel."[54]

On December 19, the Daley children and grandchildren converged at the house on Lowe Street for a Christmas celebration. This occasion was always held early so each family could be in its own home on Christmas Day itself. Father Gilbert Graham offered a home Mass and the mayor read one of the scripture selections. At the end of the ritual, Daley kissed each of his children and grandchildren. The next day, a Monday morning, Daley and Sis rose as usual, and were driven off in his official black Cadillac. In the Medill Room of the Bismarck, an old, storied hotel where machine politicians met and waited for votes to come in, the city's department heads gathered for the annual Christmas breakfast. Carols and Irish tunes played by a harpist from the Chicago Symphony wafted through the room as they waited for Daley to arrive at 8:30 and then, when he did, broke into "Danny Boy." After the eggnog and pleasantries, the group presented Daley with a gift, cleared with him in advance, of course — round-trip tickets to Ireland for Daley and Sis. He stood and offered an Irish wish: "From our home to your home we wish you one thing — good health, happiness, and a very Merry Christmas." It would later be revealed that the breakfast — what would be Daley's final meal — had been organized in the great Democratic machine tradition. It had been paid for by the Chicago taxpayers even though the city department heads who attended had been charged from $25 to $100 each to attend. It was never revealed where the extra money went.[55]

At the end of the breakfast, Daley walked through the biting wind to City Hall, where he tended briefly to paperwork at his desk. He was scheduled to see his physician, Dr. Thomas Coogan Jr., but wanted to make an appearance in Alderman Ed Vrdolyak's 10th Ward first. He set off in his limousine, heading for Mann Park, in Hegewisch, on the city's Southwest Side, where he would attend the opening of a new gym with Vrdolyak and Ed Kelly, 47th Ward committeeman and head of the Chicago Park District. Daley offered his standard fare: "This building is dedicated to the people of this great community. They're making Chicago a better city, because when you have a good neighborhood, you have a good city, and this is a good neighborhood." As the ceremonies drew to a close, Daley was given a basketball. He hunched down, and with an easy push with his right hand, the ball sailed through the basket. Vrdolyak and Kelly followed the mayor, but their shots missed. As the crowd started eating the hot dogs supplied by their alderman, Vrdolyak tried to persuade Daley to go to Phil Smidt's, a local restaurant famous for its perch. Daley declined, since he was due for his appointment in Coogan's office. He was escorted into the examination room for his scheduled electrocardiogram. Coogan did not like what he saw and started making arrangements for the mayor to be admitted to Northwestern University Hospital, a few blocks away.[56]

In the exam room, Daley called his son Michael, informed him that he was heading to the hospital, and asked Michael to call his mother. The staff in the hallway outside the room heard a crash. Coogan dashed over to Daley and then barked: "Call the emergency squad." Coogan began mouth-to-mouth resuscitation, and the paramedics began heart massage and administered drugs to start Daley's heartbeat. Physicians rushed into the crowded room. In the confusion of events, Sis Daley and several of the children waited for the mayor at Northwestern, but then rushed to Coogan's office. For an hour and a half, valiant efforts were made, but they all failed. The last rites were administered. Doctor Robert Vanecko, one of Daley's sons-in-law, agreed that the mayor was dead and nothing could be done. In fact, he had been dead since he hung up the phone with his son Michael. Dr. Coogan pronounced the time of death as 3:40 P.M.[57] Sis Daley looked at her children, and said calmly: "Now we all have to kneel down and thank God for having this great man for forty years." She took out her rosary and led the family in prayer. Throngs of reporters were assembled outside the building, clamoring for information. By the time Frank Sullivan made the announcement that the mayor was dead, everyone already knew it.[58]

In the end, Daley returned to Bridgeport — to McKeon's funeral home, across from Nativity of Our Lord Church. The neighborhood was cordoned off by Chicago police immediately after Daley's death. In keeping with the season, brightly lit Christmas trees filled the front windows of the little bungalows, but Bridgeport was in a somber mood. The Nativity of Our Lord Christmas party was canceled and, instead, about 300 parishioners gathered to say the Rosary and attend a special prayer service. The 11th Ward Democratic Organization headquarters were locked up, in honor of the greatest politician ever to emerge from them, and office hours were canceled. Only a handful of people sat drinking in Schaller's Pump, the neighborhood tavern.[59]

Daley's body lay in state at Nativity, and thousands of ordinary Chicagoans whose lives he had touched waited in the bitter cold — some for more than two hours — to gain entrance. Inside, the mayor's body reposed in an open mahogany coffin. He was dressed in a blue suit, and a black rosary lay in his folded hands. The Shannon Rovers, dressed in their signature tartan kilts and toting bagpipes, arrived to join the mourners. At the coffin, their leader, Tommy Ryan, stopped to speak to Sis Daley. "Men may come and men may go, but the name of Richard J. Daley will go on forever," he said. Mrs. Daley replied, "Tommy, he loved you." Sis Daley asked them to play one last air, and they obliged by offering up the mayor's favorite, "Garry Owen," the rousing old Irish battle hymn. Each of the mourners was personally greeted by one of Daley's four sons and three daughters, and handed a small memorial card with a black-and-white photo of the mayor and the caption, "Mayor Richard J. Daley, 1902–1976." The mourners, ushered down the center aisle to the coffin, passed by a floral wreath in the shape of a five-pointed star with a banner, "We Love You" signed "The Chicago Police Department." About 25,000 citizens walked past Daley's coffin during the nineteen-hour wake.[60]

The guests who arrived for the funeral the next day were a different crowd. As bells from Catholic churches across the Chicago Archdiocese rang out, limousines rolled through Bridgeport's narrow streets. Invited guests and dignitaries filled the church to overflowing for the funeral Mass, many of them crammed in the aisles. Nativity of Our Lord Church, which had gotten its start in a livery stable, was now host to President-elect Carter, Vice President Nelson Rockefeller, Senator Edward Kennedy, Mayor Kevin White of Boston, and Eppie Lederer, better known as Ann Landers. Daley's old foes also turned out in force to bid a final farewell, including Governor-elect James Thompson, Senator George McGovern, the Reverend Jesse Jackson, and Congressman Ralph Metcalfe. The entire Chicago City Council was present, along with just about every other political and judicial figure in the city. Many of Daley's neighbors huddled outside the church behind police barriers, listening in on loudspeakers.[61]

In the service itself, Daley's enormous impact on the world he was leaving behind was barely mentioned. At the request of the Daley family, there was no formal eulogy. "The quality of his life and his actions were his eulogy," said Father Gilbert Graham, the mayor's former pastor and longtime family friend. While the local and national media had been filled for days with memorable images from Daley's long career — the night of the 1960 presidential election, the 1968 Democratic National Convention, Daley's encounters with Martin Luther King, and his shoot-to-kill order — he was remembered inside Nativity of Our Lord as a man of simple faith. Daley had gone to church almost every day of his life, Graham noted, including the day he died. Graham also recalled that the mayor had often told him that he never needed sleeping medications because "he always had his rosary, which calmed him and prepared him for rest, no matter what the problems of the day." When Daley died, Graham said, his wallet contained pictures of his family and "a dozen well-worn prayer cards which he used every day." During the hour-long service, John Cardinal Cody of Chicago read a message from Pope Paul VI, with whom Daley had had several audiences.

The judgment of history still awaited. Daley had accomplished a great deal since the day in 1902 when he was dipped into a baptismal font in this very church. To millions of Chicagoans saddened by his passing, he embodied the spirit of their city as no man ever had — optimistic, determined, hardworking, God-fearing, and rooted in family and neighborhood. He gave them jobs, stood up for their way of life against threats from all sides, and made their city work. He had built up Chicago, leaving skyscrapers, schools, highways, and a thriving downtown to proclaim his greatness for generations. But Daley would also be remembered by millions of others, who saw in his career the dark side of modern America. They viewed him as the master of a corrupt political system, backward-looking, power-hungry, and bigoted, who ruled in the name of some groups and at the expense of others. They saw him as someone who had built a city founded on unfairness, and who was deaf to calls for change. Chicago and the world had an eternity to battle over the meaning of Daley's life and legacy, but his friends and neighbors in Bridgeport had already decided. Father Graham spoke for them when he welcomed Daley home: "May God rest this man's beautiful soul."[62]

ACKNOWLEDGMENTS

We owe a large debt to those who have written about Chicago before we did. In every generation, fine writers have emerged who have explained Chicago to the rest of the world. Theodore Dreiser, James T. Farrell, Richard Wright, Nelson Algren, Mike Royko, Gwendolyn Brooks, Lois Wille, Milton Rakove, and Dempsey Travis have all written eloquently about the city and its folkways. Roger Biles, Arnold Hirsh, Paul Green, James Ralph, and Richard Wade have all produced first-rate scholarship on the city and welcomed us to the effort.

For a book of this kind, much of the work occurs in libraries and archives. Many librarians and archivists deserve our gratitude. We were fortunate to have the help of Archie Motley at the Chicago Historical Society and Mary Ann Bamberger at the University of Illinois at Chicago. Mary Dempsey paved our way into the Chicago public libraries. The Photo Department of the *Chicago Tribune* also provided crucial assistance.

Countless people patiently shared their recollections and theories about Daley, sometimes on repeated occasions. From the Daley family to precinct captains, from the Gold Coast to the housing projects on the South Side, from Chicago to Washington, Texas, and Georgia, people were extraordinarily generous in giving us their time and their stories. Over the years, some of these have included Joanne and James Alter, William Barnett, Harold Baron, Miles Berger, Jason Berry, Robert Buono, Edward Burke, Earl Bush, F. Richard Ciccone, Tom Cokins, William Daley, Charles U. Daly, Ron and Giulianna Davidoff, Ira Dawson, Michael Dawson, Leon Despres, Anthony Downs, John Duba, Msgr. John Egan, Edwin Eisendrath, Don Haider, Julie Fernandes, Martha Fitzsimmons, Andre Foster, Richard Friedman, Gerald Frug, James Fuerst, Todd Gitlin, Bertrand Goldberg, Paul Green, Bruce Graham, Fr. Gilbert Graham, John J. Gunther, William Hartmann, David Hartigan, Arnold Hirsch, Ed Holmgren, Vernon Jarrett, Blair Kamin, Eugene Kennedy, Rick Kogan, Julian Levi, Lance Liebman, Norman Mailer, Ed Marciniak, Abraham Lincoln Marovitz, Lawrence McCaffrey, John McDermott, Paul McGrath, John McGreevy, John McKnight, Ralph Metcalfe Jr., Abner Mikva, Zoe Mikva, Kenneth Mines, James Murray, M. W. Newman, John Powell, Ed Proctor, Abe Peck, John Perkins, Alexander Polikoff, Aurelia Pucinski, Don Rose, Marvin and June Rosner, Fr. Michael Quirk, Bill Recktenwald, Dan Rostenkowski, Mary Schmich, John Schultz, Bob Secter, Charles Shaw, Barry Sheck, Seymour Simon, William Singer, Adrian Smith, John Stacks, William Stratton, Adlai Stevenson III,

David Tatel, Studs Terkel, Jerome Torshen, Dempsey Travis, Nicholas von Hoffman, Rob Warden, Meyer Weinberg, Ralph Whitehead, Hubert Will, Kale Williams, Harris Wofford, and Ray Wolfinger.

When Elizabeth moved to Chicago, she was fortunate to have able guides to this complex and storied city, including Studs Terkel and Eppie Lederer (Ann Landers), who never tire of talking about the city they love.

We are extremely grateful to our colleagues at *Time* and the *Chicago Tribune* who indulge our dual lives as journalists and historians. At *Time,* Walter Isaacson, Jim Kelly, and, of course, Priscilla Painton were a constant source of intellectual stimulation and moral support. At the *Chicago Tribune,* Howard Tyner, Ann Marie Lipinski, and Gerould Kern embody the highest standards of journalistic excellence and collegiality. We have also been privileged to work alongside talented and thoughtful colleagues at both *Time* and the *Tribune* who patiently listened to more stories about 11th Ward politics and Daley's efforts to develop downtown Chicago than we had any right to expect. A special word of thanks to John Stacks at *Time,* who roped us both into the business and has been there every step of the way.

We have been fortunate to have a fine publishing house, Little, Brown and Company, as our partners in this project. Throughout the process, Sarah Crichton has been a great ally and advisor. Jim Silberman believed in the idea and helped us to shape the book in its early stages. Roger Donald entertained us with his colorful stories of the publishing world and provided insightful suggestions about the big picture and the small details. Chip Rossetti shepherded us through the editorial stages adroitly, and Beth Davey and Katie Long cheered us with their unflagging enthusiasm. Mike Mattil's blue pencil, nuanced reading, and incisive suggestions have improved the text immensely. We are indebted to Kris Dahl, whose grasp of books and publishing, as well as her wise counsel, make her the world's best agent.

It would have been impossible to complete this book without family and friends who have provided support and inspiration over the years. Many people will find their ideas and worldview reflected in this manuscript: Caroline Arnold, Elisabeth Benjamin, Paul Engelmayer, Diane Faber, Eileen Hershenov, Amy Schwartz, Olivia Turner, Joseph Ellis, and Frances FitzGerald. Jim Kaplan shared his brilliant understanding of politics and Chicago and read every word of the manuscript twice. His belief in the project has sustained us. Barbara Taylor's values and passions have shaped the book in countless ways. Beverly and Stuart Cohen, who grew up on the streets of New York and never left, inculcated their love of cities, and Noam Cohen was always willing to share his opinions. William and Caroline, take your turns on the computer now.

NOTES

Full biblographic information for the works cited in the Notes can be found in the Bibliography.

The following abbreviations are used throughout:
CA = Chicago American
CDA = Chicago Daily American
CDN = Chicago Daily News
CD = Chicago Defender
CSM = Christian Science Monitor
CST = Chicago Sun-Times
CT = Chicago Tribune
NYT = New York Times
WP = Washington Post

Prologue

1. CBS News Report, 8/29/68.
2. CBS News Report, 8/29/68.
3. CBS News Report, 8/29/68.
4. CBS News Report, 8/29/68.
5. CBS News Report, 8/29/68; *Rights in Conflict*.
6. CBS News Report, 8/29/68; *NYT*, 8/30/68; Biles, *Richard J. Daley*, p. 160; Chester, *American Melodrama*, pp. 595–597.
7. Sinkevitch, *AIA Guide to Chicago*, p. 20.
8. *CT*, 9/4/97.
9. Jacoby, *Someone Else's House*, pp. 301–302.
10. Massey and Denton, *American Apartheid*, p. 72; Wilson, *When Work Disappears*, p. 39; *CT*, 4/12/98.

Chapter 1. A Separate World

1. Sinkevitch, *AIA Guide to Chicago*, p. 388; Koenig, *History of Chicago*, vol. 1, p. 654; *Diamond Jubilee of the Archdiocese of Chicago*, p. 399.

2. *Time*, 3/15/63; Miller, *City of the Century*, pp. 464, 506–516.
3. Sinkevitch, *AIA Guide to Chicago*, p. 387; Miller, *City of the Century*, p. 441; *Chicago Journal*, 11/12/80.
4. Sinkevitch, *AIA Guide to Chicago*, p. 388; Sinclair, *The Jungle*, p. 36; Miller, *City of the Century*, p. 203; Sinclair, *The Jungle*, p. 101.
5. Miller, *City of the Century*, p. 441; *Chicago American*, 2/12/65.
6. Kantowicz, "Church and Neighborhood," pp. 354–355; Tom Donovan, interview with the authors.
7. Skerrett, "Catholic Dimension," in McCaffrey, *The Irish in Chicago*, p. 49.
8. Fanning, "The Literary Dimension," in McCaffrey, *The Irish in Chicago*, p. 102.
9. *CST*, 8/24/68.
10. Greeley, *Neighborhood*, p. 24; *Diamond Jubilee of the Archdiocese of Chicago*, p. 401; Kennedy, *Himself!*, p. 33; Fanning, "The Literary Dimension," in McCaffrey, *The Irish in Chicago*, pp. 108–109.
11. *Chicago American*, 2/12/65; *CT*, 6/13/99; Wittke, *The Irish in America*, p. 16; *CT*, 1/13/76.
12. Wittke, *The Irish in America*, pp. 7–8.
13. Wittke, *The Irish in America*, p. 100; Shannon, *The American Irish*, p. 43.
14. *CT*, 2/26/1855, cited in McCaffrey, *The Irish in Chicago*, pp. 26, 8.
15. Shannon, *The American Irish*, pp. 28–29.
16. Greeley, *That Most Distressful Nation*, p. 42; Eugene Kennedy, interview with the authors; Rakove, *Don't Make No Waves*, p. 48; Halberstam, "Daley of Chicago," p. 26.
17. Kennedy, *Himself!*, p. 35; O'Connor, *Clout*, p. 16; Royko, *Boss*, p. 33; *CT*, 6/17/65.
18. Greeley, *That Most Distressful Nation*, p. 101; Kennedy, *Himself!*, pp. 35–36; Gilbert Graham, interview with the authors.
19. Gilbert Graham, interview with the authors; Earl Bush, in *Daley: The Last Boss* (film documentary, Barak Goodman, producer; aired on *The American Experience*, PBS).
20. *CT*, 3/28/55; Ciccone, *Daley*, p. 51; Kantowicz, "Church and Neighborhood," p. 359; Wittke, *The Irish in America*, p. 100.
21. *CST*, 9/26/68; Ehrenhalt, *The Lost City*, p. 129.
22. *CST*, 9/26/68; Fanning, "The Literary Dimension," in McCaffrey, *The Irish in Chicago*, p. 110.
23. Kennedy, *Himself!*, p. 37; Rakove, *Don't Make No Waves*, pp. 62, xx.
24. Sister Gabriel, quoted in *Daley: The Last Boss* (film); Granger, Bill, "De La Salle: Chicago's Great School," 1995 (copy on file with authors); Royko, *Boss*, p. 35.
25. "De La Salle," p. 34; Royko, *Boss*, pp. 35, 34.
26. Ciccone, *Daley*, p. 51; Centennial History, pp. 6–37.
27. Kennedy, *Himself!*, p. 41; Tuttle, *Race Riot*, p. 199; *CST*, "Mayor Daley Remembered: 10 Years After His Death, His Family Reflects," p. 10; Tuttle, *Race Riot*, p. 199; Gleason, *Daley of Chicago*, p. 130.
28. Kennedy, *Himself!*, p. 41; *CT*, 3/23/72; Fanning, "The Literary Dimension," in McCaffrey, *The Irish in Chicago*, p. 103.
29. O'Connor, *Clout*, p. 19; *NYT*, 6/27/61; *CT*, 6/28/61.
30. Tuttle, *Race Riot*, p. 102; McGreevy, "American Catholics and the African-American Migration, 1919–1970," Ph.D. dissertation (Stanford, 1992), p. 1.
31. Tuttle, *Race Riot*, p. 160; *NYT*, 8/26/63; Drake and Cayton, *Black Metropolis*, Myrdal, *An American Dilemma*, p. 1127; *NYT*, 8/26/63; Anderson and Pickering, *Confronting the Color Line*, pp. 45–46.

32. Tuttle, *Race Riot*, p. 90; Lemann, *The Promised Land*, p. 339; Grossman, *Land of Hope*, p. 205.
33. Grossman, *Land of Hope*, pp. 3–4.
34. Anderson and Pickering, *Confronting the Color Line*, pp. 45–46; Grossman, *Land of Hope*, p. 123; Myrdal, *An American Dilemma*, p. 1127; Drake and Cayton, *Black Metropolis*, pp. 81–82, 202.
35. Grossman, *Land of Hope*, pp. 168, 174; Anderson and Pickering, *Confronting the Color Line*, pp. 46, 48.
36. Shannon, *The American Irish*, pp. 4–6; Drake and Cayton, *Black Metropolis*, p. 43.
37. McGreevy, "American Catholics," pp. 22, 120; Grossman, *Land of Hope*, p. 174.
38. Grossman, *Land of Hope*, pp. 177, 179.
39. Tuttle, *Race Riot*, pp. 8–10; Grossman, *Land of Hope*, p. 179.
40. Biles, *Richard J. Daley*, p. 22; Tuttle, *Race Riot*, pp. 32, 48, 51.
41. O'Connor, *Clout*, p. 19; Kennedy, *Himself!*, p. 43; Biles, *Richard J. Daley*, p. 22; Tuttle, *Race Riot*, p. 33.
42. *CT*, 3/28/55.
43. Rakove, *Don't Make No Waves*, pp. 32-33; Erie, *Rainbow's End*.
44. Levine, *The Irish and Irish Politicians*.
45. Moynihan, "The Irish," in Glazer and Moynihan, *Beyond the Melting Pot*, pp. 224, 226–227.
46. McCaffrey, *The Irish in Chicago*, p. 62; Rakove, *Don't Make No Waves*, p. 33; Fremon, *Chicago Politics Ward by Ward*, p. 84.
47. Ciccone, *Daley*, pp. 47, 52; O'Connor, *Clout*, pp. 21–22.
48. Erie, *Rainbow's End*.
49. Rakove, *We Don't Want*, p. 251; Banfield and Wilson, *City Politics*, p. 119.
50. Banfield and Wilson, *City Politics*, p. 117; Bernard Neistein, interview, in Rakove, *We Don't Want*, p. 62; Jacob Arvey, interview, in Rakove, *We Don't Want*, p. 4; Rakove, *Don't Make No Waves*, p. 130.
51. Rakove, *Don't Make No Waves*, p. 57.
52. Guterbock, *Machine Politics in Transition*, pp. 79–80; Andre Foster, interview with the authors; Liebling, *Chicago: The Second City*, pp. 123–124.
53. Guterbock, *Machine Politics*, pp. 83–85; Andre Foster, interview with the authors.
54. Jacob Arvey, interview, in Rakove, *We Don't Want*, p. 5.
55. Fremon, *Chicago Politics Ward by Ward*, p. 180; *CT*, 3/23/72; Hampton and Fayer, *Voices of Freedom*, p. 304; Vito Marzullo, interview, in Rakove, *We Don't Want*, p. 52; *NYT*, 1/16/67; Rakove, *Don't Make No Waves*, p. 116.
56. Ciccone, *Daley*, p. 52; Paul Green, remarks in *Daley: The Last Boss* (film); Royko, *Boss*, pp. 40, 52.
57. Royko, *Boss*, p. 41; *NYT Magazine*, 9/11/66, p. 188.
58. Biles, *Richard J. Daley*, p. 23; Ciccone, *Daley*, p. 57.
59. *Chicago American*, 6/14/65; *CT*, 3/1/80; Sis Daley, quoted in *Daley: The Last Boss* (film); *Chicago American*, 6/14/65; marriage license of Richard J. Daley and Eleanor R. Guilfoyle, on file with county clerk of County of Cook, Illinois; *CT*, 3/28/55.

Chapter 2. A House for All Peoples

1. Rakove, *We Don't Want,* p. 8.
2. Allswang, *Bosses, Machines,* pp. 107–108.
3. Rakove, *We Don't Want,* p. 31; Allswang, *Bosses, Machines,* pp. 108–109; Banfield and Wilson, *City Politics,* p. 18.
4. Tuttle, *Race Riot,* p. 187; Allswang, *Bosses, Machines,* pp. 96–99, 101.
5. Gosnell, *Machine Politics,* pp. 11–12; Anderson and Pickering, *Confronting the Color Line,* p. 51; Allswang, *Bosses, Machines,* p. 110; Travis, *Autobiography of Black Politics,* p. 93; Rakove, *Don't Make No Waves,* pp. 48–49.
6. Jacob Arvey, Columbia Oral History Project, p. 21.
7. Travis, *Autobiography of Black Politics,* pp. 94–96; Rakove, *We Don't Want,* pp. 31–32.
8. *Chicago Herald and Examiner,* 10/30/29, cited in Green and Holli, *The Mayors,* pp. 103, 109.
9. Gleason, *Daley of Chicago,* pp. 169–170; O'Connor, *Clout,* p. 47; *CT,* 6/26/33.
10. Rakove, *We Don't Want,* p. 9.
11. Biles, *Big City Boss,* pp. 6–7; Gosnell, *Machine Politics,* p. 16.
12. Rakove, *We Don't Want,* p. 33; Biles, *Big City Boss,* p. 22.
13. Travis, *Autobiography of Black Politics,* p. 140; Biles, *Richard J. Daley,* p. 25; Hirsch, "Chicago: Cook County Democratic Organization and the Dilemma of Race, 1931–1987," in Bernard, *Snowbelt Cities,* p. 67.
14. Hirsch, "Chicago: Cook County Democratic Organization and the Dilemma of Race, 1931–1987," in Bernard, *Snowbelt Cities,* p. 67; *CD,* 10/20/34.
15. Drake and Cayton, *Black Metropolis,* p. 352; Biles, *Big City Boss,* p. 95; Grimshaw, *Bitter Fruit,* pp. 48–49; Ciccone, *Daley,* p. 127.
16. Drake and Cayton, *Black Metropolis,* p. 369; *CD,* 3/23/35; Travis, *Autobiography of Black Politics,* pp. 126–127, 138; Biles, *Big City Boss,* p. 94.
17. Ralph, *Northern Protest,* p. 11.
18. Ira Dawson, interview with the authors; *New York Herald Tribune,* 1/3/49; interview with John Leonard East, in Rakove, *We Don't Want,* p. 32; Christopher, *America's Black Congressmen* (New York: Thomas Y. Crowell, 1971), p. 185.
19. Travis, *Autobiography in Black Politics,* p. 169; Grimshaw, *Bitter Fruit,* p. 77.
20. Kennedy, *Himself!,* p. 90; Ehrenhalt, *The Lost City,* p. 162.
21. Christopher, *America's Black Congressmen,* p. 186.
22. Cooper, "South Side Boss," XIX *Chicago History,* 66, 68–69; Travis, *Autobiography of Black Politics,* p. 150.
23. Biles, *Big City Boss,* pp. 98–99.
24. Biles, *Big City Boss,* p. 100; Travis, *Autobiography of Black Politics,* pp. 161–162.
25. Biles, *Big City Boss,* pp. 100–101; Cooper, "South Side Boss," p. 71.
26. Ciccone, *Daley,* pp. 47–48, 50.
27. Ciccone, *Daley,* p. 58.
28. *CT,* 4/17/60; Ciccone, *Daley,* p. 60.
29. O'Connor, *Clout,* p. 59; Rakove, *Don't Make No Waves,* p. 48.
30. Ciccone, *Daley,* p. 66; Kennedy, *Himself!,* p. 68; Royko, *Boss,* p. 53.
31. Abraham Lincoln Marovitz, interview with the authors; Royko, *Boss,* p. 51.
32. *CT,* 5/12/43; O'Connor, *Clout,* p. 29; Kennedy, *Himself!,* pp. 73–74.
33. Ciccone, *Daley,* p. 61; *CT,* 4/17/60; Mathewson, *Up Against Daley,* p. 44.

34. Ciccone, *Daley,* p. 64; *CT,* 5/24/45; *CT,* 7/13/44, cited in Biles, *Big City Boss,* p. 128; *CT,* 3/25/43.
35. Ciccone, *Daley,* pp. 62–63.
36. Jackson, *Crabgrass Frontier,* p. 221; Baron, *Building Babylon;* Bowly, *The Poorhouse,* p. 18.
37. Drake and Cayton, *Black Metropolis,* p. 46; Squires et al., *Chicago: Race, Class,* pp. 99–100; Bowly, *The Poorhouse,* p. 17; Warren, "Subsidized Housing in Chicago," p. 3; Bowly, *The Poorhouse,* pp. 18, 27; Meyerson and Banfield, *Politics, Planning and the Public Interest,* p. 17.
38. Jackson, *Crabgrass Frontier,* pp. 223–224.
39. Meyerson and Banfield, *Politics, Planning and the Public Interest,* pp. 17–18; *CSM,* 5/26/47.
40. *CST,* 6/20/50.
41. *CT,* 4/19/42; *CST,* 6/20/50; James Fuerst, interview with the authors; Edward Holmgren, interview with the authors.
42. Meyerson and Banfield, *Politics, Planning and the Public Interest,* p. 263; *CST,* 4/19/42; *CSM,* 3/1/51.
43. *CST,* 6/20/50; Edward Holmgren, interview with the authors; Myerson and Banfield, *Politics, Planning and the Public Interest,* p. 287.
44. Polikoff, "Low-Rent Public Housing"; Jackson, *Crabgrass Frontier,* p. 226; Meyerson and Banfield, *Politics, Planning and the Public Interest,* p. 121; Bowly, *The Poorhouse,* p. 27.
45. Bowly, *The Poorhouse,* p. 27; Squires et al., *Chicago: Race, Class,* p. 101; Bowly, *The Poorhouse,* p. 28.
46. Bowly, *The Poorhouse,* p. 38; memo from H. A. White, housing manager, Frances Cabrini Homes, to Elizabeth Wood (on file with the authors).
47. Bowly, *The Poorhouse,* pp. 34–45; Meyerson and Banfield, *Politics, Planning and the Public Interest,* pp. 122–123.
48. Biles, *Richard J. Daley,* p. 27.
49. *CDN,* 11/4/46; Ciccone, *Daley,* p. 68.
50. O'Connor, *Clout,* p. 30; Royko, *Boss,* p. 52; *CT,* 4/8/75.
51. *CT,* 8/21/48; *CT,* 8/18/45; *CT,* 9/20/46; *CT,* 8/25/46; Hirsch, *Making the Second Ghetto,* p. 179.
52. Manchester, *The Glory and the Dream,* p. 415; McCullough, *Truman,* pp. 520–523; Ciccone, *Daley,* p. 68.
53. Kennedy, *Himself!,* p. 79.
54. Biles, *Big City Boss,* p. 135; Bowly, *The Poorhouse,* p. 46.
55. Meyerson and Banfield, *Politics, Planning and the Public Interest,* pp. 124, 141; Bowly, *The Poorhouse,* pp. 47–50.
56. James Fuerst, interview with the authors; Meyerson and Banfield, *Politics, Planning and the Public Interest,* p. 125.
57. Hirsch, *Making the Second Ghetto,* pp. 2, 76; *CD,* 12/7/46; *CT,* 12/6/46; *CT,* 12/6/46; *CD,* 12/7/46; *CD,* 12/14/46; Meyerson and Banfield, *Politics, Planning and the Public Interest,* pp. 125-126; Bowly, *The Poorhouse,* p. 50.
58. Squires et al., *Chicago: Race, Class,* p. 101; Meyerson and Banfield, *Politics, Planning and the Public Interest,* p. 126.
59. Meyerson and Banfield, *Politics, Planning and the Public Interest,* pp. 126–128.
60. Rakove, *We Don't Want,* p. 3; Berkow, *Maxwell Street,* p. 247; "Jacob M. Arvey," *New*

York Herald Tribune, 10/30/49; "Jacob M. Arvey, Democratic Boss of Chicago in the 1940s, Dead at 81," *NYT,* 8/26/77.

61. Hirsch, *Snowbelt Cities,* p. 66; Green, *Mayor Richard J. Daley,* p. 150; Whitehead, "The Ward Boss Who Saved the New Deal"; Kennedy, *Himself!,* p. 81; Rakove, *We Don't Want,* p. 12.

62. Colonel Jacob Arvey, Adlai Stevenson project, Columbia Oral History Project (Introduction by Kenneth Davis, Chicago, IL, 5/24/67).

63. Kennedy, *Himself!,* p. 76; *CST,* 10/29/47; Royko, *Boss,* p. 52; Kennedy, *Himself!,* p. 81.

64. Rakove, *We Don't Want,* p. 11; Ciccone, *Daley,* p. 74.

65. Ciccone, *Daley,* p. 74; *CT,* 12/21/48.

66. *CT,* 1/17/50.

67. Bowly, *The Poorhouse,* p. 76; Meyerson and Banfield, *Politics, Planning and the Public Interest,* pp. 23, 28, 35, 136–137; Warren, *Subsidized Housing,* p. 6; Hirsch, *Making the Second Ghetto,* pp. 223–234.

68. Warren, *Subsidized Housing,* p. 6; Meyerson and Banfield, *Politics, Planning and the Public Interest,* pp. 26, 153–187, 190–191; Granger and Granger, *Lords of the Last Machine.*

69. Meyerson and Banfield, *Politics, Planning and the Public Interest,* pp. 195–197; Hirsch, *Making the Second Ghetto,* pp. 226–228.

70. Ciccone, *Daley,* pp. 70-71, 102.

71. Ciccone, *Daley,* pp. 71, 75.

72. Ciccone, *Daley,* p. 76; *CT,* 1/9/50.

73. *CT,* 6/14/51; *CT,* 6/26/50.

74. McCullogh, *Truman,* p. 814; Ciccone, *Daley,* p. 78; Biles, *Daley,* p. 31; O'Connor, *Clout,* p. 72.

75. *CT,* 11/5/50; O'Connor, *Clout,* p. 74.

76. *Time,* 12/11/50; Mathewson, *Up Against Daley,* p. 45.

77. Rakove, *Don't Make No Waves,* pp. 90–94.

78. Mathewson, *Up Against Daley,* p. 46; Fremon, *Chicago Politics Ward by Ward,* p. 101.

79. *Time,* 12/11/50.

Chapter 3. Chicago Ain't Ready for Reform

1. Fremon, *Chicago Politics Ward by Ward,* p. 101; Royko, *Boss,* p. 61.

2. Drake and Cayton, *Black Metropolis,* pp. 470–494.

3. Travis, *Autobiography of Black Politics,* pp. 174, 170.

4. Drake and Cayton, *Black Metropolis,* p. 494.

5. Travis, *Autobiography of Black Politics,* pp. 171–172; Wilson, *Negro Politics,* pp. 54, 65 n.6.

6. Travis, *Autobiography of Black Politics,* p. 169.

7. Wilson, *Negro Politics,* p. 206.

8. *Ramparts,* 9/7/68; Ira Dawson, interview with the authors; Reed, *The Chicago NAACP,* p. 186; *Congressional Record,* 79th Congress, 1st Session.

9. Ira Dawson, interview with the authors; Grimshaw, *Bitter Fruit,* p. 108; Ehrenhalt, *The Lost City,* pp. 163–164.

10. Christopher, *America's Black Congressmen,* p. 187.

11. Interview with Edison Love, in Rakove, *We Don't Want,* p. 41.

12. Rakove, *We Don't Want,* pp. 18–19.

13. Ciccone, *Daley,* pp. 101–102, 104.

14. Mathewson, *Up Against Daley,* p. 46; Ciccone, *Daley,* p. 79.

15. O'Connor, *Clout,* p. 76.

16. Gleason, *Daley of Chicago,* p. 135.

17. *CT,* 7/22/53; Ciccone, *Daley,* p. 80.

18. Mathewson, *Up Against Daley,* pp. 47–48; Ciccone, *Daley,* p. 80.

19. Hirsch, *Making the Second Ghetto,* p. 229; James Fuerst, interview with the authors; Meyerson and Banfield, *Politics, Planning and the Public Interest,* p. 242.

20. *CD,* 5/2/53; Statement of Elizabeth Wood, 8/30/54, p. 3; Hirsch, "Massive Resistance in the Urban North," p. 526.

21. Hirsch, "Massive Resistance in the Urban North," pp. 522–523; *CD,* 8/13/53.

22. *CD,* 8/13/53; Hirsch, "Massive Resistance in the Urban North" pp. 522, 527, 531; Hirsch, *Making the Second Ghetto,* p. 81.

23. Hirsch, *Making the Second Ghetto,* p. 187; Hirsch, "Massive Resistance in the Urban North," pp. 531, 533.

24. *CD,* 2/13/54; Hirsch, "Massive Resistance in the Urban North," pp. 529, 531; *CT,* 10/3/53.

25. Hirsch, "Massive Resistance in the Urban North," pp. 528–530, 536; Bowly, *The Poorhouse,* p. 82.

26. Statement of Elizabeth Wood, 8/30/54, p. 2; *CT,* 4/15/53; Hirsch, *Making the Second Ghetto,* p. 234; *CT,* 4/17/53; Meyerson and Banfield, *Politics, Planning and the Public Interest,* p. 267 n.

27. Rakove, *We Don't Want,* p. 246.

28. *CT,* 3/1/54

29. O'Connor, *Clout,* pp. 94–95, 103.

30. Ciccone, *Daley,* pp. 97, 113–114.

31. James Fuerst, interview with the authors.

32. Statement of Elizabeth Wood, 8/30/54, p. 2; *CD,* 8/28/54; *CT,* 8/25/54; Statement of Elizabeth Wood, 8/30/54, pp. 1–3; *CT,* 8/31/53; Edward Holmgren, interview with the authors; Minutes of a Special Meeting of Commissioners of Chicago Housing Authority Held August 31, 1954; Resolution No. 54-CHA-235.

33. *CT,* 9/1/54; *CT,* 8/31/54; *CD,* 9/4/54; *CT,* 10/29/54.

34. *CT,* 10/26/54; *NYT,* 7/10/61; *NYT,* 7/31/61; *CT,* 10/12/71.

35. Edward Holmgren, interview with the authors.

36. Bowly, *The Poorhouse,* p. 83; Hirsch, *Making the Second Ghetto,* p. 236; Edward Holmgren, interview with the authors.

37. *CD,* 8/28/54; In the next decade, Trumbull Park and Lathrop kept their informal quotas of only a handful of black families. Lawndale had only two black families out of almost 130 in 1965, and Bridgeport had none. Hirsch, *Making the Second Ghetto,* p. 239.

38. *Gautreaux* case, Affidavit of Tamaara Tabb, 12/7/66; *CST,* 3/3/64.

39. "Problems and Promise of Public Housing in Chicago," speech of Jean S. Fuerst to Chicago City Club, 3/2/64.

40. *House & Home,* July 1957; James Fuerst, interview with the authors.

41. O'Connor, *Clout,* pp. 97–98; Biles, *Daley,* p. 36.

42. Ciccone, *Daley*, pp. 115–116; Travis, *Autobiography of Black Politics*, p. 206.
43. Kennedy, *Himself!*, p. 102; *CT*, 12/16/54; Mathewson, *Up Against Daley*, p. 52; *Time*, 3/7/55.
44. O'Connor, *Clout*, p. 102; *NYT*, 12/20/54.
45. Kennedy, *Himself!*, pp. 104–105; Travis, *Autobiography of Black Politics*, p. 208.
46. *CT*, 12/21/54; *Time*, 1/3/55; *NYT*, 12/26/54.
47. Gleason, *Daley of Chicago*, pp. 124–127, 196; Rakove, *We Don't Want*, p. 277.
48. Gleason, *Daley of Chicago*, pp. 196–197.
49. Gleason, *Daley of Chicago*, p. 197.
50. *CT*, 12/31/54.
51. Martin, *Adlai Stevenson*, p. 283; Rakove, *Don't Make No Waves*, p. 90.
52. Rakove, *Don't Make No Waves*, p. 69; Martin, *Adlai Stevenson*, p. 284; Gleason, *Daley of Chicago*, p. 199.
53. Kennedy, *Himself!*, p. 120; *CT*, 2/20/55; *CT*, 2/15/55.
54. Kennedy, *Himself!*, pp. 113–114; Mathewson, *Up Against Daley*, p. 53; *CT*, 2/11/55.
55. Travis, *Autobiography of Black Politics*, p. 215; Kennedy, *Himself!*
56. Rakove, *We Don't Want*, p. 252; O'Connor, *Clout*, p. 108; Johnson, *Successful Reform Litigation*, p. 482; *CT*, 2/7/55.
57. *CT*, 2/6/55.
58. *CT*, 2/22/55; *CT*, 2/1/55; *CT*, 2/7/55.
59. *CT*, 2/5/55; Ciccone, *Daley*, p. 120.
60. *Time*, 3/7/55; *CT*, 2/5/55; *CT*, 2/24/54; *CT*, 2/25/55.
61. *CT*, 2/14/55; *CT*, 2/20/55; Mathewson, *Up Against Daley*, pp. 41–42; Travis, *Autobiography of Black Politics*, p. 215.
62. Travis, *Autobiography of Black Politics*, p. 208; *CT*, 2/21/55; *CT*, 2/18/55.
63. *CT*, 2/8/55; *CT*, 2/20/55; *CT*, 2/11/55.
64. *CT*, 2/21/55; *CT*, 2/22/55.
65. O'Connor, *Clout*, pp. 114–115.
66. Biles, *Richard J. Daley*, p. 38; *CT*, 2/24/55; O'Connor, *Clout*, p. 115.
67. Ciccone, *Daley*, pp. 130–131.
68. Fremon, *Chicago Politics Ward by Ward*, p. 180; O'Connor, *Clout*, p. 114.
69. *CT*, 2/14/55; *CT*, 2/23/55; *CT*, 2/24/54; *NYT*, 3/7/55.
70. *NYT*, 12/26/54; *New York Post*, 3/14/55.
71. Rakove, *We Don't Want*, pp. 263–264.
72. Halberstam, "Daley of Chicago," p. 26; *Life*, 2/8/60; *National Observer*, 2/11/62; Rakove, *We Don't Want*, pp. 45–46.
73. *Time*, 4/18/55; Beatty, *The Rascal King*, p. 11.
74. Daniel Rostenkowski, interview with the authors; Allswang, *Bosses, Machines*, p. 21.
75. *CT*, 3/6/55.
76. *CT*, 3/4/55; *CT*, 3/10/55; Rakove, *We Don't Want*, p. 264.
77. *CT*, 3/7/55; *CT*, 3/21/55; Mathewson, *Up Against Daley*, p. 54.
78. Ira Dawson, interview with the authors; *CD*, 4/2/55; *CT*, 3/29/55; *South Deering Bulletin*, 5/7/55, 11/11/55; Hirsch, "Cook County Democratic Organization and the Dilemma of Race, 1931–1987," in Bernard, *Snowbelt Cities*, pp. 75–76; Hirsch, "Massive Resistance in the Urban North," pp. 540, 549; *CST*, 7/22/73; Gleason, *Daley of Chicago*, p. 205.
79. *CT*, 3/17/55; *CT*, 3/21/55; *Time*, 4/18/55.
80. *CT*, 3/5/55; *CT*, 3/26/55; Ciccone, *Daley*, p. 134.

81. *NYT,* 2/23/55; *NYT,* 12/26/54; *CT,* 4/5/55; *CT,* 3/6/55; Lindberg, *To Serve and Collect,* p. 286.

82. *CT,* 3/23/55; *Time,* 3/15/63.

83. Fremon, *Chicago Politics Ward by Ward,* p. 232; *Time,* 4/18/55; Biles, *Richard J. Daley,* p. 40.

84. Rakove, *We Don't Want,* p. 264; Mathewson, *Up Against Daley,* pp. 54–55.

85. Kennedy, *Himself!,* p. 122; *CT,* 2/24/55; *CDN,* 2/24/55, quoted in Biles, *Richard J. Daley; CT,* 2/28/55; *CT,* 2/27/55; *CT,* 3/30/55

86. Kalina, *Courthouse over White House,* p. 11; *CT,* 4/3/55.

87. *CT,* 3/4/55; *CT,* 4/4/55; Rakove, *We Don't Want,* pp. 264–265.

88. *CST,* 4/6/55; *CT,* 4/6/55.

89. Travis, *Autobiography of Black Politics,* p. 216; O'Connor, *Clout,* p. 121.

90. *CT,* quoted in O'Connor, *Clout,* p. 121; *New York Herald Tribune,* 7/9/60; *Time,* 2/7/55; O'Connor, *Clout,* p. 124.

Chapter 4. I Am the Mayor and Don't You Forget It

1. Riordon, *Plunkitt of Tammany Hall,* p. 23; Erie, *Rainbow's End,* pp. 15, 177, 122; Fremon, *Chicago Politics Ward by Ward,* p. 284.

2. *CT,* 4/6/55; *CT,* 4/7/55.

3. *CT,* 4/8/55; Gleason, *Daley of Chicago,* p. 215.

4. *CT,* 4/21/55; Gleason, *Daley of Chicago,* p. 217.

5. Kissinger and Booth, "Welcome to Chicago: Meet the Men Who Own It," p. 30; Grimshaw, *Bitter Fruit,* p. 93; *CT,* 4/15/55; Edward Burke, interview with the authors.

6. Ehrenhalt, *The Lost City,* p. 44.

7. Edward Marciniak, interview with the authors; Rakove, *We Don't Want,* pp. 255, 286.

8. Johnson, *Succeeding Against the Odds,* pp. 315–316.

9. Rakove, *Don't Make No Waves,* p. 60; *NYT,* 3/14/99; *CT,* 2 /24/55; Fremon, *Chicago Politics Ward by Ward,* p. 204.

10. Rakove, *Don't Make No Waves,* p. 220.

11. Fremon, *Chicago Politics Ward by Ward,* pp. 204, 284; *NYT,* 4/8/73; William Singer, interview with the authors; Rakove, *Don't Make No Waves,* pp. 214–215.

12. *CT,* 4/22/55; *CT,* 1/19/57; *CT,* 2/22/58; *CT,* 12/4/57; Fremon, *Chicago Politics Ward by Ward,* pp. 179–180.

13. Edward Marciniak, interview with the authors; Sullivan, *Legend,* p. 160.

14. O'Connor, *Requiem,* p. 22; Sullivan, *Legend,* pp. 76–77.

15. Royko, *Boss,* p. 9; *CT,* 9/7/57; *CDN,* 2/23/58.

16. Fremon, *Chicago Politics Ward by Ward,* p. 298; *Newsweek,* 7/13/70; *Chicago American,* 6/14/65; *CT,* 3/1/80.

17. Eugene Kennedy, interview with the authors; *NYT,* 5/5/57.

18. *CT,* 2/12/57.

19. *CT,* 5/16/55; *CT,* 3/1/80; *CA,* 6/14/65; *People,* 12/23/74; *CST,* 2/23/55; *CA,* 4/22/56.

20. *CT,* 4/25/55; *Life,* 2/8/60; David Stahl, interview with the authors; *CT,* 8/30/55; *CT,* 9/27/62; *CT,* 3/27/55; *CT,* 8/3/55; Fremon, *Chicago Politics Ward by Ward,* p. 299; *CT,* 12/11/57.

21. David Stahl, interview with the authors; Daniel Rostenkowski, interview with the authors; *Time,* 3/15/63; Chester, Hodgson, and Page, *An American Melodrama,* p. 107.
22. Edward Marciniak, interview with the authors; Rakove, *Don't Make No Waves,* p. 47; interview with Lois Wille, Daley, WTTV, 1986.
23. Sullivan, *Requiem,* p. xx; Ed Burke, interview with the authors.
24. Liebling, *Chicago: The Second City,* p. 125.
25. Tom Donovan, interview with the authors.
26. Tom Donovan, interview with the authors; Martha Fitzsimmons, interview with the authors; Rakove, *Don't Make No Waves,* pp. 112–113.
27. Letter of William Dawson to John S. Boyle, 1/24/50, in the William Dawson Papers, Fisk University Library.
28. Frady, *Jesse: The Life and Pilgrimage of Jesse Jackson,* pp. 186–187; Rakove, *We Don't Want,* p. 248.
29. Rakove, *Don't Make No Waves,* p. 115; Bill Recktenwald, interview with the authors.
30. Tom Donovan, interview with the authors; Affidavit of Theodore Beaureguard, *Shakman v. Democratic Organization of Cook County,* No. 69-C-2145, U.S. Dist. Ct. for the N. Dist of Illinois, E.D.; *CT,* 8/10/58; Stipulation of Fact Between Plaintiffs and Defendant Richard J. Elrod, *Shakman;* letter from James C. Murray to Raymond J. Hunt, 6/15/66, James C. Murray Papers, Chicago Historical Society, Box 233-327; 5th Ward Organization File, Leon Despres Papers, Chicago Historical Society, Box 72, Folder 2; *CT,* 8/10/58.
31. Affidavit of Leon Depres, *Shakman v. Democratic Organization of Cook County;* Affidavit of Ida Barnes, *Shakman v. Democratic Organization of Cook County.*
32. Brief of Plaintiffs, *Shakman v. Democratic Organization of Cook County,* pp. 36–37; James Murray, interview with the authors; Affidavit of Lynn Williams, *Shakman v. Democratic Organization of Cook County.*
33. O'Connor, *Requiem;* Jerry Torshen, interview with the authors.
34. Beschloss, *Taking Charge,* p. 168.
35. *CT,* 5/18/55; *CT,* 5/22/55.
36. Granger, *Lords of the Last Machine; CT,* 10/9/55; *CT,* 12/8/55.
37. *CT,* 12/5/55.
38. "Some People Are Trying to Create Tension," draft speech, Leon Despres Papers, Chicago Historical Society, Box 69-6.
39. Mayer and Wade, *Chicago: Growth of a Metropolis,* p. 376; Rast, *Remaking Chicago,* p. 26; *NYT,* 5/5/57.
40. Miller, *City of the Century,* pp. 265–266; McBrien, *The Loop,* p. 266; *CT,* 9/24/57; Miller, *Here's the Deal,* pp. 6, 76; Mayer and Wade, *Chicago: Growth of a Metropolis,* p. 452; Squires et al., *Chicago: Race, Class,* p. 154; Rust, *Remaking Chicago,* p. 27.
41. Bowen, William, "Chicago: They Didn't Have to Burn It Down After All," *Fortune,* 1/65, p. 145; *U.S. News and World Report,* 5/27/55; *CT,* 12/7/55.
42. *CT,* 5/1/55; *CT,* 9/24/55; *CT,* 5/4/55.
43. William Stratton, interview with the authors; *CT,* 4/29/55.
44. *CT,* 5/14/55; *CT,* 10/26/55; *CT,* 10/27/55; William Stratton, interview with the authors.
45. *CT,* 7/19/55; *CT,* 11/20/62; *CT,* 4/21/56.
46. *CT,* 8/9/55; *CT,* 7/1/55; *CT,* 8/25/55.
47. *CT,* 8/31/55; *CT,* 4/21/56; *CT,* 7/8/56; *CT,* 4/24/56.

48. *CT,* 7/19/55; *NYT,* 5/14/55; *CT,* 11/12/58.

49. Daniel Rostenkowski, interview with the authors; Kennedy, *Himself!,* p. 45.

50. *CT,* 9/23/58.

51. Granger, *Lords of the Last Machine; CT,* 11/23/62; *CT,* 12/4/57.

52. Peterson, *School Politics Chicago Style,* p. 11; *Fortune,* 6/62, p. 153; Edward Marciniak, interview with the authors.

53. Rakove, *Don't Make No Waves,* pp. 78–79; Seymour Simon, interview with the authors.

54. *CD,* 6/18/55; Charles Swibel interview with Nathan Thomas, summer 1986, courtesy of Professor James Ralph; Edward Marciniak, interview with the authors; Anthony Downs, interview with the authors.

55. *CD,* 6/18/55; *CD,* 7/9/55; *CD,* 7/9/55; *CD,* 8/17/57; *CD,* 10/29/55.

56. *CD,* 10/29/55.

57. Hirsch, "Massive Resistance in the Urban North," p. 549; Hirsch, *Dilemma of Race,* p. 78.

58. Gunther, *Inside U.S.A.,* p. 372; Squires et al., *Chicago: Race, Class,* p. 155.

59. Rubloff, "Central Business District Slum," in the Arthur Rubloff Papers, Box 8, Folder 13, at Chicago Historical Society; Squires et al., *Chicago: Race, Class,* p. 154; Banfield and Clark, "The Fort Dearborn Project" (second draft), in the Edward Banfield Papers, Box 7, Folder 5, Chicago Historical Society.

60. Hirsch, *Making the Second Ghetto,* p. 104; Bowen, "They Didn't Have to," pp. 145–146; Sinkevitch, *AIA Guide to Chicago,* pp. 356, 373-75.

61. Hirsch, *Making the Second Ghetto,* pp. 108–113; Bowen, "They Didn't Have to," p. 146.

62. Sinkevich, *AIA Guide to Chicago,* p. 371.

63. Statement of Holman D. Pettibone Re: Proposed Legislation in Ill. G.A. to Dissolve Chicago Land Clearance Commission, May 11, 1961, in Pettibone Papers; Hirsch, *Making the Second Ghetto,* pp. 122–125; Remarks of Ferd Kramer, Potomoc Chapter of the National Association of Housing and Redevelopment Officials, Washington, D.C., 11/18/60, in Holman Pettibone Papers, Chicago Historical Society; Bowen, "They Didn't Have to," p. 146.

64. Tom Cokins, interview with the authors; Chicago Central Area Committee, "What's Happening in Chicago," Chicago, 1958; *CT,* 9/8/57.

65. Miller, *Here's the Deal,* p. 4.

66. "Letter to Richard J. Daley from James C. Downs, Feb. 28, 1956," in Holman Pettibone Papers, Chicago Historical Society; "Statement by Mayor Daley, March 29, 1956," pp. 4–5, in Pettibone Papers; *CT,* 7/13/56.

67. *Life,* 2/8/60; *CT,* 12/20/55.

68. O'Connor, *Requiem; CT,* 1/6/56.

69. *CT,* 3/7/56; *CT,* 3/6/56.

70. *CT,* 3/7/56; *CT,* 4/6/56.

71. *CT,* 4/24/56.

Chapter 5. Public Aid Penitentiary

1. Edward Marciniak, interview with the authors.

2. Bowly, *The Poorhouse,* p. 121; "Fact Sheet Regarding CHA Projects," in *Gautreaux v. CHA* files, Businessmen and Professionals in the Public Interest; Bowly, *The Poorhouse,* pp. 19–21, 113–114, 129–130; Hirsch, *Making the Second Ghetto,* p. 241.

3. "Fact Sheet Regarding CHA Projects," in *Gautreaux v. CHA* files, Businessmen and Professionals in the Public Interest; Motion for Summary Judgment, *Gautreaux v. CHA*, No. 66-C-1459, U.S. District Court for the N. District of Illinois, in *Gautreaux v. CHA* files, Businessmen and Professionals in the Public Interest; Bowly, *The Poorhouse*, pp. 125–126.

4. Bowly, *The Poorhouse*, pp. 125, 128; *CDN*, 4/10/65; *CST*, 9/2/60; Chicago Urban League, *Public Housing: Chicago Builds a Ghetto* (1967).

5. Edward Marciniak, inteview with the authors; Bowly, *The Poorhouse*, pp. 64–65; James Fuerst, interview with the authors.

6. *CD*, 3/26/49.

7. Banfield and Meyerson, *Politics, Planning and the Public Interest*, p. 144.

8. Bowly, *The Poorhouse*, p. 126; *CDN*, 7/27/59; Bertrand Goldberg, interview with the authors; *CST*, 6/3/59; *CST*, 6/3/59.

9. *CST*, 6/2/59; Bowly, *The Poorhouse*, pp. 123–127.

10. Lewis, *Divided Highways*, p. 122; *CT*, 6/8/55; *CT*, 6/6/56.

11. Mayer and Wade, *Chicago: Growth of a Metropolis*, p. 446; Don Rose, interview with the authors.

12. Wilson, *When Work Disappears*, pp. 38–39.

13. *NYT*, 9/6/98.

14. Edward Marciniak, interview with the authors; Massey and Denton, *American Apartheid*, p. 161; Wilson, *When Work Disappears*, p. 39; Douglas Massey, Remarks at Solutions: Reinventing Public Housing, Chicago, Illinois.

15. Roemer, *Accardo*, p. 176; *Time*, 7/16/56.

16. Roemer, *Accardo*, pp. 130, 267; *CDN*, 2/11/64.

17. Edward Burke, interview with the authors; O'Connor, *Clout*, p. 114; Daley, F.B.I. Files, Correlation Summary, p. 24.

18. Paul McGrath, interview with the authors, 8/20/98.

19. *CSM*, 3/26/55; Roemer, *Accardo*, pp. 230–231; Daley, Confidential F.B.I. Files, "Memorandum to Mr. Belmont Re: Mayor Richard J. Daley"; Daley F.B.I. Files, Correlation Summary, p. 23.

20. *CST*, 6/6/66; Leon Despres Papers, Chicago Historical Society, Box 173, Folder 2; *CDN*, 2/11/64; Lens, *The Progressive*; Roemer, *Roemer: Man Against the Mob*, p. 105.

21. *CT*, 8/6/56; *CT*, 8/9/55; *CT*, 10/10/55; Sautter and Burke, *Inside the Wigwam*.

22. *CT*, 8/10/56; Biles, *Richard J. Daley*, pp. 54–55.

23. *Time*, 9/10/56; O'Connor, *Clout*, p. 142; *CT*, 8/6/56; *CT*, 8/21/77.

24. *Time*, 9/17/56; *CT*, 10/10/56.

25. *CT*, 9/1/56; *CT*, 9/21/56; *CT*, 10/5/56.

26. *CT*, 12/3/56.

27. *CT*, 11/10/56; *CT*, 1/14/57; *CT*, 12/2/56; *CT*, 11/24/56; Fremon, *Chicago Politics Ward by Ward*, p. 328; *CT*, 3/6/58; Rakove, *We Don't Want*, pp. 264–265.

28. *CT*, 1/3/57; *CT*, 1/15/57; *CT*, 3/5/57; *CT*, 3/21/57.

29. *CT*, 4/3/57; *CT*, 4/11/57; *CT*, 4/26/57; *CT*, 5/30/57; *CT*, 6/5/57.

30. CHA Press Release, "Swibel Appointed CHA Commissioner," 3/2/56; *CT*, 1/30/57; *Chicago Courier*, 11/17/62, in the Leon Despres Papers, Chicago Historical Society, Box 173, Folder 1; Bertrand Goldberg, interview with the authors; *CT*, 7/10/63; *Time*, 4/26/82; Hirsch, *Dilemma of Race*, p. 78.

31. "CHA Was in Black When I Left: Kean," *CDN*, 3/28/58; "Padding Cited in U.S. Report," *CT*, 3/27/58.

32. *CT,* 3/29/58; *CDN,* 3/28/58; James Fuerst, interview with the authors; *CT,* 3/28/58; *CT,* 11/12/97.

33. M.W. Newman, interview with the authors; Hirsch, *Making the Second Ghetto,* p. 241.

34. Deposition of Alvin Rose, *Gautreaux v. CHA* (3/3/68); Deposition of Emil G. Hirsch, *Gautreaux v. CHA* (3/3/68).

35. *CT,* 4/19/55; *CT,* 6/1/55; *CT,* 2/1/57.

36. *CT,* 6/24/57; *CT,* 6/25/57.

37. *CT,* 12/24/56; *CT,* 8/23/57; *CT,* 9/5/57; *CT,* 9/8/57; *CT,* 9/15/57.

38. *CT,* 11/14/57; *CT,* 10/15/57; *CT,* 11/5/57.

39. Hirsch, *Making the Second Ghetto,* p. 65; Hirsch, "Massive Resistance in the Urban North."

40. *CD,* 8/17/57; *CT,* 9/5/57.

41. Ralph, *Northern Protest,* p. 240; Reed, *The Chicago NAACP,* pp. 162–163; Travis, *Autobiography of Black Politics,* pp. 260–261; Reed, *Chicago NAACP,* p. 166.

42. "Open Letter to Congressman William L. Dawson," from the Executive Committee of Chicago Branch of the National Association for the Advancement of Colored People, 8/29/56, in possession of the authors.

43. Wilson, *Negro Politics,* pp. 63–64; *CD,* 12/14/57; Travis, *Autobiography of Black Politics,* p. 270; Reed, *The Chicago NAACP,* p. 189.

44. Reed, *The Chicago NAACP,* pp. 182, 189; Travis, *Autobiography of Black Politics,* pp. 261–264; Wilson, *Negro Politics,* p. 64.

45. Hirsch, *Making the Second Ghetto,* p. 139.

46. Sinkevitch, *AIA Guide to Chicago,* pp. 418–419; Horwitt, *Let Them Call Me Rebel,* p. 369.

47. Winger, "Unwelcome Neighbors," *Chicago History,* spring and summer 1992, pp. 56–73; Biles, *Richard J. Daley,* p. 13; Hirsch, *Making the Second Ghetto,* pp. 137, 135–136, 152, 153.

48. Julian Levi Oral History by Daniel Meyer, Special Collections Library, University of Chicago, pp. 46–47; Leon Despres Oral History, p. 41, Leon Despres Papers, Chicago Historical Society; Hirsch, *Making the Second Ghetto,* p. 167; Anthony Downs, interview with the authors.

49. *NYT,* 11/1/59; Horwitt, *Let Them Call Me Rebel,* p. 370; *NYT,* 11/1/59; Hirsch, *Making the Second Ghetto,* p. 161.

50. Hirsch, *Making the Second Ghetto,* p. 162; Rossi and Dentler, *The Politics of Urban Renewal,* pp. 264–65; Reed, *The Chicago NAACP,* p. 195.

51. Julian Levi Oral History, p. 81; Julian Levi, interview with the authors; Msgr. John Egan, interview with the authors; Rossi and Dentler, *The Politics of Urban Renewal,* pp. 253–263; Leon Despres Oral History, Joseph Regenstein Library, Department of Special Collections, University of Chicago, p. 39; Hirsch, *Making the Second Ghetto,* pp. 161–165, 255–260; Rossi and Dentler, *The Politics of Urban Renewal,* pp. 225–239; Baron, "Planning . . . in Black and White," in Chicago Urban League, *The Racial Aspects of Urban Planning,* 1968, n.p.

52. Fremon, *Chicago Politics Ward by Ward,* p. 204; *CT,* 3/5/58; *CT,* 4/16/58; *CT,* 4/22/58.

53. Travis, *Autobiography of Black Politics,* pp. 234; Grimshaw, *Bitter Fruit,* p. 109; Cooper, *South Side Boss,* pp. 78–79.

54. Travis, *Autobiography of Black Politics,* pp. 235–236; Ira Dawson, interview with the authors.

55. Travis, *Autobiography of Black Politics,* p. 235; Grimshaw, *Bitter Fruit,* p. 109; Cooper, *South Side Boss,* p. 81; Grimshaw, *Bitter Fruit,* p. 87.

Chapter 6. Make No Little Plans

1. Miller, *Here's the Deal,* p. 13; Mayer and Wade, *Chicago: Growth of a Metropolis,* p. 280; Sinkevitch, *AIA Guide to Chicago,* pp. 15–16.
2. *CST,* 8/23/58.
3. Banfield and Clark, *Fort Dearborn,* p. 1; Department of City Planning, Development Plan for Central Area of Chicago (1958), p. 4; Banfield and Clark, *Fort Dearborn,* p. 2; Development Plan, p. 26.
4. Tom Cokins, interview with the authors.
5. Development Plan, pp. 7, 21; Anthony Downs, interview with the authors.
6. Rubloff Papers, Box 7, Folder 4, Chicago Historical Society; Development Plan, p. 1.
7. Wilson, *When Work Disappears,* p. 13.
8. Mayer and Wade, *Chicago: Growth of a Metropolis,* p. 406; *CST,* 7/1/65; Massey and Denton, *American Apartheid,* p. 50.
9. McGreevy, *American Catholics,* pp. 109, 119; Chicago Commission on Human Relations, "Panic Peddling by Real Estate Brokers and Salesmen," in James Murray Files, Chicago Historical Society, Box 233; Massey and Denton, *American Apartheid,* p. 38; Horwitt, *Let Them Call Me Rebel,* p. 358.
10. *CST,* 7/1/65; Hauser, "Statement on the Chicago Housing Authority Proposal for Dispersed Public Housing in Chicago," 3/11/71, on file with the authors.
11. Gunther, *Inside U.S.A.,* p. 384; Ralph, *Northern Protest,* p. 48; Anderson and Pickering, *Confronting the Color Line,* p. 328; Wilson, *When Work Disappears,* p. 35.
12. Horwitt, *Let Them Call Me Rebel,* pp. 358–359, 426, 433.
13. Anthony Downs, interview with the authors; Horwitt, *Let Them Call Me Rebel,* p. 346.
14. *CT,* 10/31/58.
15. *CT,* 10/15/58; *CT,* 10/14/58; *CT,* 11/5/58; Fremon, *Chicago Politics Ward by Ward,* p. 246.
16. William Daley, interview with the authors; Rosen, *Decision-Making,* p. 30; William Stratton, interview with the authors; *CT,* 9/2/58.
17. *CT,* 9/4/58; Rosen, *Decision-Making,* p. 28.
18. Rosen, *Decision-Making,* pp. 43–47.
19. Rosen, *Decision-Making,* p. 51; *CT,* 2/20/59; *CT,* 2/24/59.
20. Fremon, *Chicago Politics Ward by Ward,* p. 187; Rosen, *Decision-Making,* p. 67.
21. *CT,* 12/8/59; Rosen, *Decision-Making,* pp. 67–69, 72; *CT,* 5/19/59.
22. *CT,* 4/14/59; *CT,* 4/15/59; see generally Bowly, *The Poorhouse;* Rosen, *Decision-Making,* pp. 81–84.
23. Rosen, *Decision-Making,* p. 81; *CT,* 5/27/59.
24. Rosen, *Decision-Making,* p. 111.
25. Rosen, *Decision-Making,* pp. 114–116.
26. *CT,* 3/21/61; *CT,* 4/19/61; *CT,* 4/20/61.
27. *CT,* 3/31/61.
28. *CT,* 4/20/61.

29. William Daley, interview with the authors; *CT,* 3/23/62; *CT,* 8/16/62; Rosen, *Decision-Making,* p. 118.
30. *CT,* 10/16/62; M.W. Newman, interview with the authors.
31. Rosen, *Decision-Making,* pp. 129–131.
32. Rosen, *Decision-Making,* pp. 131–132, 136–139.
33. Doherty, *O'Hare,* pp. 74–75.
34. Doherty, *O'Hare,* pp. 73, 76, 83–90.
35. *CT,* 5/11/55; Doherty, *O'Hare,* pp. 164, 166, 169, 171; *CT,* 10/11/55.
36. *CT,* 3/30/56; *CT,* 3/28/56; *CT,* 3/9/56; *CT,* 4/10/56; Doherty, *O'Hare,* pp. 118–119, 220.
37. Doherty, *O'Hare,* p. 242; Doherty, *O'Hare,* pp. 138–141.
38. Doherty, *O'Hare,* pp. 193–195, 214, 216; *CST,* 3/4/58.
39. *CT,* 3/14/62.
40. *NYT,* 3/10/62; *CT,* 3/23/63.
41. *CT,* 12/12/58.
42. *CT,* 12/2/58; *CT,* 12/12/58; *CST,* 12/11/58.
43. *CT,* 1/13/59.
44. *CT,* 1/9/59; *CT,* 1/20/59.
45. Lens, *The Progressive;* John Perkins, interview with the authors; *Commonweal,* April 1971.
46. Biles, *Richard J. Daley,* pp. 62–63; *CT,* 2/13/59; O'Connor, *Clout,* p. 149; *CT,* 3/17/59.
47. *CT,* 2/5/59.
48. *CT,* 1/15/59; *CT,* 1/29/59; *CT,* 2/20/59; *CT,* 3/10/59; *CT,* 4/2/59.
49. *CT,* 4/6/59; *CT,* 3/18/59.
50. *CT,* 3/1/59; *CT,* 3/13/59; *CT,* 4/3/59.
51. *CT,* 4/7/59.

Chapter 7. *Two for You, Three for Me*

1. *CT,* 9/27/58; Lindberg, *To Serve and Collect,* p. 285; Kennedy, *Himself!; CT,* 5/8/59.
2. *CT,* 5/16/59; *CT,* 11/21/59; *CT,* 5/18/59.
3. Berkow, *Maxwell Street,* p. 250; "Daley," WTTW-TV, 1986; *CT,* 5/29/59.
4. *NYT,* 7/7/59; *Time,* 7/20/59.
5. *NYT,* 7/17/59; *CT,* 8/5/59; *CT,* 10/29/59; *CT,* 11/4/59; *CT,* 11/6/59; *CT,* 11/11/59.
6. *CT,* 12/31/59; *CT,* 12/31/59.
7. *CT,* 12/19/59.
8. *CT,* 12/18/60; *CT,* 11/6/59; *CT,* 12/12/59; *CT,* 11/7/64; William Daley, interview with the authors.
9. *CT,* 1/4/60.
10. William Daley, interview with the authors; O'Connor, *Clout,* p. 150; Kalina, *Courthouse,* p. 12.
11. *CT,* 1/10/60; *CT,* 4/17/60; *CT,* 8/5/60.
12. Lindberg, *To Serve and Collect,* p. ix; Royko, *Boss,* p. 113; Biles, *Richard J. Daley,* p. 65.
13. *CT,* 1/19/60; *CT,* 1/20/60; *CT,* 1/21/60.
14. Biles, *Richard J. Daley,* p. 67; *CT,* 3/5/60; *CT,* 1/25/60; *CT,* 1/27/60; *CT,* 1/24/60.

15. *CT,* 1/31/60; Biles, *Richard J. Daley,* p. 67.
16. *CT,* 1/20/60; Lindberg, *To Serve and Collect,* p. 305; *CT,* 1/23/60.
17. Biles, *Richard J. Daley,* p. 67; *CT,* 12/19/60; Lindberg, *To Serve and Collect,* p. 309.
18. *NYT,* 3/3/60; *CT,* 2/23/60; Lindberg, *To Serve and Collect,* p. 307; *CT,* 3/18/60; *CT,* 3/14/60; *CT,* 5/11/60.
19. *CT,* 2/18/60; *CT,* 6/29/60; *CT,* 6/8/60; *CT,* 6/22/60.
20. *CT,* 4/7/60; *CT,* 4/10/60; *CT,* 5/12/60.
21. *CT,* 7/9/60.
22. *CT,* 7/8/60; Ciccone, *Daley,* p. 32.
23. *CT,* 7/11/60; *CT,* 12/6/60; White, *Making of the President 1960,* pp. 124, 167.
24. *CT,* 7/13/60; Ciccone, *Daley,* p. 44.
25. *CT,* 9/21/60; *CT,* 9/20/60; *CT,* 8/20/60.
26. *CT,* 11/8/60; Kalina, *Courthouse,* pp. 77–78; *CT,* 8/5/60; *CT,* 9/23/60.
27. Kalina, *Courthouse,* pp. 62–63, 69; *CT,* 10/12/60.
28. *CT,* 10/26/60; *CT,* 10/29/60; Kennedy, *Himself!,* p. 181.
29. *CT,* 10/28/60; Kalina, *Courthouse,* p. 76.
30. *CT,* 10/28/60; *CT,* 10/29/60.
31. Kalina, *Courthouse,* p. 65; Kennedy, *Himself!,* p. 181.
32. *CT,* 11/9/60; O'Connor, *Clout,* p. 154; Kennedy, *Himself!,* p. 184; White, *The Making of the President 1960,* p. 27; O'Donnell and Powers, *Johnny, We Hardly Knew Ye,* pp. 222–224.
33. O'Connor, *Clout,* pp. 155–58; *CT,* 11/10/60; *CT,* 11/13/60.
34. Royko, *Boss,* p. 119; Nixon, *Six Crises,* p. 391; Kalina, *Courthouse,* p. 94.
35. Kennedy, *Himself!,* p. 186; Kalina, *Courthouse,* p. 94.
36. Kalina, *Courthouse,* pp. 97–98.
37. Kalina, *Courthouse,* pp. 99–100; *CT,* 12/1/60.
38. *CT,* 11/13/60; *CT,* 12/3/60.
39. Kalina, *Courthouse,* pp. 110, 121–122; Fremon, *Chicago Politics Ward by Ward,* p. 203; *CT,* 12/1/60.
40. Kalina, *Courthouse,* pp. 132, 142–143; *CT,* 8/3/61.
41. Nixon, *RN: The Memoirs of Richard Nixon,* p. 224; O'Connor, *Clout,* pp. 157–158.
42. Kalina, *Courthouse,* p. 236 (Appendix 4).
43. Andre Foster, interview with the authors.
44. *CT,* 3/23/72.
45. Erie, *Rainbow's End,* p. 11; Kalina, *Courthouse,* p. 75; Miller, *City of the Century,* p. 466; Fanning, "The Literary Dimension," p. 103; Andre Foster, interview with the authors.
46. *CT,* 3/23/72.
47. Bill Recktenwald, interview with the authors.
48. *NYT,* 5/17/64.
49. *CT,* 9/13/72; *CT,* 9/23/72.
50. *CT,* 9/14/72; *NYWJT,* 12/9/66; *CT,* 3/23/72; *CT,* 9/16/72.
51. *CT,* 9/13/72.
52. *WP,* 11/11/68; *CT,* 3/24/72; *CT,* 3/23/72; *CT,* 9/15/72.
53. Bill Recktenwald, interview with the authors; Andre Foster, interview with the authors; *CT,* 3/24/72; *CT,* 3/23/72.
54. Kalina, *Courthouse,* p. 174.
55. Kalina, *Courthouse,* pp. 157–158, 183.

56. Kalina, *Courthouse*, pp. 214–215, 217–218, 220–221.
57. *Time*, 3/17/61; *CT*, 2/9/61; Rakove, *Don't Make No Waves*, p. 182.

Chapter 8. Beware of the Press, Mayor

1. *CT*, 1/17/61; *CT*, 1/22/61; *CST*, 12/16/60; Wofford, *Of Kennedys and Kings*, p. 90; Daniel Rostenkowski, interview with the authors; Chester, *An American Melodrama*, p. 504; Ciccone, *Daley*, p. 145.
2. *CT*, 4/21/61.
3. *CT*, 4/22/61; *CT*, 4/7/61; *CT*, 5/11/61; *CT*, 6/22/61.
4. *CT*, 3/12/61; *CT*, 6/6/61; *CT*, 6/7/61.
5. *CT*, 12/8/61; *CT*, 12/2/61.
6. Anderson and Pickering, *Confronting the Color Line*, p. 76; Ralph, *Northern Protest*, p. 14.
7. Remsberg and Remsberg, "Chicago Voices: Tales Told Out of School," in Mack, *Our Children's Burden*, p. 365; Anderson and Pickering, *Confronting the Color Line*, pp. 77, 84; Ralph, *Northern Protest*, pp. 14–15, 77.
8. Anderson and Pickering, *Confronting the Color Line*, pp. 89–90; Ralph, *Northern Protest*, pp. 15-17.
9. Meyer Weinberg, interview with the authors.
10. Anderson and Pickering, *Confronting the Color Line*, p. 90.
11. Anderson and Pickering, *Confronting the Color Line*, pp. 92, 101.
12. John Perkins, interview with the authors.
13. *CT*, 11/3/61; Travis, *Autobiography of Black Politics*, pp. 234–235; *CT*, 11/1/61.
14. *CT*, 12/2/61; *CT*, 1/3/62.
15. *CT*, 4/5/62; *CT*, 2/9/62; *NYT*, 4/12/62; *Time*, 4/20/62.
16. *CT*, 6/13/62.
17. *CT*, 5/9/62; *CT*, 5/12/62; *CT*, 6/30/62.
18. *CT*, 6/7/62; *CT*, 8/21/62; *CT*, 8/30/62; *CT*, 9/19/62.
19. *CT*, 8/29/62.
20. *CT*, 9/5/62; *CT*, 7/14/62.
21. *CT*, 10/23/62; *CT*, 11/5/62; *CT*, 10/11/62; *CT*, 11/2/62.
22. *CT*, 11/7/62.
23. *Architectural Forum* 5, pp. 62, 115–117; Sinkevitch, *AIA Guide to Chicago*, pp. 20, 34–35, 68, 69, 101, 108–109; *CT*, 5/12/93; Biles, *Richard J. Daley*, p. 47; *CT*, 6/21/63; *CT*, 5/24/68.
24. McBrien, *The Loop*, p. 33; Mayer and Wade, *Chicago: Growth of a Metropolis*, p. 462; Sinkevitch, *AIA Guide to Chicago*, p. 366.
25. Rast, *Remaking Chicago*, p. 31; Wille, *At Home in the Loop*, pp. 4–6; 1958 Plan, p. 8; Cross, Gilbert, "The House the Janitors Built," *Fortune*, 1962; Bertrand Goldberg, interview with the authors; Miller, *Here's the Deal*, p. 163.
26. John Perkins, interview with the authors; Edward Marciniak, interview with the authors; Tom Donovan, interview with the authors; *CST*, *Midwest Magazine*, 4/19/70; *CST*, 4/19/70.
27. *CT*, 1/4/63; *CT*, 12/9/62; *CT*, 12/13/62; *CT*, 12/8/62; *CT*, 12/15/62.
28. *CT*, 12/21/62; *CT*, 12/19/62.
29. *CT*, 1/12/63.
30. Biles, *Richard J. Daley*, p. 79; *CT*, 1/2/63.

31. *CT,* 2/10/63; *CT,* 1/3/63; *Time,* 3/15/63.

32. *CT,* 12/20/63.

33. *CT,* 3/14/63.

34. *CT,* 1/7/63.

35. Grimshaw, *Bitter Fruit,* p. 120; Biles, *Richard J. Daley,* p. 79; *CT,* 3/1/63; Biles, *Richard J. Daley,* pp. 79–80; *CT,* 1/10/63; *CT,* 5/16/63; *CT,* 2/6/63.

36. *CT,* 4/2/63.

37. *CT,* 3/20/63; *CT,* 3/28/63; *CT,* 3/12/63; *CT,* 3/20/63.

38. *CT,* 3/19/63; Doherty, *O'Hare,* pp. 269–270.

39. Gleason, *Daley of Chicago,* p. 339; Biles, *Richard J. Daley,* p. 82.

40. "The 1966 Bond Issues," p. 4, in Jim Murray Papers, Box 233-327, Chicago Historical Society; Hirsch, *Chicago,* p. 81.

41. *CD,* 6/15/63; *CD,* 5/11/63.

42. *Time,* 7/12/63, p.19.

43. *CT,* 7/5/63; *Time,* 4/12/63; Edward Marciniak, interview with the authors.

44. Edward Marciniak, interview with the authors; *CD,* 7/6/63.

45. *NYT,* 4/5/63; *CD,* 7/6/63; *Time,* 7/12/63.

46. *CT,* 7/7/63; *NYT,* 7/23/63; *NYT,* 7/18/63; *NYT,* 8/23/63; Ralph, *Northern Protest,* p. 26.

47. Grimshaw, *Bitter Fruit,* p. 103; *CT,* 7/13/63; *CT,* 7/12/63; *CT,* 8/24/63.

48. Rakove, *We Don't Want,* p. 253; James Murray, interview with the authors; *CT,* 9/13/63.

49. *CT,* 7/22/63; *CT,* 8/2/63; *CT,* 8/17/63; *NYT,* 8/26/63.

50. Ira Dawson, interview with the authors; Meyer Weinberg, interview with the authors.

51. Remsberg, *Chicago Voices,* p. 285; Ralph, *Northern Protest,* p. 20; Meyer Weinberg, interview with authors; Weinberg and Rich, A Report on Official Segregation in Chicago Public Schools by Coordinating Council of Community Organizations, 7/27/65; *CT,* 3/6/66.

52. Travis, *Autobiography of Black Politics,* p. 316; *CT,* 8/21/63; *CT,* 10/4/63; *CT,* 10/10/63; Ralph, *Northern Protest,* p. 20; Anderson and Pickering, *Confronting the Color Line,* pp. 117, 150.

53. Travis, *Autobiography of Black Politics,* pp. 313–314; *NYT,* 10/24/63.

54. *NYT,* 11/23/63; *CT,* 11/24/63.

55. William Daley, interview with the authors; *CT,* 7/23/63; *CT,* 7/17/63; Ciccone, *Daley,* p. 173; *NYT,* 11/17/63.

56. *CT,* 8/24/63; *CT,* 12/8/63; *CT,* 10/2/63; *CT,* 11/30/63.

57. *CT,* 1/30/64; *CT,* 4/2/64; *CT,* 4/1/64; *CT,* 4/9/64.

58. *CT,* 1/3/64; *CT,* 11/13/63; Anderson and Pickering, *Confronting the Color Line,* p. 123; O'Connor, *Requiem,* p. 27.

59. Travis, *Autobiography of Black Politics,* pp. 316–317; *CT,* 2/4/64; Usdan and Lee, *Anatomy of a Compromise,* p. 35.

60. *CT,* 2/26/64.

61. Usdan and Lee, *Anatomy of a Compromise,* p. 40; Report to the Board of Education City of Chicago by the Advisory Panel on Integration of the Public Schools, 3/31/64, pp. 6, 42; Anderson and Pickering, *Confronting the Color Line,* p. 134.

62. Travis, *Autobiography of Black Politics,* pp. 252, 322; Biles, *Richard J. Daley,* p. 100; *CST,* 6/15/69.

63. Walter Heller, Memorandum of Conversation, 11/23/63, Heller Papers, Kennedy Library; *Time,* 5/13/66, p. 25; Diary of Lady Bird Johnson, April 23, 1964, Johnson Library, Austin, Texas; Goodwin, *Remembering America,* p. 270.
64. Manchester, *The Glory and the Dream,* p. 1042.
65. Conversation of Lyndon. B. Johnson and Sargent Shriver, 2/1/64, in Beschloss, *White House Tapes,* p. 209; Anderson and Pickering, *Confronting the Color Line,* p. 168; *Time,* 5/13/66.
66. Anderson and Pickering, *Confronting the Color Line,* p. 170; Piven and Cloward, *Regulating the Poor,* p. 270; Moynihan, *Maximum Feasible Misunderstanding,* pp. 91, 131–32; *Time,* "War on Poverty," p. 28.
67. *CT,* 2/5/66; Rakove, *Don't Make No Waves,* p. 62; Halberstam, "Daley of Chicago."
68. *Time,* 7/16/65; Patterson, *America's Struggle Against Poverty,* pp. 145–146; Biles, *Richard J. Daley,* p. 105; House Committee on Education and Labor, p. 768.
69. *NYT,* 4/14/65; Biles, *Richard J. Daley,* pp. 104–105.
70. *CT,* 3/10/66; *CT,* 4/15/65; *CT,* 4/14/63; *CT,* 6/8/66.
71. *CT,* 5/18/64; *CT,* 5/20/64.
72. *CT,* 7/15/64; *CT,* 7/16/64; *CT,* 5/15/64; *CT,* 5/1/64.
73. *CT,* 8/24/64.
74. Wilson and Ferris (eds.), *The Encyclopedia of Southern Culture,* p. 211; Garrow, *Bearing the Cross,* pp. 346–347; Mann, *The Walls of Jericho,* p. 438.
75. Department of Civil Rights, Chicago Commission on Human Relations, "Report on 3309 South Lowe Avenue," Murray Papers, Chicago Historical Society.
76. *CT,* 10/7/64; Department of Civil Rights, Chicago Commission on Human Relations, "Report on 3309 South Lowe Avenue," Murray Papers, Chicago Historical Society; Biles, *Richard J. Daley,* p. 101.
77. *CT,* 9/15/64; *CT,* 10/20/64; *NYT,* 10/31/64; *CT,* 10/31/64; Ciccone, *Daley,* pp. 187–188; *CT,* 11/2/64.
78. *CST,* 11/22/64.
79. *CT,* 11/17/64; *CT,* 11/18/64; *CT,* 11/21/64; *CT,* 10/22/64.
80. *CT,* 11/24/64; *CT,* 4/21/65; Daley F.B.I. Files, Correlation Summary, p. 24; Daley F.B.I. Files, "Memorandum to Mr Belmont Re: Mayor Richard J. Daley."

Chapter 9. We're Going to Have a Movement in Chicago

1. Usdan and Lee, *Anatomy of a Compromise,* p. 66; *CT,* 1/18/65.
2. Statement by C. H. Adams III at Citizens' Schools Committee, Panel Session, 11/19/64, in C. H. Adams Papers, Chicago Historical Society, Box 6; Usdan and Lee, *Anatomy of a Compromise,* p. 74; *CT,* 5/14/65.
3. *CT,* 4/8/65.
4. *CST,* 5/14/65; *CA,* 5/28/65; Usdan and Lee, *Anatomy of a Compromise,* pp. 91–92, 94, 113; Anderson and Pickering, *Confronting the Color Line,* p. 153.
5. *CT,* 6/17/65; Anderson and Pickering, *Confronting the Color Line,* pp. 155–157.
6. "Chicago Is Facing School Aid Fight," *NYT,* 6/30/65.
7. *NYT,* 6/30/65; Anderson and Pickering, *Confronting the Color Line,* p. 159; *CT,* 6/30/65; *CT,* 7/1/65; *CT,* 6/18/65; *CT,* 6/12/65.
8. Garrow, *Bearing the Cross,* p. 400.
9. Young, *An Easy Burden,* p. 383; Ralph, *Northern Protest,* p. 29.
10. Garrow, *Bearing the Cross,* pp. 420–421; Ralph, *Northern Protest,* pp. 1, 3.

11. *CDN,* 4/16/65; *CDN,* 4/10/65.

12. *CST,* 3/8/66; *CT,* 7/7/65.

13. *CST,* 10/4/64; Bowly, *The Poorhouse,* pp. 130, 131; Monsignor John Egan, interview with the authors; Sinkevitch, *AIA Guide to Chicago,* p. 360; Bertrand Goldberg, interview with the authors.

14. Gleason, *Daley of Chicago,* p. 98.

15. *CDN,* 12/20/66; *CT,* 3/19/64.

16. July 4, 1965, Title VI Complaint of Coordinating Council of Community Organizations, Integrated Education, pp. 10–12; Meyer Weinberg, interview with the authors.

17. *New York Herald Tribune,* 4/30/65 and 5/1/65; *New York Post,* 5/2/65; July 4, 1965, Title VI Complaint of Coordinating Council of Community Organizations, pp. 15–32.

18. Anderson and Pickering, *Confronting the Color Line,* p. 178; *NYT,* 7/8/65.

19. *CSM,* 5/22/65; Anderson and Pickering, *Confronting the Color Line,* p. 178; Bernstein, *Guns or Butter; New York Herald Tribune,* 5/1/65; *New York Herald Tribune,* 4/30/65.

20. July 27, 1965, Title VI Complaint of Coordinating Council of Community Organizations, Integrated Education, pp. 24–26; Anderson and Pickering, *Confronting the Color Line,* p. 178.

21. July 4, 1965, Complaint, pp. 15–17; July 27, 1965, Title VI Complaint of Coordinating Council of Community Organizations, Integrated Education, p. 32; Weinberg and Rich, A Report on Official Segregation in Chicago Public Schools by Coordinating Council of Community Organizations, 7/27/65.

22. Bernstein, *Guns or Butter,* p. 396; Travis, *Autobiography of Black Politics,* p. 345.

23. Paul McGrath, interview with the authors; Edward Marciniak, interview with the authors; Edward Holmgren, interview with the authors.

24. Richard Wade, interview with the authors.

25. "Activists Re-Assess Movement to Integrate Chicago," *All Things Considered,* National Public Radio, 4/4/93.

26. Paul McGrath, interview with the authors; Charles Swibel, interview with Bruce Thomas and Robert Nathan, July 1986, in possession of authors; Larry O'Brien to LBJ, 8/11/65, Richard Daley Name File, LBJ Library, Austin, Texas.

27. Garrow, *Bearing the Cross,* pp. 433–434; *CST,* 7/27/65.

28. *CT,* 7/26/65; *CT,* 7/25/65; *CT,* 7/30/65.

29. *NYT,* 8/8/65; Wille, "Mayor Daley Meets the Movement," *Nation,* 8/30/65.

30. Kennedy, *Himself!,* p. 196; Letter of Al Raby to Jack Greenberg, September 18, 1965, Southern Christian Leadership Conference Papers, Atlanta, GA; *Time,* 8/13/65; *NYT,* 8/3/65.

31. *NYT,* 5/2/65; *NYT,* 4/18/65; *CT,* 7/22/65.

32. *NYT,* 4/14/65; *CT,* 12/30/65; *CT,* 12/7/65; *NYT,* 12/5/65; *NYT,* 4/18/65; *CT,* 12/24/66.

33. *NYT,* 8/19/65; Lemann, *The Promised Land,* p. 167; Biles, *Richard J. Daley,* p. 107.

34. *NYT,* 8/15/65; *Time,* 7/23/65; Harrington, "The Deserving Poor," *New York Herald Tribune,* 6/6/65.

35. *NYT,* 4/14/65; *NYT,* 4/15/65; *NYT,* 6/8/65; *NYT,* 12/2/65; *New York Herald Tribune,* 12/3/65.

36. *NYT,* 12/5/65; *NYT,* 12/7/65; *CA,* 12/7/66; conversation of Sargent Shriver and

Bill Moyers, in Beschloss, *Taking Charge: The Johnson White House Tapes,* p. 208; *New York Post,* 12/22/67.

37. *CT,* 1/11/66; *CT,* 3/24/66; *CT,* 2/26/66; *CT,* 2/17/66; *CT,* 2/19/65.

38. Manchester, *The Glory and the Dream,* pp. 1062–1063.

39. Manchester, *The Glory and the Dream,* p. 1064; Young, *An Easy Burden,* p. 380.

40. Hampton and Fayer, *Voices of Freedom,* p. 298; Abernathy, *And the Walls Came Tumbling Down,* pp. 367–368.

41. Ralph, *Northern Protest,* pp. 35–36; *CD,* 11/8–14/66; Finley, "The Open Housing Marches: Chicago, Summer '66," in Garrow (ed.), *Chicago 1966,* p. 2.

42. Garrow, *Bearing the Cross,* p. 455.

43. *NYT,* 8/15/65.

44. *NYT,* 8/15/65; Biles, *Richard J. Daley,* p. 114; *CT,* 8/17/65.

45. Anderson and Pickering, *Confronting the Color Line,* p. 164; *CT,* 9/14/65; *CT,* 9/24/65.

46. Remsberg, *Chicago Voices,* p. 285; *NYT,* 7/12/65; Anderson and Pickering, *Confronting the Color Line,* pp. 178, 179; Biles, *Richard J. Daley,* p. 115; interview of Francis Keppel, 4/21/69, in the Lyndon Baines Johnson Library, Austin, Texas.

47. Anderson and Pickering, *Confronting the Color Line,* p. 179; Bernstein, *Guns or Butter,* p. 395; interview of Francis Keppel, 4/21/69, in the Lyndon Baines Johnson Library, Austin, Texas; *NYT,* 10/17/65.

48. Telephone call between Lyndon B. Johnson and Richard J. Daley, 1/20/64, transcript in Beschloss, *Taking Charge: The Johnson White House Tapes,* pp. 168–169; Diary of Lady Bird Johnson, 4/21/64, Johnson Library, Austin, Texas; Bernstein, *Guns or Butter,* p. 396.

49. "A Chronology of Deferral," *Integrated Education,* issue 18, p. 8.

50. Bernstein, *Guns or Butter,* pp. 395–396; interview of Francis Keppel, 4/21/69, in the Lyndon Baines Johnson Library, Austin, Texas; Biles, *Richard J. Daley,* p. 16.

51. Meyer Weinberg, interview with the authors; *CT,* 10/6/65; *CT,* 10/7/65; *CDN,* 10/6/65, quoted in *Integrated Education,* p. 9.

52. Interview of Francis Keppel, 4/21/69, in the Lyndon Baines Johnson Library, Austin, Texas; *CSM,* 4/16/66; *NYT,* 12/31/65; *NYT,* 10/17/65; Kraft, "Integrating Northern Schools," *New York Post,* 11/11/65; *NYT,* 9/18/65.

53. *CT,* 10/11/66.

54. *CT,* 11/10/65.

55. *NYT,* 7/23/65; *CT,* 11/30/65; *CT,* 12/8/65.

56. *CD,* 10/9–15/65; Garrow, *Bearing the Cross,* pp. 447–448; Meyer Weinberg, interview with the authors; *CD,* 1/8–14/66.

57. Garrow, *Bearing the Cross,* p. 452; *CD,* 1/8–14/66.

58. *Civil Rights 1960–66,* p. 397; Travis, *Autobiography of Black Politics,* p. 349; Garrow, *Bearing the Cross,* pp. 456–457.

Chapter 10. All of Us Are Trying to Eliminate Slums

1. Ralph, *Northern Protest,* pp. 48–49.

2. Ralph, *Northern Protest,* p. 45; Abernathy, *And the Walls Came Tumbling Down,* pp. 362–363.

3. *Wall Street Journal,* 7/19/66; Travis, *Autobiography of Black Politics,* pp. 47, 346–347.

4. Ehrenhalt, *The Lost City,* p. 183; Travis, *Autobiography of Black Politics,* p. 354; Abernathy,

And the Walls Came Tumbling Down, p. 373; Levinsohn, "The Crusade that Failed," *Chicago Times,* May/June 1988, p. 68; Travis, *Autobiography of Black Politics,* p. 47.

5. *CD,* 1/8–14/66; *CD,* 1/22–28/66; Abernathy, *The Walls Came Tumbling Down,* p. 371; Ralph, *Northern Protest,* p. 55; Travis, *Autobiography of Black Politics,* p. 352; Young, *An Easy Burden,* p. 388; Weisbrot, *Freedom Bound,* p. 182.

6. Garrow, *Bearing the Cross,* p. 465; Abernathy, *The Walls Came Tumbling Down,* p. 371; Meyer Weinberg, interview with the authors; *CD,* 2/19–25/66; *CD,* 2/12–18/66.

7. *CD,* 1/29–2/4/66; Weisbrot, *Freedom Bound,* pp. 180–181.

8. *CT,* 1/27/66.

9. *CT,* 1/28/66; *CT,* 2/1/66; Travis, *Autobiography of Black Politics,* p. 353; *CD,* 2/12–18/66.

10. *CT,* 2/11/63.

11. Young, *An Easy Burden,* p. 392; *CT,* 3/2/66; *CD,* 2/12–18/66; *CT,* 2/12/66.

12. *CD,* 1/29–2/4/66; *CT,* 2/1/66; *CT,* 3/15/66.

13. Garrow, *Bearing the Cross,* pp. 460–461; Ralph, *Northern Protest,* pp. 73–75; *NYT,* 6/17/65.

14. *CT,* 2/26/66.

15. Ralph, *Northern Protest,* pp. 56, 57, 79; *CT,* 2/26/66.

16. *CT,* 3/4/66.

17. *CT,* 12/4/66.

18. *CST,* *Midwest Magazine,* 5/19/74.

19. *CA,* 12/17/66; *CT,* 12/18/66; *CDN,* 3/14/66; Seymour Simon, interview with the authors.

20. Travis, *Autobiography of Black Politics,* p. 357; Garrow, *Bearing the Cross,* p. 466; *CT,* 3/18/66.

21. *CT,* 4/1/66; *CT,* 3/15/66; *CT,* 3/19/66.

22. *CT,* 6/22/66; Frady, *Jesse,* p. 202; Weisbrot, *Freedom Bound,* p. 184; *CT,* 6/22/66; *CT,* 6/21/66.

23. Garrow, *Bearing the Cross,* p. 466.

24. *CD,* 3/19/66; *CT,* 3/19/66; *CT,* 3/25/66; Biles, *Richard J. Daley,* p. 122; *CT,* 3/25/66; *CT,* 3/26/66.

25. *CT,* 3/25/66; *CT,* 3/28/66; *CT,* 3/29/66.

26. *CT,* 3/8/66; *CD,* 4/16–22/66.

27. Sinkevitch, *AIA Guide to Chicago,* pp. 98–100; Berger, *They Built Chicago,* pp. 273–274.

28. *CT,* 3/20/66.

29. *CDN,* 12/23/57; John Duba, interview with the authors.

30. *CA,* 6/10/65; *CST,* 6/10/65.

31. John Gunther, interview with the authors; David Stahl, interview with the authors; *CT,* 3/20/66; "The Mayor's Whiz Kids," *Chicago Magazine,* Winter 1966, p. 61; *CDN,* 10/17/61; *CT,* 10/5/66; Biles, *Richard J. Daley,* p. 45; Rast, *Remaking Chicago,* p. 27.

32. *CT,* 4/24/66.

33. *CT,* 4/19/66; *CT,* 4/1/66; *CT,* 4/23/66; *CT,* 4/28/66; "The 1966 Bond Issues," p. 4, in Jim Murray Papers, Box 227–233, Chicago Historical Society.

34. *CT,* 4/6/66; *CT,* 4/8/66.

35. John Perkins, interview with the authors; Miles Berger, interview with the authors; Miller, *Here's the Deal,* pp. 19–22; Sinkevitch, *AIA Guide to Chicago,* p. 71; *CT,* 5/2/66; *CT,* 5/3/66.

36. *CT,* 3/22/66; *CT,* 4/1/66.
37. Peterson, *School Politics,* p. 81; *CT,* 5/7/66; Anderson and Pickering, *Confronting the Color Line,* p. 481; *CT,* 4/28/66; Travis, *Autobiography of Black Politics,* p. 358.
38. Ralph, *Northern Protest,* pp. 94–95; *CT,* 5/27/66.
39. *Time,* 7/1/66; Travis, *Autobiography of Black Politics,* pp. 359, 373; *CT,* 6/19/66; Biles, *Richard J. Daley,* p. 123.
40. Sobel, *Civil Rights 1960–66,* p. 375; Jacoby, *Someone Else's House,* p. 93; Ralph, *Northern Protest,* p. 185.
41. Sobel, *Civil Rights 1960–66,* p. 378; *Time,* 7/15/66.
42. Anderson and Pickering, *Confronting the Color Line,* p. 201; *NYT,* 7/9/66; Ralph, *Northern Protest,* pp. 101–102; Finley, *The Open Housing Marches,* p. 12.
43. Anderson and Pickering, *Confronting the Color Line,* pp. 197–198.
44. Finley, *The Open Housing Marches,* p. 8.
45. *NYT,* 7/9/66.
46. *CT,* 7/10/66; *NYT,* 7/11/66.
47. Hampton, *Voices of Freedom,* p. 306.
48. Travis, *Autobiography of Black Politics,* pp. 362–366; *CT,* 7/16/66.
49. *CT,* 7/11/66.
50. Anderson and Pickering, *Confronting the Color Line,* p. 208.
51. Hampton, *Voices of Freedom,* p. 307; Ralph, *Northern Protest,* p. 108.
52. *NYT,* 7/12/66; Anderson and Pickering, *Confronting the Color Line,* p. 208.
53. Ralph, *Northern Protest,* pp. 108–109; Biles, *Richard J. Daley,* p. 124; Travis, *Autobiography of Black Politics,* p. 365; *NYT,* 7/12/66.
54. Travis, *Autobiography of Black Politics,* pp. 374–375; Anderson and Pickering, *Confronting the Color Line,* p. 212; *NYT,* 7/18/66.
55. Anderson and Pickering, *Confronting the Color Line,* pp. 210–212; Travis, *Autobiography of Black Politics,* p. 374.
56. *NYT,* 7/18/66; *NYT,* 7/16/66; Anderson and Pickering, *Confronting the Color Line,* p. 213.
57. *NYT,* 7/16/66; *CT,* 7/16/66; *CT,* 7/18/66.
58. *CT,* 7/18/66; Ralph, *Northern Protest,* p. 111; *CD,* 8/16–22/66.
59. *CT,* 8/15/66; *NYT,* 7/26/66; Hampton, *Voices of Freedom,* p. 310; *NYT,* 7/16/66; Ralph, *Northern Protest,* p. 111.
60. *NYT,* 7/17/66; Anderson and Pickering, *Confronting the Color Line,* p. 214; Ralph, *Northern Protest,* p. 112.
61. *CT,* 8/26/66; *NYT,* 7/18/66; *NYT,* 7/20/66; Ralph, *Northern Protest,* p. 113.
62. Hampton, *Voices of Freedom,* p. 311; *NYT,* 8/6/66; Anderson and Pickering, *Confronting the Color Line,* pp. 216, 218, 223.
63. Anderson and Pickering, *Confronting the Color Line,* p. 223; "Activists Re-Assess Movement," National Public Radio; Don Rose, interview with the authors.
64. Anderson and Pickering, *Confronting the Color Line,* p. 224; Hampton, *Voices of Freedom,* p. 312.
65. *CT,* 8/3/66; Ralph, *Northern Protest,* p. 130.
66. Ralph, *Northern Protest,* p. 143.
67. Anderson and Pickering, *Confronting the Color Line,* p. 227; "Activists Re-Assess Movement," National Public Radio; Travis, *An Autobiography of Black Politics,* p. 389.
68. *NYT,* 8/6/66; Young, *An Easy Burden,* p. 412.
69. Don Rose, interview with the authors; Hampton, *Voices of Freedom,* p. 313; "Ac-

tivists Re-Assess Movement," National Public Radio; *NYT,* 8/6/66; Ralph, *Northern Protest,* p. 123; Sobel, *Civil Rights 1960–66;* Weisbrot, *Freedom Bound,* p. 183; *NYT,* 8/6/66.

70. *CT,* 7/7/66; *CST,* 7/27/66.
71. *CT,* 8/9/66; Anderson and Pickering, *Confronting the Color Line,* pp. 228–229; Ralph, *Northern Protest,* p. 144.
72. *NYT,* 8/9/66; Oudes, "The Siege of Cicero," *The Nation,* 3/27/67, pp. 398, 399; *CT,* 8/4/66; *NYT,* 8/10/66; Anderson and Pickering, *Confronting the Color Line,* p. 229; Weisbrot, *Freedom Bound,* p. 183; Hampton, *Voices of Freedom,* p. 314.
73. Sobel, *Civil Rights 1960–66,* p. 401; Ralph, *Northern Protest,* pp. 145, 151.
74. *NYT,* 8/11/66; Ralph, *Northern Protest,* p. 159; Young, *An Easy Burden,* pp. 414–415; Meyer Weinberg, interview with the authors.

Chapter 11. The Outcome Was Bitterly Disappointing

1. Ralph, *Northern Protest,* pp. 147–148, 152; *CT,* 8/11/66.
2. Anderson and Pickering, *Confronting the Color Line,* p. 271; *CD,* 8/20–26/66; John McKnight, interview with the authors; McKnight, "Summit Negotiations," in Garrow, *Chicago: 1966;* p. 122.
3. John McKnight, interview with the authors; Anderson and Pickering, *Confronting the Color Line,* p. 238.
4. *CT,* 8/18/66; Connolly, "Chicago Open Housing Conference," in Garrow, *Chicago: 1966: Open Housing Marches,* p.74.
5. McKnight, "Summit Negotiations," in Garrow, *Chicago: 1966,* p. 120, *CD,* 8/20–26/66.
6. McKnight, "Summit Negotiations," in Garrow, *Chicago: 1966,* pp. 113–114.
7. McKnight, "Summit Negotiations," in Garrow, *Chicago: 1966,* pp. 116, 241.
8. McKnight, "Summit Negotiations," in Garrow, *Chicago: 1966,* pp. 117–118.
9. McKnight, "Summit Negotiations," in Garrow, *Chicago: 1966,* pp. 119–121.
10. John McKnight, interview with the authors; McKnight, "Summit Negotiations," in Garrow, *Chicago: 1966,* p. 122.
11. *CT,* 8/18/66; McKnight, "Summit Negotiations," in Garrow, *Chicago: 1966,* p. 123; Garrow, *Bearing the Cross,* p. 508.
12. *CT,* 8/19/66; Ralph, *Northern Protest,* p. 156; McKnight, "Summit Negotiations," in Garrow, *Chicago: 1966,* p. 125.
13. McKnight, "Summit Negotiations," in Garrow, *Chicago: 1966,* pp. 124–127.
14. McKnight, "Summit Negotiations," in Garrow, *Chicago: 1966,* pp. 127–130.
15. McKnight, "Summit Negotiations," in Garrow, *Chicago: 1966,* pp. 130–131; Garrow, *Bearing the Cross,* p. 511; Anderson and Pickering, *Confronting the Color Line,* p. 250.
16. Abernathy, *And the Walls Came Tumbling Down,* p. 385; McKnight, "Summit Negotiations," in Garrow, *Chicago: 1966,* pp. 131–132, 138; Garrow, *Bearing the Cross,* p. 512.
17. McKnight, "Summit Negotiations," in Garrow, *Chicago: 1966,* pp. 132–133.
18. McKnight, "Summit Negotiations," in Garrow, *Chicago: 1966,* p. 135; Anderson and Pickering, *Confronting the Color Line,* pp. 253–254.
19. *CT,* 8/18/66; *CT,* 8/19/66; *CT,* 8/20/66; Anderson and Pickering, *Confronting the Color Line,* p. 257.

20. Anderson and Pickering, *Confronting the Color Line,* p. 254; Ralph, *Northern Protest,* p. 142.
21. Robert Warden, interview with the authors.
22. *CT,* 7/8/68; Jerome Torshen, interview with the authors; *CT,* 8/21/66; *CT,* 8/20/66.
23. *CT,* 8/20/66.
24. *CT,* 8/20/66; Yarbrough, *Judge Frank Johnson,* pp. 120–212; *CT,* 8/25/66; *CT,* 8/26/66.
25. Anderson and Pickering, *Confronting the Color Line,* p. 257; Ralph, *Northern Protest,* p. 164; *CT,* 8/23/66.
26. Weisbrot, *Freedom Bound,* p. 183.
27. Anderson and Pickering, *Confronting the Color Line,* p. 259; *CD,* 8/27/66.
28. Anderson and Pickering, *Confronting the Color Line,* pp. 262, 272; *CT,* 8/27/66.
29. McKnight, "Summit Negotiations," in Garrow, *Chicago: 1966,* p. 139.
30. McKnight, "Summit Negotiations," in Garrow, *Chicago: 1966,* pp. 139–144.
31. McKnight, "Summit Negotiations," in Garrow, *Chicago: 1966,* pp. 144–145; *CT,* 8/27/66.
32. *CT,* 8/29/66.
33. Ralph, *Northern Protest,* p. 195.
34. Anderson and Pickering, *Confronting the Color Line,* p. 274; Young, *An Easy Burden,* p. 416; Ralph, *Northern Protest,* pp. 197-98.
35. *CT,* 9/8/66; Ralph, *Northern Protest,* p. 200.
36. *CT,* 9/23/66; Ralph, *Northern Protest,* p. 207; "Activists Re-Assess Movement," National Public Radio; Levinsohn, *Crusade That Failed,* p. 71.
37. Downs, Anthony, interview with the authors; Ralph, *Northern Protest,* pp. 208–209.
38. *CT,* 9/15/66.
39. *NYT,* 11/6/66.
40. *Wall Street Journal,* 10/28/66; 11/25/66; *CT,* 10/5/66; *CT,* 11/6/66; *CT,* 10/9/66; *CT,* 10/13/66; *CT,* 11/2/66; *CT,* 10/24/66; *CT,* 10/26/66; *CT,* 11/4/66; *CT,* 11/5/66.
41. *CT,* 11/6/66; *NYT,* 11/6/66; *CT,* 11/5/66; CT, 11/3/66; *NYT,* 11/2/66.
42. *CT,* 11/9/66.
43. *NYT,* 11/10/66; *NYT,* 11/13/66; *CT,* 11/10/66; *CT,* 11/9/66.
44. *CT,* 11/27/66.
45. *CT,* 11/30/66; *CT,* 12/7/66; Abernathy, *And the Walls Came Tumbling Down,* p. 395, Ralph, *Northern Post,* p. 223.

Chapter 12. Shoot to Kill

1. *CT,* 12/7/66; *CT,* 12/10/66; *CT,* 12/30/66; Rakove, *We Don't Want,* pp. 281–282; *Wall Street Journal,* 3/31/67.
2. James Murray, interview with the authors; *Time,* 2/25/67.
3. Comprehensive Plan of Chicago, Summary Report, p. 4; *CT,* 12/15/66; *CT,* 12/13/66.
4. *CT,* 1/5/67; *CT,* 1/15/67.
5. *NYT,* 1/16/67; Garrow, *Bearing the Cross,* p. 538; *CT,* 7/22/67.
6. *CT,* 1/8/67; Grimshaw, *Bitter Fruit,* p. 124; Fremon, *Chicago Politics Ward by Ward,* p. 193; *NYT,* 1/16/67.

7. *CT,* 1/18/67; *NYT,* 1/17/67; *CT,* 1/25/67; *CT,* 2/8/67.
8. *CT,* 1/31/67; Rakove, *We Don't Want,* p. 283.
9. *Wall Street Journal,* 3/31/67; Rakove, *We Don't Want,* p. 282; *CT,* 4/5/67; *CSM,* 4/6/67.
10. *CT,* 2/10/67.
11. *CT,* 2/25/67; *CT,* 3/1/67.
12. *CT,* 3/4/67; *CT,* 3/15/67; *CT,* 3/17/67.
13. *CT,* 3/24/67.; *CT,* 4/4/67; *CT,* 3/27/67.
14. Peterson, *School Politics,* pp. 33, 36; O'Connor, *Clout,* p. 176; *CT,* 4/5/67.
15. *CT,* 5/10/67; *CT,* 4/9/67; *CT,* 4/5/67; *CT,* 4/6/67; *CT,* 4/21/67.
16. *CT,* 5/19/67.
17. *CT,* 5/13/67; *NYT,* 5/19/67.
18. *NYT,* 12/23/67; *CT,* 12/23/67.
19. *CT,* 8/16/66; *NYT,* 7/21/66; Manchester, *The Glory and the Dream,* p. 1076; Ralph, *Northern Protest,* p. 184; *New York Post,* 7/5/67; *CSM,* 9/5/67; *CT,* 12/23/67; *CT,* 8/1/68.
20. *CT,* 6/6/67; *CT,* 4/29/67; *CT,* 7/13/67; *CT,* 7/14/67.
21. Jacoby, *Someone Else's House,* p. 120; Manchester, *The Glory and the Dream,* pp. 1080–1082.
22. *CT,* 7/28/67; *CT,* 7/29/67; Biles, *Richard J. Daley,* p. 140.
23. *CT,* 7/29/67; Biles, *Richard J. Daley,* p. 141.
24. *NYT,* 11/7/67; Moynihan, *Maximum Feasible Misunderstanding,* p. 150.
25. *NYT,* 8/21/67.
26. *NYT,* 8/16/67; *CT,* 8/14/67; *Wall Street Journal,* 8/15/67; *Wall Street Journal,* 8/15/67; Rakove, *Don't Make No Waves,* p. 217.
27. O'Neill, *Coming Apart,* p. 288; Gitlin, *The Sixties,* p. 245.
28. William Daley, interview with the authors; Davidson, *Vietnam at War,* pp. 452–453; *CT,* 10/8/67; O'Connor, *Clout,* p. 194.
29. William Daley, interview with the author; Larry O'Brien, Oral History No. 23, LBJ Library; Goodwin, *Remembering America,* p. 389; WHCF, Name File (Daley), LBJ Library; David Stahl, interview with the authors.
30. Edward Burke, interview with the authors; William Daley, interview with the authors.
31. *CT,* 10/10/67.
32. *CDN,* 10/9/67.
33. *CT,* 10/9/67; *CDN,* 10/9/67.
34. *Time,* 8/30/68; Sinkevitch, *AIA Guide to Chicago,* p. 391.
35. *CT,* 10/10/67.
36. *NYT,* 12/27/67; *CT,* 12/28/67; *NYT,* 10/11/67.
37. Chester, *American Melodrama,* p. 503; Gitlin, *The Sixties,* p. 300.
38. *CT,* 4/18/68; Chester, *American Melodrama,* p. 120.
39. Chester, *American Melodrama,* p. 120.
40. Ciccone, *Daley,* p. 235.
41. Ciccone, *Daley,* p. 237.
42. O'Neill, *Coming Apart,* p. 180; *Report of the National Advisory Commission on Civil Disorders,* pp. xvii, 478.
43. Biles, *Richard J. Daley,* p. 144; *CT,* 4/5/67.

44. *CT,* 4/6/68; O'Neill, *Coming Apart,* p. 181; Manchester, *The Glory and the Dream,* p. 1128; Jacoby, *Someone Else's House,* p. 153.

45. *CT,* 4/6/68; *NYT,* 4/7/68; *CT,* 4/7/68.

46. *CT,* 4/8/68.

47. *CT,* 4/16/68.

48. *CT,* 4/17/68.

49. *CDN,* 4/17/68.

50. *CT,* 4/16/68; *CT,* 4/17/68; Jacoby, *Someone Else's House,* pp. 153–154; *CT,* 4/18/67; *CT,* 4/18/68.

51. *CT,* 4/19/68; Ciccone, *Daley,* p. 245; Earl Bush, interview with the authors.

52. Chicago Urban League, Racial Aspects of Urban Planning, n.p.; Rossi and Dentler, *Politics of Urban Renewal,* p. 262, n. 9.

53. Sander, "Study in Law and Order," p. 657; Biles, *Richard J. Daley,* pp. 149–150; *CT,* 8/2/68.

54. Gitlin, *The Sixties,* p. 321; *CT,* 8/2/68.

55. Farber, *Chicago '68,* p. 163; *CST,* 8/3/68; *CT,* 8/3/68.

Chapter 13. Preserving Disorder

1. Manchester, *The Glory and the Dream,* p. 1134; O'Neill, *Coming Apart,* p. 290; Gitlin, *The Sixties,* p. 307; *CT,* 6/6/68.

2. Gitlin, *The Sixties,* p. 322; *CT,* 6/30/68; O'Neill, *Coming Apart,* pp. 382, 383; Hoffman, *Freedom and License,* p. 59.

3. Sautter and Burke, *Inside the Wigwam,* p. 247.

4. *CT,* 8/17/68; *CT,* 8/9/68.

5. *CT,* 8/1/68; Biles, *Richard J. Daley,* p. 153.

6. Manchester, *The Glory and the Dream,* p. 1142; *CT,* 8/21/68.

7. *NYT,* 8/28/68; Farber, *Chicago '68,* p. 159; *CDN,* 8/21/68; White, *The Making of the President 1968;* Biles, *Richard J. Daley,* p. 150; Hayden, Tom, "The Battle for Survival," in *Conspiracy,* p. 164.

8. *WP,* 8/18/78.

9. *NYT,* 12/2/80; Deposition of Richard J. Daley, *Alliance to End Repression v. Rochford,* No. 74 C 3268, U.S. District Court for the N. Dist. of Illinois, p. 27.

10. Farber, *Chicago '68,* p. 160; *CT,* 8/21/68; *CT,* 8/25/68.

11. David Stahl, interview with the authors.

12. *CT,* 6/12/68; *CT,* 5/18/68; *CT,* 8/7/68.

13. *CT,* 6/28/68; *CT,* 8/17/68; *CT,* 6/20/68.

14. *CT,* 8/9/68.

15. Earl Bush, interview with the authors; *WP,* 9/9/68; *NYT,* 8/16/68.

16. White, *The Making of the President 1968,* p. 288; Biles, *Richard J. Daley,* p. 152; *CT,* 8/29/68.

17. Hoffman, "Freedom and License," in *Conspiracy,* p. 55; *CT,* 8/20/68; *CT,* 8/21/68; Hubert Will, interview with the authors.

18. *CDN,* 8/23/68; *CDN,* 8/22/68; *CT,* 8/22/68; *CT,* 8/24/68.

19. *CT,* 8/17/68; Biles, *Richard J. Daley,* p. 154; *CDN,* 8/24/68; *CT,* 8/25/68.

20. *CT,* 8/23/68; *CT,* 8/21/68; *NYT,* 8/21/68; *CDN,* 8/22/68; Chester, *American Melodrama,* p. 596; *CDN,* 8/22/68.

21. *WP,* 8/27/68; Chester, *American Melodrama,* pp. 539, 569; *CT,* 8/25/68.
22. Ciccone, *Daley,* p. 257; *CT,* 8/26/68; Chester, *American Melodrama,* p. 570.
23. Hoffman, "Freedom and License," in *Conspiracy,* pp. 58–59.
24. Biles, *Richard J. Daley,* p. 155–156; *CT,* 8/26/68.
25. *NYT,* 8/27/68; Chester, *American Melodrama,* pp. 570–571.
26. *NYT,* 8/27/68; Chester, *American Melodrama,* pp. 505, 507.
27. Biles, *Richard J. Daley,* p. 156; *NYT,* 8/28/68; *CT,* 8/28/68; Chester, *American Melodrama,* p. 513.
28. *CT,* 8/28/68.
29. *CT,* 8/28/68; Biles, *Richard J. Daley,* p. 157.
30. *NYT,* 8/29/68; *CT,* 8/30/68.
31. *Rights in Conflict,* p. 239.
32. Biles, *Richard J. Daley,* pp. 158-159; *Rights in Conflict,* p. 255; "Shana Alexander: Eyewitness," in *Law and Disorder,* n.p.
33. Hayden, *While the World Was Watching,* p. 71; Biles, *Richard J. Daley,* p. 159; *New York Post,* 8/29/68; *NYT,* 8/30/68.
34. *CDN,* 8/29/68; Chester, *American Melodrama,* p. 585.
35. *CT,* 8/29/68.
36. *CT,* 8/29/68.
37. *New York Post,* 8/29/68; *NYT,* 8/30/68.
38. *NYT,* 8/30/68; Chester, *American Melodrama,* p. 589.
39. *NYT,* 8/30/68; Chester, *American Melodrama,* p. 590; *Law and Disorder,* n.p.
40. *CDN,* 8/30/68, interview with M. W. Newman; "Dermot A. Ryan, Eyewitness," in *Law and Disorder,* n.p.; Chester, *American Melodrama,* p. 591.
41. *WP,* 8/31/68; *New York Post,* 8/31/68; Chester, *American Melodrama,* p. 592; *CT,* 8/31/68; *CDN,* 8/31/68; *Law and Disorder,* n.p.
42. *WP,* 9/10/68; *NYT,* 9/10/68; *WP,* 9/10/68; *Time,* 9/20/68.
43. "Strategy of Confrontation."
44. *NYT,* 9/5/68; *CT,* 9/16/68.
45. *WP,* 10/9/68; Chester, *American Melodrama,* p. 594; *CT,* 9/17/68.
46. *CT,* 10/8/68; *CT,* 11/8/68; *WP,* 11/14/68; *CT,* 11/14/68; *CT,* 11/14/68.
47. *CT,* 12/2/68; Mathewson, *Up Against Daley,* p. 221; *CT,* 12/2/68; *Rights in Conflict,* p. 11; *CT,* 12/2/68; Chester, *American Melodrama,* p. 603.

Chapter 14. We Wore Suits and Ties

1. *CT,* 1/9/69.
2. Biles, *Richard J. Daley,* pp. 166-167.
3. Bowly, *The Poorhouse,* p. 189.
4. Hubert Will, interview with the authors; O'Connor, *Clout,* p. 147.
5. Initial Brief of Plaintiffs in Support of their Motion for Summary Judgment and in Opposition to Defendants' Motion for Summary Judgment, *Gautreaux,* pp. 13–14; Alexander Polikoff, interview with the authors; Henderson, "Scattered Successes," *The Chicago Reader,* 10/14/94; Affidavit of Harold M. Baron, *Gautreaux v. CHA;* Initial Brief of Plaintiffs in Support of their Motion for Summary Judgment and in Opposition to Defendants' Motion for Summary Judgment, *Gautreaux,* "Controversy Over Chicago's Public Housing," *CT,* 3/14/71.
6. *CT,* 3/14/71; Initial Brief; *Gautreaux,* p. 22; *CDN,* 12/20/66.

7. *CT,* 2/12/69.
8. *CT,* 2/12/69; *CT,* 3/14/71; Bowly, *The Poorhouse,* p. 134.
9. *CT,* 3/14/71.
10. *CT,* 3/14/71; Biles, *Richard J. Daley,* p. 173.
11. Lemann, Promised Land, pp. 198–199; Biles, *Richard J. Daley,* p. 170.
12. *CT,* 2/22/72; Lemann, *Promised Land,* pp. 198–199; Biles, *Richard J. Daley,* p. 170.
13. *CT,* 2/22/72; *CT,* 2/21/72.
14. Lemann, *Promised Land,* p. 251.
15. Travis, *An Autobiography of Black Politics,* p. 253; Grimshaw, *Bitter Fruit,* p. 123; Biles, *Richard J. Daley,* p. 168.
16. *CT,* 3/10/69; *Newsweek,* 4/21/69.
17. *CT,* 3/21/68; Biles, *Richard J. Daley,* p. 174.
18. *CT,* 4/24/69.
19. *CT,* 4/4/69; *CT,* 4/6/69.
20. *CT,* 9/7/69, William Singer, interview with the authors; *CT,* 2/27/69; *CT,* 3/13/69.
21. *CT,* 9/8/69, William Singer, interview with the authors.
22. *CT,* 9/13/69; *CT,* 9/14/69.
23. O'Neill, *Coming Apart,* pp. 296–297; Biles, *Richard J. Daley,* p. 175; Schultz, *The Chicago Conspiracy Trial,* pp. 90–92.
24. *CT,* 1/25/70; Schultz, *The Chicago Conspiracy Trial,* pp. 118–128.
25. *CT,* 1/7/70; *CT,* 1/6/70; Manchester, *The Glory and the Dream,* p. 1205; Biles, *Richard J. Daley,* p. 176; Schultz, *The Chicago Conspiracy Trial,* pp. 13, 214; *CT,* 1/7/70; *CT,* 1/6/70.
26. Gleason, Daley, p. 363.
27. Travis, *An Autobiography of Black Politics,* p. 416.
28. Travis, *An Autobiography of Black Politics,* pp. 426, 432; Pearson, *The Shadow of the Panther,* p. 208.
29. Travis, *An Autobiography of Black Politics,* p. 433.
30. *Chicago Magazine,* 11/94; Biles, *Richard J. Daley,* pp. 177–178.
31. *CT,* 3/15/70.
32. *CT,* 3/21/70; *CT,* 4/5/70.
33. Biles, *Richard J. Daley,* p. 178, *NYT,* 12/27/73; Arlen, *An American Verdict.*
34. *CT,* 5/29/70; *CT,* 5/19/70.
35. Miller, *Here's the Deal,* pp. 24, 29; McBrien, *The Loop,* p. 30.
36. *CST,* 4/19/70; O'Connor, *Clout,* pp. 135–137.
37. *CT,* 7/28/70; Jacoby, *Someone Else's House,* p. 255.
38. *NYT,* 11/5/70.
39. *NYT,* 11/5/70; *CT,* 11/17/70.
40. *CT,* 12/19/70; *NYT,* 12/21/73.
41. *CT,* 12/18/70.
42. *CT,* 1/3/71; *CT,* 11/18/70; *CT,* 11/6/70.
43. *NYT,* 3/9/71; *CT,* 3/14/69.
44. Biles, *Richard J. Daley,* p. 173; *CT,* 3/14/71; *CT,* 3/9/71; *CT,* 3/14/71.
45. *CT,* 3/9/71; *CT,* 3/14/69; *New Republic,* 4/3/71.
46. *CT,* 3/14/71; *Chicago Today,* 3/11/71; *CT,* 3/11/71.
47. *CT,* 12/24/70.
48. *CST,* 3/4/71; *Life,* 3/19/71; *CT,* 1/4/71.

49. *CT,* 4/5/71; *CA,* 3/25/71.
50. Richard Friedman, interview with the authors; *NYT,* 4/8/71.
51. *NYT,* 4/8/71.
52. *CT,* 11/29/70; *CT,* 4/7/71.
53. Travis, *An Autobiography of Black Politics,* p. 449; *NYT,* 8/26/71; Biles, *Richard J. Daley,* p. 179; *Time,* 9/6/71; *CT,* 8/27/71.
54. *Chicago Magazine,* 11/94; *CT,* 9/8/71.
55. *CT,* 7/7/71.
56. *CT,* 1/3/71; *NYT,* 7/20/71.
57. *CT,* 7/22/71; Biles, *Richard J. Daley,* p. 187; William Singer, interview with the authors; *CT,* 7/24/71.
58. *CT,* 10/7/71; *CT,* 9/18/71.
59. *NYT,* 5/10/76.
60. *NYT,* 12/16/71; *CT,* 12/16/71; Biles, *Richard J. Daley,* p. 196.
61. *CT,* 7/8/71; *NYT,* 9/25/79.
62. Travis, *An Autobiography of Black Politics,* p. 285.
63. Travis, *An Autobiography of Black Politics,* p. 287; *CT,* 11/28/76.
64. *CST,* 9/29/72.
65. *CST,* 9/29/72; William Singer, interview with the authors.
66. Biles, *Richard J. Daley,* p. 189; *CT,* 11/19/70.
67. Despres papers, Chicago Historical Society; *CT,* 7/8/72.
68. *CT,* 7/9/72.
69. *CT,* 6/1/72; *CT,* 7/2/72; *CT,* 7/7/72.
70. Mailer, *St. George and the Godfather,* pp. 45–46; Biles, *Richard J. Daley,* p. 194; *CT,* 8/17/72.
71. *CT,* 10/28/72; *CT* files, Election Fraud, 6/15/74.
72. Harris Wofford, interview with the authors; Ciccone, *Daley,* p. 298; *NYT,* 10/26/72; *NYT,* 9/13/72.

Chapter 15. *If a Man Can't Put His Arms Around His Sons*

1. *CT,* 1/11/73; Daley speech, University of Chicago, 2/21/73 (on file with the authors).
2. David Stahl, interview with the authors; *CT,* 2/9/73.
3. Kennedy, *Himself!,* p. 254; *CT,* 2/15/73.
4. *CT,* 3/6/73; *CT,* 3/23/73; *CT,* 2/28/73; David Stahl, interview with the authors; *CT,* 3/15/73; *CT,* 11/23/73.
5. *Time,* 4/2/73; *CT,* 9/21/73; *CT,* 9/22/73.
6. *CT,* 5/4/73; *CT,* 1/31/73.
7. William Hartmann memo, Central Area Committee files; William Hartmann, interview with the authors; *Time,* 6/2/73; Wille, *At Home in the Loop,* p. 4.
8. *CT,* 5/23/74.
9. *CT,* 11/10/72.
10. Marciniak, *Reclaiming the Inner City,* p. 35; Edward Marciniak, interview with the authors; *CT,* 5/11/62; Arthur Rubloff Collection, Chicago Historical Society, Box 4, Folder 5; *CDN,* 11/12/60; Sinkevitch, *AIA Guide to Chicago,* p. 167.
11. *CT,* 6/15/73, Central Area Committee files; Wille, *At Home in the Loop,* p. 10; *CT,* 4/5/74; *CT,* 11/10/72; *CT,* 7/21/77.

12. Sinkevitch, *AIA Guide to Chicago,* p. 145; *CT,* 3/30/74; Wille, *At Home in the Loop,* p. 68.
13. William Daley, interview with the authors; *CT,* 11/4/73; *CT,* 3/18/73.
14. *CT,* 10/13/79; *CT,* 3/30/73; *Wall Street Journal,* 8/8/73.
15. *CT,* 11/13/74; *NYT,* 5/3/74; *CT,* 12/19/73; *CST,* 12/19/73.
16. Fremon, *Chicago Politics Ward by Ward,* p. 203; Edward Burke, interview with the authors; *CT,* 3/3/74.
17. Arthur Rubloff Collection, Chicago Historical Society, Box 4, Folder 5; *CDN,* 11/12/60; Sinkevitch, *AIA Guide to Chicago,* p. 167.
18. *CT,* 3/10/74; *CT,* 1/12/74; *CT,* 1/13/74; *CDN,* 5/2/74; *CDN,* 7/16/74; *CT,* 6/23/74; *CT,* 3/16/74; *CDN,* 3/12/74.
19. *Chicago Today,* 1/7/74; *CT,* 1/1/74.
20. *Wall Street Journal,* 1/24/74; *Time,* 2/25/74; *NYT,* 2/12/74; Kleppner, *Chicago Divided,* p. 85.
21. *NYT,* 5/13/74; *CT,* 4/2/74; *CT,* 5/7/74; *NYT,* 5/19/74.
22. *NYT,* 5/24/74; *CT,* 7/22/74; *NYT,* 5/24/74; *CT,* 4/21/74; *NYT,* 5/19/74.
23. *CST,* 7/11/74; *NYT,* 7/12/74; Biles, *Richard J. Daley,* p. 200; David Stahl, interview with the authors; *CSM,* 7/15/74.
24. *NYT,* 9/3/74, Biles, *Richard J. Daley,* p. 201.
25. *NYT,* 10/9/74; *CT,* 10/13/74; *NYT,* 10/7/74.
26. *WP,* 8/31/73; Lens, *The Progressive;* William Singer, interview with the authors.
27. *CT,* 12/22/74.
28. *CT,* 2/26/75.
29. *CT,* 2/15/75; *NYT,* 2/21/75.
30. William Singer, interview with the authors; *NYT,* 2/21/75.
31. *NYT,* 2/21/75; *CT,* 2/15/75; *CT,* 2/26/75; *NYT,* 2/21/75.
32. William Singer, interview with the authors.
33. *NYT,* 3/15/75.
34. *NYT,* 4/10/75; Edward Burke, interview with the authors.
35. William Singer, interview with the authors; Against the Crosstown, Position Paper, North River Commission, July 1972, in Leon Despres Papers, Box 69, Folder 4, Chicago Historical Society; Memo from Jim Weill, Community Legal Counsel, 4/10/70, Leon Despres Papers, Box 69, Folder 4, Chicago Historical Society.
36. Memorandum of Director William R. Mooney, Intelligence Division, B.I.S., to Deputy Superintendent Michael A. Spiotto, B.I.S., Re: Benefit Dinner Sponsored by the Afro-American Patrolmen's League, 6/8/72, copy on file with the authors; *NYT,* 6/2/75; *NYT,* 3/20/75. Documents in Chicago Historical Society.
37. *CST,* 9/10/75; *CT,* 8/16/75.
38. *NYT,* 4/19/75.
39. *NYT,* 1/6/76.
40. *NYT,* 1/6/76, *NYT,* 1/11/76; *CT,* 1/4/76; Kleppner, *Chicago Divided,* p. 86.
41. *CT,* 3/28/76.
42. William Daley, interview with the authors; Tom Donovan, interview with the authors.
43. *CT,* 11/12/75; *CST,* 2/4/76.
44. *NYT,* 4/22/76; *NYT,* 4/26/76; Massey and Denton, *American Apartheid,* pp. 161, 231.
45. *CST,* 7/28/75.

46. *NYT,* 5/4/76; *NYT,* 7/4/76; Ciccone, *Daley,* p. 309.
47. *CT,* 3/17/76, Ciccone, *Daley,* p. 309.
48. *NYT,* 3/15/76.
49. Ciccone, *Daley,* pp. 310–311.
50. *Time,* 7/21/76.
51. *NYT,* 7/15/76; *Time,* 7/26/76.
52. *CT,* 8/21/77; *CT,* 8/19/76.
53. Ciccone, *Daley,* p. 313; *Time,* 11/22/76.
54. *CT,* 11/28/76; *NYT,* 11/5/76.
55. Kennedy, *Himself!,* pp. 4–5; Gilbert Graham, interview with the authors; *CST,* 9/2/77.
56. Kennedy, *Himself!,* p. 8.
57. *WP,* 12/21/76, *CT,* 12/21/76.
58. Kennedy, *Himself!,* pp. 11, 14.
59. *NYT,* 12/22/76; *CT,* 12/21/76.
60. Kennedy, *Himself!,* p. 24; *NYT,* 12/22/76.
61. *CT,* 12/23/76; *NYT,* 12/23/76.
62. *NYT,* 12/23/76; *CT,* 12/23/76.

SELECTIVE BIBLIOGRAPHY

Archives

We made use of the following archives: Chicago Historical Society, in particular the papers of Cyrus Hall Adams, Better Government Association, Leon Despres, James C. Murray, Len O'Connor, Holman Pettibone, and Arthur Rubloff and the Red Squad. Federal court records included case files *Shakman v. Democratic Organization of Cook County* in Federal District Court Archives, Chicago, Illinois. The Federal Bureau of Investigation made Richard J. Daley's files available. We reviewed public documents at City Hall, and the Lyndon Baines Johnson Library provided rich material on Richard J. Daley.

We also consulted the Chicago Public Library, in particular its Chicago collection, and the library at Skidmore, Owings & Merrill. Businessmen and Professionals for the Public Interest generously made their *Gautreaux v. Chicago Housing Authority* case files available.

Libraries at the De La Salle Institute, University of Chicago, and DePaul University held important resources. The Mount Holyoke College library and computer center provided assistance. At Fisk University, we examined the William Dawson Papers. We utilized the Oral History Project at Columbia University. The Southern Christian Leadership Conference Papers were available at the Martin Luther King Center. The Museum of Broadcast Communications in Chicago and the Museum of Television & Radio in New York provided excellent coverage of Daley, and the 1968 convention in particular.

Articles, Pamphlets, Unpublished Documents, and Other Materials

All Things Considered. National Public Radio, May 18, 1998.
"Anatomy of a Confrontation" (City of Chicago document).
Baron, Harold. "Building Babylon: A Case for Racial Controls in Public Housing" (Northwestern University for Urban Affairs, 1971).

Chicago Urban League. *Public Housing: Chicago Builds a Ghetto* (1967).

Daley: The Last Boss, a film documentary. Barak Goodman, producer. Aired on *The American Experience* (PBS).

Diamond Jubilee of the Archdiocese of Chicago (Des Plaines: St. Mary's Training School Press, 1920).

Halberstam, David. "Daley of Chicago," *Harper's* (August 1968).

Kantowitz, Edward. "Church and Neighborhood," *Ethnicity* (7, 349–366).

Law & Disorder: The Chicago Convention and Its Aftermath. Published in Chicago by Donald Myrus and Burton Joseph.

Marciniak, Edward. "Reclaiming the Inner City: Chicago's Near North Revitalization Confronts Cabrini-Green" (Washington, DC: National Center for Urban Ethnic Affairs, 1986).

"Massive Resistance in the Urban North: Trumbull Park, Chicago, 1953–1966." *Journal of American History* (September 1995).

McGreevy, John. "American Catholics and the African-American Migration, 1919–1970" (Ph.D. dissertation, 1992).

McKnight, John. Notes on the Summit Meeting with Martin Luther King and Richard J. Daley.

"Report of the Chicago Riot Study Committee to the Honorable Richard J. Daley," August 1, 1968.

Warren, Elizabeth. *Subsidized Housing in Chicago* (1980).

Whitehead, Ralph. "The Organization Man," *American Scholar* (Summer 1977).

Interview with Charles Swibel, conducted by Bruce Thomas and Robert Nathan, July 1986, provided by James Ralph.

Books

Abernathy, Ralph. *And the Walls Came Tumbling Down: An Autobiography.* New York: Harper & Row, 1989.

Allswang, John M. *A House for All Peoples: Ethnic Politics in Chicago, 1890–1936.* Lexington: University Press of Kentucky, 1971.

———. *Bosses, Machines, and Urban Voters.* Baltimore: Johns Hopkins Press, 1986.

Anderson, Alan B., and George W. Pickering. *Confronting the Color Line: The Broken Promise of Civil Rights Movements in Chicago.* Athens: University of Georgia Press, 1986.

Arlen, Michael J. *An American Verdict,* New York: Doubleday, 1973.

Banfield, Ernest C., and James Q. Wilson. *City Politics.* New York: Vintage Books, 1963.

Beatty, Jack. *The Rascal King: The Life and Times of James Michael Curley.* Reading: Addison-Wesley, 1992.

Berger, Miles. *They Built Chicago: Entrepreneurs Who Shaped a Great City's Architecture.* Chicago: Bonus Books, 1992.

Berkow, Ira. *Maxwell Street: Survival in a Bazaar.* New York: Doubleday, 1977.

Bernard, Richard M. (ed.). *Snowbelt Cities: Metropolitan Politics in the Northeast and Midwest Since World War II.* Bloomington: Indiana University Press, 1990.

Bernstein, Irving. *Guns or Butter: The Presidency of Lyndon Johnson.* New York: Oxford University Press, 1996.

Beschloss, Michael. *Taking Charge: The Johnson White House Tapes, 1963–1964.* New York: Simon and Schuster, 1997.

Biles, Roger. *Big City Boss in Depression and War: Mayor Edward J. Kelly.* DeKalb: Northern Illinois University Press, 1995.

———. *Richard J. Daley: Politics, Race and the Governing of Chicago.* DeKalb: Northern Illinois University Press, 1995.

Bopp, William J. *"O.W.": O. W. Wilson and the Search for a Police Profession.* Port Washington, NY: Kennikat Press, 1977.

Bowly, Devereaux, Jr. *The Poorhouse: Subsidized Housing in Chicago, 1895–1976.* Carbondale: Southern Illinois University Press, 1978.

Branch, Taylor. *Pillar of Fire: America in the King Years, 1964–1965.* New York: Simon and Schuster, 1998.

Byrne, Jane. *My Chicago.* New York: W. W. Norton, 1992.

Chester, Lewis, Godfrey Hodgson, and Bruce Page. *American Melodrama: The Presidential Campaign of 1968.* New York: Viking Press, 1969.

Christopher, Maurine. *America's Black Congressman.* New York: Apollo Editions, 1971.

Ciccone, F. Richard. *Daley: Power and Presidential Politics.* Chicago: NTC/Contemporary Books, 1996.

Cronon, William. *Nature's Metropolis: Chicago and the Great West.* New York; W. W. Norton, 1991.

Davidson, Phillip. *Vietnam at War: The History, 1946–1975.* Novato: Presidio, 1988.

Drake, St. Clair, and Horace Cayton. *Black Metropolis: A Study in Negro Life in a Northern City.* University of Chicago Press, 1987.

Erie, Steven. *Rainbow's End: Irish-Americans and the Dilemmas of Urban Machine Politics, 1840–1985.* Berkeley: University of California Press, 1988.

Ehrenhalt, Alan. *The Lost City: Discovering the Forgotten Virtues of Community in Chicago in the 1950's.* New York: Basic Books, 1995.

Farber, David. *Chicago '68.* Chicago: University of Chicago Press, 1987.

Frady, Marshall. *Jesse: The Life and Pilgrimage of Jesse Jackson.* New York: Random House, 1996.

Fremon, David. *Chicago Politics Ward by Ward.* Bloomington and Indianapolis: Indiana University Press, 1988.

Garrow, David J. *Bearing the Cross: Martin Luther King Jr. and the Southern Christian Leadership Conference.* New York: Morrow, 1986.

——— (ed.). *Chicago 1966: Open Housing Marches, Summit Negotiations, and Operation Breadbasket.* New York: Carlson, 1989.

Gitlin, Todd. *The Sixties: Years of Hope, Days of Rage.* New York, Bantam, 1987.

Glazer, Nathan, and Daniel Patrick Moynihan. *Beyond the Melting Pot: The Negroes, Puerto Ricans and Jews.* Cambridge: M.I.T. Press and Harvard University Press.

Gleason, Bill. *Daley of Chicago.* New York: Simon and Schuster, 1970.

Goodwin, Richard N. *Remembering America: A Voice from the Sixties.* Boston: Little, Brown, 1988.

Gosnell, Harold F. *Machine Politics Chicago Model* (CK).

Gove, Samuel K., and Louis H. Masotti (eds.). *After Daley: Chicago Politics in Transition.* Urbana: University of Illinois Press, 1982.

Granger, Bill, and Lori Granger. *Lords of the Last Machine.* New York: Random House, 1987.

Greeley, Andrew W. *Neighborhood.* New York: Seabury Press, 1977.

————. *That Most Distressful Nation: The Taming of the American Irish.* Chicago: Quadrangle Books, 1972.

Green, Paul M., and Melvin G. Holli (eds.). *The Mayors.* Carbondale: Southern Illinois Press, 1995.

Grimshaw, William J. *Bitter Fruit: Black Politics and the Chicago Machine, 1931–1991.* Chicago: University of Chicago Press, 1992.

Grossman, James R. *Land of Hope: Chicago, Black Southerners and the Great Migration.* Chicago: University of Chicago Press, 1989.

Gunther, John. *Inside U.S.A.* New York: Free Press, 1997.

Guterbock, Thomas M. *Machine Politics in Transition: Party and Community in Chicago.* Chicago: University of Chicago Press, 1980.

Hampton, Henry, and Steve Fayer. *Voices of Freedom: An Oral History of the Civil Rights Movement from the 1950's through the 1980's.* New York: Bantam Books, 1991.

Hayden, Tom. *White the World Was Watching.* Davis, CA: Panorama West, 1996.

Hirsch, Arnold. *Making the Second Ghetto: Race and Housing in Chicago, 1940–1960.* Cambridge: Cambridge University Press, 1983.

Hoffman, Abbie, Rennie Davis, John Froines, Jerry Rubin, Bobby Seale, Tom Hayden, and Lee Weiner. *The Conspiracy: The Chicago 8 Speak Out!* New York: Dell, 1969.

Horwitt, Sanford D. *Let Them Call Me Rebel: Saul Alinsky — His Life and Legacy.* New York: Alfred A. Knopf, 1989.

Jackson, Kenneth. *Crabgrass Frontier: The Suburbanization of the United States.* New York: Oxford University Press, 1985.

Jacoby, Tamar. *Someone Else's House.* New York: The Free Press, 1999.

Johnson, John H. *Succeeding Against the Odds: The Autobiography of a Great American Businessman.* New York: Amistad, 1989.

Kalina, Edmund F. *Courthouse over White House: Chicago and the Presidential Election of 1960.* Orlando: University of Central Florida Press, 1988.

Kennedy, Eugene. *Himself!* New York: Viking, 1978.

Kleppner, Paul. *Chicago Divided: The Making of a Black Mayor.* DeKalb: Northern Illinois University Press, 1985.

Koenig, Rev. Harry C. (ed.). *History of Chicago,* vol 1. The Archdiocese of Chicago, 1980.

Kotlowitz, Alex. *There Are No Children Here.* New York: Doubleday, 1991.

Larsen, Lawrence H., and Nancy J. Hulston. *Pendergast!* Columbia: University of Missouri Press, 1997.

Lemann, Nicholas. *The Promised Land: The Great Migration and How It Changed America.* New York: Alfred A. Knopf, 1991.

Levine, Edward. *The Irish and Irish Politicians: A Story in Cultural and Social Alienation.* Notre Dame: Notre Dame University Press, 1966.

Lewis, Tom. *Divided Highways: Building the Interstate Highways, Transforming American Life.* New York: Viking, 1997.

Liebling, A. J. *The Second City.* New York: Alfred A. Knopf, 1952.

Lindberg, Richard C. *To Serve and Collect: Chicago Politics and Police Corruption from the Lager Beer Riot to the Summerdale Scandal.* New York: Praeger, 1991.

Mack, Raymond M. (ed.). *Our Children's Burden: Studies of Desegregation in Nine American Communities.* New York: Random House, 1968.

Mailer, Norman. *Miami and the Siege of Chicago: An Informal History of the Republican and Democratic Conventions of 1968.* New York: Penguin, 1986.

———. *St. George and the Godfather.* New York: New American Library, 1972.

Manchester, William. *The Glory and the Dream.* Boston: Little, Brown, 1973.

Mann, Robert. *The Walls of Jericho: Lyndon Johnson, Hubert Humphrey, Richard Russell, and the Struggle for Civil Rights.* New York: Harcourt, Brace, 1996.

Marciniak, Ed. *Reclaiming the Inner City.* Washington, DC: National Center for Urban Ethnic Affairs, 1986.

Martin, John Barlow. *Adlai Stevenson of Illinois.* New York: Doubleday, 1976.

Massey, Douglas, and Nancy Denton. *American Apartheid: Segregation and the Making of the Underclass.* Cambridge: Harvard University Press, 1993.

Mathewson, Joe. *Up Against Daley.* LaSalle, IL: Open Court Press, 1974.

Mayer, Harold, and Richard Wade. *Chicago: Growth of a Metropolis.* Chicago: University of Chicago Press, 1969.

McBrien, Judith Paine. *The Loop: Where the Skyscraper Began.* Chicago: Perspectives Press, 1992.

McCaffrey, Lawrence J. et al. (eds.). *The Irish in Chicago.* Urbana: University of Illinois Press, 1987.

McCullough, David. *Truman.* New York: Simon and Schuster, 1992.

McGreevy, John T. *Parish Boundaries: The Catholic Encounter with Race in the Twentieth-Century Urban North.* Chicago: University of Chicago Press, 1996.

Mier, Robert. *Social Justice and Local Development Policy.* Newbury Park: Sage Publications, 1993.

Miller, Donald M. *City of the Century: The Epic of Chicago and the Making of America.* New York: Simon and Schuster, 1996.

Miller, Ross. *Here's the Deal: The Buying and Selling of a Great American City.* New York: Alfred A. Knopf, 1996.

Moynihan, Daniel Patrick. *Maximum Feasible Misunderstanding: Community Action in the War on Poverty.* New York: The Free Press, 1969.

Myerson, Martin, and Edward C. Banfield. *Politics, Planning, and the Public Interest.* New York: The Free Press, 1985.

Nixon, Richard. *RN: The Memoirs of Richard Nixon.* New York: Touchstone/Simon and Schuster, 1990.

———. *Six Crises.* New York: Touchstone/Simon and Schuster, 1990.

Oates, Stephen B. *With Malice Toward None: The Life of Abraham Lincoln.* New York: Harper & Row, 1977.

O'Connor, Len. *Clout: Mayor Daley and His City.* New York: Avon, 1975.

———. *Requiem: The Decline and Demise of Mayor Daley and His Era.* Chicago: Contemporary Books, 1977.

O'Donnell, Kenneth P. and David F. Powers. *Johnny We Hardly Knew Ye: Memories of John Fitzgerald Kennedy.* Boston: Little, Brown, 1970.

O'Neil, William. *Coming Apart: An Informal History of America in the 1960's.* New York: Quadrangle Books, 1971.

Patterson, James T. *America's Struggle Against Poverty, 1900–1975.* Cambridge: Harvard University Press, 1981.

Pearson, Hugh. *The Shadow of the Panther.* Reading, MA: Addison-Wesley, 1994.

Peterson, Paul. *School Politics, Chicago Style.* Chicago: University of Chicago Press, 1976.

Philpott, Thomas Lee. *The Slum and the Ghetto: Neighborhood Deterioration and Middle-Class Reform, Chicago, 1880–1930.* New York: Oxford University Press, 1978.

Pickering, George W. *Confronting the Color Line: The Broken Promise of the Civil Rights Movement in Chicago.* Athens: University of Georgia Press, 1986.

Piven, Frances Fox, and Richard A. Cloward. *Regulating the Poor: The Functions of Public Welfare.* New York: Vintage Books, 1971.

Rakove, Milton. *Don't Make No Waves, Don't Back No Losers.* Bloomington: University of Illinois Press, 1975.

———. *We Don't Want Nobody Nobody Sent.* Bloomington: Indiana University Press, 1979.

Ralph, James R. Jr. *Northern Protest: Martin Luther King Jr., Chicago, and the Civil Rights Movement.* Cambridge: Harvard University Press, 1993.

Rast, Joel. *Remaking Chicago: The Political Origins of Urban Industrial Change.* DeKalb: Northern Illinois University Press, 1999.

Reed, Christopher. *The Chicago NAACP and the Rise of the Black Professional Leadership, 1910–1966.* Bloomington: Indiana University Press, 1997.

Rights in Conflict: The Violent Confrontation of Demonstrators and Police in the Parks and the Streets of Chicago During the Week of the Democratic National Convention (New York: Bantam, 1968).

Report of the National Advisory Commission on Civil Disorders. New York: Bantam Books, 1968.

Riordon, William L. *Plunkitt of Tammany Hall.* New York: Alfred A. Knopf, 1968.

Rivlin, Gary. *Fire on the Prairie: Chicago's Harold Washington and the Politics of Race.* New York: Henry Holt, 1992.

Roemer, William F. *Accardo: The Genuine Godfather.* New York: Donald I. Fine, 1995.

———. *Roemer: How the F.B.I. Cracked the Chicago Mob.* New York: Balantine Books, 1989.

Rogers, William Warren, et al. *Alabama: The History of a Deep South State.* Tuscaloosa: University of Alabama Press, 1994.

Rosen, George. *Decision-Making Chicago Style: The Genesis of a University of Illinois Campus.* Champaign: University of Illinois Press, 1980.

Rossi, George, and Robert A. Dentler. *The Politics of Urban Renewal: The Chicago Findings.* New York: The Free Press, 1961.

Royko, Mike. *Boss: Richard J. Daley of Chicago.* New York: Dutton, 1971.

Sautter, R. Craig, and Edward M. Burke. Foreword by Richard M. Daley. *Inside the Wigwam: Chicago Presidential Conventions 1860–1996.* Chicago: Loyola University Press, 1996.

Schultz, John. *The Chicago Conspiracy Trial.* New York: Da Capa Press, 1993.

———. *No One Was Killed.* Chicago: Big Table, 1998.

Shannon, William V. *The American Irish.* New York: MacMillan, 1966.

Sinclair, Upton. *The Jungle.* New York: Signet, 1905.

Sinkevitch, Alice (ed.). *AIA Guide to Chicago.* San Diego: Harcourt Brace, 1993.

Sobel, Lester (ed.). *Civil Rights 1960–66.* New York; Facts on File, 1967.

Spear, Allan H. *Black Chicago: The Making of a Negro Ghetto, 1890–1920.* Chicago: University of Chicago Press, 1967.

Squires, Gregory D., Larry Bennett, Kathleen McCourt, and Philip Nyden. *Race, Class, and the Response to Urban Decline.* Philadelphia: Temple University Press, 1987.

Sullivan, Frank. *Legend: The Only Inside Story about Mayor Richard J. Daley.* Chicago: Bonus Books, 1989.

Teaford, Jon C. *The Rough Road to Renaissance: Urban Revitalization in America, 1940–1985.* Baltimore: Johns Hopkins University Press, 1990.

Travis, Dempsey. *An Autobiography of Black Politics.* Chicago: Urban Research Press, 1987.

Tuttle, William M. *Race Riot: Chicago in the Red Summer of 1919.* New York: Atheneum, 1970.

White, Theodore H. *The Making of the President 1960.* New York: Atheneum, 1961.

————. *The Making of the President 1968.* New York: Atheneum, 1969.

Wille, Lois. *At Home in the Loop: How Clout and Community Built Chicago's Dearborn Park.* Carbondale: Southern Illinois University Press, 1997.

Wilson, Charles Reagan, and William Ferris (eds.). *The Encyclopedia of Southern Culture.* Chapel Hill, NC: University of North Carolina Press, 1989.

Wilson, James Q. *Negro Politics: The Search for Leadership.* New York: The Free Press, 1960.

Wilson, William Julius. *When Work Disappears.* New York: Alfred A. Knopf, 1977.

Wittke, Carl Frederick. *The Irish in America.* New York: Russell & Russell, 1956.

Wofford, Harris. *Of Kennedys and Kings: Making Sense of the Sixties.* New York: Farrar, Straus & Giroux, 1980.

Yarbrough, Tinsley. *Judge Frank Johnson and Human Rights in Alabama.* Tuscaloosa: University of Alabama Press, 1981.

Yessne, Peter. *Quotations from Mayor Daley.* New York: Putnam's Sons, 1969.

Young, Andrew. *An Easy Burden: The Civil Rights Movement and the Transformation of America.* New York: HarperCollins, 1996.

INDEX

604

Index